THE SOVIET COLOSSUS

THE SOVIET COLOSSUS

COLOSSUS

HISTORY AND AFTERMATH

SEVENTH EDITION

MICHAEL KORT

M.E.Sharpe
Armonk, New York
London, England

The EuroSlavic and Transroman fonts used to create this work are © 1986–2010
Payne Loving Trust. EuroSlavic and Transroman are available
from Linguist's Software, Inc., www.linguistsoftware.
com, P.O. Box 580, Edmonds, WA 98020-0580 USA, tel (425) 775-1130.

Library of Congress Cataloging-in-Publication Data

Kort, Michael, 1944–
 The Soviet colossus : history and aftermath / by Michael Kort. — 7th ed.
 p. cm.
Includes bibliographical references and index.
ISBN 978-0-7656-2386-7 (cloth : alk. paper) — ISBN 978-0-7656-2387-4 (pbk. : alk. paper)
1. Soviet Union—History. 2. Russia—History—Nicholas II, 1894–1917. I. Title.

DK246.K64 2010
947.084—dc22   2009038897

Printed in the United States of America

The paper used in this publication meets the minimum requirements of
American National Standard for Information Sciences
Permanence of Paper for Printed Library Materials,
ANSI Z 39.48-1984.

∞

IBT (c)   10   9   8   7   6   5   4   3   2   1
CW (p)   10   9   8   7   6   5   4   3   2   1

for
Eleza and Tamara
and
in memory of
Victor Kort

ARCTIC OCEAN

ARCTIC CIRCLE

CHERSKY RANGE

Magadon

Petropavlovsk

CENTRAL
SIBERIAN
PLATEAU

SEA OF OKHOTSK

Angara River

Yakutsk

FEDERATION

Lena River

Amur River

YABLONOVOY RANGE

Lake Baikal

Bratsk

Irkutsk

Vladivostok

THE FORMER
SOVIET UNION

Contents

Preface to the Seventh Edition   xi
Acknowledgments   xiii

PART I
THE FUNDAMENTALS OF RUSSIAN HISTORY

1. Prologue   3
2. The Autocratic State   8
3. The Nineteenth-Century Crisis   19
4. The People   26
5. The Intelligentsia: Strangers in a Strange Land   32

PART II
THE END OF THE OLD ORDER

6. Capitalism Comes to Russia   47
7. The Revolutionaries Regroup   54
8. The Final Years and Last Stand   73

PART III
LENIN'S RUSSIA

9. 1917: Russia's Two Revolutions   91
10. Into the Fire: The Civil War   114
11. New Policies and New Problems   142

PART IV
STEELING THE REVOLUTION

12. Bolshevism Without Lenin   175
13. The Revolution From Above   199
14. Trial by Fire: The Great Patriotic War   248
15. Stalin's September Songs   264

PART V
THE SOCIALIST SUPERPOWER

16. Khrushchev: Reforming the Revolution   283
17. The Brezhnev Era: The Graying of the Revolution   317
18. Gorbachev: From Restructuring to Deconstruction   360

PART VI
THE RUSSIAN FEDERATION

19. The Russian Devolution   409
20. Russia in the Twenty-First Century   440

Chronology   460
Selected Readings   473
Index   481
About the Author   503

Preface to the Seventh Edition

When the first edition of *The Soviet Colossus* was completed in 1984, the Union of Soviet Socialist Republics stood imposingly as a troubled but immensely powerful and seemingly durable military superpower. By the time the second edition of the book appeared in early 1990, the USSR, after five years of perestroika and democratic reforms, had undergone change beyond what anybody had expected a few years earlier. However, while badly shaken by the pace and extent of change, the Soviet state and its vast imperium still seemed likely to survive, even if in a drastically altered form.

The third edition of *The Soviet Colossus* appeared as a witness to the shocking collapse of the Soviet Union, at one time the flagship of international Communism, the world's largest country, one of the planet's two nuclear superpowers, history's first and mightiest totalitarian state, and a country whose social system was based on an ideology that at the peak of its influence governed the lives of one-third of the world's population and commanded the adherence of numerous intellectuals the world over. Yet this colossus crumbled over the course of a few short years and meekly ended up being proclaimed out of existence. The fourth through sixth editions of this book, retitled *The Soviet Colossus: History and Aftermath,* carried the narrative through a decade and a half of the post-Soviet era, by which time it was clear that Russia's exit from Communism had not been an escape from the serious troubles that sprang from the Soviet experience and, further, that having left that experience behind, Russia was not evolving into a Western-style democratic, capitalist society.

The seventh edition of *The Soviet Colossus* continues the methodology of the earlier editions, which focused first on the historical background that shaped Russia before the Bolshevik Revolution and then on pivotal turning points that led in turn to the establishment of the Bolshevik dictatorship, the development of Stalinist totalitarianism, the reforms and counterreforms under Khrushchev and Brezhnev, the dramatic changes that swept the country under Mikhail Gorbachev, and, in 1991, the pathetic end of the great experiment

Lenin and the Bolsheviks so confidently began in 1917. Regrettably, the 1990s did not see a successful transition to a democratic society and a functioning market economy but a spasmodic descent into a morass of political dysfunction, economic hardship, social disorder, unchecked criminality, and corruption on a massive scale. During the first decade of the new century, Russia under the leadership of Vladimir Putin has seen the establishment of greater order and an economic recovery, but at the price of the evolution of an authoritarian political system. In this edition, that apparent turning point is the subject of a new chapter, which covers Putins' presidency and the first year of his tenure as prime minister. There are also revisions throughout the text as well as condensations of certain sections in order to keep this book at a manageable length.

A few explanatory words about dates and the spelling of Russian names. By the nineteenth century, the Julian calendar used in Russia until February 1918 trailed behind the modern Gregorian calendar by twelve days, and by the twentieth century, by thirteen days. All dates in this volume prior to February 1918 are given according to the modern Gregorian calendar (with Julian-style dates, when needed, in parentheses). The spelling of Russian names is always a problem since transliteration is an inexact science at best. My standard has not been one of the various imperfect systems of transliteration currently in use, but rather the injunction to make the text user-friendly to this volume's typical reader, who probably does not know Russian. This has been done in large measure by using the most familiar spellings of famous or common names ("Trotsky" not "Trotskii") and the spelling of less well-known names as they appear most frequently in the mainstream American press. Thus (aside from in the endnotes and bibliography, and when referring to Aleksandr Solzhenitsyn), I use "Alexander" and "Alexei" rather than "Aleksandr" and "Aleksei." Sometimes there are inconsistencies regarding the name itself: Russia's tsars are called "Nicholas" or "Paul" since that is what American students are accustomed to seeing in their textbooks, while other Russians with the same name are called "Nikolai" or "Pavel." Some Russian intellectuals who emigrated to the West and published major works there become "Paul" (Milyukov) and "Nicholas" (Berdyaev)—the names that appeared on their books—instead of "Pavel" and "Nikolai." In most cases I have opted for "Peter" rather than "Petr," "Pyotr," or something similar. All of this will not satisfy the purist, but I think it will make it easier on the reader.

There is also the matter of what to call territories and peoples in the wake of post-Soviet name or spelling changes. When dealing with the period up to December 31, 1991, I refer to "Belorussia," which in the text becomes "Belarus" on January 1, 1992. The people who live in that region are called Belarusians throughout the text. The country known today as "Ukraine" is called "the Ukraine" prior to January 1, 1992, and I use the conventional spelling "Kiev" throughout the text for the city, now often spelled "Kyiv," that is its capital. Communism is spelled with a lower case "c" when referring to that concept in the generic sense and with a capital "C" when referring to the Soviet variant and its various offshoots. Finally, from 1917 until 1946 top-level Soviet government officials were called "commissars"; thereafter they became "ministers." To avoid unnecessarily wordy sentences, beginning in Chapter 15, which covers the period in which that change occurred, the term "minister" is used exclusively.

Acknowledgments

In writing the first edition of this book, I received invaluable help from Robin King, who read the entire manuscript and then spent many additional hours helping me rework large parts of it. I benefited from the expertise of Norman Naimark and Jeremiah Schneiderman and from the support and skills of Alex Holzman, my editor at Scribner's. I relied heavily on what I learned from William L. Blackwell, who guided me through my graduate studies at New York University. Many people helped me with one or more of the earlier editions of this book, and I have acknowledged them there; at this point I would like once again to mention Richard Ellman, Jay Corrin, John Zawacki, the late Zvi Meth, and the late Brendan Gilbane, for twenty-five years the dean of the College of General Studies at Boston University. No editions of *The Soviet Colossus* would have been written without the constant support and encouragement of the late Frederick M. Koss, for many years the chairman of the Social Science division at the College of General Studies, a wise and humane man, and a warm mentor and friend.

In preparing the past several editions, I received extensive help from William Tilchin, whose close and careful reading of large parts of the manuscript prevented innumerable errors from finding their way into print. My thanks to Robert Wexelblatt for critiquing several lengthy chapters of this edition and, as he has done in the preparation of earlier editions, for untangling mangled prose over the phone at almost any hour of the day or night.

I am grateful once again to Patricia Kolb, editorial director at M.E. Sharpe and my editor through the past five editions of this book, who has brought to this project her vast knowledge of Soviet affairs as well as her sound judgment, patience, and sense of humor. Ana Erlić and Makiko Parsons capably shepherded this edition through the labyrinth that lies between writing and publication. Therese Malhame did an excellent job copyediting the manuscript.

I would like to thank Yevgeny Yevtushenko for permission to reprint several lines from two extraordinary poems that brilliantly illuminate so much about

Soviet history: "Stalin Heirs" and "Half Measures." I am most grateful to Robert Conquest for taking the time to consult with me on the latest scholarship dealing with Stalin's Great Terror.

Special thanks to Florence Chvat for insightful criticism and moral support. I will always owe my parents, Paula and the late Victor Kort, far more gratitude than I can ever express. Since our childhood, Judith Kort Leider, my sister, has provided by example my most valuable lessons in how to face life's problems with courage and dignity. My daughters, Eleza and Tamara, who have grown up through the writing and rewriting of this book, remain the projects of which I am by far the proudest. My wife, Carol, took time from her own work to proofread and discuss with me, over and over again, many parts of this latest edition, an enormous undertaking for which I am deeply grateful. She remains through all editions of every book and for forty-one years my essential source of joy and common sense in everything I do.

Part I
The Fundamentals of Russian History

Dedicated to Peter the Great, Falconet's 1782 statue of the *Bronze Horseman*, in St. Petersburg's Senate Square, was commissioned by Catherine the Great. (Painting by Vasily Ivanovich Surikov)

1
Prologue

There was a dreadful time, we keep
still freshly on our memories painted;
and you, my friends, shall be acquainted
By me with all that history:
A grievous record it will be.

—Pushkin

For seven decades, the Union of Soviet Socialist Republics (USSR) was the colossus among the nations of the world. It sprawled over 6,000 miles from Central Europe across the breadth of Asia to China and the Pacific shore, and well over 2,000 miles from the semitropical Asian heartland in the south to frozen Arctic wastes extending toward the North Pole. Its influence stretched yet further into Europe, Asia, Africa, and even the Americas. Like the Russian Empire it succeeded, which an enthusiastic Russian nationalist once called "a whole world," the USSR, whatever one thought of it, surely was more than just another country. It stood like a giant astride the frontier between Europe and Asia and, although at its core European, was geographically and culturally a part of Asia as well. By the 1980s, over 280 million people lived within its vast borders, about 51 percent of them ethnic Russians, or "Great Russians," as they are sometimes called. The Russians are the most numerous of a group of peoples known as the East Slavs, who have lived in the region that eventually became the European part of the USSR for well over 1,000 years. Aside from the Great Russians, the USSR was populated by two other East Slavic peoples, the Ukrainians and the Belarusians (Belorussians); by Latvians, Lithuanians, Estonians, Armenians, Georgians, Azeris, Moldovans (Moldavians), Jews, and others in Europe; and by Uzbeks, Kazakhs, Kyrgyz, Tajiks, Tatars, Turkmen, and many others in Asia—well over 100 distinct national and ethnic groups in all. Its expanse was considerably more than twice that of Canada, its nearest competitor: over 8.5 million square miles comprising one-sixth of the world's land surface. And the USSR's power dwarfed even its size. Armed with a hydra-headed nuclear arsenal, it was the second-greatest military power in history, possessing an ability to annihilate that, while calculable, was unimaginable.

The USSR's core, like that of the fallen empire upon whose foundations it was built, was Russia and the Russian people, and its size and strength in many ways were a tribute to the Russian people's ability to endure and survive an almost endless gauntlet of hardships. Nature has imposed the most constant and inescapable of these. Most of Russia lies within the central and eastern portion of the great Eurasian plain. It is the largest such feature on the globe, stretching from Western Europe deep into Asia and Siberia, broken only by a low mountain range—the Urals—that is more of a landmark than a barrier to human or natural forces. The plain's major geographic feature is an extensive river system that for centuries was the region's main highway. Along the rivers laced between the Baltic and the Black seas, the East Slavs, ancestors to the Russians, Ukrainians, and Belarusians, first developed their civilization and national life.

To the north of the Eurasian plain are Arctic wastes whose winter winds annually sweep over the land to freeze most human activity no less than they freeze the rivers and lakes. A succession of mountain ranges—from the Caucasus in the west to the ranges of central and eastern Asia—demarcate the plain's southern boundary. To the east lie the highlands and mountains of eastern Siberia, where some of the coldest temperatures in the world have been recorded. The plain itself is divided into three main vegetation zones: the frozen, scrubby tundra in the north; the largest forest in the world, amounting to 20 percent of the world's total timber resources, in the center; and the steppe, the windy, often dry prairie containing Russia's richest soil, in the south.

Overwhelming in size and potential, this is a hard land, a northern land too distant from the Atlantic Ocean to benefit from the moderating Gulf Stream breezes that waft over the western fringes of the plain inhabited by other nations. The resulting climate is as severe as it is extreme. Winters are long and frigid. Summers are short and hot. The resulting short agricultural season is made even more precarious by other natural idiosyncrasies. In the spring the accumulated winter snows melt rapidly and run off as floodwaters, inundating rather than irrigating the farmers' fields. Rain falls most plentifully on the poor, thin soils of the forest zone, while the rich, black earth to the south must rely on sparser and often unreliable or ill-timed allotments. Although Russia is endowed with a treasure trove of natural resources, like most treasures these resources have been to a large extent out of reach, either too remote or too poorly located to be put to use. Only modern technology has made them exploitable. All this has forced the Russian people to expend their energies to produce a precarious existence that in the best of times generally meant a tolerable poverty. Bad times often have forced them to endure the intolerable.

Nature has placed at least one other crushing hardship on Russia. The Eurasian plain has no natural borders to separate its rival peoples or block invaders from the east or west. Russian history therefore is scarred with wars and invasions that repeatedly exacted their price in human misery when the Russians either fought each other, attempted to expand at the expense of their neighbors, or themselves were the victims of intruders. The period after the founding of the first East Slavic state—the tenth through the twelfth centuries—witnessed a cycle of ebb and flow, with the East Slavs cast both as aggressors and as victims. The next era was much harsher, as nomadic invaders from Asia increasingly pressured and eventually destroyed the weakened East Slavic state. From the middle of the thirteenth century until well into the fifteenth century no formally independent East Slavic or Russian state existed. By contrast, between 1700 and 1900 Russia was on the offensive in a large majority of its wars.

Most other nations, at least those that have survived, have enjoyed greater respites from the battlefield. Western Europe suffered through waves of invasions, but each wave was comparatively short-lived. By the eleventh century they had subsided, leaving most major European nations to develop in relative safety, sheltered by a semblance of natural boundaries and their own balance of power. The most favorably located were the English, whose ability to develop institutions of self-government owes a considerable debt to the narrow but stormy channel that insulated them from their neighbors.

Most fortunate of all were the ex-Europeans and their descendants who became citizens of the United States. America and Russia did have one thing in common: an open frontier. The American West and Russian Siberia were both sparsely populated lands inhabited by backward, poorly organized peoples unable to offer serious resistance to colonization. But here the similarity ends. No powerful enemy lurked behind America's western frontier or, for that matter, its eastern border. Thousands of miles of ocean protected the new nation to the east—and once it reached the Pacific, to the west—during its early stages of development. The frontier and the riches it contained meant only opportunity, and if conquering it imposed hardships and sacrifice on settlers and pioneers, this was only a price that individuals had to pay in order to take possession of the new land. One may not agree with the famous thesis of historian Frederick Jackson Turner that the frontier created American democracy, but it is hard to deny an important link between the nature of that frontier and the economic, social, and political achievements of the American people.

How different was the Russian experience. No oceans protected it, nor for long periods could its various rulers. The road was always open for invaders from Asia and Europe, and it was often taken. The invasions from the east reached a macabre and ferocious crescendo with the Mongol conquest of the thirteenth century. The descendants of these conquerors—whom the Russians called Tatars—settled on the southern portion of the steppe and made Russia's southern frontier a source of unrelieved misery. For centuries the Tatars, who established a state called the Golden Horde, ravaged the Russian land and its people. Not even Moscow in the distant northern woods was safe. As late as 1571, when Ivan the Terrible, one of Russia's most powerful rulers, was at the height of his power, a huge Tatar force besieged Moscow, burned down most of the city, and carried off tens of thousands of prisoners.

Even after Moscow was made safe from the Tatars, the conflict with them did not end. The struggle against the Tatars and later the Turks for control of the rich black soil of the steppe consumed 300 years. Meanwhile, in the west there were other formidable foes, including the Poles, Lithuanians, Swedes, and Germans. Between the mid-thirteenth and fifteenth centuries, besides forty-five wars with the Tatars, Russia fought forty-one wars with the Lithuanians, thirty wars with the German crusading orders, and a total of forty-four more with Swedes, Bulgarians, and other enemies. The approximate total of foreign invasions during this period was 160. In the 200 years that followed, fully eighty-five were spent in six wars with Sweden and twelve with Poland.

All this the Russians endured, and more. In doing so they saved more than themselves; they helped save the centers of Western civilization that so frequently ignored or despised them. Already at the dawn of Western culture and even before there were people known as Russians, in 512 B.C., the inhabitants of the Eurasian plain made the region's first contribution, however reluctantly or unwittingly, on behalf of the West. These accidental allies were the Scythians, a nomadic warrior people with an artistic flair they expressed in magnificent works of gold, who controlled the steppe for about 500 years. The Scythians indirectly helped a struggling Athens when the armies of Persia's Darius the Great pursued them deep into the endless plain. In the intervening centuries, much of the fury of invading Asian nomads was spent in Russia, sparing the luckier Europeans to the west. The Russians to an extent also protected their neighbors to the west from themselves. Russian endurance and the terrible winter of 1812 destroyed Napoleon's Grand Army and helped restore the balance of power fundamental to the European state system. In 1914, in the opening days of World War I, the Russian thrust into eastern Germany forced the Germans to transfer troops to the eastern front and left them unable to mount sufficient force in the west to take Paris. And in World War II, once Hitler finally turned his Nazi war machine against his former Soviet ally, the hard-pressed Western democracies received vital help when two-thirds of the German army first became bogged down and then was bled, frozen, and eventually crushed in the heart of Russia.

Russia had to build its state and institutions during centuries of conflict and calamity. Those who are critical of the form these took are missing the point; it is a tribute to the Russian people's courage and tenacity that they had the time and energy to build anything at all. Russia by its very setting was a land of extremes. No less than the extraordinary precautions they have always taken as individuals against the harsh weather, the Russians as a group had to use extreme measures to survive as a people. The institutions they eventually created for this purpose extorted a terrible payment from the nation they preserved: the political, civic, and economic freedoms that Westerners have come to take for granted.

Russia, then, was different from the West in many important ways. Among the critical European historical developments Russia missed were the Renaissance and the Reformation, both so important in shaping Western culture. All subsequent Western achievements were regarded in Russia with a mixture of fascination and fear, stopped at the border, so to speak, and searched for possible subversive qualities. Even in the periods when some Western ideas and institutions were embraced by certain Russians, their impact was limited. Russia's traditions remained dominant, transforming imports, sometimes beyond recognition, to conform to local conditions.

The great Bolshevik Revolution was supposed to fundamentally change Russian life. But any revolution, no matter how drastic its ends or means, inevitably reflects the historical legacy of a nation's culture, customs, attitudes, and institutions. In Russia that harsh legacy undoubtedly shaped the Bolshevik Revolution, even as the revolution so painfully transformed Russia itself. That is why, before examining the history of the USSR, we turn to a brief survey of the historical legacy inherited by the nation—or world—that was Russia before 1917.

2

The Autocratic State

The Tatars were unlike the Moors; having conquered Russia,
they gave her neither algebra nor Aristotle.

—Pushkin

In modern times Russia has been thought of as a monolithic colossus, weighed down by its oppressive social structure and autocratic government and therefore forever lagging socially, politically, culturally, and technologically behind Europe. It was not always so. During the ninth century the first East Slavic state developed along what was called the river road, a web of rivers forming a natural link between the Baltic and Black seas. A rather loose association of principalities with its center at Kiev on the southern reaches of the Dnieper River, Kievan Russia, as that state is usually called, flourished by virtue of its control of what had become the major trade route linking Europe with the civilizations to its east. This path became a thoroughfare after Arab expansion in the Mediterranean cut Europe's traditional means of access to the Middle East and the lands beyond. By the eleventh century Kiev was the largest city in Eastern Europe, a city of sufficient size, culture, and beauty to rival Constantinople, the glorious capital of the Byzantine Empire.

Because of the importance of foreign trade, Kievan culture was, for its day, relatively cosmopolitan and urban. Most of the population, of course, earned its living from subsistence agriculture, and although there was a large number of slaves in Kievan Russia, the bulk of the peasantry was free. Kiev was only one of numerous well-developed East Slavic towns that, like their European counterparts, had developed organs of self-government. Called *veches*, these councils shared power with assemblies of nobles and princes of Kievan Russia. There were some significant regional political differences. Nonprincely authority was strongest in the more developed areas of Kievan Russia: the *veches* enjoyed their greatest influence in the northwest and the nobles theirs in the south and southwest. In the northeast, a less-developed frontier area, princely authority predominated. This regional division became important *internal warfare*

→ decline of Kievan Russia be cause of atide of Eastern nomads &

later when foreign invasions shifted the center of gravity in Russia to precisely those areas where centralized princely government was strongest.

Religion was another factor that eventually assumed political importance. Late in the tenth century, Kievan Russia adopted Orthodoxy, the eastern branch of Christianity imported from the Byzantine Empire to the south. Most of Europe at that time followed Roman Catholicism. Those countries, like Russia, that were Orthodox found a major barrier separated them from their Catholic neighbors.

Whether measured by economic development, cultural achievement, or political institutions, Kievan Russia compared favorably with most of Europe. Although a frontier between Europe and Asia, Kievan Russia was not a back-water. Its culture carried most of the same seeds for growth as the European states. But in Kievan Russia these still-tender shoots were under the constant pressure of the nomadic peoples pushing into the European steppe from central and eastern Asia. By the twelfth century the disunited Kievan polity, weakened by internal feuding and warfare between contending princes, was unable to stem the invaders. They swept across the southern steppe, rendering both the trade route to Constantinople and the farming population of the southern steppe increasingly insecure. Trade and the cities dependent on it declined, and the population itself began to migrate to the relative security of the northeast. Another blow to Kievan Russia was the opening of a more direct trade route to the east via the Mediterranean Sea, a process that began as early as the eleventh century and accelerated after the Fourth Crusade of 1204.

THE MONGOL CONQUEST

Catastrophe followed decline. After an exploratory campaign, the Mongol armies, ruthless masters of cavalry warfare, burst out of Asia in 1237 to deliver to the Russians the worst blow they would ever receive. It would take them more than 200 years to recover their independence.

The actual conquest took three dreadful years. In Ryazan, the first city to fall, a witness recorded that "not an eye was left open to weep for those that were closed." Six years after Kiev was burned to the ground, a papal envoy found only 200 houses standing amid a landscape of wreckage and ruin. Many other cities suffered a similar fate. As much as 10 percent of the entire population may have been enslaved. The region's best craftsmen and artisans were deported thousands of miles to the east to serve the Mongol ruler, the dreaded khan. At home the quality of crafts and buildings dropped precipitously.

The Mongol conquest played a role in several long-term developments. Battered by the wholesale destruction of the conquest and bled by generations of subsequent exploitation, the Russian economy fell behind the economies of the West. Since the thirteenth century Russia has labored with a legacy of economic backwardness. Once independence was regained in the fifteenth century, a fundamental task of the state became to catch up with a rapidly advancing Europe. It has been a centuries-long chase that is far from over. The Mongol conquest also cut many of Russia's ties with Byzantium and, more significantly, with the West. While the West was enriched by Humanism and the Renaissance, Russian cultural development was stunted and considerably brutalized by poverty, oppression, and isolation. Another important development was the threefold division of the East Slavic people. Those who lived in the northeast and paid tribute to the Mongols came to be known as the Great Russians. Eventually they accounted for just over 70 percent of the East Slavs. In the west, two groups subject to the Lithuanians and the Poles emerged: the Belarusians, or White Russians, and the Ukrainians, or Little Russians. The former would comprise about 5 percent of East Slavs, the latter slightly less than 25 percent. Although these groups generally had as much uniting as dividing them, their differences at times have loomed large and emerged as powerful centrifugal forces in their history, strong enough, in the post-Soviet era, to divide them into three independent states.

Most important, the Mongol conquest had a major influence on the development of the Russian state. The next centuries would be the incubation period for a new political phenomenon: the Russian autocracy. The Mongols, to be sure, were not the only force behind this development. The old Kievan princes had enjoyed a great deal of power, especially in the northeast. Kievan Russia had also inherited the concept of caesaropapism—the idea that the monarch should exercise both temporal and spiritual powers—from the Byzantines. But these phenomena had been balanced by the power of the nobility and the city *veches*, particularly in certain western and southern cities. The extreme pressures during two centuries of Mongol domination virtually destroyed the *veches* and gravely weakened the power of the nobility in most of Russia. The field was largely left to the princes, and eventually to only one prince.

Although the Mongols ruled Russia indirectly, their state provided a model for its Russian princely puppets to follow. Power was centralized far beyond anything that had existed in Russia or would be achieved by the so-called absolute monarchies of Europe. The ruler, or khan, was in fact an absolute sovereign. All of his subjects were bound to serve his state. He was the sole owner of all land; all others held land on condition of service to the state. A grotesque form of equality was realized by the denial of freedom to all. The state's job was to maintain order and security and collect taxes necessary for those purposes. The state did not serve society; the state dominated it.

THE RISE OF MOSCOW

As agents of the Mongol khan, the Russian principalities tended to adopt their master's administrative methods. They also competed for the khan's favor, a critical factor in the struggle for survival. The most successful in this treacherous political roulette proved to be the princes of a small state in the remote northeast. A minor village during Kievan times, it gained importance as refugees from the endemic violence in the south swelled its formerly insignificant population. Its favorable location near the sources of the Volga and Oka rivers aided its economic growth. Blessed with a line of princes who were long-lived, intelligent, ruthless, and—perhaps most important of all—lucky, this tiny state grew and became stronger during the dark days of the fourteenth and fifteenth centuries. It proved best able to adapt to the conditions of Mongol rule and incorporate the basic tenets of Mongol government. Outstripping its more venerable and often more cultured rivals, it became the core of the new Russian state and society. It unified and eventually recast Russian society; its history became Russia's history. This was Moscow.

Muscovite society took shape under the most severe conditions. The principality lived under constant threat of foreign enemies: the Tatars to the south and east, the Lithuanians to the west, and the Swedes and German knights to the northwest. As if this were not enough, the Russian princes fought ninety wars among themselves between the mid-thirteenth and mid-fifteenth centuries. Survival meant the full mobilization of scarce resources in order to extract the maximum for state use. The affliction that would torment Russia into the twentieth century—the discrepancy between what Russia needed to compete with powerful rivals and the resources that were available to do the job—plagued Moscow from the start. With only scarce resources and primitive tools at their disposal, its princes were impelled to resort to compulsion to meet the state's needs. The enormity of the problems and the extreme measures used to solve them gave birth to the two fundamental institutions of Russian life: autocracy and serfdom.

To do its Sisyphean task, the Muscovite state grew until it could muster more power than its enemies, including the dreaded and hated Tatars. In the process it grew stronger than the society it was obliged to protect, finally acquiring the power to mold that society to serve state purposes. This meant in practice the destruction of all competing centers of power within the realm and the regimentation of most of the population. It meant taking control of most aspects of Russian life, leaving virtually no space for private activity. Through sheer energy and force, the state became the owner of most of the nation's wealth. As the distinguished Russian historian Vasily Kliuchevsky put it: "The state waxed fat, while the people grew lean."[1]

Seemingly a theme in Russian history: more than a theme, a fact of life

Control was even extended to people's minds. Absolute authority required avoiding unfavorable and therefore dangerous comparisons with life elsewhere. Russia had to be quarantined from subversive ideas, the most dangerous of which came from the West. Russia became highly insular and xenophobic; the few foreigners admitted to the country were forced to live apart from the native population. Foreign travel for Russians was extremely restricted; it was not the Communists but the regime they overthrew that first employed the technique of forcing Russians who traveled abroad to leave their families behind. Ever suspicious, the Russian state became the proprietor of an increasingly active political police and a pioneer in the use of terror to control society.

AUTOCRACY AND SERFDOM

The Russian autocratic state coalesced in the fifteenth and sixteenth centuries, especially during the reigns of Ivan III, the Great (1462–1505), and Ivan IV, the Terrible (1533–1584). Ivan the Great earned his title from Russian patriots because he completed the job of unifying Russia under Moscow's leadership and, in 1480, formally restored the nation's independence by renouncing allegiance to the Tatars. He gave his statement substance by mobilizing a large army that compelled an invading Tatar force to retreat rather than risk battle. Ivan also began the task of destroying the power of the old nobility, known as the *boyars*, the last remaining genuine obstacle to absolute autocratic power in Russia.

By the time Ivan the Great finished his considerable labors, all potential challengers to autocratic power other than the *boyars* had been eliminated. The Russian Orthodox Church, consistent with its Byzantine inheritance of caesaropapism, endorsed the state's expanding power. The loss of their independence had eliminated the princes as rivals to Moscow. Ivan's conquests also had destroyed the powers of the few remaining town *veches*. The somber finale came in 1478 with the annexation of the city-state of Novgorod, home of Russia's most powerful *veche*, and the removal of its bell, for generations its symbol and clarion, to permanent exile in Moscow.

The *boyars* were undermined by the creation of a new class of nobles. Unlike the *boyars*, who held their titles and estates on the basis of heredity, the new nobles held their estates, called *pomesties*, and their titles solely on the basis of service to the state. The *pomestie* nobles became the backbone of autocracy's huge military establishment and of the state apparatus. In some cases, creating *pomestie* nobles simply required parceling out newly conquered lands to loyal functionaries. But the process often became sticky, and bloody, involving forcible evictions and mass deportations. This did not deter Ivan in the least. Having conquered Novgorod, he dispossessed over 8,000 landlords of their hereditary estates and deported and resettled them on *pomesties* in outlying reaches of his expanding realm. Their old estates went, again on a conditional basis, to Ivan's reliable servants from Moscow. Ivan repeated this process several times as the few remaining independent Russian principalities fell under his control.

Ivan IV, the Terrible, finished what his grandfather began. Early in his reign Ivan immodestly promoted himself from Grand Prince of Moscow to Tsar (Caesar) of all the Russians. But tsar or not, the *boyars* still remained a powerful force in Ivan's dominions. His grandfather's methods having proven only partially successful, Ivan IV resorted to even more violent measures. He launched a legendary reign of terror that, with varying severity, lasted almost a quarter of a century. One of its victims, by the tsar's own hand, was his son. Another of Ivan's notable rampages occurred in Novgorod, where thousands of people were slaughtered and the once-proud city leveled. Ivan also gave Russia its first political police: the fanatical and deadly *Oprichnina*.

The *boyars* were decimated. The new nobility that emerged was a pliable tool of the state. Ivan had granted the nobility hereditary title to its estates, but at a price: an equally hereditary lifetime state service obligation. Genuine local self-governing bodies had been replaced by state institutions that were part of a centralized administrative structure. The country's enormous size and primitive communications limited the state's control, but Ivan the Terrible had largely made good his claim to being an absolute ruler. Barely a century after the Tatar yoke had finally been cast off, Russia had been resubjugated by its own autocracy.

It is important to realize how different this state of affairs was from what has ever existed in Western Europe. European travelers in Russia continually were struck by the absolute and arbitrary nature of the tsar's powers compared to that exercised by European monarchs. The early sixteenth-century ambassador of the Holy Roman Empire, hardly a bastion of democracy, had a typical reaction when he reported: "In the sway which he holds over his people, he surpasses all the monarchs of the whole world." In Europe the monarch's political power and property were separate; no such distinction existed in Russia. The tsar ruled the land as if he owned it, a claim no European monarch dared make. Unlike in Europe, the rule of law did not inhibit the Russian state. In short, in Europe even those with "divine" right to rule shared power with some of their subjects; in Russia they did not.

The Russian state, with its gargantuan military and administrative establishments to feed, had a voracious appetite that the primitive Russian economy could not satiate. This imbalance gave birth to the "grim monster, savage, gigantic, hundred mouthed, and bellowing" called serfdom. These words of

Alexander Radishchev, the eighteenth-century writer credited with being Russia's first revolutionary, aptly describe the most important social institution in Russia's history. Serfdom ended the peasantry's ability to take advantage of Russia's open plain, where new land and escape from Moscow's authority lay just over the eastern or southern horizon. The serfs were confined to the place of their birth and subject to the authority of their landlords. They were therefore readily available to serve the state's needs, whether to pay its taxes, fight in its army, or work on its building projects. Enserfing the peasantry alleviated an urgent labor shortage that had forced landlords to compete for peasants. The *pomestie* nobility was guaranteed a stable labor supply for its estates, thereby freeing it to render its service to the state.

Serfdom developed gradually, more or less parallel with the rising power of the autocracy. Over the course of about 150 years beginning in the late fifteenth century, Russian peasants were reduced to virtual slavery, subject, at the whim of their landlords, to being sold (sometimes without their families), tortured, jailed, exiled, forced to marry, forbidden to marry, and removed from the land. Their lot included a host of other deprivations and hardships as well. The Russian serfs, unlike the medieval European serfs, enjoyed almost no enforceable rights. If they were better off than slaves, as some claim, the Russian serfs still suffered from burdens slaves did not endure: slaves, at least, were spared the obligations of paying taxes and serving in the military.

The only compensation, if one assumes that misery does indeed love company, was that the serfs were not alone. The Law Code of 1649, which governed Russia for almost 200 years, froze the nation into several hereditary groups called estates. The service nobility, distinguished by its ability to abuse others even as the state abused it, headed the list of the tsar's subjects. Seven categories of townsmen and four of peasant serfs followed. Less significant were a shrinking number of free men and several varieties of slaves. The situation then and 200 years later was best summed up by Mikhail Speransky (1772–1839), himself the compiler of a later law code and the close advisor to two tsars: "In Russia I find only two estates: the slaves of the sovereign and the slaves of the landlord."

EXPANSION, SECURITY, AND WESTERNIZATION

Whatever its internal conditions, Russia was not to be confined to lands occupied by the Russian people. Independence for Russia soon meant subjugation for other nations. On the borderless Eurasian plain, there was no logical place to stop once a nation had acquired more power than its neighbors. The lack of natural frontiers meant that any area conquered immediately required yet another annexation to protect its security. Russia therefore quickly became a multinational empire, and eventually so many peoples were overrun that the Great Russians comprised less than half the empire's population. Russia came to be called, with some justification, the "prison house of nations."

Expansion was really nothing new for Russia; it was a basic component of the nation's history. Since Kievan times the Russians' East Slavic ancestors had been colonizing the empty or thinly settled regions of the forest and steppe beyond their own territory. Even when nomadic hordes were driving them from the southern steppe, the Russians were expanding into the forests of the northeast. By the 1560s, a more powerful Russia was aggressively on the move. The road westward was still blocked by powerful European states, while to the south the mighty Ottoman Empire held sway, but in the east the old Tatar states were decaying rapidly. During Ivan the Terrible's lifetime, Russians established themselves in western Siberia; within barely sixty years they had reached the Bering Sea. Later Russia accumulated the power to surge westward as well, so that while ominous, it was not entirely an exaggeration to claim, as a Russian newspaper did on the eve of World War I, that "after a thousand years, [Russia] is still on the march to its natural boundaries."

The Russian people benefited as little from their nation's rise to empire as the people they subjugated. The demands of governing a sprawling empire and alien peoples reinforced the state's autocratic tendencies. The new lands provided estates for additional legions of *pomestie* nobles who served the burgeoning needs of the state. But destruction of non-Russian power on the eastern steppe removed the main obstacle that had hemmed in the restless Russian peasantry. The nobility thus faced a ruinous loss of already scarce labor essential for farming its estates. The state reacted by tightening restrictions on the peasantry's freedom of movement. In a bitter reversal of the American frontier experience, available and accessible free land resulted in less, not more, freedom for those who actually farmed it. As their country's power rose, the Russian peasants sank deeper into serfdom. Somehow, even when Russia won, the Russian people lost.

By the seventeenth century Russia was master of its own house and increasingly master of parts of the Ukraine in the west and its more backward neighbors to the east. The autocracy had survived a dangerous succession crisis when the old royal line degenerated and died out shortly after Ivan the Terrible's death. It had expanded the ranks of the *pomestie* nobility and imposed state service upon it, and its new law code issued in 1649 had placed strict regulations on the entire population, especially the hapless serfs.

But Russia was not secure. Even in the sixteenth century, before the runaway advances of the industrial revolution, Russia lagged far behind the West in technology and organization, and therefore in power. Even its most formidable rulers met defeat when confronted with Western strength. Ivan the

Terrible was beaten in his exhausting twenty-five-year campaign to expand westward to the Baltic Sea. Peter I, the Great, was routed by a numerically inferior army of Swedes on the shores of that same Baltic in 1700. Competing with the West—and geography and the nature of the international state system left the Russians no choice but to compete—required first learning from the enemy. Learning required contact of all sorts, thereby enabling Western ideas about everything from philosophy to politics to penetrate Russia. The state's great unsolved dilemma after 1700 was how to import the Western technology that could be used to build up the autocracy while excluding the influences that might corrode and eventually destroy it. As the West developed its technology and produced new political and social ideas, Russia's difficulties worsened.

The impact Western Europe had on Russia has become known as Westernization. It later became a worldwide phenomenon in the wake of the spectacular rise of European power after 1600; Russia was one of the first societies to face its consequences, and thus the necessity of formulating a response. Westernization in Russia has meant different things to different people. To liberal-minded Westerners who feared the Russian autocracy and to some idealistic Russians who hated it, Westernization should have been an all-encompassing process of economic, political, and social modernization that would transform and democratize Russian society. To the Russian autocrats and their supporters, Westernization meant modern science and technology only. Any ideals or values potentially subversive to the autocracy would be filtered out, like so many pollutants.

PETER THE GREAT

This was precisely the attitude of Peter the Great, Russia's first systematic Westernizer. Peter spent much of his time learning from Europe, and he made his country do the same. His grandiose goals made this imperative. Like Ivan the Terrible, Peter was determined that Russia become a major European power. He therefore began a military buildup. The bloated armed force Peter created strained Russia's already arthritic fiscal, administrative, and social structures beyond their capacities. But despite its size, that force initially proved to be inadequate against the Europeans to the west and, for that matter, the Turks to the south. Russia clearly needed thorough modernizing.

The attitude of most of Russian society posed an equally difficult problem for Peter. Steeped in its own traditions, Russia had no desire to change. Not inclined to persuasion in any case, Peter used the Russian state's traditional method of force and repression to accomplish his Westernization objectives. He decided what was necessary and made sure that it was done; after a rebellion early in his reign the youthful tsar served as his own chief executioner. The ironic and terrible truth is that under Peter, Russia's first experience with modernization called forth cruelty that even exceeded Ivan the Terrible's madness.

Westerners were imported to provide the knowledge and skill for Peter's many projects; the Russians supplied the sacrifices. Russia's first modern industries were built and staffed by thousands of conscripted state peasants—unfree peasants living on state-owned land—who were attached to the factories for life, as were their descendants. The Russian people benefited little from these modern marvels. Peter's factories and mines served his war machine. The state was their chief promoter, either as the direct owner or through loans, subsidies, tariff protection, and—frequently—coercion designed to encourage private entrepreneurs. The state, with its burgeoning military sector, also was the main market for the new products. A new levy, the soul tax, was instituted to exploit Peter's subjects more efficiently; only the nobility and the clergy escaped this heavy new burden. Serfdom now bore down more uniformly and even more cruelly on the Russian peasants. Russia's upper classes were hounded into submission by the *Preobrazhenskii Prikaz*, Peter's dreaded and deadly political police. The central government's administrative apparatus was rationalized according to Western models so that it could better implement Peter's arm twisting and bone breaking, while a brand new navy and a modern army were shaped from the inchoate Russian military mass. Spiritual matters were attended to by stripping the Orthodox Church of its independence. It simply became part of the state apparatus.

The payoff came quickly in battlefield victories that established Russia on the Baltic coast. It is a proper tribute to Peter that when he built his capital there on pilings sunk into disease-infested swampland, the new city rose on the corpses of thousands of conscripted serfs who died laboring for their tsar. Peter quite logically called his city St. Petersburg; others, just as logically, called it "the city built on bones."

Peter the Great accomplished much of what he intended, pushing Russia's boundaries westward and erecting an updated absolutist state in place of the antiquated, rickety older model bequeathed to him. He established Russia's first industrial base and did more than anyone else to develop the nation's industry prior to the late nineteenth century. Russia's first experiment with Westernization had dramatically strengthened the autocracy, better enabling it to control the country while resisting Western social and political influences. Peter had served the Russian state, if not the Russian people, well. The state had a political police force and even directly controlled the nation's spiritual affairs. It now was the world's most formidable entrepreneur, its largest land-lord, employer, and capitalist. Peter certainly never intended it, but he provided an example for those who 200 years later would murder his descendants, destroy tsarism, and, by imposing sacrifices that not even he had demanded, give Russia more power than he could ever have dreamed possible.

RUSSIA AND EUROPE

Yet Peter's accomplishments soon began to erode. Insulated Russia could not keep pace with its intellectually more vibrant neighbors in the freer West. Merely borrowing technology meant that after a generation or two Europe was ahead again and the borrowing process had to be repeated.

Westernization also created new problems while it solved others. No matter how hard the state tried to prevent it, a thin layer of Russian society was exposed to and transformed by Western thought and culture. Members of this Westernized elite, whether they supported or opposed the autocracy, thus became alienated from the vast majority of the nation. Russia was being split into two unequal and mutually uncomprehending parts.

How to compete with Europe without becoming like Europe was a dilemma the Russian autocracy never solved. The horns of this dilemma fatally gored or crippled most significant reform plans when their inevitable implications—placing limits on the power of the autocracy—became clear. Because of this, for much too long, no reforms were undertaken to bring about the end of serfdom. To the contrary, during the second half of the eighteenth century serfdom's geographic reach was expanded. But during the nineteenth century the pressures on Russia intensified as the pace of European progress quickened. However selectively Russia modernized, subversive European influences were slipping in and corroding the autocracy and the social structure upon which it rested. By the middle of the century, fundamental changes, most notably the abolition of serfdom, could no longer be put off. By the end of the century, it was clear that the reforms adopted had not been enough. In order to understand how Russia did change and, more important, how it failed to change, it is necessary to glance at a few key developments in the nineteenth century, the last century that the crisis-ridden autocracy and the society it dominated managed to survive.

NOTE

1. Vasily Kliuchevsky, *Kurs russkoi istorii*, Vol. 3 (Moscow, 1937), p. 11.

3

The Nineteenth-Century Crisis

*One more century of the present despotism
will destroy all the good qualities of the Russian people.*

—Alexander Herzen (1851)

Russia the same

The amazing thing about nineteenth-century Russia is that the country changed so much while remaining fundamentally the same, with old problems left unresolved. During the course of the century Russian culture would flourish, serfdom would be abolished, and major reforms would overhaul the legal system and rural government. Economic development would make the empire the world's fifth-largest industrial power. Yet Russia's population remained overwhelmingly rural. The peasantry found its new freedom limited by an atavistic web of legal limitations and by wretched poverty. The traditional chasm between the ignorant masses and the educated elite widened rather than shrank, Westernization having created in Russia two separate cultures and societies. Meanwhile, although in 1762 Tsar Peter III freed the nobility from its obligation to serve the state, the autocracy retained a monopoly on power that it exercised through an ever-expanding bureaucracy. Tsarism was housed in an elegant capital city with an opulent court, but Russia remained poor and exhausted from her struggle to match the power of more advanced and prosperous European competitors.

Russia moved forward in spite of an autocracy that expended most of its strength in a quixotic crusade to contain the winds of change blowing in from all sides. All of the men who sat on the throne, whatever their differences in personality or style, were committed autocrats. One, Alexander II, instituted unprecedented reforms, including the abolition of serfdom. These reforms contained the potential to set Russia on the course of development that had occurred in the West. But in the end even he remained a loyal disciple of his heritage, like the Alexander and Nicholas who preceded him and the Alexander and Nicholas who succeeded him.

It is probably not unfair to say that Russia, faced by mounting challenges

19

and weighed down by increasingly obsolete social and political institutions, wasted the first half of the nineteenth century. The country's rulers, who were the logical products of a senile political order, refused to consider social change as a solution to the nation's difficulties. Alexander I (1801–1825), the conqueror of Napoleon, talked of reforms but instituted few. Eventually he became an unbalanced mystic, and he died without an heir. His death was the signal for what is known as the Decembrist uprising, a rebellion led by army officers from the nobility who wanted to make Russia a constitutional monarchy. Unlike the blindly violent peasant uprisings of earlier centuries, this was a revolutionary upheaval with a number of modern programs for political change. It was a forerunner of and inspiration for things to come. The immovable autocracy finally had a serious rival, a revolutionary movement that, if not irresistible, at least proved irrepressible. The rest of the century and the first part of the next one would be punctuated by an intermittent but unending duel between these two uncompromising forces.

THE REIGN OF NICHOLAS I

The Decembrist uprising permanently stained the reign of Alexander's successor, Nicholas I. Nicholas suppressed the rebellion and spent the next thirty years trying to keep the clock from moving. Commentators have not been kind to Nicholas. His nickname was the "knout." While there were signs of life, especially regarding economic development, the satirist Mikhail Saltykov-Shchedrin captured a central aspect of his country's reality during the second quarter of the nineteenth century when he glumly described it as a "desert landscape, with a gaol in the middle." Even Nicholas's supporters despaired of him, including one who lamented that "the main failing of the reign of Nicholas Pavlovich was that it was all a mistake."

Mistaken or not, Nicholas was determined to restore stability to Russia. He had good reason to be not only determined, but also frightened. Many of the Decembrists belonged to some of Russia's most venerable noble families. In 1826, only one year into his reign, Nicholas's fears found their institutional expression in the Third Section of the Imperial Chancellery, the innocuous name for what became Europe's most feared and pervasive secret police. Although Russia had known secret police organizations before, the scope of the Third Section's activities was something new. During previous reigns, the secret police had largely limited itself to searching out political enemies of the monarch and for years at a time had been abolished by one ruler or another. The Third Section proved to be far more durable and probed the work of writers, journalists, historians, and others for the slightest deviation from what the government considered the acceptable norm. This created an

Censorship from varying political & ideological sources has been a part of Russian society from Nicholas Pavlovich to the end of the Soviet Empire

atmosphere of suspicion in Russia unlike anything found elsewhere in Europe at the time.

Nicholas gave Russia a model for the modern secret police that became a fundamental fixture of Russian life until the last decade of the twentieth century. He also gave Russia its first comprehensive censorship code and a criminal code containing fifty-four pages of political crimes. Historian Richard Pipes has called this code "a veritable charter of an authoritarian regime . . . to totalitarianism what the Magna Carta is to liberty."[1] Between organizing the Third Section and compiling the new criminal code, Nicholas also found time to proclaim a catechism of beliefs for his subjects. Called "Official Nationality," this new formula defined loyalty to Russia on the basis of three principles: autocracy, orthodoxy, and nationality. Autocracy reaffirmed the absolute power of the throne. Orthodoxy asserted the role of the Russian Orthodox Church as the nation's official religion. Nationality stressed the special nature of the Russian people and devotion to the nation's traditions and the status quo. To make sure the people got the message, the government sponsored its own corps of journalists—the despised "reptile press"—to extol Russian virtues and condemn the subversive liberal and democratic notions filtering in from Europe. Meanwhile, the complex demands of controlling an enormous nineteenth-century empire not permitted to govern itself encouraged the expansion of Russia's already overgrown bureaucracy.

But time would not stand still, not even for a tsar. Capitalism was taking root in Russia and beginning to tear fissures in the agricultural economy based on serfdom. The spread of education and European ideas overwhelmed even the efforts of the Third Section to keep Russia ideologically pure. By the middle of the century a new class of intellectuals had emerged, an extraordinarily brilliant group that initiated the "Golden Age" of Russian literature, a period of towering achievement that lasted into the 1880s. Pushkin, Lermontov, and Gogol wrote their major works during Nicholas's reign, while Turgenev, Dostoyevsky, and Tolstoy made their first appearances on the literary horizon. Some of Russia's writers, led by literary critics like Vissarion Belinsky, produced another important, albeit largely political, creation: a tradition of opposition to the autocracy. Hounded by the Third Section and the censors and denied the right to a meaningful role in Russian political life, a significant part of the educated elite turned against the autocracy and made literature and art vehicles to express that opposition. The inability of the Russian state to win the loyalty of a large portion of its educated citizens was a critical factor in undermining the autocracy and the social order it was committed to defend.

Nicholas's obsession with repressing liberal or reformist ideas did not stop at Russia's frontiers. It led him to intervene in European affairs, earning Russia the epithet "the Gendarme of Europe." The apparent growth of Russian power finally led the Western powers to oppose by force Russian schemes against the Ottoman Empire. The resulting Crimean War, which broke out in 1853, ended in disaster for the backward Russian army. Nicholas himself did not survive the war; neither did many of his policies. The war, already lost by 1855, was concluded in 1856 by Nicholas's son, the new tsar, Alexander II. Russians were shocked by their nation's inability to defend itself against the small but modern forces the Europeans had sent against it. Russian backwardness had again led to military defeat, and the realization that drastic reform was necessary reached even the tsar and his advisors. Russia had to modernize in order to compete with Europe, something it could not do so long as serfdom continued to stifle economic development. No less important, the extent and seriousness of peasant discontent threatened the entire social order. These imperatives produced the era of the Great Reforms. *Zemstvos / rural self-gvt. — limited*

ALEXANDER II AND THE GREAT REFORMS *→ independent judiciary*

On March 3 (February 19), 1861, Alexander II abolished serfdom in Russia. Whatever the shortcomings of his edict, and there were many, it remains the greatest single act of emancipation in history. More than 20 million serfs on private estates were freed from the authority of their landlords, five times the number of slaves liberated by Abraham Lincoln in the United States two years later. The Emancipation Edict was followed by several other major reforms, the most important of which were the establishment of organs of rural self-government called *zemstvos* and the reform of the legal system. The latter created for the first time in Russia an independent judiciary based on the Western model. Other important measures reformed town government and the system of military service.

The Great Reforms opened an era of Westernization unique in Russian history prior to the Gorbachev era of the 1980s. Russia had "Westernized" before, primarily under Peter the Great, and would again under the Communists, but in both those cases "Westernization" meant only physical modernization: new factories, industrial techniques, administrative techniques, and the like. The relationship between the people and the state remained the same. The Great Reforms were different, perhaps not in their intent, but definitely in their results. Although the peasants remained subject to numerous legal restrictions, the abolition of serfdom did make the economy more flexible and hence helped promote industrial and commercial development independent of state control and interference. The establishment of an independent judiciary put a small dent in the arbitrary nature of the state's authority. One of the main differences between Russian and Western societies had been that in the West—even in the "absolute" monarchies—citizens were protected from the

West
• Rule of law
  — Customs & legal precedent
  Sort of safeguard people
  Under absolute rule

Russia
Tsar is arbitrary and absolute ruler

THE NINETEENTH-CENTURY CRISIS ⚒ 23

state by legal norms and rules. In short, those societies were governed by the rule of law. Naturally, the development of the rule of law varied from era to era and state to state, but the situation in Europe stood in dramatic contrast to the untrammeled, arbitrary, and virtually absolute authority of the Russian state. For the most part this remained the case even after the judicial reform, but a crucial seed for change had been planted and had begun to germinate. The question was whether it would have the proper climate in which to grow. Complementing this development was the limited self-government introduced in the towns and in the countryside. Again, actual self-government as known in the West remained a distant goal, but for the first time since the days of the *veches* Russia had institutions upon which it might someday be based.

Nonetheless, it is essential to remember that however bright the reforms shone in contrast to the dark background of centuries of inertia, the autocracy had no intention of seeing their democratizing potential realized. Alexander II may have been called the "Tsar-Liberator," but he was a tsar first, determined to maintain all of his autocratic powers. His goals were economic development and the strength it produced, not democracy. In this he was no different from Peter the Great. His response to a group of nobles who shortly after the emancipation petitioned him for an elected national assembly was typical of his outlook; Alexander threw them into prison. Hopes that the tsar would "crown" his reforms with a constitution and make Russia a genuine constitutional monarchy proved to be illusions. After a Polish rebellion in 1863 and an attempt on his life in 1866, Alexander began to chip away at his reforms. Hope turned to disappointment and then despair, feeding the revolutionary fervor among Russia's educated youth. That fervor cost the Tsar-Liberator his life. In 1881 he was assassinated by a small group of young revolutionaries whose members believed the tsar's violent death would spark a nationwide socialist upheaval.

ALEXANDER III AND THE "COUNTERREFORMS"

The new tsar, Alexander III, was the perfect ruler to preside over a policy of reaction. Alexander III illustrated his attitude toward political reform when he issued a manifesto declaring he would discuss his empire's destiny only with God. When the latter was not available, Alexander relied on Konstantin Pobedonostsev, a steadfast reactionary who denounced democracy, a free press, public education, and even inventions with remarkable vigor. His advice included telling the tsar that a bloody revolution was preferable to a constitution.

Guided by Pobedonostsev, Alexander III weakened or gutted many of the Great Reforms. His "counterreforms" included drastic restrictions in the authority and representative nature of the *zemstvos* and on the independence of the judiciary. The tentative steps taken toward self-government and the rule of law were now rapidly retraced in a race back to bureaucratic and police rule. At the same time, in an attempt to unify his multinational domains, Alexander intensified the pressures on millions of non-Russian minorities through a policy of forced Russification. Poles, Ukrainians, and others suffered, as did religious minorities, but the most victimized were the Jews. They now were caught in an inexorably tightening vise of deep-seated popular anti-Semitism and government-imposed discrimination. The main result of the regime's harsh treatment of non-Russian minorities was that the revolutionary movement, until Alexander's time an almost exclusively Russian enterprise, received a massive dose of new non-Russian recruits. Several of the key men who helped bring Vladimir Ulyanov (Lenin), himself a Russian, to power in 1917 and who played pivotal roles in his government were non-Russians, including Lev Bronstein (Trotsky), an atheist Jew, ignorant and contemptuous of the traditions of his ancestors, who organized the Bolshevik coup and the Red Army; Felix Dzerzhinsky, a Pole of aristocratic birth, driven by a militant hatred of social privilege and a fanatical devotion to the revolution, who became the first head of the Soviet secret police; and Joseph Dzhugashvili (Stalin), a rebellious Georgian seminary student turned revolutionary and a man of unlimited ruthlessness and ambition, who eventually emerged as Lenin's successor.

Alexander III fastened on Russia a bureaucratic and police rule more intense than the country had ever known. The most important vehicle for this was the notorious decree of August 14, 1881.[2] This "Statute Concerning Measures for the Protection of State Security and the Social Order," an allegedly temporary measure that remained in force until 1917, immediately subjected large parts and eventually most of Russia to regulations similar to martial law. The authorities and police now were specifically permitted to arrest, imprison, fine, and exile citizens, close down businesses, ban public meetings of all kinds, and turn people over to military courts. No trial or other legal proceedings were necessary. Public employees could be fired without cause and, under certain circumstances, elected officials dismissed and the *zemstvos* closed down. As if this were not enough, in 1882 the police received even more power. Now people placed under what was blandly called "overt surveillance"—and it could happen to anyone—became virtual police prisoners, their every move and activity subject to police approval. The long list of disabilities ranged from being barred from several fields of employment to being forbidden to move without permission or join a private organization. These people could be searched at any time and denied their mail. Meanwhile, the political police was reorganized and renamed the *Okhrana*, a term that would become synonymous with the most sinister and sophisticated secret police machinations.

Thus, at a time when most European nations were broadening popular participation in the political process, a development deemed essential for mobilizing national strength, political life in Russia in effect was rendered illegal. At the dawn of the twentieth century, the bureaucracy and police still ruled in Russia.

Alexander III did enjoy some successes. He managed to reign without a foreign war and his economic policies promoted impressive industrial growth. Yet his repression had only stalled, not destroyed, the revolutionary movement. At his death in 1894, a new revolutionary generation already had made its debut. Left to deal with this and other mounting problems was the tragicomical figure Nicholas II. At his coronation as the ruler of one-sixth of the world's land surface he confided, "I know absolutely nothing about matters of state." When his reign was brought to its sudden end in 1917, he could have made the same statement without fear of contradiction.

The reign of Nicholas II marked the final failure of the autocracy to reform adequately in the face of increasingly rapid social and economic change. Out of that failure came a political struggle between a huge reactionary state and a tiny revolutionary minority. The question that immediately arises is why these two forces—a corroded autocracy and a motley collection of revolutionaries—dominated the political stage between 1825 and 1917, with the rest of Russian society serving as little more than so many set pieces. Why, unlike in the West, was there no powerful counterweight in the middle to the combatants at the extremes? What were the different classes of Russians doing while the battle raged that would decide their fates?

NOTES

1. Richard Pipes, *Russia Under the Old Regime* (New York: Charles Scribner's Sons, 1974), p. 295.

2. The name of this decree reflects the date it was issued according to the Julian calendar. It was issued twelve days later according to the modern Gregorian calendar.

4

The People

Your majesty has 130,000,000 subjects.
Of them barely more than half live, the rest vegetate.

—Sergei Witte to Nicholas II (1898)

Most Russians, it turns out, were just trying to survive. In the second half of the nineteenth century five-sixths of the Russian people were still peasants. Very few of them had managed to rise above the level of bare subsistence. From the early eighteenth century until 1861 the peasantry fell into two major groups: serfs and state peasants. Serfs were bonded to land owned by private landlords and were subject to their authority. The serf therefore served two severe masters: the state and the landlord. The major obligations owed the state were high and often confiscatory taxes and, if the serf was unlucky, what amounted to a lifetime of military service. The debt to the landlord was paid either in labor in the landlord's fields or by payment in kind or in money. The state peasants, created by Peter the Great in the 1720s from the approximately 20 percent of the peasantry that somehow had avoided serfdom, lived on state-owned land. They also were bonded to the land but, serving only one master, and a more distant one at that, were somewhat better off than the serfs. Because of government policies and better overall economic conditions, the state peasants increased in number faster than the serfs and actually slightly outnumbered them by the last decades of serfdom. Aside from their interminable struggle with the elements, the state peasants' major worry was that they might lose their modest status. Until emancipation, state peasants could be given to private landlords, in which case they became serfs, or conscripted as laborers to industrial enterprises. This latter fate frequently was worse than enserfment. The conditions of their emancipation under a separate law issued in 1866 left them better off than the ex-serfs in several important respects, but as time went on the overall problems and misfortunes the two groups shared dwarfed these differences, making them little more than varying degrees of

Serfs — or military service — State peasants
(handwritten margin notes)

- bound to landlord & state
- Confiscatory taxes (even after 1861)
- landlord's debt was paid in the fields or by money

State peasants
- slightly better off
- taxes still high
- bound to state land
- could be sold into serfdom
- or made to work in Industrial factories

misery. Most peasants, both before and after emancipation, also shared the obligatory status of being members of village communes, institutions of limited self-government that primarily assisted the state in regulating peasant life and guaranteeing tax collections.

By the time serfdom finally was abolished, it had brutalized most of the Russian people and disfigured Russian life. To appreciate the extent of the damage, the reader who understands the festering effects of slavery on American society that lingered after the Emancipation Proclamation needs only to recall that serfdom was for centuries the most pervasive institution in Russia, not a "peculiar institution" confined to one region and ensnaring only a minority of the population. Slavery had been the major cause of the American Civil War, and the problems left unsolved by emancipation and Reconstruction cast a shadow on many aspects of American life well into the twentieth century. Similarly, emancipation in Russia was incomplete and left unsolved many of the worst problems associated with serfdom. As historian G.T. Robinson has noted, "the Emancipation of the 'sixties contributed powerfully to the making of the Revolution of 1917."[1]

THE PEASANTRY AFTER EMANCIPATION

The problem with the emancipation was its narrow scope: it simply freed the serfs from the authority of the landlords without addressing the gap between the peasantry and the rest of Russian society. The emancipation was limited because the government feared the peasantry and continued to concern itself primarily with the interests of the landed nobility. Post-emancipation peasants at best were second-class citizens. They were still subject to the authority of special courts and to corporal punishment. The individual peasant could leave the land only with great difficulty. He was forced to remain a member of his commune and remained subject to its authority.

The most damaging aspect of emancipation was its economic shortcomings. Emancipation took a primitive, unproductive, and inflexible rural economy and actually exacerbated some of its problems. In 1861, the landlords' estates were divided between the landlords and the peasants, the former getting about two-thirds of the land—mainly because in addition to their share of the farmland they retained most of the pasture and forest areas—and the latter the rest. That smaller portion came at a very high price. Peasants were sold land that they were unable to choose at inflated prices they were unable to negotiate. The landlords retained the best land. Because the ex-serfs did not have the available cash to pay for their land, the government paid the landlord, and peasants were given forty-nine years to repay the government. The installments were called redemption payments. This arrangement, combined with high taxes, turned virtually all ex-serf peasant families into bad financial risks unable to meet their obligations. The arrears mounted each year until, in 1905—two famines, innumerable rural riots, and one unprecedented revolutionary upheaval later—the government finally got the point and abolished the redemption payments and cancelled the debts they had caused. In comparison to what the former serfs received in 1861, the former state peasants in 1866 were given larger land allotments at lower prices. They at least initially were able to satisfy their basic needs.

Another serious problem was the failure to change the inefficient system of peasant land tenure. In most parts of Russia, land was still owned and controlled by the commune (or *mir*). Each peasant household held an allotment consisting not of a unified plot, but a series of strips, often as many as twenty or thirty and as narrow as six feet in width, scattered over the countryside. The impossibility of farming efficiently under such conditions was increased by the custom of periodically redistributing the land. This eliminated the incentive to make any long-term improvements. But the commune was a time-tested instrument for controlling and taxing the peasantry, and so it was retained after 1861 (and again in 1866) and given the additional critical job of assuring that the redemption payments were met. The commune remained an albatross around the neck of the peasantry, choking attempts to increase rural productivity.

In some respects emancipation actually made things worse. As serfs, the peasants at least had access to the forest and the meadowland of the landlord's estate. This provided essential supplements to what the peasant could earn from farming, including important resources such as firewood. These benefits were lost when the landlord was granted most of these lands in the 1861 settlements. Meanwhile, the population of Russia increased rapidly during the second half of the nineteenth century, turning what already was a land shortage into a crisis. The average peasant land allotment dropped by almost a quarter in the last twenty-five years of the century. Additional hardship resulted when the growth of industry undermined the cottage industries that provided a margin of survival for many peasant families. Finally, harsh government tax policies squeezed the peasants even further. The rural standard of living declined until, in 1891, when the harvest failed with so many families living right at the subsistence level, Russia experienced one of the worst famines in its history. More than peasants died this time, however; so did patience with the autocracy. Disgust and shame swept through large sectors of educated Russian society. Many members of the younger generation turned to revolutionary groups sprouting up in the universities.

Emancipation, then, had not materially helped the majority of the peasantry. As the twentieth century was about to begin, the peasants still lived "worse than cattle . . . they were coarse, dishonest, dirty, and drunken." Anton Chekhov, the great playwright and author who provided this unkind but accurate description in 1897, did not blame his countrymen for their crudeness. Their lives, he explained, were dominated by "crushing labor that made the whole body ache at night, cruel winters, scanty crops, overcrowding; and no help and nowhere to look for help." Such miserable people were hardly likely to concern themselves with common political matters or issues of governmental reform. "For the peasant," historian Richard Charques observed, "all the constitutional government in the world mattered less than an acre of land."[2]

THE NOBILITY

[handwritten marginal note: Russia's autocracy had, knowingly or not, pitted it's nobility against it's peasants, with the state in the middle protecting (badly) the former against the latter]

No less absorbed by the struggle to survive was the Russian nobility. Even before losing its serfs in the emancipation, the nobility, unable to manage its own affairs, became totally dependent on the autocracy. Ivan the Terrible had shattered its political power in the sixteenth century. Peter the Great had debased the nobility even further, and a temporary rise in its fortunes in the second half of the eighteenth century, when it had freed itself of state service and received a charter enumerating its rights from Catherine II (1762–1796), had not lasted long. Catherine's successor, her mad son Paul, revoked much of what his mother had granted, proving that charter or no charter, the nobility was incapable of protecting itself from the tsar. It was equally incapable of protecting itself from the lowly peasantry, a point driven home by the great rebellions led by Stenka Razin in the seventeenth century and by Yemelyan Pugachev in the eighteenth century. Even in quiet times, the nobility knew that only the autocracy stood between it and the sullen and seething serfs.

Even more debilitating, most of the nobility, its titles notwithstanding, was poor. Primogeniture—the passing of an estate intact to the eldest son—did not exist in Russia. Estates therefore were continually divided among an ever-increasing number of noble sons. The government estimated that ownership of at least 100 serfs was necessary to live like a gentleman, yet fewer than 20 percent of the nobility had that many. Historian Richard Pipes has concluded that 98 percent of the nobility lacked an income from its estates adequate for a "decent living."[3] The backwardness and low productivity of the countryside had impoverished not only the peasantry but the nobility as well. Its only recourse to supplement its income was bureaucratic work provided by the government. Even this did not help enough; by 1861 the nobility had mortgaged over 75 percent of its serfs. It had a fitting literary symbol: Ilya Ilyich Oblomov, the novelist Ivan Goncharov's fictional character who wakes up in the morning and spends most of the day deciding whether to get out of bed.

After emancipation, the nobility was totally unprepared to cope without its serfs. Despite governmental attempts at resuscitation, the nobility just became sicker and sank deeper into debt. By the end of the century it had sold one-third of its remaining land and mortgaged much of the rest. During the new century the decline became more rapid.

THE MIDDLE CLASS

In Europe the decline of the landed nobility was accompanied, and in fact hastened, by the rise of the middle class. The growth of Europe's middle class in turn had been promoted by the increase in trade and the relative security and freedom that existed in the European cities. In Russia few of these conditions existed. The country's isolation had retarded its economic development, and what economic opportunities did exist had been hoarded or closely regulated by the omnipresent Russian state. Not until after the Emancipation Edict did the Russian economy develop to the point where a genuine commercial and professional middle class began to emerge. It grew significantly during the period of rapid industrial growth in the 1880s and 1890s. But the Russian middle class was only a tiny part of society as a whole. Like the nobility, it faced an overwhelmingly powerful state that blocked its attempts to exert political influence. And like the nobility it was dependent on the state for protection, in this case from foreign competitors and from another class it had created through its own efforts: the small but militant Russian proletariat. Westerners and certain Westernized Russians who wanted Russia to follow the European capitalist and parliamentary path of development pinned their hopes on Russia's middle class. These hopes proved to be too heavy a burden for this fledgling and weak class, caught between the unyielding autocracy and the angry masses.

THE PROLETARIAT

"The working class? I know of no such class in Russia," Pobedonostsev commented less than twenty-five years before Lenin and the Bolsheviks would seize power in the name of that class. At the time Pobedonostsev spoke, the working class, several million strong, certainly existed, but barely. It labored under incredibly oppressive conditions. The working day at the close of the nineteenth century often ranged from twelve to as many as eighteen hours, the legal limit of eleven and a half hours notwithstanding. Many workers lived in rotting tenements so crowded that people had to sleep in beds in shifts; others made their homes on the floors next to the machines they tended. Labor unions were illegal. For their efforts, the workers watched their real wages fall during the entire period between 1860 and 1900.

The ex-peasants who suffered so much in Russia's factories did have one advantage over their rural compatriots. Russia's late start in developing industry meant that when factories were finally built, often with European capital and expertise, they reflected the latest in technology and economy of scale. Therefore, although small in number in 1900—about 3 million—the Russian proletariat was concentrated in large factories clustered in a few industrialized regions. These workers, accessible to and often influenced by university students ready to enlighten them about revolution and socialism, developed a surprising cohesiveness and solidarity. Because everything was so concentrated, a well-organized strike could spread very quickly and became extremely disruptive. And because the proletariat was so wantonly exploited and had so little to lose, it responded to calls for drastic action and change.

THE NON-RUSSIANS

Finally, centuries of Russian expansion had created an empire that by the late nineteenth century was only one-half Russian. Many of this vast collection of peoples, some closely related to the Russians and others totally alien from them, opposed not only the tsarist regime but Russian imperial control over their lands and lives. Intensified repression during these years only increased ethnic consciousness and inflamed discontent across the non-Russian parts of the empire. All of these problems played into the eager and passionate hands of a tiny group of secular crusaders who called themselves revolutionaries.

NOTES

1. Geroid Tanquary Robinson, *Rural Russia Under the Old Regime* (Berkeley: University of California Press, 1967), p. 65.
2. Richard Charques, *The Twilight of Imperial Russia* (New York: Oxford University Press, 1958), p. 27.
3. Richard Pipes, *Russia Under the Old Regime* (New York: Charles Scribner's Sons, 1974), p. 295.

5

The Intelligentsia: Strangers in a Strange Land

Is this normal? Everything is abnormal in our society.

—Dostoyevsky

The revolutionaries emerged from a new segment in Russian society created by the spread of education and Western ideas. Called the intelligentsia, this was a group with no real counterpart in the West. The Russian intelligentsia of the nineteenth century should not be confused with what are called intellectuals— well-educated and cultured people who may but do not necessarily have any particular interest in politics. The Russian intelligentsia's main concern, by contrast, was politics. It is probably best defined as that group of Russians whose members combined a certain level of education and awareness with a social conscience and a commitment to making significant changes in Russian society. It was also true that those who fit this description were odd men out in nineteenth-century Russia: "Foreigners at home and foreigners abroad," in the words of Alexander Herzen, one of their number. Their education and political commitment had made the members of the intelligentsia strangers in their own land, cut off by their expanded horizons from the ignorant and superstitious masses and stifled and hounded by an autocracy that would not let them implement their ideas for improving their country. These conditions and the resulting alienation did not exist in the West, where, whatever the social imperfections, the gap between educated elite and the general popula-tion was smaller and the opportunity to participate in the political process was greater. Aside from what it reveals about Russia's problems, this alien-ation was of fundamental historical importance because it created in Russia the first significant group independent of the autocracy and therefore able to challenge it.

The intelligentsia was a polyglot group that varied within a given genera-tion and from one generation to another. It therefore espoused a variety of solutions to Russia's problems. Russia's earliest modern revolutionary thinker, Alexander Radishchev, in the 1790s called for the abolition of serfdom and for a republic that would guarantee individual rights. The Decembrists, Russia's first active revolutionaries, split into two main groups. The majority wanted some sort of constitutional regime based on Western models, while others advocated a centralized dictatorship. In the 1830s and 1840s, some members of the intelligentsia wanted change based on old Russian traditions, others called for a democratic federal republic, and a small minority urged a conspiratorial revolution or a vast peasant upheaval. Beginning in the 1860s, opinion was split for several decades between those putting faith in the peasants and those trusting only members of the intelligentsia itself as capable of making a revolution. Of course, this debate over the type of change needed and the means of accomplishing it went on for so long and shifted ground so many times because for decades *nothing* seemed to work.

Nevertheless, over time, the intelligentsia underwent important changes that intensified the frustration and alienation of many of its members and therefore its determination to make a revolution. Its history really begins in the 1830s and 1840s. Its members then were predominantly nobles whose exposure to Western society made them ask searching and subversive questions about their backward, poverty-stricken, and repressive homeland. These nobles were divided into two categories. A conservative group called the Slavophiles wanted reforms to be based on what it believed was Russia's indigenous traditions. Opposed to this was a liberal group called Westerners, who felt that Russia had to follow the European model of development. As education spread, the intelligentsia expanded and changed. Beginning in the 1840s and particularly after 1860, the noble intelligentsia was reinforced and eventually engulfed by elements from the nonnoble classes. These new recruits included, among others, the sons of priests, who abandoned dedication to God for dedication to society; the children of lower-level civil servants; and, later, the sons and daughters of the Russian middle class. The Russian word for these people—*raznochintsy*—literally means "people of various ranks." This new generation, the "sons" of Ivan Turgenev's classic novel *Fathers and Sons*, often had known poverty and physical deprivation as well as alienation and tended to be far more radical and uncompromising than its elders, Turgenev's "fathers," in both its political goals and the methods by which it proposed to achieve them. The "sons," who came to the fore in the 1860s, and the generations that followed them, constituted what may be called the revolutionary intelligentsia.

The theories and programs developed by the revolutionary intelligentsia tended to be absolutist, unrealistic, or both. This happened because for decades the intelligentsia lived and worked in a vacuum. At no time prior to the 1890s did it have any meaningful contact with a broader audience. The peasants were beyond reach and, unlike in the West, there was no substantial middle class to provide an interested and active public. The result was that theory remained untempered or modified by the necessity of winning widespread support or by the opportunity of being put into practice. These theories were further hardened by the repression to which the revolutionary intelligentsia was subject. In short, nineteenth-century Russian conditions made for political abstractions, not practical politics.

At no point did the revolutionary intelligentsia make up more than a small portion of Russia's educated elite. But the minority that did belong, like Gideon's army, made up for its lack of numbers by an indefatigable courage born of faith. It was appalled by the poverty, inequality, and injustice that pervaded Russian life and driven by a passion to rectify everything that was so terribly wrong. Split into factions, divided by ideological disputes, isolated by distant places of exile and prison walls, the revolutionary intelligentsia was united by an iron determination to do good. Somehow it would make a revolution that would destroy the old society and replace it with one without fault. In the face of seemingly impossible odds, the revolutionary intelligentsia persisted, and, after several generations marked by poverty, imprisonment, exile, hard labor, and sometimes untimely death, it made its revolution and seized power. Then, like the bee whose very act of attacking and stinging its victim is suicidal, the revolutionary intelligentsia found that its success soon sealed its own doom.

SLAVOPHILES AND WESTERNERS

The intelligentsia, revolutionary or not, faced two critical problems: deciding what the ideal Russia should look like and devising the means to implement the desired changes. During the 1830s and 1840s, the Slavophiles and Westerners debated the first issue. Influenced by German idealism, which stressed the uniqueness of each individual nationality, the Slavophiles looked backward into Russia's history. They felt that Russia had once been a much better place, a spiritual and harmonious society that was disrupted by the reforms of Peter the Great. The spiritual and cooperative instincts of the people had been reflected by their religion—Orthodoxy—and by the peasant commune. The latter supposedly had been a spontaneous creation of the peasants themselves. Russia's problems could be traced, the Slavophiles argued, to Western influence in general and to Peter's reforms in particular. Soulless Western rationality had to be driven out of Russia and the old national spirituality restored to its proper place. Serfdom had to go, but not tsardom. Instead, the pre-Petrine benevolent and paternal monarchy had to be restored. A benevolent autocracy, not a legalistic constitutional or parliamentary regime, was the most suitable form of government for Russia. And once Russia had returned to its moral ways, the Slavophiles added, it could teach the world how to live.

The problem was that this Slavophile vision was a fantasy. The key Slavophile–Westerner battles were fought over the history of the peasant commune, and the Westerners produced convincing evidence that the commune as it existed in the nineteenth century was largely a mechanism of taxation and social control connected with the evolution of serfdom. The Westerners, however, had problems of their own, best illustrated by the difficulties encountered by Alexander Herzen, possibly the most brilliant of the generation that entered the political stage in the 1830s. Herzen was an ardent Westerner—until he learned about the West firsthand. Like the other early Westerners, he was strongly influenced by French socialist thought and himself espoused a vague sort of socialism. After going into exile in Western Europe in 1847, Herzen witnessed the revolutions of 1848 that swept across large parts of the continent before collapsing. Herzen was demoralized by these failures. Socialism had not triumphed. Capitalism and all the exploitation associated with it now seemed entrenched in Europe. To Herzen, the Western path of capitalism and materialistic bourgeois values was as unacceptable as what existed in Russia.

It was at this point that Herzen took a leaf from the Slavophiles and rediscovered the Russian peasantry and its commune. Unlike the Slavophiles, however, Herzen did not want to use the commune to recreate a version of Russia's idealized past. Instead, it was to become the springboard for Russia to leap over the wilderness of capitalism into the promised land of socialism. Russia's backwardness, once a curse, now became a virtue because it had preserved the venerable commune. In the process, the Russian peasant—brutal, miserable, superstitious, and greedy—was transformed into an instinctive socialist. Some of the ease with which Herzen executed his theoretical gymnastics is perhaps explained by his virtual ignorance about how the Russian peasant really lived. At any rate, the belief that socialism in Russia could be realized on the basis of peasant collectivist instincts and the commune without first going through the horrors of capitalism later acquired a more elaborate theoretical framework and a name: populism. It became and remained the dominant political creed of the intelligentsia for the rest of the nineteenth century. For a long time, until its spectacular but Pyrrhic victory of assassinating Tsar Alexander II in 1881, populism had the stage to itself, an era long enough to stamp the revolutionary movement with important characteristics it never really lost.

Having opted for a socialist Russia, Herzen faced another problem. How would the new social order be put into place? What would move the heretofore immovable autocracy, and what form of government would take its place? A fellow nobleman, Mikhail Bakunin, put his faith in the creative power of a nationwide violent peasant upheaval. Other Russian socialists issued similar calls, but not Herzen. A basically humane and moderate man, he saw little that was positive in mass destruction and warned his comrades that "whenever somebody's blood is spilled, somebody's tears will flow." He had the same reaction to those who were ready to resort to a revolutionary dictatorship once the autocracy had been overthrown. These people, Herzen complained, were guilty of "Peter the Greatism," a reference to the tyranny and suffering that occurs when the power of the state is used to impose "progress" on an unwilling people.

CHERNYSHEVSKY AND THE "NEW MEN"

Herzen never found a means for realizing the revolution and socialism, and the search was continued by populist revolutionaries who followed him. But a critical change took place. Some important members of the new generation of populists discarded Herzen's reservations and scruples and replaced them with a pitiless, unflinching outlook known as nihilism. Nihilism rejected all existing values and institutions as being hopelessly corrupt or useless. Conventional standards of behavior or ethics were abandoned in favor of an absolutist moral code that justified any means to help achieve the end of revolution. Because all existing institutions were condemned as rotten, destruction for its own sake was transformed into a creative act. Nihilists did believe in progress, placing enormous faith in the ability of modern science and the scientific method to solve social problems. Yet in fact they recognized as valid only those scientific discoveries and theories that seemed to support revolutionary political goals. Finally, nihilism emphasized the crucial revolutionary role of a self-appointed elite that had mastered these revolutionary tenets.

It is true that very few of the revolutionaries from the 1860s on called themselves nihilists, but the nihilistic code developed during that decade put its brand on an important segment of the Russian revolutionary tradition. The linchpin of the new attitude was that everything could and should be subordinated to the revolution, morality included. Traditional values and standards of behavior had to give way if they interfered with the imperative of revolution, regardless of the pain involved. Nikolai Chernyshevsky, the single greatest hero for two generations of revolutionaries, including many populists and a Marxist named Vladimir Ilyich Lenin, warned his fellows that their path was not a pristine one:

all a means to an end:
Revolution & (supposedly) the greater good

This highroad of History is not a sidewalk of the Nevsky Prospect. It passes all the way through open fields, dusty and muddy; at times it cuts across marshes or forests. If one shrinks from getting covered with dust and dirtying one's boots, then one should never enter into public activity. This is a salutary occupation if one is really inspired by the idea of the good of mankind, but it is not a particularly clean occupation. *However, there are different ways of defining moral purity.* (Italics added.)

Chernyshevsky and many of his comrades defined moral purity as anything promoting the revolution, even if terrible suffering resulted. If the people had to sink even deeper into misery to get them to act, so be it. In discussing the Emancipation of 1861, Chernyshevsky commented that "it would have been better if the extreme reactionaries had their way over the reform and liberated the peasants without land: there would have been an immediate catastrophe." And once the revolution came, what if certain roadblocks required that the new progressive rulers employ even greater oppression than had the reactionary autocracy? "Does it really matter?" Chernyshevsky asked. After all, peaceful and calm development is impossible, for "without convulsions there could never have been a single step forward in history."

The revolutionary imperative caught more than morality in its net. Art and beauty also had to do their part. In the 1840s, Vissarion Belinsky—"furious" Vissarion, as he justifiably was called—formulated the thesis that literature was obligated to carry a progressive message. Because in Russia writers were the "only leaders, protectors, and saviors from the desolation of the autocracy," a writer could be forgiven an "inferior" book that was poorly written, but never a "harmful" one that carried the wrong political message. Chernyshevsky insisted that it was the responsibility of all writers to address the proper social and political issues; art for art's sake, in his opinion, was "useless." A leading literary critic of the next generation, Dmitry Pisarev, went further, declaring that literature was a waste of time. "I utterly reject the notion of art having in any way promoted the intellectual or moral advancement of mankind," he intoned.

The ultimate manifestation of the intelligentsia's deification of the revolution was its subordination of the Russian people, supposedly the reason for all this trouble, to that end. The peasantry might be idealized as the instinctive carrier of socialism, but was in reality credited with little more than instinct. It had to be led and molded by the self-appointed elite. Chernyshevsky was convinced that "the mass of the population knows nothing and cares about nothing except its material advantages." This indifference, he added, was what created the possibility for an effective leadership to institute change. Chernyshevsky summed it all up in a sentence Peter the Great or Pobedonostsev might have used: "The mass is simply the raw

Populists, in creating their new state, wanted power for themselves Citing peasant ignorance & immobility. It seems to me that they were not truly interested in making Russia better, just in changing who is in charge

material for diplomatic and political experiments. Whoever rules it tells it what to do and it obeys."

Chernyshevsky was not alone in his beliefs. Before him, the Decembrist Pavel Pestel proclaimed his intention to organize a centralized revolutionary police state, and Vissarion Belinsky endorsed the brutal methods of Peter the Great, whom he characterized as a "hero and demigod." After Chernyshevsky, the populist Peter Tkachev insisted that a revolutionary minority had to do the job of changing Russia, because if the people were allowed to do what they wanted, "you will soon discover that they won't do anything new." The people, Tkachev warned, "can never save themselves." Therefore the revolutionary minority, by virtue of its "superior intellectual and moral development," had to hold power. A generation later Vladimir Lenin echoed these sentiments when he insisted the professional revolutionaries had to lead the working class to socialism because the masses, on their own, could develop only reformist, or what he called "trade union," consciousness.

Bolshevik Communist believed this idea as well

In Russia this may be true because they know nothing else & have never had the opportunity to try anything else

Chernyshevsky also provided the model of what a revolutionary life should be, a contribution that won him the adoration of several generations of revolutionaries. He created that model in an artless and tendentious novel called *What Is To Be Done?* a book Lenin admired so much that he used the same title for his first major political pamphlet. Chernyshevsky's book is filled with heroes and heroines ready to endure anything for the cause. One of them, Rakhmetov, engages in constant exercise and eating regimens to prepare himself for his destiny. Not even sleep gives him pause, for this magnificent revolutionary specimen sleeps on a bed of nails. These were not ordinary people, Chernyshevsky stressed. They were "superior beings, unapproachable by the likes of you or me." His "New Men" were "as the caffeine in tea, the bouquet of noble wine, they give it its strength and aroma. They are the flower of the flower of men, the motor of motors, the salt of the salt of the earth."

Beneath the purple prose, Chernyshevsky's "New Men" emerge as a caste of new revolutionary supermen saving the downtrodden and hapless masses. As such, why should they not be permitted to employ any and all means to achieve their noble ends? Chernyshevsky had no problem with this; neither did many of the activists of the 1860s and 1870s who strove mightily to become in reality what Chernyshevsky could only write about. There were some, however, who dissented from this line of thinking. A number of influential revolutionary thinkers, such as Herzen and after him Peter Lavrov and Nikolai Mikhailovsky, strenuously warned against the dictatorial implications of such an attitude. In fact, the ultra-elitist tendency exemplified by Chernyshevsky and Tkachev was a minority opinion in every phase of the Russian revolutionary movement, as it was in the 1870s, when Lavrov's influence was paramount. But it remained a powerful undercurrent, its failures notwithstanding, in the wake of the majority's own failures and the unsuppressible gnawing fear that something had to be done soon lest Russia follow the capitalist-parliamentary path of the West.

Rejection of the West, even by men like Herzen and Lavrov, turned out to be extremely important. Russian history provided no example of how to keep the state under control. Western Europe did, but Herzen, Lavrov, and many other Russian revolutionaries rejected Western parliamentary and legal institutions as being tools of bourgeois exploitation, just as they rejected the capitalist economic institutions with which they were associated. Mikhailovsky came closest to advocating a constitutional regime; he even discussed the matter with some prominent liberals in 1879. But these discussions reached no agreement. In short, the prevailing attitude among the revolutionaries of all stripes was opposed to the political system spawned in the West no less than it was to the one spawned in Russia. Presumably there was a third possibility for governing a large modern society, but finding it turned out to be a puzzle the Russian revolutionary movement never solved, a failure that had momentous and terrible implications for the Russian people.

CONSPIRACY

By the 1860s, after a quarter century of writing and reading, the intelligentsia finally was ready to act. Its revolutionary crusade had begun, but for a long time it would be a lonely crusade. The revolutionary intelligentsia may have been ready for action, but the peasantry, the class whose mass strength was to supply the revolution's power, was not. Its horizons bounded by poverty, ignorance, and superstition, the peasantry remained loyal to its "Little Father," the tsar. The first phase of the active struggle against tsarism has a neatly defined beginning and end: 1861, the year Tsar Alexander II liberated the serfs; and 1881, the year revolutionaries assassinated the Tsar-Liberator. What occurred in between was less tidy, as the revolutionaries waged a fruitless and frustrating struggle to spark the great uprising they needed to create a socialist Russia.

It might seem incongruous that the emancipation itself pushed the intelligentsia to active struggle, but it was precisely the Emancipation Edict's limits and the burdens that it put on the peasantry that extinguished the last flickering hope that satisfactory change could be accomplished by tsarist reform from above, a hope held until 1861 even by figures like Herzen and Chernyshevsky. Subsequent events brought further disappointments, driving some revolutionaries to extreme theories and desperate measures.

During the mid-1860s many revolutionaries were arrested, an experience that convinced those still in the fray that only the most tightly organized conspiratorial party could succeed against the autocracy and its political police. This elitism also received a boost when the people failed to answer the revolutionary clarion. Peasant disturbances that occurred between 1861 and 1863 in the wake of disappointments related to the emancipation soon faded. In 1866, the peasantry responded to an assassination attempt against Alexander II, by a group calling itself "Hell," by choosing to believe a rumor that the attempt was a plot by landlords angry over the loss of their serfs. Instead of rebelling, peasants demonstrated in support of the tsar and even beat up a few radical students.

Among the new leaders who emerged after this debacle were two men who further promoted the revolutionary movement's elitist and conspiratorial disposition: Sergei Nechaev and Peter Tkachev. Although they briefly worked together, they are important for different reasons. Nechaev carried the concept of revolutionary morality with its logic of the ends justifying the means to its ultimate and scandalous conclusion. To promote the revolution, Nechaev was quite willing to use blackmail, extortion, and, in one case, even murder, not against the oppressors but against his fellow revolutionaries. Among the victims of his lying and deceit were Herzen, Mikhail Bakunin, and the prominent populist Mark Natanson. There also was an unlucky agricultural student named Ivanov, whose murder Nechaev arranged because Ivanov openly doubted him. Nechaev had proclaimed that the revolutionary was a "lost man," a person with "no feelings, no attachments, not even a name of his own." When he wrote these words his fellow revolutionaries did not react adversely; when he lived by them they were horrified and ashamed. But it was easier to repudiate the man and his individual actions than to deal with the problem of revolutionary zeal leading to amoral and corrupting actions, a problem that haunted the Russian revolutionary movement long after Nechaev, who was convicted of murder and died in prison, was in his grave.

Peter Tkachev was a populist without any faith in the peasantry's ability to consummate the revolution. His great fear was that a delay in the revolution would force Russia to follow the European path of development and lose its chance to skip capitalism and jump directly to socialism. He therefore focused on the specifics of how the intelligentsia could seize power as quickly as possible.

Tkachev developed, to a far greater degree than had been done before, a program for a revolution organized and led by a centralized, disciplined party of revolutionaries that would implement socialism by means of a minority dictatorship. First and foremost, he emphasized that only the most tightly organized party could have any chance of success:

If organization is necessary for a large and strong party, it is undoubtedly even more indispensable for a weak and small party, for a party which is only beginning to be formed. Such is the position of our social revolutionary party, and for it the problem of unity and organization is a problem of life and death. . . .

The masses would be involved and their support would be sought, but only as followers being told what to do. Finally, once power had been seized, the party would keep that power for itself and use force, if necessary, to set up its utopia since, as Tkachev saw it:

The revolutionary minority must be able to continue its work of revolutionary destruction in those spheres where it can hardly reckon on the genuine support and assistance of the popular majority. That is why it must possess might, power, and authority.

GOING TO THE PEOPLE

All this plotting and scheming about setting up conspiratorial parties and revolutionary dictatorships did not escape criticism, especially after the scandal caused by Nechaev's sinister and bloody machinations. In Peter Lavrov, the revolutionaries of the 1870s found a more restrained counsel. Lavrov echoed Herzen's criticism of reliance on an omnipotent state to build a new society. Russia had experienced more than enough of overpowering states, Lavrov argued. Russia's revolutionaries should rather base their actions on moral and ethical principles that recognize that the revolution had to be made *by* as well as *for* the people. A dictatorship, regardless of what it called itself, would be "hostile to a socialist system of society." It would corrupt "even the best of people" and leave the basic problem in Russia unsolved. "Dictatorship," Lavrov warned, "is torn from the hands of the dictators only by a new revolution."

Lavrov's criticism of revolution by conspiracy and dictatorship appealed to an intelligentsia chastened by the Nechaev episode. So too did his call to "go to the people," to go into the villages and turn the peasants into revolutionaries by propaganda that addressed their everyday needs. The assumption was that the peasants were socialists by an instinct who simply had to be made aware of their true feeling by enlightened emissaries.

In 1874, without the benefit of any central organization or direction, 2,000 students descended on the countryside armed with their revolutionary fervor and faith in the socialist potential of the peasant. What these youths found instead during their "Mad Summer" were desperately poor farmers suspicious of the intruders from the universities and overwhelmingly convinced of the goodness of their tsar. They had no interest in or instinct for socialism. Rather they aspired to acquire more land and become prosperous capitalists in their own right. Adding injury to insult, the peasants proved quite willing to betray the students to the police. For many young revolutionaries the summer that began so full of hope proved to be a way station to years in prison and Siberian exile.

The disaster of 1874 was followed by a smaller and equally unsuccessful revival in 1875. Faith in the peasants' socialist instincts received a justified blow from which it never fully recovered. Thus in 1876 a group of revolutionaries in the Chigirin district in southern Russia was discovered inciting revolution not with a socialist program, but with a forged manifesto in which Alexander II allegedly called on his people to rise against the evil nobility and bureaucracy. The Chigirin affair was doubly embarrassing to the revolutionary movement, both for what it said about the new lack of confidence in the peasantry and, more important, for what it said about the ethics of the revolutionaries involved. They were, after all, using fraud and deceit against the very people they were supposedly leading in a noble cause.

The defeats in the countryside in 1874 and 1875 were followed by defeats in cities in 1875 and 1876, when the police succeeded in destroying revolutionary organizations in Moscow and the southern port city of Odessa. These organizations had represented the first effort to radicalize Russia's small but growing factory working class. The final blow dealt to the revolutionaries of the 1870s was a series of trials in 1877 and 1878. These resulted in harsh sentences for many of the young idealists who had been swept up by the ubiquitous tsarist police net.

All of this revived conspiratorial tendencies and engendered a new cynicism among the revolutionaries concerning the ability of the people to act for themselves. The trauma of 1874 and 1875 ran deep. More and more revolutionaries were becoming panicked by the realization that they had to succeed before the natural course of events transformed Russia into a capitalist society with a strong bourgeoisie. This terrible prospect would end the flickering hopes that Russia might leap directly from backwardness into socialism. Once the bourgeoisie was entrenched, a socialist revolution, the populists felt, would be far more difficult to achieve.

TERROR

The new weapon employed to avoid the specter of capitalism was terror, specifically the assassination of selected state officials. Terror eventually became the main political tactic of a newly formed secret party, Land and

Freedom, organized in 1876. The hope was that assassination could disrupt the functioning of the state and cause its collapse. For a while the government seemed genuinely stymied and confused by the new turn of events. Repression was increased. In 1879, the country was divided into what amounted to six military districts, but still the terrorists could not be stopped. Nevertheless, the primacy of terror as a political weapon was not universally accepted, and Land and Freedom split over the issue in the summer of 1879. One faction, calling itself Black Repartition, remained committed to propaganda; it soon metamorphosed into Russia's first Marxist group. The other, the People's Will, reaffirmed the use of terror and decided to go for broke: it would assassinate Tsar Alexander II. Presumably, with its head cut off, the entire tsarist system would collapse.

The People's Will, a small, militant sect rather than a political party, was a laser beam focused on the tsar. As its name implied, the People's Will maintained that the "downtrodden state of the people" gave it both the right and the obligation to act in their place. The group accepted as permissible any means that led to its revolutionary ends. In early 1880, the People's Will blew up the tsar's dining room in the Winter Palace, killing eleven people and wounding more than fifty, but Alexander was not present when the explosion took place. This was the closest the organization came to success between late 1879 and early 1881 in six failed assassination schemes, several of which did not get beyond the planning stage. Then, on March 13 (March 1), 1881, decimated by the arrests of its top leadership, the remnant of the People's Will staged the group's desperate last hurrah. Two young assassins each threw a bomb at Alexander. The first device, thrown at the tsar's carriage as it passed down a St. Petersburg street, did Alexander no harm but caused him to step down from the safety of his vehicle to check on those who had been injured; the second, thrown from close range at his feet, where he was more accustomed to seeing his subjects bow down, fatally wounded the Tsar-Liberator.

The assassination of Alexander II brought two eras to a close. The first was the period of reform initiated by the autocracy. Alexander II may have vacillated and even undermined some of his own reforms, but they were still momentous. The new tsar, Alexander III, instituted an era of repression and reaction reminiscent of the reign of Nicholas I. Progress toward broadening the political process in Russia came to a screeching halt for twenty-five years.

The assassination also marked a turning point in the revolutionary movement. The members of the People's Will who had survived to kill Alexander II did not long survive their triumph. They were quickly rounded up and hanged. The police-state measures introduced in 1881 and 1882 kept things quiet for the rest of the decade. Yet silence did not mean the absence of meaningful activity. A new generation of revolutionaries was thinking about what had gone wrong. Some of them began to look beyond the peasantry and conspiracy by isolated groups of revolutionaries to a changing society that was producing new agents and possibilities for revolution. They spoke about dialectics, historical materialism, and the proletariat. Marxism, the quintessence of revolutionary thought, had come to Russia.

Part II

The End of the Old Order

The Russian imperial family in 1913, surrounding Nicholas II, the last tsar. (Photograph from the London Illustrated London News and Sketch)

6

Capitalism Comes to Russia

*I . . . shall preserve the principle of autocracy as firmly and as
unflinchingly as did my late unforgettable father.*

—Nicholas Romanov, Tsar of Russia, 1895

*The Romanov Dynasty will end with Nicholas II.
If he has a son, the son will not reign.*

—Vasily Kliuchevsky, Russia's leading historian, 1895,
upon hearing Nicholas's comment

More than just a century was drawing to a close in Russia by the 1890s. The
iron tentacles of Western Europe's industrial revolution finally had reached
eastward into Russia, taken hold, and torn irreparable fissures in traditional
Russian society. Although many Russians refused to acknowledge what was
happening—from revolutionary populists who dreamed of a peasant socialist
Russia spared the ravages of capitalism to arch-conservatives and reactionaries who were determined to preserve Russia's hallowed traditions—their
visions and commitments were helpless to stop capitalist development. The
old dreams and days were numbered, the countdown having begun several
decades earlier with the emancipation of the serfs.

Two crucial factors shaped the development of Russian capitalism: the
disproportionate role played by foreigners and the direct involvement of the
state. Foreigners played such a pronounced role because Russia lacked
the capital resources and technical skills necessary for extensive industrial
development. Foreign investment eventually accounted for one-third of the
total industrial investment in Russia, with a particular concentration in such
basic industries as iron, coal, chemicals, and oil production. Foreign loans to
the Russian government also provided the capital the state needed when it took
over the job of building Russia's railroad network in the 1880s. As always in
Russia, the state mobilized the nation's resources because no institution or

social class was able to do the job. In fact, despite the gradual development of a Russian bourgeoisie after 1860, the state's role in the national economy increased with each passing decade between 1861 and 1900.

THE BURDENS OF BACKWARDNESS

Actually, Russia's military and strategic priorities, not economic development per se, determined the state's policies. After 1862, the autocracy actively began to encourage railroad construction. The Crimean War had made it clear that a modern railroad network was needed to move Russian troops and supplies quickly to future battlefields. It also would tie the sprawling empire together, thereby promoting both the government's authority and economic activity. Unfortunately, the cost put an intolerable burden on the already strained state treasury. Foreigners would not risk investing in Russian railroads unless their debts were guaranteed by the state, and since the autocracy barely managed to cover its normal expenditures, it was forced after 1862 to rely heavily on foreign loans to meet its expanding obligations. These loans further compounded Russia's financial troubles, since more foreign investment and loans could be lured into Russia only if the government was solvent and the local currency reasonably stable. The government therefore had to balance its budget and, to protect its currency, maintain a favorable balance of trade. When in the 1880s the government decided that the empire's strategic and economic needs would be better served if it built the necessary railroads itself, the huge costs of direct railroad construction made balancing the budget still more difficult.

The difficulty of balancing the budget was compounded because agriculture, still the main source of wealth in Russia, had made relatively little progress in the decades immediately after the emancipation of the serfs. Some advances had been made in raising Russia's chronically low agricultural productivity, as a few landlords managed to modernize and raise the productivity of their estates. Grain exports tripled between 1861, when serfdom was abolished, and 1880. Yet the agricultural landscape as a whole remained a bleak patchwork of backward noble estates and inefficient peasant allotments, and the value of the grain exports themselves was reduced by abundant crops flooding the international market from new foreign sources, particularly the United States.

The state's financial tangle therefore became a noose around the necks of the Russian peasantry, the group that still bore most of the tax burden. First, the soul tax was raised by 80 percent. Later, when that tax was abolished, the government placed taxes on most things the peasants needed or wanted, including matches, tobacco, and alcohol. The continuing quest for a favorable balance of trade resulted in an unrelenting export of grain. Even in a *famine* year, 15 percent of the grain harvest might be exported. It is hardly a wonder that the public dubbed these shipments "starvation exports." One minister of finance, Ivan S. Vyshnegradsky, who deserved more credit for candor than compassion, summed up the policy when he observed that "We may go hungry, but we will export." Russian peasants bore the burden of that policy.

Still, the statistics looked reasonably good. Along with railroad construction, Russia's coal and iron industries registered impressive growth. Banking and credit institutions prospered. Russia's factory working class grew at an unprecedented rate.

None of this helped the autocracy. It staggered from financial crisis to financial crisis. Each finance minister in the first three decades after the emancipation—Mikhail Reutern (1862–1878), Nikolai Bunge (1881–1886), and the quotable Mr. Vyshnegradsky (1887–1892)—ended his tenure in failure. By the end of Vyshnegradsky's term, it was clear that only a far stronger economy than Russia had been able to build could generate the productivity and revenues needed to remain a great power. Vyshnegradsky was working toward that end when in 1891 he had the tsar enact a high tariff designed in part to protect and foster the growth of Russian industry. But Vyshnegradsky's taxes left the peasants with virtually no reserves. Bereft of its grain reserves, the country experienced one of the most terrible famines in its history. Aside from the horrors of the famine itself, Russia and the world were treated to a sordid sideshow when the government tried to limit its bad press and protect its credit rating by minimizing the seriousness of the situation. For a time, the government prevented private relief efforts, insisting that they were unnecessary. Reality soon forced the regime to relent. It also moved the autocracy to resort to the most vigorous industrialization policies since the days of Peter the Great in an effort to break the chain of backwardness and poverty that kept Russia bound in constant crisis.

THE WITTE SYSTEM

The man who led that effort was the new finance minister, Sergei Yulevich Witte. Witte was the outstanding Russian statesman of his generation and among the most competent that tsarist Russia managed to produce during its last century. Yet his career as finance minister ended as it began, with Russia in deep crisis. Russia was starving when he assumed office in 1892. In 1903, when he was dismissed from his post, southern Russia was experiencing a massive series of industrial strikes, parts of southwestern Russia had been shaken by large peasant riots just the year before, and the entire country stood less than two years away from a full-fledged, though ultimately unsuccessful, revolutionary upheaval. Paradoxical as it might seem, from the point of view of social stability and the survival of the autocracy he served, it was not only

Witte's failures, but his very successes, that made things worse. Nothing better illustrates the difficulties Russia faced than Witte's successes and debacles as finance minister between 1892 and 1903.

Witte, as Peter the Great before him and Joseph Stalin after him, was driven by a sense of the urgent need to industrialize. The new finance minister felt that Russia faced far more than a military or financial problem. Despite the progress of the past thirty years, Russia in 1892 was still predominantly an agricultural, peasant country. Its rivals in Western Europe, by contrast, were modern industrial powers, and although Russia was politically independent, its economic relationship with Western Europe was of the classic colonial type. Russia served Europe as a market for industrial goods and a source of raw materials. "International competition does not wait," Witte warned. If Russia did not overcome its backwardness and awaken from its "economic slumber lasting two centuries," it would be overwhelmed by its more advanced competitors. Russia's military situation would become untenable because in an industrial age the ability to produce modern machines translated directly into military power. Beyond that, the increasing foreign ownership of Russia's economy "may gradually clear the way also for the triumphant political penetration by foreign powers." In other words, Russia easily could become another India or China—colonized or carved up by the industrialized West.

Modern industrial capitalism, Witte argued, was the solution to Russia's most pressing problems. Although he expected that ultimately private enterprise could be stimulated to the point where it could guarantee Russia's further progress and prosperity, he believed that for the moment only the autocracy had the resources to take the initiative. Industrialization, Witte insisted, could best be promoted by massive railroad construction. This would stimulate the metallurgical and fuel industries, and these in turn would stimulate light industry, a pattern that already had occurred in Western countries. Such a chain reaction would give Russia an industrial base sufficient to compete with Western industries and, by dramatically expanding Russia's productivity, would generate enough revenue to end at last the state's chronic deficits.

Railroads were the basis, not the totality, of Witte's program. He also implemented a broad series of supporting measures. These included providing subsidies and credits for key industries, building technical and engineering schools, promoting banking, using the state's purchasing power to support certain industries, protecting Russia's fledgling industries behind the tariff of 1891, and putting the Russian ruble on the gold standard, to name only a few. The last measure, by guaranteeing the stability of Russia's currency, enabled Witte to attract large amounts of foreign capital to Russia in the form of new industrial investment. It also enabled him to borrow more than ever before and thereby balance the government's budget, now stretched to the breaking point by his railway building projects and the growing needs of Russia's military establishment.

The results were spectacular by any standard. During Witte's tenure as finance minister, Russia's industrial production doubled, growing at an annual rate of over 8 percent, the highest rate of growth of any of the major powers. Oil production almost tripled, propelling Russia to first place in the world. Coal production more than doubled, pig iron production tripled, and total railroad track mileage grew by 73 percent. Most of European Russia's rail network was completed, as was most of the Trans-Siberian Railroad, then, as now, the longest railroad in the world.

PROBLEMS OF INDUSTRIALIZATION

The problems associated with this rapid growth and change were hardly less daunting. The treadmill of borrowing more and more to meet skyrocketing expenses moved even faster, and running to keep up with it meant imposing higher taxes on the peasantry, even higher than those of the pitiless Vyshnegradsky. Witte admitted that the exports squeezed from the peasantry came "not out of excess but out of current needs." In 1897, his export program finally earned Russia enough gold to enable him to put the ruble on the gold standard. However, the next year Russia again experienced famine. The famine passed, but not the problems that had caused it. Despite periodic famine, the population had increased 50 percent during the past thirty years. Most of that increase took place in the countryside, correspondingly increasing the misery there. Continued low productivity meant that the average peasant family earned barely half of what it needed to survive from its land allotment. Witte, despite some small gestures, had done nothing of consequence for the peasantry. This failure left the overwhelming majority of Russians in an ugly mood.

Added to peasant discontent was a rapidly growing and utterly miserable urban proletariat. The Russian proletariat of the late nineteenth century was exploited in the classic fashion of factory workers in the early stages of industrialization, but conditions were even worse in Russia than they had been during corresponding stages in the West. The few laws on the books protecting workers were rarely enforced. Workers were denied the right to form trade unions or to strike. Nobody could doubt where the government's sympathies lay, least of all the workers, whose strikes increasingly included political as well as economic demands. The strikes hit a peak in 1897, the year Witte triumphantly put Russia on the gold standard. The government's response, aside from an ill-enforced law mandating an eleven-and-a-half-hour day, was repression. During Witte's tenure the use of troops to suppress strikes and demonstrations was *twenty-seven* times greater than ever before. Witte's success in building Russian industry, it turned out, had created in the growing proletariat a volatile element that was all the more dangerous because, unlike the peasantry, it was concentrated at the centers of power in Russia—including St. Petersburg and Moscow. This enabled the workers to organize, often with the help of eager members of the revolutionary intelligentsia. Witte's failures in the countryside, combined with his successful industrializing works, helped bring Russia's social problems to a boil.

TSARISM AND THE MODERN WORLD

Against all of the turbulence stood the autocracy. Although the social instability resulting from the emancipation had magnified the autocracy's weaknesses, this antiquated institution in a modern world remained the most important factor holding Russian society together. A satisfactory understanding of what happened to that society therefore requires an examination of how the autocracy functioned—and malfunctioned—as the old century waned and the new one dawned, bringing with it new and greater challenges.

Perhaps the most noteworthy characteristic of tsarism during these years was how it embodied two normally exclusive features: extreme centralization and chaos. Far too much depended on the tsar himself. Although he was advised by an appointed body called the State Council, the tsar alone could make laws. While such centralization, if nothing else, might be expected to produce order and consistency, such was not the case. The ministers who carried out the tsar's orders were rival freelancers more than colleagues. Each reported individually to the tsar, where he did his best to defend his turf. A Western-type cabinet, where consultation and cooperation might produce coordinated policy directions, did not exist in Russia.

Because the tsar had so much power, the qualities of the individual who wore the crown were of vital importance. Alexander III, who reigned from 1881 to 1894, had few virtues, but at least he was a strong ruler able to stick to and enforce his reactionary policies, however misguided they might have been. His son, Nicholas II, had most of his father's faults and none of his strengths. Nicholas's reign began in disaster, marked its midpoint in 1905 with catastrophe, and closed in 1917 with the annihilation of tsarism. The pattern of ineptitude was set in 1896 when hundreds of people were killed during a riot by an enormous crowd celebrating his coronation. At a time when rival foreign powers were broadening their political bases, Nicholas dismissed the idea of sharing political decision making with popularly elected representatives as "senseless dreams." Having inherited his father's generally narrow-minded advisors, Nicholas added to this group a coterie of misfits and charlatans that included his unbalanced wife, Alexandra, and her confidant and spiritual masseur—the drunken, debauching, and ignorant but hypnotically compelling self-proclaimed "holy man" Grigory Rasputin. As a rule, Nicholas continued his father's policies, whether they were constructive, as in the case of Witte's industrialization program, or destructive, as with the notorious Russification programs that embittered so many of his subjects. Where Nicholas deviated from Alexander's path, it usually was for the worse. Alexander III at least had followed a cautious foreign policy that kept Russia out of war. Nicholas's more aggressive policies led Russia into two wars. The first—the Russo-Japanese War—shook the autocracy to its foundation and forced it to institute major reforms; the second—World War I—tore Russia apart and cost Nicholas his throne and his life.

As Nicholas had promised, there was no deviation on the issue of sharing the autocracy's power with its subjects. On this question there was considerable agreement among Nicholas's advisors, from the reactionary Konstantin Pobedonostsev to the forward-looking Witte. Pobedonostsev wanted to preserve the autocracy's prerogatives so that it could prevent progress; Witte wanted to use those same powers to promote progress. In this regard Witte, again, was a worthy successor to Peter the Great and a harbinger of Joseph Stalin. He argued forcefully that the spread of *zemstvo* self-government eventually would subvert the absolute power of the autocracy, failing until 1902 to see the wisdom of political reform. Secure in his conviction that industrialization would solve all of Russia's difficulties, Witte ignored the country's political problems even longer than he ignored its agricultural crisis. Even Witte, the best the old system could produce, a man who had vision and realized that the twentieth century had arrived, was not prepared to modernize Russia's dangerously deficient political institutions.

By the time Witte did see the need for reform, his tenure as finance minister was coming to an end. An international economic slump beginning in 1899 had slowed Russian industrial expansion. In 1902, large peasant disturbances rocked the Ukraine, while the next year a massive wave of strikes swept the south. All of this was grist for Witte's many enemies, including bureaucrats he had brushed aside and powerful landlords whose interests he had ignored. Witte was further weakened by his opposition to Russia's aggressive Far Eastern policy, which he feared might lead to war and disaster. In August 1903, Nicholas II dismissed his most competent advisor.

Witte's departure from the scene was soon followed by the first sustained appearance at center stage of a group with another approach to modernizing Russia, an approach that required the destruction of the autocracy and most of what Witte was trying to preserve. After frustrating and painful decades of enacting morose melodrama in underground shadows, the revolutionary intelligentsia, acknowledged at last by some of the aroused masses, finally would get its chance to perform great drama in the sunlight.

7

The Revolutionaries Regroup

*It is more pleasant and useful to go through
the experience of revolution than to write about it.*

—Vladimir Lenin

*Don't be too hard on Lenin. I think that much of his strange behavior
can be simply explained by the fact that he totally lacks a sense of humor.*

—George Plekhanov

The revolutionaries got their chance to strike at the autocracy because the economic and social developments that took root during the 1890s also allowed
their movements to regenerate and mature. The famine of 1891 had provided
the impetus to reorganize. The next several years witnessed a slow revival of
activity flowing in two distinct political currents. The old populist tendency was
being replenished by new recruits. By 1901, this new generation of believers
in peasant socialism had organized a new party, the Socialist Revolutionaries
(SRs). At the same time, the growth of industry and a factory proletariat led
other revolutionaries to organize around Marxism, a new theory imported from
Western Europe that proclaimed socialism would be achieved when the proletariat, not the peasantry, rose in revolution. Like their colleagues in Western
Europe, these people called themselves Social Democrats (SDs).

Economic and social changes meant that the revolutionary intelligentsia
no longer was completely alone in its desire to change Russia. A growing and
militant proletariat, a peasantry exposed to subversive ideas by a rising level
of literacy and improved communications, an angry and restive collection of
non-Russian minorities antagonized by Russification, and a growing number
of liberal-minded professionals in both the cities and the rural *zemstvos* all
potentially constituted a broader audience for varying parts of the intelligentsia's revolutionary message. That disparate audience, if unified, held the
potential to become the decisive political force in Russia.

The SRs were worthy heirs to Russia's native revolutionary tradition. The terror campaign by their fearless "combat section" against the government after the turn of the century claimed many more victims than the legendary efforts of the People's Will. Aside from directing their message to the peasantry, the largest and traditionally the most troublesome group in Russia, the SRs also had some success organizing among the small but growing factory working class. But the SRs had serious weaknesses. Their program was more relevant to an agricultural Russia than to one that was rapidly industrializing. Like the peasantry itself, the party was diffused and disorganized. Yet it had the largest following in Russia of any political party in 1905 and again in 1917, so whatever its limitations in being able to act decisively, its reputation in both revolutionary and police circles was formidable.

MARXISM COMES TO RUSSIA

Although populism was enjoying a rebirth, it no longer had the revolutionary field to itself. By the 1880s the Russian intelligentsia had discovered Marxism, the revolutionary theory that was to become, in one or another of its multiple permutations, the central article of faith for twentieth-century revolutionary socialists all over the world. Marxism's great appeal to the Russian revolutionaries was that it opened a new road to revolution and socialism. Back in the 1840s, Karl Marx postulated that society passes through certain stages of economic organization as the human race develops its technology and increases its ability to produce what it needs to live. Focusing on Western Europe, Marx traced societal evolution from ancient slavery through medieval feudalism and modern industrial capitalism. In each phase of development, there was a struggle between those who controlled the wealth of society and those who did not, what Marx called the "class struggle." When combined with improvements in technology and the resulting changes in the way goods were produced, the class struggle eventually led to the destruction of a given social order and the birth of a new, more advanced order.

It was under capitalism that something unprecedented happened: the development of the technology and productive capacity sufficient to give every person a high standard of living. Of course, under capitalism the minority haves (the bourgeoisie) were still exploiting the majority have-nots (the factory working class, or proletariat) so that although the universal good life was technically possible, it remained an unfulfilled promise. But because the proletariat worked in huge factories where hundreds and even thousands of workers had to cooperate, it was learning from its day-to-day experience about the collective nature of the process that produced all of society's wealth. Eventually, led by a vaguely defined group called "communists," the proletariat would unite and overthrow the bourgeoisie. Society would then go through a transition period guided by a "dictatorship of the proletariat," a form of government Marx mentioned several times but never concretely defined or described. It would soon reach socialism, a nonexploitative society in which the ownership of social wealth, like the productive process itself, was collective. Then "communism," a system that functioned so smoothly that each person could work "according to his ability" and be remunerated "according to his need," would be achieved. The completion of this process would bring the end of human misery and strife.

The good news about all this, aside from its rosy prognosis of harmony and well-being, was Marx's claim that his predictions rested on a scientific study of history. This study demonstrated that the human race was inexorably moving toward socialism. The bad news was that there were no shortcuts to the promised society. It was necessary to go through all the preliminary historical phases. This meant Russia would have to go through capitalism, something that all populists and their SR successors desperately wanted to avoid. For years the advocates of peasant socialism had devoted much of their time trying to prove that Russia could skip capitalism and jump directly into socialism. Yet Russia's Marxists, or at least some of them, also had a problem with the capitalist historical phase. Russia, after all, at best was in the early stages of capitalism, which meant that Russian Marxists were in for a long wait as capitalism ran its natural course. That Marx had ambiguously suggested Russia, under certain circumstances, might skip capitalism only added fuel to a multisided debate that raged well beyond the November 1917 revolution that supposedly brought socialism to Russia.

A large part of Marxism's appeal in Russia resulted from frustration among certain populists. They felt that two generations of failure were enough. The peasants, from their hostility to the "going-to-the-people movement" of the 1870s to their generally negative reaction to those who tried to help them during the famine of 1891–1892, seemed hopeless as a revolutionary force. Terror had produced some sparks and many corpses, but little else. On top of that, by the late 1880s and certainly by the 1890s, it was becoming clear that capitalism had come to Russia. Dreams of peasant socialism were fading against a background of railroad lines and factory smokestacks, while in the countryside capitalist practices such as production for the market and renting land increased economic differentiation among the peasantry. Meanwhile, new dreams were born as the fledgling Russian working class began to discuss revolutionary socialist theories in the 1870s. By the 1880s, these workers were starting to rattle their factory walls with strikes. Far more massive strikes followed during the next decade. All of this lent even more weight to the formidable Marxist scholarly works detailing and analyzing the development of European capitalism.

Russian Marxism was born in the 1880s among the Russian émigré community in Switzerland. Its godfather was George Plekhanov, a former populist of aristocratic background. Plekhanov marshaled impressive evidence demonstrating the growth and spread of capitalism in Russia and, based on that evidence, argued that Russia would have to go through a capitalistic phase before reaching socialism. This would require the overthrow of the reactionary autocracy and its replacement by a regime run by the bourgeoisie. As it had in Western Europe, capitalism would create the essential preconditions for socialism, including the proletariat, a genuine revolutionary class. Populist dreams of jumping directly from backwardness to socialism were just that, dreams, Plekhanov maintained.

Plekhanov also issued a warning to those who would jump over historical stages, a warning sounded before him by Friedrich Engels, Marx's lifelong collaborator. He cautioned that if a minority seized power before historical developments had prepared the ground for socialism, either it would have to watch the economic equality it decreed erode in the face of economic scarcity, or it would have to assume control of all aspects of the economy. The latter would require dictatorial methods and would result in what Plekhanov called "Inca Communism," a society in which an all-powerful elite controlled the lives of a mass of slaves. When Plekhanov wrote these words in 1883—the year Marx died—his warning was directed at his conspiratorial populist opponents. It is unlikely he imagined that a generation later some of his fellow Marxists would warrant the same criticism.

LENIN, MARXISM, AND THE RUSSIAN REVOLUTIONARY TRADITION

Until the turn of the century, Plekhanov was the recognized leader among Russian Marxists. Then practical control of the movement began to pass to members of a new generation schooled in underground work inside Russia during the 1890s. Slowly the movement grew, but as it did, it began to crack. The most important fissure emerged because of the gap between Russia and Europe and, consequently, between the political approaches available in each area. The fundamental question was whether Russian Marxism would be cast in a traditional European or a native Russian mold. At first Plekhanov had done most of the molding. After 1900, a new leader would emerge to take over the job: Vladimir Ilyich Ulyanov, better known by his revolutionary nom de plume, Lenin. It is impossible to understand the Russian Revolution and the society that emerged from it without first understanding Lenin and his political incarnation, the Bolshevik Party. While Leninism, like any other political movement, went through different phases, its unchanging foundation may be discerned by examining the personality of its founder, his use of Marxism, and his debt to the Russian revolutionary tradition from which he sprang.

Vladimir Ilyich Ulyanov was born in 1870 in Simbirsk, a town on the Volga River in central Russia. He was the second son in a family of six children. His mother, the daughter of a physician, grew up in a prosperous and cultured home. She spoke German, English, and French and was an accomplished singer and pianist. His paternal family had risen from serfdom to hereditary nobility in three generations and was a mixture—not unusual for that part of Russia—of Russian and Asiatic (mainly Kalmyk) lineage. Ilya Ulyanov, Lenin's father, was a respected official in the ministry of education whose rise through the ranks had earned him noble status. His well-educated and intelligent wife added yet another element of culture and refinement to what was a comfortable middle-class home.

Although Lenin was not born to be a revolutionary, as his Soviet biographies would have it, a family crisis and his own personality certainly prepared him for the profession. When Vladimir was seventeen, his older brother, Alexander, was executed for complicity in a plot to assassinate Tsar Alexander III. This tragedy exposed Vladimir to his brother's illicit world and began to loosen the moorings linking him to tsarist society. The social ostracism his family suffered, a difficulty aggravated by his father's untimely death several years earlier, embittered and further disoriented the teenager.

Lenin's personality was marked more than anything else by an iron determination to achieve his goals and an extraordinary ability to concentrate. As a youth he gave up skating because it interfered with his studies. Later "addictions" he would attempt to overcome, although not entirely successfully, were chess and music, the former because it was too time-consuming and the latter because he thought it weakened his will. He once told a friend, "I can't listen to music too often. It affects your nerves, makes you want to say stupid things and stroke the heads of people who create such beauty while living in this vile hell."

Fellow revolutionaries, themselves fiercely motivated, were struck by Lenin's overpowering will. One told Lenin that in contrast to "the greyhound" Plekhanov, "you are like a bulldog: you have a deadly grip." Lenin never let go because he was convinced that he knew best, that the only possible road to socialism in Russia was the one he had charted. In a tightly knit world populated by many people who were sure they were right on any given issue, Lenin's conviction of his infallibility stood out. One unsympathetic colleague concluded that he was "constitutionally incapable of digesting opinions different from his own." Plekhanov eventually became so exasperated with his former protégé that his advice to fellow delegates at a party congress in 1906 simply was "on all issues, vote against Lenin."

Leninism was an adaptation of Marxism to Russia's Political & social Climate

There was yet another element
mitment to the revolution left no r
might be necessary to achieve it. In
peasants because the forces driving
were promoting capitalism and were
he was capable of ordering mass exe
group, including workers and peasan
Lenin, the brutality of the hated capita
sures, regardless of the pain they caused
interests of the proletariat. This was a the _____ ___al
life. In 1908 he wrote that the Paris Comm ___minated its
enemies." After the Bolsheviks seized powe ___ ınat shirking extreme
measures, including executions, was "a mistake . . . impermissible weakness,
pacifist illusion" that would disarm and defeat the revolution.

Leninism probably is best summed up as an adaptation of Marxism to
Russian conditions by fusing traditional Marxism and the Russian revolutionary tradition. Lenin never accepted the model and political approach of
contemporary Western European Marxist parties, the strongest of which was
the German Social Democratic Party. Those parties operated in countries with
parliaments and constitutional safeguards and were able to function legally.
They were allied to and supported by powerful trade union movements.
While they ultimately stood for socialism, Western Social Democratic parties
generally made concessions and deals associated with parliamentary politics,
avoided an all-or-nothing attitude, and devoted their energies to achieving
democratic reforms and step-by-step improvements of the working class's
economic conditions. In short, traditional Marxist rhetoric about revolution
notwithstanding, Western Social Democratic parties in practice worked for
evolutionary change.

In Russia, a group of Social Democrats called "Economists" adopted an
analogous approach. The Economists contended that Social Democrats could
best advance their cause by focusing on the proletariat's specific economic demands rather than on political revolution. After 1903, when the Russian Social
Democrats finally managed to organize a functioning political organization,
a faction of that organization—the Mensheviks—continued to base political
actions in Russia on Western formulas. Unlike the Economists, who believed
socialism would evolve through incremental reforms, the Mensheviks still
believed that a revolution was necessary to establish socialism. However, the
traditional Marxist scenario called for a long capitalist period in Russia, and
therefore the Mensheviks were not concerned with the immediate problems
of seizing and holding power.

Lenin, of course, accepted the basic Marxist tenets regarding historical

e role of capitalism, its overthrow by the proletariat, and
of communism. He was, however, more than just a Marx-
oremost, Lenin was a revolutionary. Throughout his career, he
ated his determination to let nothing, including Marxist theory, come
een him and the revolution he craved. As he put it, Marxism should not be
"dogma," but a "guide to action." Lenin recoiled from anything that might
postpone the socialist revolution, be it economic prosperity, social reform, or
Marxist theory. Like Peter Tkachev before him, Lenin's worst nightmare was
that, given a chance, Russian capitalism might become stabilized. The chances
for a socialist revolution then would be severely compromised or even lost.
Lenin therefore, while still professing Marxism, wound up trying to circum-
vent the Marxist tenet that Russia had to have a bourgeois revolution and a
subsequent lengthy period of capitalist development before it would be ready
for its socialist revolution. His career after 1900, in fact, is best understood as
a quest for a shortcut to a socialist revolution in Russia. Although intellectually
a Marxist, temperamentally and spiritually Lenin was the heir to the militant
populist tradition of Chernyshevsky, Tkachev, and Nechaev.

LENIN'S "PARTY OF A NEW TYPE"

In order for Russia and its revolutionaries to avoid the long trip through a
capitalist purgatory, Lenin had to develop a practical political vehicle able
to undermine the autocracy and secure political power. He also had to make
adjustments in Marxist theory to compress the waiting period between the
bourgeois and socialist revolutions. Lenin's vehicle was what he called his
"party of a new type." He described it and made it a viable institution, as
will be seen, between 1900 and 1904. Both his concept of that party and the
way he operated it quickly made Lenin the focus of bitter controversy. His
adjustments to Marxist theory, likewise a source of controversy, took longer.
In fact, for a long time Lenin was not sure exactly where Russia could make
its shortcut to socialism and how it could be justified in Marxist terms, and his
theoretical juggling therefore continued even beyond the Bolshevik seizure
of power in 1917.

Lenin's revolutionary career began in earnest in 1893 with his arrival in St.
Petersburg. A short trip to Europe in 1895 to meet Plekhanov and other leaders
of Russian Marxism in exile was followed, after returning home, by his arrest
in December of that year, fourteen months of prison, and then exile to Siberia
from 1897 to 1900. Since conditions of imprisonment and internal exile for
political dissidents under tsarism were not remotely as harsh as they were to
become after 1917, Lenin was able to study, write, and maintain contact with
his comrades in Russia and Europe. When he emerged from his cold Siberian

cocoon in 1900, Lenin had mature...
mark on international Marxism an...

Shortly after his release from Sib...
an exile that would last, with the exc...
1906, until 1917. The Russian Socia...
ray. An attempt to set up a nationwide...
when most of the participants in what i...
Congress were arrested before they c...
After 1901, many young members of the...
organized Socialist Revolutionaries, who...
fied a youthful urge for action. Others we... ...ving liberal
movement. The Russian working class wa... ...g some leaders of its
own: practical-minded workers more concerned with wages and working
conditions than with political revolution. What was worse, the Economists
agreed with them.

Lenin, along with Plekhanov and many others, was horrified by Economism. He and his colleagues claimed that by focusing excessively on the proletariat's immediate economic needs, many of which could be satisfied by moderate reforms, the Economists were denying the essence of what Marxism, supposedly a revolutionary doctrine, stood for. If Economism was not stamped out, Lenin feared, the emphasis on piecemeal economic improvement and gradual reform would blot out the goal of revolution. Russian social democracy then would undergo a transformation from a revolutionary movement into a reformist political party, much like what had happened to German social democracy.

Lenin's fears about the dangers Economism posed to the revolutionary movement reflected deeper fears about Russian society and the overall prospects for a socialist revolution. In contrast to Marx, who expressed an optimism and faith in the historical process, Lenin has been called a revolutionary pessimist who lacked faith in those forces. In 1900, he certainly had good reason to be pessimistic. He could see no class capable of making a socialist revolution in Russia. As a Marxist, Lenin rejected the populist conception of the peasantry as Russia's revolutionary force, but while other Marxists had turned wholeheartedly to the working class, Lenin's revolutionary temperament was frustrated by that class's emphasis on wages and working conditions at the expense of explicitly revolutionary goals. He was further distressed when the Economists gave the workers' attitude their theoretical blessing. Also, the liberal movement in Russia was growing stronger, and although it opposed the autocracy, it opposed socialism at least as much. To save the revolution from its enemies across the breadth of the political spectrum, Lenin proposed his "party of a new type."

→ overcome obstacles

his new party would have to overcome two obstacles
...ed. The first was the Russian state, which still denied its
right to political activity. In this case, Lenin, like all Russians,
victim of his country's autocratic tradition. The second obstacle,
...y enough, was the Russian people themselves, specifically the proletariat. Here Lenin's difficulties arose not because the proletariat wanted to
put any limits on his political activity, but precisely because *Lenin* wanted
to control the *proletariat's* political activity. In this case, Lenin was the heir
to the elitist tradition of the Russian revolutionary intelligentsia. Lenin's
solution to both problems was to advocate a tightly organized, conspiratorial, and hierarchical party, one that could insulate itself from police spies
and, perhaps more important, avoid contamination by insufficiently militant
political ideas.

Lenin was on solid ground when it came to the problem of revolutionaries surviving in the face of the autocracy and ubiquitous police. As he noted
while still in Siberia:

> Against small groups of socialists seeking shelter up and down the broad
> Russian underworld stands the gigantic machine of the powerful contempo-
> rary state. . . . [I]n order to carry on a systematic struggle against the govern-
> ment we must bring our organization to the highest point of perfection.

Any political organization, Lenin repeatedly argued in the years that followed, that could not protect itself against infiltration by the police would
quickly be destroyed. It went without saying that a broad-based, open political
party on the model of the German Social Democratic Party, as favored by
many Russian Marxists, would be unequipped to survive in Russia's rigorous
political climate.

No less dangerous to Russian social democracy, Lenin believed, were the
workers and the Social Democratic leaders themselves. The problem was
that both were untrustworthy. While Marx and Engels had believed that the
proletariat would develop naturally a socialist and revolutionary outlook, or
"consciousness," as a result of the conditions it faced, Lenin had far less faith
that the workers would see the light. The workers, he warned, if allowed to
follow their "spontaneous" inclinations, inevitably would forsake revolution
for "petty bourgeois" reformist objectives such as better wages. The proper
"social democratic consciousness"—as opposed to the unrevolutionary and
therefore dangerous "trade union consciousness"—that directed the proletariat
toward revolutionary action was not a product of its own thinking, but of the
intelligentsia's. It was a harsh and gloomy assessment, to Marxist ears at
least, to pronounce that the class allegedly destined to save the world could

not think for itself, but Lenin simply had no use for the workers if they did not enlist in the revolutionary struggle as he defined it. The workers, Lenin's good friend Maxim Gorky once observed, "are to Lenin what minerals are to the metallurgist."

Lenin also found that many members of the intelligentsia were no more helpful than the politically unaware workers. In their willingness to give priority to the workers' economic demands, even if only in the short run, Lenin's erstwhile colleagues were guilty of "subservience to spontaneity," in other words, of allowing those who were unqualified to dictate policy. Page after page of *What Is To Be Done?* (1902), Lenin's major work on how to organize a Russian Social Democratic Party, denounced the Economists for that error.

The key to saving the movement lay in organization. Harking back to his Russian revolutionary roots, Lenin stressed that what was needed was not an organization of workers on the Western European model—which to Lenin meant an organization limited to reformist objectives—but a conspiratorial, centralized phalanx of revolutionaries, a party cut from Chernyshevsky's cloth and sewn together according to Tkachev's pattern. Lenin's own conduct as a revolutionary, his total professional dedication, his readiness to sacrifice his personal life, or anyone else's, to the cause, and his demand that others do the same, was pure Chernyshevsky. As Lenin once put it, Chernyshevsky's *What Is To Be Done?* taught him "what a revolutionary must be like, what his rules must be, how he must go about attaining his goals, and by what method and means he can bring about their realization." Lenin's model for his party closely resembled Tkachev's; it is not for nothing that Lenin frequently told his followers to study populism's leading theorist of a conspiratorial, elite political party. Russia's new Marxist party had to be composed of professionals. As early as 1900, in discussing what he called the party's "urgent tasks," Lenin stressed the need to train people "who shall devote to the revolution not only their spare evenings but the whole of their lives." Of course, this formula excluded the type of armchair socialist Lenin loathed. It also excluded most proletarians who, after all, spent the greater part of their lives making a living in the factories.

As already noted, Lenin's professional revolutionaries were to be organized in a conspiratorial, centralized, and hierarchical network. Such an organization, Lenin wrote in *What Is To Be Done?* faced a political struggle "far more extensive and complex" than the workers' economic struggle and "must of necessity be not too extensive and as secret as possible." All authority was to rest with a central committee. It not only would issue policy orders to be carried out without question by local committees but also would have the power to organize and disband those committees, as well as to select and, if need be, remove their leaders. Those at the lower levels, Lenin stressed in an article written several months after the publication of *What Is To Be Done?* were to consider themselves as "agents" of the central committee, "bound to submit to all its directives, bound to observe all laws and customs of this army in the field into which they have entered and which they cannot leave without permission of the commander." The military metaphor was hardly accidental. Lenin was not interested in building a political party in the conventional sense of that term; instead, his goal was to create an organization capable of waging—and winning—a war for political power.

It must be emphasized that although the party was to be made up primarily of intellectuals, Lenin rejected the idea that the party could function without the proletariat. As both a Marxist theorist and revolutionary tactician, Lenin recognized that such isolation in an era of mass politics would doom his party to failure. The party had to make every effort to organize in the factories and to win influence in whatever groups the proletariat might be able to form. But the party, not the working class, would determine the proper doctrine and make all the decisions. Bertram D. Wolfe has aptly summed up the relationship between Lenin's party and the proletariat, noting that "it [the party] is to use that numerous and closely packed class as its main battering ram in its struggle for power, but is itself to supply the doctrine, the watchwords, the purposes, the commands."[1]

If the party was to tell the working class what to do, and the party's central committee was to govern the party, the logical question was how the central committee itself was to make its decisions. Lenin's problem was how to reconcile two divergent and often contradictory imperatives: the need for absolute discipline and unity of action and the desire to maintain democracy within the party. Unity and discipline were vital if the party was to overcome the heavy odds facing it. Internal democracy was a tradition and commitment that no self-respecting Marxist of that era could openly flout. Marxism, after all, still drew its primary strength and leadership from countries where democratic values held sway among both workers and intellectuals. Lenin called his solution to this problem "democratic centralism," a term he first used in 1905. Under democratic centralism, full discussion and vigorous debate could precede any decision, but once the majority decided, every party member was bound to obey, regardless of his personal views. By the same token, all decisions made at the center were binding on all other party units. Democracy in this case was assured because, presumably, those at the center had been elected from below and because genuine debate preceded all decisions.

Democratic centralism turned out to be far more centralist than democratic. Rarely was there a shortage of debate under Lenin's leadership, but in a party whose leaders either lived in exile or underground in Russia, these debates took place within a tiny circle. In reality, membership in the central committee, supposedly determined by elections at the lower levels or by party congresses, generally was determined by cooption: the standing committee simply selected new members whenever necessary. As for debate at the rank-and-file level, Lenin stressed it could not be allowed to undermine the party's overall strength. In particular, in 1906 he wrote that this imperative ruled out "*all* criticism which disrupts or makes difficult the *unity* of an action decided on by the Party." In short, the discipline and unity Lenin demanded constituted yet another powerful regimenting force in an already centralized power structure.

None of this lack of democracy bothered Lenin. The exigencies of survival meant that fineries like elections simply would have to wait for a more auspicious time. Anyhow, he wrote in *What Is To Be Done?* the party had "more than democracy"; it had "complete comradely confidence among revolutionaries." Lenin did not worry that the lack of democratic controls would lead to corruption. Good revolutionaries, he pronounced, "feel their responsibilities very keenly." He was quite sure, in any case, that the working class would understand that the cause was more important than the "toy forms of democracy."

MARXIST CRITICS OF LENIN

Other revolutionaries, no less dedicated or radical than Lenin, disagreed. Yuli Martov, Lenin's friend and colleague in the 1890s and subsequently the leader of the Mensheviks, called the author of *What Is To Be Done?* a dictator. Pavel Axelrod, a veteran Social Democrat of impeccable credentials—he was one of the few leaders of working-class origins—denounced what he called Lenin's "theocratic" party. He compared it to the Jacobin party of the French Revolution, the party that had attempted to impose a minority dictatorship on France by means of its notorious Reign of Terror.

Even foreign revolutionaries joined in the assault. Rosa Luxemburg, a passionate revolutionary active in the movements of three countries, known for both her unquestionable radicalism and her devotion to the working class, attacked Lenin in an article written in 1904 called "Leninism or Marxism?" She deplored the "pitiless centralism" in Lenin's thinking that recalled the elitism of the pre-Marxist Russian revolutionary movement. Lenin's party, she warned, would stifle, not educate the Russian working class, exactly the opposite of what Marxists should want for the class upon which all hopes for socialism depended. What good was it to have the central committee be the "only thinking element in the party"? Socialism could be realized only on the basis of a working class able to think for itself. Lenin's party, Luxemburg complained, would "enslave" the young working-class movement in a "bureaucratic straitjacket"; the movement would become an "automaton manipulated by a Central Committee." She concluded:

> Let us speak plainly. Historically the errors committed by a truly revolutionary movement are infinitely more fruitful than the infallibility of the cleverest Central Committee.

This was damaging criticism, coming as it did from such a respected colleague. The most devastating criticism, however, came from the pen of a brilliant young firebrand named Lev Davidovich Bronstein, who two years earlier had taken the underground pseudonym Leon Trotsky:

> Lenin's methods lead us to this: the party organization first substitutes itself for the party as a whole; then the central committee substitutes itself for the organization; and finally a single "dictator" substitutes himself for the central committee.

These words, written in 1904, left Lenin unmoved, but after his death they would haunt his successors. Trotsky's criticism turned out to be a chillingly accurate prediction of the history of Lenin's Bolshevik Party and, therefore, of doom for so many of its most devoted members, among them Trotsky himself.

BOLSHEVIKS AND MENSHEVIKS

Although it would take several decades for Lenin's methods to lead to the end that Trotsky predicted, they did lead to an immediate split in the fledgling Russian Social Democratic Party. During July and August 1903, fifty-seven delegates representing various Social Democratic groups met at what they called their party's Second Congress in deference to the ill-fated 1898 meeting. During the course of the sweltering three-week summer affair that began in Brussels and ended in London, the newly organized party split into two factions. One, led by Lenin and committed to his view of party organization, called itself the "Bolsheviks," or "majority." The other, supported by a number of brilliant Social Democrats who often found it difficult to work together, accepted the label "Mensheviks," or "minority." Its most prominent member, and the closest thing it had to a leader, was Martov. Lenin's claim to the "majority" label was based on a series of votes taken at the congress after a number of delegates sympathetic to Martov's faction had walked out to protest an earlier decision. Until that walkout Lenin's supporters had been in the minority, as they would be within the party for much of the period from

1903 to 1912, at the end of which the two factions finalized their split and became separate parties. Lenin's Bolsheviks nonetheless kept the "majority" designation they had appropriated at the Second Congress and the prestige it yielded, providing a measure of both sides' political instincts and of the reliability of the titles politicians and political parties give themselves.

Despite the patch that seemed to cover it for nine years, the fissure that emerged between the Bolsheviks and Mensheviks at the Second Congress was unbridgeable. The initial dispute at the congress—over the requisites for membership in the party—occurred because there existed two diametrically opposed concepts of what the party should be. Martov's relatively loose membership requirements reflected his vision of a mass Western-type party composed of sympathizers and workers, not just of the stalwarts manning the party machine. Lenin's strict, demanding qualifications pointed to the elite revolutionary phalanx he had outlined in *What Is To Be Done?* After his defeat on this issue at the start of the congress, the subsequent walkout of delegates transformed Lenin's forces into a majority, an advantage he used without pity or compromise to pass rules mandating a centralized party organization staffed, as far as possible, with his allies and supporters. Lenin's tactics shocked not only Martov, who protested about "martial law within the party," but many others, including Trotsky and even Lenin's mentor, Plekhanov. The Second Congress, convened amidst tears of joy after years of waiting, ended in bitterness and division.

Lenin's outlook reflected a critical difference between himself and the Menshevik leadership. His conduct was the practical realization of the Russian revolutionary tradition's will to power at any cost. Lenin accepted the concept that the ends justified the means. Echoing Chernyshevsky, Lenin wrote that there were no absolute standards governing revolutionary activity. Allegations that such standards existed were a "deception" and a "fraud." "Everything that is done in the proletarian cause is honest," Lenin insisted. His ferocious verbal and written attacks against fellow Social Democrats shocked many Russian and European Marxists. Nor did Lenin shrink, as did many Social Democrats, from employing criminal means such as extortion, fraud, and bank robbery to fill party coffers or from associating with criminal elements helpful in executing these projects. Lenin called bank robberies "expropriations," arguing that any refusal to accept them and similar activities as legitimate revolutionary tactics was "petty bourgeois snobbery." Besides, he added, in response to the queasiness many felt in consorting with less than honorable elements, "Sometimes a scoundrel is useful to our party precisely because he is a scoundrel."

Before the seizure of power in 1917, such tactics got Lenin into trouble with his Social Democratic colleagues, who even set up a special court to investigate his conduct. Lenin survived this challenge, but many would say he did less well when dealing with the consequences of his actions after 1917. In any case, barely a decade after his death, one of the men who rose to prominence by organizing some of Lenin's "expropriations," a taciturn Georgian named Joseph Stalin, launched a bloodbath that claimed almost every one of Lenin's associates still alive at the time. Another of Stalin's victims, at least according to many revolutionaries and observers with some sympathy or respect for Lenin, was Leninism itself.

The Mensheviks were different. Their interpretation of Marxism affirmed that Russia would follow directly in the footsteps of its Western neighbors. The coming revolution therefore was to be what Marxists called a bourgeois revolution led by Russia's small but growing middle class, the group that was the basis of Russia's liberal movement. The role of the proletariat and its representative, the Social Democratic Party, would be to support the liberals in their struggle against the autocracy and permit them to take power. Then, while the bourgeoisie ran things, the proletariat would go into opposition. Since Russia's bourgeois regime-to-come would mirror the capitalist societies in the West, the Russian Social Democratic party should begin to organize a broadly based party on the Western model. The Mensheviks recognized the necessity of maintaining an underground organization as long as the autocracy survived, but for them this was just a temporary requirement that would disappear when the Russian body politic became like the capitalist democratic regimes in the West.

LENIN'S BLUEPRINT FOR REVOLUTION

While the Mensheviks were preparing for a bourgeois democratic regime in Russia, Lenin was building a party capable of seizing power. Yet, as a Marxist, how could Lenin justify this approach when accepted Marxist wisdom mandated that backward Russia first pass through its bourgeois democratic historical phase? Eventually he made two modifications or additions (some have understandably called them revisions or distortions) to Marxist theory beyond those already in *What Is To Be Done?* that together pointed the way to a historical shortcut to a Marxist seizure of power in Russia. Lenin's first modification focused on Russia itself. In *Two Tactics of Social Democracy*, written in 1905, he postulated that Russia's peasantry—actually the country's poor peasants—a social class Marxists traditionally rejected as hopelessly reactionary, would be the proletariat's ally in the coming revolution that would overthrow tsarism, albeit in a distinctly subordinate role. That alliance would then establish a regime with the tongue-twisting title "revolutionary democratic dictatorship of the proletariat and the peasantry." This regime would be democratic in a class sense, Lenin argued, because it represented the great majority of the people. However, because of Russia's social and economic realities—that is, Russia's economic backwardness—it initially would not be able to introduce socialism. Instead, it would destroy the last vestiges of the old regime, a campaign that would include radical reforms, such as the redistribution of land to the peasantry and an eight-hour day, designed to improve the condition of the masses and clear Russia's social and political landscape for the building of socialism. At the same time, this regime would be "precisely a dictatorship" of the "mass over the few" with unlimited power, a state of affairs that was absolutely necessary to smash the continued resistance and counterrevolutionary efforts of the landlords and bourgeoisie. And most important, although in technical Marxist terms Russia would still be in the unavoidable bourgeois democratic historical phase of development, Lenin's revolutionary democratic dictatorship of the proletariat and the peasantry would render the bourgeoisie helpless and place Marxist hands—which undoubtedly meant those of Lenin and his followers—firmly on the levers of state power.

Since a revolution in a Russia that was still 80 percent rural could not be successful without peasant support, Lenin's new strategy was a brilliant political stroke. It both embodied and expanded Lenin's fundamental disagreement with the Mensheviks regarding any compromise or cooperation with Russian liberalism, the political movement of the bourgeois class enemy, whose success would strengthen capitalism and indefinitely postpone the socialist revolution.

Lenin's second post–*What Is To Be Done?* modification of Marxism was international in scope and came much later in his career. He eventually concluded that special conditions arising both in Russia and abroad had made it possible for Russia to begin its socialist revolution before socialist revolutions broke out in the industrialized countries of the West. This inversion of classic Marxism did not come easily, even to Lenin, notwithstanding his previous modifications of Marx's precepts. The key to this change was the phenomenon Lenin and other Marxists called imperialism. In *Imperialism: The Highest Stage of Capitalism*, written in 1916 in the midst of World War I, and in assorted articles and speeches during 1917 and 1918, Lenin explained that capitalism had survived longer than Marxists expected because it had become a global system—imperialism—in which the main European capitalist powers exploited less developed countries worldwide. Imperialism had delayed the world socialist revolution, as it had allowed the bourgeoisie of the advanced capitalist countries to use some of the enormous wealth they had acquired abroad to improve conditions for the proletariat at home. But imperialism could give capitalism only a temporary reprieve. Indeed, the competition among imperialist powers had led to the great war that was tearing Europe apart and brought the continent's leading capitalist powers to the brink of revolution.

One implication of Lenin's theory of imperialism was that world capitalism was most vulnerable in the relatively backward capitalist countries, where social and economic problems were most acute. In other words, the first socialist revolution might occur not in an advanced capitalist country, as standard Marxist theory held, but in a relatively backward capitalist country such as Russia. It seems clear in this regard that by 1917 practice was driving theory. Specifically, Lenin concluded that the fall of tsarism in March (February) 1917 and the chaos that followed had opened the door for a Bolshevik seizure of power in the immediate future, and that act had to be justified in Marxist terms. Interestingly, Lenin does not seem to have fully formulated his rationale for Russia being the first country to make a socialist revolution until early 1918, that is, *after* the Bolsheviks actually had seized power in the name of the proletariat. In any event, when he finally provided his initial explanations for the Bolshevik seizure of power and the establishment of a socialist regime, they were hardly models of sophisticated Marxist dialectical analysis. For example, in March 1918 he informed the delegates to the Bolshevik Party's Seventh Congress that because of the "zigzags of history," a "more backward" capitalist country, Russia, "has proved to be the one to start the socialist revolution." References to zigzags soon evolved into what Trotsky called Lenin's "lapidary formula" that Russia had been the "weakest link" in the chain of world imperialism and therefore the place where that chain broke and the world's first socialist revolution took place. Meanwhile, Lenin also stressed that the Bolshevik Revolution alone would not and could not guarantee the victory of socialism. Russia still lacked the industrial base and technical skills to build a socialist society. The help Russia needed would require a socialist revolution in Western Europe, exactly what Lenin expected would follow now that the Russian proletariat had shown the world how to get the revolutionary ball rolling.

A final theoretical guidepost to Lenin's shortcut to a socialist revolution in Russia—his analysis of the state—did not require any modification of classical Marxism. Lenin's major work on this topic was *The State and Revolution*, written during 1917 but not published until after the Bolshevik Revolution. This pamphlet has a distinctly utopian tinge unique among Lenin's writings. Several parts are devoted to demonstrating how easy it would be for the proletariat to run major institutions once the capitalists were overthrown. Because so much of the job consisted of "watching and bookkeeping," Lenin envisioned the bulk of the transition being accomplished within twenty-four hours. For a man with a reputation of being a pessimist, this certainly was an upbeat scenario, one that could be used after November 1917 to further explain and justify the Bolshevik seizure of power.

The key point in all of this is that Lenin's concern with theory, while sometimes intense, always remained secondary to his concern for action. In this crucial respect, Lenin was fundamentally different from most of his Marxist comrades. As he put it, paraphrasing the great German poet Goethe, "Theory, my friend, is gray, but green is the eternal tree of life." Indeed, any close reading of Lenin's works reveals a maze of theoretical contradictions he apparently felt no need to resolve. While many of his rivals thought like academics, Lenin thought like a general. If circumstances dictated a change in strategy or tactics, Lenin adjusted, however awkward that adjustment might be from the perspective of Marxist theory. If an opportunity arose suddenly, as it did in the fall of 1917, Lenin seized it and forged ahead, allowing Marxist theory—in this case, the thesis that the first socialist revolution would take place in an advanced capitalist country—to catch up later. Leon Trotsky, his right-hand man in the glory days of 1917, summed up Lenin's genius when he observed that the essence of Leninism lay in "revolutionary action."

A word must be said about Lenin and power. Lenin did not want power for its own sake or as a trophy to satisfy his vanity. Other than his unshakable conviction that he was always right, Lenin was devoid of personal vanity. After 1917 he lived in modest circumstances, even continuing to wear an old coat bearing a bullet hole from a 1918 assassination attempt. He derived no pleasure from seeing his name in lights. At large public meetings and party congresses he cut an inconspicuous figure when he was not on the rostrum. A typical photograph finds a rumpled Lenin surrounded and almost obscured by other disheveled delegates. He had no desire to have monuments to himself or cities named after him. Even his detractors admit that he would have been horrified by the cult of adoration his successors built after his death, an enterprise that resulted in his body being mummified and used as a sort of holy relic for Communist pilgrims and believers. Lenin had no time for anything but revolution. His goal was the destruction of capitalism and the building of socialism. His monument was to be his good deeds.

For most of the years before 1917 it looked as if there would be no socialist monuments in Russia. For years the debates among Russia's revolutionaries were so many tempests in a teapot. Their political parties were little more than frightened mice, forever hiding in the shadows and crevices of Russian society, occasionally emerging to lead a strike or demonstration before being chased underground again by the cat's claws of the tsarist political police. Tsarism continued to have its problems, but it hung on and even managed to implement a few reforms in the bargain. If any forces were gaining strength, they were the forces of capitalism, not socialism. And among the revolutionary parties, the Bolshevik Party, its name notwithstanding, remained a distinctly minority tendency. To any objective observer, it must surely have seemed that only a totally unpredictable and massive historical accident would enable Russia's assorted revolutionary parties to realize even their most limited objectives.

Lenin therefore was justified in fearing that he would be denied a chance to build socialism in Russia. Hopes were raised during the great upheaval that shook the country during 1905 and 1906, but the tsarist regime weathered the storm. Lenin and most of Russia's leading revolutionaries fled back into exile while those who remained in Russia burrowed deeper underground. Wherever they were, Russia's revolutionaries were further than ever from their goals.

NOTE

1. Bertram D. Wolfe, *The Russian Revolution and Leninism or Marxism?* (Ann Arbor: University of Michigan Press, 1961), p. 13.

8

The Final Years and Last Stand

In politics there is no vengeance; there are only consequences.

—Prime Minister Peter Stolypin (1906)

*He will leap over history; and great will be the tumult when he does so.
He will leave the earth: the very hills will crumble from the fear
assailing them, and this fear will make the native plains arch
themselves into hills . . . and Petersburg shall sink.*

—Andrei Bely (1913)

Russia's 1905 Revolution took almost everyone by surprise. In hindsight, perhaps it should not have. Russia had been staggering from crisis to crisis ever since the economic slump that began in 1899 slowed Witte's development program to a crawl. In 1902 a wave of peasant disorders shook the Ukraine, and in 1903 strikes that started in the oil-producing city of Baku on the Caspian Sea spread at an unprecedented scale across southern Russia. These strikes were particularly disturbing to the authorities because they shattered what had been an extraordinarily sophisticated attempt by the autocracy to control and direct industrial discontent. Beginning in 1901, under the leadership of a police official named Sergei Zubatov, the government actually had been organizing workers into worker associations controlled by the police. Zubatov, a revolutionary turned police official who envisioned himself serving both the workers and the state that oppressed them, somehow had convinced his superiors that his "police socialism" could direct the proletariat's energies away from dangerous political concerns to a less-threatening concentration on wages and working conditions. The old order would then be left intact. Zubatov enjoyed considerable success in organizing his associations and, for a time, instilling them with patriotic fervor. Once he collected 50,000 workers to lay wreaths at a monument of the Tsar-Liberator Alexander II. Unfortunately for Zubatov, the workers had ideas of their own about liberation. They exploded out of control in 1903, making police socialism and Zubatov's career their first casualties.

While the workers and the peasants were striking and rioting and the revolutionaries were spinning their new political webs, a liberal movement, a new force in Russian politics, was growing. Unlike the Socialist Revolutionaries and the Social Democrats, the liberals' main goals were a constitution and a parliamentary regime similar to those in the capitalist West. The liberal economic program, far from endorsing one or another form of socialism, envisioned the further evolution and expansion of capitalism as well as social reform. The liberals drew their strength from the country's growing number of professionals and industrialists—Russia's long-awaited bourgeoisie—and from a small but active group of progressive-minded landlords. In 1902, an influential liberal journal, *Liberation*, began publication, although its editor, a former Marxist but now a leading liberal thinker named Peter Struve, wisely published the journal from the safety of Western Europe. Shortly after *Liberation* made its debut, Struve met in Switzerland with a number of other prominent like-minded figures to establish the Union of Liberation, in effect Russia's first liberal, albeit illegal, political party. Struve also contributed to a seminal collection of scholarly essays that likewise appeared in 1902 in a volume titled *Problems of Idealism*. The twelve contributors to *Problems of Idealism* included some of Russia's most distinguished intellectuals, such as the philosophers Nicholas Berdyaev and Sergei Bulgakov and the eminent legal scholar Pavel Novgorodtsev. Their essays ranged widely, but all were grounded in the fundamental Western liberal principles requiring society to recognize the autonomy of the individual and operate according to the rule of law. It was their hope that in the new century Russia would finally undertake reforms to meet those standards. Organization efforts in moderate and liberal circles quickened during the next two years and in 1905 produced two new political parties: the Constitutional Democrats (Kadets), the more liberal and militant of the two, and the Octobrists, a moderate group more inclined to compromise with the tsarist regime.

Russia's liberals faced a cruel dilemma from the start. They wanted to end autocratic rule but feared a revolution would sweep them away along with the tsar. They also were caught in a political vise. The liberals represented very few Russians. On one side, the peasants and workers, poor and hungry, had no understanding of or patience with liberal preoccupations with moderate reform and orderly, legal, and often excruciatingly slow parliamentary procedures. Many revolutionaries, including Lenin, bore them a deep-seated hatred and contempt. On the other side, the autocracy refused to accept even the most moderate limits on its power, a posture that not only at times impelled some liberals to resort to illegal methods but also brought the nation closer to the revolution that meant the end of all their hopes.

By 1903 Russia was in turmoil. The government's response was increased repression, exploitation of popular bigotry, and, finally, a blunder into war. Repression included the increased use of troops against strikers and protesters. In its attempt to direct popular discontent away from itself, in 1903 the government resorted to the old and vicious ploy of exploiting the endemic anti-Semitism of the Russian people. When a pogrom (a riot in which Jews were beaten, robbed, and murdered) broke out in the town of Kishinev (now Chişinău), instigated by a reactionary newspaper editor whose publication was heavily subsidized by the government, neither the central government nor local authorities did anything to stop it. Forty-nine Jews were killed and over 1,500 houses and businesses damaged or destroyed. Dubbed an "anti-revolutionary counteraction" by the anti-Semitic Interior Minister V.K. von Plehve, the Kishinev incident and more than two dozen subsequent pogroms failed to counter the slide toward revolution and did not subside when it broke out. Just as the peasant and worker disturbances of 1902 and 1903 were a prelude to the upheaval of 1905, the earlier pogroms were only a harbinger of the horrors 1905 would bring for Russia's Jews. A two-week reign of terror during the fall of that year engulfed over 600 Jewish communities, leaving more than 3,000 dead, thousands more wounded or crippled, 1,500 children orphaned, and millions of rubles lost to vandalism. In the Black Sea port of Odessa alone 300 Jews were murdered, several thousand injured, and 40,000 left economically destitute.

Von Plehve had one other scheme for quieting popular discontent: what he called a "small victorious war." Russia was pursuing an aggressive foreign policy in the Far East designed to win control of the northeastern Chinese province of Manchuria and the kingdom of Korea. Here the Russians ran into the rising power of the Japanese Empire. Fighting began in February 1904 when the Japanese, without declaring war, attacked the Russian naval base at the Manchurian city of Port Arthur. The Russo-Japanese War of 1904–1905 resulted in a string of Russian defeats, while at home it produced privation and hardship. The disasters of 1904 ultimately engulfed von Plehve, who was assassinated after six months of defeats in his "small victorious war."

The autocracy's obvious incompetence, now thrown into even higher relief, spurred new demands for reform. Liberals and moderates, including distinguished members of the nobility, pressed their demands for meaningful political changes, including some form of national legislative assembly. The campaign culminated in a series of public meetings transparently disguised as banquets, held in defiance of governmental orders. All these efforts met with rejection from the tsarist authorities.

The scales finally tipped in 1905. Russia's factory workers, short of food and out of patience, were not inclined to banquets. Because of a rather bizarre situation that could have occurred only in tsarist Russia, the proletariat's ability to organize in St. Petersburg had been given a boost by, of all things, a police agent: a handsome, eloquent, egotistical, and highly emotional Orthodox priest named Father George Gapon. Gapon's credits eventually included associations with numerous revolutionaries, including Lenin, as well as dealings with government officials and police. In the spring of 1904, he managed to get von Plehve's support for a Zubatov-type police union in St. Petersburg. By late December the union had become involved in a strike that soon spread citywide. At this point Gapon decided that his flock, wives and children included, should make a direct appeal to the tsar at his Winter Palace. On January 22 (9), 1905, an enormous crowd of about 30,000, wearing their "best dress" and armed with religious icons and a humble petition for relief that Gapon personally planned to deliver to Nicholas II, approached the Winter Palace. It was met not by Nicholas but by mounted Cossacks and armed infantrymen, a force one officer described as "twelve thousand bayonets and sabers." The soldiers were ordered to fire directly into the defenseless crowd, and an estimated 200 people were killed and hundreds more wounded in the carnage that followed. January 22, 1905, justly went down in history as "Bloody Sunday."

THE 1905 REVOLUTION

Bloody Sunday ignited what became the 1905 Revolution. While the tsar's military forces continued to lose battles to the Japanese in the Far East, the empire was engulfed by strikes, riots, meetings, peasant rampages, assassinations, and mutinies by military personnel. New organizations, from a Peasant Union to an umbrella liberal group called the Union of Unions, sprang up. The cries for a constitution and legislative assembly swelled and were not silenced by either the tiny concessions the tsar was willing to make or the end of the war in September 1905, a denouement brilliantly negotiated by Sergei Witte, whom the tsar had recalled to government service in June. Russia remained locked in turmoil, and by October the pressures became too great to be contained. A series of strikes that began in Moscow spread to St. Petersburg and ballooned into a general strike. On October 26 (13) the workers of St. Petersburg organized a Council—or Soviet—of Workers' Deputies. The Soviet, led by Mensheviks, soon included representatives from all over the city. It also included members of the revolutionary intelligentsia, the most notable of whom turned out to be Leon Trotsky. Cornered by encroaching chaos and pressured by key advisors, most prominently Witte, Nicholas II finally reached what he called his "terrible decision." On October 30 (17), 1905, he issued a document drafted by Witte known as the October Manifesto, promising his subjects basic civil rights and a parliament with genuine legislative powers. The autocracy, that centuries-old immovable object, at last had been budged.

Although tsarism teetered on the brink that October, it managed to survive. Nicholas II appointed Witte prime minister. The October Manifesto won the tsar and his government some allies among progressives and liberals, although most of them, now organized into the Kadet Party, demanded even more concessions. But a significant minority, including a number of leading landlords and industrialists, were satisfied with the manifesto and formed their own "Octobrist" Party as a demonstration of their support. In early December of 1905 the government already was strong enough to arrest the entire St. Petersburg Soviet. At the end of the month it successfully crushed a Bolshevik-led uprising in Moscow. Restoring order throughout the vast empire took longer, but the job was done, brutally and efficiently, by troops returned from the Far East. The government also enlisted the aid of reactionary gangs of thugs, called the Black Hundreds, to attack selected targets and mount pogroms against its old scapegoat, the Jews. Meanwhile, Nicholas increasingly marginalized Witte, even while keeping him on as prime minister to use his prestige to negotiate a huge loan from France. Correctly convinced that the tsar had no further use for him, Witte resigned in May 1906, leaving high office for the second, and last, time.

On the political front, the generalities of the October Manifesto were made concrete by the empire's new "Fundamental Laws," issued by Nicholas on May 6 (April 23), 1906. Many liberals were deeply disappointed by the tsar's narrow interpretation of his manifesto. He retained the great majority of his traditional powers. The tsar still appointed all government ministers, and they continued to be responsible only to him. He maintained complete control over foreign policy and the military part of the state budget and could veto all legislation. Under Article #87 of the Fundamental Laws, the tsar could promulgate emergency laws while the parliament—called the Duma—was not in session, although such laws required the Duma's eventual approval to remain in force. The tsar also could dissolve the Duma and call new elections at his pleasure. The Duma was elected according to a formula that discriminated in favor of the landlords and peasants and against the working-class and urban population, a safeguard that did not prevent the elections to the first two Dumas from producing a majority hostile to the autocracy. After dissolving each Duma in turn, the government in June 1907 used Article #87 to drastically revise the electoral law even more in favor of the empire's landlords, its most conservative class. In addition, the Fundamental Laws established a second legislative chamber above the Duma called the State Council. Half of its members were appointed by the tsar and half elected by various privileged groups, such as the clergy and the *zemstvo* nobility. The State Council could block any Duma legislation and was, in essence, another client serving the throne.

In short, the political system created by the new Fundamental Laws fell far short of Western conceptions of a parliamentary system. Russia was, as historian Richard Charques aptly put it, only a "semi-demi-Constitutional Monarchy,"[1] but even that was a dramatic change. A legislature with limited but real powers did exist, populated by representatives from various political parties enjoying legal status for the first time. In the Duma, along with reactionary parties committed to their tsar and his goal of reversing his "terrible decision," liberals of various stripes mingled with Mensheviks, Socialist Revolutionaries, and even Bolsheviks.

Notwithstanding the Duma's limitations, Russia made significant strides forward between 1906 and the outbreak of World War I in 1914. A 1908 law mandated the achievement of free, compulsory primary education by 1922. There was also progress in expanding secondary and higher education. Russian industry grew rapidly, although at a slower rate than during the boom years of the 1890s. Despite uneven progress, by the outbreak of World War I Russia ranked as the world's fifth-largest overall industrial power.

STOLYPIN AND THE "WAGER ON THE STRONG"

Russia also saw significant developments in agriculture. The man behind them was Peter A. Stolypin, Russia's prime minister from mid-1906 until his assassination in 1911. Stolypin's job was not an enviable one. When he took office, Russia was still gripped by widespread peasant disorders. Various revolutionary groups were attacking government officials in a deadly campaign of revolutionary terror. The Socialist Revolutionaries alone assassinated more than 4,000 government officials between 1906 and 1910. In response to the crisis Stolypin unleashed what amounted to a government reign of terror on the countryside. Special courts tried and executed people within twenty-four hours of their arrests. These "field courts-martial" claimed over 1,000 lives between August 1906 and April 1907, and this represented only a fraction of the executions carried out by the government between 1905 and 1908. Combined with the imposition of martial law wherever it was deemed necessary, these instant trials and the hangings that followed, the so-called Stolypin neckties, did their job. Order was restored and Stolypin was then free to get on with an even more difficult charge: overhauling Russian agriculture in a generation.

The Stolypin reforms were an attempt to complete, as rapidly as possible, what the emancipation had begun over forty years earlier. Despite some progress in certain areas, almost two generations after the emancipation rural Russia remained poor, inefficient, volatile, and a threat to the dynasty. Land hunger remained the hallmark of the Russian peasant, still bound to backward farming techniques and his commune. Stolypin hoped to solve all these problems by turning the commune-bound Russian peasant into an independent farmer similar to farmers in Western Europe or the United States. If the autocracy, he reasoned, helped peasants to acquire their own independent, consolidated farms, they would become far more productive and—equally important—conservative supporters of the tsar's regime. The monarchy, for the first time in generations, would have a broad, solid base of social support. Some peasants, many in fact, would fail once they were cast out on their own. Stolypin nonetheless felt that the potential gains in productivity and support from the successful peasants would far outweigh any difficulties that might arise from those who failed. Russia and the monarchy, he emphasized, could be strengthened only if they relied not "on the drunken and the weak, but on the sober and the strong."

The heart of Stolypin's "wager on the strong" was legislation that released peasants from membership in their communes, allowed them to claim their land allotments as private property, and, finally, permitted them to consolidate their scattered parcels into one plot. Other reforms promoted peasant resettlement in sparsely populated regions of central Asia and Siberia, eliminated the remaining legal restrictions on the peasantry, and provided financial help to buy land. When he began his program in 1906, Stolypin asked for twenty years of peace, after which, he promised, Russia would be "unrecognizable." This was a bold boast, but there were many who believed that this tough, able, and single-minded servant of the tsar might succeed where so many others had failed.

The "strong" peasants Stolypin was counting on often were called "kulaks"—the word "kulak" means "fist" in Russian—a term that varied in meaning according to the circumstances in which it was used. Often the term meant simply an efficient, hardworking, and prosperous peasant who employed hired labor and normally had acquired more land than his fellow villagers. The term also could have a pejorative connotation, as kulaks often lent money to their neighbors at high rates and had various other avenues to take advantage of them. Either way, their achievements and economic status made kulaks the most influential people in Russia's peasant villages.

A decade after Stolypin began his work the Russian countryside was indeed changing. About half of all peasant households in European Russia held their land under individual ownership. Approximately 10 percent had consolidated their plots. It was a good start, but the race already was being lost. By 1916 Stolypin had been dead for five years, and Russia, two terrible years into World War I, was beginning to crack under the strain of defeat at the front and discontent at home.

The outbreak of the war was not the only impediment to the Stolypin reforms. Like Witte before him, Stolypin had to contend with the entrenched reactionary forces. Reactionary nobles and bureaucrats tried to thwart Stolypin's attempts to extend the *zemstvos* to Russia's western provinces. Their constant harassment undermined the prime minister's authority, both with the population at large and with the tsar. At times, however, Stolypin had only himself to blame for his troubles. A devoted nationalist and advocate of Russification, Stolypin carried out repressive and discriminatory policies that antagonized, among others, millions of Finns, Poles, and Ukrainians. Russification was hardly conducive to the twenty years of peace Stolypin said he needed.

Another source of Stolypin's difficulties was his failure to enlist the support of moderate, progressive political elements. The Kadets were determined to turn the Duma into a genuine parliament with powers far beyond those specified in the Fundamental Laws. Their attitude placed them in direct confrontation with Stolypin and the government. The more moderate Octobrists accepted the limits on the Duma and initially hoped to be able to cooperate with the prime minister and even join with him in governing the empire. In return, during discussions shortly after the dissolution of the first Duma in July 1906, they demanded seven (out of thirteen) cabinet posts be reserved for individuals from outside the tsarist bureaucracy. Stolypin considered these demands excessive and turned them down. The Russian government continued as before to be based on nothing more representative than the corrupt and despised bureaucracy.

The failure to broaden the regime's political base created problems for Stolypin, but he was still able to govern, albeit with some difficulty. In 1907, after the dissolution of the second Duma, he invoked Article #87 and then rewrote the electoral law. As a result, the next Duma was sufficiently conservative and pliable to enable the government to work with it. The real losers were the moderates and liberals. The autocracy, having used small concessions to win breathing space and recover its footing, continued to be a barrier to progress. There were some differences of opinion about what to do. The Octobrist leadership clearly feared the Russian masses more than it objected to the Russian autocracy. More militant Kadet politicians, in particular the distinguished historian Paul Milyukov, the party's leading figure, at first had been ready to flirt with the revolutionaries. Milyukov hoped that the revolutionaries could be used to batter down the autocracy, after which the liberals would govern in a parliamentary and republican Russia. Later, however, he became more fearful of revolution and was willing to settle for a genuine constitutional monarchy. The liberals' dilemma and their inability to function as an independent force was a direct function of the weakness of the

Russian bourgeoisie, an observation made many times by political pundits of varying leanings. As Nicholas Berdyaev, a former Marxist turned conservative religious philosopher, put it: "In Russia it was not the communist revolution but the liberal bourgeois revolution that proved to be a utopia."

THE REVOLUTIONARIES ASSESS THE 1905 REVOLUTION

In the aftermath of the 1905 defeat, however, the prospects of any revolution seemed, if not utopian, at least remote. During the period of upheaval the Socialist Revolutionaries had enjoyed some success in organizing peasant uprisings, but army troops had crushed them. Subsequently, in 1917, unable to agree on a new revolutionary strategy, the party split into two parts. The Social Democrats, already divided in 1905, attempted to learn some lessons from the revolution's defeat. These lessons are important because of what they reveal about the Bolsheviks and Mensheviks and because they turned out to be the difference between success and failure when, much to everyone's surprise, the revolutionaries were given a second chance in 1917.

During 1905, the Mensheviks, insisting that they were involved in a "bourgeois" revolution, tailored their activities to fit that revolution. They welcomed the formation of the St. Petersburg Soviet, declaring that it was the nucleus of a broadly based workers' party. The Mensheviks readily cooperated with other socialist groups inside the Soviet and with liberals outside the Soviet. They had, for example, joined in the liberal "banquet campaign" of 1904 and, at the Social Democrats' Fourth Congress in 1906, they advocated an alliance with the Kadets. In their view, the defeat of the 1905 Revolution proved that the proletariat still had to bide its time and build its strength. Russia's next revolution still would have to be "bourgeois." Only afterward, as Russian capitalism matured and the proletariat grew, would the proletariat's chance for power come.

Lenin and the Bolsheviks also had a lesson to learn. Their performance during the 1905 Revolution was not impressive. Lenin did not even make it back to Russia until November. During the early months of 1905, when it seemed possible that the tsarist regime might collapse, Lenin had doubted the chances of achieving a socialist revolution. Later he equivocated about the St. Petersburg Soviet. On the one hand, he went beyond the Mensheviks and asserted that the Soviet could be the embryo of a transitional revolutionary government. On the other hand, Lenin distrusted any mass, spontaneous institution that he and his Bolsheviks could not control. The Bolsheviks, in fact, played a relatively minor role in the St. Petersburg Soviet. They were more active in the Moscow Soviet, especially in leading it into an armed uprising in late December 1905. But that bloody failure hardly added to the Bolsheviks' or Lenin's luster.

Amid the rubble of the 1905 failure, Lenin honed his two weapons: Marxist theory and revolutionary technique. Out of the realization that the Russian proletariat on its own was too weak to make a revolution arose Lenin's idea of a proletarian–peasant alliance (led by the proletariat, of course) and a concerted effort to develop a platform that would appeal to the peasantry. Lenin also worked hard on practical matters. Originally, he favored boycotting the Duma elections, but he reversed himself when he concluded that the Duma, whatever its weaknesses, could be an excellent soapbox. In 1906, a variety of pressures, including strong sentiment for unity among the rank and file of both factions, forced him to agree to heal the Bolshevik–Menshevik split. Lenin went through the motions, all the while maintaining a separate Bolshevik organization. When he finally engineered a formal party split in 1912, he seized the organization's funds and records. Finances, always a problem during the dark days after 1905, were seen to by a variety of questionable measures including fraud, extortion, counterfeiting, and a famous series of bank robberies. These activities got Lenin into trouble not only with the Mensheviks but also with the entire European socialist movement, which in effect censured him for conduct unbecoming of a revolutionary.

Lenin remained undeterred. Neither these activities nor his faction's association with the criminal elements sometimes required to carry them out embarrassed him. Nor was he disturbed when those who could not accept his leadership left the party. During the difficult years between the 1905 Revolution and the outbreak of World War I in 1914, the Bolsheviks shrank in size and remained isolated on the political fringe. Yet through it all Lenin never lost sight of his goal. At the outbreak of the war many Marxists forgot their revolutionary priorities and rallied instead to their respective national colors. Others opposed the war from a pacifist perspective and worked to restore the peace. In sharp contrast to both of these positions, Lenin and a few other militants called for turning the conflict into a revolutionary war. This was the message of his book *Imperialism: The Highest Stage of Capitalism.*

The calls by the left for a negotiated peace or a revolutionary war— depending on which group was making the call—fell on deaf ears. Like battered boxers who refuse to fall, the belligerent powers remained on their feet, and the war dragged on. Even Lenin became demoralized. "We of the older generation may not see the decisive battles of the coming revolution," he told a Swiss audience in January 1917. Within two months the Russian autocracy collapsed.

RUSSIA ON THE EVE OF WORLD WAR I

Because of the momentous changes that were to overwhelm Russia after the revolutionary year of 1917, historians have tried to sort out the multiple causes of tsarism's collapse. Pared down to its essentials, the question is whether Russian society was headed for a new stability or toward disintegration in the decade prior to World War I. In other words, did the war destroy a viable society or simply hasten a fractured society's impending collapse? It is, ultimately, a question without a conclusive answer, as World War I was a cataclysm of overwhelming power that in social terms shattered the strong as well as the weak, killed the healthy as well as the sick, toppled the sturdy as well as the unstable, and swept away the deeply rooted as well as the tenuously held. And prewar Russia was a huge conglomeration of all of these.

Certainly there had been progress. In the half century since emancipation, Russia's entire social order had begun to change under Western influences. This was an unprecedented development for a country that historically had done everything it could to exclude all Western influences except for technology. Beginning in the 1860s local government and the judiciary were reformed, education created a vast new reading public receptive to Western ideas, capitalism sank deep roots, and entirely new classes similar to those in Europe developed. The pace of change quickened in the 1890s. In the generation between 1890 and 1914, Russia experienced one of the highest industrial growth rates in the world. On the eve of World War I, only the United States, Germany, Great Britain, and France stood ahead of Russia as industrial powers. Additional progress marked the decade prior to the war. In the countryside, the Stolypin reforms began to shape a new, independent, and prosperous peasantry whose conservatism might have become a vital new prop for the monarchy. Even the monarchy itself changed. After 1905, Russia finally had a parliament of sorts with real, if severely limited, powers. Censorship was eased.

The generation before World War I also witnessed a flowering of Russian culture, the "Silver Age," a worthy successor to the glorious Golden Age of Pushkin, Dostoyevsky, and Tolstoy. Although the Silver Age produced no single figure equal to those giants, it did create for an audience larger than ever before a marvelous diversity of outstanding literature, music, theater, and art. Regardless of the empire's other difficulties, Russian high culture, studded with a kaleidoscopic array of brilliant artists in virtually every medium, stood with the best Europe had to offer. In music, Peter Tchaikovsky, perhaps the greatest of all Russian composers, died in 1893, but Silver Age composers such as Sergei Rachmaninoff, Igor Stravinsky, and Alexander Scriabin achieved international, and lasting, renown. Fyodor Chaliapin, the legendary operatic basso, gave triumphal performances in venues from Moscow to Milan's La Scala to the United States. In ballet, Russia produced not only many of the outstanding dancers of the age, but some who surely were among the best of all time, most notably, but not exclusively, Vaslav Nijinsky and Anna Pavlova, of whom a famed teacher (an Italian, not a Russian) to many of the era's top dancers said, "Pavlova has that which can be taught only by God." Among the many talented Russian prose writers and poets who came of age in the generation before World War I were Andrei Bely, Alexander Blok, Anna Akhmatova, and Ivan Bunin. (In 1933, thirteen years after joining many of his colleagues and opting for exile in the West in the wake of the Bolshevik Revolution, Bunin became the first Russian to win a Nobel Prize in literature.) Painters Vasily Kandinsky, Marc Chagall, and Kazimir Malevich, to name but a few, also reached prominence during the Silver Age. Meanwhile, the Moscow Art Theater, founded in 1898 and led by the pioneering director Konstantin Stanislavsky, was staging the great dramas of Anton Chekhov—at once Russia's premier playwright and short story writer—beginning with *The Seagull*, the play that gave the theater its symbol. The theater also presented the works of Maxim Gorky and other Russian playwrights, as well as works by ancient Greek dramatists, Shakespeare, and contemporary European playwrights such as Henrik Ibsen. Russia during its Silver Age also arguably produced in Sergei Diaghilev the greatest art impresario of all time, the man who just before the turn of the century gathered a galaxy of avant-garde luminaries around the publication *The World of Art*. A decade later Diaghilev fused the genius of some of Russia's best dancers, composers, musicians, and artists in a dance company called the Ballets Russes, whose performances, beginning in Paris in 1909, with their unprecedented and breathtaking multimedia blend of music, art, and dance, dazzled and amazed European audiences. And all this barely serves as a highly selective introduction to Russia's Silver Age.

But this impressive new social landscaping rested astride deep and shifting societal fault lines. Russian industry progressed, but only by producing a poverty-stricken proletariat along with its manufactured products and, until the Stolypin reforms, by living off governmental policies that worsened conditions in the countryside. Trade unions, legalized in 1906, still labored under severe restrictions and remained weak. Meanwhile the workers remained dissatisfied. After a decline in labor militancy and strikes between 1906 and 1910, the tide of unrest began to rise again. Strikes doubled in 1911. In 1912, the country again trembled with shock and anger when workers at the Lena gold fields in Siberia, on strike to improve their miserable wages and shorten their 5 A.M. to 7 P.M. workday, had their strike violently broken by troops at the cost of 170 dead and almost 400 wounded. More than 725,000 workers struck in that year. In 1913, 887,000 workers went out. And 1,250,000—out of a *total* workforce of barely 3 million—struck in the *first half* of 1914 to back up their demands both for economic improvements and for potentially much more dangerous political reforms.

There simply had not been enough progress to assuage all the pain. When measured on a per capita basis, Russia was losing rather than gaining ground relative to its European competitors. In the fifty years between 1860 and 1910, Russia was unable to overtake even Spain or Italy, much less the real industrial powers, in that vital measure of industrial progress. In 1900, Russian per capita production had been one-eighth that of the United States and one-sixth that of Germany; on the eve of the war those figures were one-eleventh and one-eighth, respectively. In 1913, Russia produced only one-tenth as much coal and barely half as much steel as Great Britain, a country with less than half Russia's population. Over half of the empire's industrial equipment still had to be imported.

In agriculture the situation was no better. The Stolypin reforms produced poor peasants as well as more prosperous ones by removing the protective cloak of the commune. Agricultural production rose significantly between 1900 and 1913, but the average Russian could hardly have noticed. Exports of grain were on the average 50 percent higher in the last several years before the war than during the first years of the century, and a rising percentage of the crops that remained in Russia were industrial crops, like cotton, that fed machines rather than people. In fact, it is likely that the average Russian in 1914 had no more to eat than his counterpart had in 1860.

Other problems plagued the empire. Millions of its non-Russian subjects hated the regime. So did many Russians who felt the weight of state oppression because they chose to practice a form of Christianity other than the officially endorsed Russian Orthodoxy. The dangerous cleavage between the educated few and the uneducated masses still remained unbridged. Most of the elite continued to be alienated from the official political process. And all the tsar's subjects also still chafed under the dead weight of the ubiquitous Russian police. In short, the government teetered on an eroding foundation.

WORLD WAR I

It was under these conditions that Russia entered the inferno of World War I. Although the causes of the war are complex and are still debated, much of the blame must go to the rivalries between the Great Powers and the frustrated nationalist sentiment in Central Europe and the Balkans. Russia's involvement in the war is one thing for which Nicholas II and his government cannot be blamed. It is difficult to imagine how any Russian government committed to traditional national foreign policy goals could have avoided the fatal plunge that claimed all

Europe's Great Powers, each of them seemingly gigantic lemmings rushing to a raging sea. Yet there were people in every capital who understood the colossal folly of what was happening and feared the worst. In Russia, no one saw through the glass darkly more clearly than Peter N. Durnovo, a former police official and minister and member of the State Council. In February 1914, six months before the war's outbreak, Durnovo sent a memorandum to Nicholas II in which he predicted, with eerie accuracy, what would happened if Russia, with its deep class divisions, was exposed to the battering ram of military defeat:

> In the event of defeat . . . social revolution in its most extreme form is inevitable. . . . The trouble will start with the blaming of the Government for all disasters. In the legislative institutions a bitter campaign against the Government will begin, followed by revolutionary agitations throughout the country, with Socialist slogans, capable of arousing and rallying the masses, beginning with the division of land and succeeded by the division of all valuables and property. The defeated army, having lost its most dependable men, and carried away by the tide of primitive peasant desire for land, will find itself too demoralized to serve as a bulwark of law and order. The legislative institutions and the intellectual opposition parties, lacking real authority in the eyes of the people, will be powerless to stem the popular tide, aroused by themselves, and Russia will be flung into hopeless anarchy, the issue of which cannot be foreseen.

The war began, as wars often do, with a patriotic rally to the colors. Soon, however, modern twentieth-century warfare began to exact its price. The war strained even Europe's most advanced industrial economies to their limits, and Russia now paid dearly for its backwardness. To the two colossal burdens the old regime had borne before 1914—the unequal competition with the highly industrialized Western powers and the immense strain caused by rapid social and economic change in the face of limited political change—was added the supreme test of World War I. Russia's semi-industrialized economy, pushed beyond its limits by the skyrocketing demands of modern warfare and the demoralization caused by military defeats, began to fall apart. Economic dislocation generated tremendous social discontent and turmoil. The political system, still an antiquated bureaucratic relic despite the limited reforms of the past fifty years, was woefully overmatched.

It took about a year for Russia's economy to falter seriously. Russia was unable to export to Germany, once its most important customer but now its mortal enemy, and at the same time was compelled to increase imports to feed its hungry war machine. The resulting enormous trade imbalance produced severe inflation. Yet all the imports were not enough to meet Russia's needs. Geography and history seemingly had conspired again by placing Russia's enemies—Germany,

Austria-Hungary, and Turkey—between itself and its allies in Western Europe. The partially successful enemy blockade caused Russia to suffer grave shortages of raw materials and vital industrial machinery that could not be produced at home. Production fell in several key industries. The eventual mobilization of 15 million men disrupted both industrial and agricultural production, while the enemy's occupation of Russia's economically advanced western regions added to the economic difficulties and also created a massive refugee problem.

Distributing those resources that were available became another unsolvable problem. Russia's railroad system, inadequate in peacetime, was swamped by the vastly larger wartime burden. Eventually it began to deteriorate as worn-out equipment was not replaced. It took until mid-1915 for significant shipments of military supplies from Russia's allies in the West to arrive at the far-northern ports of Arkhangelsk and Murmansk; then much of that desperately needed materiel was stranded there, hundreds of miles from any Russian army, because of land transportation bottlenecks. Arkhangelsk, ice-bound half of the year, had only an inadequate single-track railway line linking it to Moscow (until the line was double-tracked later in the war), while ice-free Murmansk had no railroad at all until a line linking it to St. Petersburg was completed in late 1916. Equally serious, consumer goods disappeared in the wake of industry's conversion to military production, and the peasantry, unable to find goods to buy, began to hoard the food it produced. Over time the unavailability of manufactured goods and farm machinery caused agricultural production to decline. The cities began to lack food. As it turned out, it was a food shortage in Petrograd (as the capital now was called, instead of the Germanic St. Petersburg) that sparked the crisis that brought down the monarchy in 1917.

The government's almost unbelievable incompetence exacerbated the crisis. Russia was unprepared for war. One year after the outbreak of fighting, one general lamented that "No amount of science can tell us how to wage war without ammunition, without rifles, and without guns." To enforce sobriety and presumably thereby enhance the war effort, Russia in August 1914 became the world's first country to enact a national prohibition. Liquor, of course, continued to flow illegally. What dried up was the government's supply of money. Its single largest source of revenue in 1914 was the state liquor monopoly; the Russian people's excessive alcohol consumption produced 30 percent of what were understandably dubbed "drunken budgets." The disastrous results of Russian prohibition were pointed out by an exasperated member of the Duma budget committee who complained, "Never since the dawn of history has a single country, in time of war, renounced the principal source of its revenue."

The war overmatched Russia's political leadership. The men Nicholas appointed to head his council of ministers during the war were ignorant, incompetent, senile, or all three. One, J.L. Goremykin, a senile man in his mid-seventies, was labeled by a colleague as one of the "worst products of the Russian bureaucracy." His successor, N.D. Golitsin, actually begged Nicholas to find somebody else for the job. That probably was the best advice Golitsin ever gave, considering that he was, as the economist and historian Michael Florinsky has noted, "entirely without experience in state affairs."[2] As bad as these men were, they were better than Rasputin, whose influence over the empress and her weak-willed husband increased with each crisis-packed year. When Nicholas went to the war zone in the fall of 1915 to take over direct command of the army, a blunder that directly tied him to every military failure, the empress and her sinister spiritual advisor made important decisions of state back in the capital. By 1916, Rasputin controlled most important ministerial appointments. Men who could barely help themselves now were chosen to lead Russia in its moment of dire emergency. The empress, meanwhile, displayed her lack of political acumen by calling for the exile to Siberia of leading Duma members. Not surprisingly, although unfairly, both she and Rasputin were widely accused of treason.

Support and sympathy for the monarchy were evaporating. By the end of 1916 Russia's military losses, which cannot be fixed with certainty because of incomplete records, probably exceeded 6 million: about 1.5 million dead, at least 2 million wounded, and more than 2.5 million captured or missing. Rasputin's assassination in December of that year eliminated him, but not the leadership vacuum. The tsar's refusal to consider reforms proposed by leading Duma moderates and liberals embittered and alienated many potential allies. During January and February of 1917 strikes and demonstrations rocked Petrograd. Disorder increased nationwide as well. Prophecies of doom and rumors of upheaval were everywhere.

Yet Tsar Nicholas II remained unperturbed. He was oblivious both to the immediate crisis and to historical developments that dictated that by 1917 even the Russian tsar would have to respond to his people's needs and demands if he was to win their support and survive. When warned by a foreign diplomat that he had to regain his people's confidence, Nicholas rejected the well-intentioned warning. The problem, he insisted, was that the people had to regain *his* confidence. The tsar, trapped in a changing and unfriendly world he did not understand, chose to live instead in a world of his own. Meanwhile, the Romanov dynasty was sliding ever closer to the abyss.

NOTES

1. Richard Charques, *The Twilight of Imperial Russia* (New York: Oxford University Press, 1958), p. 30.
2. Michael Florinsky, *The End of the Russian Empire* (New York: Collier Books, 1961), p. 90.

Part III

Lenin's Russia

Joseph Stalin, Vladimir Lenin, and Mikhail Kalinin at the Eighth Congress of the Communist Party of the Soviet Union, March 1919.

9

1917: Russia's Two Revolutions

Surely some revelation is at hand;
Surely the Second Coming is at hand; . . .
And what rough beast, its hour come round at last,
Slouches toward Bethlehem to be born?

—William Butler Yeats

With all your body, all your heart and mind, listen to the revolution.

—Alexander Blok

Claim too great freedom, too much license,
and too great subjugation shall befall you.

—Alexis de Toqueville

The fifty-six years between 1861 and 1917 represented an unprecedented period in Russian history, the only era under the tsars when Western influence was pervasive in Russia and not confined to economic development projects, technological and scientific imports, or a sampling of Western intellectual delicacies by the educated elite. The society as a whole was changing as Europe seemingly was pulling Russia, inch by inch, across the Urals in a social, cultural, and economic sense. The events of March 1917 opened up new vistas for change along Western lines by eliminating the autocracy, the greatest obstacle to that process. Yet those events also created opportunities for long-suppressed forces oriented in completely different directions to tug and pull on Russia. In the middle of a world war, the main battle for the Russian people suddenly shifted to the home front, where the central issue was not the country's relations with foreigners, but how Russians would relate to each other.

THE MARCH (FEBRUARY) REVOLUTION

The remarkable thing about the revolution that put an end to the 300-year-old Romanov dynasty and the even older Russian autocracy is the relative ease with which it all finally happened.[1] In March (February) 1917 the exhausted and exasperated Russian people went on strike, vented their anger in demonstrations and riots, and engaged in street fighting for about a week in their capital city, and the old political order collapsed. The stage for these events had been set between January and the first week of March by strikes and fuel shortages that had closed factories throughout Petrograd, including the huge Putilov manufacturing complex, a center of working-class militancy. Then, on March 8 (February 23), large crowds of hungry strikers clamoring for bread joined with demonstrators celebrating International Women's Day and turned the center of Russia's capital into a scene of mass antigovernment protests. By midday 100,000 workers were on strike, and within two days about 200,000 workers were demonstrating in the streets. Nicholas commanded that order be restored, but troops sent to do the job refused to shoot down their countrymen and soon mutinied instead. The mutiny spread quickly; suddenly there was no authority in the capital loyal to the tsar. On March 11 (February 26), word reached Petrograd that Nicholas II had dissolved the Duma. A majority of its members defied the tsar and refused to disperse. The next day, March 12 (February 27), a group of leading Duma members set up a Provisional Committee of the Duma to cope with Russia's crisis, as the tsar obviously could not. Also on March 12, in the very same building that had housed the Duma and now housed the Provisional Committee, a self-appointed contingent of workers, soldiers, and members of the revolutionary intelligentsia organized what they ultimately called the Petrograd Soviet of Workers' and Soldiers' Deputies, an institution evoking memories of the short-lived 1905 St. Petersburg Soviet but whose purpose was still unclear. On March 15 (March 2), after hours of negotiations with the leaders of the Petrograd Soviet that had started late the previous night, the Provisional Committee of the Duma declared itself Russia's Provisional Government. Nicholas II, stranded on his royal train because nobody would follow his orders, stood completely alone. Everyone he spoke with, including his most trusted military officers, told him that his time was up. On March 15 the tsar bowed to the reality of the situation by abdicating on behalf of himself and his hemophiliac son in favor of his brother, the Grand Duke Michael. When Michael refused the throne the next day, the Romanov dynasty, which had begun just over 300 years earlier with a luckier Michael, came to an end.

The revolution that ended the Romanov dynasty, while over quickly, was nonetheless often a violent affair. Armed gangs looted shops and broke into the houses of the well-to-do to pillage and rape. Soldiers in Petrograd and sailors at nearby naval bases expressed years of pent-up rage by murdering their officers, sometimes with great brutality. There was bloody street fighting in the capital between mutinous soldiers, supported by armed civilians, and the police. Mobs hunted down and murdered police who were attempting to escape the rising tide of rebellion they could not control. In Petrograd about 1,500 people were killed or wounded. Yet the level of violence, however frightening to those who witnessed it, seems relatively minor compared to the seismic political upheaval Russia was experiencing, and it certainly pales in comparison with what was to come. In any event, the removal of the autocracy did not eliminate the myriad of problems that had precipitated the revolution. Russia remained mired in an unsuccessful and unpopular war that had bled the nation and left its battered army barely able to fight. The economy was dangerously close to collapse. In the cities and towns food was scarce. Industrial production was declining. Peasant land hunger remained unsatiated. And the autocracy's collapse, even as it solved one problem by eliminating a derelict system of government, posed a new one in its place—the task of replacing the old regime with one that could cope with the country's mounting distress.

DUAL POWER

The removal of the Romanovs created a tremendous power vacuum. In the wake of the collapse of a political order of 300 years standing, no group had a legitimate claim to govern. The result was a peculiar and unstable situation that came to be called "dual power." Two institutions shared political authority, insomuch as any authority existed at all: the Provisional Government—Russia's self-proclaimed interim government—and the Petrograd Soviet. The Provisional Government was the creature of leading Duma moderates and liberals. As such, it lacked any enthusiastic support from the bulk of the Russian people. Because of its commitment to establishing a Western-type parliamentary system in a country inexperienced with and suspicious of representative government, the Provisional Government faced long odds from the beginning. Its indecisiveness and mistakes quickly lengthened those odds.

The Provisional Government's chances of success were further diminished by the presence of the Petrograd Soviet of Workers' and Soldiers' Deputies. The Soviet was a hybrid political species, combining the trappings of a government, a political convention, and a mob. Composed of representatives from the factories and military units in and around the capital, the Soviet lacked both a consistent formula for selecting its membership and a defined area of responsibility or jurisdiction. Nonetheless, its strategically placed popular support gave it more power than the Provisional Government. The Soviet's status was further complicated by the attitude of the Mensheviks and the Socialist Revolutionaries, the two socialist parties that controlled it from March to September. According to Menshevik thinking, which the SRs at the time did not challenge, the Soviet could not aspire to political power because Russia was going through its "bourgeois" revolution. The Soviet's historically mandated task was to permit the bourgeoisie to govern while it served as a nongovernmental guardian of the revolution and the interests of the working masses.

Because of support from the workers and soldiers of Petrograd and from hundreds of soviets that quickly sprouted up all over the country, the Petrograd Soviet soon made its influence felt, mainly at the expense of the Provisional Government's credibility and its efforts to set Russia's house in order. The Soviet itself accomplished little that was constructive. Dual power really meant the Provisional Government had very little power.

Meanwhile, the bulk of the population—the land-hungry peasants, the exploited and hungry factory workers, the oppressed and agitated national minorities, and the weary and demoralized soldiers (themselves largely peasants)—confronted the Provisional Government with demands for re-forms that they hoped would improve their lives. Many of these demands the government could or would not meet, while what it could do satisfied very few people. It did, for example, abolish all religious, national, and class discrimination; eliminate many of the oppressive aspects of military disci-pline; and guarantee a wide range of civil and political liberties. These were significant advances, and even a cynic like Lenin admitted that Russia had become the "freest country in the world." Yet none of these decrees raised anybody's standard of living. The peasants still did not have their land. The workers still faced inadequate wages, ruinous wartime inflation, employer lockouts, and food shortages. The national minorities still lacked the autonomy or independence they craved.

This was bad enough, but besides their demands for immediate measures to improve their lives, Russia's masses were raising more fundamental and dangerous issues. Their hatred for those above them went far beyond the tsar, his bureaucracy, and the nobility; it encompassed all of Russia's economic and social elite, including those who staffed the new government and the intellectuals who ran Russia's various political parties, whatever their pro-testations or political orientation. The average peasant or worker did not trust any government and saw a plot where often there was mainly hesitation or ineptitude. Thus, when elections to the promised Constituent Assembly were postponed, largely because of technical difficulties, many people were sure that the delay was an upper-class conspiracy. Many local soviets openly opposed the Provisional Government and its attempt to establish some central authority in Russia to replace the fallen tsar.

For the bulk of the Russian people, freedom meant an escape from the governmental authority that always had perpetuated their misery. It meant the right finally to take what they wanted and needed without regard for the priorities of any government, irrespective of whatever well-intentioned gentlemen staffed it or what noble ends it proclaimed. As historian Marc Ferro has observed, Russia's masses seemed to want "not a better government, but no government at all."[2] In such a context, there was no popular mandate for representative government as it existed in the West. The peasants frequently did not even know what viewpoints the various political parties held.

In order to understand the complexity and chaos that followed the March Revolution, it is helpful to understand three divisions that marked Russia's political life. The first divided Russia's privileged classes into two camps, moderate/liberal and socialist, and was in large part responsible for the tense relationship between the Provisional Government as originally constituted and the Petrograd Soviet. By making it more difficult for anyone to govern, this cleavage helped open the door to further upheaval. At the same time, by 1917 the gap was closing in some places as Russia's political ground shifted, bringing some socialist parties closer to the liberal camp and in turn distancing those same parties from more radical socialist groups.

The second division was the old dichotomy between Russia's privileged elite—including those elements running both the Provisional Government and the Petrograd Soviet—and the masses. In 1917, however, this division had a new and crucial dimension: the masses finally had the means to become politically articulate. During the course of the year, the Russian people, for the first time in their history, established a great variety of mass organizations in which they participated directly and through which they projected considerable political power. These organizations—local soviets, factory committees, soldier committees, peasant committees, the Petrograd Soviet itself, and the like—activated and mobilized enormous numbers of people at the bottom of Russia's social pyramid. The nature of the resulting tension was fairly straightforward. The Russian masses increasingly demanded far more radical social changes than the Provisional Government or the Soviet's leadership were willing to sanction. This inevitably weakened the Provisional Government and discredited the Socialist Revolutionaries and Mensheviks, the parties that controlled the Soviet, exposing them to charges that they were insufficiently revolutionary to lead the aroused masses. This division also furthered the likelihood of another upheaval.

The third division was between those parties that had a response tailored to take advantage of the increasing turmoil and those that did not. As the masses became more frustrated and radical during 1917, most of the major political parties, including the Kadets, the SRs, and the Mensheviks, attempted to restrain them. The Kadets, of course, along with the somewhat more conservative Octobrists, supported a constitutional parliamentary regime and free enterprise. The SRs and Mensheviks, notwithstanding their revolutionary rhetoric, had mellowed during the past decade and increasingly accepted democracy. They were evolving into moderate socialist parties similar to those found in the West. Among Russia's major political groups, only Lenin's Bolshevik Party, which until 1917 had been relegated to the far fringes of Russian political life, militantly rejected the regime that had emerged after tsarism's collapse and was prepared to pander to and incite the angry masses. Concerned only with winning power, untrammeled by scruples, and indifferent to the devastating impact of the war on the country and its people, Lenin from the minute he arrived in Petrograd in April demagogically exploited Russia's turmoil to position the Bolshevik Party to seize power. The gulf between the Bolsheviks and the other socialist parties was crucial, for the Bolsheviks, unlike those parties that tried to contain the growing disorder, were not swamped by the rising revolutionary wave; instead, they were in a position to ride it to power.

THE PROVISIONAL GOVERNMENT

The Provisional Government that the Bolsheviks eventually overthrew was more provisional than a government. Because it shared the stage uneasily with the upstart Soviet, the Provisional Government was called the "half power." Yet even that pejorative term was overly generous. The new government drew most of its support from Russia's professional classes and the progressive elements of the nobility and business community, a thin and fragile layer of Russian society. It drew no strength from what were increasingly the real arbiters of power in Russia: the crowds of workers and soldiers in the capital who had first attacked the autocracy, the army that had been unwilling to come to the old regime's rescue, and the peasants.

Moreover, the new government's leading members were ill-suited to swim in a rising and treacherous revolutionary tide. Prince George Lvov, the prime minister, was a *zemstvo* notable and prominent Kadet who had earned a national reputation for his wartime role mobilizing thousands of volunteers and institutions to supply the army with food, medicines, and other necessities the government was unable to provide. When it came to exercising political leadership, however, Lvov was hopelessly naive and fatally incapable of decisive action. He was overshadowed by several members of his cabinet from the start. Among them was Foreign Minister Paul Milyukov. The leader of the Kadets and a distinguished historian, Milyukov understood academic historical debates better than the immediate crisis posed by masses banging at the gates. The minister most closely identified with the masses was the SR lawyer Alexander Kerensky, who held the justice portfolio. He unfortunately was far better at talking to the masses than at listening to them. Kerensky also was a member of the Soviet's executive committee. As the only person during the early days of the revolution who was a member of both the Provisional Government and the Soviet, Kerensky provided an initial, though ineffectual, link between the two bodies. Later, when more SRs and Mensheviks from the Soviet joined Kerensky in the government, this link became a chain that dragged down these socialist parties when the Provisional Government went under.

The Provisional Government's haplessness was established even before it officially assumed power. In the negotiations of March 14–15 with the Soviet prior to the government's formation, its leaders had agreed to several conditions, including the abolition of all police organs and their replacement by a militia with elected officers, that made it exceedingly difficult for the new regime to assert its authority. Even more damaging was a decree on March 14 by the Petrograd Soviet called Order Number One. The socialists who ran the Soviet issued Order Number One without consulting with the liberals and moderates who were about to form Russia's new government. Officially addressed to the garrison of the St. Petersburg military district, its influence quickly spread beyond the capital to other military units, including those at the front. At a time when anarchy threatened to engulf Russia and powerful enemy armies occupied large parts of its western provinces, Order Number One effectively destroyed the government's control over its army. The Soviet was concerned lest the army be used by conservative forces to crush the revolution. Order Number One therefore stipulated, among other things, that the "lower ranks" of all Petrograd district military units elect committees and choose representatives to the Soviet. It also stated that the Soviet rather than the government was the ultimate authority to which the military was responsible. Order Number One eliminated what was left of the army's fighting ability and shackled the new government before it took a single step. Barely a week after Nicholas's abdication, the man who was supposed to be in charge of the armed forces, Minister of War Alexander Guchkov, summed up his problems and those of his government:

> The Provisional Government possesses no real power and its orders are executed only insofar as this is permitted by the Soviet of Workers' and Soldiers' Deputies, which holds in its hands the most important elements of real power. . . . It is possible to say directly that the Provisional Government exists only while this is permitted by the Soviet of Workers' and Soldiers' Deputies.

The Provisional Government bore other burdens as well. The moderates and liberals who initially staffed it wanted Russia to embrace legal and parliamentary institutions similar to those found in the West. They therefore mandated that a nationally elected Constituent Assembly had to determine the country's constitution and permanent form of government. This made sense given the political system the Provisional Government hoped to establish and also was in accordance with the conditions its leaders had accepted in their negotiations with the Soviet. However, it left the current government stuck with its tenuous "provisional" status. The Provisional Government further undermined its position when it insisted that certain other major reforms also had to await the convocation of a Constituent Assembly, as only such a body would have the proper mandate to promulgate these fundamental changes in Russian life. The impatient peasants therefore were told they would have to wait for their land. The national minorities—aside from the Poles, who were promised independence—were informed that their autonomy would have to wait. The government's position was further compromised when the advent of the Constituent Assembly was postponed because of the difficulties involved in arranging the elections. By the time the Constituent Assembly finally did meet, in January 1918, the Provisional Government already had been overthrown.

The Provisional Government meanwhile compounded its problems when it reaffirmed Russia's commitment to the Allied war effort and aims. By 1917, while there was no clear national consensus on the war, the nation clearly was war-weary, and the Soviet's call late in March for a peace "without annexations and indemnities" probably represented what the largest number of Russians supported. Sentiment was different in the government, where the leadership was highly nationalistic and sympathetic to the Allied cause. These leaders, particularly Milyukov, assumed that the masses shared their enthusiasm for a vigorous new war effort to secure Constantinople and the Dardanelles from the Ottoman Empire or spheres of influence in China. They could not have been more wrong. The disturbances that followed Milyukov's announcement of his foreign policy forced his and Guchkov's resignations in mid-May. The cabinet then was reorganized, with five Mensheviks and SRs joining that body and Kerensky becoming minister of war. The government, now a coalition of liberals and socialists, did not learn from Milyukov's fate. Instead, it began planning an offensive against the Germans and Austrians, which resulted in a disastrous defeat.

Finally, while it planned to fight the mighty Germans, the Provisional Government was too weak to ensure order at home. It was unable to replace the old tsarist administrative apparatus, which had disintegrated. Some policies made a difficult job even harder. For example, as per the March 14–15 agreement with the Soviet, the police were replaced with a voluntary militia, which neither helped restore order nor strengthened the regime. As part of its blanket amnesty for political prisoners, the government allowed avowed foes of democracy who were openly determined to overthrow the new regime to return to Russia. All this only made things easier for the government's enemies.

THE PETROGRAD SOVIET

While the Provisional Government was stumbling along, the Petrograd Soviet had problems of its own. It was a chaotic body, made up of about 1,500 deputies elected by factories and military units in and around the capital. Continual elections in the factories and military units meant that the Soviet's composition was always in flux. Many of those in attendance at any given meeting were not elected by anyone, but, as in the case of members of the revolutionary intelligentsia, simply were admitted by the Soviet or even self-appointed. In this chaos, real decisions could only be made by the Soviet's executive committee, a body dominated not by workers or soldiers but by members of the politically more experienced intelligentsia.

From March to September of 1917 the Soviet was controlled by a coalition of Mensheviks and Socialist Revolutionaries. The Mensheviks and SRs, like the liberals in the Provisional Government, while free from tsardom, were still prisoners of their own ideology. The loosely organized SRs—their leader Viktor Chernov once referred to his party as a "herd"—generally deferred to the Mensheviks. They, in turn, deferred to dog-eared Marxist revolutionary blueprints, which defined the current revolution as being "bourgeois." Therefore, the socialists and their political instrument—the Soviet—would not take power, regardless of the ineptitude and weakness of the Provisional Government. Compelling practical considerations reinforced this conclusion among the Mensheviks and SRs, particularly the fear of a violent reaction by the propertied classes and the army against any socialist bid for power. So the Soviet contented itself with supporting the Provisional Government in its efforts to implement social reform, while at the same time making sure, as it did with Order Number One, that neither the government nor any other potentially unfriendly player could threaten the working masses. While this stance in theory protected the working classes, in practice it had the more immediate effect of subverting the Provisional Government's efforts to restore order in Russia and govern.

LENIN'S APRIL THESES

Russia thus lingered in a political vacuum. As Prince Lvov observed, a government possessing "authority without power" faced a Soviet representing "power without authority." This situation was too unstable to survive for very long; it created an opportunity for any politician perceptive and ruthless enough to exploit it. That politician was Lenin. Although he certainly was not expecting the revolution when it occurred, and at first assumed it was merely an Allied-orchestrated plot to preclude a separate Russian–German peace, he quickly realized his chance had come. Yet he could only gaze at it from afar, for March 1917 found Lenin marooned in Switzerland. After several frustrating weeks he managed to reach Russia, courtesy of the German government, which decided to grant him and several other revolutionaries safe passage home in the expectation that such people would further disrupt things in Petrograd and drive Russia from the war. In the short run Lenin did not disappoint them; in the long run he astounded not only his unwitting benefactors, but many others as well.

One of the reasons Lenin was in such a hurry to get back to Russia was that the Bolsheviks on the scene, notwithstanding his years of effort to set his party apart from the other socialist groups, were behaving like everyone else. Led by Lev Kamenev and Joseph Stalin, the Bolsheviks in Russia had accepted the prevailing view that the current revolution was "bourgeois" and socialists consequently should abstain from power. Worse, these Bolsheviks actually were discussing reunification with the Mensheviks, a prospect that threatened the political machine Lenin had been building for fifteen years. The day he set foot in Russia in mid-April, Lenin repudiated any thought of cooperation with the Provisional Government. The next day, in a dramatic statement that left even his most avid supporters stunned, Lenin spelled out his position in what are known as his April Theses.

The April Theses were designed to restore the Bolsheviks' ideological militancy and set them apart from their rivals. Lenin's major points were no support for the "imperialist" war effort; no support for the Provisional Government; the transfer of "the entire state power to the Soviets of Workers' Deputies"; confiscation of the landed estates for the benefit of the poor peasants; and, to indelibly distinguish the Bolsheviks from Social Democratic parties that had "betrayed socialism and deserted to the bourgeoisie," a change in the party's name to the "Communist Party." Lenin's program, whatever its failings in terms of traditional Marxism—he was, after all, closing down Russia's bourgeois revolution after barely a month—was closer to the racing popular pulse than that of any other political party. Certain refinements made it even more so. These included support for what was called "workers' control," a vague concept that to some meant worker participation in management decisions in the factories and to others meant a complete takeover of those factories, an ambiguity Lenin did not bother to clarify. The Bolsheviks also unequivocally endorsed the right of national self-determination for all of Russia's ethnic groups.

Along with a program that had an immediate appeal to so many, the Bolsheviks had slogans the people could understand: "Land," "Bread," "Peace," and "All Power to the Soviets." They also translated the sympathy these slogans aroused into tangible support by organizing more effectively than anyone else in key mass associations such as urban soviets, factory committees, and soldiers' committees. That effort included arming their supporters whenever possible; it yielded the factory worker militia known as the Red Guards and groups of soldiers and sailors who provided the party with vital military muscle. With Lenin at the helm, the Bolsheviks also had the Russian politician who proved best able to navigate the country's treacherous and unpredictable revolutionary rapids.

THE BOLSHEVIKS GAIN STRENGTH

Against a background of government ineptitude, the vacillation of the Mensheviks and the SRs, the continued decline of living conditions, and their own organizing efforts, Bolshevik strength began to grow. In March they had fared very poorly in the elections to the Petrograd Soviet, winning only about fifty of approximately 1,500 seats. However, over the next several months their strength in the Soviet grew steadily. That upward curve was reflected in elections to the First All-Russian Congress of Soviets, which was comprised of representatives from soviets all over the country. When the Congress convened in the capital in mid-June, the Bolsheviks had 15 percent of the delegates, although once again the SRs and the Mensheviks had an overwhelming majority.

The Bolsheviks also were doing well in the streets. Ironically, they, the alleged elitists, were proving to be the best practitioners of the new art of mass politics. In mid-June the Bolshevik leadership scheduled an antigovernment demonstration to take place while the Congress of Soviets was in session, an event that would have included armed soldiers from pro-Bolshevik regiments, but was forced to cancel it under pressure from the Menshevik and SR majorities in the Petrograd Soviet and the Congress of Soviets. The Menshevik/SR leaders of the Petrograd Soviet then staged a demonstration of their own, only to find that Lenin's organizers had been hard at work at the grassroots level and that slogans on the placards indicated that most of the more than 400,000 workers and soldiers who showed up supported the Bolsheviks. Bolshevik strength meanwhile grew in the urban soviets, the burgeoning trade unions, the factory committees set up in the plants and shops, and the military units. The soldiers were particularly important; the Bolsheviks remembered that the 1905 Revolution failed when the army remained loyal to the tsar. This time Lenin intended to have the army on his side, or at least to neutralize it, and the concerted Bolshevik effort among the troops reflected this concern. Overall, between March and August the Bolshevik Party grew more than tenfold, from 20,000 to about 250,000 members.

Credit for the Bolsheviks' success must go to Lenin. Since 1902 he had worked to create an elite political organization that would stand apart from Russia's other socialist parties. It had not been an easy task, as his troops several times had drifted toward reconciliation with the Mensheviks. In 1917, Lenin again faced that same old problem as well as poor discipline in the ranks. His April Theses, in fact, initially had been rejected by the party leadership because most Bolsheviks considered them too radical; it took Lenin almost a month to get his way.

Once Lenin got the party on course, it was a continual struggle to keep it there. After he had to flee Petrograd in July to avoid arrest, controlling his party was like steering a kite in a swirling wind. He sometimes was unable to control his Central Committee. Ironically, though, Lenin's struggle to maintain party discipline reflected a source of Bolshevik strength. The party was not yet, as it would become and remain, a monolithic and bureaucratic automaton. The tremendous growth of membership during 1917 had changed it from an exclusive, insulated elite into something of a mass party, with many new and expanded local committees and cells often operating quite independently. Decisions in these local bodies often reflected actual feelings of the rank and file. At times this mass base was even more radical than Lenin himself. That was why in June the party leadership, fearing it might lose influence among militant workers and soldiers, had planned the armed demonstration that, had it not ultimately been cancelled, would have been a direct challenge not just to the government but to the Congress of Soviets. In short, the party's new mass base gave Lenin a direct reading on the pulse of the nation. As the spring of 1917 turned into summer, that pulse was beating faster.

The situation was similar at the top levels of the party. Because Lenin made the Bolsheviks into what was clearly the most revolutionary party in Russia, it attracted numerous talented and impatient radicals from other parties. These were not yes-men; if they had differences with Lenin they did not hide them. They thereby added not only their skills but an element of awareness and flexibility to the party's resources.

By far the most important of these newcomers was Lenin's long-time critic, Leon Trotsky. His assets included not only extraordinary organizational and oratorical skills but also his theory of "permanent revolution." According to Trotsky, the peculiar characteristics of Russia's development—in particular, the weakness of its bourgeoisie, which lacked the strength to hold on to political power for any length of time—and the possibility of spreading the revolution to Western Europe meant that Russia, despite its backwardness, could flash right through the "bourgeois" revolution to a socialist revolution. This, of course, was basically what Lenin was trying to do. Trotsky, who suddenly metamorphosed from one of Lenin's most caustic critics into one of his most unabashed admirers, later wrote that without Lenin there never would have been a Bolshevik revolution. He certainly was correct, but it is also hard to imagine how Lenin could have succeeded without Trotsky, the man who actually organized the Bolshevik seizure of power and then created, "out of nothing," as Lenin put it, the Red Army that successfully defended the Bolshevik government against a long list of opponents in a brutal civil war.

As 1917 wore on, permanent revolution changed from a political dream to a real possibility. The spring of 1917 had been both literally and figuratively the springtime of the revolution, a time of relative optimism and goodwill. Most people seemed willing to give the new government a chance to prove itself. Even the peasants, in part because increased demand for food had benefited many of them economically and because they expected that the government would soon sanction their takeover of the landed estates, generally held back from violent action. By the summer, hopes and optimism, like spring flowers, were beginning to wilt. The mood in Russia had changed.

THE JULY DAYS

The failure to respond to that change was fatal, both to the Provisional Government and to the Mensheviks and Socialist Revolutionaries. These two parties had entered the government after Milyukov's resignation because they hoped to forestall collapse and the threat of civil war. They thereby unintentionally tied their fates to that shaky regime. While the Provisional Government was embarrassed and bruised in May and June, beginning in July it suffered debilitating wounds. Ever since May, Kerensky in his capacity as minister of war had been preparing an offensive against the Central Powers, in the hope that military victories would both further Russia's national interests abroad and rally support for the government at home. A man whose reputation owed more to his hyperbolic language than to any political or military acumen, Kerensky went to the front to rally his troops with advice such as "Forward to liberty! . . . Forward to Death." The Russian troops, devoted to their country through it all, amazingly were still ready to try again. After a two-day artillery bombardment, on July 1 (June 18) they moved forward, briefly, against Austrian forces before being battered by a German counterattack. The offensive quickly collapsed. The army then mercifully began to crumble; 700,000 men deserted during the summer and fall. As Lenin put it, the soldiers "voted with their feet" for peace.

Some troops expressed their feelings in other ways. In mid-July, even before news of the most recent Russian defeat had reached Petrograd, soldiers from several army units stationed in the city mutinied because of fear they would be transferred to the front. These troops were joined first by militant, pro-Bolshevik workers and then, after some hesitation, by the Bolshevik leadership. The mutiny, which began on July 16 (July 3), became a Bolshevik-led uprising against the Provisional Government known as the July Days.

Considering the Bolsheviks' triumph less than four months later, the immediate results of this three-day upheaval were deceptive. Several hundred people were killed in the fighting, which lasted until July 18. The government succeeded in gathering loyal soldiers to defeat the uprising and was then able to turn on the Bolsheviks. Hundreds of party members were arrested, along with several top leaders. The party newspaper was closed, and Lenin, a warrant out for his arrest, fled the capital and went into hiding. His reputation was seriously tarnished by revelations that his party had accepted money from the German government. Lenin, as earlier "expropriations" had demonstrated, did not care where his money came from. He considered himself no more in debt to the German government than he was to the Russian banks from which his party had previously "expropriated" funds. At any rate, intervening events would cause this embarrassment to be largely forgotten by autumn, while the German money helped the Bolsheviks regain their strength.

The Provisional Government and its Menshevik and SR ministers survived the July Days, and a few days after the fighting ended Kerensky succeeded Lvov as prime minister. But Kerensky's disastrous military offensive had cost the government crucial public support. In early August he revamped the cabinet by adding more moderate socialists as ministers, with little noticeable impact on the government's effectiveness. As for the Mensheviks and SRs, their growing commitment to the government placed them more than ever against the rising tide of popular revolutionary sentiment. The Soviet probably could have taken power in July and formed an all-socialist coalition government. Such a move quite likely would have ended Lenin's hopes for an exclusively Bolshevik seizure of power. Yet despite the urging of the respected Menshevik leader Yuli Martov, the Soviet did not act, much to the chagrin of the workers and soldiers roaming the streets of the capital. A famous scene that took place during the July Days in front of the Soviet's headquarters illustrates how out of step with the popular mood the Mensheviks and SRs were falling. When a mob appeared to demand that the Soviet take power, Viktor Chernov, the SR leader and current minister of agriculture in the Provisional Government as well as a leading member of the Soviet, tried to calm the crowd. One demonstrator shook his fist in Chernov's face and screamed: "Take power, you son of a bitch, when it is offered to you." Chernov was saved from injury and possibly from death only by Trotsky's intervention.

The Bolsheviks' recovery from the July Days was almost as rapid as had been their eclipse. In early August, the party's Sixth Congress, held in the capital, testified to a growing and well-managed organization, even during its leader's imposed absence. The overall situation in Russia during the late summer increasingly favored those who stood for change. Food shortages in the towns and industrial centers continued unabated. Factories closed, unable to obtain supplies. Sometimes owners closed them because of labor unrest, much of which was instigated by Bolshevik-led factory committees. In the villages, militant peasant committees sprouted up while people with radical political sympathies took over the leadership of the traditional peasant communes, leaving much of rural Russia in a state of upheaval. The wait for land was over. Afraid of missing their chance if they did not act and reinforced by armed deserters coming home from the front, peasants now seized the landlords' land and property, sometimes killing the landlords in a process that continued well into 1918. These activities were organized by the communes, which also forced many of the independent farmers who had emerged under the Stolypin reforms to return to the communal fold. The Bolsheviks also benefited from the backlash against Kerensky's failed military offensive. Workers, peasants, and soldiers increasingly demanded an immediate peace, something the government, with its commitment to the Allies, could not deliver.

THE KORNILOV AFFAIR AND ITS AFTERMATH

All of this naturally frightened the middle and upper classes. As the masses moved to the left, the propertied classes shifted to the right. Many people now became sympathetic to the idea of a military dictatorship as the only hope of restoring order and preventing a complete social upheaval. Kerensky also determined that order had to be restored if his government was to survive. To do this he turned to his newly appointed commander-in-chief, a brave but politically inept Cossack named Lavr Kornilov. But Kornilov, who according to a fellow tsarist general had "the heart of a lion but the brains of a sheep," marched to a different drummer—the concerns of frightened conservative and moderate Russians and worried Allied diplomats. He decided to suppress all the revolutionary forces, from the moderate socialists in the Soviet to the militant Bolsheviks in the streets. Early in September, after a confusing and rather tragicomic series of moves and countermoves by the bumbling general and the hysterical prime minister, Kornilov marched on the capital to take charge. Kerensky managed to defeat this clumsy military coup, but only by turning to the Bolsheviks for help. The desperate Provisional Government released Bolshevik leaders from prison and supplied arms to the party's Red Guard militiamen. While thousands of Red Guards prepared to defend

Petrograd, emissaries sent to agitate among Kornilov's troops succeeded in destroying their morale and provoking a mutiny. Crucial help also came from other sources, including the pro-Menshevik railway workers.

The Provisional Government was saved, but hardly safe. On top of all its old unsolved problems, it had incurred the wrath of many army officers who previously had been willing to take its orders. Additional trouble came from the areas inhabited by non-Russians, from the Baltic Sea to the Ukraine to Central Asia, where nationalist sentiment and impatience were building. By September, the Provisional Government existed by an apparent act of political levitation, for it was impossible to discern its sources of support.

Prime Minister Kerensky remained as ineffectual as ever. The best he could do was organize a monthly series of conferences and large meetings: the Moscow State Conference in late August, the Democratic Conference in late September and early October, and the Pre-Parliament in late October. Kerensky's performance at the Moscow State Conference exemplified his weaknesses as a political leader. His opening speech, as historian William Henry Chamberlin has observed, "conformed to a familiar pattern: loud phrases which covered up feeble and irresolute actions."[3] Despite warnings about Bolshevik intentions, Kerensky did nothing to hinder Lenin's minions after the Kornilov affair. He did little about governing Russia, now sinking into chaos in the wake of rioting, looting, and a host of criminal activities. In his closing speech to the Moscow State Conference, the prime minister became so emotional that he almost collapsed.

Bolshevik strength was meanwhile approaching a critical mass. By August the party controlled several important soviets, including the one at the important Kronstadt naval base in the Gulf of Finland, less than twenty miles from Petrograd. In mid-September, the Bolsheviks became the majority in the Petrograd Soviet; they took control of the Moscow Soviet a few days later. About two weeks after the party's triumph in the capital, Leon Trotsky, the man who had led the revered 1905 St. Petersburg Soviet in its final days, became president of the Petrograd Soviet. As in 1905, Trotsky's ascension was quickly followed by dramatic events. This time, however, those events would carry him not to prison, but to power.

THE ORDER OF THE DAY

While Trotsky was the visible star in Russia's political firmament during October and early November, the hidden force moving key elements into place was Lenin. Like Trotsky, Lenin believed that a golden opportunity had arrived with the rapid decay of the Provisional Government and the political paralysis of the Mensheviks and SRs, an opportunity that might not come again. Only

Lenin could convince the party leadership that the time had come to seize power. This job was much harder than one might have expected because the party's Central Committee remained, as it would for a few more years, a body that could achieve a genuine consensus only through debate and persuasion. Lenin's political genius in 1917 and in the crises of the next four years lay not only in his ability to choose a viable course of action, however dangerous or ruthless, but also in carrying his party along with him. He probably had a more difficult time convincing his Central Committee to take power than the party had seizing it. He observed, after all, that the latter was like "picking up a feather"; controlling a Central Committee of egotistical and willful men was more like wrestling with an octopus.

Lenin's campaign to win support for a seizure of power began in late September. It was made more difficult because he remained in hiding in Finland, which prevented him from meeting with his Central Committee colleagues in Petrograd. Lenin's opening salvo consisted of two letters—a third followed two weeks later—to the Central Committee in Petrograd. The first letter began: "The Bolsheviks, having obtained a majority in the soviets of workers' and soldiers' deputies in both capitals [Petrograd and Moscow], can and *must* take power into their own hands." The Central Committee, to put it mildly, was not convinced. Trotsky later recalled that no one supported Lenin's urgent demand when its members first discussed his letters. Nikolai Bukharin, at the time one of the group's most militant members, remembered that "We were all aghast." Rather than prepare for an uprising, Lenin's colleagues decided to forestall any violent actions by workers and soldiers. Apparently in several subsequent meetings the Central Committee did not even discuss its leader's stunning proposal.

The battle dragged on for a month. The opposition to Lenin in the Central Committee was led by two previously loyal lieutenants, Grigory Zinoviev and Lev Kamenev. They doubted that the country would follow the Bolshevik lead, noting that while a majority of workers and many of the soldiers would support the party, "everything else is questionable." They wanted to wait for the upcoming Second Congress of Soviets, where they expected a Bolshevik majority. The party then could come to power without resorting to an armed coup. That analysis produced Lenin's third letter, a furious harangue that argued that to await the Congress of Soviets "is complete idiocy or complete treason." Inaction would make the Bolsheviks "miserable traitors to the proletarian cause," especially since with a well-planned immediate attack "the chances are a hundred to one that we would succeed." Lenin went so far as to resign from the Central Committee to protest its lack of action. His colleagues ignored his resignation even more completely than his protests against their policies.

In the long run, far more was at stake than the question of when and how to take power. The underlying issue was how that power would be exercised and what would be the basis of Bolshevik rule. Zinoviev and Kamenev did not expect the Bolsheviks to rule alone but to lead a socialist coalition commanding the support of a majority of the Russian proletariat and peasantry. By predicating a Bolshevik government on winning the support of a majority in the Second Congress of Soviets, Lenin's dissident lieutenants injected a democratic component into their conception of Bolshevik power. Lenin, in contrast, wanted the party to seize power alone and to rule alone. By choosing to rely on his claim that the Bolsheviks represented the best interests of Russia's toiling masses without waiting for them to express their opinion on the matter through elections, and by his insistence on using force to come to power regardless of any electoral results, Lenin made dictatorship the basis of his proposed regime.

Lenin succeeded in swinging the Central Committee most of the way to his side when he finally came to Petrograd for a meeting on the night of October 23 (10). The committee, without fixing a precise date, voted 10–2 that an armed seizure of power was "the order of the day." Zinoviev and Kamenev dissented. They both promptly protested the decision to the party at large and leaked the news of the planned coup to the press. That Lenin, shortly after the seizure of power a few weeks later, was willing to forget this outrageous breach of party discipline and accept the two recalcitrants back into the party's good graces is testimony both to his ability to put practical politics above vindictiveness or spite and to the give and take that characterized Bolshevism in 1917. That the Provisional Government reacted barely at all to the advance notice of a plot to destroy it is testimony to its advanced state of decay. No wonder seizing power was as easy as "picking up a feather."

The final debate—over the precise timing of the coup—Lenin actually lost. He wanted immediate action. At one point in October he warned, "Every day lost could be fatal. History will not forgive us if we do not take power now." But Lenin's entreaties ran up against the judgment of Bolshevik leaders working directly with rank-and-file members in Petrograd who insisted on a delay until the convening of the Second Congress of Soviets in early November, where they expected to have a Bolshevik majority. These leaders cited strong evidence that the masses in the capital and other urban centers would oppose a coup by the Bolsheviks acting alone. In addition, acting in concert with the Second Congress satisfied the consciences of those Bolsheviks who had retained at least a minimal commitment to the democratic traditions of European Marxism and were therefore loath to seize political power without some kind of expression of support from the working class, whose vanguard they claimed to be.

Even Trotsky, whose credentials as an impatient and fearless firebrand were incontestable, disagreed with Lenin on the key issue of timing. Trotsky reasoned that if the Bolsheviks waited for the Second Congress of Soviets to convene and endorse their overthrow of the Provisional Government, the coup would win an important measure of legitimacy. He believed such an endorsement was essential if the Bolsheviks were to avoid strong popular opposition, particularly from the soldiers in Petrograd. At the same time, Trotsky was not leaving that endorsement to chance. By now president of the Petrograd Soviet, he was manipulating the process of delegate selection to the upcoming congress by increasing the representation of soviets and army units where the Bolsheviks held a majority at the expense of soviets and army units where other parties predominated. As he reassured a deeply worried Lenin at the crucial October 23 Central Committee meeting— without convincing him in the slightest of the wisdom of delaying the coup—"We are convening a Congress of Soviets in which our majority is assured beforehand."

THE NOVEMBER (OCTOBER) REVOLUTION

The Bolsheviks actually had no detailed plan for a coup until Kerensky forced their hand. On the evening of November 5 (October 23), his cabinet proclaimed a state of emergency. It ordered that the Soviet's newly formed Military Revolutionary Committee be dissolved (an eminently reasonable demand since Trotsky was using that committee to organize the Bolshevik coup), as well as the closure of two Bolshevik newspapers and the arrest of several party leaders, most notably Trotsky. A few hours after midnight Kerensky dispatched his few remaining loyal troops to occupy strategic positions in the capital and close down the Bolshevik printing plant that produced its newspapers.

Kerensky's moves did little more than provide Trotsky with an excuse to strike under the pretext that the "Petrograd Soviet is in direct danger." During the night and predawn morning hours of November 6–7 (October 24–25), Bolshevik detachments, including sailors from the Kronstadt naval base, had no trouble seizing most of the key points in Petrograd. So smoothly did the operation proceed that nobody really noticed. As historian Lionel Kochan notes:

> Petrograd's *dolce vita* was not interrupted. Guards officers clicked their spurs and engaged in gay adventures. The sound of wild parties burst from private salons of elegant restaurants. The electric current was switched off at midnight but heavy gambling continued by candlelight.[4]

The official announcement of the Provisional Government's overthrow, issued by the Soviet's Military Revolutionary Committee, came at 10:00 A.M. on November 7 (October 25). The only real fighting in the capital, and it was minimal, occurred the night of November 7–8 (October 25–26). It began on November 7 at about 9:30 P.M. when the cruiser *Aurora*, under Bolshevik control and strategically positioned in the Neva River, opened fire on the Winter Palace, seat of the Provisional Government. The mighty *Aurora* was firing only blanks, and probably fired only one shot, but the noise had an intimidating effect and turned the warship into a revolutionary icon. Bolshevik Red Guards gradually occupied the Winter Palace without serious opposition and at about 2 A.M. on November 8 arrested the Provisional Government ministers, although missing Kerensky, who had fled Petrograd beforehand in a car provided by the U.S. embassy. It had taken only twenty-four hours and a few hundred casualties to depose Russia's government and bring the Bolsheviks, who only months before were a tiny political sect, to power. No wonder an exhausted Lenin commented to Trotsky that the whole process "makes you dizzy."

THE FAILURE OF THE RULE OF LAW AND DEMOCRACY IN RUSSIA

The Provisional Government's collapse marked the failure of a decades-long effort to establish Western democratic political life in Russia. That effort was severely handicapped from the start by Russia's historical legacy. By the start of the twentieth century, Western concepts of private property, the rule of law, and parliamentary government had started to take root in Russia, but those roots still were shallow. Only a few elite groups—the professional middle class, the business community, and progressive elements of the nobility—had any interest in or inclination toward parliamentary democracy. That thin layer of Russian society proved to be too fragile a foundation to support a parliamentary regime during the turmoil of 1917. Most Russians had little interest or confidence in constitutional and democratic representative institutions. The peasants wanted land, the proletariat wanted workers' control, the soldiers wanted to go home, the national minorities wanted autonomy, and none of them cared how they achieved their respective goals. When the Provisional Government could not deliver right away on these crucial bread-and-butter issues, Russia's masses turned against it.

The Provisional Government failed because, aside from the burdens imposed by history, it also was limited by nationalistic obsessions, legalistic and democratic inhibitions, and unimaginative leadership. Because of nationalism it locked itself into a war it could neither win nor end, with disastrous results. It refused to decree the reforms most urgent to the bulk of the population because that would have violated legal norms such as property rights. Staying in the war made it impossible to arrest the spreading economic collapse. This, in turn, left the Provisional Government incapable of controlling Russia's masses, who, liberated at last from their tsarist fetters, were running wild. Nor could the Provisional Government cope with the Bolsheviks and their determined will to power.

Will, of course, hardly explains the Bolshevik triumph. In ordinary times, the Bolsheviks would have remained where they were before March 1917, isolated and irrelevant, on the fringes of Russian political life. But these were not ordinary times. The Bolsheviks turned out to be the Russian political party best suited to a revolutionary environment that demanded adaptability, ruthlessness, and a demagogic instinct for the new phenomenon of mass politics. In Lenin the party had a leader ready to exploit any opportunity and flexible enough to adapt to changing circumstances. The Bolsheviks tailored their program to appeal to the masses—the workers, soldiers, peasants, and non-Russian nationalities—especially as those groups became more militant and impatient during the summer and fall. Because during the early months of 1917 new local Bolshevik organizations sprang up and grew too fast to be dominated by the party's central apparatus, those organizations reflected the sentiments of their rank and file and therefore kept the leadership abreast of the popular mood. Superior organization enabled the Bolsheviks to build their strength and ultimately win control of key urban soviets and worker and military committees. Because of Lenin's concern for the nuts and bolts of seizing power, the Bolsheviks also organized their own armed units, which were essential to the November success.

Lenin and the Bolsheviks had more going for them than will and political skill. It seems fair to say that luck played a major role in their eventual success. During 1917 Lenin made his share of errors, including the abortive uprising in July that very nearly brought the Bolsheviks to grief. The party constantly was distracted by its internal squabbles, which lasted right up to the seizure of power. Lenin and the Bolshevik Party were rescued from these disabilities by circumstance—in particular, the complete collapse of authority—and the more serious and numerous errors and internal squabbles of their opponents. As historian Robert V. Daniels has pointed out:

> The stark truth about the Bolshevik Revolution is that it succeeded against incredible odds in defiance of any rational calculation that could have been made in the fall of 1917. . . . Lenin's revolution . . . was a wild gamble, with little chance that the Bolsheviks' ill-prepared followers could prevail against the military force that the government seemed to have, and even less chance that they could keep power even if they managed to seize it temporarily.[5]

Lenin took that gamble because in reality he had little choice. He understood that a military coup was the only way his militant but small Bolshevik sect could ever achieve the absolute power he demanded and that dictatorship was the only way the party, or any group for that matter, could permanently hold that power. What drove the Bolsheviks forward into the maelstrom was the tradition of the Russian revolutionary intelligentsia to which they were heirs, a tradition that transmuted everyday popular protests and hopes for a better life into cosmic visions of a revolution that would transform Russia, and the world, into a socialist utopia. It was those visions, and the ability to justify any means to attain them, that enabled the Bolsheviks to generate force far beyond what their numbers or resources suggested was possible and ultimately gave them a fighting chance to win their wild gamble. Their November victory in turn was testimony to the rather un-Marxist reality that in times of society-wide upheaval and the collapse of order, pivotal decisions by a few individuals, rather than collective actions by masses of people, can be decisive in determining who wins and who loses the contest for power.

The Provisional Government's fall and the Bolshevik seizure of power marked a momentous historical watershed—the end of the social, economic, and political process of Westernization that, particularly since 1861, had been recasting ever greater parts of Russian society. The Bolshevik Revolution reversed Russia's direction, and the country embarked on a new path that would widen the gap with the West to the greatest extent since the time of Peter the Great. Perhaps the most important consequence of the Bolshevik victory was that it postponed for seven decades the effort to establish a society based on the rule of law, private property, and parliamentary democracy in Russia. That effort, to be sure, was a struggle against the odds from the start. During its short life the unsteady Provisional Government legalized all political parties, ended censorship, abolished the secret police, guaranteed freedom of the press, legalized trade unions and the right to strike, and took many other progressive steps. However, lacking a broad social base on which to ground their parliamentary edifice, the new government's supporters, devoid of experience and deficient in skill, were forced to navigate stormy and treacherous political seas, driven relentlessly by the winds of war and social turmoil, that lay between the Scylla and Charybdis of the antidemocratic extreme right and left. During 1917 they managed to avoid being wrecked by the former, only to be swamped by the latter.

Still, while the Provisional Government lost out in Russia in November 1917, Bolshevism's ultimate triumph was hardly inevitable. Most of the country, if not committed to formal parliamentary democracy, wanted some kind of multiparty government based on the soviets. The Bolsheviks owed much of the support for their November coup to their ability to wrap themselves in the soviet mantle. When their intent to rule alone became clear, many of those who had supported the new regime turned against it. Once these elements sided with others opposed to a Bolshevik dictatorship, the stage was set for a bitter struggle, one that brutalized the country and gravely worsened the odds of sparing the Russian people the misery of a regime far harsher than the one they had overthrown in March. In light of the suffering that would follow during the next seven decades, the debacle of the first of Russia's two revolutions in 1917, and the resultant failure to establish a parliamentary regime based on the rule of law in the land once ruled by tsars, must rank as one of the great disasters of the twentieth century.

NOTES

1. According to the Julian calendar in use in Russia prior to February 1918, Russia's two 1917 revolutions occurred in February and October, respectively. That is why the revolution that overthrew Tsar Nicholas II is often called the "February revolution," while the Bolshevik Revolution is referred to as the "October revolution." This volume refers to both revolutions according to the modern Gregorian calendar.

2. Marc Ferro, "Aspirations of Russian Society," in *Revolutionary Russia,* edited by Richard Pipes (Garden City, N.Y.: Doubleday, 1969), p. 196.

3. William Henry Chamberlin, *The Russian Revolution*, Vol. 1 (New York: Grosset and Dunlap, 1965), p. 203.

4. Lionel Kochan, *Russia in Revolution, 1890–1918* (London: Granada Publishing, 1970), p. 276.

5. Robert V. Daniels, *Red October: The Bolshevik Revolution of 1917* (New York: Charles Scribner's Sons, 1967), p. 215.

10

Into the Fire: The Civil War

There is nothing unhappier than a civil war,
for the conquered are destroyed by,
and the conquerors destroy, their friends.

—Dionysius of Halicarnassus

How do I live?—That is not a pleasant tale.

—Maxim Gorky, 1919

The revolution that brought down the Provisional Government in November 1917 was very different from the upheaval that overthrew the autocracy in March. The March Revolution erupted spontaneously among the Petrograd workers and soldiers; as it spread from the capital it became a nationwide phenomenon, albeit chaotic and without a unifying focus, involving millions of people. The November Revolution, by contrast, was a *Bolshevik* revolution, a planned coup d'état executed by a single political party. The Bolsheviks at the time certainly had significant support in Russia, particularly among workers and military personnel, and only a few Russians were saddened to see the Provisional Government fall. Still, the Bolsheviks, their party name notwithstanding, never spoke in any sense for more than a distinct minority of the Russian people, and most of the support they enjoyed in November 1917 was an endorsement of their apparent role as defenders of the multiparty soviets, not of any intention to rule alone as dictators of Russia. Their seizure of power was certain to be challenged.

The new regime had several broad objectives during its first few months. The most urgent need was to relieve some of the immediate pressures threatening it, specifically those caused by the unending war and rising peasant discontent. Hardly less vital in terms of survival was to bring some order to the chaos engulfing the nation, a situation the Bolsheviks themselves had done

114

much to foster between March and November. In effect, this meant containing and even in part reversing the revolution that had been spreading for eight months. Finally, the Bolsheviks were anxious to use their newly acquired power to make some drastic changes; they had come to power, after all, not simply to rule, but to remake Russia into a socialist utopia.

Whatever the Bolsheviks' eventual plans, the odds were stacked heavily against their staying in power. They physically controlled only a small part of the country, and their easy triumph in Petrograd was not repeated elsewhere. For example, it took almost a week of fighting, in which more than 1,000 people died, before Bolshevik forces won control of Moscow. Until they made peace with the Germans, the Bolsheviks faced a powerful military force that occupied Russia's western territories and was capable of marching on Petrograd and unseating them. The country's non-Russian minorities posed a serious problem: nationalism and the desire for independence were rampant— particularly in the west, among the Finns and Poles; in the southwest, among the Ukrainians; and in the south, among the people of the Caucasus. Even where ethnic Russians lived, near-anarchy prevailed. Peasant discontent had boiled over in the countryside. The economy was in a shambles. Serious shortages of basic necessities, including food, continued unabated. A long list of political groups opposed the November coup, although for the time being most seemed to be in shock and immobilized. Like the late Provisional Government, Russia's new Bolshevik regime was plagued by problems on all sides that in one combination or another could easily sweep it away.

SECURING THE BOLSHEVIK BEACHHEAD

Although Lenin's decisive actions in November may have created the impression that he and his fellow Bolsheviks had a well-thought-out program to realize their goals, the reality was quite different. Subsequent events were to demonstrate that Lenin, the man who had sought power for so long, actually had no concrete plans once he got it. Efforts to plan ahead, of course, were complicated because the Bolsheviks came to power in a country that met none of the traditional Marxist prerequisites for a socialist revolution. Prior to 1917 Lenin had thought about this problem in a general sense and therefore postulated that any advance toward socialism under a Marxist regime in backward Russia would depend on two crucial factors: support from proletarian regimes in Western Europe after the expected socialist revolutions there and a proletariat–peasant alliance in Russia. Trotsky thought along similar lines, although he ignored the Russian peasantry and staked everything on the "direct state support of the European proletariat." Yet these minimal conditions were not fulfilled. There were no successful socialist revolutions in Western

Europe after the Bolshevik Revolution, and serious problems arose in Russia with both the peasantry and the proletariat.

Still, the November victory initially bolstered Lenin's somewhat dormant faith that in a revolutionary situation "the people are capable of performing miracles." Lenin was convinced that his party was about to fulfill a historic role as the spark for a world socialist revolution, and with that in mind, he was not about to let some unexpected difficulties in Russia get him down. A key component of his faith in "miracles," however, was that they could take place only under his direction, and that conviction led directly to his regime's first crisis. The trouble began the moment the Bolsheviks seized power. An armed coup by a single group clashed head-on with the general assumption among socialists both inside and outside the Bolshevik Party that any socialist government in Russia would be a coalition of the various socialist parties. Immediate negotiations to establish a socialist coalition therefore were exactly what Menshevik leader Yuli Martov urgently proposed to the Second Congress of Soviets just after it opened shortly before 11 P.M. on November 7 (October 25). His motion was seconded by a Bolshevik delegate, and the congress—whose membership of 670 included about 390 Bolsheviks and their sympathizers— passed it unanimously. At this uncomfortable point Lenin and his supporters had a stroke of luck when most of the Mensheviks and Socialist Revolutionaries, after denouncing the Bolshevik coup as a "criminal venture," walked out of the congress. The walkout was an enormous blunder. "By quitting the congress, we ourselves gave the Bolsheviks a monopoly of the Soviet, of the masses, of the Revolution," a leading Menshevik later dejectedly recalled. Martov, left with only a small band of supporters, failed in a second lonely and desperate attempt to get the congress to support a socialist coalition. He and his supporters then also walked out, reeling from Trotsky's famous and savage taunt:

> You are miserable bankrupts, your role is played out; go where you ought to go—to the dustbin of history!

Devoid of most dissenters, the congress, at about 5 A.M. on the morning of November 8 (October 26), overwhelmingly adopted a manifesto called "To All Workers, Soldiers, and Peasants" endorsing the Bolshevik seizure of power.

When the congress reconvened that night, Lenin presented it with two decrees designed to bolster support for the new regime and give it urgently needed breathing space. They announced what millions of Russians desperately were waiting to hear. The Decree on Peace called for immediate negotiations to end the war and made it clear that the Bolsheviks were prepared to negotiate with the Central Powers if the Western Allies did not respond to their call. The Decree on Land abolished all private ownership of land; the land was to be turned over to the use of those who tilled it, the millions of peasants who in any event were in the process of seizing the country's large estates.

The congress approved those decrees and one other of fundamental importance: it established an all-Bolshevik government called the Council of People's Commissars, or *Sovnarkom*. Lenin was the new government's chairman. But the issue of the government's composition was far from settled. A few days after the Second Congress of Soviets endorsed Lenin's all-Bolshevik government, the Bolshevik Central Committee, at a meeting from which Lenin and Trotsky were absent, unanimously supported the idea of a socialist coalition government. Lenin could not have been more furious. While some felt a coalition was the best way to represent the popular will, to Lenin it meant "hesitation, impotence, and chaos." It certainly meant his personal power and influence would be diminished. Lenin's first battle to maintain his Bolshevik regime now began. It was an uphill struggle, for although Lenin had Trotsky's support, he was outvoted on the coalition issue even within his most intimate circle. Additional pressure developed when the Executive Committee of the powerful railway workers union (*Vikzhel*), one of the key groups that had brought General Kornilov to grief in September, placed itself at the head of the struggle for a socialist coalition. *Vikzhel* was responding to widespread popular sentiment that, significantly, came not only from virtually all the socialist parties—including the SRs, Mensheviks, Jewish Bund, and Polish Socialist Party—but from rank-and-file workers' and soldiers' organizations. Soldiers at the front, wounded veterans at home, and many factory committees all joined to protest against what they viewed as a usurpation of power by the Bolsheviks. Even workers in the solidly pro-Bolshevik working-class districts added their protest.

In an attempt to sabotage the pro-coalition forces in his party, Lenin was reduced to stalling and negotiating on the basis of demands he knew were unacceptable to the other socialist parties. His tactics did not impress some of his comrades; on November 17 (4), five of them, including Zinoviev and Kamenev, resigned from the Central Committee. Four members of the government also resigned, three of whom (Viktor Nogin, Alexei Rykov, and Vladimir Milyutin) had the distinction of having quit both the party's Central Committee and the government. As Lenin's *Sovnarkom* comrades parted company with him, they issued a dire warning to their stubborn leader: "Other than this [a coalition government] there is only one policy: the preservation of a purely Bolshevik government by means of political terror."

At this point his opponents' ineptitude, already in evidence on November 8, again came to Lenin's rescue, this time in the Mensheviks' handling of the negotiations for a coalition. At one point they demanded the exclusion of the victorious Bolsheviks from the coalition. Later they suggested leaving Lenin and Trotsky out of the government. Such empty posturing did little beyond helping Lenin to regain control of his Central Committee. He won the support he needed and slipped out of his political corner on December 1 (November 18) when he agreed to admit the Left Socialist Revolutionaries (Left SRs), a faction that had split off from the main SR group, as junior partners in his government. This shotgun marriage between unequal partners lasted barely four months. At the same time, the Bolsheviks closed ranks. As was becoming a habit they would repeat later under far worse circumstances, Kamenev and Zinoviev returned to the fold ready to atone for their ideological sins.

BUILDING THE ONE-PARTY STATE, 1917–1918

Although by December 1917 Lenin had a government in place that was reasonably close to what he wanted, its position remained extremely insecure. Prior to November, Lenin had subordinated everything to seizing power. That accomplished, Lenin concentrated all his party's strength on holding power. More than anything else, it was this ability to focus like a laser on his target that distinguished Lenin from both his rivals and colleagues and made him a figure of historic importance.

Lenin did not wait for trouble to come to him. Never bothered by democratic niceties, he quickly struck against the new regime's opponents. On November 9 (October 27), the fledgling Bolshevik government suppressed the non-socialist press. Early in December, "revolutionary tribunals" were set up to dispense justice, short of the death penalty, to opponents of the regime. (In June 1918, the tribunals received the right to dispense capital punishment.) Also in December, the Kadets, who were preparing to take their seats in the long-awaited Constituent Assembly, found their party outlawed and their leaders denounced and under arrest as "enemies of the people." Most important of all, the work of that very busy month was crowned on December 20 (7) by the decree establishing the "Extraordinary Commission for Combating Counterrevolution and Sabotage," or Cheka. Thus the Russian secret police, not yet cold in the grave it had occupied since March, was reincarnated, albeit in a revolutionary rather than a reactionary body. It was an event of fundamental importance in the history of Soviet Russia, for it immediately placed the new regime above the law. Meanwhile, beginning with the one-week battle to secure Moscow, the Bolsheviks used the last eight weeks of 1917 to extend their control over most of Russia's major cities.

In their struggle to solidify their control, the Bolsheviks had to contend not only with alleged "enemies of the people" but with the people themselves, or at least with the proletariat. Lenin had faced this problem before. Prior to 1917, in order to make the revolution he wanted, he had deemed it essential to oppose what he called "spontaneity," the proletariat's tendency to concentrate on bread-and-butter issues rather than on the intelligentsia's revolutionary goals. Once in power, in order to preserve the revolution he wanted, Lenin had to prevent the workers from using their new-found strength to satisfy what they considered their own interests at the expense of what Lenin considered the legitimate objectives of the revolution.

The Bolsheviks were in large part to blame for this problem. During the anarchic months between March and November of 1917, the party had supported the spread of "workers' control." The workers attempted to realize their control through factory committees set up in the plants, usually with chaotic results. Where factory committees attempted merely to participate in decision making, friction between workers and owners often disrupted production. Where workers took over enterprises and tried to run them, they frequently lacked the technical skill to manage them or mismanaged them because they cared only about immediate improvements in their standard of living.

Prior to November, workers' control served Bolshevik interests by adding to the chaos undermining the Provisional Government. Yet even then, Lenin had written that workers' control belonged "side by side with the dictatorship of the proletariat and *always after* it." Once in power, the Bolsheviks found it vital to restore economic order before the economy collapsed completely and brought them down with it. This meant curbing workers' control, although the new government lacked the strength to challenge the workers directly. So, as historian E.H. Carr put it, the Bolsheviks worked instead to make workers' control "orderly and innocuous by turning it into a large-scale centralized public institution."[1] The effort began with the establishment of a hierarchy of factory committees in which local factory committees were directly responsible to higher councils in charge of an entire locality and ultimately to an "All-Russian Council of Workers' Control." The trade unions, whose leadership felt threatened by the free-wheeling factory committees, enlisted with the government in this effort. Although this particular bureaucratic scheme yielded few immediate results, the government began to manage key industries and to limit workers' control through the spreading branches of yet another new highly centralized bureaucratic institution, the Supreme Council of the National Economy (*Vesenkha*), set up in December 1917. Workers' control was giving way to Bolshevik control.

Bolshevik control during these early months was not particularly revolutionary, at least from a Marxist perspective. The emphasis was on restoring discipline and stability, not on a headlong rush to socialism. Proclaiming an eight-hour day was hardly a fire-breathing step. The land decree of November 8, which had deprived nonpeasants of their landed property but done nothing to promote the Marxist goal of collectivized agriculture, was confirmed by a law issued in February 1918. *Vesenkha* was given extensive powers over industry, but it took only small steps toward establishing a socialist economy.

Other early measures, to be sure, were more radical. In November, armed units seized control of Russia's state bank after its management refused to advance money to the new government on the grounds that the Bolsheviks had taken power illegally. In December all private banks were nationalized. This assault on Russia's banks, aside from striking a blow against a hated capitalist institution, was an important survival mechanism. It gave the Bolsheviks access to gold coin and tsarist-era rubles, which unlike the billions of rubles the Bolsheviks were printing, were not virtually worthless. This enabled Lenin's government, at a time when it was barely clinging to power, to pay its Cheka employees, Red Guards, and other security and military personnel with currency that actually had value, which in turn helped maintain their loyalty. Meanwhile, in February all tsarist foreign debts were repudiated. There also was some nationalization of industry, but with the exception of the merchant marine, nationalized in January 1918, and the sugar and oil industries, nationalized in May and June, respectively, such things were decided on a case-by-case basis. During its first several months in power the Bolshevik regime nationalized a number of large mines and factories, including the enormous Putilov manufacturing complex in Petrograd. Altogether, fewer than 600 enterprises were nationalized through June of 1918, many of them taken over by local soviets or worker groups.

All this was consistent with an economic policy that initially was limited in scope. Lenin felt that the regime's immediate objective should be "state capitalism," a highly centralized economy under strict state supervision. The state would nationalize the country's most advanced capitalist enterprises such as the banks, railways, and the largest factories and mines, but the economy as a whole would remain largely under private ownership. State capitalism was to be a measured step toward socialism, not an immediate revolutionary leap to a fully socialist economy. This made some sense, at least when the guideposts with which the new regime had to work are considered. Marxism offered little practical help when it came to economic planning. As Lenin noted ruefully in 1918, "Nothing has been written about it in the Bolshevik textbooks, and there is nothing in the Menshevik textbooks either." The best guide available, and the one Lenin was using, came from a rather unlikely source: the sophisticated combination of private enterprise and state planning developed in capitalist Germany during World War I.

THE CONSTITUENT ASSEMBLY

Along with their restraint in economic policy, the Bolsheviks made one involuntary and very short-lived concession to democracy. Despite some attempts to intimidate other parties, the Bolsheviks permitted a generally free nationwide election, Russia's first, conducted under universal and equal suffrage. The Provisional Government, after several false starts, finally had set the elections to the Constituent Assembly for November 25 (12), 1917. Of course, by election day (it actually took two weeks to complete the balloting, given Russia's vast size) the Provisional Government had been overthrown by the Bolsheviks. This in effect turned the election into a referendum on the Bolshevik regime. Lenin was uninterested in how the people of Russia might want to be governed and in fact feared that his Bolsheviks would be swamped in an election inevitably dominated by Russia's peasant majority. He repeatedly warned his colleagues that permitting the elections was "a mistake, an obvious mistake for which we shall pay dearly." But the Bolshevik government dared not cancel the long-promised election. As expected and feared, the Bolsheviks decisively lost the election. The peasant-oriented Socialist Revolutionaries secured a plurality of 41 percent of the votes against an impressive, but still second-place, Bolshevik total of 24 percent. Bolshevik strength was concentrated in the cities and in military units. The other parties trailed, splitting the remainder of the vote.

The Bolshevik government reacted swiftly. First it postponed the convocation of the assembly. On January 18 (5), 1918, the day the assembly finally opened at the Tauride Palace, Bolshevik Red Guards attacked unarmed pro-assembly demonstrators with machine guns and bayonets, leaving the capital's streets littered with dead and wounded. Many workers were among the casualties, a fact that eroded the regime's working-class support as the news of the killings spread during the following days and weeks. Inside the palace itself, the Constituent Assembly's SR majority, bolstered by Menshevik support, made it clear that its vision of a vast democratic federal Russian republic had no room in it for a Bolshevik dictatorship. The Bolsheviks made it even clearer that their vision of a Bolshevik Russia left no room for any political rivals. Viktor Chernov, elected the assembly's president, recalled that when he spoke from the podium, Bolsheviks in the hall met "every sentence of my speech . . . with outcries . . . often buttressed by the brandishing of guns." In the end, which came less than twenty-four hours after its convocation, the Constituent Assembly was dispersed by force in what Lenin bluntly and accurately called a "complete and frank liquidation of the idea of democracy by the idea of dictatorship."

The Constituent Assembly caused hardly a ripple as it went down. Most Russians, exhausted by almost a year of upheaval, were preoccupied with the immediate tasks of finding personal security and sustenance amid the turmoil and lacked the energy to come to the assembly's defense. For Lenin, extinguishing the sole political institution in Russia that reflected a nationwide consensus did not violate any revolutionary principle because "the republic of the Soviets is a higher form of democratic organization than the usual bourgeois republic with its Constituent Assembly." Obviously, lower bourgeois forms had to give way to higher socialist forms.

RUSSIA LEAVES THE WAR

Although the Bolsheviks disposed of the Constituent Assembly rather easily, their regime probably could not have survived had it not solved the problem of getting Russia out of the war. While many of his most able associates, including his right-hand man, Trotsky, could hardly bear the thought of negotiating with the German emperor and his generals, Lenin knew better. The failure to bring peace had contributed mightily to the Provisional Government's demise, and the virtual disintegration of the Russian army since the summer of 1917 had left the Germans and their allies virtually unopposed at the front. The Bolsheviks, Lenin insisted, had to make peace if they were to survive.

Lenin had almost as much difficulty on this issue with his party comrades as he did with the Germans. Between December 1917, when an armistice was signed, and February 1918, only a minority of the party leadership was willing to accept the harsh German peace terms. One faction, led by Nikolai Bukharin, favored carrying a quixotic "revolutionary war" into Western Europe, oblivious to the fact that the means for such a campaign did not exist. Another group, led by Trotsky, advocated an oxymoronic "neither war nor peace" formula, a strategy that salvaged revolutionary pride while leaving everything, including the revolutionary government in Russia, in both limbo and danger. Lenin was forced to go along with his comrades' stalling and grandstanding until the Germans ran out of patience in February and began a rapid advance that soon threatened Petrograd and the regime's very existence. With their capital hurriedly transferred to the relative safety of Moscow, the Bolsheviks reluctantly yielded to Lenin and accepted peace terms worse than those they previously had rejected. At the Treaty of Brest-Litovsk, signed on March 3, 1918, Russia gave up over 1 million square miles of territory containing over 60 million people and huge chunks of its industrial plant, natural resources, and farmland. Lenin justified these concessions by saying he expected the coming revolution in Germany to render the treaty null and void. More to the point, the Bolshevik regime, the beachhead of the world socialist revolution, had survived.

SOVIET RUSSIA BETWEEN REVOLUTION AND CIVIL WAR

Although the Treaty of Brest-Litovsk gave the Bolsheviks some breathing room, it deeply angered many patriotic Russians. The treaty's enormous concessions to the Germans caused the Left SRs, who also opposed Bolshevik attempts to foster class war against prosperous peasants, to withdraw from the government that same month. Still, by the middle of 1918, the Bolsheviks had some accomplishments to show for their first several months in power. They had taken Russia out of the war. Important institutions to defend the regime and extend its power had been organized, including the Cheka and, after Trotsky's appointment as commissar of war in March, the Red Army. There even had been some significant reforms. The Bolshevik regime, among other things, had overhauled marriage and divorce laws, abolished legal discrimination based on sex, decreed the separation of church and state, taken energetic measures against gambling and prostitution, adopted the Gregorian calendar used in the West, given illegitimate children the same rights as everyone else, and even reformed and simplified the Cyrillic alphabet used to write Russian.

The regime also had plenty of problems, some unanticipated. The Bolsheviks were not daunted by continued opposition from Russia's propertied classes; that was expected. What they did not expect was losing the support of the working classes and soldiers. Yet by the spring of 1918 that is exactly what happened in the wake of repressive policies and continued economic decline. The situation was clear to Lenin in April 1918 when he published an article called "The Immediate Tasks of the Soviet Government." As he had done before and would do again, Lenin blamed the problem of flagging support not on his regime but on the flawed revolutionary commitment of the working class. His solution? Having explained that the amount of coercion necessary in the transition from capitalism to socialism "is determined by the development of a given revolutionary class," Lenin declared that a regime charged with that historically crucial task "may assume the sharp forms of a dictatorship if ideal discipline and class-consciousness are lacking." Russia's working class and soldiers meanwhile were not impressed with Lenin's analysis: in elections to local soviets across European Russia held during April and May, they gave overwhelming majorities to the Mensheviks and Socialist Revolutionaries. The Bolsheviks hung on to their majorities in Moscow only through electoral fraud and in Petrograd by postponing the elections.

In March 1918, the Bolsheviks had officially renamed their organization the Communist Party. In July they gave Russia a new name, the Russian Soviet Federated Socialist Republic, and its first Soviet constitution, a document that in one breath condemned all exploiters, extolled the toiling masses, and promised a world socialist revolution. Soviet Russia's constitution also had a practical side. It disenfranchised all the old "exploiting" classes. Among those who could vote, some were more equal than others: the votes of urban residents, among whom the Bolsheviks had their strongest support, counted five times as much as votes of rural residents.

The constitution also established a new governing structure, a network of soviets beginning with directly elected local soviets and proceeding upward via indirect elections to an All-Russian Congress of Soviets. Whatever its merits or flaws, the new constitution was not put into practice. By July the country was on the brink of a new ordeal. As if the cumulative hardships of world war and revolution were not enough, Russia was about to undergo the extreme travail of civil war.

THE CIVIL WAR

The seeds for civil war were planted when Lenin set up his all-Bolshevik government in November 1917. They began to germinate during the last weeks of 1917, when several tsarist generals and conservative politicians began organizing anti-Bolshevik military units in the Ukraine. Fighting between pro- and anti-Bolshevik forces began by February 1918. Bolshevik repression meanwhile fueled opposition to the regime, especially on the political left. In April, a massive Cheka raid on anarchist headquarters resulted in hundreds of arrests. On June 14, the Mensheviks and Socialist Revolutionaries, duly elected by Russia's toiling masses to represent them, were expelled from the soviets.

In early July, the embittered Left SRs attempted to overthrow the Bolshevik regime. The government quickly suppressed their ill-planned revolt in Moscow. Shortly thereafter it quashed a haphazard series of uprisings in several other towns. By then the civil war was heating up; among its first victims were the former tsar and his family, executed on the night of July 16–17 to prevent their liberation by anti-Bolshevik forces. On July 29, the government proclaimed that "the socialist fatherland is in danger," in effect officially announcing a state of civil war. The Left SRs, while failing to overthrow the Bolsheviks, did somewhat better at their old trade of assassination, much to the misfortune of the German ambassador to Russia, murdered on July 6, and Mikhail Uritsky, the chief of the Petrograd Cheka, gunned down on August 30. Lenin, also a Left SR target on August 30, got away with a serious bullet wound. The Bolsheviks responded by unleashing the Cheka to conduct a massive wave of arrests and executions, marking the beginning of the Red Terror that lasted until the end of the civil war.

The civil war would have devastating effects on Russia, costing millions of lives and laying waste to the economy. The damage undoubtedly was worse than anything Lenin and even his most militant colleagues expected. Yet it is inescapable that Lenin and most of his lieutenants not only expected civil war but saw it as integral to the revolutionary process. Thus in April 1918 Lenin asserted in "The Immediate Tasks of the Soviet Government":

Every great revolution, and a socialist revolution in particular . . . is inconceivable without internal war, i.e., civil war, which is even more devastating than external war, and involves thousands and millions of cases of wavering and desertion from one side to the other, which implies a state of extreme indefiniteness, lack of equilibrium and chaos.

Trotsky, with his usual gift for hyperbole, agreed. During a debate over seizing grain by force from the peasantry in June 1918 he stated: "Yes, long live civil war! Civil war for the sake of the children, the elderly, the workers and the Red Army, civil war in the name of direct and ruthless struggle against counterrevolution." To the Bolsheviks, as one local leader put it, "Civil war is the same as class war." Historian Orlando Figes has ably summed up the outlook of Lenin and the party leadership:

Lenin himself was doubtless convinced that his party's best hope of building its own tiny power base was *to fight a civil war.* Indeed he often stressed that the reason why the Paris Commune had been defeated was that it had failed to launch a civil war. . . . Of course Lenin could not have foreseen the full extent of the civil war that would unfold . . . if he had, he might have thought again about using civil war to build up his regime. But even so, it is surely true that the Bolsheviks were psychologically prepared for a civil war in a way that could not be said of their opponents.[2]

The civil war, which would have been bad enough had the Russians been allowed to fight it out by themselves, was made worse by outside intervention. The Allies intervened when the Bolsheviks made peace with Germany and thereby left the latter free to concentrate its full military might against the Allied armies in the west. The Allied intervention initially was limited to protecting military supplies stored in several Russian ports and considered to be in danger of falling into German hands, but the Allies also wanted to get a Russian government in power that would wage war against Germany. Another important motivation was to overthrow Bolshevism in Russia before it could spread westward. Thus, between March and June of 1918, British, French, American, and Japanese troops landed on Russian soil.

In May an extraordinary incident escalated the intervention. While Russia had still been fighting alongside the Allies, it had organized a large group of Czech and Slovak prisoners of war, about 40,000 in all, into the so-called Czech Legion. These former soldiers of the Austro-Hungarian Empire were switching sides in an attempt to liberate their homeland from the Hapsburg monarchy. They were in the process of traveling eastward across Russia via the Trans-Siberian railroad for evacuation at the port of Vladivostok and transfer to Western Europe when fighting developed between the ex-POWs,

whom the Bolsheviks feared and attempted to disarm, and the newly organized Red Army. The Czech victories in these skirmishes were a convincing
demonstration of Bolshevik military weakness and therefore encouraged both
anti-Bolshevik Russians and the Allies. During the summer of 1918, French,
British, and Japanese troops reached Russia in larger numbers. They were
joined by more American forces, the latter dispatched in part to monitor the
troops of the territorially ambitious Japanese in Siberia.

REDS VERSUS WHITES

The number of foreign troops actually present in Russia was never very large.
Their main purpose was to support the various native anti-Bolshevik governments and armies scattered throughout the country. Collectively known as the
"Whites," as opposed to their "Red" Bolshevik opponents, these disparate
groups had only their opposition to the Bolsheviks in common. They ranged
in political outlook from SRs and Mensheviks to monarchists. The Whites
had some advantages in the struggle, including better and more professional
officers, skilled cavalry forces, and better access to food supplies because of
the agricultural areas they controlled. But they never were able to establish a
united force; at one point the Whites were divided into eighteen governments
and factions. The closest they came to organizing a functioning government
was a fractious liberal–socialist coalition known as the Directory, which was
established at a conference of anti-Bolshevik groups in September 1918 but
did not actually begin operating until October. The Directory lasted barely a
month. Conservative forces overthrew it and turned to a former tsarist naval
officer, Admiral Alexander Kolchak, as their "Supreme Ruler."

Real power among the Whites rested with a series of ex-tsarist officers.
The most important were the alleged Supreme Ruler Admiral Kolchak,
whose supremacy lasted only a year, General Anton Denikin, and General
Peter Wrangel. Various other generals ineffectively tried to aid the cause. The
Whites' military difficulties often resulted not only because the considerable
distances between their different armies prevented adequate coordination,
but sometimes because the generals' mutual rivalries and suspicions came
between them.

Disunity was only part of the Whites' problem. Poorly disciplined troops and
military incompetence helped drag the White cause down. So did the burden
of having to fight from Russia's periphery while the Bolsheviks controlled
the country's heartland, including Petrograd and Moscow and most of Russia's industrial and population centers. White armies separated by hundreds
or thousands of miles were always trying to link up. The Reds, by contrast,
were able to shuttle troops and materials along compact interior lines of com-

munication. The Whites also did a poor job of organizing local administration as their armies advanced. This made it very difficult to supply their troops with vital food and equipment. Their brutal repression of workers in industrial areas they controlled sent production into an unstoppable downward spiral. Foreign aid did little to redress these disadvantages. The Allies, often divided among themselves and plagued by a war-weariness that produced, among other things, a mutiny among French sailors dispatched to the Black Sea to help the Whites, provided neither reliable nor adequate help. The stigma of being associated with foreigners outweighed whatever aid the Whites received and allowed the Bolsheviks to pose as patriotic defenders of Mother Russia.

Most important, it proved impossible for the Whites to win a civil war without popular support, and they offered very little to the Russian masses. Many peasants had grown to hate and fear the Bolshevik government for fomenting class war in the villages and seizing grain by force, but at least the Bolsheviks appeared to have endorsed what peasants cared about most: the right to the land they had seized in 1917 and 1918. Meanwhile, some White factions endorsed the new order in the countryside, others equivocated, and still others insisted the estates be returned to their former owners. So the peasants, when they favored anyone at all, opted for the Bolsheviks. The Whites also alienated most of the minority nationalities by insisting their new Russia once again would be a centralized, "united and undivided" state. At key points guerrilla warfare by peasants and non-Russian minorities therefore undermined White campaigns, particularly those of Kolchak and Denikin, the two commanders with the best chances to defeat the Bolsheviks. It is perhaps symbolic of the Whites' futility that Kolchak, their leading figure and a respected naval officer, took up the struggle against the Bolsheviks in Siberia, thousands of miles from any navigable sea.

Still, the Bolsheviks were not that formidable themselves, and thus the civil war dragged on for almost three years. In a country already bled by four years of world war and revolution, the civil war became, as historian William Henry Chamberlin wrote in his classic history of the period, a time "when hunger, cold, disease, and terror stalked through the country like the Four Horsemen of the Apocalypse."[3] Both Red and White forces spread their terror across the land in a desperate struggle for supremacy—and they did not have the field to themselves. Bands of peasant guerrillas known as "Greens," driven by motives ranging from anarchist ideals to outright banditry, fought both the Reds and the Whites and ravaged the countryside and the towns. Class war, largely fomented by the Bolsheviks, raged in the villages in what historian Louis Fisher aptly called "a civil war within a civil war."[4] The dissolution of normal restraints also produced violent struggles between the poor and propertied classes in the cities and towns. Among the most victimized people in Russia were the Jews, who suffered terribly from pogroms at the hands of both the Whites and Greens as well as from the political terror of the Reds. Russia's civil war truly marked, as Chamberlin put it, "one of the greatest explosions of hatred, or rather hatreds . . . ever witnessed in human history."[5]

To this catastrophe the Allies added their troops and, even worse, a blockade that denied relief to the suffering Russian people. Regardless of which side one supported, almost every person in Russia had to fight cold, hunger, and disease. People endured ruthless speculation, corruption, inflation, and merciless competition for what little was available. As Chamberlin reported:

> The law of survival of the fittest found its cruelest, most naked application in the continual struggle for food. The weaker failed to get on the trains to the country districts, or fell off the roofs, or were pushed off the platform, or caught typhus and died, or had the precious fruits of the foraging taken away by the . . . hated guards who boarded the trains as they approached the cities and confiscated surplus food from the passengers.[6]

Those who did not starve lived in constant danger of freezing to death because of a lack of fuel. Entire houses were dismantled and used as firewood; wooden pavements met the same fate. When that was not sufficient, people gathered together to warm their living quarters with their body heat. Cold and hunger left many vulnerable to diseases, with medical care and supplies rarely available. The sick taken to hospitals fared little better than those left on their own; inside the hospitals, patients were freezing to death.

LENIN AND HIS LIEUTENANTS

In the midst of such misery, it stands to reason that neither the Bolsheviks nor their rivals enjoyed much popularity. Victory went to the Bolsheviks because they were better able to mobilize and organize whatever support they had as well as the few resources available to them. The key to their success was Lenin. His performance during these years was the high point of his career and a tribute to his skills as a political leader. He displayed a highly accurate sense of what was possible and what the Bolsheviks' priorities had to be. Like his colleagues, Lenin was driven and sustained by the vision of exporting the revolution; unlike many of them, he was not blinded by that vision. The first priority was to preserve Bolshevik power in Russia, the international revolution's beachhead. That was why, in February 1918, Lenin had insisted that the Bolsheviks accept the onerous Brest-Litovsk treaty, and throughout most of the civil war he maintained similar restraint and focused on the battle at home. His one serious lapse occurred late in the war when the Red Army tried unsuccessfully to carry the revolution into Poland. Fortunately for Lenin, most of the Bolsheviks' organized domestic enemies already had been vanquished, and his regime therefore did not become a casualty of that defeat.

Above all, Lenin gave the Bolsheviks unity. That alone was an accomplishment. The tremendous strains between 1917 and 1921 led to heated debates, bitter personal rivalries, and breakdowns in discipline—but not a party split. At critical points Lenin's stature and authority as the party's leader and the organizational structures he developed were indispensable in giving the Bolsheviks the crucial unity their enemies lacked.

Lenin's leadership would have meant little without energetic, devoted, and often fanatical followers. The most important was Trotsky, a man with superb skills as a propagandist and organizer. Also invaluable was Yakov Sverdlov, who until his death from influenza in 1919 served brilliantly in a number of important posts, among them that of party secretary. Meanwhile, Joseph Stalin was an efficient troubleshooter, not bothered by the ruthless means he used to save the regime. Many others lower in the party hierarchy made impressive and often unlikely contributions—people like Mikhail Tukhachevsky, the former tsarist second lieutenant of noble origins turned Red Army commander, and Mikhail Frunze, a tough labor organizer whose quick mastery of military science enabled him to best both Kolchak and Wrangel. Other noteworthy men were Felix Dzerzhinsky, a Pole of noble blood who devoted his every fiber to making the Cheka a deadly weapon of the workers' state, and Leonid Krasin, a leading Bolshevik until 1908 and an excellent engineer, whose return to the fold late in 1917 brought the Bolsheviks invaluable technical and organizational expertise. At still lower levels the party had dedicated and effective organizers and expert propagandists, anonymous veterans seasoned by years of underground work, able to exploit class antagonism and White mistakes for the Red cause. Although the Bolsheviks certainly had their share of corrupt and incompetent cadres, in a struggle where attrition was high and talent was scarce, they still had a decisive edge over the Whites.

In the end, victory depended not only on superior leadership and personnel, but on the ability to organize and apply force. The Bolshevik regime could not have survived without its Red Army, a fighting force Leon Trotsky conjured up from scratch during the early months of 1918. Building the Red Army required burying certain revolutionary principles. It was, to be sure, very different in some respects from traditional armies. Military pomp was eliminated and officers were far closer to their men. In other respects, however, military tradition ruled. Conscription was reintroduced as the Bolsheviks abandoned their ideas about a "voluntary" people's militia. The election of officers, once a Bolshevik slogan, was eliminated, while the death penalty for desertion was restored.

Trotsky added a few revolutionary wrinkles of his own. He found a creative solution to the Red Army's acute shortage of qualified officers: recycling old tsarist officers. Many of them readily volunteered to serve, but, to prevent any change of heart, Trotsky hounded them with what were called political commissars. These were trusted party functionaries attached to military units to ensure the loyalty of officers and spread propaganda among the troops. Trotsky also took the added precaution of holding as hostages the families of his ex-tsarist officers. Nor did Trotsky hesitate to use force to maintain discipline in the ranks. In the summer of 1918, for example, he restored order to a regiment that was disintegrating in the middle of a battle by executing more than twenty soldiers, including the commander and a political commissar. He also issued orders that the political commissar and commander of any unit retreating without authorization be shot and that any dwelling found sheltering a deserting Red Army soldier be burned to the ground. Although such orders were not always carried out, they served as a powerful deterrent to a Red Army soldier considering either retreat or a permanent farewell to arms.

The Red Army was hardly perfect. Only those units with a large percentage of workers were reliable. Constant conflicts erupted between the officers and political commissars who shadowed them, as well as between Trotsky and various party members who resented his arrogance and highhandedness. Many units lacked even shoes for their soldiers, and desertion was a constant problem. The Reds, like the Whites, lost more troops to disease than to the enemy. Nonetheless, the Red Army grew quickly and learned how to fight well enough to defeat the Whites, the Greens, and the various other groups opposing the Bolsheviks.

THE CHEKA AND THE RED TERROR

In Russia, terror was a time-honored weapon among the revolutionaries. Lenin embraced it many times, both before and after 1917. In a typical pre-1917 statement he advocated a "real, nationwide terror which reinvigorates the country." He endorsed its use frequently in the months after the seizure of power. In the heat of the civil war battles he endorsed "revolutionary violence" against uncooperative elements of the working classes. Lenin's attitude became even more extreme when he discussed the peasantry or bourgeoisie. His language is laced with words such as "merciless" and "pitiless" and his policy recommendations filled with calls for gratuitous violence.

One of his more notorious, but not atypical, commands went out in August 1918 to hard-pressed Bolsheviks in the town of Penza, where peasants were resisting the seizure of their grain:

> Comrades! The kulak uprising in your five districts must be crushed without pity. . . . You must make an example of these people. (1) Hang (I mean hang publicly, so the people will see it) at least 100 kulaks, rich bastards, and known bloodsuckers. (2) Publish their names. (3) Seize all their grain. (4) Single out the hostages per my instructions. . . . Do all this so that for miles around people see it, understand it, tremble, and tell themselves that we are killing the bloodthirsty kulaks and that we will continue to do it.

Kulaks, priests, "White Guardists," and other "unreliable elements" were to be confined in a concentration camp to be set up outside the town. Lenin was also prepared lest any Penza Bolsheviks display faintheartedness in carrying out his orders, telling local party leaders to "find tougher people."

Lenin's colleagues echoed his views. Trotsky, who prior to 1917 was critical of many of Lenin's methods, during the civil war advocated the "guillotine" for enemies of the revolution and explicitly justified any means to achieve the party's revolutionary ends, which he insisted represented the apotheosis of human progress. Nikolai Bukharin, thinking beyond the limited horizons of the civil war to the brave new socialist world to come, opined that "coercion in all its forms, starting with execution . . . is . . . a method of creating Communist mankind out of the human raw material of the capitalist epoch." Dzerzhinsky called for "massive terror" and was an early advocate of setting up concentration camps. Zinoviev called for a "socialist terror" that would "get rid" of the 10 million Russians he estimated opposed the Bolshevik regime. Although some Bolsheviks opposed political terror, they were in the minority and did not influence policy.

Given these attitudes, the conduct of political terror was a logical development for the Bolsheviks. The Cheka, set up on December 20, 1917, began modestly; by March 1918, its staff numbered only 120 and had conducted only one execution. The pace then quickened. In April the Cheka struck at the anarchists, a group that between March and November of 1917 had cooperated with the Bolsheviks. By the summer, amid the opening salvos of the civil war, the restraints on the Cheka had dissolved. More than 350 people were shot in the city of Yaroslavl, a town north of Moscow, after an uprising there in July led by SR notable Boris Savinkov and at least an additional 1,000 in Petrograd and Moscow as the Red Terror began after the August assaults on Uritsky and Lenin. After a two-month binge lasting into the fall during which at least 10,000 to 15,000 people were executed, the Cheka had claimed more lives than *all* tsarist security forces in the previous *century*. Estimates of the Cheka's total executions during the civil war run into the hundreds of thousands.

The Cheka's growth between 1917 and 1922 was nothing short of phenomenal. By June of 1918 it had 12,000 employees, by the end of that year about

40,000. By the end of the civil war the Cheka and the security troops it controlled numbered more than 250,000 personnel. More important than numbers, however, was the expanded scope of its activity. The Cheka's original mandate was to root out the regime's enemies: the counterrevolutionaries, saboteurs, enemy agents, and speculators. In doing so, driven by revolutionary fervor and unrestrained by law, by 1922 the Cheka had penetrated virtually every area of life in Soviet Russia. It was active in assuring the food supply, in maintaining transport, in policing the Red Army and Navy, in monitoring the schools, and in ensuring that vital industries continued to function and deliver essential materials to the state. It hunted down speculators and hoarders, sometimes cordoning off entire neighborhoods during its massive search operations. It surrounded villages and shot peasants resisting the forced requisitions of grain, often leaving the peasants who remained alive without enough to eat. It even suppressed strikes by factory workers, the presumed rulers of the "workers' state."

When the government decreed compulsory mass labor in October 1918, the Cheka managed that vast enterprise. Sometimes it prevented workers from leaving their posts. At other times it tore peasants from their farms to do extremely difficult and perilous jobs. One of the first and largest compulsory labor projects was the conscription of 120,000 peasants and workers to bolster Moscow's defenses against advancing White armies. During the fall of 1918 the Cheka also was assigned to set up a network of forced labor and concentration camps, some in the frozen Arctic north. These camps contained not only "exploiters" but workers and peasants, whose appalling death rate was matched only by the steady influx of new prisoners.

The Cheka was not merely a secret police. With the Bolshevik regime locked in a struggle for survival and compelled to mobilize a society uprooted and exhausted by war, revolution, poverty, and disease, the Cheka became a major and pervasive instrument of Bolshevik rule. This was, to say the least, inherently corrupting. All sorts of unsavory characters found their way into the Cheka's ranks, people attracted by violence and spoils. Even many who began as honest individuals were corrupted by the unrestrained power they wielded at a time when people gave up the accumulated treasures of a lifetime for food or favors. Torture, rape, and theft were commonplace as the Cheka went about its job, as one supervisor put it, of "trying to wipe out the bourgeoisie and the kulaks as a class." The many reports to the Central Committee make it clear that Lenin and the other Bolshevik leaders knew what was going on. One of them chronicled events in Yaroslavl:

> Safe in the knowledge they cannot be punished, they have transformed Cheka headquarters into a huge brothel where they take bourgeois women. Drunkenness is rife. Cocaine is being used widely among the supervisors.

Aside from the corruption it infused into the regime as a whole, the Cheka contributed enormously to skewing the party's relationship to the working class, its presumed social base, a relationship that increasingly became based not on shared interests but on the force the party was able to muster to bend the workers to its will. The Cheka, in fact, did not even defer to regular party authority; it was responsible only to the highest leadership. Aside from the dangerous leeway this situation gave the Cheka functionaries, it enabled the party leadership to ignore not only the will of the population at large but at times strongly felt sentiments within the party itself.

WAR COMMUNISM

The civil war was not only a military and political struggle: it was an economic one as well. After November 1917, the economy continued to deteriorate. The impact of the harsh winter of 1917–1918 and the disruption of food production caused by the expropriation and division of the large estates intensified food shortages in the months after the Bolshevik coup. As industrial production dropped, in part because of fuel and food shortages and in part because of the chaos caused by workers' control, the peasants found little to buy and began hoarding their produce. The Treaty of Brest-Litovsk cut off food and fuel from the Ukraine, Russia's breadbasket, since it left that vital area under German occupation. The fighting during the summer of 1918 further limited available supplies and added to the general misery. The deepening crisis threatened to leave the cities and the Red Army without adequate resources, undermining the regime's ability to defend itself.

The Bolsheviks responded by mobilizing the entire economy for the war effort. Their policy had two central components. First, instead of relying on the marketplace to provide the resources necessary to fight the war, the state took direct control over as much of the economy as possible. Second, it used force as the primary means for making this economic system function. Other major characteristics of this policy included the mobilization and impressment of labor on a vast scale and the attempt, largely unsuccessful, to suppress all private trade. Eventually the Bolsheviks even tried to eliminate money as the primary means of exchange and replace it with a system of state rationing. No overall plan or framework ever existed; many drastic and desperate measures were concocted on the spur of the moment. These diverse measures even lacked a collective name; only in retrospect did they come to be known as "War Communism."

War Communism in essence was an unstable combination of cold and often cruel expediency born of the civil war crisis and utopian visions of recreating Russian society as a socialist wonderland in the Marxist equivalent of six biblical days. Because of the magnitude of the crisis, expediency predominated. War Communism's first harbinger was the "food dictatorship" decree of May 1918, which called for using force and class warfare in the villages against the wealthier peasants, or kulaks, to assure the delivery of grain to the state monopoly at fixed prices. In June, "Committees of the Poor" were organized in the villages to expand the war on kulaks and speculators. They were joined two months later by machine-gun-equipped "Food Requisition Detachments" from the cities. They seized not only grain and other food but other necessities such as horses and wagons. This was all-out war against the kulaks, and the Food Requisition Detachments were prepared for battle: official instructions specified that each detachment consist of at least seventy-five men and "two or three" machine guns and that these units be deployed "in such a manner as to allow two or three detachments to link up quickly." These campaigns immediately reached well beyond the kulaks to peasants of lesser means, an inevitable development since to Lenin and his comrades any peasant who opposed Bolshevik policies was by definition a kulak and therefore a class enemy deserving no quarter. Bereft of produce to sell, food to eat, tools to work with, and money to buy the necessities of life they could not produce themselves, the peasants were left to fend for themselves as best they could. This was hardly the way to preserve the proletarian–peasant alliance Lenin had postulated as essential to building socialism in Russia.

On June 28, 1918, the government issued the decree generally recognized as marking War Communism's unofficial inauguration. In a display of stunning audacity, the Bolsheviks nationalized all of Russia's large-scale industry, which included factories, mines, and other enterprises. The unenviable job of managing that unwieldy conglomeration fell to *Vesenkha*. Endowed with extensive powers to run and reorganize industry, *Vesenkha* grew into a bulging bureaucratic apparatus of over forty departments. The government also created new institutions to mobilize resources, the most important of these being the Council of Labor and Defense. In November 1920 the Bolsheviks extended nationalization to small factories using machines and employing more than five workers, or ten people if a shop did not use machines. That decree notwithstanding, the government lacked the manpower to bring many nationalized factories under effective state control.

Besides the plundering of the peasantry and the seizing of Russia's industries, War Communism involved subjecting the population at large to various forms of compulsory labor. This concept, first put into practice in the fall of 1918, encompassed the Cheka's labor and concentration camps. It also included conscripting peasants to cart wood and clear railroad tracks of snow. Subsequently, additional groups of civilians, those with special skills and those working in certain critical fields, were mobilized for the war effort. Beginning in 1920, all citizens became subject to conscription for "socially useful work in the interests of socialist society." People from all walks of life found themselves putting up buildings, constructing roads, and doing agricultural work at the state's behest. Little was overlooked; one mobilization called for women aged eighteen to forty-five to do "socially useful work" by sewing underwear for the Red Army. The most controversial measure was Trotsky's short-lived attempt to establish "labor armies" subject to military discipline by shifting to civilian projects army units no longer needed for fighting.

These intensified restrictions on the population inevitably meant a marked deterioration in the workers' ability to defend their interests against the state. Workers' control and the collegial administration of industrial enterprises associated with it soon gave way to one-man management under the eye of the *Vesenkha* bureaucracy. One innovation in controlling workers was the introduction of labor books in which all jobs held by a given individual were recorded. Strikes were forbidden, and armed force was used against those who defied the ban. Special disciplinary courts fined workers or sentenced them to hard labor, and sometimes the authorities cut the already meager rations of recalcitrant workers. Under War Communism the trade unions steadily lost much of their independence. All of this was backed up by a swift and severe enforcement of the law, much of it handled by the ubiquitous Cheka.

In a strict economic sense, War Communism at best yielded meager results and at worst was disastrously counterproductive. Nationalization, for example, resulted in an enormous bureaucracy rather than increased production. Industrial production, beset by poor management, inadequate food for the workers, and shortages of materials, continued to plunge despite the government's best efforts.

Matters were no better in food production. The peasants responded to the grain requisitions first by hoarding their food, then by growing enough only for their own needs, and finally by armed resistance. In some regions, the area sown dropped by over 70 percent. In early 1919 an effort was made to bring order to the grain-collection process by requiring peasant villages to deliver grain and other foodstuffs to the state according to strict quotas. This more systematic method of confiscation did little good, and the cities remained woefully short of food. Equally demoralizing, the bulk of the food that was available reached its hungry consumers through the black market at ever-inflating prices. Urban inhabitants responded by fleeing to the countryside. Moscow lost half of its population, and Petrograd more than two-thirds. For far too many individuals it did not matter where they moved; between January of 1918 and early 1921, perhaps 5 million people died from hunger and disease.

War Communism nonetheless had its defenders. Many Bolsheviks considered it the first experimental stage in the transition to socialism. Perhaps to some extent this type of thinking represented coating unpalatable social medicine with ideological sweeteners, but beyond that War Communism definitely appealed to the more impatient advocates of overhauling Russian society, who liked using nonmaterial incentives, such as "socialist competition" between groups of workers, to spur production. These militants viewed nationalization of industry, the suppression of private trade, and taking control of agriculture as measures essential to building a planned socialist economy, and they were happy to see them implemented, even under difficult conditions. In a classic example of beauty being in the eyes of the beholder, many party enthusiasts viewed paying workers in kind, a measure necessitated by runaway inflation, as a positive step toward a socialist economy free of the evil of money.

These sentiments were widespread. They were reflected in the idealistic party program adopted at the Eighth Party Congress in 1919. They were clearly in evidence late in 1920, when Lenin himself was arguing for yet harsher economic measures, including an unworkable plan to control the sowing and harvesting of over 20 million peasant households. And they were still very much alive in 1921, when Lenin, having become convinced that rising popular discontent and rebelliousness meant War Communism had to go, encountered considerable opposition among his colleagues to proposals for different economic policies. Yet whatever its failures as a long-term economic program, War Communism was a success as an emergency measure for scrounging up what little was available to supply the Red Army and cities with enough resources to enable the Bolshevik regime to survive during the worst years of the civil war.

THE NON-RUSSIAN MINORITIES

Along with the military victory they achieved between the summer of 1918 and the fall of 1920, the Bolsheviks enjoyed surprising success in reattaching the non-Russian parts of the defunct Russian Empire to the new Soviet state. The Bolsheviks' policy regarding the non-Russian nationalities was two-sided. Sympathizers might call it dialectical; cynics would call it hypocritical. On November 15 (2), 1917, the Bolsheviks boldly announced in their "Declaration of the Rights of the People of Russia" the equality of all peoples of Soviet Russia and their right to self-determination, including the right to secede. In practice, as illustrated by what happened in Finland and the Ukraine, attempts to secede were met with claims that "counterrevolutionaries" were behind such activities. Simultaneous attempts to subvert the new regimes and to invade their territory followed. The pattern was similar elsewhere. As soon as they had the strength, the Bolsheviks tried to assert their control over the non-Russian parts of the old empire. In Finland, Estonia, Latvia, and Lithuania they failed. In Ukraine (by far the most important prize), Central Asia, Siberia, and the Caucasus they succeeded.

Still, the November declaration never quite lost all of its propaganda value, especially against the background of White declarations of "Russia: one, great, and indivisible." The situation that developed mirrored what occurred with the peasantry: the minorities feared and hated the Bolsheviks but dreaded the Whites even more.

WAR WITH POLAND

The serious fighting between the Reds and the Whites lasted from the summer of 1918 until the fall of 1920, although the decisive battles were fought in 1919. By November 1920, General Wrangel, the leader of the last significant White force, was defeated; his final task was to evacuate 150,000 White soldiers and civilians from what was to be a Soviet Russia. By then the Bolsheviks had turned their attention to Poland. During the spring and summer of 1920, two ancient enemies with new, grandiose plans once again collided on the broad Eurasian plain. The Poles, hoping to detach Belorussia and the Ukraine from their giant eastern neighbor and reduce it to a second-rate power, had attacked Russia in April. By June the invaders had met defeat. A tantalizing vision then began to dance in Bolshevik heads: the possibility of exporting their revolution to the west. This meant pursuing the defeated Polish army westward in the expectation that the arrival of the Red Army would ignite a socialist uprising in Poland and that this in turn would spread the revolutionary flame to Germany and the rest of Western Europe. But Lenin and his comrades miscalculated. The Poles did not rally to the red Russian banners but to the forces defending their long-suppressed and cherished dream of an independent national life. In August they stopped the Red Army, in a battle few thought they could win, at the gates of Warsaw.

THE LEGACY OF THE CIVIL WAR

The defeat at Warsaw ended three years of civil war and left the Bolsheviks with half a loaf. There would be no quick export of the revolution. Prior to the debacle at Warsaw, two Communist uprisings had failed in Germany and a Communist regime collapsed in Hungary, after surviving for 133 days during 1919 as the "Hungarian Socialist Federated Soviet Republic." In March 1921, another quixotic uprising quickly sputtered out in Germany. Meanwhile the Bolsheviks still ruled in Russia, solitary but steadfast guardians of the revolutionary flame.

That international isolation was compounded by the party's internal quarrels and its estrangement from the population of Russia. The policies and methods that won the civil war for the Bolsheviks had made the party increasingly authoritarian and led to organized opposition within its ranks. A key requirement during the civil war, as in any war, had been rapid decision making, something the cumbersome nineteen-member Central Committee could not do. Therefore, the Eighth Party Congress, meeting during March 1919, set up two bodies subordinate to the Central Committee: the Politburo (Political Bureau) and Orgburo (Organizational Bureau). They joined another new arm of the Central Committee—the Secretariat. Although the Politburo was supposed to report to the Central Committee, the presence of Lenin, Trotsky, and Stalin among its five members meant that it immediately became the party's policy-making body. The Orgburo and the Secretariat implemented those policies. As such, they also acquired considerable power, particularly the Secretariat, whose responsibilities included assigning, promoting, and checking on officials throughout the party. In effect, these three bodies soon supplanted the Central Committee.

Critics at the Eighth Congress had protested that these new bodies would further centralize power and destroy party democracy. Their fears were well founded, but the future they feared already had arrived. The three new organs were merely the crystallization of tendencies dating from the Bolshevik coup. By 1919, as Robert Service notes in his study of the party during its first years in power:

> Hierarchical discipline and obedience were now accepted on a scale and with a speed which made an amazingly abrupt contrast with the organizational looseness of early 1918. It had taken merely a few months for customs of collective deliberation and democratic accountability, which had seemed so solidly entrenched, to succumb to radical erosion.[7]

This did not bother Lenin at all. As the civil war wore on he became less and less tolerant of dissent and increasingly disillusioned with the masses, particularly the proletariat. Their sin went beyond merely refusing to give the Bolsheviks wholehearted support; sometimes they actually opposed the party's plans. The masses' failure to see the light was, in Lenin's eyes, sufficient cause to deprive them of their right to determine their own fate. In 1919 he stated that "we recognize neither freedom, nor equality, nor labor democracy if they are opposed to the interests of the emancipation of labor from the oppression of capital." Lenin further explained that the masses' "low cultural level" meant that the soviets could only be "organs of government *for* the working people," rather than "*by* the working people" (emphasis added). Real decisions would be made by the "advanced elements of the proletariat," who naturally were synonymous with the membership of the Bolshevik Party.

Lenin was hardly alone in his disillusionment with the working masses. His critics within the party who insisted that the party respect working class opinion, notwithstanding their eloquence or passion ("Comrade Lenin," one of them asked him at the Ninth Party Congress in 1920, "do you think the salvation of the Revolution lies in mechanical obedience?"), remained a distinct minority. The majority, taken aback by the widespread hostility to the party, convinced by their own ideological passions that they represented the people's best interests, separated from the masses by the privileges that went with being part of the governing elite, and entrenched by the party's suppression of any political opposition, also often lost patience with Russia's workers and peasants. Most party cadres were quite prepared to use the Cheka or other armed forces to suppress independent proletarian institutions such as factory committees or to ignore the local soviets. At the same time, if the party could be made more efficient by abolishing elective offices or even entire local committees, many would not object. Not a dictatorship of the proletariat as Marxist theory called for, but a Bolshevik Party dictatorship over the proletariat, was rising on the ruins of the fallen old regime.

The ferocity of the civil war accustomed the party to ruling by fiat or from behind the barrel of a gun. The most obvious example of this development was the behavior of the Cheka, but similar tendencies existed in virtually every party and state institution. The Bolshevik Party had placed itself above the law and the will of the population. It increasingly thought of itself in militant military terms: fighting battles, attacking fortresses, viewing those who disagreed as enemies or traitors. This method of rule, the "War Communism model," as some have called it, did not disappear when the civil war was won and War Communism abolished in 1921; it fused seamlessly with the fundamental authoritarian thrust of Leninism and became a part of the party's guiding set of principles.

Probably the most insidious aspect of Bolshevik policy as it evolved during the civil war was the practice of demonizing and systematically assaulting entire populations: what the Bolsheviks called "class war." The key point about class war is that it was not an integral part of the battlefield struggle against the Whites; rather it was a fundamental part of Bolshevik social engineering and the party's mission to build a new socialist world. It became routine to murder groups of people strictly on the basis of class in the name of the revolution. As one Cheka leader informed his officers in 1918, "We are exterminating the bourgeoisie as a class." This meant the Cheka's investigations into anti-Soviet activity did not need to bother with evidence about what a person had said or done. The determinants of guilt were "what class he comes from, what are his roots, his education, his training, and his occupation." Members of the peasantry, aristocracy, and bourgeoisie all were at risk as members of the so-called "possessing classes." Historian Nicolas Werth has chronicled some of the mass executions, strictly along class lines, perpetrated by the Bolsheviks between 1919 and 1921:

> In Kharkiv [Kharkov] there were between 2,000 and 3,000 executions in February–June 1919, and another 1,000–2,000 when the town was retaken again in December of that year; in Rostov-on-Don, approximately 1,000 in January 1920; in Odessa, 2,000 in May–August 1919, then 1,500–3,000 between February 1920 and 1921; in Kyiv [Kiev], at least 3,000 in February–August 1919; in Ekaterinodar, at least 3,000 between August 1920 and February 1921; in Armavir, a small town in the Kuban, between 2,000 and 3,000 in August–October 1920. The list could go on and on.[8]

The gruesome culmination of civil war–era class war occurred in southern Russia along the Don and Kuban rivers, where the largely Cossack population had sided against the Bolsheviks. The Cossacks' decision was not surprising since the Bolsheviks already had classified them as "kulaks" and "class enemies." In January 1919 the Central Committee adopted a secret resolution asserting that "we must recognize as the only politically correct measure massive terror and a merciless fight against the rich Cossacks, who must be exterminated and physically disposed of, down to the last man." The resolution was not fully implemented, but what was done was dreadful enough. During 1919 and 1920, out of a population of about 3 million, the Bolshevik regime killed or deported an estimated 300,000 to 500,000 Cossacks. Mass murder in the service of the revolution had approached the nether world of genocide.

Finally, along with the War Communism model came an important group of practitioners, for the civil war years witnessed the rise to prominence of a new type of party cadre: the tough, ruthless functionary unencumbered with ideological inhibitions and willing to use whatever measures were necessary to complete his assignment. At best, these cadres fit the popular image of the gruff, leather-jacketed commissar rushing from emergency to emergency on his motorcycle. At worst, they were thugs and killers, deeply hated by ordinary people just trying to survive. Workers in a factory in the city of Perm undoubtedly spoke for many ordinary Russians when they passed a resolution demanding that "all the leather jackets and caps of the commissars should be used to make shoes for the workers." The newly minted commissars penetrated all levels of the party as its membership swelled from 250,000 at the start of the civil war to three times that number at the end. At the top echelon they were represented by Joseph Stalin, who by 1921 had become one of the party's three or four most powerful men. Thus, as the party began its struggle to reshape Russian society during the civil war, the war in turn reshaped the party itself, in a way that would have enormous historical significance.

NOTES

1. E.H. Carr, *The Bolshevik Revolution*, Vol. 2 (Baltimore: Penguin, 1966), p. 75.

2. Orlando Figes, *A People's Tragedy: The Russian Revolution, 1891–1924* (New York: Penguin, 1998), p. 616.

3. William Henry Chamberlin, *The Russian Revolution*, Vol. 2 (New York: Grosset and Dunlap, 1965), p. 335.

4. Louis Fisher, *The Life of Lenin* (New York: Harper and Row, 1964), p. 356.

5. Chamberlin, *Russian Revolution*, p. 356.

6. Ibid., p. 345.

7. Robert Service, *The Bolshevik Party in Revolution* (New York: Barnes and Noble, 1979), p. 110.

8. Nicolas Werth, "A State Against Its People: Violence, Repression, and Terror in the Soviet Union," in Stéphane Courtois et al., *The Black Book of Communism: Crimes, Terror, Repression*, translated by Jonathan Murphy and Mark Kramer, consulting editor Mark Kramer (Cambridge, Mass., and London: Harvard University Press, 1999), p. 106. Many of the examples of civil war terror are taken from this account.

11

New Policies and
New Problems

We have failed to convince the broad masses.

—Lenin, 1921

Soviet Russia emerged from four years of revolution and civil war with a regime that historically was the first of its kind: a one-party state whose leaders were committed to using absolute dictatorial power to reconstitute society according to a preconceived utopian vision. The Bolshevik Party that controlled the Soviet state was not a traditional political party as understood in the West, but rather a self-appointed phalanx of revolutionary crusaders unwilling to tolerate opposition or dissent from either rival political groups or the population at large. Marxism and its prophecy of a perfect communist society provided the ideological rationale for any and all violence and repression necessary to keep the party in power. In terms of political institutions, the Bolshevik Party's complete control over the state—really the fusion of what are normally two separate entities, with the state transformed into an administrative arm of the party—and the dictatorial nature of the regime as a whole amounted to a new political hybrid, the party-state.

Along with having created the party-state, by 1921 the Bolsheviks could take satisfaction in the progress they had made in implementing the social revolution that gave meaning to their existence and struggles. Russia's former ruling and propertied classes had been shattered. Either they had been scattered to the winds—more than 2 million members of the nobility, business and professional classes, bureaucratic elite, and intelligentsia had emigrated—or they remained in Russia largely as dispossessed and despised remnants of what contemptuously were called the "former classes," often reduced to selling off the last of their possessions bit by bit as they struggled against the odds to survive in a new and hostile world. In the cities, the businesses and homes of the wealthy and the middle class were in the hands of the Bolshevik-controlled state, while in the countryside the estates of the departed landlords had been divided and distributed among the peasants.

In addition, Bolsheviks now had a new opportunity to shore up their regime. Since the end of 1917 the government had been seizing precious metals and valuables, worth billions of dollars at today's prices, from various sources in Russia. The largest single prize was the tsarist strategic gold reserve, but plunder from private banks, safe deposit boxes of the wealthy, Orthodox churches and monasteries, and other sources added to that trove. The intent was to use these resources to help finance the revolution by selling them abroad and using the proceeds to purchase weapons, military supplies, and other essential materials. However, during the civil war the Allied blockade, maintained by the British navy, made it virtually impossible for Soviet Russia to export or import anything. By the spring of 1920 British policy toward the Bolshevik regime had changed, and London was no longer enforcing the blockade. The Baltic Sea, the best route to and from Russia, was open for trade, allowing huge quantities of gold (supplemented by other precious metals and jewelry) to head west from Russia and supplies of all kinds—rifles, machine guns, artillery, military uniforms, saddles, vehicle spare parts, locomotives, even airplanes—to head east from Europe. Military supplies began arriving in Russia in large quantities by the end of 1920, too late for the key battles of the civil war or the conflict with Poland, but just in time to help the regime deal with a growing wave of uprisings by the Russian people. According to one estimate, in less than two years beginning in May 1920, the Bolshevik government sold more than $350 million dollars in gold—about $35 billion at today's prices—in Europe in exchange for a huge cornucopia of urgently needed goods. These supplies were used almost exclusively to strengthen the regime, and especially the Red Army, not to relieve the dreadful conditions, including famine, under which millions of people in Soviet Russia were living. As noted below, the job of famine relief was left to Western organizations.

Despite what Lenin and his colleagues had achieved, the end of Russia's civil war left the Bolshevik government facing urgent and menacing problems. In 1921 Russia's economy hit bottom. Agricultural production was less than half of what it had been in 1913, the last full year of peace before World War I. Industrial output had declined even more, to about a fifth of the prewar level. Coal production stood at 10 percent of its former level, pig iron production at 3 percent. Russia's railroad network barely functioned. Very little food reached the cities; in Petrograd workers doing heavy labor received less than 1,000 calories a day, far beneath the 1,600-calorie daily requirement of an average person. During the fighting perhaps 7 million people had been killed in combat or died from hunger and disease; in the first years of peace, 1921 and 1922, one of the worst famines in Russia's history claimed 5 million more victims. The factory working class, supposedly the social base for the Bolshevik regime, had suffered enormous losses. Between 1917 and 1921, attrition from combat, hunger, and disease, and flight to the countryside in search of food, had reduced its numbers from about 3.5 to perhaps 1.5 million. Although finally at peace for the first time in seven years, Soviet Russia and its long-suffering people, as the historian Isaac Deutscher has written:

> stood alone, bled white, starving, shivering with cold, consumed by disease, and overcome with gloom. In the stench of blood and death her people scrambled wildly for a breath of air, a faint gleam of light, a crust of bread. "Is this," they asked, "the realm of freedom? Is this where the great leap has taken us?"[1]

The people did more than just ask questions: they rioted, went on strike, and rebelled. As the White military threat evaporated during 1920, peasants all over Russia vented their bitterness against the hated Bolshevik food requisitions, labor mobilizations, and generally cruel treatment by staging numerous uprisings against the victorious Reds. There were significant rebellions in the eastern Ukraine, western Siberia, the Volga region, the northern Caucasus, and in other areas, as well as literally hundreds of small-scale revolts. The Bolsheviks responded by employing the Cheka and the Red Army to crush the various insurgencies. They operated without mercy, burning whole villages, seizing hostages, and shooting rebel prisoners. The most serious peasant uprising, lasting from mid-1920 until mid-1921, occurred in Tambov province astride the Volga River, about 200 miles southeast of Moscow. It took a Red Army force of 100,000 men, whose tactics included using poison gas to flush the peasant rebels from their hiding places and incarcerating 50,000 people in concentration camps, to extinguish the rebellion. Commanded by Mikhail Tukhachevsky, the army relied heavily on weapons and supplies imported since 1920, from saddles for cavalry troops to spare parts for trucks to airplanes used for surveillance and area bombing. Restoring order in the Tambov region also required the termination of War Communism and cancellation of grain requisitions, which took place in March 1921 and reduced popular support for the rebels.

Meanwhile, thousands of workers went on strike in the cities, where Socialist Revolutionary and Menshevik influence was again on the rise. The most important strikes took place in Petrograd in February 1921; they were broken by the Red Army and by denying striking workers ration cards. The multiple wellsprings of discontent produced such a steady flow of new worker and peasant prisoners that the Cheka had to open thirteen new forced labor camps in addition to the 107 it had operated during the civil war. The proletarian–peasant alliance Lenin had often hoped for now existed. The bitter irony was that this inchoate association was forged from a common misery and shared opposition to the Bolshevik dictatorship. Lenin in effect admitted this early in 1921 when he glumly told his colleagues: "We have failed to convince the broad masses."

THE KRONSTADT REBELLION

The uprisings and strikes of 1920 and 1921 were ample proof of how right Lenin was. Yet nothing seemed to shake the party's confidence—until Kronstadt. The Kronstadt naval base, located on an island in the Gulf of Finland near Petrograd, had long been a revolutionary hotbed and Bolshevik stronghold, the "pride and glory of the revolution," according to Trotsky. During the civil war the Kronstadt sailors furnished the Bolsheviks with reliable cadres on every front. Although the war took its toll and many veteran revolutionaries were replaced by new peasant recruits, Kronstadt in 1921 remained a vivid symbol of both the revolutionary movement as a whole and of the November Revolution in particular.

Irrespective of its status as the revolution's pride and glory, Kronstadt was not immune to the distress and disillusionment sweeping Russia. On March 2, 1921, as the Bolsheviks were preparing to meet at their Tenth Party Congress to chart their revolution's future, the Kronstadt sailors broke with them and elected their own Provisional Revolutionary Committee. The garrison's demands for freedom of political activity for all socialist parties, elections to the soviets based on free and secret ballot, and an end to the privileged position of the Communist Party (as the Bolshevik Party officially was called after 1918) amounted to demanding abolition of the Bolshevik dictatorship in favor of a multiparty socialist regime.

The Kronstadt sailors had thrown down the gauntlet. Their program, after all, sounded very much like the promises of 1917 and corresponded closely to the most widely held conception of what Russia's socialist government should be. At the same time, the rebellious garrison was a rallying point for a broad spectrum of anti-Bolshevik sentiment. Fearful that impending warm weather would melt the ice in the gulf and make the Kronstadt island fortress impregnable to infantry, the Bolsheviks, after five days of fruitless negotiations, attacked the men they still called their "blinded sailor-comrades." A terrible civil war was now succeeded by political fratricide. As was the case in the Tambov rebellion, recently imported weapons, including airplanes used to bomb the rebel fortifications, played an important role in suppressing the Kronstadt uprising. Historian Isaac Deutscher described the macabre end of the ten-day battle:

White sheets over their uniforms, the Bolsheviks advanced across the Bay. They were met by hurricane fire from Kronstadt's bastions. The ice broke under their feet; and wave after wave of white-shrouded attackers collapsed into the glacial Valhalla. The death march went on. From three directions fresh columns stumped and fumbled and slipped and crawled over the glassy surface until they too vanished in fire, ice, and water. . . . Such was the lot of these rebels, who denounced the Bolsheviks for their harshness, . . . that for their survival they fought a battle which in cruelty was unequaled throughout the civil war. The bitterness and rage of the attackers mounted accordingly. On 17 March, after a night-long advance in a snowstorm, the Bolsheviks at last succeeded in climbing the walls. When they broke into the fortress, they fell upon the defenders like revengeful furies.[2]

Thousands died on both sides, and several thousand surviving rebels were executed or sent to living deaths in concentration camps. For the victorious survivors it was at best a bitter memory; for many of them it was a haunting, lingering nightmare. Lenin, Trotsky, and other Bolsheviks defended their actions at Kronstadt as essential to preserving the revolution, but many Bolsheviks were deeply shaken by what they had done to save their party's dictatorship. Lenin made a point of defending the battle and subsequent massacre on several occasions, almost to the point of protesting too much. As for Trotsky, even as late as August 1940, the final month of his life, he was still defending the "tragic necessity" that took place at Kronstadt.

Kronstadt, the graveyard for thousands of men and many ideals, drove the final nail into the coffin of War Communism. In the face of rising peasant disturbances, the Bolsheviks were ambivalent and divided about this policy in any case, and Lenin himself apparently concluded in February 1921 that it had to go. Kronstadt, by making it clear that popular discontent was a threat to the regime's very existence, convinced most Bolsheviks that Lenin was right.

THE NEW ECONOMIC POLICY

The decision to scrap War Communism was made in 1921 at the same Tenth Party Congress the Kronstadt uprising had so rudely disturbed. The attending Bolsheviks, their victories over the Whites and rebellious sailors notwithstanding, had little to cheer about. Their plans, like their country itself, lay in ruins. Neither of the two conditions Lenin had set for building socialism in Russia stood fulfilled. No socialist revolution had occurred in Western Europe, and at home the expected proletariat–peasant alliance in support of the Bolshevik regime did not exist. At least for the time being, nothing could be done about instigating a socialist revolution in Western Europe, but something absolutely had to be done about relations with the peasantry. Above all, Russia's economy had to be revived. First and foremost this meant that food production had to be increased, something only the peasantry could accomplish. Since the use of force between 1918 and 1921 had achieved precisely the opposite results, the only logical alternative was to discard the ineffective stick for the untried carrot. The New Economic Policy (NEP) was the result.

With the NEP, the Bolsheviks abandoned an economic policy based on centralized control and force in favor of one relying primarily on the marketplace and traditional market incentives. Its cornerstone was the abolition of forced food requisitions, which were replaced by a progressive and rather moderate tax, initially levied in kind and later, beginning in 1922, in cash. The peasants were free to consume what remained or sell what they wished on the open market. This system once again made it worthwhile for the peasant to produce as much as possible, and under the NEP, despite primitive farming methods and technology, Russian agriculture recovered rapidly. For 5 million citizens, the recovery came too late. They died during the dreadful famine of 1921–1922, when sharply reduced sowing, the consequence of years of war and forced requisitions, combined with drought to produce the worst harvest in decades. Not even help from the non-Communist Russians and volunteer organizations from the capitalist West, all enlisted by the desperate Bolsheviks, could contain the tragedy.

The "strategic retreat," as Lenin rather defensively called the NEP, was hardly a complete turnabout. Rather, it created what generally is called a "mixed economy," one with elements of socialist state control and free enterprise. In the mixed economy of the NEP, the regime still controlled the economy's so-called "commanding heights." The state managed foreign trade, the banks, the transport network, and the largest industrial enterprises, which employed over 80 percent of Russia's factory workers. These enterprises were organized in a series of "trusts." Significantly, state factories soon were expected to show a profit rather than look for state aid and were run by individual managers, not worker committees. In some cases those managers were "bourgeois specialists," technocrats who had attained their positions in pre-revolutionary times or even former owners of nationalized industries. Planning continued, particularly under the aegis of *Vesenkha* and a new body, the State Planning Commission (*Gosplan*).

None of this could stop the free enterprise proliferating in the vast economic valleys beneath and between the commanding heights. The NEP meant that the Bolsheviks had to accept the spread of a hated enemy, private business. It quickly became the vibrant and vital part of the NEP economy. Marketing peasant surpluses required private trade, which was duly legalized shortly after the Tenth Congress adjourned. The small traders who immediately sprang up to market agricultural production and establish other small businesses were caustically dubbed "Nepmen." The Communists despised and feared them as bad seeds ready to sprout into full-blown capitalists and subjected Nepmen to a gauntlet of discrimination and interference: the state took 50 percent of their profits in taxes; they faced discrimination in obtaining credit or supplies; local officials burdened them with class-based surcharges on rents and public utilities; the licenses and leases they needed to do business often were revoked; and they were harassed by the police and subject to arrest for what the regime arbitrarily deemed "speculation." Still the Nepmen proliferated. Soon there were few areas in the economy where their services were not needed or their influence was not felt. At the same time, the economic and political conditions under which Nepmen worked offered little incentive for long-term invest-ment that might ultimately produce expansion and economic growth. What made sense was to turn a quick profit and, if it suited one's personality and pocketbook, to immediately enjoy the fruits of one's labor in the restaurants, nightclubs, and theaters of Russia's major cities. Most Nepmen, of course, barely eked out a living from tiny stalls or as petty traders and were unlikely to haunt fashionable urban night spots.

Common sense dictated that nationalization of small enterprises be undone, further increasing the ranks of the Nepmen. Thousands of small factories and shops were returned to their former owners or leased to other entrepre-neurs. These businesses quickly became the nation's main source of essential consumer goods. The process did not stop there. Free enterprise brought in its wake a free labor market. In the countryside, although the state retained legal title to the land, free enterprise sank deeper roots as a series of decrees eventually allowed individual peasants to lease land in addition to their allot-ments and to hire wage laborers. Capitalism, not socialism, held sway where most Russians lived and worked. Economic necessity also led the Bolsheviks to negotiate with foreign capitalist governments, which resulted in a trade agreement with Great Britain in 1921 and a broad economic and political pact with Germany in 1922.

The NEP was quite successful as a policy of recovery. It relieved the worst of Russia's economic shortages by 1923 and restored the economy to a sem-blance of health by 1925. Ironically, its very successes greatly distressed the Bolsheviks. They, after all, had made their many sacrifices to build *socialism*, not a quasi-capitalist society of peasant entrepreneurs and Nepmen. Notwith-standing the many restrictions it had placed on the Nepmen, the party shared Lenin's fear that freedom of trade would lead to the "victory of capitalism, to its full restoration." In order to prevent this and to keep Russia from slipping from their control, Lenin and his comrades tightened the nation's political reins. That effort began in 1921 at the same fateful Tenth Party Congress that had given birth to the NEP.

THE TENTH PARTY CONGRESS: PARTY UNITY
AND DICTATORSHIP

The Tenth Party Congress was the point at which the Bolsheviks first became caught in their own net of repression. Although the party had preserved its exclusive hold on power, it was sharply divided over the measures it had used and what it should do next. The various strains of discontent had coalesced into two main groups: the Democratic Centralists and the Workers' Opposition. The Democratic Centralists, made up largely of Bolshevik intellectuals, criticized the party's increasingly centralized and undemocratic structure, including the growing practice of appointing cadres to local leadership posts formerly filled by election. The Democratic Centralists also objected to the stifling of free discussion within party organs. In effect, the Democratic Centralists complained, these developments were turning the party into a governing bureaucracy distinguished by rank and privilege.

While the Democratic Centralists were a serious annoyance, Lenin and his closest colleagues were more worried about the Workers' Opposition, a faction with strong support among trade union workers and therefore a group with considerable potential influence. It was led by Alexander Shlyapnikov, a veteran Bolshevik of working-class origins, and by an ex-Menshevik and 1917 convert to Bolshevism named Alexandra Kollontai, the party's best-known feminist and somewhat notorious advocate and practitioner of free love, whose list of lovers included Shlyapnikov. The Workers' Opposition opposed replacing workers' control with one-man management and employing the so-called bourgeois specialists in managerial positions. It also had something more ominous to worry about: the party leadership's attempts to strip the trade unions of their autonomy and turn them into little more than arms of the state. The Workers' Opposition wanted the trade unions to control industry.

It is important to keep in mind that while both opposition groups complained about conditions *inside* the party, neither was concerned about democracy *outside* the party. The fates or rights of the Mensheviks or Socialist Revolutionaries, to say nothing of the Kadets, were of little importance to most Bolshevik dissidents. They did not, in other words, question the party's dictatorship; they simply wanted more democracy for the party membership. It was their oxymoronic article of faith that the party could be democratic internally while imposing its dictatorship on the rest of Russia.

Lenin, meanwhile, was concerned only about the well-being of the party dictatorship. While allowing debate, Lenin as party leader always had been unwilling to accept compromise and unhesitatingly did what was necessary to get his way. His attitude was no different in March 1921. The party had an enormous country to govern and unity was critically important. He therefore told the congress that the time had come "to put an end to opposition now . . . to put a lid on it, we have had enough of oppositions."

Lenin's majority passed two resolutions to get the job done. The first, denouncing "syndicalism and anarchism," condemned the Workers' Opposition and its ideas about trade union independence and control over industry. Lenin's efforts in getting this resolution passed were made easier by Trotsky, who independently presented a resolution that would have totally abolished the independence of the trade unions and made them organs of the state. Lenin then was able to pose as a moderate by proposing a compromise that only deprived the unions of *most* of their independence and placed them under tight party control. While some trappings of independence remained, particularly in terms of dealing with private employers, the substance of their independence was eliminated.

A second resolution—"On Party Unity"—was more encompassing. Rather than merely muzzling one specific distasteful opinion, its target was *any* group holding a point of view different from that of the leadership. "On Party Unity" banned the formation of "factions," as organized dissident groups were called, within the party. Those opposed to the party leaders were proscribed from organizing to present their views. Dissenters could speak, but only as isolated voices in a chorus conducted by the leadership. This resolution was given teeth by a secret amendment permitting the Central Committee to expel anyone guilty of "factionalism" from the party. If the offender in question sat on the Central Committee, expulsion required a two-thirds majority.

Considerable uneasiness attended the banning of factions, a step that went beyond the traditional limits of democratic centralism. The expulsion amendment remained unpublished for two years, hidden from the party as a whole like some mutilation one hopes will become less hideous over time. Karl Radek, an articulate veteran propagandist and organizer, verbalized the doubt that plagued many of the delegates as they voted for Lenin's resolution. "In voting for this resolution, I feel that it can well be turned against us, and nevertheless I support it," Radek admitted. Trotsky once wrote of Radek that he "exaggerates and goes too far." Unfortunately for both men and for so many of their comrades, in voicing his opinion this time, Radek did not go nearly far enough.

The party's first extensive purge, initiated in the summer of 1921, reinforced the steps taken at the Tenth Congress. It cut the party's membership of 700,000 by more than a quarter. By 1924, further purging had cut the party's ranks by half. Although the purges' expressed purpose was to root out careerists and opportunists who had joined the party for personal advancement and was therefore not officially directed at "factionalism," they eliminated many dissenters and thus served to intimidate those who remained.

While political activity inside the party was being circumscribed, outside the party it was eliminated altogether. During the civil war the Mensheviks and the SRs had been allowed a precarious and marginal existence; in 1921, both parties were completely suppressed. Twenty-two SR leaders were tried for counterrevolution in 1922. Although the irregular proceedings and indefensible sentences associated with these trials paled compared to what was to come under Stalin in the 1930s, the SR trials, with their trumped-up charges and propagandistic grandstanding by the prosecution, were the direct ancestors of Stalin's notorious show trials.

Also in 1922 the Cheka was officially abolished, only to rise again immediately as the State Political Administration, or GPU (after 1923 the Unified State Political Administration, or OGPU). Unlike the Cheka, the GPU was a regular branch of the state administration, an important boost in status for the secret police as an institution and an unmistakable reassertion of the principle that the Bolsheviks would rule without deference to the public will. The GPU, unlike the Cheka, had the right to arrest party members, a telling sign of the times and of things to come.

The years 1921 and 1922 thus marked an important watershed in the development of the Bolshevik Revolution. During those years Lenin and his comrades in the party leadership settled the fundamental question of whether the Soviet regime would reach an accommodation with the people or rule over them. Any genuine accommodation would have required the abolition of the Bolshevik dictatorship because by 1921 not even the most faithful had any illusions about the regime's popularity. Zinoviev even estimated that 99 percent of the workers were anti-Bolshevik. This estimate was excessively pessimistic, but both Lenin and Trotsky, men of more resolve and self-confidence than Zinoviev, admitted that the party had lost the support of the masses. Trotsky reflected the leadership's response to this problem when he pronounced that the party's historical mission bound it to "retain its dictatorship, regardless of the temporary vacillations" of the working masses. In other words, the party would decide what the proletariat needed and would enforce its decisions, regardless of what the workers thought about the matter.

The developments of 1921 and 1922 were not by themselves sufficient to decide the ultimate course of the Bolshevik Revolution, at least in terms of its denouement as Stalinist totalitarianism. The point is that a critical mass of repression was building as events unfolded from year to year. Thus 1917 was the year of the torpedoed socialist coalition government, 1918 the year of the forcibly disbanded Constituent Assembly, mid-1918 through late 1920 years of civil war and ruthless class war, and 1921 the year of strangled opposition within the party. These measures in turn created the need for a permanent and pervasive secret police and led inexorably to events like the Kronstadt and Tambov uprisings and the decision of the Tenth Party Congress to ban factions. One by one they produced the major building blocks for what was becoming a new autocracy over the people of Russia, one far more severe than that of the fallen tsars.

The one-man tyranny predicted by Lenin's critics was still some years away. But the tyrant was close by. In 1922, with Lenin's strong support, Joseph Stalin was appointed to a newly created post: general secretary. This gave him control of the Secretariat, with its enormous patronage powers. In addition, Stalin was the only Bolshevik sitting on the Central Committee, the Politburo, the Orgburo, and the Secretariat, the party's four main power centers. Aside from the physically declining Lenin, he was already the most powerful man in Soviet Russia.

Meanwhile, by maintaining its dictatorship at all costs, the party painted itself into a political corner. As the debates at the Tenth Party Congress made clear, the party was deeply divided. The Democratic Centralists and Workers' Opposition could not challenge the leadership, but they did raise a disturbing question: would the party dictatorship being imposed on Russia lead to dictatorship within the party itself? If it did not, the existing divisions might widen until they caused a party split, a development that would threaten the Bolshevik dictatorship. The Workers' Opposition was particularly dangerous in this regard because of its strong roots among the trade union rank and file. More worrisome was the danger of debate leaking outside the party sanctum. After all, the spectacle of open debate carried out by organized factions within the party would set an example for everyone in Russia. So the Bolsheviks unavoidably were forced to deny to themselves what they had denied to others. Their dictatorship was coming home to roost.

SOCIETY AND CULTURE DURING THE NEP

During the civil war the Bolsheviks developed the habit of viewing their struggle to build socialism in military terms. Even when the fighting was over, they often referred to civilian activities in terms of battles on the economic, political, or social "fronts" or used language such as "storming" this or that objective, controlling "commanding heights," and so on. Given their objectives and methods, the military metaphor remains a useful prism through which to view Bolshevik activity, even during the relatively quiescent 1920s. Thus, while Bolshevik political policy during the NEP years may reasonably be described as an unrelenting offensive against dissent, and economic policy as the seizure of designated strategic bastions while temporarily conceding others to groups that were considered class enemies, social and cultural policy during that era amounted to what historian Vladimir Brovkin has called "low intensity warfare."[3]

The Bolsheviks took this approach not because of a lessened commitment to effecting total change but because of the limited resources they had available to accomplish their ambitious agenda. In fact, much of the 1920s was devoted to building up the party and various auxiliary organizations so that more sustained offensives could be resumed in the near future. The party itself was reinforced by two recruitment drives—the "Lenin Enrollment" of 1924 and the "October Enrollment" of 1927—that swelled its membership to 1.7 million by the end of the decade. In addition, the Bolsheviks focused on building mass organizations. Their job was to extend the reach of the party's propaganda message and tentacles of control to tens of millions of people outside its ranks and thereby broaden and stabilize the regime's narrow and shaky base of support. These "transmission belts" included trade unions (which had 10 million members by 1930), antireligious organizations, the party's Women's Department (*Zhenotdel*), youth organizations, and sports clubs. No transmission belt was more important than the Young Communist League, or Komsomol. Founded in 1918 for people aged fourteen to twenty-eight, the Komsomol had the crucial job of indoctrinating the next Soviet generation as a whole while also serving as the party's main recruiting and training vehicle for new members. It expanded rapidly in the 1920s, reaching a membership of more than 1 million by the middle of the decade.

An important objective of Komsomol indoctrination was to break the younger generation's ties to religion, an effort that was part of the regime's overall struggle against religious belief. As militant Marxists and devout atheists, Lenin and his comrades hated religion, but they believed any attempt to completely uproot centuries of tradition was premature and unwise. Russian Orthodoxy and other religions therefore were subjected to a war of attrition rather than an all-out assault. Aside from distributing propaganda in the form of antireligious films, books, and newspapers, the Soviet regime employed tactics such as confiscating property, forcibly closing houses of worship, banning religious instruction, disrupting and mocking religious ceremonies or celebrations, denying state employment to people who worshipped publicly, and arresting and sometimes executing members of the clergy. The Bolsheviks tried to undermine their main religious enemy, the Russian Orthodox Church, in a variety of ways. They briefly sponsored an alternative organized by a group of reformist clerics called the "Living Church," but it won very few adherents. In 1925, when the Orthodox Church's patriarch died, the regime refused to allow the election of a successor. A broader attack on religion in general came after 1925 from enthusiasts organized into the "League of the Militant Godless." However, these campaigns, while weakening Russia's religious institutions, remained limited; the state's full weight did not fall on religion until the NEP itself was abolished.

The Bolshevik education system at first was a curious amalgam of state control, ideological straitjacketing, and progressive reform. Many distinguished educators, damned for their "bourgeois" origins or sympathies, were driven from their posts or chose to leave Russia. Thousands of ordinary teachers became targets of campaigns to impose ideological correctness; those who refused to bend sufficiently, or who came from particularly suspect social backgrounds, such as the former landlord class, were fired. Not all was negative, however, as the regime simultaneously mounted an intensive campaign to eliminate illiteracy. Its new educational system stressed technical subjects and expertise in order to create skilled cadres for the new order. In order to break down old customs and habits deemed hostile to the new order, many modern practices considered "progressive" in the West were introduced, including coeducation at all levels, genuine student self-government, abolition of examinations, and liberalized discipline. In 1918 university education had been opened to all young people over the age of sixteen; that reform lasted only until 1922, when high school diplomas again became required for university admission. Meanwhile, the universities lost their autonomy and were placed under state control.

As militant Marxists, the Bolsheviks believed that no institution inherited from the past inhibited the efforts of the party and its auxiliary organizations and thereby blocked the road to socialism more than the "bourgeois family." It was the key transmitter of the despised and dangerous old values from one generation to another. As one of the drafters of the regime's 1918 family code put it, "The family must be replaced by the Communist Party." This, a party expert on education opined that same year, would enable the Soviet regime to "rescue children from the harmful effects of the family" and "nationalize them." During the 1920s many true-believing party activists, including those who were married and had children, tried to live according to their beliefs. Bolshevik husbands and wives dedicated themselves to party work, leaving their children in the care of others. They took pride in adopting a Spartan lifestyle and paying little attention to their living quarters or acquiring material possessions. When it came to the rest of society, where Marxist visions regarding human relations did not prevail, the Bolsheviks had to tread carefully. Still, they tried to loosen traditional family ties through two family codes issued, respectively, in 1918 and 1926. Both codes, for example, minimized the authority of fathers, made divorce easy, and encouraged children to disobey their parents. Meanwhile, children in the Komsomol were taught that loyalty to building socialism took precedence over loyalty to the family.

The world of literature and the arts during the NEP years was a study in contrasts. Many of Russia's leading cultural figures, unable to endure the constricted intellectual environment at home, went into exile in the half-decade after the Bolsheviks came to power. The long list of exiles by choice included Ivan Bunin, the first Russian writer to win the Nobel Prize for literature (in 1933); Ilya Repin, the great realist painter whose "The Volga Boatmen," "The Religious Procession in Kursk Province," and "Ivan the Terrible with the Body of His Son" are among the most famous of all Russian paintings; Marc Chagall, a pioneer of modern art who is recognized as one of the twentieth century's outstanding painters; Vasily Kandinsky, Russia's first purely abstract painter; and Maxim Gorky, the radical novelist and playwright, longtime friend of Lenin, and sometime Bolshevik sympathizer, who could no longer stomach, among other things, the regime's repression of intellectuals and persecution of non-Bolshevik socialists. (Gorky returned home in 1931.) Those who left voluntarily were joined by others the regime deported during 1922–1923, among them the eminent philosopher Nicholas Berdyaev and about eighty distinguished writers, engineers, scientists, religious thinkers, and social scientists. According to Lenin, whose idea this was, the deportations would help "cleanse Russia for a long time to come."

Artists and intellectuals who remained found that the state controlled most literary and artistic outlets, and the regime used that leverage to politicize cultural expression as much as possible and censor what it considered politically unacceptable or dangerous. The state also spawned cultural organizations to push its revolutionary line, although sometimes they got out of control and had to be shut down. Such was the fate of *Proletkult*, an organization of militant ideologues and artists dedicated to creating a genuinely "proletarian" literature. *Proletkult* was intensely intolerant of other tendencies in literature and of artistic freedom in general. Its zeal eventually made it a nuisance rather than a useful tool of the state, particularly when it claimed total authority in its area of interest and demanded freedom from party control. *Proletkult* therefore was disbanded in 1923. By then the regime preferred to rely on several arms of the state and party bureaucracies, which often worked closely with the secret police, to make sure that artistic expression remained within tolerable ideological bounds. These bureaucratic watchdogs paid especially close attention to Russia's few remaining private printing houses, theaters, and similar associations. Thus in 1923 the Main Repertoire Committee (MRC), which operated under the authority of the Central Committee, reported that its "first priority" was to remove "all that garbage which had flooded our cinemas" prior to its formation the year before. Foreign films were especially vile, and indeed dangerous, as "almost all of them" were "contaminated by petty bourgeois ideology." Evidence of this included their defense of marriage and the family and the fact that in many of these films "almost everywhere you hear [the] fox trot." The MRC also turned its watchful ideological eye to the theater, banning dozens of plays for various offenses during its first few years in operation, among them the Moscow Art Theater's production of *The Brothers Karamazov*, deemed reactionary because it promoted Christian humility. Other plays that ran afoul of the MRC and were closed down included Oscar Wilde's *Salome*, for being "decadent-aesthetic," and *An Ideal Husband*, found guilty of affirming bourgeois parliamentary ideas.

Despite the state's monopoly of all forms of communication, the NEP era had its creative side. Supporters of the regime and its ideals in the artistic community, the foremost among them being poet Vladimir Mayakovsky, expressed their enthusiasm through genuinely interesting work, in Mayakovsky's case through a wide range of writings and his remarkable propaganda posters. Certain non-Communist writers, dubbed "fellow travelers" by Trotsky, who expressed varying degrees of sympathy as opposed to support for the regime, also initially enjoyed considerable, if precarious, artistic freedom. Some fellow travelers gathered together in a small group called the "Serapion Brotherhood." Their goal was to preserve complete artistic freedom. The best known of this talented group was Yevgeny Zamyatin, whose career in a way epitomizes the fate of artistic freedom during the 1920s. As early as 1921, his essay "I Am Afraid" stressed the urgency of opposing official dogma. Far better known is *We*, a brilliant anti-utopian novel that anticipated the work of Aldous Huxley and George Orwell. *We* was denied publication in Soviet Russia, and Zamyatin and many of his friends and associates came under increasing attack as the 1920s wore on. While many bowed to the pressure, Zamyatin was among the few to stand firm; in 1931 he was fortunate enough to be allowed to emigrate.

The relative freedom of the early 1920s even lured back some émigrés. Two who returned in 1923 were Ilya Ehrenburg, who at various points in his long career as a novelist and journalist found himself both out of favor and serving as an apologist for Stalinism, and Alexei Tolstoy, who ended up as a Stalinist hack. Some major literary figures who did not support the regime, like the poet and novelist Boris Pasternak and Osip Mandelshtam, generally acknowledged as Russia's greatest twentieth-century poet, never left Soviet Russia but managed to keep working. Average citizens, however, did not necessarily get a chance to appreciate that work; most of Pasternak's prose remained unpublished in the Soviet Union during his lifetime.

Considerable creativity survived in the state-controlled theater and cinema, both of which the regime used extensively to deliver its propaganda message to a mass audience. The theater's outstanding director, Vsevolod Meyerhold, was extremely innovative in using his medium to create "proletarian" art and bring the arts to the Russian masses. Sergei Eisenstein was Russia's most distinguished movie director. Two of the films he made in the 1920s—*The Battleship Potemkin*, the story of the dramatic mutiny by sailors on a warship in 1905, and *Ten Days That Shook the World*, an adaptation of the account of the November Revolution by American journalist John Reed—constitute a remarkable synthesis of political propaganda and artistic achievement.

When looked at as a whole, cultural life in the 1920s often appears to shine brightly, especially when contrasted with the quarter-century of fearsome darkness that followed under Stalin. This is an illusion arising from the failure to view events in a sufficiently broad historical context. During the 1920s the Soviet state already was casting an increasingly ominous shadow of censorship and suppression over the country's cultural life. The artists who illuminated that environment were not the first lights of a proletarian cultural renaissance, as their pro-Bolshevik members would have had it, but merely the flickering remnants of Russia's far richer and infinitely more diverse pre-revolutionary Silver Age. Rather than being artistic pioneers in a fledgling Marxist utopia, as Mayakovsky hoped, they were forlorn and ultimately doomed survivors of the carnage of the revolution and civil war and the haphazard government interference and repression of the NEP era, shipwrecked in an inhospitable brave new world. Thus Nadezhda Mandelshtam, the wife of Osip Mandelshtam and herself the author of two riveting volumes of memoirs about life under Stalin, years later rejected any "hankering after the idyllic twenties." Far from being "idyllic" or in any way progressive, she wrote in the memoir she called *Hope Against Hope*, that decade constituted a period "in which all the foundations were laid for our future": the dreadful era of totalitarian rule in the 1930s, when freedom of expression was extinguished along with the lives of countless cultural luminaries, including that of her husband.

NON-RUSSIANS IN THE SOVIET UNION

Bolshevik nationalities policy also oscillated between flexibility and repression during the 1920s. The Bolsheviks were unyielding, their official doctrine notwithstanding, when it came to the question of self-determination. Those peoples formerly subject to the tsars who established their independence after 1917 did so only because the Bolsheviks lacked the power to stop them. However, the Bolsheviks did grant considerable cultural autonomy to the non-Great Russians still citizens of the Soviet state, which from December 1922 officially was known as the Union of Soviet Socialist Republics (USSR). The cultural autonomy issue was extremely important since non-Russians accounted for just under half of the Soviet population. Ukrainians and Belarusians, Slavic peoples with their own territory and languages, received opportunities long denied them by the tsars to use their languages and develop their native cultures. Soviet Russia's 3 million Jews found that the state harassed their religion as it did others, but the Bolsheviks did make anti-Semitism a crime and permitted a considerable range of secular cultural self-expression in Yiddish, although, significantly, not in Hebrew. The Bolshevik regime even helped develop written languages for numerous illiterate tribes scattered across Asia. Finally, when a new constitution was adopted in 1924, it was based on the principle of federalism and provided for four constituent Soviet republics in the USSR: the Russian, Ukrainian, Belorussian, and Transcaucasian Soviet Federated Socialist Republics.

All this consideration given the minority nationalities served a greater purpose. Spreading education, regardless of the language used, spread the new socialist gospel as well. Yiddish, for example, was used as a tool to wean Jews away from their religion, an endeavor aided by mass closings of synagogues and the activities of a special unit of the Communist Party called the *Yevsektsiya*, or "Jewish section." At the same time, Hebrew was suppressed by the mid-1920s because the Communists insisted it was, simultaneously, the language of the Jewish bourgeoisie, of religion, and of Zionism, the latter already having been outlawed in 1919. Soviet Muslims were taught how to write their various languages, but in a newly developed Latin script rather than in an Arabic script in order to isolate them from Muslims across the border. (Later, in order to link the Muslims more closely to the Slavic majority, a Cyrillic script replaced the Latin one.) Although the Union of Soviet Socialist Republics supposedly was a federal state with each "union republic" enjoying the right to secede, real power was exercised by the centralized and unitary Communist Party. As for the right to secede, it would only be honored if the initiative came from the "proletariat," a rather unlikely development since the regime automatically classified all such agitation as "bourgeois."

THE NEP, SOCIALISM, AND CAPITALISM

The Bolsheviks' relative success in dealing with the various non-Russian nationalities contrasted with the difficulties they had with the economy. It soon became clear that the party's ambitions for beginning a planned economy and industrial development were faltering. The NEP, no less than War Communism, was a product of dire necessity. Unlike War Communism, which at least looked like socialism to many Bolsheviks, the NEP had little redeeming value from a socialist point of view. It deeply offended Marxist sensibilities to allow a widespread revival of capitalism in Soviet Russia. Particularly galling were the broad and increasing concessions to the peasantry, the class that to Marxists represented everything that was obscurant and reactionary. Yet there was little choice. Denied aid from Europe because the anticipated socialist revolution there had not materialized, the Bolsheviks were forced to rely on what the peasantry produced at home. In practice this meant unpalatable concessions such as allowing the more prosperous peasants to lease additional land and hire wage laborers.

In industry the picture was equally demoralizing. Small-scale and light industry had been largely turned over to private entrepreneurs or cooperatives. Only Russia's large-scale heavy industry remained in state hands. Yet this sector, hampered by the loss of foreign skills and capital as well as the emigration of native managerial and technical personnel, showed the slowest recovery rate in the Russian economy. Heavy industry drained the state budget and in return produced inadequate supplies of goods at excessively high prices. Even the light industry that produced consumer goods failed to reach 50 percent of its prewar production by 1923. The result was the so-called scissors crisis (named for a graph Trotsky used to illustrate the problem) of that year, during which the prices of scarce industrial goods soared relative to plentiful agricultural products. The danger that farmers would refuse to market their produce under such unfavorable conditions led the government to compel the state-run industries to lower their prices, even at the expense of industrial wages. On top of that, the decision to close some inefficient plants caused unemployment. Party leaders were distressed by these developments: after only two years of the NEP, the "workers' state" was being forced to sacrifice the proletariat's economic interests, as well as the ability of state-run industry to earn profits needed to create capital for future development, to the interests of the despised peasantry. Industrial workers in state-run enterprises found the situation intolerable. Their wages languished well below pre-1914 levels, but the Soviet state denied them the right to bargain for higher wages. The wages the workers did receive often were paid late. Adding insult to injury, their new Bolshevik bosses frequently treated them no better than the departed bourgeoisie and used the privileges that came with positions of authority to live lavish lifestyles while the workers struggled just to get by. When a wave of strikes broke out in 1923, the regime called in the GPU. Meanwhile, the Nepmen were looking more and more like a fledgling bourgeoisie. No wonder some cynics called the NEP the "new exploitation of the proletariat."

THE BOLSHEVIK REVOLUTION AND THE WORLD

The Bolsheviks tended to blame many of their domestic problems on international developments, particularly their unenviable position as the lone socialist state making its way in a capitalist world. That situation was not entirely unforeseen. Back in 1906 Trotsky had warned of a scenario that party leaders by the early 1920s feared might soon come to pass:

Without the direct state support of the European proletariat, the working class in Russia will not be able to maintain itself in power and convert its temporary supremacy into a lasting socialist dictatorship. We cannot doubt this for a moment.

Lenin made much the same point numerous times in the wake of the seizure of power. However, the years immediately after the revolution seemed to belie these concerns. Intoxicated by their own success, the Bolsheviks believed the potential for a world proletarian revolution was there and in 1919 set up an organization to promote it: the Communist International (Comintern). The Bolsheviks called their creation the Third International to distinguish it from the reformist Second International, the organization of the world's Social Democratic parties. An equally important distinction was that the members of the Second International were independent political parties; from the start the Third International was dominated by the Russian Communist Party, the only member that was not a newly formed, marginal sect. That control was officially spelled out by the twenty-one conditions imposed on all member parties at the organization's Second Congress in 1920. Each member party was obliged to organize itself along centralized Bolshevik lines, adhere to ideological positions as defined in Moscow (allegedly by the Comintern's Executive Committee but actually by the Bolshevik Politburo), and stand ready to help the "Soviet Republics" in their struggle against "counterrevolution."

In contrast to initial Bolshevik expectations, the period between 1919 and 1924 brought defeat and disappointment, not a European revolution. Throttled in the West, the Comintern began considering an end run around the European capitalist bulwark. At its "Congress of Peoples of the East," held in September 1920 in Baku, a city on the western shore of the Caspian Sea where Europe ends and Asia begins, delegates expressed the hope that the European capitalist states could be undermined by nationalist revolutions in their Asian colonies. Baku's Asiatic atmosphere seemed to cast a spell on the European-bred Soviet leaders who organized the conference. Zinoviev, the Comintern's chairman, issued a call for a "holy war" against British capitalism, while Bela Kun, former leader of the defunct "Hungarian Socialist Federated Soviet Republic," offered the distinctly non-Marxist thesis that communism could be established in an economically backward country that did not even have an industrial proletariat. Aside from dramatic rhetoric, the conference yielded little for the Bolsheviks or their would-be protégés: the colonial revolt against the West was still a generation away. A "Congress of Toilers of the East" held in Moscow in 1922 did no more than the Baku meeting to change that fact.

Actually, the Bolsheviks did not set a very good example for aspiring

European or Asiatic revolutionaries. They made some efforts to foment unrest abroad, but at the same time the failure of those efforts compelled them to enter into normal relations with other nations in a world they seemed unable to change. After years of war and blockade, Soviet Russia desperately needed to trade with the outside world. The Bolsheviks had to accept a sort of diplomatic NEP. This meant that the Comintern's other members had to moderate their behavior. In 1921 they were ordered to abandon plans to seize power in the immediate future and instead gather their strength for what would be a long struggle. More important, during 1920 and 1921, the Soviet government signed peace treaties with Estonia, Latvia, Lithuania, Finland, and Poland on Soviet Russia's European frontiers and with Turkey, Persia, and Afghanistan on its Asian borders. These treaties enabled the Soviet regime to secure most of its enormous flank and break the diplomatic isolation that had lasted for the duration of the civil war.

The Soviets capped their successful diplomatic campaign of 1920–1921 on March 16, 1921, when they reached a trade agreement with Great Britain. Until then, hostility to Bolshevism and the Soviet regime's cancellation of tsarist debts and nationalization of foreign property had precluded any commercial, much less diplomatic, relations with the major European powers. Once the British broke ranks, the other European powers concluded their own agreements with the Soviet Union.

Neophyte Soviet diplomacy achieved another dramatic success in 1922. Germany and Soviet Russia were pariahs in Europe, the former because it had been branded by the victorious Allies as being responsible for World War I and the latter because it declared war on capitalism in the name of revolutionary socialism. Both nonetheless were invited to attend a major economic conference at Genoa in April 1922. Neither country was able to get what it wanted from the victorious but parsimonious Allies, Soviet Russia's unrealized objectives being a loan and diplomatic recognition. So at the nearby resort of Rapallo the two outcasts reached their own agreement, announcing on April 16 that they had established diplomatic and commercial relations and renounced all claims against each other. Aside from the shock this treaty of pariahs produced in the West, where the view somehow persisted that these two former great powers could be ignored and abused without catastrophic consequences, the Rapallo agreement facilitated secret military cooperation between Soviet Russia and Germany. That cooperation enabled Germany to evade the disarmament strictures of the Versailles treaty and provided Soviet Russia with much needed experience in modern military techniques, including armored and aerial warfare.

It took a bit longer, until 1924, for the rest of Europe to fall into line. Then, convinced that the Soviet regime was going to last and anxious for access to the Russian market, most major European states, including Great Britain, France, and Italy, granted the Soviet Union diplomatic recognition. The Soviets meanwhile continued their unique brand of foreign policy. They combined normal diplomatic relations with subversion against capitalist states, although after 1921 diplomacy predominated and the Comintern was leashed to Russian national interests: that is, promoting international revolution was subordinated to defending the Soviet state.

LENIN AND HIS REVOLUTION

A more intractable and important problem, and the one that took the largest share of Lenin's time during his last years, lay much closer to home. By 1922, Lenin was worried that something was terribly wrong with Bolshevism. Perhaps being incapacitated by his first stroke in May of that year and therefore forced to observe from the sidelines gave him a new perspective on his regime. In any case, the founder and builder of the Bolshevik Party sensed that his prized political machine was beginning to run out of control. He used the term "bureaucratism" to describe what bothered him. Lenin's concerns were not the growth of bureaucracy per se and phenomena commonly associated with it, such as red tape and an impersonal method of operation, although these tendencies certainly disturbed him. Instead, Lenin was deeply worried about the basic relationship between the governing party and the people it governed. Bureaucratism to Lenin meant the growing gulf between officialdom and the people, the tendency of officials to surround and insulate themselves with privileges and to focus on their own interests rather than on those of the public they supposedly served. It meant abusive treatment of the powerless by the powerful, sometimes to the point of physical violence. Simple corruption also fell under the damnable rubric of bureaucratism. In short, bureaucratism was the domination and exploitation of the Soviet people by their Bolshevik government.

All this was a terrible shock to Lenin, who, for all his hard-headed realism, seems to have believed in many of the ideals he wrote about in *The State and Revolution.* Bureaucratism to Lenin was one of the most hateful aspects of "bourgeois" and especially tsarist society and high on the list of things slated for extinction after the revolution. Unfortunately, it had not taken long for Lenin's regime to succumb to creeping bureaucratism. In part this reflected the transformation of the Bolshevik Party from a revolutionary phalanx into an administrative apparatus attempting to govern an enormous, poor, and troubled country that did not share the party's goals. One aspect of this was the changing nature of the party's membership as it became flooded by careerists: upwardly mobile people not interested in what they could do for the cause, like revolutionaries who had joined in the old days, but in what the cause could do for their personal advancement. But something more fundamental was at work. Because the Bolsheviks were determined to rule alone and considered any challenges to their policies seditious, the party automatically cut itself off from the people it governed. As the party solidified what was increasingly its arbitrary power, it became corrupted by that power.

This syndrome was not new to Russia. In tsarist times there had been no political or legal checks on the autocracy—hence the tyranny of the tsarist bureaucracy. In Lenin's Russia there likewise were no checks on the Soviet dictatorship. Therefore the same phenomenon appeared, although this time it was a revolutionary rather than a reactionary bureaucracy that bore down on the people and enforced the decisions of a ruling clique responsible only to itself.

Lenin's battle against bureaucratism actually began as early as 1919 with the creation of a watchdog commissariat called the Workers' and Peasants' Inspectorate (*Rabkrin*). *Rabkrin*'s job was to root out corruption and waste in other governmental agencies. Within the Communist Party, a series of "control commissions" headed by a Central Control Commission was assigned the same job after 1920. *Rabkrin*'s chief was none other than Joseph Stalin. This new commissariat, of course, was no more responsive to the will of the population at large than any other part of the state bureaucracy. Stalin used it to promote his own political fortunes. By the time this dawned on Lenin in 1921, *Rabkrin* had become one of the most detested arms of the hydra-headed Soviet bureaucracy. The same can be said for the work of the control commissions, which did more to suppress dissent than to fight bureaucratism and bring the party closer to the masses.

Lenin's offensive against bureaucratism went into high gear in 1922. He focused on several areas of misconduct, all of which, not incidentally, were linked to Stalin, the man initially assigned to fight the scourge. By mid-1922 Stalin had acquired enormous power by placing himself at every key point of Lenin's party and, although few realized it, was already the second most powerful man in Soviet Russia. Lenin attacked Stalin for two major offenses: his unsatisfactory performance as *Rabkrin*'s chief official and his part in a shocking episode that occurred in Georgia, a small country on the southern slopes of the Caucasus Mountains originally absorbed by Russia in the late eighteenth century but independent since 1918.

Lenin had sanctioned Soviet Russia's reconquest of Georgia in early 1921. This action broke no precedent, but rather was part of the process of reassembling most of the patrimony, Russian and non-Russian, once ruled by the tsars. Besides, Georgia was being governed, and governed well, by, of all people, the Mensheviks, who made no secret of their distaste for Lenin and his Bolsheviks. ("We prefer the imperialists of the West to the fanatics of the East," said Georgia's president, Noah Zhordania.) The reconquest, against courageous resistance, and the subsequent ousting of a democratically elected regime, did not bother Lenin at all. He was, after all, suppressing Mensheviks himself in Moscow. What followed was another matter. The Communists sent from Moscow to oversee the establishment of Bolshevik rule treated their Georgian Communist comrades no better than they treated other Georgians. Local Georgians, whatever their political leanings, were given no real input into deciding how Georgia should be governed, and they were particularly disturbed by the decision to merge their homeland with other Transcaucasian regions into a "Transcaucasian Federated Republic." News of a long list of abuses, including using physical violence rather than comradely debate as a means of persuasion, reached Lenin. He reacted by condemning the ranking Moscow emissary on the scene, a Georgian named Sergo Ordzhonikidze. Equally important, Lenin strongly criticized Ordzhonikidze's boss, General Secretary Joseph Stalin, himself also a Georgian.

LENIN, STALIN, AND BUREAUCRATISM

Having found Stalin at so many trouble spots (the two men also clashed over the proposed new constitution and issues involving foreign trade), Lenin merged his struggle against bureaucratism with an attempt to limit Stalin's power. Both efforts were complicated by Lenin's deteriorating health. The last eighteen months of his life resembled the struggles of a drowning man. Three times strokes dragged him down. Twice he struggled up to renewed political activity. His first stroke occurred on May 22, 1922. After five months Lenin was back on the job, although at a reduced level of activity and effectiveness. A second stroke in December left Lenin partially paralyzed and temporarily unable to speak. Just as his campaign against Stalin seemed to be getting in high gear, Lenin suffered a third stroke on March 7, 1923. This time he remained an invalid until his death in January 1924.

Had Lenin lived, he might well have succeeded in removing Stalin; overcoming political opponents was a skill Lenin had mastered. He would have had a far more difficult time with bureaucratism. Not only was this a foe Lenin never had faced before and a phenomenon that far transcended any one man or group of men, but Lenin himself was a central part of the problem. While he was battling bureaucratic tendencies with one hand, he was buttressing them with the other. Lenin chose Stalin to be general secretary in large part because he wanted more effective internal party administrative controls after oppositionists embarrassed the leadership at the Eleventh Party Congress, held in March 1922. One of the worst moments at the congress occurred when Lenin defended the Bolshevik dictatorship over the working class on the grounds that the Russian proletariat was too weak to rule because it had disintegrated as a class during the recent difficult years. Alexander Shlyapnikov's caustic reply must have hurt as only the truth can: "Vladimir Ilyich said yesterday that the proletariat as a class, in the Marxian sense, did not exist [in Russia]. Permit me to congratulate you on being the vanguard of a non-existent class." For his efforts to combat what may fairly be called Lenin's bureaucratic tendencies, Shlyapnikov was dropped from the Central Committee and had his views condemned in a special resolution at the congress. He was not, as Lenin wanted, expelled from the party. That job, as well as Shlyapnikov's subsequent liquidation, was done by Stalin.

Lenin meanwhile reinforced the party's dictatorship over the proletariat in several ways. After the Tenth Party Congress, the trade unions functioned, but with clipped wings. By 1922 the soviets were purged of Mensheviks and Socialist Revolutionaries and increasingly subject to directives from the Bolshevik leadership. The secret police was an integral part of the regime. The number of concentration camps in Russia almost tripled to 355 between 1921 and the end of 1923, in part because of an influx of dissident workers, peasants, and socialists of various types. Not even party members were safe. Many dissidents were expelled in the purge of 1921. Those who remained politically active after their expulsion ran the risk of arrest; some dissidents who were not expelled complained bitterly of house searches, mail seizures, and attempts at entrapment by undercover agents.

Lenin militantly supported all of this. In February 1922, he urged intensified repression against the "political enemies of Soviet power and the agents of the bourgeoisie (specifically the Mensheviks and SRs)." He wanted what he called "model trials" staged to intimidate potential dissidents and for propaganda purposes. Over the long term, Lenin had strict requirements for Soviet Russia's proposed new criminal code: "The paragraph on terror must be formulated as widely as possible, since only revolutionary consciousness of justice can determine the conditions of its application." Defendants, in other words, should have as little recourse as possible to legal rights and guarantees. If Lenin was concerned about bureaucratism—that is, about Soviet life becoming more authoritarian and arbitrary—he certainly had an odd way of showing it.

Still, Lenin did try to do something about the deterioration of the Bolshevik regime. As 1922 wore on, he railed against both Stalin and bureaucratism while at the same time trying to prevent another crisis: a split and struggle for power among his chief lieutenants. Late in the year he hurled two major salvos at Stalin: a critique of *Rabkrin* in August and a denunciation of "dominant nation chauvinism"—in other words, of Stalin's handling of the Georgian affair—in

October. Lenin also tried to rally others to his cause. Twice he unsuccessfully urged Trotsky to become vice-chairman of *Sovnarkom*, a post that would have made him Lenin's number one deputy and greatly strengthened his political standing. Lenin also urged that he and Trotsky form a "bloc against bureaucracy in general."

LENIN'S "TESTAMENT" AND FINAL ARTICLES

Lenin's second stroke hit in mid-December of 1922. It was immediately followed by the most important of Lenin's writings during these years, his "Testament," written late in December, to which a "Postscript" was dictated on January 4, 1923 (both kept secret from most party leaders until 1924). The "Testament" was a critique of each of the major party leaders. It implied that Lenin did not want any one man, but rather a collegium, to succeed him. None of his lieutenants was quite fit. Stalin already had too much power and might not use it well. Bukharin was ideologically suspect. Zinoviev and Kamenev had caved in during the crucial days of 1917. Trotsky, Lenin's apparent favorite and the "most capable" man of the group, also had serious flaws. Lenin also suggested enlarging the Central Committee to a total of 50 to 100 members. Such a step, Lenin hoped, would help prevent a split among the party leaders, in particular between Trotsky and Stalin.

Lenin's "Postscript" went further than his "Testament." One thing absolutely had to be done, he warned. Because Stalin was "too rude," a characteristic "unbearable in the office of General Secretary," Lenin urged that he be removed and replaced by someone "more patient, more loyal, more polite, and more attentive to comrades, less capricious, etc."

Although already gravely ill, Lenin soldiered on. By now he was floating all sorts of ideas to keep the party dictatorship he had built from degenerating into a modernized version of the late tsarist autocracy. "How We Should Reorganize *Rabkrin*," Lenin's instructions to the upcoming Twelfth Congress, was published on January 15, 1923. His key point, aside from urging that *Rabkrin* be drastically reduced in size, again was that the party must renew its ties with the working class. He suggested that 75 to 100 "workers and peasants" be elected to the Central Control Commission, which at times would meet jointly with the Central Committee. In "Better Fewer, But Better," published on March 4, Lenin went still further. He stressed that the party had to tap not only the workers' revolutionary spirit, but also the skills and culture of Soviet Russia's educated, nonparty people.

Lenin put much of his remaining energy into a speech attacking Stalin he planned to give to the Twelfth Congress. He also sent a note to Trotsky on March 5 urging him to carry the offensive against Stalin at the congress and a note to Stalin in reaction to the latter's extremely rude treatment of Nadezhda Krupskaya, Lenin's devoted wife and indispensable aide of twenty-three years. A bitterly angry Lenin threatened to sever all personal ties with Stalin if an apology were not immediately forthcoming. Two days later, Lenin suffered his third stroke.

LENINISM AT A DEAD END

Lenin's last stand came too late. His Central Committee already was split. The so-called Stalin–Zinoviev–Kamenev triumvirate was pitted against Trotsky. Stalin meanwhile was using the general secretary's immense patronage power so effectively that he already had more leverage in the party than any other of Lenin's would-be heirs. His supporters, in alliance with those of Zinoviev and Kamenev, controlled the Twelfth Congress in April 1923, which Lenin could not attend because of his poor health. Stalin used a reorganization plan that on the surface conformed with Lenin's desire to bring new blood into the party to place his cronies in key party and state positions. By the end of 1923, as Lenin was barely clinging to life, Trotsky was so isolated that he decided to put aside his own authoritarianism and demand a return to what he called "intra-Party democracy."

Much more was wrong with Lenin's efforts than timing. His campaign against bureaucratism was as feeble as his health. It focused on individuals or symptoms rather than on the Bolshevik system as a whole. For example, in "Better Fewer, But Better" he suggested that only the most dedicated people—"the best elements" or "really enlightened elements"—should be recruited for the state or party apparatus. To combat inefficiency and intolerable behavior, Lenin felt an enormous education effort was needed to raise the Bolshevik level of "culture." Initially, even "real bourgeois culture" would be an improvement, although in another article ("On Cooperation") Lenin looked forward to what he called a "cultural revolution."

Unwilling to grab the bull by the horns—that is, to admit that any dictatorship, even a Bolshevik dictatorship that presumed to represent the "people," meant oppression, corruption, and hence bureaucratism—Lenin grasped at straws. In 1923, he even turned to the proletariat, the very same class that since 1902 he had insisted was inept and unconscious and needed his "vanguard" to lead it along. Now it was the vanguard that needed help. That is why Lenin suggested adding 75 to 100 ordinary working people to the Central Control Commission and having the Commission meet in joint session with the Central Committee. Presumably, the proletariat's very presence in the inner sanctums of power would somehow clear the stagnant air that was suffocating socialism. By a process Lenin did not elaborate on, proletarian honesty and purity would restore revolutionary fervor and purity to his bureaucratized Central Committee.

Lenin's hopes were misplaced. Individuals could not alleviate problems that were rooted in the nature of the regime. For example, after his death thousands of workers were added to the party in the Lenin Enrollment, but their selection and placement were determined by the very people who controlled the levers of the party bureaucracy. The whole process thus served Stalin's interests rather than Lenin's objectives and strengthened the very forces Lenin opposed.

Lenin's dilemma was that he wanted to invigorate the party but would not permit genuine criticism of his policies from within the party, to say nothing of suggestions from outside it. He wanted the proletariat to improve the party but would not let the proletariat judge the party. It might "vacillate," in Trotsky's words. He would not even let the proletariat have its own independent trade unions, only unions controlled by the increasingly corrupt Bolshevik Party. He wanted to prevent the party from ruling arbitrarily and cruelly but would not allow it to be subject to laws and legal norms that could have restrained it.

Lenin, in reality, could undertake no genuine reform. To do so would have limited the party's freedom of action and raised the possibility of its losing power, thereby violating the prime directive underlying everything he had done since November 1917. Given his commitment to untrammeled Bolshevik power, Lenin was no more capable of reversing the advance of bureaucratism that was destroying his dream than he was of stopping the arteriosclerosis that was killing him.

As for Lenin himself, the lion went out like a lamb. In December 1923, the avowed atheist spent an evening with family and friends around a Christmas tree as gifts were exchanged. On January 19, Krupskaya read him Jack London's short story "Love of Life." It tells of a sick man, dying of hunger and unable to walk, who survives a life-and-death struggle with a starving wolf and somehow reaches safety. Lenin greatly enjoyed the story; possibly he took hope from it. Two days later, not yet fifty-four years old, the living embodiment of Bolshevism was dead.

Lenin's death gave birth to a secular cult, promoted by his successors, which led to his being revered by millions of true believers. His career spawned a debate among serious observers and students of the Bolshevik Revolution, both Marxist and non-Marxist, that outlived the Soviet Union. To what extent, the debate runs, was Lenin responsible for the totalitarian society that developed in the Soviet Union under Stalin? Did Lenin prepare the way for Stalin, or was Stalinism a betrayal of the ideals and practices that have come to be called Leninism?

Some of Lenin's achievements are largely beyond debate. By modifying, some might say mutilating, Marxism, he adapted it to the Russian political environment. His elite "party of a new type" gave Marxism the protective armor it needed in tsarist Russia and provided a model for Marxists in many other countries. To this he added two key political insights: the concept that Russia's poor peasantry could play a revolutionary role as a junior partner allied to the proletariat, and his analysis of the revolutionary opportunities imperialism had created for Russia. Lenin also had extraordinary gifts of decisiveness, timing, and flexibility. In combination with his ruthlessness and readiness to gamble, these characteristics made Lenin an unsurpassed master at winning and holding power.

Power, however, was not an end in itself for Lenin; it was a means to an end. While it is difficult to know precisely what Lenin had in mind when he talked about "socialism" and "communism," it seems fair to say that he envisioned a collectivist society with a high standard of living based on advanced technology that would provide a wide range of opportunities for all individuals. This was the vision in *The State and Revolution*. It also seems fair to say that Lenin did not spend his life working for a revived autocracy bearing down ever more heavily on the Russian people through a new bureaucratic machine. This is the meaning of his struggle against "bureaucratism" and why he expressed his fear about the revival of the old Russian bureaucratic tradition with a "Soviet veneer." It also accounts for his eleventh-hour struggle against Stalin.

Stalin's rise to power resulted in a tyranny over the Russian people far worse than Lenin or almost anyone else could have imagined in the 1920s. Yet the evidence is compelling, indeed overwhelming, that Lenin, whatever his intentions, prepared the way not just for Stalin the dictator, but, more fundamentally, for the totalitarian system associated with his name. Before 1917, Lenin created a political party with an ethos that in the name of revolution justified many activities that repelled many other revolutionaries. That ethos also heartily endorsed a regime based on force so long as it was a "proletarian dictatorship" committed to socialism. Lenin's highly centralized party also required all members to subordinate themselves completely to the collective—all members, that is, except the leader.

The key to Stalin's rise to power was the interaction between Bolshevik theory and practice and the extreme strains and harsh conditions of the period between 1917 and Lenin's death in 1924. In order to stay in power during those difficult years, Lenin initiated or approved virtually every political institution or process that Stalin later used to establish his dictatorship: the authority of the Politburo and the tentacles of the Secretariat; the rule that forming a "faction" within the party was tantamount to treason; the Central Committee's power to expel party members simply for actively disagreeing with the leadership; the party purge to control dissent; the party's control of every branch of state; the party's attempt to control every institution in Russian life, leaving no room for anything that opposed the Bolshevik dictatorship; and a secret police operating above the law as an integral part of Soviet society. Lenin's government also engaged in brutal and widespread repression, established and then expanded a network of concentration camps, staged outrageous political show trials, and wrote a criminal code that gave the state almost unlimited repressive powers. Stalin's collectivization program had its roots in Lenin's anti-kulak policies during the civil war. As Dmitri Volkogonov pointed out in his groundbreaking biography of Lenin—having cited Lenin's August 1918 outburst: "Merciless war against these kulaks! Death to them!"—Stalin the collectivizer "had no need for new slogans—they had already been prepared for him."[4] Even Stalin's policies of deporting entire national groups during World War II had their precedents in Lenin's deportation of hundreds of thousands of Cossacks from their homes along the Don and Kuban rivers during the civil war. All of this explains why Alexander Yakovlev, a key figure in the unsuccessful effort to reform the Soviet Union between 1985 and 1991, had this to say about Lenin and Stalin: "The truth is that in his punitive operations Stalin did not think up anything that was not there under Lenin: executions, hostage taking, concentration camps, and all the rest."[5]

A vitally important product of the centralism Lenin infused into Bolshevism and of the harsh measures used to maintain the party's dictatorship after November 1917 was the steady narrowing of the party's decision-making structure. Overwhelming power became concentrated in a tiny group of men holding a few key bureaucratic levers. Because of this, the Bolshevik Party was a pyramid standing on its point rather than on its base and therefore vulnerable to sudden jolts. In practice this meant it was possible that after Lenin was gone, one of the leaders at the top might seize power from the others and impose his will on the party as a whole. This, in fact, is what happened, and there is every reason to consider it a natural outgrowth of Bolshevism. Trotsky had predicted as much back in 1904.

That the man who won the post-Lenin power struggle was Stalin, a monstrously warped individual whose crimes included mass murder on an unprecedented scale, both on behalf of and against the party, cannot be seen as an inevitable consequence of Bolshevism. But it cannot be considered unlikely, either. The political structure Lenin had built was made to order for such a dreadful denouement to occur. In that sense, Lenin must be judged responsible for Stalin and what occurred after Stalin took control of the party.

Beyond that, and even assuming someone other than Stalin had won the struggle for power, in establishing a regime based on force rather than on popular consent and the rule of law, Lenin reached a political dead end. Force, expedience, and ruthlessness served him well in seizing and holding power.

However, they were futile and counterproductive for achieving anything remotely resembling the socialist society envisioned by Marx and Engels. Ironically, Lenin's successful quest for power made his use of it a failure. As historian Rolf H.W. Theen has pointed out, Lenin

> was unable to recognize that he could not manipulate Russian society as he had manipulated his party and at the same time hope to develop the mutual trust between the ruled and the ruler which is the foundation and *conditio sine qua non* of any civilized government.[6]

The idea of a revolutionary state overhauling Russia by force was neither new nor uniquely Lenin's; Russian revolutionaries from Tkachev to Trotsky had endorsed the concept. Lenin's contribution was to develop the basis for such a state in practice. In doing so, he went beyond what traditional Marxism suggested was possible and ran into the precise dilemma some Marxists had predicted. Before Lenin was born, Friedrich Engels, writing about Thomas Münzer, a sixteenth-century visionary with communistic notions, commented that Münzer's actions "paved the way to a social system that was the direct opposite of what he aspired to." A case can be made that the same was true for Lenin.

If Lenin would be unhappy about sharing Münzer's fate, he might take posthumous comfort in knowing that he played a pivotal role in preventing Russia from developing into a Western-style capitalist and parliamentary society he so hated, at least for the duration of the twentieth century. For the Bolshevik Revolution in the end guaranteed one thing: that Russia's course of modernization would follow a different path than any other nation had taken before. Lenin must be judged on the basis of the burdens that path imposed on the people he promised he would lead to a better world.

NOTES

1. Isaac Deutscher, *The Prophet Unarmed. Trotsky: 1921–1929*, Vol. 2 (New York: Vintage, 1965), p. 1.

2. Isaac Deutscher, *The Prophet Armed. Trotsky: 1879–1921*, Vol. 1 (New York: Vintage, 1965), pp. 513–514.

3. Vladimir Brovkin, *Russia After Lenin: Politics, Culture, and Society, 1921–1929* (London and New York: Routledge, 1998), p. 20.

4. Dmitri Volkogonov, *Lenin: A New Biography*, edited and translated by Harold Shukman (New York: Free Press, 1994), p. 197.

5. Alexander N. Yakovlev, *A Century of Violence in Soviet Russia*, translated by Anthony Austin (New Haven and London: Yale University Press, 2002), p. 20.

6. Rolf H.W. Theen, *Lenin* (Princeton, N.J.: Princeton University Press, 1973), pp. 139–140.

Part IV

Steeling The Revolution

Kliment Voroshilov, Vyacheslav Molotov, Joseph Stalin, and Nikolai Yezhov, overlooking the newly opened Moscow-Volga Canal, built by prison labor. After presiding over the great purge, Yezhov himself was eventually tried and executed and his image was erased from this 1937 photograph.

12

Bolshevism Without Lenin

It's a struggle for the throne—that's what [it is].

—Stalin, 1923 or 1924

If Lenin were alive now, he would be in one of Stalin's prisons.

—Krupskaya, 1927

Lenin's death left the Bolshevik Party politically orphaned. In the past, whatever the problems it faced, the party had known who its leader was. Suddenly, Lenin was gone; only the problems that had sapped his last strength remained. Replacing Lenin would have been extremely daunting under any circumstances. Devising coherent policies for dealing with the multiple forms of corruption in the party and the disturbing tendencies in the NEP would have been difficult even with Lenin at the helm. After January 1924, the party faced the Herculean task of performing all these tasks simultaneously.

Because the Bolsheviks never before had to choose a leader, the process became lengthy, disorderly, and disruptive. This was not because of any formal arrangements or offices that Lenin held. He had been the chairman of the *Sovnarkom*, but he held no titles within the party that distinguished him from other members of the Bolshevik leadership. His formal status on the Politburo and Central Committee was like any other member's. Neither body had a chairman and both decided issues by majority vote, votes Lenin sometimes lost.

Nevertheless, the man who listed his party role as merely "member of the Central Committee" was irreplaceable. He was the heart and soul of the Bolshevik Party, its founder, and the only leader it had ever known. He also was the linchpin of the Soviet regime; while he was still healthy no major decisions were implemented without him. He wielded almost dictatorial power by persuasion rather than force and was able to do so because his political stature dwarfed that of every other party leader. It loomed so large that many of his colleagues could not conceive of governing without him.

THE LEADING CONTENDERS

Although Lenin's mystique prevented any of his lieutenants from openly claiming the right to succeed him, this did not prevent several of them from struggling for position and power against each other even while the ailing leader still lived. Two men dominated the unofficial battlefield: Leon Trotsky and Joseph Stalin. Trotsky was the best-known Bolshevik after Lenin. The revolution, and his place in it, was his life. A Jew by birth, Trotsky once re- sponded to an anti-Semitic taunt about whether he was "a Jew or a Russian" by pronouncing himself "a Social Democrat, that is all." A brilliant polemicist and orator, Trotsky also was a superb organizer and administrator and capable of both fearless and ruthless conduct. Revolutionary situations brought out the best in him. During the 1905 Revolution he clearly eclipsed Lenin as a revolutionary leader, rising to the chairmanship of the celebrated St. Peters- burg Soviet and defending himself heroically at his trial after the revolution was suppressed. His performance in 1917 was even more impressive. Again he became chairman of the soviet in what was then called Petrograd and was instrumental in putting that vital body at the service of the Bolsheviks. Trotsky was Lenin's right-hand man during the revolution and civil war. He headed the Petrograd Soviet's Military Revolutionary Committee, which actually planned the Bolshevik coup, and then, among other things, forged and directed the Red Army. After the civil war, Trotsky continued to sit on the Politburo and serve as the commissar of war. Until 1923, he seemed to be Lenin's logical successor.

Yet for all his incomparable skills as a revolutionary, Trotsky was an inept politician. A longtime critic of Lenin who did not join the Bolsheviks until July 1917, Trotsky did nothing to assuage the bruised feelings of many veteran party members who resented his meteoric rise to the top. Trotsky could be intoler- ably aloof and insufferably arrogant. Who else would have read French novels during meetings of the Politburo while his enemies sniped at him? During the civil war his high-handedness and ruthlessness made him additional enemies within the party, even as his Red Army was defeating the Whites. Trotsky did, to be sure, enjoy wide popularity in the party, but he proved unable to organize his supporters into an adequate power base by ensconcing them in strategic places in the growing party apparatus. Thus, after the Tenth Party Congress, several of his supporters were removed from the Central Committee and his loyalists lost control of both the Secretariat and the Orgburo, the two bodies that soon became the fulcrum of Stalin's strength. Trotsky also was hamstrung by his obsession with history and his place in it. He therefore refused to rely on the Red Army during the struggle for power because, in his Marxist eyes, this would have made him a Russian equivalent of Napoleon Bonaparte, the French general (and later emperor) whose coup restored order and protected the interests of the bourgeoisie after the French Revolution. Finally, Trotsky grossly underestimated Stalin. Even after Stalin had banished him from the party and from Russia, Trotsky could do no more than grant his victorious opponent the dubious status of being the party's "outstanding mediocrity." It was Lenin who raised Trotsky up and made him a leading Bolshevik. Without the "old man's" support, Trotsky, his talent, popularity, and personal charisma notwithstanding, stood on a shaky political base.

Joseph Stalin was born Joseph Dzhugashvili in a village in Georgia, a small country in a polyglot part of the Russian Empire between the Black and Caspian seas known as Transcaucasia. Stalin (which means "man of steel" in Russian) was the only leading Bolshevik whose class background made him one of the masses. Born into poverty, he was the victim of a particularly brutal childhood, enduring terrible beatings from his drunken father until the latter abandoned his family. Despite this, young Joseph, highly intelligent and endowed with an excellent memory, excelled in a local church primary school and won a scholarship to a seminary in Tiflis, the Georgian capital. There he met more mistreatment at the hands of obscurant monks until he rebelled and, in 1899, was expelled after failing to take the examinations that would have enabled him to graduate. By then, having joined the local branch of the Social Democratic party the year before, Stalin had already launched his revolutionary career.

Stalin's childhood experiences left their mark on his personality and on how he operated as a revolutionary. As a young man he could be lively, engaging, and even charismatic. An excellent organizer and skilled conspirator, Stalin was determined to lead, and between 1900 and 1905 he established himself as a prominent figure in the turbulent and fragmented Transcaucasian Social Democratic underground. But Stalin was also vicious, conniving, hostile, and domineering. "Koba," as he was known in the revolutionary underground, alienated many of his colleagues. Years later, in Siberian exile, Stalin made a similar negative impression on several Marxists from other parts of Russia. In the unforgiving Transcaucasian revolutionary world, which had more than its share of cutthroats, Stalin stood out for his ruthlessness and readiness to resort to violence and criminal acts. Extortion, running protection rackets, and kidnapping were among the weapons he used to intimidate employers in labor disputes, finance revolutionary activities, or enhance his own position in the movement. Stalin recruited criminals into the revolutionary groups he led and cooperated with outright criminal gangs. As historian Simon Sebag Montefiore has aptly noted, Stalin "preferred rogues to revolutionaries."[1] While it was accepted practice among revolutionaries to eliminate police informers in their ranks, Stalin dispensed with the normal practice of investigation and ordered executions based on his suspicions alone.

Stalin's most significant activity during this early stage of his revolutionary career was organizing robberies, with Lenin's enthusiastic approval, to fill the empty Bolshevik coffers. These "expropriations," as their supporters preferred to call them, led Lenin to take his first serious notice of young Koba. Others were less impressed. After organizing his most famous "expropriation," a June 1907 bank robbery in Tiflis during which homemade grenades left several guards and bank employees literally blown to pieces and a total of about forty dead, Stalin apparently was expelled from the Menshevik-controlled Trans-caucasian Social Democratic organization. Meanwhile, he saw to it that the bulk of loot from that robbery, several million dollars in today's money, was delivered to Lenin. Some of Stalin's fellow Georgians referred to him as a *kinto*, an insulting Georgian term connoting a combination of street tough and petty thief. He certainly was a man devoid of many usual human sensibilities and restraints and was capable of extraordinary cruelty.

Like his personal background, Stalin's revolutionary background differed from that of the other top Bolshevik leaders. While Lenin and the others lived as émigrés in Western Europe, Stalin spent virtually his entire pre-1917 revolutionary career as an underground worker inside Russia. Lenin, Trotsky, Zinoviev, and the rest, all well-educated and exposed to European life and culture, tended to be cosmopolitan and internationally oriented. Their lives were not easy, but they were spared much of what the underground workers at home had to endure. Hardened by poverty, hounded by the secret police, betrayed by informers, and tempered by prison and Siberian exile, the "prac-ticals" working in the trenches in Russia in many ways were a tougher breed than their leaders living in Europe. Their lives left them unconcerned with the ideological fineries that so intrigued men able to spend hours in European libraries or cafes. "Practicals" tended to be parochial in their outlook, more concerned with a revolution in the Russia they knew than one that might sweep across countries they had never seen.

Whatever his faults or limitations, Stalin nevertheless possessed important talents and strengths. He was efficient and tough, a good choice for any dif-ficult or unsavory job. Stalin was also an excellent actor, able to ingratiate himself with people and even charm them when necessary. The list of those he impressed includes not only Lenin but sophisticated world leaders such as Winston Churchill and Franklin Roosevelt. In a party of garrulous intel-lectuals, Stalin knew when to keep silent. Among comrades who reveled in displaying their erudition, he carefully concealed his knowledge. Stalin also had an acute sense of political timing and a sixth sense for his opponents' weaknesses. Perhaps that is why Nikolai Bukharin, one of the brilliant intellectuals he bested in the struggle for power, called him not only "Genghis Khan" but a "devil."

Stalin tended to side with Lenin in party disputes as early as 1901, and became a steadfast Bolshevik immediately after the 1903 party split. By 1907 he was the leading Bolshevik in Transcaucasia. His rise in the central Bolshevik organization nonetheless was slow until 1912, when Lenin, his ranks depleted by defeats and hard times, promoted the man he called a "wonderful Georgian" to the newly formed Bolshevik Central Committee. This promotion was followed by Lenin's bringing Stalin to Europe for six weeks to write a major pamphlet on the nationality problem in Russia. Shortly after his return to Russia in 1913, Stalin was arrested and exiled to Siberia, where he remained until freed by the March 1917 Revolution. He did not play a particularly visible role in the great Bolshevik triumph in November, but he was a key member of the party's leadership team and was appointed commissar of nationalities in Lenin's original cabinet. The civil war, which created such opportunity for clever and ruthless people, propelled him to the top echelon. By 1921, Stalin headed two commissariats—nationalities and *Rabkrin*—and sat on both the Politburo and Orgburo. Aside from enjoying Lenin's confidence, his party jobs and position at the head of two commissariats gave him considerable clout. Upon becoming general secretary in 1922, Stalin indisputably was the politician with the most direct control of the rapidly growing party apparatus. The man a prominent eyewitness to the events of 1917 once described as a "gray blur, which glimmered dimly and left no trace" was beginning to leave his indelible mark.

THE "STRUGGLE FOR THE THRONE"

The struggle for power had several phases. From late 1922 until January 1925, most of the senior Bolshevik leadership united against and defeated Trotsky. The core of this anti-Trotsky conglomeration—it was too diverse and internally divided to call it an alliance—was the "Triumvirate" composed of Zinoviev, Stalin, and Kamenev. From its inception in late 1922, the Triumvirate was the party's strongest organizational bloc. It fell apart as soon as Trotsky was defeated because Stalin was hard at work undermining his partners and they in turn feared his growing power. Their fears were justified; by 1925 Stalin had bolstered his considerable organizational strength by allying himself with three other Politburo members: Nikolai Bukharin, Alexei Rykov, and Mikhail Tomsky. These men were the leading advocates of continuing the moderate NEP policies of tolerating and even encouraging private peasant enterprise and the small-scale capitalist enterprise of the Nepmen. Since Zinoviev and Kamenev attacked these policies, and because they immediately found themselves a minority in the party as a whole, their faction was called the Left Opposition. Stalin's alliance with the party's moderate or "right" wing easily defeated the Left Opposition and its successor, the so-called United Opposition, a quickly hatched combination of the Zinoviev–Kamenev and Trotsky factions that rose from the ashes in 1926 only to sink back down in defeat by December 1927. The final phase was the showdown between Stalin, who rather suddenly emerged as a critic of the Bukharin–Rykov–Tomsky economic policies, and the general secretary's latest ex-allies, collectively known as the Right Opposition. This phase spanned much of 1928 and 1929 and ended in complete victory for Stalin.

STALIN'S ADVANTAGES

Stalin was aided in what he called the "struggle for the throne" because each of his opponents had serious political weaknesses. Zinoviev, the only man who fought Stalin on his own terms by trying to manipulate the bureaucratic apparatus, had considerable political and oratorical skill and a formidable array of party and nonparty posts. Lenin's closest associate in the decade before 1917, Zinoviev was a Politburo member, head of the Leningrad party organization, and chairman of the Comintern. He also had the unswerving support of the third triumvir, Lev Kamenev. Kamenev, the powerful boss of the Moscow party organization, so closely and consistently orbited his friend that the two men became Bolshevism's binary star, locked into the same positions and, as it turned out, the same fate. Yet Zinoviev, for all his power and oratorical skills, was a mediocrity. Many of his "comrades" criticized him for his cowardly behavior during the fall of 1917. Once in power, he proved to be eminently corruptible. By 1921 he was not above delaying an entire railroad train to suit his convenience or ordering railroad cars full of passengers detached to accommodate his personal parlor car. Kamenev meanwhile raced through Moscow in a Rolls-Royce. Like most of the other Bolshevik leaders, Zinoviev and Kamenev underestimated Stalin. However, they both also hated Trotsky for having replaced Zinoviev as Lenin's right-hand man, a hatred that prevented them from turning to Trotsky to block Stalin until it was too late.

Nikolai Bukharin was an outstanding theoretician and an able economist. He was a member of the Politburo and popular among the party elite. A man whose interests ranged from reading to collecting butterflies, Bukharin was far better suited for the rarefied world of intellectual discourse than for combat in the political trenches, something he demonstrated conclusively in his ineffectual struggle against Stalin in 1928–1929.

These men compounded their individual weaknesses by failing to unite their strengths. Although Stalin's power initially was something of a political iceberg largely hidden in the stormy Bolshevik factional seas, by the summer of 1923 it loomed large enough to worry Zinoviev and several other leaders. They hatched a scheme to limit the general secretary's power by converting the Secretariat from Stalin's personal preserve into a body composed of several of the top leaders. But the plan was stillborn because Zinoviev and his cohorts lacked the resolution to see it through. First they readily accepted an alternative compromise offer from Stalin, and then they failed to use the supervisory powers the compromise gave them. After Zinoviev took the lead in attacking Trotsky in 1923 and 1924, Trotsky stayed in his tent when Stalin moved against Zinoviev and Kamenev in 1925. By the time Trotsky and Zinoviev joined forces, they were too weak to stop Stalin. In 1928, a desperate Bukharin was unable to get Kamenev to help him forge an anti-Stalin alliance while, true to form, several important Trotsky supporters joined up with Stalin after 1929 because they agreed with his plans for rapid industrialization. All of this allowed Stalin room to divide, conquer, and destroy his opponents one by one.

Stalin also benefited from a mystique that surrounded the party. It was rooted in Lenin's conception of a vanguard party that was the only agent capable of blazing a path to socialism. That vanguard therefore required absolute unity, an imperative that gave birth to democratic centralism. The concept of unity, venerated in 1903 and beatified in 1921 at the Tenth Party Congress, was canonized after 1924. It became a devastating weapon the majority could use against the minority or "opposition." The accusation of "factionalism" became a mark of Cain that delegitimized any attempt to criticize the leadership. Thus the Triumvirate used it against Trotsky; Stalin and Bukharin used it against the Left Opposition and United Opposition; and Stalin used it against the Right Opposition. Equally telling, the shimmering party mystique seemed by itself to hypnotize and thereby immobilize oppositionists. The outstanding—but not the only—example of this occurred when Trotsky, a fearless critic of Lenin and democratic centralism before 1917, drew back from the fray with Stalin in 1924 when he proclaimed that he accepted his party "right or wrong" because "history has not created other ways for the realization of what is right."

Lenin left behind some practical tools that Stalin found useful, including the expulsion provisions of the 1921 resolution "On Party Unity," the party purge, and the party machine itself. While he made effective use of the first two, the key to his strength was his control of the party machine through the Secretariat. Stalin used the Secretariat to shift opponents to where they could do the least harm and move supporters to where they could do the most good.

One key tactic involved the selection of party secretaries at the provincial, town, and district levels. They supposedly were elected by the corresponding party committees, but the Secretariat interfered in that process by "recommending" the nomination of pro-Stalin loyalists. This practice, already widespread by 1923, enabled the Secretariat to control many party organizations at all levels. This in turn enabled Stalin's supporters to dominate the selection of delegates to the party congresses, and it was the party congress that elected the Central Committee, which in turn elected the Politburo. This meant that although Stalin did not win firm control over the Politburo until late 1929, the power he exercised through the Secretariat made him the Politburo's dominating figure as early as 1924.

The party's transformation from a revolutionary elite into a governing bureaucracy also aided Stalin. It became an organization one joined to make a career rather than a revolution. In 1924 Stalin engineered the so-called Lenin Enrollment, which brought more than 200,000 new members into the party. Because most of them were workers, Stalin was able to present this maneuver as consistent with Lenin's desire to combat bureaucratism. In fact, it allowed the general secretary to pack the party with thousands of raw and malleable recruits. The Lenin Enrollment and subsequent recruitment drives literally revamped the party, which grew from 386,000 members in 1923 to about a million in 1927 and to more than 1.5 million in 1929. At the same time, the old revolutionary veterans were disappearing. In 1922, only half of the 24,000 who dated from early 1917 remained; only 8,000 were left in 1929. Indeed, by 1929, barely one-quarter of the party's membership antedated the 1924 Lenin Enrollment. One old-guard leader summed up the situation when he observed that "I am not exaggerating when I say that the activist of 1917 would find nothing in common with his 1928 counterpart." All of this strengthened the machine politician adept at bureaucratic manipulation and formulating simple or even simplistic formulas at the expense of the idealist who relied on his intellectual brilliance to inspire revolutionary enthusiasm. The mass of new, young, and inexperienced Bolsheviks was a surging tide made to order for raising a man like Stalin and sinking a man like Trotsky.

The failure to defend the "democratic" component of democratic centralism—that is, the tradition of genuine debate that preceded a decision—gave Stalin another boost. Each of his rivals proved quite prepared to suppress dissent within the party when in the majority, only to rediscover the virtues of dissent and democracy within the party when in the minority. Trotsky militantly supported suppressing the Workers' Opposition in 1921. In 1923, however, he denounced the Triumvirate for authoritarianism in a long article called "The New Course." In 1923, the most avid defender of party unity was Zinoviev. Two years later, when he, too, realized the merits of democracy, he was trenchantly informed by Vyacheslav Molotov, one of Stalin's closest associates, that "When Zinoviev is in the majority he is for iron discipline. . . . When he is in the minority . . . he is against it." Even the comparatively gentle Bukharin was as guilty of suppressing dissent as anyone else, to the point of demanding penalties for the defeated Left after 1927 that were even harsher than those suggested by Stalin.

Another important cog in Stalin's political juggernaut was his link with the secret police and his readiness to use it against his rivals. During the civil war Stalin had worked closely with Felix Dzerzhinsky, head of the Cheka, and by 1923, the GPU, as Dzerzhinsky's secret police was then known, already was doing Stalin's bidding. Among its services was to harass and eventually arrest M.G. Sultan-Galiev, a party leader who opposed Stalin's nationalities policies in 1923, and to fan out across Moscow to collect copies of Lenin's damning "Testament" after it was distributed to members of the Central Committee gathered for the Thirteenth Party Congress in 1924. Prior to Lenin's death Stalin already was using his formidable resources to keep party leaders, including Lenin, under surveillance. Stalin, the former *kinto*, also used the secret police to beat up members of the opposition in 1927. Enlisting twentieth-century technology in his cause, he even used electronic bugs to spy on the conversations of his colleagues.

Stalin also found strength in unexpected quarters. Five days after Lenin's death and the day before his funeral, the general secretary delivered a speech to a large party gathering, subsequently known as the "Lenin Oath," which proved to be a stunning success for a man not known as a public speaker. Sounding more like a church litany than a tribute to a revolutionary and atheist, and replete with vows to honor the dead man's wishes, Stalin's verbal genuflections and pledges to the departed Lenin did not impress many other Bolshevik leaders. But unlike Marxist-laden hyperbole spouted by his rivals, Stalin's awkward speech spoke clearly and comprehensibly to the unsophisticated party membership at large and, after being published, to the general public, and so it became an important stake in Stalin's claim to be Lenin's leading disciple.

The events surrounding Lenin's death and funeral were part of a growing secular cult devoted to the fallen leader. All of Lenin's would-be successors contributed to its development in one way or another—Kamenev, for example, proclaimed that there was "only one antidote against any crisis, against any wrong decision: the teaching of Vladimir Ilyich"—but none did so as much as Stalin or exploited it as successfully for his own ends. The cult received a major boost when the Politburo voted to embalm Lenin's body and display it in a mausoleum in Red Square, a decision that had Stalin's strong backing. This particular decision outraged some Bolshevik notables, including Trotsky and

Kamenev, who finally found something to agree on, albeit in a losing cause. Krupskaya also opposed this morbid idea, and it is fair to say that Lenin, had he had one, would have been spinning in his grave. Meanwhile, Petrograd was renamed Leningrad, another posthumous honor Lenin certainly would rather have done without.

The struggle for power also saw Stalin reveal heretofore unknown theoretical talents. For years Trotsky had been known as the theorist of "permanent revolution," the doctrine that linked any hope for achieving socialism in Russia with the spread of the revolution to the industrialized countries of the West. This doctrine had considerable appeal in 1917, but by 1924, when hopes for a revolution in the West seemed dead, it was not what most party members wanted to hear. They wanted to be assured that their own efforts at home could guarantee success, which is exactly what Stalin did. In 1924, his book, *Problems of Leninism*, outlined his reassuring theory of "socialism in one country," the idea that Russia could build a socialist society regardless of what happened in the West. *Problems of Leninism* made Trotsky look like an overly pessimistic prophet of gloom in contrast to the upbeat Stalin. It also established Stalin as a major Marxist theorist, giving him another key leadership credential he previously had lacked.

STALIN TRIUMPHANT

Despite all of his assets, Stalin could have been stopped, especially if Trotsky had acted firmly during 1923 and 1924. Historians remain perplexed as to why he did not. Perhaps it was his failing health—he suffered from a long series of fevers of unknown origin—or his reluctance to declare his ambitions while Lenin was still alive. Perhaps he simply lacked the discipline, will, and stamina required to build a political organization and govern a country. Whatever the reasons, Trotsky let his opportunities pass. He ignored Lenin's wishes and failed to attack Stalin at the Twelfth Party Congress in 1923. Although the Triumvirate controlled a majority at the congress, Trotsky's position was strong. He was still immensely popular with the rank and file and had several excellent issues to exploit, including the Georgian affair, the Secretariat's abuses of power, and Lenin's hostility toward Stalin. A concerted attack probably could have won the day, but Trotsky let this chance pass with barely a murmur.

Trotsky let his next chance pass equally quietly. When Lenin died on January 21, 1924, Trotsky was in the Caucasus for a rest cure. Incredibly, he missed Lenin's funeral for reasons that remain unclear, as he certainly had time to get back to Moscow for the event. Trotsky thus cast another shadow over his political future while Stalin used the opportunity to seize the spotlight with his "Lenin Oath" speech.

After that, only one real trump remained to Trotsky: Lenin's "Testament." Lenin's wife, Krupskaya, had kept the document secret until the eve of the Thirteenth Party Congress, at which point, on May 21, 1924, it was read to a Central Committee plenum. This was a moment of truth. There was little that Stalin could do; he sat feeling "small and miserable," an eyewitness recorded, while others considered his fate. He offered to resign. Trotsky, once again, did nothing, but the fear of what he might do if Stalin were demoted became the latter's safety net. Zinoviev, still more afraid of Trotsky than of Stalin, saved the general secretary. Lenin's fears had proved unfounded, Zinoviev announced; Stalin should be left at his post. So he was. The "Testament" was suppressed; Stalin survived.

Trotsky's defeat was virtually assured after the "Testament" episode. His subsequent attempts to speak against the Triumvirate at the Thirteenth Party Congress were drowned in jeers. It was a new kind of party congress, run according to the new Stalinist script. Debate and genuine decision making were banished in favor of prefabricated speeches, prepackaged decisions, and organized abuse. Even Krupskaya was driven from the podium when she tried to criticize the new leadership. After the congress, Trotsky's slide continued; in January 1925, he yielded his position as commissar of war, his last bastion of power. Trotsky now sat only as an isolated lame duck on the Politburo.

With Trotsky relatively powerless, Stalin locked horns with Zinoviev and Kamenev in a short, fierce battle that ended with Stalin's overwhelming victory at the Fourteenth Party Congress in December 1925. The congress was an awesome demonstration of the Secretariat's power. Only the Leningrad delegation escaped its control. For the first time, Stalin was able to promote several of his loyalists, including Molotov, to the Politburo in place of demoted oppositionists. The sad saga of the United Opposition followed. In successive waves in 1926 and 1927 its leaders lost all their important posts, including their seats on the Politburo. On November 7, 1927, Trotsky and Zinoviev led street demonstrations in Moscow and Leningrad in a last desperate attempt to bring their case to the workers. A far more formidable and ruthless foe awaited them than the government they had overthrown on that day in 1917. The demonstrations were broken up, and the two men, each of whom at one point had been Lenin's closest associate, were expelled from the party. Trotsky was evicted from his Kremlin apartment. At the Fifteenth Party Congress that December, lesser oppositionist leaders were expelled as well; a thorough purge of several thousand lower-ranking dissenters followed. Zinoviev and Kamenev caved in as they had before and would again. After humbly recanting, they were allowed back into the party to endure more abuse. Not Trotsky. In January 1928 the still-defiant ex-Bolshevik was deported from Moscow, in the middle of the night to avoid any demonstrations, and shipped into Siberian exile. The next year he was banished from the Soviet Union altogether. Still, Trotsky's trumpet of criticism continued, although it blared from ever more distant shores—eventually Mexico—until 1940. Then, having already taken almost everything from his hated rival—his power, his homeland, even his children—Stalin had an assassin take Trotsky's life.

After disposing of his critics on the left, Stalin wasted little time in undermining those on the right who had helped tip the balance of power in his favor in the recently completed battle. As usual, he was calculating and flexible. His latest ex-allies-turned-opponents had considerable strength: Bukharin headed the Comintern and edited *Pravda*, the party newspaper; Rykov chaired the *Sovnarkom*; Tomsky headed the trade unions; and all three sat on the Politburo. But they could not match Stalin's organization, willpower, cunning, and pure ruthlessness. By the end of 1929 the Right had lost most of its important posts and was politically defeated. When he officially celebrated his fiftieth birthday on December 21, 1929, Stalin was securely in place as Lenin's successor and leader of the Soviet Union.[2] Stalin was not, to be sure, the absolute dictator he would someday become. His position and ability to rule depended on the support of other powerful members of the Politburo. Yet, that limitation notwithstanding, he had won the struggle for the Bolshevik throne.

THE BOLSHEVIKS AND THE NEP

Along with the question of who would lead the party, Lenin's death had left unanswered the equally vexing question of the fate of the NEP. Lenin had frankly called the policy a "retreat," and when it was implemented it was difficult for many Bolsheviks to see the numerous concessions made to capitalist enterprise as anything else. Given the party's raison d'être of building socialism, it was clear that the retreat had to be a temporary one.

However, in the course of this retreat Lenin's views moderated. He began to think in terms of progress over the long haul. He suggested that peasants be encouraged to form autonomous cooperative institutions and that education had to be a primary means of consummating the "cultural revolution" essential to building socialism. One of Lenin's last articles, significantly entitled "On Cooperation," outlined these new ideas. They clearly complemented antibureaucratic themes Lenin was developing, particularly his criticism of Stalin. But Lenin's death left these matters for his colleagues to unscramble.

In strict economic terms, by 1925 the NEP had done its job. Agricultural production, including the all-important grain crop, was approaching its 1913 levels, and the Soviet people were eating tolerably well. Industrial production also showed progress, with overall production just under three-quarters of 1913 peak levels. Key industries such as coal mining and fabric production stood at 90 percent or more of their highest prewar levels. Steel and pig iron production, respectively, reached 75 percent and 60 percent of their 1913 levels.

This impressive overall recovery did little to dispel Bolshevik discomfiture with the NEP, since much of the progress had been bought at the price of continued concessions to private enterprise. The most galling measures were the ones granting peasant farmers the right to rent more farmland and hire workers without restrictions. Furthermore, the industrial picture was hardly a reason for rejoicing. Recovery was based almost entirely on repairing the old factories and infrastructure damaged between 1914 and 1921. Relative to the West, Russian industry was still backward, inefficient, and unproductive. It was unable to meet urban and peasant consumer needs; neither could it produce the necessary profits to finance new capital investment that was needed, particularly in heavy industry, before any real progress could be made toward a modern industrialized economy.

There was no agreement about where funds for that investment could be found. Little was available from the agricultural sector, the traditional source of government revenue over the centuries. Its recovery was more complete than that of industry, but its future was hardly inspiring. Russian agriculture as of the mid-1920s was dominated by 25 million small, inefficient peasant allotments, most of them communally held under the control of the *mirs*. In fact, more peasants held their land in this way, as opposed to owning it privately, than in 1917. The old three-field system and division of allotments into strips subject to reapportionment still prevailed in many areas. Perhaps 20 percent of all peasants used the ancient *sokha*, or wooden plow, causing one demoralized official observer to complain of how often he saw "a wretched wooden *sokha*, dating from the flood, . . . often dragged along by a miserable yoke of lead oxen or by the farmer, or even his wife."

The revolution was in part to blame for this state of affairs. The Bolshevik regime had legalized and promoted the expropriation of the large estates and even some of the largest peasant holdings and their redistribution among peasants with little or no land. This meant that the most modern and productive units, those large and efficient enough to use modern machines and methods and produce a large surplus, had disappeared, and with them much of the marketable grain that had made prewar Russia one of the world's largest grain exporters. By the mid-1920s, slightly less grain was being produced by a slightly *larger* rural population divided into *more* and *smaller* allotments, while a larger percentage of that grain was staying on the farm and being consumed by the peasants who had grown it. And much of the grain that was marketed went into the private sector of the Nepmen to serve consumer needs in the growing cities and towns rather than state policy interests. So Russia, which in 1913 had 12 million tons of grain to export in exchange for foreign goods, including industrial equipment, had only 2 million tons available in 1925–1926, 2.1 million tons in 1926–1927, and 300,000 tons, or almost nothing at all, in 1927–1928.

At the top of the rural social structure, the concessions to private peasant enterprise were producing a growing class of prosperous kulaks, whose development indicated to some nervous Bolsheviks that capitalism might overrun the countryside. Though the kulaks actually were quite poor by Western standards—a typical kulak might farm enough land to justify hiring one worker and perhaps also own all of two horses and two cows—they looked prosperous to the many of their neighbors who had much less. While the Bolsheviks wanted to see Russian agriculture based on collective socialist principles, the kulak was undeniably an incipient capitalist and an example most of the peasantry wanted to follow. He had no love for the Bolsheviks, a party of urban functionaries lacking any knowledge of or sympathy for peasants like himself. The kulaks, a statistically small but socially and economically significant group accounting for approximately 5 percent of the peasantry, produced about 20 percent of the country's marketable grain, which they refused to sell when the government's price was too low. They also exerted a growing influence on their fellow peasants, an unpleasant reality reflected in elections to rural soviets of 1925, when only about 10 percent of the successful candidates were Communist Party members. In the mid-1920s only about 1 percent of all peasant households lived on government-run collective farms, large units in which, according to Marxist plans, many peasant families combined their land and resources and worked together. In short, the Soviet government wanted the peasants to live one way, but they overwhelmingly preferred to live another way. This did not bode well for the *smychka*, the presumed revolutionary bond between the proletariat and the peasantry proclaimed by Lenin as the cornerstone of the NEP.

The core of the problem was that by the mid-1920s the NEP was at an impasse. Socialism required overcoming economic scarcity, and that in turn required a modern industrialized economy. Unfortunately, the capital essential to achieve this was not available. Soviet Russia's backward industry could not produce it. Neither could its agricultural sector. The government might have found a partial solution by encouraging the kulaks to create large-scale capitalist farms, but this would have been an odd posture for a "socialist" regime. The capitalist West was not interested in investing in Soviet Russia, as Lenin had hoped it would. And the failure of the revolution to spread to the West meant there were no advanced socialist countries to bail out the local cause, as Lenin had insisted was necessary if socialism was to survive in Russia.

The economic noose slowly began to tighten in 1926 and 1927, in part because the continuing struggle for power left economic policy in a lurch. Enforced low prices for industrial goods produced by state-run industry (Trotsky wanted them raised) helped create a demand for products that Russia's inefficient industries could not meet. This left the peasantry with nothing to buy in exchange for its grain, a "goods famine" that after 1926 became a seemingly permanent part of the NEP landscape. Even worse, to save money the government, though split on the issue, in 1926 lowered the price it was willing to pay for grain. The peasants responded by refusing to sell their crop until the price was raised, leaving the government without the grain it needed to feed the cities, much less use for export. More confusion resulted from another policy change noticeable by 1927: the decision to strangle the nonagricultural private sector, which many Bolsheviks continued to view as a potential womb for the rebirth of capitalism. By 1928, crippled by confiscatory taxes and other measures, that sector was in a tailspin.

THE INDUSTRIALIZATION DEBATE

All of this lent credence to Stalin's arch-rival, Leon Trotsky, whose critical voice still echoed clearly even as his political star was fading. Trotsky for several years had been warning that the NEP was leading Soviet Russia to an economic dead end. His thinking was based on the theories of a brilliant party economist, Yevgeny Preobrazhensky, who in 1925 summed up his ideas in a work called *The New Economics*. Preobrazhensky argued that under capitalism the necessary capital for the Industrial Revolution was accumulated by exploiting the working class and forcing it to live in poverty, a process, following Marx, he called "primitive capitalist accumulation." He theorized that because socialists had seized power in Russia before a modern industrial base existed, they would have to do something similar. Since capital accumulation would be done under a socialist regime, Preobrazhensky called this process "primitive *socialist* accumulation." But who would bear the burden of this accumulation? Not the workers, said Preobrazhensky. For one thing, there were far too few of them. For another, one could hardly expect the "workers' state" to exploit its leading class. The source, as usual in Russia, would have to be the peasantry. Preobrazhensky stated this could be done through high taxation and by replacing the market with a network of state monopolies that would charge high prices for the consumer and industrial goods the peasants bought and pay low prices for the agricultural products they produced. By imposing what Preobrazhensky called "forced savings" on the peasantry, the Bolsheviks could shift productive resources from the private to the socialist sector of the economy, and this in turn would enable the Bolshevik-controlled state to rapidly build a modern socialist industrial base. Once socialist industry was sufficiently developed, the Bolshevik state would have the resources to promote the voluntary collectivization of Russia's farms. Peasant and Nep-man capitalism would no longer be a threat, and Russia would cease to be vulnerable to Western economic and military might.

The Achilles' heel of this analysis was the attitude of the peasants. They wanted to prosper, not make sacrifices to achieve the goals of urban Bolshevik visionaries. The price and taxation policies of "primitive socialist accumulation" would certainly cause the peasants to withhold their crops from the market; that alone would cripple Bolshevik industrialization efforts. Neither Preobrazhensky nor Trotsky could explain how to implement this program without encountering massive peasant resistance. Several decades later a sympathetic American economist dubbed their intractable problem the "Preobrazhensky Dilemma."[3]

At the other end of the Bolshevik spectrum stood the defenders of the NEP, led by Bukharin. They insisted that the NEP worked and only needed modification. Bukharin believed that the key to success was balanced growth. He suggested that lower industrial prices would encourage the peasants to produce more while, in turn, their purchases of agricultural implements would stimulate industry. As industry grew, predicted Bukharin, it would provide the peasantry with more agricultural implements and machines at lower prices, thereby increasing both the ability and desire of Russia's farmers to produce more food. A continuous upward cycle would result. Bukharin also stressed the need to stretch available resources through careful planning.

Bukharin's theory came with its own dilemma. Private enterprise would not be seriously restricted, and the rate of economic and industrial growth would necessarily be slow. Bukharin's slogans did little to make these unsavory facts more palatable to many Bolsheviks. In 1925 he urged the peasants to "enrich yourselves," a remark he quickly had to repudiate. He suggested that Russia would have to grow at the "speed of a peasant nag," an unedifying prospect for Bolsheviks, who considered themselves dynamic revolutionaries, not country-bumpkin teamsters. Still, Bukharin remained confident. The party's control of the economy's key areas, such as large industry and the banks, would enable it to limit the growth of small-scale capitalist enterprise, which would be confined mainly to filling the gaps left by the socialist sector. Meanwhile, the peasantry, if treated properly, would cooperate and become an ally rather than an adversary.

There was a prophetic urgency to Bukharin's analysis. He certainly was no democrat, as his political tactics against the Left demonstrated. Still, he desperately wanted to avoid an all-encompassing dictatorship. Bukharin feared that the breakneck industrialization advocated by the Left would lead to a Leviathan-type state that would crush all human freedom. He had written about the dangerous growth of state power in the advanced industrialized societies of the capitalist West and felt that socialist societies were not immune to that phenomenon. Bukharin was in good company; fear of the state was a thread in socialist thinking that ran back to Karl Marx, and it was shared by many in the Bolshevik old guard. That is why Marxists wanted the state to "wither away."

Preobrazhensky and Bukharin represented only two views in a multisided "Industrialization Debate" that took place in Soviet Russia during the 1920s. The many economists of varying persuasions who took part produced an array of questions and policy suggestions that mark the birth of development economics. Preobrazhensky and Bukharin were the leading lights in this group, but they shone as part of a small galaxy of stars who lit a new path in economics. They were, however, personally soon to be extinguished: almost all were imprisoned, and many executed, during Stalin's reign of terror in the 1930s.

Stalin meanwhile used the Industrialization Debate as a field in which to maneuver politically. While the others argued principles, he built his organizational strength. Although Stalin sided with Bukharin after 1925, he was careful never to embrace Bukharin's ideas too closely. Stalin rejected the "enrich yourselves" slogan and had the Fourteenth and Fifteenth Congresses, both of which he controlled, endorse expanded industrialization efforts. In fact, the same Fifteenth Congress that expelled the Left from the party endorsed a large part of its industrialization program and called collectivization "the principal task of the party in the villages," something that at the time was certainly news to Bukharin. Stalin played his cards so well that even as the Left and Right drew closer together in their theoretical outlooks, he still was able to play them off against each other. By the time Bukharin realized who his real enemy was, an epiphany that took place in 1928, he had already helped cripple his potential allies.

THE END OF THE NEP

Between 1927 and 1929, derailed by policies born of Bolshevik hostility, the NEP reached a dead end. During 1927 the government had begun a serious attempt to formulate a comprehensive economic plan, a job undertaken by the State Planning Commission (*Gosplan*). At the same time, major new investment projects in mining, iron and steel mills, railroads, and hydroelectric dams drained resources from the economy as a whole and intensified the "goods famine." To pay for all of this, the government raised taxes on the peasants and Nepmen and accompanied those taxes with discriminatory practices that made it increasingly difficult to do business. None of this helped in the crucial area of grain procurements, where near disaster loomed. By January 1928 procurements trailed the previous year's by 25 percent (although recent research suggests that Stalin may have falsified these figures to bolster the case for collectivization). This situation the general secretary would not tolerate. Since the peasants were unwilling to sell their grain at the government's unrealistically low price, he decided to take it. Armed with a law against "speculation," Stalin ordered that peasant grain stocks be seized by force. Called the "Urals-Siberian method" because of Stalin's personal tours to those areas, this virtual reign of terror during the early months of 1928 also was implemented in other major agricultural areas, including the Volga region, Ukraine, and North Caucasus. Roads were blocked, houses searched, and peasants arrested while their grain was carted away. By the fall of 1928 the government was seizing the land and property of many prosperous kulaks in the countryside, as well as the goods and shops of large numbers of Nepmen in the cities and towns. Meanwhile, shortages forced the regime to begin rationing bread and other foods.

The Stalinist offensive against the peasantry took place in the face of strong opposition from Bukharin and other supporters of the NEP. Because in 1928 Stalin had not yet solidified his control of the party, he had to compromise with Bukharin and his allies, who included important Politburo members. One concession was to characterize the Urals-Siberian method, which Bukharin denounced as "military–feudal exploitation," as an emergency measure. Stalin's concessions were short-lived. By 1929 the general secretary was strong enough to launch a frontal attack against Bukharin and the moderates, now branded as the "Right deviation." By the middle of the year, the Right was finished as a political force, leaving Stalin free to dispatch 100,000 party cadres to the countryside to implement his Urals-Siberian method on peasant farms nationwide. The results were dramatic: the amount of grain collected in 1929 was double that of 1928. In effect, the methods of War Communism had returned to the countryside, bringing with them a violent and chaotic end to the NEP.

THE BOLSHEVIK REGIME AND THE PEOPLE

The dilemma the Bolsheviks faced in dealing with the economic problems posed by the NEP was only one of many difficulties that plagued their regime. Simply put, by the late 1920s the Bolsheviks had failed to win the population, or even a significant percentage of it, to their cause, a failure that signaled a threat to their grip on power. The situation probably was most urgent in the countryside, where most of the people still lived. The 1925 elections to rural soviets were only the tip of an iceberg of troubles the Bolsheviks faced in dealing with the peasantry. Despite efforts to build up the party during the 1920s, by the end of the decade there were only 330,000 full-time party workers organized into about 23,000 party organizations scattered over the vastness of rural Soviet Russia. Most decisions that mattered to the rural population were made by 350,000 peasant communes, to which more than 90 percent of the peasantry belonged and over which the Bolsheviks had scant if any influence. Rather than turn their fates over to the regime by joining government-run collectives, the peasants were demonstrating their ability to organize their own independent cooperatives to buy machinery, market their produce, and purchase consumer goods. Increasingly independent-minded, they bitterly resented government interference in their lives and in the local economy, in particular the regime's policies of controlling prices by having state agencies pay low prices for grain while charging high prices for machines and consumer goods produced by state-controlled industries. As one peasant in the Moscow region asked rhetorically, "What kind of free trade is it when they [the government] control the prices?" Tax increases introduced in 1926 on prosperous peasants and a new discriminatory electoral law that same year that disenfranchised many kulaks only heightened the tension between the peasants and the regime. Notwithstanding government prohibitions, peasants continued their efforts to set up peasant unions independent of Bolshevik control to represent their interests. During the late 1920s there also were growing numbers of attacks on Bolshevik property and party cadres. Despite the 1926 anti-kulak electoral law, the 1927 elections in the countryside resulted in yet another severe Bolshevik defeat. For the Bolsheviks, the situation was nothing less than a crisis. As historian Vladimir Brovkin has noted, as the 1920s were drawing to a close, the regime faced a process "of the withering away of the Communist Party in the countryside."[4]

The record was not much better with other social groups. Bolshevik hopes that women, liberated by the new regime from the inequalities and restraints of the past, would enlist in the struggle for a socialist future were disappointed. In the countryside, peasant women, when elected to local soviets, defended traditional peasant values as resolutely as did their men. Women in the cities and towns showed little interest in emulating the model of the ascetic, asexual new Soviet woman, dressed in unflattering masculine clothes (including heavy leather coats and boots), whose private life, including her family, took second place to building communism. Urban women with access to information from abroad were far more interested in sexy, fashionable clothes, Western films, and the 1920s dancing rage in the West, the fox-trot. Wherever they lived, women in Soviet Russia had little use for permissive Soviet family divorce laws, in particular a law enacted in 1926 that doubled the divorce rate and left thousands of women and their children without any means of support. As for proletarian women, like their male counterparts they resented government attempts to increase their work output without a corresponding increase in wages.

Nor was the youth of Soviet Russia enamored with Bolshevik ideology. The Komsomol, whose membership was intended as the recruitment pool for future Communist Party members, had trouble attracting recruits committed to the cause. The bulk of its new members during the 1920s were young men from the countryside whose main motivation in joining often was to escape rural poverty by becoming part of the governing establishment. Young urban workers who joined in frequently did so in the hope that they might add some excitement and social experiences to their dreary workaday lives. Komsomol members, to the distress of high-ranking party leaders, frequently showed more interest in partying and drinking than in Leninism or socialist construction. As one report in Leningrad put it, local Komsomol activists "were not interested in political education, but in organizing dancing parties instead." This hardly distinguished them from their peers in the general population. Young urban workers, males and females alike, preferred jazz, fashionable clothing, the latest dances, and other facets of Western popular culture to party propaganda. As for the Bolshevik assault on traditional values and "bourgeois morality," Soviet Russia's youth often translated that into sexual promiscuity, which both shocked and distressed ideologically committed party cadres. In rural areas where traditional values continued to hold sway among the young, religious congregations attracted far more adherents than the Komsomol.

The majority of Russia's intelligentsia—its artists, writers, scientists, engineers, professors, and the like—had opposed the Bolshevik Revolution. A decade later those who remained in Soviet Russia had not been won over to the cause, especially as the party persisted in maintaining a dictatorship that left little room for artistic or intellectual freedom. By the mid-1920s, some of those who had initially supported the Bolshevik seizure of power—in particular artists who detested pre-revolutionary traditional "bourgeois" life and considered themselves revolutionaries of one sort or another—were becoming disillusioned by a regime that showed little sympathy for their radical, avant-garde artistic ideas and increasingly confined them and their art to delivering the Communist Party's version of the truth. Thus the poet Sergei Yesenin, whose initial revolutionary zeal had turned to despair, committed suicide in 1925, leaving a final poem written in his own blood. Vladimir Mayakovsky, who probably was more closely identified with the revolution than any other artist, managed to ward off total disillusionment for the entire 1920s and the duration of the NEP. In 1930, however, at the age of thirty-seven, he shot himself, lamenting in his last major, and unfinished, poem that he had set "my heel on the throat of my own song."

Of all the Bolsheviks' failures to win popular support in the 1920s, none could be more troubling than their strained relationship with the working class. After all, the party's self-declared status as the vanguard of the proletariat had been the justification for the Bolshevik Revolution and, for the party member-ship, remained the ultimate source of legitimacy for the Soviet regime. But the working class was not thriving under that regime. Wages in inefficient state industries remained depressed, languishing at barely half pre–World War I levels. The members of what supposedly was the new ruling class could not form independent unions to represent them against the state, were fired for trying to organize or for any other breaches of state-imposed discipline, and were constantly harassed by the secret police. Their new Bolshevik bosses, if anything, treated them even more harshly than their departed capitalist bosses. Workers bitterly resented management attempts to increase their workload and output without increasing wages. As a result, the anger and strikes of the early NEP years did not subside. In 1925, attempts to speed up the pace of work led to a massive strike in the textile industry that forced the regime to abandon its plans. In 1927 a group of workers at the Putilov factory, in 1917 one of the hotbeds of revolution, unanimously issued a declaration that said, "What we need is butter, not socialism." More than two-thirds of the 400-plus workers who unanimously backed that declaration were party members. Another ominous sign of the times as far as the regime was concerned was working-class humor. For example, one joke repeated widely among workers said that the letter "m" had been abolished. Why? Because "there's no meat, no margarine, no manufactured goods, and no milk, and there's no point in keeping the letter 'm' just for the sake of a single name: Mikoyan." (Mikoyan was a high-ranking Soviet official.) In the fall of 1928, in the wake of food shortages that earlier in the year had sparked protests and riots in Moscow and several other cities, another wave of strikes and protests rocked the country. Even angrier than the workers with jobs who went on strike were the large numbers of unemployed. One of them expressed a widely held sense of resent-ment when he commented during a rally in 1926 that "There are two classes today: the working class and the Communists, who have replaced the nobles and the dukes." Although the Bolsheviks certainly retained some support among the proletariat, their overall standing with that vital class as a whole was a cause of deep concern.

Even the party itself was part of the problem of Bolshevism's relationship to society. The problem was ironically dialectical: the party bureaucracy was—depending on the time and place—at once too distant and too close to the population at large. The excessive distance, dating from the earliest days of the revolution, was a direct function of the party dictatorship. Once in power, party cadres had used their positions to live better than the poverty-stricken masses surrounding them. With no popular check on their power, top leaders often lived in luxury; further down the line lower-level functionaries took what they could get, whether these were the best living accommodations, food unavailable to the general population, bribes from Nepmen or prosperous peasants, or opportunities to embezzle local party funds or tax revenues. The range of opportunities available, running from luxury in the midst of poverty to personal pleasure, was summed up by a party journalist when he referred to the "car-harem syndrome." Or, as historian Moshe Lewin observed, after the seizure of power, the Bolshevik Party

> became a class apart, isolated from the masses, enormously privileged and enjoying a standard of living such that its members were soon being described as "satraps" and the "new aristocracy."[5]

At the same time, low-level party cadres sometimes developed the bad habit of getting too close to those they governed, of identifying with people from whom they often were distinguished by little more than having recently acquired a party card. This appears to have been especially true in rural areas, where local cadres, isolated from their party comrades in the cities, frequently were either sympathetic to the peasants or involved with them in profitable business deals or other types of personal relationships. It was not unusual for local party organizations to borrow money from independent peasant cooperatives, often without the expectation that those loans would be repaid. This type of symbiosis between the presumed representatives of the working class and their class enemies in the countryside was yet another warning to the Bolshevik leadership in Moscow that something had to be done about the NEP, and quickly.

BOLSHEVISM AND THE REVOLUTION

By 1929 the Bolshevik Party faced unavoidable decisions. Its entire reason for existing was to seize power and use that monopoly of power to transform Russia into an industrially advanced socialist society. In 1921, in order to maintain its power, the party had been forced to compromise, institute the NEP, and postpone implementing its socialist vision. In the eight years that followed, the NEP had failed to produce the economic surplus essential for building the modern industrial infrastructure that all Marxists agreed socialism required. Making matters considerably worse, social classes whose interests conflicted fundamentally with Bolshevik socialist goals—in particular the prosperous peasantry but also the Nepmen—had gained strength and coherence. Even in the cities and among the proletariat, the party's roots were dangerously shallow. Thus, even if the Bolshevik Party, while continuing the NEP, proved capable of maintaining its one-party dictatorship, it clearly would have only a tenuous grip on society as a whole and therefore would lack the requisite control over the country's resources to mount the all-out industrialization drive its raison d'être demanded.

It has been argued since Bukharin first made the case in the 1920s that the NEP could have provided the basis for industrialization *and* socialism. It certainly is indisputable that Stalin's methods of the 1930s, aside from their dreadful human costs, were extremely wasteful, and the Industrialization Debate of the 1920s suggests that far less violent and brutal methods might have achieved impressive results. For example, recent research suggests that Bukharin's methods would have produced much higher production in agriculture during the 1930s than was actually achieved, in part because the tremendous losses of farm animals, especially draft animals needed for plowing and other heavy work, would have been avoided. According to one computer model, by *not* collectivizing, the Soviet Union by 1940 would have enjoyed an agricultural output 10 percent higher than what was achieved via collectivization; that increase in turn would have fed an economy at least 29 percent larger than what was achieved by Stalin's methods. That most economists working for the party advocated a course far different from the one Stalin took is by itself significant.

The problem with this analysis, at least from a Communist Party perspective, is that any pattern of economic development emerging from an NEP framework, even if impressive in terms of absolute growth, would have been radically different from the Bolshevik socialist vision and, in addition, would have compromised the party's ability to transform society along socialist lines beyond the serious limits that prevailed in 1929. After all, the NEP framework unavoidably required increasing autonomy for a peasant class that firmly believed that it, not the Soviet state, was and should continue to be the master of Russia's agricultural land. This in turn, as the experience since 1921 demonstrated, would have required free markets, and, of course, the Nepmen and their private businesses. In direct opposition to this scenario, the Bolshevik vision of Soviet Russia's future required that industrialization take place under direct and total state control and that the party, not the kulaks and the Nepmen, determine economic priorities. This vision in turn demanded rapid and enormous inputs of resources into heavy industry and therefore a radical change in power relationships in the countryside, where the peasants and what they produced had to be brought under state control. Such wrenching change could be accomplished only by the use of massive force unprecedented in scope, whether by Stalin or by another party leader. If the party leaders were to remain true to their bedrock Leninist impulse and vision of totally transforming society, which had impelled them to seize power in the first place—that is, if they were to remain Communists in practice as well as in name—they could not accept as permanent the NEP retreat that was creating a social and economic reality increasingly incompatible with that vision.

Stalin's final triumph in the struggle for power in 1929 was more than simply an example of skilled bureaucratic manipulation. Beginning when he coined the concept of "socialism in one country" in 1924, he had been building his credentials as the man best suited for leading the party in the construction of socialism. Between 1927 and 1929, his policies of attacking the kulaks and Nepmen and committing vastly increased resources to state-controlled industrialization projects were supported by a majority of party leaders and activists. Stalin's political victory meant that the Bolshevik Party, as in the days of Lenin, again had a leader prepared to use whatever force was necessary to achieve its fundamental goals. That, inevitably, meant an end to the NEP. For party militants, it meant the end of a frustrating era of compromise and marking time and a return to the heroic forge-ahead spirit, and violent methods, of War Communism. For Soviet Russia, it meant spectacular economic advances in a very short time—although in retrospect hardly as impressive as they once seemed—but only at an incalculable, horrible human cost.

NOTES

1. Simon Sebag Montefiore, *Young Stalin* (London: Weidenfeld & Nicolson, 2007), p. 175.

2. Stalin actually was born in December 1878 but subsequently gave the false 1879 date, for unknown reasons.

3. Alexander Erlich, "Preobrazhenski and the Economics of Soviet Industrialization," *Journal of Quarterly Economics* 64 (February 1950), pp. 80–81.

4. Vladimir Brovkin, *Russia After Lenin: Politics, Culture, and Society, 1921–1929* (London and New York: Routledge, 1998), p. 170. This section relies heavily on Brovkin's pathbreaking monograph.

5. Moshe Lewin, *Russian Peasants and Soviet Power: A Study of Collectivization*, translated by Irene Nove with the assistance of John Biggart (New York: Norton, 1968), p. 189.

13

The Revolution From Above

Although the Bolshevik Revolution took place in 1917, the party did not fully revolutionize Russian society until the 1930s. Despite the extensive changes that took place between 1917 and 1929, on the eve of Stalin's triumph the country was strikingly similar to what it had been on the morrow of Lenin's revolution. In 1929, the Soviet economy was still dominated by small-scale and backward peasant agriculture. Its industrial sector, notwithstanding the socialized "commanding heights," still could not meet the nation's needs and lagged behind the modern industrial establishments in the West. Russia, in fact, had basically the same industrial base that had existed in 1913. In short, in 1929, the majority of the population lived much as they had before 1917.

Ten years later the picture was dramatically different. Collectivization had transformed Soviet agriculture. The Soviets had built a new industrial infrastructure, one that at long last had the potential to be competitive, at least in terms of military power, with the industrial economies of Western Europe. The balance between the rural and urban sectors was changing rapidly in favor of the latter. Soviet Russia also had a largely modernized military force. An unprecedented reign of terror had produced a thorough social revolution of its own. After a decade of what Stalin called his "revolution from above"—

sometimes called the "second" Bolshevik Revolution—very few Soviet citizens lived as they had before.

The economic transformation of that decade is of historic importance, for Soviet Russia's system of economic development, based on a planned, state-controlled economy, would become a serious alternative to the free enterprise Western model for many unindustrialized nations from the 1930s until the 1980s. The economic modernization and growth during the decade after 1929 is relatively easy to chronicle. What cannot adequately be described is the catastrophic human cost of the Soviet "revolution from above." Millions of human lives were sacrificed, millions more damaged beyond repair, an entire nation terrorized. And what is even more difficult to comprehend is how the building and the brutality, the achievement and the agony, the grandiose and the grotesque, all were locked together in an inseparable embrace, whirling like a surrealistic dynamo to generate a new Soviet Russia.

Astride it all stood Stalin, the coldly calculating *Vozhd* (leader) who, like the biblical Pharaoh, hardened his heart to human suffering as he pushed ever harder to build the Soviet pyramids he considered so vital to the state and the revolution. Yet, while Stalin eventually accumulated power as absolute as that of any monarch or dictator in history, imposing many of his dreams, fears, and hatreds upon the Soviet Union, it is vital to remember that the Stalin era resulted from a confluence of several broad historical currents. World War I had been only the latest of many crises to punish Russia for its backwardness, thereby compelling the state once again to undertake a program of rapid modernization. Stalin was part of a tradition stretching from Ivan the Terrible through Peter the Great and Alexander II into the twentieth century. At the same time, Stalin's revolution from above went far beyond anything Russia had seen, or suffered through, before. This was possible for several reasons. The severe crises of the early twentieth century had shattered the old society, scattered the old elites, and brought a new elite to power, one far more vigorous and with far more ambitious goals than the ruling class it replaced. Meanwhile, the social upheaval that brought this new elite to power had broken down many traditional moral restraints in society as a whole. These conditions encouraged the new ruling elite to employ radical measures of unprecedented scope and severity to achieve its goals and enabled it to find many collaborators among the population at large ready to implement those measures, whatever suffering they caused. All of these factors were necessary to produce "Stalinism," which belongs in a category of horrific twentieth-century totalitarian systems along with Hitler's Germany, Mao Zedong's China, and Pol Pot's Cambodia. In each case calamity and social disintegration paved the way for those who would recast society according to visions that left no room for dissent or for entire categories of human beings deemed unfit to live in the new world to come. In the case of the Soviet Union, Stalin's personality certainly was pivotal as a catalyst and shaper of events, but he got his chance to play such an enormous role because a long series of powerful shocks and wrenching twists had prepared the historical stage and provided a large supporting cast.

THE FIRST FIVE-YEAR PLAN

Although there is no formal date that inaugurates the Stalin era, a convenient reference point is the adoption of the Soviet Union's First Five-Year Plan in April 1929. The 1,000-page plan was the first document of its kind, a comprehensive attempt to coordinate an entire economy to promote rapid industrialization and economic growth. The economists produced two serious options, a "minimum" and an "optimum" plan. While virtually all the Soviet Union's economic experts felt that the minimum version's hefty projected increases represented the maximum realizable goals, the Central Committee adopted the optimum version. Not only did the optimum version call for quantum leaps in production—industrial production was to rise by 250 percent, heavy industry by 330 percent, coal, pig iron, and electricity by two, three, and four times, respectively—but there were also optimistic projections for consumer goods and agriculture. The plan was declared operational as of October 1928, five months before it was adopted and several more months before it was completely prepared. In the summer of 1929 its targets were raised further. Then, at the Sixteenth Party Congress meeting in June and July of 1930, the goal was set of achieving what was already impossible to achieve in only four years.

In reality, Stalin's economic program was not a viable plan in the sense of taking what was available, organizing it as efficiently as possible, and striving for realistic goals. Rather it was a series of gigantic mobilization campaigns, often uncoordinated and sometimes in conflict with each other. The impetus came partially from the enthusiasm the regime was able to generate but mostly from brute force and terror on a horrendous scale. If the First Five-Year Plan was anything at all, it was a propaganda piece signaling the regime's intention to push the nation ahead at a reckless speed, regardless of the costs. The optimum version's original goals were unrealizable. They depended on simultaneously achieving a 110 percent increase in industrial productivity, a 30 percent drop in fuel consumption, and a 50 percent drop in construction costs. They also required ideal weather conditions and optimum agricultural production, high prices for Russian agricultural exports, and low defense spending, among other things. None of these prerequisites were met. All kinds of bottlenecks developed after the first year of the plan (1928–1929), the only year the projected production increases were reached. When that happened, Stalin and his Politburo, no longer restrained by any organized opposition and driven by a fanatical desire to transform Soviet Russia in a decade, reacted with a vengeance. They raised, rather than lowered, the goals and intensified the pressures to meet them. "We are bound by no laws. There are no fortresses the Bolsheviks cannot storm," was Stalin's motto. "Objective conditions" could not be permitted to block the attainment of the party's goals. Stalin's program went well beyond the measures Bukharin had denounced as "military–feudal exploitation." As historian Robert Daniels has observed, the economic policies of the revolution from above "accorded more with the economics of Ivan the Terrible than with those of Karl Marx."[1]

It is difficult to say precisely what accounted for the insistence on these unattainable objectives. The decisive factor certainly was Stalin himself, as his insatiable ego and indomitable will refused to let what he considered the pedantic computations of economists and the petty desires of the people sabotage the realization of his objectives. But there also was a great deal of support for these goals in the Communist Party as a whole. Party members from the Politburo on down, at least those with some knowledge of their country's history, knew how Russia had paid for lagging behind the West. They knew that the West had intervened against them during the civil war and, as Marxists and Bolsheviks, they felt an urgency to transform Soviet Russia into a proletarian society with an industrial base adequate to support a socialist way of life. Many doubters and dissenters, including supporters of Bukharin, were removed from positions of leadership in the purge of 1929–1930, which hit rural organizations, where sympathy for the peasantry was greatest, especially hard. Therefore, the party was ready, even eager, to pursue the goals, however unrealistic, its *Vozhd* and Politburo set.

COLLECTIVIZATION

The first people to find this out were the peasants. Between 1929 and 1932, they were torn from their homesteads and pushed, pulled, driven, and lured into collective farms. Collectivization engulfed the majority of the Soviet people and hence was an enormous revolution in itself. It is important to realize that although the Bolsheviks had been discussing collectivization for years, the actual implementation of the project was not carefully thought out or prepared. Instead, Stalin and his colleagues suddenly turned to all-out collectivization after struggling to wrest sufficient agricultural products from the peasantry during the harvests of 1928 and 1929. This lack of preparation helped produce the mixture of chaos and brutality that made collectivization such a human and economic catastrophe.

The First Five-Year Plan, adopted in the spring of 1929, projected that by 1933 slightly less than 20 percent of the peasantry would be collectivized, supposedly on a voluntary basis without resorting to violence. By the fall, that objective no longer satisfied the party leadership. Stalin's procurement campaigns had disrupted agriculture enough so that the 1929 harvest was less than that of 1928. There were severe shortages not only of grain but of vital industrial crops such as hemp. The peasants' refusal to deliver their crops to the state because of low prices made matters worse. Things quickly became so bad that as early as June, the government had threatened peasants with imprisonment, confiscation of property, or deportation to a remote area if they failed to fulfill certain production obligations.

The industrialization drive that began with the First Five-Year Plan made everything even more urgent. New industrial projects had swollen the labor force more than initially expected because labor productivity was lower than anticipated and additional workers had to be hired. These workers had to be fed. Stalin's "Urals-Siberian" method relieved some of the pressure during the summer of 1929, but the grim reality was that Russian agriculture, largely because of government interference, was in a downward spiral. Something had to be done before the 1930 harvest or the entire industrialization plan would be in jeopardy.

Stalin and the Politburo decided on full-scale collectivization. The gargantuan enterprise of overhauling the lives of most of Soviet Russia's peasants was to be completed in three years. In the key grain-producing areas the target was one or two years. As if that were not enough, the bulk of the job was to be completed "in the months, weeks, and days ahead."

Beginning in December 1929, the full power of Stalin's coercive machinery descended on the countryside, spearheaded by the OGPU and its heavily armed military units. It also included the regular army and eventually more than 150,000 urban cadres, among them the elite "25,000ers" (actually just over 27,000 volunteers), a carefully screened phalanx of workers committed to remaining in the countryside to run the new collective farm system. This force was assisted locally by poor peasants who were encouraged to wage class war on their more prosperous neighbors and on any peasants who somehow lacked sufficient enthusiasm for the idea of having their entire lives uprooted. Sometimes a serious attempt was made to persuade peasants to join the new collectives, but "no" was not taken for an answer. Villages were invaded by these various government-sponsored gangs, whose methods included house-to-house searches for seed and supplies. The assault often was extended beyond land and crops to include the closing of thousands of churches, destruction of church property, and assaults against local clergy. Villages that resisted these intruders were surrounded and attacked with machine guns. Often the tenacity of the resistance required the intervention of the Red Army. In perhaps 2,000 cases peasants organized and took up arms to defend their farms and way of life. The strongest resistance, and thus the government's most severe repression, was in the Ukraine. The following eyewitness account is indicative of what happened:

> In 1930, in the Dniepropetrovsk region thousands of peasants armed with hunting rifles, axes, and pitchforks revolted against the regime. . . . NKVD units and militia were sent. For three days . . . a bloody battle was waged between the revolting people and the authorities. . . . This revolt was cruelly punished. Thousands of peasants, workers, soldiers, and officers paid for the attempt with their lives, while the survivors were deported to concentration camps. In the villages of Ternovka and Boganovka . . . mass executions were carried out near the *balkis* (ravines). The soil of this region was soaked in blood. After the executions, these villages were set on fire.[2]

The collectivization campaign quickly careened out of control as cadres, fired by enthusiasm or fear of the party's wrath in the event of failure, strove to outdo each other in reaching or exceeding their targets. By March 1930, less than three months into the campaign, almost 60 percent of the Soviet Union's peasants—about 15 million households totaling 70 million people— had been driven from their homesteads into collective farms. But the resulting chaos was so widespread that even Stalin, pressured by several of his closest colleagues who had toured the countryside and seen firsthand what was happening, had to give ground. On March 2, he published an article in *Pravda* called "Dizzy with Success." Using what was to become a typical tactic, Stalin shifted the blame for what he had ordered from himself to others. In this case, the hapless culprits were party cadres who allegedly had exceeded their instructions, having become intoxicated by the great victories the party was winning and, hence, "dizzy with success." To underscore the point, some cadres were singled out for punishment. At the same time, the government did not prevent a mass departure from the collectives that left less than a quarter of all peasant households on the regime's new farms. Those who left the collectives, however, did not do so for long. The government had made a temporary tactical retreat, not changed its overall strategic objective. Soon the collectivization offensive was on again in full force. By 1932, two-thirds of all peasants were collectivized; by 1936 the figure reached 90 percent. Stalin and the Soviet state had won the collectivization war.

The price of the victory was high. Breakneck speed and the resultant disorganization, so characteristic of the First Five-Year Plan in both industry and agriculture, caused extensive destruction of property and cost many human lives. Newly collectivized peasants found that no one, least of all the urban cadres who were in charge, knew anything about how to manage this new approach to farming. Production plans and workable remuneration systems did not exist. Frequently, valuable farm implements or scarce machines taken from their original owners were ruined by lack of proper care. Many farm animals died for the same reason. The urban party functionaries caused more havoc when they refused to listen to the "backward" peasants. Their blunders included requiring peasants to sow wasteland or meadow land and undertaking ill-conceived agricultural experiments. Forced sowing campaigns produced careless work by demoralized peasants. Weeds rather than crops soon covered hundreds of thousands of acres, particularly in the Ukraine, the nation's traditional breadbasket.

Overwhelmed by the state's coercive power, peasants resisted as best they could. They destroyed their crops, tools, and animals rather than give them up to the collectives. Sometimes they consumed their slaughtered animals in enormous eating orgies that literally left them sick. This peasant tragedy was an economic disaster. As a result of mismanagement and deliberate destruction, almost half the nation's cattle, more than half its horses, about 60 percent of its pigs, and almost two-thirds of its sheep and goats did not survive collectivization and the First Five-Year Plan. It took decades for Soviet agriculture to make up these losses and the food and power the missing animals would have provided. Meanwhile, overall production in agriculture dropped by 20 percent and did not reach pre-collectivization levels until the eve of World War II. In 1953, the year of Stalin's death, grain production was below the level reached in 1913.

DEKULAKIZATION

Collectivization was made much worse by its companion project, what the regime called "dekulakization," or, in its franker moments, the "liquidation of the kulaks as a class." It is not entirely clear why Stalin and the Politburo made this murderous and destructive decision. The party, to be sure, had long discussed what to do with the kulaks, but liquidation on such a massive scale was something new. Perhaps the Politburo reasoned that destroying the kulaks would make it easier to bend the rest of the peasantry to the party's will. What is clear is that the result was mass death as millions of people were uprooted and sent to live in inhospitable places under dreadful conditions.

In 1929 the kulaks amounted to perhaps 5 percent of the peasantry. They were not only the most prosperous and influential peasants but also the best and most efficient farmers, whose skills presumably would have been an asset to the proposed collective farms. Instead, all kulaks, from the heads of households down to the infant children, were excluded from the new collectives. They were rounded up according to quotas initially set by the Politburo for the entire country and then applied all the way to the village level. Some people, usually labeled "counterrevolutionary kulak activists" because of their prominent roles in opposing collectivization, were executed or sentenced to labor camps. The greatest number of kulaks were deported to remote parts of the country. A few remnants were left where they were to become impoverished pariahs, consigned to live on marginal land of no use to the state. Wherever they were or wherever they went, the kulaks were thoroughly broken first. These peasant farmers, who had done little more than rise from abject poverty through hard work and thrift, were left with nothing. One police report recorded that kulaks were left "in their underclothes, for everything was confiscated, including old rubber boots . . . women's drawers . . . 50 kopeks worth of tea . . . pokers, washtubs, etc. . . . . Kulak families with small children were left without any means of feeding themselves."

Many kulaks, often entire families, committed suicide. The deportees were shipped under inhuman conditions to European Russia's frigid far north, the forests of Siberia, the Urals region, the dusty steppes further east, or the deserts of Central Asia. As one former Bolshevik, who himself ended up in Siberia, recalled:

> Trainloads of deported peasants left for the icy North, the forests, the steppes, the deserts. These were whole populations, denuded of everything; the old folk starved to death in mid-journey, newborn babies were buried on the banks of the roadside, and each wilderness had its crop of little crosses of boughs of white wood.[3]

Some of the trains were so long and densely packed that it took two locomotives to move them, one to push and one to pull. Inside the boxcars, those who died of thirst or disease did so on their feet; there was no place to fall down.

Once they reached their bleak destinations, some of the men were separated from their families and sent to labor camps; many did not survive the forced marches through frozen wastes to these hellish places. The majority of the deportees who were spared the camps, including women and children, did only minimally better, even though technically they were not prisoners or camp inmates who officially had been denied their freedom. They were deposited in remote outposts called "special settlements." In many cases, however, literally nothing was there. Instead of towns or villages with shelters in which to live, "special settlers" found only bare ground, the open steppe, or marshy forests. Thus an OGPU report in 1931 noted that 40 percent of the settlers in western Siberia lived in "makeshift huts, dugouts, barracks, etc." One witness described what he saw upon his arrival at a Siberian special settlement:

> At the foot of many slopes something had been dug that looked from a distance like garbage dumps. Out of them black beings emerged, adults and children, it seemed, and followed us with their eyes.
> "What are they? Human beings?" I stupidly asked.
> "These are called . . . special migrants," our new authority on local affairs began to explain. "There are thousands of them, many thousands. For the most part they are forgotten. They are sent here as voluntary deportees. They won't let them into the camps or barracks. If you want to eat, you've got to work; if you don't want to, you might just as well dig yourself into the earth. There is little difference."[4]

The kulaks were utterly destroyed as a class, but they did not suffer and die alone. All sorts of peasants were sucked into the maelstrom with them. Often it was difficult to distinguish a kulak from his neighbors, or even to be sure of one's own class status, for that matter. Thus the story was told of one peasant busily "dekulaking" on one side of a village while his own homestead was being "dekulaked" on the other side. It was enough to be unenthusiastic about collectivization (or to have the wrong enemy or something that someone else coveted) to be labeled a kulak. In some cases, at a loss as to how to meet their assigned quota, peasants held village meetings and chose their local "kulaks"; in other cases "kulaks" were chosen by lot. According to Stalin's own testimony, millions of human beings were uprooted and vast numbers of them died. Official records show that one-third of all peasants deported during 1929–1930 had died by January of 1931 from exposure, lack of food, and disease. That did not deter the Soviet regime in the least. According to OGPU records, during 1930–1931 about 400,000 peasant families—more than 1.8 million people—were deported and exiled to special settlements. Within a year, only 1.3 million special settlers remained on official rolls. To be sure, many thousands had fled, but deaths certainly accounted for much of that decrease. Indeed, the Politburo at the time was informed that the death rate in many settlements among children under eight was 10 percent per *month*.

"EXECUTION BY HUNGER"

Most of the kulaks were dispossessed and sent to their grim fates in special settlements or labor camps between 1930 and 1932. What followed in some of the places they had left behind was equally horrible. Bad weather and the raging turmoil of collectivization combined in 1932 to produce a poor harvest, the second in a row. Despite reduced quantities of grain on the farm, particularly in the Ukraine and the North Caucasus, key breadbaskets that traditionally provided half the country's marketable grain, quotas for grain deliveries to the state remained as high as or higher than in previous years. In fact, in 1930, the first year after collectivization, the state took 30 percent of the crop in the Ukraine and 38 percent in the North Caucasus, versus the 15 to 20 percent the peasants had marketed during the NEP. In 1931, when the crop was smaller, the figures for the Ukraine and the North Caucasus were 41.5 and 47 percent. By 1932, bereft of the food they had grown, the peasants of the Ukraine and North Caucasus began to starve. People ate cats, dogs, field mice, bark, and even horse manure in a desperate struggle to stay alive. ("Yes, the horse manure. We fight over it. Sometimes there are whole grains in it," a peasant woman told a shocked party worker.) They ate animals that had died of disease. Even cannibalism occurred. In some areas infant mortality approached 100 percent; in others entire villages starved. Meanwhile, the OGPU seized grain from starving peasants and moved it to the country's ports so it could be exported. Army units were deployed to keep starving peasants from eating unripened crops in the field, a crime that fell under the expansive rubric of an August 1932 decree on "theft of state property" or "kulak sabotage." Peasants bitterly called the decree the "ear law," since many convicted under its provisions had taken only a few ears of corn or stalks of rye from the collective farm fields. Those who managed to get their hands on a few seeds of unripened grain without being caught often died anyway because such seeds were indigestible to weakened and ravaged bodies. Thousands of peasants defied police attempts to keep them out of the towns, where they begged for food, lay listless, and died. As one eyewitness recalled:

> And no matter what they did, they went on dying, dying, dying. They died singly and in droves. They died everywhere—in yards or streetcars and on trains. There was no one to bury these victims of the Stalinist famine.[5]

The best estimates are that 7 million people died in the terror-famine of 1932–1933: 5 million in the Ukraine, 1 million in the North Caucasus, and 1 million elsewhere in the Soviet Union, mostly in the Lower Volga area. Unlike in 1921–1922, the government made no effort to stop the famine and every effort to prevent news of it from reaching the nation at large and the West. Grain taken from the collectives according to government quotas was used to feed the burgeoning urban industrial labor force; it continued to be exported for foreign exchange, whose value apparently exceeded that of human life at home. Far from trying to relieve the famine, the evidence suggests that Stalin and the Politburo allowed it to continue and thereby help them break peasant resistance to collectivization, particularly in the Ukraine. More than five decades later a survivor of events in the Ukraine aptly called Stalin's policy "execution by hunger."[6]

THE COLLECTIVE FARM SYSTEM

From the depths of 1933 there was no place to go but up. The defeated peasants were compelled to accept collectivization, which they, not without some justification, viewed as the return of serfdom. The victorious government likewise yielded a bit in order to make its new system work, if not efficiently, at least predictably. It was a system that remained remarkably stable until the demise of the Soviet Union almost six decades later. While some peasants worked as wage-earners on huge state-run farms called *sovkhozy*, the majority lived and worked on collective farms called *kolkhozy*. These smaller units supposedly were independent and collectively owned by those who lived and worked there. Actually, the party controlled the *kolkhozy* through party members who held the leadership positions on the farms. Each peasant's individual income was determined according to his or her share of the collective's profits, each share being determined by the number of "labor days" a person earned. The peasants were not paid until the state had taken its share of the farm's production, at a very low fixed price, and resources were set aside for planting, reserves, and other needs. Another institution, the Machine Tractor Station (MTS), for years also fed at the trough before the membership of the collective. The Machine Tractor Stations (abolished in 1958) supplied the *kolkhozy* with heavy agricultural machinery, in theory because it was more efficient for several farms to share these expensive and complex machines. In reality, the Machine Tractor Station was another lever of control, since it took a large percentage of the crop (generally around 15 percent) in exchange for services that often were of questionable quality.

Yet despite all these controls, the Soviet government never was able to get the system to work effectively. Instructions and orders handed down from party authorities to the farms often produced confusion, emphasis on the wrong crops or techniques, and apathy rather than increased yields. Even more important, peasants were paid so poorly for their work in the collectives that they frequently did not bother to work efficiently.

What did produce results were the garden plots and farm animals left to each peasant family. These Stalin had to tolerate almost from the start. In 1930, at the height of the collectivization campaign, peasants were allowed to keep tiny garden plots for their own use, a concession confirmed by a law issued in 1935. Peasants were permitted to raise what they could on these plots and, beginning in 1932, to sell whatever surplus they could produce in local markets. Another concession in 1934 allowed each peasant household to keep a small number of farm animals such as cows, pigs, and poultry. Given the price the government was willing to pay for what it took from the collectives, a price that for many years was below what it cost the collectives to produce these crops, the peasants never could have survived without their private plots and livestock. Neither, in fact, could the nation because these so-called private plots, amounting to only 3 to 4 percent of the Soviet Union's farmland, and the peasantry's farm animals over the years produced 25 percent of the country's total agricultural output, including at least a third of its fruit, milk, meat, eggs, and vegetables.

Despite the appalling human cost, from the government's point of view collectivization was a success. It gave the regime the leverage it needed to procure the grain necessary to feed the growing industrial labor force and to export in return for industrial machinery. Beginning in 1930, the regime drastically increased its grain procurements over previous levels and kept them there, despite poor harvests for several years and the unfair and inadequate price it was willing to pay for what it took. Once the peasants were under the heel of collectivization, there was nothing to keep the regime from taking an average of almost 40 percent of the agricultural harvest from the mid-1930s until Germany invaded the Soviet Union in 1941. In effect, the Communist regime, like the tsars but much more so, put the bulk of the burden for industrialization squarely on the peasantry's back.

However, agriculture became a drag on the Soviet economy. In 1929, the leadership apparently hoped that collectivized agriculture would soon provide it with one-third of the capital needed for industrialization. The subsequent disasters made this impossible. At best, only extreme exploitation of the peasantry kept the agricultural sector from disrupting the industrialization plans. It is also true that during the 1930s all Soviet citizens, not only the peasants, suffered enormously because the peasants produced so little. After Stalin's death, matters improved, but nothing the regime did ever enabled the Soviet Union to feed itself. A country that under the tsars was a leading grain exporter was turned into the world's largest grain importer. Collectivization remained not only a yoke on the Soviet peasantry, but an albatross around the neck of the entire country.

THE INDUSTRIALIZATION DRIVE

Agriculture was so ravaged because it was treated as only a means to an end. The paramount goal of Stalin's revolution from above was industrialization: to build, at any cost, an industrial base capable of supporting a modern military establishment. This meant that heavy industry—iron, steel, coal, machine tools, electric power, and the like—was fed virtually every available resource at the expense of everything else, devouring five-sixths of all investment during the First Five-Year Plan. Consequently, these industries grew tremendously during the 1930s.

The industrialization drive might have been more successful were it not for the excessive speed at which it took place. Reckless haste produced bottlenecks, shortages, and enormous waste. Precious supplies delivered to a given project often lay unused because other vital materials were unavailable. Since heavy industry could not be permitted to lag behind, the nonfavored sectors were squeezed even more to make up for what had been wasted. In the course of a decade the Soviet Union did become an industrial giant, but a grossly deformed one, at once heavily muscled to produce armaments, yet too weak to provide many basic human needs, let alone pleasures, for most of the population. Housing, consumer goods, and agriculture were ignored.

Stalin's enthusiasm for gigantic projects also added to the general misery. He seemed convinced that bigger was better—one critic complained that Stalin wanted "a canal that could be seen from Mars"—and that human will could be harnessed to overcome any obstacle. Some of the projects eventually succeeded, like the great Dneprostroi hydroelectric dam on the Dnieper River, the largest waterpower project in Europe at the time, and the construction, from scratch, of the steel complex of Magnitogorsk at the southern edge of the Ural Mountains. Others were expensive and tragic fiascoes, like the Baltic–White Sea canal, built in less than two years at the cost of tens of thousands of lives. Triumphantly finished ahead of schedule, the canal proved to be too shallow to serve as a military transport route, its main strategic purpose.

Stalin also raised production targets at will. Fairly typical was his tripling a tractor production target to 170,000; less than 50,000 actually were produced. Some grandiose schemes, such as Stalin's dream to change Russia's climate by planting a huge forest belt, mercifully were never begun. At best, these projects tied up valuable resources for excessive periods of time until they became productive and relieved some of the pressures on the nation. At worst, precious resources were squandered. Of less concern to Stalin and his colleagues were the hundreds of thousands of human lives that these expensive musings destroyed.

All of this—the ravaging of agriculture, the wasteful destruction of resources, the gigantic projects—played havoc with the plans that were supposed to guide the industrial drive. The first two Five-Year Plans actually were little more than propaganda billboards. Real planning was done over one- or at best two-year periods. Even at this level, planners labored under extreme hardships. Resources allotted for one project often were suddenly diverted to a "priority" project or to the most favored projects being built by what were called "shock methods." Since quantity—producing the specified tons of steel, tons of coal, or numbers of tractors—was the main criterion for judging success or failure, the tendency was to churn out large amounts of poor-quality, often useless goods. Whatever was produced, whether it served any useful purpose or not, counted toward fulfillment of the plan. Another persistent problem was the poor quality of the workforce. Hastily recruited, ill-trained, poorly paid, constantly browbeaten and threatened, the new Soviet industrial proletariat was so unproductive that many additional workers had to be recruited and trained in a desperate attempt to meet the regime's targets. This inevitably led to budget overruns, higher costs, and greater demands on increasingly scarce social services.

Against this background it should not be surprising that very few major targets were reached during the first two Five-Year Plans (1929–1937). Nonetheless, the achievements were impressive in the key target areas of heavy industry. Steel production rose from 4 to 17 million tons, oil from 11.7 to 28.5 million tons, coal from 35.4 to 128 million tons, and electricity from 5.1 billion kwh to 36.2 billion kwh. Important new industries were created, among them automobile, aviation, tractor, and chemical, as were several entirely new industrial complexes. Many new sources of raw materials were developed, particularly east of the Ural Mountains and in Siberia. Transport was significantly improved, mainly by additions to the canal and railroad networks. Some small strides even were made in expanding light industries that produced consumer goods, although these remained a very poor relation to heavy industry. Overall, heavy industry grew by 400 percent. The industrialization drive, precisely because it was planned and controlled by a central authority, yielded vital economic and strategic benefits beyond purely quantitative growth. Because a significant proportion of this development was located in the central and eastern regions of the country, it both contributed to the economic advancement of these previously backward regions and made the new industrial plants and resources safer from foreign attack. Planning also yielded economic benefits because industrial installations were located closer to essential raw materials. Soviet Russia, despite the suffering and waste, built a viable modern industrial base in a decade. By 1941 the industries built during the 1930s were producing a full range of modern weapons, including some of the world's best tanks, artillery, and tactical rockets. After World War II those industries provided the basis for even greater growth that made the Soviet Union, until it was surpassed by Japan in the 1980s, an industrial power second only to the United States.

FULFILLING THE FIVE-YEAR PLANS

One question that logically arises regarding the industrialization drive of the 1930s is how so much was built in the face of such enormous chaos and waste.

Several factors help account for this. The narrow focus on heavy industry was a two-edged sword. It caused imbalances and shortages, but it also meant that those projects most vital to a modern industrial infrastructure were completed, even if a great deal was sacrificed along the way. It was much easier to get all those steel mills built if no attention was paid to providing the steel workers with shoes or housing them and their families in decent dwellings.

The enthusiasm and dedication that Stalin and his propaganda machine were able to generate helped spur production. Many urban cadres gave their best efforts to the collectivization drive, and were capable of extreme cruelty in carrying out their orders, because they believed they were participating in the birth of a socialist utopia. The same enthusiasm was evident at many of the great construction sites such as Magnitogorsk, where an American engineer, somewhat hyperbolically, observed how "construction work went on with a disregard for individuals and a mass heroism unparalleled in history"; he added that the "battle" to build that great steel complex claimed more casualties than the Battle of the Marne. It proved possible to stimulate additional effort through such campaigns as socialist competition of labor, in which rival groups tried to outdo each other, and through the famous (or notorious) Stakhanovite movement. The latter got its name from a coal miner named Alexei Stakhanov, who, in 1935, with help from the management of his mine, organized his team of workers so that in one shift he was able to mine fourteen times his quota of coal. The world's largest propaganda machine turned Stakhanov's effort into a national event in order to inspire the rest of the nation. The honors and material rewards that went to overachievers like Stakhanov quickly produced a host of "Stakhanovites." However, although the state glorified these people, the proletariat often did not, since their extraordinary feats were used as excuses to raise the norms and quotas of ordinary workers.

Far more important was what the economist Naum Jasny has called the "strangulation" of consumption.[7] Stalin and his planners could invest—and waste—as much as they did only because the Soviet people were denied the fruits of their excruciatingly hard labor. Jasny estimates that per capita income dropped by 25 percent for urban workers and 40 percent for rural workers in the generation after 1928. During the worst years of the 1930s, the drop almost certainly exceeded 50 percent. Housing for the rapidly expanding urban working class simply was not built. Instead of the promised consumer goods, the people received rations, shortages, long lines, and high prices. The price system, in fact, was the regime's best revenue-raising tool. All goods were subject to a "turnover tax," a levy collected not just once, but several times as a product moved from its origins as raw material to the state-run retail outlet. This made it possible to exploit both the producer and the consumer at the same time by paying the former next to nothing, adding on a stiff turnover tax, and charging the latter an astronomical price. High prices unfortunately were the least of the average citizen's problems, since low agricultural productivity and the neglect of consumer-goods industries meant that often nothing was available at any price. According to economist Alec Nove, "1933 was the culmination of the most precipitous peacetime decline in living standards known in recorded history."[8]

The industrialization drive also was helped by compromises and concessions made during the Second Five-Year Plan (1933–1937). These changes came at an opportune time. Collectivized agriculture was in a shambles. Many large and expensive projects stood unfinished and unproductive. The mad rush to create an industrial labor force out of uneducated peasants had resulted in enormous losses of expensive and complex machinery that had been operated by unqualified personnel. The regime responded by modifying its emphasis on expansion and quantity. Growth rate targets for industry were reduced and more attention was paid to consolidation and quality. This was manifested in greater attention to the training of workers, efforts to improve technical education, a determined attempt to finish the huge projects started during the First Five-Year Plan, and better managerial techniques. There were also administrative reorganizations, including the overhaul of the railroad administration by Lazar Kaganovich, one of Stalin's most ruthless and effective henchmen and a key troubleshooter during collectivization. Concessions made to the peasantry regarding private plots and livestock allowed agriculture to partially recover from the disastrous levels of 1931 to 1933. The result was what Jasny called the "three good years" of 1934 to 1936, a period that yielded the most impressive growth rates of the great industrialization drive of the 1930s.

One frequently overlooked contribution to the Soviet industrialization drive came from abroad. As with the previous Russian efforts to build modern industry since the time of Peter I, Soviet industrialization under Stalin required Western technology and expertise. American firms like International Harvester, Ford, General Electric, and DuPont participated in major Soviet industrial projects. The Dneprostroi hydroelectric dam and the Magnitogorsk steel complex, two of the giant showpieces of the First Five-Year Plan, each had critical American input: an American engineering firm designed and supervised construction of the Dneprostroi dam and another provided designs for the Magnitogorsk steel mills. While economic depression was gripping established but stagnant industries of the capitalist world, American and European companies eager for business and thousands of individuals seeking jobs were providing vital technical expertise to the new and expanding industries of the Communist world.

The most important force behind the industrialization drive was coercion on a monumental scale. During the 1930s, the Soviet labor force, largely recruited from the peasantry, was brutally exploited and regimented. With little to hold them in the way of incentives, these workers made a habit of moving from job to job in search of tolerable wages and working conditions. The workers' state therefore made simple absenteeism a criminal offense, later reinforcing that law by stipulating that being twenty minutes late to work constituted absenteeism. Theft of collective farm or state property became a capital offense. After 1932, workers and other urban residents had to carry internal passports, a form of control dredged up from the tsarist past. These passports were denied to peasants, in effect tying them to the land as in the days of serfdom before 1861. In 1938 came the notorious labor books. They contained a record of every job a worker had held, and it was impossible to get a job without producing one's book. In 1940 all workers were frozen in their jobs.

The proletariat was not alone in its misery. The managers, engineers, and technocrats above them toiled under the same whip hand. Since most of them were of "bourgeois" origin, they were a convenient scapegoat for the many failures that plagued the industrialization drive, failures that were the consequences of the regime's own irrational policy decisions. A series of public show trials between 1928 and 1933, often accompanied by executions and long prison terms, blamed the nation's economic difficulties on "wreckers," "saboteurs," and the like. These trials, orchestrated to the drumbeat of large propaganda campaigns, undoubtedly convinced many people that their economic problems could be blamed on these "bourgeois" specialists rather than on the regime's errors. The sentences the defendants received deprived the Soviet economy of valuable talent and drove many of those not arrested to seek the relative safety of positions with little responsibility, which wasted their skills. Meanwhile, executions of many other "bourgeois" specialists took place in secret, often without the benefit of any trial.

FORCED LABOR AND THE GULAG

The quintessence of the exploitation and force that fed Stalin's new economic machine was the largest slave labor empire the world had yet seen. Compulsory labor had a long history in Russia, and it continued to exist after the Bolshevik Revolution. However, under Stalin it expanded exponentially and intensified qualitatively, reaching staggering proportions in terms of both size and cruelty. Stalinist forced labor, like so many other institutions, has its roots in the Lenin era. Forced labor and concentration camps were part of the Bolshevik arsenal for winning the civil war. After the Bolshevik victory, the concentration camps were retained as places of punishment for opponents of the regime. The specific idea of using slave labor to build a new socialist industrial economy dates from the mid-1920s. Important advocates included Felix Dzerzhinsky, chief of the OGPU, and G.L. Pyatnikov, whose responsibilities as the head of *Vesenkha* included economic development. Their goal was to find a way to develop and exploit mineral resources in the country's remote and inhospitable regions, and one way, they both agreed, was to "make better use of prisoners." The OGPU by then had what in effect was a laboratory for developing its forced labor techniques, a small group of prison camps aptly named the Northern Camps of Special Significance (SLON), established at the site of a former monastery in 1923 on an island in the frigid White Sea. Stalin was deeply interested in these matters from the start. With the beginning of the industrialization drive and collectivization in 1929, the Politburo under Stalin's leadership adopted a resolution titled "On the Utilization of the Labor of Criminal Prisoners." It officially endorsed the idea of setting up a large network of these camps for exploiting natural resources and settling remote regions containing those resources. Slave labor would be used to help build socialism.

The Soviet Union's existing labor camp network expanded quickly, initially with the influx of hundreds of thousands of dispossessed kulaks. As Stalin and the Soviet leadership saw it, forced labor had several important advantages in facilitating industrialization. It would be cheap, since it cost very little to maintain workers whose lives were considered expendable. Forced labor also could be used as a substitute for machines, since the workers had no choice about the jobs they did. The most severe discipline could be enforced to get the work done. Finally, forced laborers could be moved to remote, resource-rich areas that free workers would shun. This was especially true with regard to skilled workers and technical specialists (mining engineers, for example), who, after being deprived of their freedom for alleged "wrecking" and similar offenses, provided essential technical expertise at Gulag mining, construction, and industrial projects. These were valuable assets to a regime in a country so short of food, machines, and other factors vital to the industrialization drive.

Economic calculations above all else governed the treatment of prisoners; to the Soviet regime, labor camp inmates were an economic resource, not human beings. Their worth was calculated in units of labor, and prisoners who could not fulfill their work quotas received reduced rations, a system that starved people who already were physically weak and became the largest cause of death in the camps. When modifications were made, it was for economic reasons. Thus, in 1938 when Lavrenty Beria, a member of Stalin's inner circle, became responsible for the forced labor camps and ordered that food rations be increased, his objective was to increase efficiency and thereby production by cutting the death rate and the labor losses it caused, not to improve the prisoners' lot. From the 1930s through the early 1950s, the primary goal of the labor camp managers was to make those camps "profitable" and increase their contribution to Stalin's five-year plans and the building of the Soviet version of socialism.

Millions of people, mostly men but also large numbers of women and children, labored in these camps. Beginning in 1934 they collectively were known as the Gulag (the acronym for Chief Administration of Camps), a special department set up by the People's Commissariat of Internal Affairs, or NKVD, which that same year also absorbed the OGPU. The best available estimate of the total number of people who spent time in the Gulag (and pre-Gulag) labor camps and "colonies" (camps administered by local rather than central Gulag authorities) between 1929 and Stalin's death in 1953 is about 18 million. At least 6 million people at one time or another during that period were confined to the special settlements, which also were under Gulag authority.[9] The area under the Gulag's control was equally astounding. One division, the Dalstroi, which included the notorious Kolyma gold mines in eastern Siberia, by itself controlled an area four times the size of France. Smaller Gulag camps were almost everywhere, from every major Soviet city to the country's most remote and forsaken regions.

Slave labor worked on the most formidable and dangerous projects of the First and Second Five-Year Plans, especially in construction and mining. Slave laborers mined gold, iron, and coal, built canals and railroads, harvested lumber in the frozen north, constructed hydroelectric stations, helped to build the Magnitogorsk steel center, and built an entire port city, the notorious Magadan, in one of the most inhospitable regions of eastern Siberia to service Stalin's gold mines in the Kolyma region. Gulag labor increased production of gold in the Kolyma from 511 kilograms in 1932 to 5,515 kilograms in 1934 and to 33,360 kilograms in 1936, causing one Soviet official to gush with unfettered enthusiasm, "Never, in the most feverish years of the capitalist gold rush that included all the metal taken out of Alaska, did a territory give up as much gold as that produced this year by the new Kolyma region." Gulag labor was crucial to opening up Siberia's coal, oil, and gas deposits for exploitation. Its role in the Soviet economy grew throughout the 1930s. A partial list of its share of the Soviet Union's production of metals by the start of the 1940s reads as follows: 46.5 percent of the nickel, 76 percent of the tin, 60 percent of the gold. The Gulag at that point also produced 25.3 percent of the Soviet Union's lumber, was a major producer of coal, and accounted for 13–14 percent of the county's capital construction projects. Slave laborers worked on numerous other types of industrial projects as well, including many run by other state authorities. During World War II the Gulag became a key part of the military effort. It organized hundreds of special labor colonies to serve defense industries and produce tanks, airplanes, ammunition, and other military supplies. Gulag workers built aircraft factories, metallurgical complexes, and airfields. The Gulag also provided the army with soldiers: about 1 million prisoners, out of about 5 million who passed through the camps and colonies during the war, were released and immediately sent to the front.

This pattern continued after the war as Gulag workers were mobilized to rebuild the country's shattered infrastructure. Working almost exclusively with hand tools, as they had before the war, in 1949 Gulag workers mined almost 100 percent of the Soviet Union's platinum and diamonds and more than 90 percent of its gold. The Gulag's overall share of the country's industrial production that year exceeded 10 percent, and in 1950 Gulag labor accounted for more than 10 percent of all the residential construction in Moscow. The Soviet Union's crash project to build an atomic bomb also relied heavily on Gulag slave laborers, who did everything from mining uranium under appalling conditions to building the structure that housed the country's first nuclear reactor.

The cost in human life in all of this was staggering. Many prisoners did not even survive the trip to the camps. Of the 16,000 prisoners sent during its first year of operation in 1932 to Kolyma, the "land of the white death," fewer than 10,000 reached the region alive, and only half of them survived the following year. In 1933 a slave ship headed for the Kolyma gold mines became stuck in the Arctic ice; when it finally reached its destination in 1934, *every one* of its 12,000 prisoners was dead. (The ship was repaired.) In the Pechora region in northern European Russia, no less than 1 million people died between 1937 and 1941 alone. In the four war years that followed, more than 2 million inmates died in Gulag camps and colonies; the toll rises even higher when it includes deaths in special settlements and other Gulag units. Annual mortality rates of 10 to 20 percent were common in the Gulag, and higher rates were not unknown. In certain lumber camps few prisoners survived for more than two years. During 1942–1943, the mortality rate for the Gulag as a whole reached 25 percent; in other words, a quarter of the entire camp population died in a single year. The Gulag camps killed more people than the regime executed; their ghastly toll is unknown, but obviously ran into the millions. This account of working conditions eloquently explains why:

> We were forced to work in temperatures of –40 degrees [F]. Rain and snow storms were disregarded. We had to cut trees in the forests even when the snow was waist deep. Falling trees hit the workers, who were unable to escape in the snow. In the summer . . . men had to stand knee deep in water or mud for 10

or 12 hours. . . . Influenza, bronchitis, pneumonia, tuberculosis, . . . malaria, and other illnesses decimated our ranks. . . . The men continually had frozen extremities and amputation due to frostbite was common. . . . The men were compelled to work by force. . . . Camp authorities would force the prisoners to work by beating, kicking, dragging them by their feet through mud and snow, setting dogs on them, hitting them with rifle butts, and by threatening them with revolvers and bayonets.[10]

Against this regimen, inmates received a food ration of 1,400 calories per day, a level calculated for people who were confined to a prison cell and did no physical labor. The renowned novelist Aleksandr Solzhenitsyn, who spent eight years in Gulag camps after World War II, described a typical death. After suffering from innumerable diseases and their ravages—the rotting teeth, bleeding gums, ulcerated legs, decaying and peeling skin, diarrhea, and the like—a dying man

> grows deaf and stupid, and he loses all capacity to weep, even when he is being dragged along the ground behind a sledge. He is no longer afraid of death; he is wrapped in a submissive rosy glow. He has crossed all boundaries and has forgotten the name of his wife, of his children, and finally his own name too. Sometimes the entire body of a man dying of starvation is covered with blue-black pimples like peas, with pus-filled heads smaller than a pinhead—his face, arms, legs, his trunk, even his scrotum. It is so painful he cannot be touched. The tiny boils come to a head and burst and a thick worm-like string of pus is forced out of them. The man is rotting alive.
>
> If black astonished head lice are crawling on the face of your neighbor on the bunks, it is a sure sign of death.[11]

There was one division of the Gulag where these dreadful conditions did not prevail. Shortly after taking over as head of the NKVD (and therefore the Gulag) in 1938, Lavrenty Beria ordered the establishment of what were called special design bureaus to house prisoner scientists and engineers. During the next fifteen years several thousand individuals were imprisoned in these bureaus, called *sharashkas* by the prisoners. Their number included some of the Soviet Union's most talented scientific and technological personnel whose alleged crimes consisted of fabrications such as "sabotage of socialist construction." Interestingly, for some the *sharashkas*, whatever their obvious indignities, quite literally were lifesavers. Most notably, aeronautical engineer Sergei Korolev was doing exhausting manual labor in the Kolyma gold mines when he was assigned to a *sharashka* in Moscow. A rocket designer of true genius, Korolev after the war became chief of the Soviet space program and designed the rockets that, among other things, put the world's first artificial satellite and human being into orbit. Another famous *sharashka* prisoner was Andrei Tupalov, one of the world's most gifted airplane designers, whose service to his country's aviation program spanned decades. There were *sharashkas* in Moscow, Leningrad, and many other cities during World War II, and their inmates designed a variety of advanced weapons that were used against the Germans. These scientific prison laboratories continued to work after the war until finally being abolished after Stalin's death.

The Gulag was an ocean of human misery. Mixed in were not a few drops of bitter irony, most notably that the Gulag also was an economic failure. To be sure, a lot of projects were completed and a great deal was produced, but rarely as cheaply or in as timely a fashion as promised. The Kolyma mining operation provided gold that Moscow used as foreign exchange to pay for equipment needed for the industrialization drive. Overall, however, it turned out that slave labor was both inefficient and wasteful. It was expensive to uproot millions of peasants and ship them to remote places, and it also was costly to build camps and staff them with guards. Most labor camps, burdened by sick and dying prisoners, were disorganized and unproductive. A study done in 1941 revealed that in construction and assembly work Gulag labor was only half as productive as free labor, one reason why Gulag projects often failed to meet their goals. Overall, a reasonable estimate is that Gulag labor was about 50 to 60 percent as productive as free labor. Meanwhile, even with its seemingly endless supply of unskilled laborers, the Gulag needed modern equipment, skilled workers, and technical specialists to complete many of its projects, all of which raised costs. Making matters worse, the erroneous belief that slave labor was so cheap encouraged the regime to authorize ill-considered projects that wasted enormous amounts of resources. The White Sea Canal is the best known of these fiascos—more than seven decades after its completion the History Channel made it the subject of a lengthy segment during a program on engineering disasters—but it is only one of many. Another blunder was the Salekhard-Igarka Railroad. Built in the late 1940s and early 1950s through hundreds of miles of arctic swamps at the cost of many lives and billions of rubles, it literally led nowhere when it finally was abandoned. Other so-called dead railroads likewise never moved an ounce of freight or a single passenger: by 1938 the Soviet Union had about 3,000 miles of unfinished railway track. It also had many additional miles of completed track that were used rarely or not at all. Numerous other major projects also were abandoned, including several ill-conceived hydroelectric installations cancelled after Stalin's death. While Stalin was alive false claims and exaggerations concealed many of these failures. However, in the end nothing could change the fact that the Gulag forced-labor system, aside from being a monstrous moral crime, also was an economic sinkhole that on balance hurt rather than helped Soviet industrialization and economic development. It remained what one expert has called "a kind of narcotic for the economy" until it finally was dismantled in the decade after Stalin's death.[12]

A MILITARIZED SOCIETY

The Soviet Union did not just become an industrial society during the 1930s; it also became a militarized one. A militarized society is not defined simply in terms of quantity—that is, a society that devotes an abnormally large percentage of its resources to the military—although this certainly is a characteristic of such a society. More fundamentally, it is a matter of quality: a situation, as historian David R. Stone has put it, in which a society is economically, culturally, and psychologically organized for war and lacks "clear boundaries between military and civil life."[13] Civilians can still be fully in control in a militarized society—in particular, the military can be subordinated to civilian political authority—as in fact was the case in the Soviet Union both during and after Stalin. Nonetheless, it is the military that has first call on a nation's most vital resources, from its best scientists, to its technologically most advanced factories, to its most valuable natural resources, and anything else of importance. It is the needs of the military that drive economic policy: the military is served first and the civilian sector of the economy gets what is left. This situation is what evolved in the Soviet Union during the 1930s, and it remained a fundamental feature of Soviet life until the end of the Soviet regime.

The militarization of the Soviet Union was entirely consistent with the logic of the Bolshevik Revolution. As with so many fundamental features of Stalinism, it was rooted in Leninist assumptions. After November 1917 Lenin fully expected that in the end the struggle between socialism and capitalism would be decided by war. As he told his colleagues in 1918, "international imperialism," with its "highly organized military technique . . . could not under any circumstances, on any condition, live side by side with the Soviet Republic." Lenin never changed his mind on this point, even as he recognized after 1921 that the immediate military threat to the Soviet regime had receded. The threat would remain until socialist revolutions swept away the world's capitalist regimes. These assumptions remained fundamental to the Bolshevik outlook after Lenin's death, as the party leadership indicated in 1925 when it warned that "bourgeois Europe is pregnant with new imperialist wars." This was not rhetoric; it was an ideological axiom and one of the few points on which the bitter rivals Stalin and Trotsky agreed. The Soviet Union had to be prepared for the great and inevitable military challenge ahead.

In terms of government policy, the imperative of being prepared for a decisive war with the capitalist world acquired additional urgency because of the assessment of what that war would be like. In the wake of World War II, Soviet strategists, like their counterparts in the West, assumed all future modern wars would be total wars. They would call on and test the full strength, economic as well as military, of every society involved because modern armed forces depended on advanced industrial economies to produce the weapons and other materials needed to wage war. This in turn meant there was no longer a distinction between the battlefront and the home front; civilians and their productive efforts were as vital to winning modern war as soldiers.

Following this logic, Soviet military planners as early as the mid-1920s were insisting that the Soviet economy had to be mobilized for war and generating plans to accomplish that end. Given the all-encompassing nature of this task, economic mobilization for war had to be done during peacetime and integrated into economic planning. Only in this way would the Soviet Union be ready when the inevitable armed conflict came. Of course, this also meant that the Soviet Union, whose economy was woefully backward compared to the modern capitalist states of the West, had to do everything possible to catch up economically and technologically with those states. Industrialization and military power were inseparably linked.

These priorities were built into the First Five-Year Plan, and they produced tangible results in terms of modern weapons such as artillery, machine guns, and tanks. In 1932 and again in 1936, in part in response to perceived threats from Japan and Germany, there were sharp increases in military spending. Another sharp spike upward took place between 1938 and 1940. By 1940, the Soviet Union had seven times as many soldiers and, more important, twenty times as much military equipment as it had possessed only a decade earlier. Most important of all, by then every sector of the economy and every part of the country had been integrated into military preparations, and the Soviet Union stood ready to mobilize all its resources for war if it came. A military-industrial revolution had produced a huge, modern socialist war machine.

All of this had an enormous impact on World War II and the subsequent great Cold War struggle between the Soviet Union and the United States. In terms of World War II the results were mixed. The focus on building so many weapons during the early 1930s left the Soviet Union with vast stores of outdated weapons when it was attacked by Germany in June 1941. However, outdated weaponry was not the Soviet Union's main problem as it faced the Nazi onslaught. Many Soviet weapons were a match for their German counterparts. Rather, the military disasters that occurred during the first year of the war were the result of shocking leadership failures, above all Stalin's stubborn refusal during the months prior to the June attack to allow his generals to deploy their troops for battle when German forces were massing along the Soviet Union's western border. That said, the Soviet Union weathered the initial Nazi storm. It then could call on its vast capacity to produce weapons and supplies and strike back at the Germans, something it could not have done without the buildup of the 1930s. Yet in the longer run, the Soviet Union's overgrown military sector became a serious liability that drained the country's civilian economic sector for decades. After World War II, despite overall economic growth, the size of the military sector was an important factor in Moscow's inability to provide its people with a standard of living comparable to what existed in the West. In that sense, the militarization of Soviet society, even if it helped win World War II against Germany, became an economic dead weight in the next great challenge, the Cold War competition with the United States, and ultimately contributed to the exhaustion of the Soviet economic system and the eventual collapse of the Soviet Union itself.

INTELLECTUAL, CULTURAL, AND SOCIAL LIFE

The industrialization drive was the core of Stalin's revolution from above, but it did not define its limits. Bolshevik ideology also demanded a fundamental recasting of Russian society into a new socialist mold. The requisites of the industrialization drive and the ideology of the nation's leadership meant that the state inevitably intruded into virtually all areas of life. While this occasionally had a positive effect (such as improving education), overall it meant that a suffocating cloud of repression, rote, and uniformity enveloped Soviet Russia's cultural, scientific, and spiritual life for a generation.

The First Five-Year Plan had a far-reaching effect on education. The various liberalizing reforms of the 1920s were largely done away with and replaced with a stress on technical achievement, discipline, and heavy, unrelenting indoctrination. Technical education received the most attention because of the state's burgeoning need for specialists to staff the growing industrial infrastructure. At the same time, the needs of a modernized economy required a broad-based effort, and the spread of free primary education led to a dramatic drop in illiteracy during the 1930s.

If a case can be made that Stalin's education policy produced some progress, his cultural policy was a giant step backward. This was particularly true in what may be called mass or popular culture. It took the form of a secularized religiosity; cultural historian James H. Billington has aptly called this phenomenon the "revenge of Muscovy." As Billington observes, instead of "icons, incense, and ringing bells" Stalin's Russia had "lithographs of Lenin, cheap perfume, and humming machines"; instead of "omnipresent calls to [the] worship of Orthodoxy" there was the "inescapable loudspeaker or radio with its hypnotic statistics and the invocations to labor"; instead of "priests and missionaries" there were Stalin's "soldiers of the cultural army," all united, as in Ivan the Terrible's time, by "the believer's cry of hallelujah in response to the revealed word from Moscow."[14]

Culture was just another conscript for the campaign to build socialism. It marched under the dreary banner of "socialist realism." According to Stalin, "The artist ought to show life truthfully. And if he shows our life truthfully, he cannot fail to show it moving to socialism. This is and will be socialist realism." In reality artists were not to depict things as they were, but as the state wanted them to be. They were expected to produce propaganda that served the ends of the state, not art that expressed their untrustworthy inner feelings. They were to compose patriotic, upbeat music, paint prosperous and plump collective farmers and enthusiastic and heroic factory workers, and write novels extolling the new socialist work ethic. In novels, plays, and movies, heroes and heroines acted out positive themes in settings crowded with self-sacrifice, enthusiasm for the Five-Year Plan, and unlimited devotion to the greatest of all leaders, Comrade Stalin. Writers, in particular, said Stalin, were "engineers of the human soul," and properly engineered souls were crucial to the building of socialism. All of this left little room for genuine art. Although Soviet artists produced some worthwhile work, socialist realism suffocated most attempts at genuine artistic expression.

The social sciences also suffered grievously. History was rewritten to suit the needs of Stalin and the state, from questions concerning the origins of the Russian state to the history of the Bolshevik Party. Interestingly, the traditional Marxist historical school favored under Lenin, which was extremely critical of Russia's tsarist past, was suppressed in favor of an approach stressing selected aspects of the past useful to Stalin. Russian expansionism, for example, suddenly became a progressive historical force beneficial to the people it enveloped, while tyrants like Ivan the Terrible and Peter the Great became great builders and statesmen. The history of the Bolshevik Party was rewritten right down to the participants' memoirs. It emerged unrecognizable to anyone who had been active when Lenin was alive. The entire movement and the revolution itself became the exclusive work of Lenin and his magnificent right-hand man, Stalin, with occasional input from the masses. All others receded into the background or, like Trotsky, into ignominy.

Nor did the natural sciences remain unscathed. How could it be otherwise when so many of the best scientists were imprisoned or murdered for having the wrong political outlook, or simply for having the wrong enemies? The worst destruction occurred in biology and genetics, where Trofim Lysenko, a charlatan without serious scientific training, became the leading authority because of his theory that environmentally acquired traits could be passed to succeeding generations. Lysenko's field was agriculture, and his main goal was to shorten the growth period of crops so they could be harvested before the onset of cold weather, one of the gravest threats to crops in most of the Soviet Union. He believed this could be done by subjecting seeds to moisture and cold before planting, a process he called "vernalization." Lysenko's crackpot theories received an enthusiastic reception from Stalin for two reasons. First, they promised miraculous results for Soviet agriculture. Second, they meshed well with the Bolshevik goal of creating what was called the "new Soviet man," that is, people who would enthusiastically embrace life according to the dictates of Marxist-Leninist ideology and who presumably would emerge over time once the proper social and economic conditions were in place. At one point Lysenko announced he had converted winter wheat into spring wheat, a spurious claim that turned out to be based on exactly one plant of uncertain genetic stock. Making matters worse, many of Lysenko's critics—serious scientists and agricultural specialists—were dismissed from their jobs, and some of them were arrested. The most notorious single example of this involved Nikolai Vavilov, one of the world's most distinguished biologists, a man whose travels in the service of his remarkable research and reputation spanned the globe. For criticizing Lysenko, Vavilov was arrested in 1940. He died of malnutrition in prison in 1943. Lysenko's pseudoscientific theories, of course, were absurd, but that did not prevent them or their author from wreaking havoc on Soviet biology, genetics, and agronomy from the late 1930s until the early 1960s.

Personal matters also came under increased state scrutiny and regimentation. The sudden drop in the birthrate during the 1930s—it fell by one-third— was dealt with by reinstating the old ban on abortion. Other policies included far stricter divorce standards and attempts to promote stable and authoritarian family life. Children and young people were regulated ever more rigorously by the pyramid of organizations (Young Octobrists, Pioneers, and the Young Communist League, or Komsomol, in ascending order) that supervised and indoctrinated them until they were about thirty and eligible to join the party itself. Attempts to restore some of the social order disrupted by the industrialization drive included making children liable to punishment as adults from the age of twelve. The ideal child not only joined the appropriate youth organization, but gave it and the state his primary loyalty. The hero to emulate after 1932 was Pavlik Morozov, a fourteen-year-old peasant youth who had denounced his father for supposedly being a kulak.

THE NON-RUSSIAN MINORITIES

Stalin's policies caused considerable harm to the Soviet Union's non-Russian nationalities. Cultural autonomy in any genuine sense was dangerous to Stalin for two reasons. It could easily reinforce the centrifugal forces in the multi-national Russian (now Soviet) empire, and it might provide living examples of alternative social systems. The 1930s therefore witnessed intensive and extensive Russification. In the Ukraine, home to over 30 million non-Russian Slavs, cultural policies included the arrest of leading Ukrainian intellectuals, the Russification of the Ukrainian language, and the required study of Russian in the schools. Similar programs were implemented in Belorussia. The Jewish community, a traditional victim of the Russian state, suffered severely. Anti-Semitism resurfaced, Jewish culture was largely suppressed, and Jews increasingly were excluded from key positions in the party and state bureaucracies. Overall, although certain forms of non-Russian cultural expression were permitted, everything had to take place within the context of the new "Soviet" nationality, a formula that meant the domination of Russian language and culture. Anything outside that context was "bourgeois nationalism."

The regime used a variety of weapons to suppress ethnic sentiments among the minority nationalities. In 1930, it began its show trials of Ukrainian artists and intellectuals; during 1932–1933, Stalin allowed famine to work as a bludgeon to break Ukrainian resistance to collectivization. Collectivization devastated the way of life of the Muslim Kazakhs, while colonization by ethnic Russians turned some nationalities into minorities in their own homelands. Russia under Stalin was a very difficult and often dangerous place for any non-Russian ethnic group desiring genuine self-expression, even worse than it had been under the tsars.

COMMUNIST INEQUALITIES

Other vestiges of the tsarist past also found a place in Stalin's revolution from above. During the 1930s the regime reintroduced various forms of hierarchy that had been eroded or eliminated by the revolution. Soviet society became as hierarchical as Russian society had been during tsarist times. These hierarchies included a full range of wage differentials based on categories of work and elite classes of workers such as Stakhanovites. In 1931, the idea of equal wages was demoted from a socialist ideal to "petty bourgeois egalitarianism." Piece rates frequently replaced straight salaries. Economic differentials began to approach those of capitalist countries. Whereas an ordinary worker might make 150 rubles a month, an engineer made 500 rubles, a shock worker—someone able to exceed his quota—as much as 2,000, and a high state official more than 5,000. Below the workers stood the peasants, confined to a second-class status reminiscent of serfdom, and below them the slave laborers. Ranks, complete with uniforms, reappeared in the civil service, while military ranks similar to the tsarist pattern returned to the armed forces. Aside from salary and rank,

Soviet citizens were distinguished by their access to goods and services. The "new proletarian aristocracy," as some uncharitably but not inaccurately called the Communist Party, enjoyed a wide variety of privileges. Members of the party's upper crust shopped in special stores stocked with goods unavailable elsewhere, sent their children to exclusive schools, and received the best social services, not the least of which was adequate medical care. They enjoyed private cars, country villas, fine restaurants, and even servants. At the other extreme, the slave laborers had literally nothing, not even hope.

Although it is undoubtedly true that under Stalin a great deal changed, one thing did not. Power, as always, continued to corrupt, and when power was as close to being absolute as it was in Stalin's Russia, there was a corresponding degree of corruption. By the 1930s, the Bolshevik revolutionary asceticism that had once governed the lives of many party members was a thing of the past. A vast gap in living standards had opened up between the Communist Party elite and the general population in a society officially committed to socialism. At the very top, among the men closest to Stalin, former revolutionaries lived like princes. During the 1930s, when there were no funds to build housing for the proletariat and millions had to crowd together in filthy substandard quarters, Leningrad party boss Sergei Kirov lived in a magnificent apartment equipped with the most modern appliances and electrical equipment from abroad, including one of only ten huge General Electric refrigerators imported into the Soviet Union from the United States. The Moscow home of Henrik Yagoda, Stalin's NKVD chief from 1934 to 1936, was equally grand. As one visitor later recalled, it was "beautifully equipped. . . . One of the rooms was furnished in the Asiatic style, with carpets on the walls, divans, and thick rugs on the floor." When Anastas Mikoyan, a top Stalin aide for many years, was not in his comfortable Kremlin apartment, he shared a country mansion with several top party leaders about twenty miles from Moscow. Mikoyan's rural residence was part of a magnificent estate that had once belonged to an industrialist against whom Mikoyan had organized strikes before the revolution. Stalin's daughter, Svetlana, described it as:

> exactly as its exiled owners left it. On the porch is a marble statue of a dog. . . . Inside are marble statues imported from Italy. The walls are hung with Gobelins, and downstairs the windows are of stained glass. The garden, the park, the tennis court, the orangery, and the greenhouses are all exactly as they have always been.[15]

Many of Russia's new rulers could hardly believe they had achieved so much. Abel Yenukidze, a draftsman before 1917 who came up the ladder with his longtime friend and patron, Stalin (who later had Yenukidze shot), apparently spent much of his time comparing his new lifestyle with how the tsars used to live. Not even the privations of World War II were allowed to get in the way of the Communist Party elite's good life, as an American general observed at a luncheon during the height of the conflict, when so many ordinary Soviet citizens were starving:

> The centerpieces were huge silver bowls containing fresh fruit specially procured from the Caucasus. . . . Beautifully cut glass ran the gamut from tall thin champagne glasses, through those for light and heavy red wines, to the inevitable vodka glass. . . . There were bottles the entire length of the table from which the glasses could be and were filled many times. Interspersed among the bottles were silver platters of . . . fresh large grained caviar, . . . huge delicacies. . . . Knives, forks, and spoons were of gold, and service plates of the finest china heavily encrusted with gold. The whole spectacle was amazing and called to mind the banquet scene in Charles Laughton's movie *Henry VIII*.[16]

All this reveling inevitably had a touch of frenzy, for the revelers never knew if and when the secret police would step in and end it all. After Stalin began the massive wave of arrests that terrorized the Soviet Union during the mid-1930s, people lived for the moment, as the end often came without warning. One prisoner who survived Stalin's camps reported seeing women in prison still dressed in the tattered remnants of their luxurious evening dresses. Apparently, like so many Cinderellas, they did not even make it home before their world disappeared in a flash.

The corruption peaked with the general secretary himself. On some levels Stalin always lived modestly. His wife, until her suicide in 1932, rode the streetcar to the industrial academy where she was a student. Over the years Stalin's wardrobe consisted mainly of old tunics and pants topped by his signature greatcoat and cap that dated from the civil war. Yet no tsar ever lived better. As historian Nikolai Tolstoy observed, "There was no whim, however extravagant or eccentric, which the state budget could not be brought to indulge."[17] Stalin, his simple public image notwithstanding, enjoyed several magnificent estates, a fleet of luxury cars, and many other luxuries. His more private pleasures included viewing pornographic movies seized from the Nazis during World War II. When Stalin left the Kremlin en route to one of his nearby country homes, he traveled in a heavily armed convoy along wide avenues specially built to ensure a safe trip.

All of this actually was the lesser part of the corruption, for as historian Roy Medvedev and others have reported, party leaders could and did get away with kidnapping, rape, and murder.[18] It is with good reason that Stalin felt the need to assert that "equality has nothing in common with Marxian socialism."

Whatever the merits of that statement, it is reasonable to conclude that in its uncontrollable power and the moral and material corruption that accompanied it, the Communist Party of the Soviet Union (CPSU) had much in common with its presumed ideological opposite, the National Socialist (Nazi) Party of Germany. Corruption, it would appear, knows no ideology.

THE GREAT TERROR

In one regard the CPSU stood alone. Between 1936 and 1938 it became simultaneously both an agent and a victim of what is referred to as the "great purge" or, more aptly, the "great terror." Prior to the mid-1930s, terror—a term that in the Soviet context refers to the use of massive, indiscriminant violence—clearly was the main force behind Stalin's revolution from above. As such, terror was the core of that revolution, the force that held its various component parts—in industry, agriculture, culture, and so on—together. Then something happened deep inside that plasmatic, unstable core. It exploded, becoming a raging super-nova, expanding in all directions seemingly at the speed of light, enveloping everything in sight as it reached the four corners of the vast Soviet universe that had given it life. By the time the terror ran its course, large parts of Soviet society were seared beyond recognition; others, most tellingly the party's Leninist old guard and much of Stalin's new guard, were vaporized almost entirely. New orders of society were created out of the cataclysm as it tore old ones apart. The great terror eventually ended, but it left large, sometimes enormous remnants, including the burgeoning Soviet system of labor camps, a black hole into which millions continued to disappear until the 1950s. Other elements, including the most fortunate members of the Brezhnev–Andropov generation of party cadres, survived beyond the 1950s to become the managers and later the masters of the new society forged in the crucible of Stalin's great terror.

"Why? What for?" were the questions of the era, scratched into innumerable prison walls and transport vehicles by uncomprehending victims. It is difficult to provide definitive answers. There are only partial and at times speculative responses to those simple, forlorn inquiries that became the epitaph for so many.

Terror was nothing new to Bolshevism; it was built into the new Soviet order from the start. Lenin used terror to destroy opponents of the regime and as a means of mass coercion, especially against the peasantry during the civil war. Between 1917 and 1924 the Soviet regime relied heavily on terror, and most Bolsheviks accepted it as a legitimate political weapon. Equally important, Lenin also institutionalized terror in the form of the secret police. What changed under Stalin was the scope of the task at hand and, correspondingly, the scale of the terror. When the party went beyond fighting for power to re-casting society in a new socialist mold, terror became not only a logical but a primary tool in the face of an overwhelmingly reluctant population. Because the job of recasting an entire society was so much more massive than simply beating back enemies, the use of terror was exponentially greater after 1929 than in Lenin's day. In fact, the terror employed in the collectivization drive was so dreadful that many Bolsheviks recoiled from it once collectivization and the great construction projects of the First Five-Year Plan were completed. As for party purges, they were a periodic occurrence, the latest round hav-ing led to the expulsion of 450,000 people during 1932–1933. Still, by 1933 the general hope was that the worst, in every sense, was over. Instead, a far greater terror and purge lurked just ahead.

The Bolshevik legacy provided the basic ingredients for the great terror. The essential catalyst, however, was the nature of the man in power, for just as there would not have been a Bolshevik Revolution without Lenin, there would not have been a great terror without Stalin. Stalin, an incessant plotter himself, seems to have been convinced of innumerable plots against him, conspiracies which in his mind could best be quashed by striking first, not just against the individuals involved, but against entire categories of people that might produce opponents of his regime in the future. He worried that his defeated opponents, from Bukharin and Rykov to Zinoviev and Kamenev to the exiled Trotsky, might somehow get together to attempt a return to power. Stalin's fears were reinforced because during the early and mid-1930s he did not yet have absolute power. To be sure, Stalin was the dominant figure on the Politburo, a body composed entirely of his supporters, but his power was not total. The Politburo as a collective body still remained something of a force in Soviet politics, and on rare occasions a member stood up to Stalin. This seems to have been true of Sergo Ordzhonikidze, a fellow Georgian and long-time colleague who headed the commissariat of heavy industry, and possibly of Leningrad party boss Sergei Kirov. During the mid-1930s Ordzhonikidze on several occasions attempted to protect economic managers he needed to run important industries from repressive policies ordered by Stalin. He also tried to protect old cronies from Georgia who had run afoul of the general secretary. In addition, Kirov disagreed with Stalin on several occasions, including in February 1934, just after the Seventeenth Party Congress, when he refused Stalin's proposal that he leave his Leningrad post and move to Moscow. It is possible that Stalin did not favor the more moderate economic policies of the Second Five-Year Plan. He also seems to have been disturbed by certain events at the Seventeenth Party Congress, his hand-picked "Congress of Victors," which took place during January–February 1934. Much of what happened behind the scenes cannot be documented from official records of the congress. Yet there is evidence of a widespread desire among party leaders for consolidation and moderation, at least regarding the industrialization drive. Thus Kirov, an excellent orator and, unlike Stalin, an ethnic Russian, was well received when he told his fellow delegates, "The main difficulties are already behind us." There are also reports that Kirov received the greatest number of votes in the balloting for the Central Committee, while Stalin received the least. (All candidates were elected, as there was only one candidate for each seat, and the official congress records, probably falsified, report only a handful of the alleged 270 anti-Stalin votes.) Several memoirs also refer to an incipient plan to replace Stalin with Kirov as general secretary, although if such a plan did exist Kirov did not encourage it. Indeed, recent research strongly indicates that, as historian Oleg Khlevniuk has put it, Kirov when all was said and done was very much "Stalin's man."[19] What is clear among all these shadows is that the outlook of the remaining members of the Bolshevik old guard who remembered Lenin, combined with the general sentiment among many of Stalin's own loyalists that the time had come to moderate the pace and the harshness of the revolution from above, would deny Stalin the absolute power he craved.

All that said, the reasons for launching the great terror went deeper. Stalin did not distinguish between his personal power and security on the one hand and the security of the Soviet state and the fate of the Bolshevik revolution on the other, and there were good reasons to believe that tens of millions of people would welcome a change of regime. After all, the revolution from above had produced enormous social dislocation and widespread discontent, especially in the countryside. Beyond these understandable concerns, Stalin, despite his victories over his opponents, detected "anti-Soviet elements" and activities everywhere. Over time party bureaucrats up and down the chain of command had established their own networks and carved out small fiefdoms, which allowed them to strengthen their political positions and also meet their obligations to the regime. To Stalin this constituted an ominous "independence from the Central Committee." There were more than 1 million former party members, expelled during the 1920s and 1930s, scattered across the country. That they were powerless, and in many cases actually supported and worked for the regime, did not matter to Stalin; it was intolerable that they existed at all. All of this, at least to the hyper-suspicious and insecure Stalin, was dangerous and unacceptable, at once a threat to his power and to the revolution he was using that power to further. Nor was Stalin alone in his paranoid dread that there were, as he complained in 1937, "enemies in the army, in the staff, even in the Kremlin." These fears were shared and encouraged by key members of his inner circle such as Molotov, Kaganovich, and Kliment Voroshilov, a crony since the civil war days. Terror had been used to make the revolution and then to establish the fundamental institutions of the Soviet Union. Now, Stalin seems to have reasoned, it would be used again against a new set of targets to destroy the remaining opponents of his regime and obstacles to building his version of socialism, and thereby to forever secure the achievements of Bolshevism.

If the Bolshevik legacy and Stalin's personal agenda provide some explanation for the impetus behind the great terror, they do not explain how such a horror could engulf an entire society. The great terror required the active participation of hundreds of thousands of people. There were, to be sure, many thugs and killers in Soviet Russia, and Stalin made good use of them, but criminals alone could not provide enough manpower to staff the gigantic apparatus that ran the terror. That required a multitude of people who in normal times would have been quite content to go about their customary business. But the 1930s in Soviet Russia were not normal times. Society had been torn apart by relentless and extraordinary violence that began with World War I and ran through the 1917 revolutions, the civil war, collectivization, and the industrialization drive. People by the millions were torn from their traditional social moorings and morality. And they were bombarded by a new morality—the revolutionary morality of Bolshevism—that justified extreme measures for the sake of the revolution. These otherwise ordinary people therefore were available to serve as informers, police, administrators, guards, and executioners in the terror apparatus, much as they had been during collectivization. Some did so because they believed they were building a modern socialist Russia, as Stalin may well have believed himself. Others participated simply to better their lives and advance their careers. And, of course, many participated out of fear, making victims of others lest they become victims themselves.

In 1934 Stalin began to prepare his new campaign, this time against many of the very people who had brought him to power and carried out the revolution from above. The main goal, especially when the new terror and purge peaked during 1937 and 1938, was vast: to eliminate any individual or group either hostile or in any way *potentially* hostile to himself and his closest collaborators. The secret police, since 1934 part of the NKVD, was reorganized and new personnel brought in. A shadowy but vital body, the Special Section of the Central Committee, became more active. Headed by A.N. Poskrebyshev, Stalin's personal secretary, the Special Section functioned as Stalin's private secretariat: his personal eyes and ears that spied on all party and state agencies, including the NKVD, and carried out some of his most secret projects. Finally, in December 1934, the Soviet Union was shocked to hear that its beloved Comrade Kirov had been assassinated. Stalin calmed a nervous nation by intervening directly in the investigation, a prudent step because some evidence published since his death, including remarks by Nikita Khrushchev, suggests that Stalin gave the order to have Kirov eliminated. Even if that is not the case, and the evidence is not conclusive, Stalin without a doubt made the most of the opportunity that murder created.

A wave of hysteria swept the country as the press filled with stories of legions of anti-Communists, foreign agents, disloyal Communists, unscrupulous Trotskyists, and similar menaces. About 40,000 alleged plotters were arrested in Leningrad alone, while thousands of "Japanese spies" were uncovered in eastern parts of the country. Several hundred thousand people were deported to the Gulag. Draconian new laws made children over twelve liable to capital punishment and gave almost unlimited scope to the crime of counterrevolution. Zinoviev and Kamenev were arrested (again), tried, and convicted of "moral responsibility" for Kirov's murder. Stalin may also have been involved in the deaths of two important Bolsheviks who opposed further purges: V.V. Kuibyshev, a Politburo member who died in 1935, and Maxim Gorky, the famed writer and friend of Lenin, who died in June 1936. A tidal wave of denunciations, arrests, deportations, and executions was building.

Such was the prelude. The great terror became a full-fledged public spectacle with the first of the famous show trials of leading Bolsheviks. Between August 1936 and March 1938, almost every prominent member of the surviving Bolshevik old guard went on trial for plotting against Lenin and/or Stalin. To believe such charges one would have to accept the contention that virtually every member of the Leninist leadership, excepting, of course, Stalin, aligned himself with foreign capitalists, counterrevolutionaries, and other enemies of the workers' state. The arch-villain in this gallery of Bolshevik rogues was Trotsky, whose evil web at once allegedly ensnared Hitler, the emperor of Japan, Zinoviev, Kamenev, and Bukharin, to name but a few, quite a tribute to a man who proved incapable of building a political organization in the 1920s when it really counted. Thus Andrei Vyshinsky, the prosecutor at these trials, was able to link, in one sentence, the "Rightists, Trotskyists, Mensheviks, Socialist Revolutionaries, bourgeois nationalists, and so on and so forth." The language of the trials reflected the quality of the charges and the supporting evidence. The accused, who included the pride of the party and Lenin's Politburo, were a "foul-smelling heap of human garbage," the "scum and filth of the past," "hateful traitors" who "must be shot like mad dogs." They were spared nothing; they were even forced to join the cheerleading against themselves. Hence Zinoviev's remarkable political odyssey: "My defective Bolshevism became transformed into anti-Bolshevism and through Trotskyism I arrived at fascism." This type of statement typified the most remarkable fact about the trials: every single man in the dock confessed to his crimes.

There were three show trials. In August 1936, Zinoviev and Kamenev were tried with fourteen men of lesser rank. All were executed. In January

1937, seventeen former supporters of Trotsky, all of whom had repented and joined with Stalin after Trotsky's defeat, took their turn in the dock. Thirteen were executed; the rest disappeared into the camps. The grand finale in March 1938 featured Bukharin, Rykov, and Nikolai Krestinsky, all former members of Lenin's Politburo, as well as Henrik Yagoda, the former head of the NKVD, and seventeen others of varying stature. All but three were shot; the survivors vanished forever into the camps. In between these extravaganzas, Stalin's police found time to secretly arrest, torture, and execute the cream of his military establishment for treason and spying, including the civil war hero and chief of the general staff, Mikhail Tukhachevsky.

The linchpin of the Moscow trials was the confession. The Bolshevik luminaries in the dock described, often in excruciating detail, a host of crimes ranging from sabotage to murder to treason in which they supposedly participated. Only one, Nikolai Krestinsky, dared to retract his confession in open court, an error he quickly corrected after an additional night with the NKVD. One can understand why Stalin wanted confessions since there was no other evidence of any kind to back up the charges. Also, by getting his once-mighty victims to confess and demean themselves, Stalin totally discredited not only them, but any version of the "truth" other than his own. The confessions gave the trials surprising credibility, not just in the Soviet Union, where the people were under constant bombardment from the state-controlled media, but in the West, where various sorts of Marxists and other left-leaning intellectuals, who had access to reliable information that belied the entire spectacle, chose to accept what they heard from Vyshinsky rather than to think for themselves and know better.

One of the nagging questions about the show trials is why so many hardened revolutionaries who had once stood up to the mighty tsarist empire broke like eggs and spilled out their fabricated confessions to Stalin. A variety of factors were involved. Some veteran Bolsheviks had lived their lives only to serve the revolution and the Communist Party, and it was possible to convince them to render the party one more service, even in their disgrace. Many forlornly hoped to save their wives and children if they cooperated. Some, like Bukharin, apparently hoped that by confessing in general terms, while at the same time denying many of the key details of the charges against them, they could obliquely make the point that the charges themselves were false. If all else failed, confessions were obtained from stubborn defendants through the use of relentless and sophisticated torture.

As bad as the show trials were, they were only the smallest tip of an iceberg the size of the Soviet Union itself. The great purge decimated the nation's elites. No group suffered worse than the Communist Party, particularly its old guard. Aside from Stalin, five members of Lenin's April 1917 Central Committee survived into the 1930s. Stalin killed them all. Seventeen of Stalin's colleagues who served on the Central Committee elected in September 1917, the Central Committee that made the Bolshevik Revolution, lived into the 1930s. None survived Stalin's terror. Stalin's own supporters, the people who had given him victory in 1929, did not fare much better. The purges claimed 70 percent of his hand-picked Central Committee at the "Congress of Victors" and 1,108 of the 1,966 delegates at large. They swept through the middle and lower ranks of the party several times, sometimes wiping out the leadership of a locality three or four times. Estimates of Communist Party deaths range from 200,000 to a million, a count that probably makes Stalin the greatest killer of Communists in history. (His only rival for that title is fellow Communist dictator Mao Zedong of China.) Whatever the exact total, the party was unable to recruit members fast enough to make up its losses.

The armed forces were ravaged because Stalin feared that the Soviet military leadership, which was critical of the purges, might unite and overthrow him. Three out of 5 marshals, 14 out of 16 top army commanders, all 8 admirals, and 131 out of 199 divisional commanders perished. Half of the country's military officers—more than 35,000 men—were imprisoned or shot. Not even the NKVD itself was safe. It was purged several times. Yagoda, its chief since 1934, lasted until 1936. His successor was Nikolai Yezhov, a criminal psychopath by any reasonable standards. He ran the purge during its peak years, so that the entire period came to be called the *Yezhovshchina*. Yezhov was eliminated in 1938 in favor of Lavrenty Beria. Down the rat hole also poured the Soviet Union's artists and writers, people like Boris Pilnyak, Isaac Babel, Yuri Olesha, Osip Mandelshtam, Vsevolod Meyerhold, and uncounted others.

And yet even this represents merely the headlines of a story millions of lives long. Stalin's drive for absolute power and security meant that the entire nation, not merely the party or a particular social class, like the peasantry, had to be terrorized into complete submission. In the NKVD, he had available for this purpose the world's largest secret police organization. By the mid-1930s, fed by the collectivization and industrialization campaigns, the NKVD had grown into a behemoth. It not only controlled the secret police, but ran prisons, managed and guarded the labor camps, controlled the regular police, guarded the borders, and had its agents planted virtually everywhere people gathered— from factories, collective farms, and railroad stations to libraries, theaters, apartment houses, and parks—to spy on and terrorize a nation of 150 million people. It had its own military units equipped with heavy artillery and tanks. The NKVD's roster of employees numbered in the hundreds of thousands. Its ubiquitous network of informers swelled that number even further so that its administrative expenses may have totaled two-thirds of the amount spent by all the other branches of the state apparatus put together.

The great terror hit its peak between mid-1937 and the end of 1938. The timing seems to be related to the cloud of war that was gathering in Europe because of the growing power and menacing posture of Nazi Germany. At least that is the testimony of Molotov, at the time the Soviet prime minister and probably Stalin's closest aide, who four decades later insisted that "1937 was necessary. . . . We were driven in 1937 by the consideration that in the time of war we would not have a fifth column." Therefore, on July 2, 1937, the Politburo passed a resolution called "Concerning Anti-Soviet Elements." Four weeks later the NKVD dutifully responded with its notorious Order No. 00447, authorizing the arrests of a long list of "contingents" including former kulaks, members of any opposition parties, former tsarist officials, "terrorists," "spies," and anyone deemed "socially dangerous." The order mandated quotas for every province, territory, and republic, with those arrested to be divided into two categories: those to be shot and those to be sent to the camps for eight to ten years. Local officials were permitted to show their devotion to the cause by requesting additional quotas, something many of them made sure to do lest they themselves end up on one of the arrest lists because of questionable loyalty. The campaign, originally scheduled to run a total of four months, lasted four times that long. Nobody knows how many people were arrested and executed during this period of terror extraordinary even by Stalinist standards. The official records currently available suggest that during 1937–1938 the NVKD arrested 1.6 million people and executed about 700,000, but these figures, as historian Oleg Khlevniuk has pointed out, reflect only partial access to NKVD records and thus constitute only "the minimal starting point" regarding an accurate and complete count of the victims. Even at this starting point, it means that in the Soviet Union 1,500 people *per day* were executed between August 1937 and November 1938. Since additional hundreds of thousands of people in prisons and labor camps died from maltreatment and because some executions were not recorded on accessible lists, a reasonable but quite possibly incomplete estimate of deaths at NKVD hands during 1937–1938 is 1 to 1.2 million. Meanwhile, aside from the NKVD arrest and execution campaign, between 1937 and 1940 Soviet courts convicted more than 7 million people of various offenses.[20]

Between 1936 and 1938 nobody in the Soviet Union could ever feel safe. The nights were the worst, since the NKVD preferred to operate in the shadows, but the days were not much better. Solzhenitsyn has chronicled what Soviet citizens had to anticipate as they tried to go about their daily lives:

> They take you aside in a factory corridor . . . and you are arrested. They take you from a military hospital with a temperature of 102. . . . They take you right off the operating table. . . . In the Gastronome—the fancy food store—

you are invited to the special-order department and arrested there. You are arrested by a religious pilgrim whom you have put up for the night "for the sake of Christ." You are arrested by the meterman. . . . You are arrested by a bicyclist who has run into you on the street, by a railway conductor, a taxi driver, a savings bank teller, the manager of a movie theater.[21]

As with the show trials, there were no objective standards of truth, no standards for guilt or innocence. Most people never knew why they were arrested or, almost as frightening, why their neighbors were arrested and they were not. While still free, people denounced each other without rhyme or reason in order to demonstrate their loyalty.

Once arrested and put through the NKVD's mill, people confessed to anything and denounced anyone in a desperate attempt to win a small measure of mercy; it is not difficult to understand why. Bodies and spirits were damaged and broken beyond repair. The system worked well enough to bring most of the main figures to trial and get innumerable others involved in other cases to "confess" to virtually anything the human imagination could dream up. Few could resist the notorious "conveyor," a series of continuous interrogations under bright lights that often lasted for several days or, if necessary, several weeks. Even more devastating was continuous interrogation combined with sleep deprivation that often went on for many months. Men were made to stand for ten or twenty hours as their legs swelled up, or until they collapsed, or to sit on hot pipes until their skin was burned. Others were tied under a strip of wood that was then pounded with an axe until the victim's internal organs were destroyed. Additional methods included beatings with rubber truncheons and empty bottles, the breaking of limbs, which were then left unset, and kicking a person's teeth out. If all this failed, and it rarely did, a man's family could be threatened. One witness recorded how women and girls were "beaten to a pulp. . . . Their hair was torn from their scalps, their fingers broken, their toes crushed, their teeth knocked in, temples crushed, skin broken open." Often the beatings destroyed their internal organs. They might also be raped. A prisoner's child could be killed outright. No wonder that one expert interrogator reportedly could brag that "If Karl Marx himself fell into my hands, he'd confess to spying for Bismarck."

Most of those arrested wound up in Stalin's labor camps. There they entered a turbulent world increasingly disorganized by the arrests of many camp officials, mass executions, and rising mortality rates from overwork and generally deteriorating conditions. The terror literally deformed Soviet society. Since the great majority of purge victims were males, by the 1950s in the age groups most affected by the great terror there were less than four males for every six women, a ratio comparable to the age groups most affected by World War II.

The great terror roared ahead until the end of 1938. By then the upward spiral was becoming dangerous even for Stalin. The spreading net of denunciations, as each prisoner had to denounce someone, if not several people, threatened to pull in so many people that Soviet society might have broken down altogether. The economy was badly disrupted as party cadres, technicians, planners, and people with an endless variety of essential skills were arrested. Economic growth plummeted to a small fraction of what it had been between 1934 and 1936. The economic disruption reached even into the Gulag, which lost many important administrators to the terror, among them the director of the Dalstroi. Stalin therefore ended the slaughter in his typical way: he blamed others for it. The Politburo conveniently resolved that under Yezhov the NKVD had been guilty of "gross inadequacies and distortions." Yezhov therefore was replaced in December 1938 by Beria, who proceeded to purge the organization. Yezhov himself was arrested in April 1939 and shot in February 1940. Stalin thus both deflected the blame for the terror from himself and preempted the possibility that the secret police could threaten him. He could not, at least initially, do much for the economy: it remained paralyzed from the effects of the great terror until late 1940. Nor did terror as a system of managing society come to an end. The newly cleansed NKVD remained in place. Under Beria it simply functioned in a more systematic manner, arresting enough people to keep the population under control rather than totally disrupting all life with haphazard arrests. The camps also remained; they were, among other things, an essential part of the state's economic policy. Stalinist terror, in fact, could still reach around the world. In August 1940 an NKVD agent in Mexico murdered Trotsky as the exiled revolutionary labored to complete his biography of Stalin. Although the great terror was over, what one historian has appropriately called the "lesser terror" lasted until Stalin's death in 1953.[22]

THE REVOLUTION FROM ABOVE, THE PARTY, AND SOVIET SOCIETY

The end of the great terror marked the consolidation of Stalin's virtually absolute power. He had not only eliminated all real, potential, or imagined personal rivals, but also had subordinated the party to his personal dictatorship. After 1938, the party was mainly a transmitter for enforcing Stalin's personal will. Much like the nobility under Ivan the Terrible or Peter the Great, the party under Stalin was a caste without any rights; it rendered service to the sovereign in return for privileges. Party officials continued to control the other major Soviet bureaucracies—the army, the secret police, and the state bureaucracy—but it was Stalin rather than the Politburo or Central Committee as a whole who decided important policy.

The party served Stalin in another way. It provided his personal dictator-ship with revolutionary legitimacy. Yet even here the party and the memory of Lenin and Marx were superseded by what amounted to a cult dedicated to the glorification of Stalin. He was pictured as the world's greatest genius, a man whose expertise and ability in every area exceeded anyone else's. Anyone in the Soviet Union who accomplished anything—the pilot who set a speed record, the scientist who discovered something, the production team that set an output record—gave credit to Stalin for inspiring the accomplish-ment. Stalin's name and likeness were everywhere. Two dozen cities began the list of places named after him. Coins bore his profile, songs glorified his name, the national anthem paid him tribute. His list of titles (Great Leader of the Soviet People, Great Helmsman, Leader of the World Proletariat, etc.) seemed to go on forever. A statue on top of Mt. Elbrus summed things up by proclaiming "On the highest peak in Europe we have erected the statue of the greatest man of all time." In effect, Stalin legitimized his rule by turning himself into a secular deity. (A typical song gushed that "We give Thee our thanks for the sun Thou hast lit.") His cult was a true measure of the extent to which Stalin, rather than the party, ruled in the Soviet Union. The Soviet people had been bent to Stalin's will.

Aside from the incalculable suffering it caused, the great terror also did other damage. It deprived the economy of thousands of invaluable special-ists and rendered those who remained free unable to make decisions for fear of the consequences, which contributed significantly to the stagnation that marked the period from 1937 to 1940. It also left the Soviet military virtually bereft of experienced senior officers, which helped the Germans come close to victory on the eastern front during 1941–1942. Finally, the great terror also marked a revolution in the composition of the country's leadership. The Bolshevik old guard, including many loyal Stalinists, was liquidated, as were several layers of cadres that originated after 1924. Some of Stalin's original cronies did survive, the most important being Molotov and Kaganovich, as well as some lesser lights like Mikoyan and Voroshilov. Of them, only Molo-tov, who under Stalin served as prime minister and foreign minister, had any stature at all when Lenin ran the party. Around them were the new men who earned their spurs during the 1930s: Andrei Zhdanov, Kirov's replacement in Leningrad; Lavrenty Beria, like Stalin a Georgian, who at various points in his notorious career headed the NKVD, managed the deportations to Siberia of several minority peoples during World War II, and ran the Soviet Union's atomic bomb project after the war; Georgy Malenkov, an important member of the Secretariat and Stalin's heir apparent during the dictator's last years; and Nikita Khrushchev, an efficient satrap in the Ukraine and in Moscow, and Stalin's eventual successor. Others who rose from obscurity as the killing opened up opportunities were Georgy Zhukov, Soviet Russia's greatest general in World War II, and, in the next generation, Leonid Brezhnev and Alexei Kosygin, the duo who succeeded Khrushchev.

The social revolution that accompanied the purges went far deeper than the party's upper ranks. Stalin's scorched-earth purging finished the job of decimating the Westernized layers of Russian society, a process that had begun with the Bolshevik Revolution and accelerated during the civil war and Stalin's revolution from above. They were replaced by people mostly of peasant origin, largely untouched by Western culture. The ascendancy of these new men—tough, ruthless, either poorly educated or possessing a narrow technical education, and completely loyal to the tyrant who had raised them up—meant that Russia was turning away from Westernization and reverting to many of its earlier, homegrown ways. When one adds to this Stalin's brutal treatment of his servitors, the terror of the 1930s represents a critical point in what economist Alec Nove called the "revival of . . . the Asian-despotic element in the Russian tradition,"[23] the tradition of Ivan the Terrible and Peter the Great.

Stalin's new men were far better suited to the new (or old) environment than their predecessors. The latter, better educated and more cosmopolitan, were too independent. Although many supported Stalin quite enthusiastically, they recoiled from his worst excesses, as evidenced by the events of 1934. Stalin's new men had no such qualms. They and many thousands below them were in fact the beneficiaries of the purges, which for them provided the route to power and privilege. They therefore were loyal to the system. Thus the purges, while doing so much damage to the Soviet Union, provided Stalin and his system with the base of support necessary to survive the great strains and challenges that lay ahead in World War II and the postwar period.

STALINIST TOTALITARIANISM

Out of the fire and brimstone of the Stalin's revolution from above emerged a new phenomenon: a totalitarian society. Totalitarianism was not possible prior to the technological advances of the twentieth century, which created new and unprecedented means for controlling the lives of millions of people. In a totalitarian society, the party-dominated state, or party-state, is the paramount force. It uses modern technology to control not only the armed forces and all operational weaponry, but all means of communication and every institution of society's economic, intellectual, cultural, and political life. All human activity and every citizen are considered to be at the service of the party-state. Stalin's Russia was not a perfect totalitarian society, but it came closer than any other contemporary competitor (e.g., Nazi Germany or Fascist Italy) and was more perfectly totalitarian than it was anything else (e.g., socialist). Society was molded by the Soviet party-state with its numerous bureaucratic tentacles, whose ultimate weapon of control was terror carried out by the secret police. No independent institutions were permitted to exist, nor was the party-state limited by the rule of law. Not just political life, but economic, social, and cultural activities that elsewhere were private matters were controlled by the pervasive bureaucracy, which also controlled all newspapers, magazines, book publishers, radio stations, and other information outlets. Access to jobs, education, housing, vacations, medical care, and much more depended on decisions made by bureaucrats of the party-state.

There was simply no way for the average citizen to effectively oppose the multiple levels of control the party-state possessed. There were, of course, some limits to that control, if for no other reason than that 1930s communications and transportation technology—especially in the vastness of the Soviet Union, which in many technological areas lagged behind the times—could hardly keep tabs on all the activities of an entire society. This was true in factories and on construction sites, where in the 1930s workers were in demand and managers were willing to bend all sorts of rules to attract additional workers or keep those they had. Workers were prepared to change jobs if, for example, they could raise their wages by being placed in a higher skill category or find better housing or working conditions. Thus in 1930 the average Soviet factory worker found a new job every eight months. Even though the rate of labor turnover decreased during the Second Five-Year Plan (1933–1937), in its last year almost a third of all workers took a new position every three months. On the collective farms, peasants worked their private plots and sold the surpluses from that work outside state-controlled networks. And inevitably, as in any system, there was corruption as local officials and managers—either to do their jobs under conditions of extreme scarcity or for personal gain—relied on ties of friendship, kinship, or simple mutual need to get around party-state controls. Still, these were tiny cracks and crevices in a huge block. The flaws and foibles in the Stalinist totalitarian system did not change its basic nature or the fundamental reality of the party-state's domination of society.

It was therefore a bitter irony that in 1936, as the great terror that represented Soviet totalitarianism at its most extreme was gathering steam, the Soviet Union received a new constitution that proclaimed socialism, the crucial stage just before communism, had been achieved. The "Stalin Constitution," put forward as the world's most democratic, contained an extensive list of individual rights and gave the Soviet Union an elaborate federal structure that seemed to protect the various minority nationalities. It provided for a bicameral legislature called the Supreme Soviet, elected by direct suffrage. The Supreme Soviet was divided into a Soviet of the Union, elected by the population at large, and a Soviet of Nationalities, elected by the different nationalities according to their administrative status (i.e., each "union republic" selected twenty-five deputies, while lesser national administrative units had correspondingly lower representation). There were now eleven union republics, ranging from the Russian SSR, the most populous, to the diminutive Kyrgyz SSR. The fundamental point, however, is that the constitution provided no legal mechanism to protect all these rights and contained several crucial disclaimers that rendered them all so much window dressing. Thus, notwithstanding the enormous difference in status between the population at large and the party elite, all Soviet citizens shared the same position of being essentially powerless vis-à-vis the totalitarian party-state.

THE INNER CIRCLE

One thing the great terror affected in an important way but did not fundamentally change was Stalin's personal system of rule. From his first days in power Stalin governed through a small group of about twenty cronies and collaborators he had gathered around him. The original group included Molotov, Kaganovich, Voroshilov, Ordzhonikidze, Mikoyan, and others of lesser rank, although over time some faces changed. For example, for several years during the 1930s, until his fall in 1938, Nikolai Yezhov belonged to the group. In 1937 Ordzhonikidze departed via suicide when tension between himself and Stalin over the great terror became unbearable. In 1938, having demonstrated in Georgia his unmatched ability to purge and murder, Lavrenty Beria was called to Moscow and inducted into Stalin's inner circle. These Soviet bosses lived in close proximity to Stalin and each other, often in the Kremlin; they socialized, relaxed in country homes, and vacationed with each other and their respective families; they were connected by long-standing friendships and often by ties of marriage. At the same time, they were also deeply divided and pitted against each other by jealousies, suspicions, and rivalries. Controlling and manipulating it all was Stalin. He doled out material rewards such as lavish apartments, fancy cars, and money, and skillfully encouraged the personal divisions that made his top lieutenants rivals and hence more dependent on him. With the onset of the great terror, Stalin added the element of permanent insecurity to life in the inner circle. Henceforth, in addition to providing material favors, he imprisoned a wife or had a brother shot to keep his magnates in line, or simply destroyed one of them according to his political agenda or personal whim. Stalin's top lieutenants maintained their positions through total loyalty and constant genuflection, although from the mid-1930s on not even that was enough to guarantee survival. The center of power of the regime that supposedly was building the world's first communist society was a patrimonial preserve with characteristics of a feuding Caucasian mountain clan, scheming Mafia family, and conspiratorial royal court. It stayed that way as long as Stalin lived.

STALINISM IN HISTORICAL CONTEXT

Stalinism as a social system was a historically unprecedented combination of state-imposed social change, state terror against the population as a whole, and individual tyrannical rule. Historian Robert C. Tucker has suggested three major forces that converged to produce the political, economic, and social phenomenon known as Stalinism: the legacy of traditional Russia, the legacy of Bolshevism, and what Tucker calls the "mind and personality of Stalin."[24]

Traditional Russia left a legacy laced with heavy burdens. Backwardness, poverty, and outside threats had produced the old Russian autocracy, a regime that mobilized the nation's resources in its struggle to survive. That state developed a tradition of "revolution from above," a process of mobilization and change imposed regardless of the cost or resistance involved. Its leading practitioners were Ivan the Terrible, who destroyed the old nobility and secured the autocracy; Peter the Great, Russia's first industrializer; and Alexander II, the "Tsar-Liberator"—admittedly far more benign in both his methods and policies than his two predecessors—who abolished serfdom. After 1917 Soviet commissars faced many of the same problems that had confronted the tsars, and the old tradition of revolution from above, an idea that intrigued Russian revolutionaries from Pestel to Tkachev to Lenin, was a natural model for Stalin. The major difference between Stalin and the tsars is that Stalin had far more power at his disposal and a much more radical vision for change. Like Ivan, only more thoroughly, Stalin secured autocratic rule. Like Peter, but more comprehensively, Stalin promoted industrialization, using force as his major tool, and imposed state service on all Russians without any compensatory rights. Like Alexander II, Stalin revolutionized Russian agriculture, but whereas Alexander abolished serfdom, Stalin in effect restored it. Stalin also turned to many other relics from the past—the use of ranks in civilian and military life and internal passports, for example—not because of nostalgia, but because old cultural habits were not easily shed and old methods seemed applicable to problems and conditions that themselves were not entirely new.

Stalin's revolution from above was far more dynamic and comprehensive than anything the tsars ever attempted. This in large part was due to the second wellspring from which Stalinism drew—its Marxist/Bolshevik heritage. Russia's reforming tsars had only wanted to make certain changes, albeit sometimes very large ones, in order to keep the basic Russian system intact.

Stalin, drawing from the legacy of Marx and Lenin, wanted to overhaul society completely. This all-encompassing goal was reinforced by Bolshevik morality, which justified any measure or use of force so long as what was being done served the Revolution. From Bolshevism also came the idea of a centralized, dictatorial party, which both contributed to the establishment of a one-man dictatorship and was invaluable in the industrialization drive. The general thrust of Bolshevik ideology and the experience of War Communism created a constituency within the party receptive to the measures used during collectivization and the First Five-Year Plan.

Collectivization and the industrialization drive had roots in both tsarist history and Bolshevik ideology, as did the overall concept of revolution from above. The purges and use of terror also had both old Russian and Leninist pedigrees. However, it was because of Stalin personally that these policies took the shape they did and were pushed as far as they were. As political scientist Stephen Cohen has put it, Stalinism was "excess, extraordinary extremism"[25] in every respect, so much so that in certain ways, at least after 1934 and the onset of the great terror, it was qualitatively different from its antecedents. Unlike the other party leaders who had been Lenin's lieutenants, Stalin truly knew no limits. That is one reason he had to eliminate them before completing his revolution from above. Stalin's personality was a key force in forging a social system built on unrelenting terror, and not until that personality was eliminated with his death in 1953 could the system undergo significant change.

Beyond the influence of traditional Russia, Bolshevism, and Stalin himself, Stalinism in an important sense was also a product of circumstance. Circumstance in this case was both the consequences that flowed from a dictatorial elite's attempt in the twentieth century to overhaul a society according to a preconceived socialist vision and the relative backwardness of that society. Stalin's revolution from above, particularly the state's takeover of the entire Russian economy, was only possible with twentieth-century technology. The extent of this takeover was unprecedented in Russian history and a critical factor in changing the pre-twentieth-century autocratic state into a twentieth-century totalitarian one. This is precisely what Bukharin feared would happen and why he opposed first Trotsky and then Stalin during the 1920s. Given the enormous job the state had undertaken and the modern technological tools at its disposal, a powerful totalitarian thrust would have existed no matter who was leading it. Also, the level of what could be imposed on the country was heightened by the particular conditions existing in the Soviet Union during the 1930s. The country's economic backwardness and the fever pitch of building that resulted from trying to overcome it created an atmosphere in which brutality was accepted in the name of the god of progress. These in turn produced institutions (e.g., the Gulag) required to get the job done. To a certain extent they even produced Stalin, for the unsophisticated party cadres, drawn from Russia's uneducated population and locked in a battle with the people, naturally looked almost unquestioningly to their *Vozhd* for guidance, much as their even more ignorant forefathers had looked to their "little father," the tsar. In other words, both the background of the party rank and file and the circumstances in which they found themselves impelled them to accept the strong hand of an absolute authority or dictator. As political scientist Severyn Bialer has observed, by creating such a violent and all-encompassing upheaval in a backward society, Stalinism "created its own conditions," which distinguished it from what had come before.[26]

However, because the industrialization drive had achieved its basic goals and in the process had created an entire new elite of educated and sophisticated people, it became increasingly difficult to sustain certain aspects of the 1930s totalitarian system, and major changes became unavoidable. Stalin's very successes, in other words, meant that certain parts of the regime he built became obsolete, even while he lived and worked feverishly to preserve them.

NOTES

1. Robert V. Daniels, *The Conscience of the Revolution* (Cambridge, Mass.: Harvard University Press, 1965), p. 358.

2. Victor Kravchenko, *I Chose Justice* (New York: Scribner's, 1950), pp. 99–100.

3. Victor Serge, *Memoirs of a Revolutionary, 1901–1941*, translated by Peter Sedgwick (London: Oxford University Press, 1963), p. 247.

4. David J. Dallin and Boris I. Nicolaevsky, *Forced Labor in Soviet Russia* (New Haven: Yale University Press, 1947), pp. 42–43.

5. Fedor Belov, *The History of a Collective Farm* (New York: Praeger, 1955), pp. 13–14.

6. See Miron Dolot, *Execution By Hunger: The Hidden Holocaust* (New York: Norton, 1987).

7. Naum Jasny, *Soviet Industrialization, 1928–1952* (Chicago: University of Chicago Press, 1961), p. 9.

8. Alec Nove, *An Economic History of the USSR* (Middlesex, England: Penguin, 1969), p. 207.

9. These figures are only estimates. There are no precise numbers with regard to the Gulag and forced labor during these years, as many records were subsequently destroyed and others are incomplete or otherwise tainted. Several recent scholarly works have supplied updated statistics based on new research. The figures mentioned here are from Anne Applebaum, *Gulag: A History* (New York: Doubleday, 2003), pp. 580–581. I have also relied on Galina Mikhailovna Ivanova, *Labor Camp Socialism: The Gulag in the Soviet Totalitarian System* (Armonk, N.Y.: M.E. Sharpe, 2000)ꞏ Oleg V. Khlevniuk, *The History of the Gulag: From Collectivization to the C Terror* (New Haven: Yale University Press, 2004); and Paul R. Gregory aⁿ

Lazarev, eds., *The Economics of Forced Labor: The Soviet Gulag* (Stanford: Hoover Institution Press, 2003).

10. Dallin and Nicolaevsky, *Forced Labor in Soviet Russia*, pp. 37–38.

11. Aleksandr Solzhenitsyn, *The Gulag Archipelago Two* (New York: Harper and Row, 1975), pp. 210–211.

12. Oleg Khlevnyuk, "The Economy of the Gulag," in *Behind the Façade of Stalin's Command Economy: Evidence from the State and Party Archives,* edited by Paul R. Gregory (Stanford: Hoover Institution Press, 2001), p. 128. (This is the same Oleg Khlevniuk mentioned in note 8 as author of *The History of the Gulag.* The spelling here follows the transliteration used in the book in which "The Economy of the Gulag" appears.)

13. David R. Stone, *Hammer and Rifle: The Militarization of the Soviet Union, 1926–1933* (Lawrence: University of Kansas Press, 2000), p. 9. This section relies heavily on Stone's comprehensive monograph. See also Mark Harrison, "Providing for Defense," in Gregory, *Behind the Façade of Stalin's Command Economy*, pp. 81–110.

14. James H. Billington, *The Icon and the Axe* (New York: Vintage, 1970), pp. 532, 538.

15. Svetlana Alliluyeva, *Twenty Letters to a Friend*, translated by Priscilla Johnson McMullan (New York: Harper and Row, 1967), p. 27.

16. John R. Deane, *The Strange Alliance: The Story of Our Effort at Wartime Cooperation with Russia* (New York: Viking Press, 1947), p. 14.

17. Nikolai Tolstoy, *Stalin's Secret War*, translated by George Saunders (New York: Holt, Rinehart and Winston, 1981), p. 37.

18. Roy A. Medvedev, *Let History Judge*, translated by Colleen Taylor (New York: Vintage, 1971), p. 368.

19. Oleg V. Khlevniuk, *Master of the House: Stalin and His Inner Circle*, translated by Nora Seligman Favorov (New Haven and London: Yale University Press, 2009), p. 109. This discussion draws on Khlevniuk's latest findings.

20. See Khlevniuk, *The History of the Gulag*, pp. 165–167, 304–305. For more on the question of the statistics involving the Gulag see Robert Conquest, *The Great Terror: A Reassessment* (New York and Oxford: Oxford University Press, 1990), pp. 484–489, an updating of his magisterial 1968 book on the subject that has brilliantly withstood the test of time. Conquest further updated and revised his estimates in a review of Edwin Bacon's *The Gulag at War: Stalin's Forced Labour System in Light of the Archives* (London: Macmillan; New York: New York University Press, 1994), which appeared in the *Times Literary Supplement*, February 24, 1995, and in several subsequent commentaries. Bacon's superb book includes a comprehensive analysis of the conflicting assessments of the size of the Gulag and total arrests and executions during the Stalin era (see especially pp. 36–38). Among the many assessments Bacon considers are those of Olga Shatunovskaya, a member of the 1960 Central Committee commission that investigated the death of Sergei Kirov, and Nikolai V. Grashoven, the head of the Russian Ministry of Security commission for rehabilitation that did its work more than thirty years later. Comparable figures come from Dmitri Volkogonov, a former Soviet general who had unprecedented access to Soviet archives for his biographies of Stalin and Lenin. See his *Stalin: Triumph and Tragedy*, edited and translated by Harold Shukman (Rocklin, Calif.: Prima Publishing, 1992), p. 524. Most of the terror and Gulag statistics in this volume are based on the work of Conquest, Bacon, Khlevniuk, Anne Applebaum, Galina Ivanova, Steven Rosefielde,

and Michael Ellman. I have also relied on Stéphane Courtois et al., *The Black Book of Communism: Crimes, Terror, Repression*, translated by Jonathan Murphy and Mark Kramer, consulting editor Mark Kramer (Cambridge, Mass., and London: Harvard University Press, 1999), in particular the section by Nicolas Werth, "A State Against Its People: Violence, Repression, and Terror in the Soviet Union." For additional assessments on the incompleteness of the available statistics on death by NKVD execution or as a result of conditions in the Gulag camps, see Applebaum, *Gulag: A History*, pp. 583–584 and Ivanova, *Labor Camp Socialism*, p. 117.

21. Aleksandr Solzhenitsyn, *The Gulag Archipelago, 1918–1956: An Experiment in Literary Investigation*, vols. 1–2, translated by Thomas Whitney (New York: Harper and Row, 1973), p. 10.

22. See Michael Parrish, *The Lesser Terror: Soviet State Security, 1939–1953* (Westport, Conn.: Praeger, 1996).

23. Alec Nove, *Stalinism and After* (London: George Allen and Unwin, 1975), p. 62.

24. Robert C. Tucker, "Stalinism as Revolution from Above," in Robert C. Tucker, ed., *Stalinism: Essays in Historical Interpretation* (New York: Norton, 1977), p. 78.

25. Stephen Cohen, "Stalinism and Bolshevism," in Tucker, ed., *Stalinism*, p. 12.

26. Severyn Bialer, *Stalin's Successors* (Cambridge, England: Cambridge University Press, 1980), p. 47.

14

Trial by Fire:
The Great Patriotic War

*Millions of men perpetrated against one another such innumerable
crimes, deceptions, treacheries, robberies, forgeries, issues of false monies
deprecations, incendiarisms and murders as the annals of all the courts of
justice in the world could not muster in the course of whole centuries,
but which those who committed them did not at the time regard as crimes.*

—Leo Tolstoy

Although the Soviet Union did not live in a friendly world during the 1920s, it
was not a world that posed the direct threats the Bolsheviks had faced immediately after the revolution. The Soviet Union, to be sure, had no real friends,
only acquaintances offering a degree of toleration that varied from country to
country and year to year. There also was no shortage of vocal ideological opponents to the Soviet system in every Western country. This enabled Stalin to
raise the specter of war when it suited him in his political struggles, although
in truth during the 1920s none of the world's military powers was ready for
war. The onset of the Great Depression in 1929 and the resulting domestic
turmoil in the advanced capitalist countries, if anything, worked to the Soviet
Union's advantage. Western businessmen began to knock at the Soviet Union's
door to sell the heavy machinery so vital to Russia's industrialization drive.
All in all, the decade after the civil war was a breathing space in which the
party leadership was able to go about its business without undue concern for
what its critics in the West were planning.

STALIN AND SOVIET SECURITY

This tolerable, if not tranquil, situation changed during the early 1930s. The
Soviet Union became one of many nations with new security problems.

Germany and Japan, the former an industrial giant held down by the dead weight of the Versailles settlement and the latter a rapidly growing military and economic power hamstrung by the European colonial web that covered large parts of Asia, began to challenge the world order they resented. What followed, particularly with regard to Germany, did little credit to any of the world's major powers. Courage and foresight were in short supply everywhere, including the Soviet Union.

Stalin, to be sure, wanted security and peace during the 1930s as much as anyone. However, his definition of national security was skewed, as it focused first and foremost on his personal power and rule. Sometimes, as when he brought the Soviet Union into the League of Nations in 1934, his needs and national interests coincided. At other times, particularly when he purged the army or when he persecuted and murdered foreign Social Democrats and Marxists of various stripes for fear they might help galvanize opposition to him at home, Stalin's needs were directly opposed to those of the nation as a whole.

Stalin's concern for his own power also played havoc with the Marxist goal of a world socialist revolution. He simply did not want to see a socialist revolution under circumstances he could not control. Such an event, after all, might demonstrate that there was an alternative to his form of socialism and consequently threaten his throne. Stalin could not say that publicly, of course, but the role foreign Communist parties were expected to play was made clear by the Sixth Comintern Congress in 1928. It proclaimed that the litmus test for revolutionaries was their readiness to "defend the USSR," a formula that really meant complete subservience to Stalin's orders and interests. This primacy of Stalin's personal interests is essential to understanding Soviet foreign policy in the 1930s and Stalin's share in the chain of events and blunders that led to World War II and its attendant horrors.

Stalin was most successful in dealing with the Japanese. During the early 1930s, while absorbed in the industrialization drive, he made concessions to them while at the same time working to flank them by improving relations with the United States and Chiang Kai-shek's Nationalist regime in China. Moscow achieved an important success in 1933 when the United States finally recognized the Soviet Union, almost sixteen years after the fall of the Provisional Government. Later Stalin was able to build up his Siberian army sufficiently to defeat the Japanese in 1939 in a short, fierce border war, a defeat that helped convince them to sign a neutrality treaty with the Soviet Union in 1941 and shift their territorial ambitions from eastern Siberia to Southeast Asia.

Stalin's greatest problems were in Europe, where the gears of his private war against independent Marxists ground against the gears of the Soviet

Union's national interests. There is no doubt that Hitler's rise to power was facilitated by Stalin's insistence after 1928 that German Communists make political war on that country's Social Democrats. This strategy, which was linked to Stalin's battles against his domestic opponents within the party, prevented a Social Democratic–Communist alliance in Germany precisely at a time when Hitler's strength was increasing in the wake of the Depression. Trotsky's warnings about the Nazi threat in Germany only reinforced Stalin's determination to stay his course. In 1933, with the German Communists still at the throats of the Social Democrats, Hitler became the German chancellor. Within a year he was shipping Communists and Social Democrats alike to his concentration camps. In the end, some German Communists would have the dubious distinction of being imprisoned in both Hitler's and Stalin's camps before the two totalitarian dictators finally passed from the scene.

The same situation arose during the Spanish Civil War of 1936–1939. During that conflict between the democratically elected republican government and fascist rebels supported by Hitler and Mussolini, the Soviet Union was the only nonfascist nation to give significant help to the republican cause. However, that help soon deteriorated into a search-and-destroy operation that Stalin's NKVD waged against anarchists and especially Trotskyites fighting on the antifascist side. With friends like Stalin, the embattled Spanish republic hardly needed enemies. Despite heroic resistance, it fell to Francisco Franco's fascist legions in 1939. Stalin, meanwhile, having tested some of his new weapons, withdrew his people and material support. By purging and murdering many of the agents he had sent to Spain, he also made sure that none of the potentially infectious Trotskyite or anarchist viruses spread from the western edge of Europe to the "Socialist Fatherland."

THE NAZI THREAT

The burning issue in Europe during the 1930s was how the various powers were going to deal with Hitler once he began his efforts to rebuild German military might and reverse the results of World War I. Again, it must be stressed that none of the powers did themselves credit. Britain and France either did nothing, or they attempted to appease Hitler by allowing him to remilitarize the Rhineland in 1936, annex Austria in March 1938, and dismember Czechoslovakia later that year. The last concession, made at the Munich Conference in September 1938, gave the word "appeasement" a pejorative meaning and added to several languages the word "Munich," meaning an unconscionable and unjustified surrender in the face of threats. The United States, ready only to moralize about international aggression, stood by while the Germans and Japanese blithely went about their expansionism.

Stalin, ever cautious and deceitful, tried to play the diplomatic game both ways. He may have felt more comfortable working with Hitler, a fellow dictator, than with the Western democracies, despite Hitler's unabashed call for creating *Lebensraum* (living space) for the German "master race" by expansion to the east. Stalin continued Soviet–German military cooperation until Hitler ended it in 1933, and there seem to have been secret German–Soviet contacts between police and government officials during 1933 and 1934. Meanwhile, nonaggression pacts signed during 1932 with France and several states on the Soviet Union's immediate western flank (Poland, Estonia, Latvia, and Finland) moved Moscow a few steps closer to the mainstream of European diplomacy. In 1934 the Soviet Union took a larger step when, with strong French support, it gained admission to the League of Nations while also becoming an advocate of "collective security." In 1935 the pace picked up. The Comintern dutifully reversed itself and called for "popular front" tactics, that is, cooperation between Communists and other nonfascist parties against the common fascist menace. This led to the establishment of a short-lived socialist government in France in 1936. Moscow also signed mutual assistance treaties with France and Czechoslovakia, the latter a small, vulnerable state wedged along Germany's southeastern border. Under these agreements, the Soviet Union committed itself to come to Czechoslovakia's aid in the event of German aggression, provided the French did the same.

The road to war, a four-year odyssey that stretched to 1939, is far too complex to cover in detail here. Suffice it to say that Hitler continued his aggressive and disruptive behavior and none of the major powers did anything about it. Meanwhile, the Soviet Union's position generally improved in the east and deteriorated in the west. After 1937 the Japanese became bogged down in a futile attempt to conquer China, and the Soviets triumphed over them in the short undeclared war Tokyo and Moscow fought along the Mongolian–Manchurian border during the spring and summer of 1939. The Soviet victory in the Far East, confirmed by a truce in September, was testimony to the Red Army's skill in tank warfare. In a negative development, Germany and Japan signed the "Anti-Comintern Pact," an anti-Soviet document, in November 1936. In the west, Hitler annexed Austria in March 1938. In September came the Munich Conference, a meeting among Germany, Italy, France, and England from which both Czechoslovakia and the Soviet Union were excluded. Prior to the conference the Soviets offered to honor their 1935 commitment to defend Czechoslovakia against Germany if the French did likewise. This the French did not do; instead, they joined with the British in caving in to Hitler at Munich, thereby forcing the Czechs to cede to Germany a strategically vital border area inhabited mainly by ethnic Germans. This left Czechoslovakia militarily indefensible. Further annexations of most of what remained of

Czechoslovakia soon followed, as well as a new series of German demands on Poland. At this point, Britain and France, realizing that appeasement could not satisfy Hitler, finally took a stand and threatened to go to war if Germany violated Polish sovereignty.

THE NAZI–SOVIET PACT

Darkening war clouds shrouded the diplomacy that followed. Stalin, no doubt, was fed up with the weakness of the West and feared, with some justification, that the Western powers hoped to turn Hitler eastward against the "Bolshevik menace." In May 1939 the Soviet dictator took an important step. He replaced Maxim Litvinov, his urbane and effective commissar of foreign affairs, who happened to be Jewish and therefore unsuited for dealing with Hitler, with Vyacheslav Molotov, a tough and tenacious negotiator and member of the Politburo inner circle. By August the Soviet Union was negotiating with the Germans on the one hand and the British and French on the other. The latter seemed to believe that the Nazis and the Communists, archenemies according to their ideologies and propaganda, could never get together. The two Western powers therefore negotiated with the Russians with a shocking lack of urgency. But Stalin (and Hitler) calculated in terms of power politics, not ideology, and this was what impelled the Soviet dictator to favor an agreement with Berlin. A pact with Germany could buy Stalin the time he needed to rebuild his military strength, so damaged by his own purges, while allowing him to wait while the capitalist democracies and the fascists slugged it out and weakened each other.

Stalin, in fact, was thinking well beyond the approaching war, which a Soviet agreement with Germany would guarantee, to a postwar Europe with a radically altered balance of power. As he told his Politburo colleagues in a meeting on August 19, 1939, the past twenty years had demonstrated that Communists could not come to power in a European country without a "great war." Germany currently was prepared to acquiesce to Soviet expansionist ambitions in the Baltic and the Romanian province of Bessarabia, while war between the Germans and the Western democracies would destroy Poland and open to Moscow a sphere of influence in Eastern and Central Europe that would include Romania, Bulgaria, Hungary, and even Yugoslavia. As for Germany itself, if it lost the coming war, as Stalin expected, a Communist revolution would "inevitably follow." That in turn could create an opportunity Kremlin strategists could exploit, if they prepared for it in advance. The Soviet Union, by supplying Germany with raw materials and food, should seek to enhance that country's ability to fight—while using native Communists in Britain and France to "disorganize and demoralize" their armies—and thereby prolong the war "as long as possible so that an exhausted and debilitated England and France are in no condition to destroy a Sovietized Germany."

Such was the thinking, defensive in the short run but ultimately aggressive and expansionist, that led the Soviet Union to cut a deal with a regime that previously had given every sign of being its mortal enemy. On August 23, 1939, a diplomatic bombshell exploded in Europe as the USSR and the German Third Reich announced a nonaggression pact. Along with a public expression of friendship, the two powers secretly agreed to divide Poland and much of Eastern Europe between them. Hitler was now freed from the nightmare that had haunted generations of German military strategists: a war on two fronts. His only formidable enemies now lay in the west. Within ten days real bombshells came raining down on Europe as German troops crossed the Polish border, and World War II began.

The Stalin–Hitler pact of August 1939 gave the Soviet Union almost two years of breathing space while the Nazis, their eastern flank secured by their new Soviet allies, brutally and efficiently conquered most of Western Europe to the shores of the English Channel. Stalin was a good ally. There was tension between the two totalitarian giants, but no more than subsequent tensions between the Soviet Union and the Western democracies in the so-called Grand Alliance they hastily forged when Hitler invaded the Soviet Union in June 1941. From August 1939 to June 1941, the Soviet Union supported the German Reich diplomatically, provided it with naval bases, and punctually delivered the raw materials Hitler needed to storm Western and Central Europe, right up until the last moment. Thus when Hitler launched his war against the Soviet Union on June 22, 1941, Nazi armor rolled past Soviet trains filled with oil, grain, and other raw materials that had been en route to Germany. No wonder that Hitler called Stalin "indispensable" and "a hell of a fellow," while Mussolini pronounced Stalin to be a "secret fascist."

THE SOVIET UNION AT WAR

Whatever Stalin was in Hitler's eyes, the Soviet leader used his two years of grace to do more than please Germany's dictator. The Soviet Union intensified its military buildup. It developed such major new weapons as the T-34 tank and the Katusha rocket launcher. New defense plants were built deep in the interior, away from the menacing armies in the west. But the buildup was badly flawed. The armed forces, decimated by the purges, were commanded either by Stalin's incompetent old cronies, men like Kliment Voroshilov and Semyon Budenny, or by inexperienced and inadequately trained officers whose promotions resulted solely from the liquidation of those above them. The military buildup also was hampered because many of the Soviet Union's best scientists and engineers, including experts in both rocketry and airplane design, were languishing in prisons or labor camps. Many older industrial plants dangerously close to the western border remained vulnerable. Moreover, Soviet military units in the western part of the country were left exposed and unprepared for combat, even when hard intelligence warned Stalin of the precise day the Germans were planning to attack during the spring of 1941.

In the Soviet Union, the cataclysm known in the West as World War II is usually referred to as the "Great Patriotic War." The Soviets fought that war as part of what Winston Churchill called the "Grand Alliance" (others called it the "Strange Alliance"), an uneasy partnership with the United States and Great Britain, which in turn was the core of a broader coalition of more than twenty countries that joined in the desperate struggle against Nazi Germany and its fascist allies. The Nazi–Soviet part of that war was a titanic clash that, in Hitler, finally produced for Stalin an adversary who matched him in cruelty, cynicism, duplicity, and determination. Not only Stalin's regime, but Russian national life, was at stake in a war the Soviet Union nearly lost.

As terrible as it was, though, killing millions of Soviet citizens and up-rooting tens of millions more, the Great Patriotic War actually changed the Soviet Union very little. It was not an earthquake that permanently alters the landscape, but more a monstrous hurricane that sweeps in, does incalculable damage, and then passes, leaving the survivors to mourn the dead and rebuild in a manner that resembles as closely as possible that which was destroyed. By surviving, the Stalinist system was tempered and strengthened, and the repressive and hierarchical structure of Soviet society was consequently reinforced.

This surprised many people, who mistook Stalin's various small conces-sions to rally the nation to the war effort as signs that a period of relaxation and reform would follow the war. They did not understand that Stalin, while laboring so hard to avoid a two-front war against both Germany and Japan, in reality fought two wars between 1941 and 1945, one against the Nazi war machine and one against the Soviet people. The latter, aptly called "Stalin's Secret War" by historian Nikolai Tolstoy, was surreptitiously carried out by the NKVD to ensure that the Soviet people could not mount any challenges to their government. Ironically, during the war Hitler was also fighting his own secret war: his campaign of extermination that some have called his "War Against the Jews." The great difference between the two dictators is that while Hitler lost one of his wars—his battle against the Allies—Stalin won both of his. Hitler's secret war therefore was completely exposed; Stalin's remained a secret. Hitler's brand of murderous totalitarianism was destroyed; Stalin's survived.

Stalin made better preparations for his secret war than he did for the Soviet

Union's war with the Germans. When the Red Army claimed the Soviet Union's share of Poland in 1939 in accord with the August 23 pact, 230,000 Polish troops were rounded up and deported. They included 15,000 officers, all of whom the NKVD shot. In 1943 the Germans announced they had discovered the bodies of more than 4,000 of the officers in the Katyn Forest near the Russian city of Smolensk; the announcement added yet another sore point to the many tensions that existed between the Soviet Union and its democratic partners in the Grand Alliance. Meanwhile, of the total of 230,000 Polish soldiers taken prisoner in 1939, only 82,000 were alive by the summer of 1941. At least 400,000, and perhaps as many as 1 million Poles were deported to the Gulag.[1] When in 1940 the Soviet Union occupied Latvia, Lithuania, and Estonia, three small countries on its western border, the NKVD moved in with detailed lists of whom to arrest. The operation was so well planned that the smallest details—when and how to make arrests, what the arrestee could take with him, even how the police should handle their weapons—were covered in the instructions the NKVD agents carried. More than 130,000 people were deported without so much as perfunctory legal procedures.

One aspect of Stalin's preparations, his dealings with Finland, went less well. Because the Finns refused to grant territorial concessions and military bases Moscow wanted, Stalin sent his purge-riddled Red Army into Finland. For months during the winter of 1939–1940, Finland's small military forces held Stalin's army, navy, and air force at bay, killing more than 125,000 Soviet troops and destroying more than 1,000 airplanes, as against losses of 62 of their own aircraft. Eventually the Soviet Union's enormous resources and Stalin's willingness to accept appalling casualties in frontal assaults prevailed, and in March 1940 the Finns were forced to sue for peace. Stalin got the bases and territory he wanted. More important, he began a massive effort to reorganize and reequip the Red Army, whose inadequacies had glared so brightly in the Finnish winter twilight.

The job was not completed in time, in part because Stalin refused to believe that Hitler would break his word so soon and attack the Soviet Union. Stalin received numerous detailed warnings of German war preparations during early 1941, including an urgent handwritten note in May, the month he took over from Molotov as Soviet prime minister, from General Georgy Zhukov, the newly appointed chief of the general staff. When Germany struck on June 22, 1941, Stalin refused to be the bearer of bad news and ordered Molotov to broadcast the official announcement of the invasion to the nation. For most of the next week Stalin worked round the clock with his top civilian and military advisors, but nothing could stop the string of defeats on every front. In the early morning hours of June 29, overwhelmed by the uncontrollable crisis, Stalin apparently suffered a nervous breakdown. He retreated to the solitude of his nearby country home, where he stayed until Molotov, Beria, and a few other Politburo comrades arrived on the night of June 30. The distraught dictator, slumped in an armchair, seems to have assumed his uninvited guests had come to arrest him; instead Molotov, Beria, and the others reassured him that he was still in charge. Stalin did not recover his equilibrium sufficiently to address his anxious people until July 3, by which time the Germans were deep into the Soviet Union and the military disaster was well under way. So was the Nazi slaughter of Jews, who because of Soviet censorship and propaganda had no warning about either the impending German invasion or the Nazis' attitude toward them. Stalin's main achievement was having survived the first weeks of the war still in power. By June 1941, there simply was no one left capable of thinking the unthinkable: that Stalin could be replaced. The purges and terror had done their job.

Bolstered by the element of surprise, superior generalship, and better equipment in the initial battles, the Germans might have won the Nazi–Soviet war. A combination of factors, none of which can be credited to Stalin, prevented this. The Nazis made both military and political errors. At key points Hitler interfered with the military operations, overruling his generals and dissipating advantages his forces held. He weakened his forces poised before Moscow in August 1941 in order to attempt to take the Soviet oil wells in the Caucasus, a maneuver that failed and left the German troops facing Moscow unable to take the city. Hitler's blunders at the battle of Stalingrad during the winter of 1942–1943 produced an even greater debacle. The Germans could have by-passed Stalingrad, the former Tsaritsyn, which Stalin had renamed for himself after serving there during the civil war. But the Führer was determined to take the "City of Stalin" at all costs. Instead the Germans suffered a crushing defeat, their first on the European continent, a defeat considered by many military experts to be the turning point of the war. In the summer of 1943, Berlin took too long to launch the crucial Battle of Kursk, allowing the Soviets to prepare powerful defenses that German armored forces could not breach. The Soviets won this titanic clash, the largest tank battle in history, in which more than 3 million men took part. After their defeat at Kursk, the Germans were unable to mount another major offensive in the Soviet Union.

Perhaps more important, the Nazis squandered the support they might have had from the Soviet population. In many places, particularly in the Ukraine and Belorussia, German troops were greeted as liberators from the hated Communist regime. Millions of Soviet citizens suddenly had some hope. The peasants hoped for freedom of religion and the dissolution of the collective farms, the most hated single institution in Soviet Russia. Many ethnic Russians, Ukrainians, and others were ready to fight the Soviet government they loathed, if the Germans would only arm them. Among them was General Andrei Vlasov, a captured officer who apparently had both considerable military skill and popular appeal. Many German civilian and military experts urged a policy that would exploit this vast reservoir of goodwill, but Hitler would hear nothing of such thinking. To him the Slavic *Untermenschen* (subhumans), although not slated for extermination like the Jews, were fit only for slave labor, deportation, or repression. The collectives were not dissolved, prisoners of war were brutally mistreated, and the population at large was terrorized. By 1942 the Russians under German occupation had learned their terrible lesson and were resisting their would-be conquerors with considerable effect. By the time Hitler recognized his mistake in 1944, it was far too late to do anything about it.

Aided by the brutal Russian winter that helped stall the Germans at the gates of Moscow in 1941 and the effectiveness of newly installed commanding officers—including Zhukov, commander of Soviet troops in the Far East before becoming chief of the general staff, and K.K. Rokossovsky, plucked from a labor camp—the Soviet government survived the defeats of 1941 and 1942. American Lend-Lease shipments also arrived to help stem the German tide. This aid was particularly important in providing the Red Army with motor vehicles needed to match the German army in mobility. Most of all, the Soviet Union and Stalin were saved by the Soviet people. It was the average citizen's stunning heroism and ability to endure that saved Leningrad, where in a 900-day siege 1 million people died, more than 600,000 of them from starvation. Soviet resistance at Stalingrad during the dark winter of 1942–1943 was equally remarkable, as the Red Army yielded 90 percent of the totally destroyed city inch by inch but never broke. Although losses of territory, livestock, and farmland cut agricultural production in half between 1940 and 1943, an inadequately fed, clothed, and housed labor force, further weakened by military conscription, gradually managed to raise industrial production levels after the severe drop caused by the invasion. It was a painful process, but by 1944, largely on the basis of domestic production, but also because of vital supplies sent by the United States under its Lend-Lease program, the Red Army was better equipped than the German *Wehrmacht*. This was possible in large part because during 1941 and 1942, under the worst of conditions, the Soviets succeeded in dismantling and transporting hundreds of factories eastward beyond the reach of the Germans.

As the fighting raged along a thousand-mile front, the Jewish population caught behind German lines was engulfed by the Nazi campaign, known today as the Holocaust, to exterminate the Jewish people. The killing in the Soviet Union was spearheaded by specially recruited and trained units called *Einsatzgruppen*, which relied primarily on machine guns to massacre their victims. The *Eizatzgruppen* were assisted by other German military and police units and often by local collaborators. The most notorious single massacre took place September 1941 in the Ukraine at a ravine outside Kiev called Babi Yar, where more than 33,000 men, women, and children were murdered in just two days. During 1941 alone the Nazis systematically murdered 90,000 Jews at Babi Yar and more than 500,000 Jews on Soviet soil. By the end of the war the death toll from shootings and deportations to death camps was more than 2 million. This was about a third of all Jews murdered in the Holocaust and more than 60 percent of all Jews living on Soviet-controlled territory, including territory taken from Poland after Stalin's pact with Hitler in August 1939, that German forces overran during World War II. The bulk of those who survived did so because they managed to flee eastward ahead of the German army.

The Soviet regime could do little to protect its civilians from Nazi terror and genocide. Meanwhile, its conduct of the war was marred by senseless and brutal treatment of its own soldiers. Although Stalin was to promote himself to "Generalissimo," he showed little talent for military strategy. Zhukov, the Soviet Union's most famous soldier and the real architect of its successful military strategy during the war, succinctly summed up matters in 1956 when he angrily complained to several of Stalin's associates and successors: "You people collaborated with Stalin in driving the troops like cattle to the slaughter." Indeed, on Stalin's orders Soviet military authorities often carried out the slaughter themselves. They executed more than 157,000 of their own soldiers—"fifteen divisions were decimated by our own side," disabled World War II veteran Alexander Yakovlev bitterly recalled decades later—virtually all of whom were guilty of nothing more than being captured and then escaping from enemy prisoner of war camps or being resourceful enough to break through German lines after their units had been encircled.[2] Stalin's greatest contribution to the military effort was to stay out of it and let Zhukov run things, a restraint the generalissimo frequently failed to display.

STALIN AS NATIONAL LEADER

It was as a political leader that Stalin excelled. Once the "man of steel" recovered his nerve, Stalin gave the nation a focal point. He directed the war effort from the Kremlin. Exhortations for more work and sacrifice were cleverly framed in terms of "Mother Russia" and "fatherland," Slavic pride, and other references to traditional Russian patriotism. Little was heard of the "socialist fatherland" or other aspects of Communist ideology. Stalin reached an accord with the Russian Orthodox Church. It received the right to elect a patriarch for the first time in thirty years, and in return, it blessed the Soviet leader and his regime in their struggle to defend Russia. In 1942 the army commanders in smaller units finally were rid of the political commissars, the party functionaries with whom they had shared authority and whose interference often had been detrimental to Soviet military operations, while political commissars attached to larger military units had their authority drastically reduced. Even the peasants got something: restrictions on their private plots were eased, while higher agricultural prices enabled them to raise their miserable standard of living and even to save a little. These may in reality have been little more than crumbs, but Stalin doled them out so skillfully to his materially and spiritually starved people that they seemed like bountiful loaves of bread.

STALIN AS DIPLOMAT

Where Stalin really excelled was in his dealings with the Allies. He not only impressed men like Roosevelt and Churchill, but it is hard not to feel that he got the best of them in their mutual dealings. Churchill, to be sure, had few illusions about Stalin; the English leader was a longtime anti-Communist crusader. FDR was different. He mistakenly felt he could befriend and manipulate the man he called "Uncle Joe."

Until Stalingrad, Stalin was unavoidably cast in the role of supplicant. He was desperate enough in 1941 to plead for British and American troops to fight the Germans on Russian soil, a plan he quickly abandoned when the initial emergencies passed. He was more insistent that the Allies land forces in France to open a "second front" and relieve some of the pressure on the Red Army. This the Allies proved unable to do until June 1944, by which time the Red Army, at appalling cost, had turned the tide in the east and was pushing beyond Soviet borders into Eastern Europe. As a result, not only was Stalin after 1943 able to negotiate from a position of strength provided by his advancing Red Army, but he was able to exploit Western guilt over having been unable to hit the Germans directly while the Russians bore the brunt of the fighting between 1941 and mid-1944. He also earned some goodwill by dissolving the Comintern in 1943.

Stalin used all of his geopolitical and psychological advantages to extend Soviet influence over large parts of Eastern Europe. The United States and Britain naturally resented this. Britain (and France) had gone to war in 1939 in part because Hitler's gains in those same areas threatened the European balance of power. This struggle over Eastern Europe, which focused initially on Poland, caused tremendous tensions within the Grand Alliance, whose only real glue, as postwar events were to demonstrate, was the mutual Nazi enemy. For his part, Stalin always feared that his allies might make a separate peace with Germany that would deny the Soviet Union what he felt were its rightful gains after the suffering it had endured in turning back the Germans. There was, of course, no basis for Stalin's fears; it was only Stalin himself, in 1943, who briefly considered the idea of making a separate peace with the Nazis.

Stalin scored his first major diplomatic victory during his first meeting with Churchill and Roosevelt in Teheran during November 1943. There, despite the embarrassing revelations in April of the Katyn Forest massacre, Stalin won acceptance of the Polish–Soviet border he wanted, one that was considerably to the west of the 1939 border. He also finally got a firm commitment to establish the long-awaited second front on French soil the following spring. In return, the Soviet Union committed itself to join the war against Japan once Germany was defeated.

Stalin won further concessions during 1944, as the Red Army swept the Germans out of the Soviet Union and drove them back toward Germany. When the Soviet leader met with Churchill in the Kremlin in October 1944, the British prime minister, hoping to save what he could, proposed a deal that gave the Soviet Union predominant influence in Romania (90 percent) and Bulgaria (75 percent), gave it equal influence with the West in Yugoslavia and Hungary, and gave Britain and the United States predominance in Greece. Stalin accepted that formula without saying a word. Later some of these figures had to be revised in the Soviet Union's favor, owing to the Red Army's rapid advance.

In February 1945 came the Yalta Conference, the most important Allied meeting of the war. By then the Red Army occupied large parts of Eastern Europe, while the Western Allies were struggling in their arena. The United States, which had not yet tested its atomic bomb, was more anxious than ever for the Soviet Union to enter in the war against Japan and also join in establishing a postwar international peacekeeping organization to be called the United Nations. Churchill headed a totally exhausted nation, while FDR was a dying man with two months to live. In return for very small concessions, Stalin accomplished most of his agenda. The Polish–Soviet border was moved westward, Poland getting formerly German territory as compensation for its losses to the Soviets. More important, a Soviet-sponsored group of Polish Communists, diluted ever so slightly with representatives from a British-sponsored non-Communist Polish government in exile, was in effect established as the new Polish government. The Soviets were to permit "free and unfettered" elections in Poland, an event that, had it transpired, would have meant the ouster of Stalin's puppet regime. Stalin, who never took this commitment seriously and assumed that no one else did either, naturally did not honor this part of the Yalta agreement. The Polish question soon became one of the key issues that launched the Cold War.

Plans for the occupation and denazification of Germany also were made at Yalta. In addition to the substantial territory that was to be turned over to

Poland, the Soviet Union took a small piece of Germany on the Baltic coast for itself and joined the United States, Britain, and France in a four-power occupation of what remained. The Soviet Union also remained in control of Latvia, Lithuania, Estonia, and other territories annexed between 1939 and 1941 in agreement with the Germans. The Yalta Conference thereby solidified Soviet power in the heart of Europe, a state of affairs that included a solid grip on the eastern part of Germany. It also gave the Soviets a de facto veto over any attempt to reunify Germany. This situation was inherently unstable because it left the ultimate disposition of Germany, with its enormous industrial resources and technologically skilled population, in limbo, which in turn became another key issue that led to the end of the Grand Alliance and the start of the Cold War.

STALIN'S SECRET WAR

Germany's defeat in World War II brought the full horror of Hitler's secret war against the Jews to world attention. By contrast, the Soviet Union's spectacular victory over the Nazis created a halo that obscured Stalin's secret war. In truth, however, that war, while different from Hitler's in intent and target, also claimed millions of lives. There were other parallels as well. Each war originated in the recesses of the respective dictator's mind. Hitler was driven by his all-consuming hatred for Jews, Stalin by his obsession with potential threats to his power. Each secret war hurt its respective nation's war effort. Hitler used thousands of elite SS troops, invaluable railroad cars, and other resources needed for the war effort to speed up the extermination campaign even as the Allies closed in from the east and west. Stalin also used large numbers of troops and guards for various repressive and murderous tasks, including guarding millions of innocent men who otherwise would have been available to fight the Germans.

Stalin's war against the Soviet people was fought on many fronts. When the Germans first invaded, the NKVD murdered thousands of Gulag prisoners rather than let them and their potential testimony fall into enemy hands. Millions of other people were deported to the Gulag. Aside from those deported from Poland and the Baltic states before June 1941, the NKVD sent at least 1 million Ukrainians to the Gulag after the fighting began. This type of deportation was not new. But during the war, the Soviet regime broke new ground by deporting entire national groups. This was justified by a new legal innovation: blaming an entire nation for collaboration with the enemy on the part of some of its members. Approximately 1.5 million people, comprising all or most of the Soviet Union's Chechens, Ingush, Karachai, Balkars, Kalmyks, Crimean Tatars, Meskhetians, and Volga Germans were deported; perhaps one-third of them died. These operations were swift—the Crimean Tatars were given fifteen minutes to collect their belongings—and so well concealed that news of what happened to some of these small nations did not reach the West for years. Thus, to the horror of the deportations themselves must be added the chilling fact that it was possible to drop entire nations, as historian Robert Conquest has observed, down a "memory hole."[3]

In the camps themselves, the population swelled to the peak levels of the purge years. Conditions, eased briefly after 1938, sank to the rock-bottom levels of the 1930s. Mortality rates soared. When possible, the camps were switched to war production. Slave labor was used for military construction projects such as border defenses, airfields, and fortifications, including some of those at Stalingrad. More than 1 million prisoners, including people who had completed their sentences, were sent from the Gulag camps directly to the front. Once there, more than 400,000 of these unfortunate people were organized into "penal battalions." These units were used for mass frontal assaults against heavily fortified positions and for clearing minefields—by marching through them. To push them forward, special NKVD troops followed behind to shoot anyone who hesitated or tried to retreat. The NKVD troops also killed the wounded. These "barrier troops" additionally served behind the lines of regular units to prevent any "unauthorized retreats" by shooting anyone who took a step backward without permission.

Adding to the toll of the dead were the prisoners of war and civilians who managed to survive the brutal conditions in the German labor and concentration camps. To Stalin they were "traitors," and as such they were either shot upon repatriation or shipped by the hundreds of thousands to the Gulag. Overall, recent estimates put the Soviet Union's wartime losses at 27 million people. The Nazi invaders obviously killed or indirectly caused the deaths of most of those millions. Yet the Stalin regime, through its deportations, purges, Gulag camps, military tactics that ignored human losses, and other measures, also killed millions. All this the Soviet people endured, and still they managed to fight their war from Leningrad, Moscow, and Stalingrad to Berlin. It was a collective act of courage and endurance on a titanic scale that lent new truth to the old saying, "Only the Russians can conquer Russia."

THE GREAT PATRIOTIC WAR AND SOVIET MEMORY

World War II, which exacted the greatest human toll of all the calamities in Russia's history, left a wound a nation wide and generations deep. Like the painful wounds and scars millions of citizens carried in their individual lives, the war experience became an integral part of the Soviet Union's postwar life. Each year May 9, Victory Day, marked a solemn day of remembrance, but it was only twenty-four hours of what for many was a recollection lasting all year. Almost every town in the western part of the Soviet Union built its war memorial, and for those who did not come to one of these shrines, an endless stream of books, films, theater productions, songs, and reminiscences about the war came to them. This obsession was in part a product of propaganda, as both Stalin and his successors used the victory over the Nazis as vindication of the Communist system and the sacrifices made to build it. But it was no less a reflection of the genuine feeling and emotion of the Soviet people. For millions of them World War II was both the best and the worst of times, an era when Stalin's tyranny abated slightly and the desperate national defense effort created a unity and comradeship that enabled the country to survive the unspeakable horrors of war and Nazi atrocities.

There was, however, a demon lurking behind the saintly memory of World War II: some of that memory was a lie. A short-lived reevaluation of the war began after Nikita Khrushchev, at the Twentieth Party Congress in 1956, criticized Stalin's wartime leadership for having cost enormous unnecessary suffering. A far more thorough and painful reassessment took place three decades later. Soviet citizens then were confronted with, among other things, their country's barbaric treatment of returning prisoners of war and costly blunders by military commanders, even at the legendary battle of Stalingrad. Often the revelations were too much to bear. One war veteran spoke for many when he complained that they "will end with our national values and everything which represents the spiritual pride of the people toppling into the abyss." His complaint, while poignant, ultimately had to be futile, for as the distinguished Chinese writer Lu Xun observed more than a decade before Russia fought its Great Patriotic War, "Lies written in ink cannot obscure a truth written in blood."

NOTES

1. On these statistics see Nicolas Werth, "A State Against Its People: Violence, Repression, and Terror in the Soviet Union," in Stéphane Courtois et al., *The Black Book of Communism: Crimes, Terror, Repression*, trans. Jonathan Murphy and Mark Kramer, consulting editor Mark Kramer (Cambridge, Mass., and London: Harvard University Press, 1999), pp. 208–209; and Andrzej Paczkowski, "Poland, the 'Enemy Nation,'" in ibid., pp. 372–373.

2. Alexander N. Yakovlev, *A Century of Violence in Soviet Russia*, edited and translated by Anthony Austin (New Haven and London: Yale University Press, 2002), p. 174. Thousands more Soviet soldiers were executed without any kind of formal proceedings. By contrast, the United States Army executed about 125 soldiers during the war, almost all for violent crimes against civilians or fellow soldiers. One soldier was executed for desertion, in a case that remains controversial to this day.

3. Robert Conquest, *The Nation Killers* (London: Macmillan, 1970), p. 67.

15

Stalin's September Songs

I told you that I am becoming a conservative.

—Joseph Stalin, 1943

The eight years between the end of World War II and Stalin's death in 1953 witnessed two major developments. On the international scene, the Soviet Union joined the United States as one of the world's two superpowers, and the two countries became embroiled in a potentially catastrophic confrontation, destined to outlive Stalin by more than three decades, known as the Cold War. Domestically, the postwar years were a period of conservative retrenchment as Stalin struggled to keep intact the system his policies had forged during the 1930s.

WORLD WAR II AND SOVIET POWER

World War II greatly enhanced Soviet power. It destroyed or gravely weakened most of Russia's traditional rivals. Germany and Japan, the great powers on its immediate flanks, were totally defeated. Britain and France, supposedly among the winners, were exhausted by their victory. Meanwhile, the fortunes of war carried the Red Army into the heart of Europe. The Red Army drove the Nazis from Poland, Romania, Bulgaria, Czechoslovakia, and Hungary, and it controlled a large part of Germany itself. After 1945, it continued to occupy those territories for varying periods of time, while native Communist resistance movements controlled Yugoslavia and Albania. A strong Communist movement with a powerful army controlled a large part of China, while the Communist parties of France and Italy had large followings and were major players in the political life of those two Western European countries. The Soviet Union's power also was magnified because its totalitarian government was able to demand further sacrifices from its people in order to rebuild and expand the nation's heavy industrial sector and pursue the development of new weaponry.

The Soviet Union's enormous new power was not without its pitfalls. It caused great concern in the West, contributed to the dissolution of the Grand Alliance that had defeated Nazi Germany, and thus became the key factor that precipitated the Cold War. The former allies already were seriously at odds by early 1945. This should not be surprising. The alliance was a shotgun marriage of unlikely partners, born of Nazi aggression. Mutual suspicions between the partners had already been rampant during the war. When the tide had turned in 1943, British Prime Minister Winston Churchill desperately concocted military and political strategies to get British and American armies into Eastern Europe before the Soviets. Churchill's plans ran afoul of geopolitical and military obstacles and America's determination to place strictly military matters, rather than future political considerations, at the head of the wartime agenda. Still, there was growing fear in the American camp of escalating Soviet power. During the war, such considerations were subordinated to the immediate task of defeating Germany and Japan, but they became a major concern once victory became certain. As for Stalin, he was no less suspicious of the Western powers than he was of anybody else. He had lived in a self-concocted fear of a separate Western–German peace and was convinced that the American–British delay in establishing a second front was part of a plot to weaken the Soviet Union by leaving it to fight the Germans alone as long as possible.

These tensions, which first surfaced during the wartime conferences, particularly at Yalta, became open disputes at the first conference following Germany's surrender, held from mid-July to early August 1945 in Potsdam, a suburb of Berlin. The conferees managed to agree on most issues concerning the occupation of Germany and on the Soviet Union's entry into the war against Japan, but they disagreed about everything else, from Stalin's failure to fulfill his Yalta pledge to hold "free and unfettered" elections in Poland to who would control the Black Sea straits. It is probably appropriate that the atomic bomb, the symbol of the Cold War, was successfully tested for the first time by the United States the day before the Potsdam Conference began. When later in the conference American President Harry Truman casually told Stalin that the United States had "a new weapon of unusual destructive force," the Soviet leader, thanks to his efficient spy network, knew Truman was referring to the atomic bomb. If Stalin needed any more fuel for his fear of the West, America's possession of this awesome new weapon more than filled the bill.

THE FATE OF EASTERN EUROPE

Whatever his fears, Stalin's foreign ambitions after World War II were extensive. To be sure, the Soviet Union was too exhausted to march westward to the Atlantic, as some initially feared. Rather, as Molotov put it many years later, Stalin's policy was "to expand the borders of the Fatherland as much as possible." In 1945 the area of possibility was Eastern Europe. Stalin therefore pushed his armies westward as fast as he could in the last months of the war, taking enormous losses in the process, in order to occupy as much territory as possible as a potential buffer against the West. He was committed both to retaining the territorial gains he had won during the period of the Nazi–Soviet pact and to ensuring that no governments hostile to the Soviet Union could establish themselves in the rest of Eastern Europe. This would enhance the Soviet Union's strategic defensive position and also insulate the Soviet people from the outside world. Beyond that opening position, Stalin was flexible—quick enough first to use the opportunities created by the advance of the Red Army to expand Soviet influence in Eastern Europe and then, when the West began to object to his activities and tensions began to rise, to clamp down on the countries within his grasp while he had the chance.

Some of Stalin's ambitions were thwarted by Western resistance during 1945 and 1946, including his plans for a role in the occupation of Japan, joint control with the Turks of the Black Sea straits, and a permanent presence in oil-rich Iran. Nonetheless, Stalin had a great deal to show for his efforts in the years immediately after the war. As Molotov proudly noted, "They [the Western leaders] woke up only when half of Europe had passed from them." Germany, even if the West tried to put it back together, had been permanently weakened by losses of territory and resources to Poland and the Soviet Union. The Soviet occupation zone in eastern Germany gave Moscow direct control over almost 30 percent of what remained of Germany and a formidable position from which it might, given the right circumstances, influence the future of the country as a whole. Furthermore, by 1945 the Soviets had installed a puppet Communist-dominated regime in historically anti-Russian Poland, the country that twice in half a century served as Germany's main invasion route eastward. As pressures built with the West, Stalin, using a combination of treachery, threats, and pure force, succeeded in establishing a series of Communist-controlled regimes in countries occupied by the Red Army along the Soviet Union's western and southwestern flank. Poland, the major prize, was completely under Communist control before the dust of World War II had settled. Hungary, another country with little fondness for the Russians, maintained some vestiges of political pluralism until mid-1947; thereafter, Communist control was total. In Romania and Bulgaria, Communist control was firm by early 1945 and all opposition eliminated by 1947. Meanwhile, as early as 1945 native Communists relying largely on their own resources and efforts had brought Yugoslavia (a country the Red Army occupied only partially, withdrawing completely in 1945) and Albania into the Soviet camp.

The lone holdout was Czechoslovakia, the only country in the region with a democratic tradition. It also had a powerful and popular Communist party and a history of friendship with the Soviet Union. This was not enough for Stalin. Undisguised pressure and the not-so-carefully disguised murder of Foreign Minister Jan Masaryk closed the book on Czechoslovakian democracy and genuine independence in February 1948. Less than three years after German Nazism was driven from Eastern Europe, Russian Communism had overwhelmed the region quickly, cruelly, and thoroughly.

These Soviet gains were a bitter pill for the West to swallow. One of the causes of World War II had been the West's determination to prevent Germany from dominating Eastern Europe and thereby upsetting the traditional European balance of power. Now suddenly the Soviet Union, a power considered by many to be a threat as great as Nazi Germany had been to Western freedoms, was firmly in control in key areas from which the Germans had been dislodged at such great cost. But Western protests meant little to Stalin. He had not interfered in the areas his 1944 agreement with Churchill allotted to the West—in Greece, for example—and therefore felt free to do what he wanted in what he considered the Soviet Union's sphere of influence. Moreover, the Soviet Union was in a strong position; the Red Army still occupied much of the territory from which it had driven the Germans and was not about to leave.

This did not mean that Stalin did not have some very big problems. In Yugoslavia, he caused them himself. Yugoslavia was firmly under the control of a local, very pro-Soviet Communist, Joseph Broz Tito. Having come to power on his own, Tito was an independent actor who could, and sometimes did, ignore Stalin's orders. Stalin was not satisfied with Tito's loyalty; the Soviet dictator wanted complete and direct control. To feel safe, Stalin required puppets, not allies like Tito, whose very independence suggested that there were other methods than Stalin's for maintaining Communist rule. But Stalin's attempt to reduce Tito and Yugoslavia from independence to dependence ended in complete failure in 1948. The result was a formal split between the two Communist leaders and their countries. Tito then in effect was compelled to set Yugoslavia on a course that made it an anomaly in the postwar world: a Communist state that was neutral in the Cold War. Stalin's response was a series of purges in the satellite nations to extinguish all embers, real or imagined, of "Titoism." The iron curtain, which Winston Churchill in 1946 said had descended across Europe, clanged down even harder after Tito bested Stalin two years later.

THE COLD WAR

By 1948 Stalin had much greater problems than his ex-comrade Tito. The United States, the other superpower, increasingly encouraged by concerned leaders in Britain and France, was moving into the power vacuum in Europe. Stalin apparently lived in secret terror of an attack by the United States— the world's only nuclear power until the Soviets tested their first bomb in 1949—keeping Moscow's air raid defense on twenty-four-hour alert. But the United States had more than just atomic bombs with which to frighten the Soviet Union. It was overall American strength and the threat to use it that forced Stalin to drop his expansionist plans regarding Turkey and Iran in 1946. In early 1947, when the exhausted British indicated that they were no longer able to support the anti-Communist side in the Greek civil war, the United States stepped into the breach, announcing a policy that came to be called the Truman Doctrine. The Truman Doctrine committed Washington to providing the anti-Communist governments of Greece and Turkey with military and economic aid and to preventing Communist takeovers elsewhere. Several months later, an article in the authoritative journal *Foreign Affairs* signed by "X" (American Soviet expert George Kennan) outlined America's overall policy toward the Soviet Union. Henceforth, the United States would maintain a policy of "long-term, patient but firm and vigilant containment" vis-à-vis its Communist rival. The United States, in other words, intended to block any attempt the Soviet Union made to expand its influence. In the wake of the Communist coup in Czechoslovakia, the United States implemented a massive economic aid program called the Marshall Plan to rebuild Western Europe's war-shattered economy. This was particularly troubling, as Stalin was counting on continued European weakness to give the Soviet Union breathing space and freedom of maneuver in its foreign policy. A weak Western Europe, after all, meant a safer Soviet Union. Equally disturbing, by 1948 it was clear that the Western powers were planning to fuse their occupation zones in Germany to create an independent country and, in addition, willing to permit their former enemy to rebuild its industrial might.

Aside from his moves in Eastern Europe, Stalin responded to the West in September 1947 by resurrecting the Comintern in a new guise, the Communist Information Bureau (Cominform). In 1948 he responded more forcefully by attempting to discredit Western, and especially American, resolve. His point of attack was Berlin. The former German capital actually was located more than 100 miles inside the Soviet occupation zone, but, like Germany as a whole, it had been divided into four occupation zones. In June 1948 Stalin blockaded Berlin, hoping to force the Western powers to halt their plans for Germany and to abandon the city. Stalin hoped to convince the German people in both the Soviet and Western zones that they could not rely on the West and therefore should seek whatever accommodation the Soviet Union was willing to offer. That accomplished, he hoped to erode American influence in the rest of Western Europe. The West stood firm. It avoided both an ignominious retreat and the frightening prospect of firing the first shot of a potential third world war by airlifting supplies over Stalin's blockade. War with the United States was something the Soviet Union, still repairing the damage from the struggle against Nazi Germany, could not afford, so the planes flew without a Soviet shot being fired. When Stalin gave up in May 1949 and lifted his blockade, his problems were worse than in 1948, for on April 4, 1949, the North Atlantic Treaty Organization (NATO), a military alliance of eleven Western nations led by the United States, was formed in Washington.

The chain of events between 1945 and 1949, beginning with the Yalta Conference, left Europe divided into two hostile halves, a Soviet-dominated bloc in the east and an American-led bloc in the west, and marked the opening phase of the forty-five-year-long conflict known as the Cold War. The Soviet bloc even had its own version of the Marshall Plan, Council of Mutual Economic Assistance (COMECON), or Molotov Plan, set up in January 1949. If this was a tense and uncomfortable state of affairs, at least by 1949 it was possible to say that the situation in Europe was relatively stable.

The same was not true in the Far East, where developments were further intensifying the Cold War. In October 1949, after a three-year civil war, Communist rebels led by Mao Zedong completed their conquest of China, the world's most populous nation, and announced the founding of the People's Republic of China (PRC). This development did not particularly please Stalin. Mao had won his victory without extensive Soviet help, controlled his own party and army, and was quite independent of Stalin—and Tito already had given Stalin more than his fill of independent Communist leaders. The Soviet dictator would have preferred a non-Communist China kept weak and divided by a strong Communist presence. Whatever Stalin's preferences, the West, especially the United States, was horrified. In one blow, 25 percent of the world's population "went Communist." The successful Soviet test of an atomic bomb in August of 1949, several years earlier than all predictions, intensified Western anxieties.

Then came North Korea's invasion of South Korea in June 1950. The former was a Soviet puppet state that occupied the Korean peninsula north of the 38th parallel, the part of Korea occupied by the Red Army in 1945; the latter, located south of the 38th parallel, was an American-backed authoritarian regime thinly masked by a veneer of democratic institutions. The United States flatly blamed the Soviet Union for the invasion—correctly, as it turned out. Stalin had approved the North Korean invasion plans and then provided his Asian ally with the arms it needed to launch its attack. The United States intervened immediately, first with air strikes and, when South Korean forces still could not stop the North Korean offensive, with ground troops. The American troops that defended South Korea did so under the auspices of the United Nations. That was possible because in June of 1950 the Soviets were boycotting the United

Nations to protest that organization's refusal to admit the PRC. They therefore missed crucial Security Council meetings that authorized the military defense of South Korea. The U.N. forces in Korea, which included small contingents of troops from several American allies, turned the tide of battle in their favor in September. In November, to stave off a total North Korean defeat and the destruction of that Communist regime, the PRC intervened in force. The war dragged on near the 38th parallel until several months after Stalin's death in March 1953, helping to guarantee that the Cold War, intensified even further by the American–Soviet race to develop a hydrogen bomb, would remain dangerously acute even after Stalin passed from the scene.

THE CONSERVATIVE DICTATOR

Whatever its faults or failures, Soviet foreign policy after World War II was dynamic, even revolutionary. In the Eastern European countries he controlled, Stalin imposed entirely new social systems based on the Soviet model. This included the Communist Party's monopoly of political power, purges, terror, concentration camps, planned industrialization, and collectivization. Significantly, collectivization was pursued much more slowly in the satellite countries than had been the policy in Soviet Russia. Only in Bulgaria was more than half the arable land collectivized by 1953. At the same time, as one of the world's two nuclear powers, the Soviet Union enjoyed a status in international affairs that matched or exceeded that achieved by Russia after the Napoleonic Wars.

By contrast, Stalin's internal policies were conservative and, in a sense, even reactionary. Most of his efforts were directed toward restoring and preserving the system that had evolved prior to 1941. His difficulties in this regard came from several sources. During the war millions of Soviet citizens—either as prisoners of war, displaced persons, victorious soldiers, or inhabitants of territory overrun by the Germans—had come into contact with foreign ideas, or, even worse, had actually seen the way people lived outside the Soviet Union. The war had forced Stalin to relax certain controls in order to win popular support for the defense effort. More important, Stalin's revolution from above had produced a new generation of highly educated specialists, people who wanted the type of security Stalin had never been willing to grant. This new generation staffed the huge and complex bureaucratic machine that ran the country, a machine whose very complexity made it increasingly difficult for its creator to control. Much of what Stalin did during his last years may therefore be explained as an attempt to manage that apparatus by using a combination of violence and threats to keep its most powerful elements off balance and pitted against each other.

MASS ARRESTS AND DEPORTATIONS

There also were very direct challenges to Stalin's way of doing things, and even to Soviet power itself. In the Baltic states of Lithuania, Latvia, and Estonia, as well as in the western Ukraine, areas that had not been part of the Soviet Union between the world wars and that had been occupied by the Germans during much of World War II, the attempt to reestablish Soviet control after the war met determined resistance. Thousands of Soviet troops died fighting local partisans after the Red Army had driven the Germans out. Repeating tactics it had used since 1939, the NKVD turned to mass deportations to quell opposition. In May 1946, during a forty-eight-hour dragnet called "Operation Spring," almost 37,000 Lithuanian men, women, and children were arrested and deported; they were categorized as "bandits, nationalists, and families of these two categories." By the end of the year the deportation total in Lithuania reached 80,000. In 1949, almost 95,000 additional people were deported from Lithuania, Latvia, and Estonia. Recent research by Nicolas Werth indicates that as a result of wartime and postwar deportations and arrests, by 1953 "10 percent of the entire Baltic population was either deported or in a camp." The western Ukraine, Werth reports, "was finally 'pacified' at the end of 1950, after forced collectivization of the land, the displacement of whole villages, and the arrest and deportation of 300,000 people."[1]

Meanwhile, by 1946 the Gulag, already filled to the brim with newly deported soldiers, partisans, and nationalists of various stripes, was boiling over. Several major uprisings involving thousands of prisoners rocked Stalin's slave labor empire between 1946 and 1950. These revolts were crushed, but unrest continued to simmer in many parts of the Gulag into the new decade.

Stalin's defensive measures began with approximately 5 million soldiers, POWs, slave laborers, and refugees, all of whom had spent part of the war outside the Soviet Union. It was an episode with many victims and no heroes, at least among the Western leaders who acquiesced to Soviet demands. Hundreds of thousands of people of all types who were left behind Western lines when the fighting ended did not want to return home. They were forced to go back because the Western powers wanted to ensure the safe return of their nationals behind Soviet lines and were still trying to avoid an open split with Stalin. They therefore made every effort to honor the Yalta agreements calling for the return of all displaced persons to their respective countries. Many of the people subject to these agreements committed suicide rather than return to the Soviet Union. Some tore their clothes off in a vain attempt to stay where they were. Allied soldiers had to force others into trains and trucks at gunpoint or with rifle butts and bayonets. Still others fought with the troops ordered to ship them eastward; some begged the troops to shoot them. Between 1945 and 1947 about 2 million Soviet citizens, and several thousand people who had left the Soviet Union before 1921 and therefore had never been Soviet citizens, were shipped eastward, and into Stalin's clutches. They were joined by 3 million more people brought back from territory occupied by the Red Army.

These unfortunates did not receive a gracious welcome at home. Stalin was determined not to repeat Russia's experience after the Napoleonic Wars, when soldiers returning from their victorious campaign in the West brought back enough subversive ideas to foment the Decembrist uprising of 1825. To Stalin, anyone's presence in the West, regardless of the reasons, was proof that he or she was a traitor. So the returnees were quarantined as soon as they touched native soil. Some were executed outright, sometimes behind the warehouses on the docks where they had just landed. Most were shipped directly to newly established "filtration" camps. From there the majority, mainly women and children, were allowed to go home, but many of the men ended up in army disciplinary battalions or in what were called "reconstruction battalions." An additional 360,000 were sent to Gulag labor camps or into exile as special settlers. Of course, there were some collaborators with the Nazis among those shot or deprived of their freedom, but most of the returnees were completely innocent of any crime; they were murdered or sent to living deaths because the regime decided that they had committed "treason against the fatherland" or simply were "socially dangerous."

ECONOMIC RECOVERY

World War II had left huge sections of the Soviet Union in ruins. A British correspondent described the landscape he observed in the western part of the country shortly after the war ended:

> To travel, painfully slowly, by train from Moscow to the new frontier at Brest-Litovsk in the days after the war was a nightmare experience. For hundreds of miles, there was not a standing or a living object to be seen. Every town was flat, every city. There were no barns. There was no machinery. There were no stations, no water towers. There was not a solitary telegraph pole left standing in all that vast landscape. . . . In the fields, unkempt, nobody but women, children, very old men could be seen, and these worked only with hand tools. In winter it was even more uncanny. Then the blanket of snow quite concealed what tiny vestiges of life remained. . . . Smolensk stood, a ruin, on its hill. Minsk, the great capital of Byelorussia, simply was not there—only a plain of snow, broken by meaningless hummocks.[2]

In cold statistical terms, aside from the staggering human losses, 70,000 villages, 100,000 collective farms, 40,000 miles of railway, and half of all urban housing had been entirely or partially destroyed. None of this deterred Stalin. When he spoke to the nation on February 9, 1946, many in his audience undoubtedly were expecting their leader to promise them some relief. Instead, they heard that the forced march of economic development of the 1930s would be resumed. Soviet Russia still lived in a hostile world, Stalin told his people, and this meant that the traditional emphasis on industrial development and heavy industry would continue. Collectivized agriculture would be preserved. Stalin's goals were as grandiose and oppressive as ever. Steel production would have to reach 60 million tons by 1960 (versus 12 million in 1945) and coal production 500 million tons (versus 150 million in 1945). Other targets for heavy industry were equally ambitious.

Actions followed these words. The lax practices of the war were abolished. Agriculture was the hardest hit; the wartime expansion of private peasant plots was reversed, and *kolkhozy* were forced to deliver grain and other produce to the government at extremely low prices, often at less than the costs of production. That was not even the worst of it. Every peasant household, for example, was obligated to deliver 200 liters of milk per year to the state, this when over half the peasant households had no cow. The number of workdays each peasant owed the collective was raised, as were taxes. To better supervise all this, the state ordered that the *kolkhozy* be merged into larger units, a process that decreased the total number of collectives by more than half. The currency reform of 1947 substituted one new ruble for ten old ones, thereby effectively wiping out the savings some peasants had accumulated during the war. Nor was there investment in agriculture that might have boosted its chronically low productivity. As in the 1930s, nothing was allowed to get in the way of Stalin's agricultural policies, and the consequences again were dreadful. In 1946, a summer drought struck the Ukraine and several Russian provinces, severely reducing the grain harvest. In a repeat of what occurred in 1932, the regime refused to lower crop collection targets in the affected areas. And again the result was famine, which this time claimed at least 500,000 lives. Once again Stalin refused to take any action to ease the crisis, despite the appeals of Nikita Khrushchev, who was in charge of the Ukraine at the time. All news of the famine and its victims was suppressed.

In the next few years agricultural production did manage a slow recovery, reaching its overall 1940 level by 1949, but considerable hunger still stalked both the cities and the countryside. By 1952 Soviet agriculture still produced less grain and potatoes, its two major crops, than in 1940. In fact, total grain production was less than it had been under Nicholas II in 1913. Meanwhile, in the cities privation remained the rule. Workers in the immediate postwar years endured low wages and intensified labor discipline and lived in war-damaged housing. In 1949 real wages were less than half of their 1940 level. As was the case during the 1930s industrialization drive, Gulag forced laborers did many of the most difficult jobs. The Gulag administration also supplied hundreds of thousands laborers to other Soviet agencies. Overall, between 1950 and 1952 the Gulag reached its peak in terms of its share of Soviet industrial production.

It may seem hard to imagine how any regime could have demanded such sacrifices from its people after the war and survived. Such were the advantages of totalitarianism. Because of these sacrifices the immediate postwar years produced spectacular economic growth. By 1953, steel and pig iron production were about double their 1940 levels. Oil production was up by two-thirds over 1940, coal by 100 percent. By 1960 Stalin's steel and coal targets were reached and that for oil was exceeded. No less important, the Soviet Union managed to rearm with modern weapons, particularly after 1949. This was facilitated by a surge in capital investment in military infrastructure and in industries producing arms and military technology, which rose by 60 percent in 1951 and by an additional 40 percent in 1952. Top priority went to the atomic bomb project, which beginning in 1945 absorbed enormous resources. Stalin put Beria in charge; his job was to get results regardless of the costs, human or otherwise. More than 450,000 people worked on the project, half of them mining uranium under literally lethal conditions. Led by physicist Igor Kurchatov, Soviet scientists built an experimental nuclear reactor in Moscow and in December 1946 achieved their first controlled nuclear reaction. Meanwhile, a special laboratory to design a bomb, Arzamas-16, was established 240 miles east of Moscow. A nuclear reactor to produce the plutonium needed for a bomb, built at breakneck speed by a labor force of 70,000 on the eastern slopes of the Urals, began operation in mid-1948. In August 1949, aided by information from spies who had penetrated the wartime American nuclear project, Kurchatov and his colleagues successfully tested the Soviet Union's first atomic bomb, a virtual copy of the world's first atomic bomb the United States had tested four years earlier.

By Stalin's death in 1953, the Soviet Union possessed not only atomic bombs but an array of new land, air, and sea weaponry that included guided missiles; it also was only a few months away from successfully testing its first prototype hydrogen bomb (the United States had tested a thermonuclear device in 1952). Finally, during the Fourth Five-Year Plan (1946–1950), some progress was made in producing consumer goods. Although these continued to be in very short supply and life remained extremely difficult, the miserably low living standards slowly began to rise. Overall, aided by industrial booty taken from Germany as war reparations immediately after the fighting stopped and by its economic exploitation of its European satellites, the Soviet

Union's economy grew rapidly during Stalin's final eight years. It thus was able to support the Soviet Union's superpower pretensions.

THE *ZHDANOVSHCHINA*

No less than Western military or economic strength, Stalin feared Western ideas, which accounts for his treatment of millions of returnees after the war. Yet even with the returnees out of the way, Stalin was convinced that the rest of the Soviet population had been contaminated by Western ideas during the war. He therefore decided to launch an ideological offensive to vaccinate every Soviet citizen against Western intellectual germs. This campaign against Western influence of all sorts has gone down in history as the *Zhdanovshchina,* after Andrei Zhdanov. From the time of Kirov's murder until his own death from heart disease and alcoholism in 1948, Zhdanov was Stalin's satrap in Leningrad. He began his comprehensive campaign against Western influence in 1946 with a vicious attack on two of the Soviet Union's leading writers, Anna Akhmatova and Mikhail Zoshchenko. Zhdanov called Akhmatova a combination of "a whore and a nun" because of her concern with inner spirituality and art for art's sake. Zoshchenko, perhaps the Soviet Union's leading humorist, was the "scum of the literary world." The campaign spread to theater and film, and from there to music, philosophy, economics, and beyond. The great composers Prokofiev and Shostakovich were informed that their music was too "bourgeois," while Sergei Eisenstein was compelled to admit that part two of his classic film *Ivan the Terrible* was "worthless and vicious" because it was too critical of Ivan and his murderous police. Yevgeny Varga, the country's leading economist, was denounced for failing to foresee the presumed impending postwar American depression, an event that never occurred.

The list goes on. Jazz was banned. Trofim Lysenko flourished as the destructive dictator of Soviet genetics. Everything Russian was extolled vis-à-vis the West. Russian expansion under the tsars was deemed progressive. It was revealed that previously unheralded Russian geniuses invented innumerable things before Western tinkerers falsely received credit for their achievements. Russian, as Stalin himself hinted when he intervened in an academic debate on linguistics, was the language of the future. Zhdanov's death in August 1948 brought relief only to his political rivals. The *Zhdanovshchina,* stripped only of its masthead, forged ahead, as Stalin, its motive power, continued to hatch his plots in the Kremlin.

THE BLACK YEARS OF SOVIET JEWRY

Another aspect of the *Zhdanovshchina* was its revival of anti-Semitism. Stalin seems to have always borne an animus toward Jews. There were clear anti-Semitic overtones in his struggle against Trotsky. He became furious when two of his children married Jews, and the presence of numerous Jews among the Bolshevik old guard Stalin so loathed and feared did little to moderate his hostility toward that minority. Many Jews were dismissed from sensitive positions in the state and party apparatus during the 1930s, a process that culminated in Litvinov's removal as foreign minister in 1939. Still, these elements of bigotry and discrimination did not coalesce into a coherent policy for many years. However, after the war—during which the Nazis murdered more than 2 million of the 5.25 million Jews living in the Soviet Union as of 1941—the Soviet government embraced anti-Semitism as closely as had any bigoted monarch in the days of the tsars.

There seem to have been several immediate causes for Stalin's anti-Semitic campaign. Soviet Jews probably had more contacts abroad than most other ethnic groups. In fact, during the war Stalin had even used this resource, sending his hand-picked "Jewish Anti-Fascist Committee," headed by the great Yiddish theater actor Solomon Mikhoels, to drum up support for the Soviet Union in the West. A special attack on Jews, particularly on the community's intellectual elite, therefore grew naturally out of the overall campaign against Western influences. Equally important, if not decisive, the establishment of the State of Israel in 1948, which Stalin had initially supported in order to undermine the Western powers in the Middle East, and the enormous enthusiasm it evoked from Soviet Jews unnerved Stalin, the potentate of a multinational empire.

The result was a frontal assault on the Soviet Jewish community. The period from 1948 to 1953 is aptly known as the "Black Years of Soviet Jewry." It began with the murder of Mikhoels in January 1948. Later that year hundreds of Jewish intellectuals, including the remaining leaders of the Jewish Anti-Fascist Committee, were arrested. Some were shot immediately, the others sent to prison. Fifteen members of the Jewish Anti-Fascist committee were tried for treason and espionage in 1952; one died during the proceedings while thirteen others were shot and one sent to a labor camp after their inevitable convictions. All these people were "rootless cosmopolitans" whose knowledge of and love for Western culture made them un-Russian, unpatriotic, and unreliable. Virtually all the Jewish community's communal institutions—theaters, newspapers, the remaining synagogues—were shut down. Thousands were arrested. Finally, in January 1953 nine doctors, seven of them Jewish, were arrested for allegedly murdering Zhdanov and plotting to kill other top Soviet officials. No one can tell for sure where the "Doctors' Plot" would have led, but there is evidence suggesting that Stalin intended to deport Soviet Jews en masse to Siberia.

THE OLD MAN

During his last years, Stalin's mental state began to deteriorate markedly under the impact of hardening of the arteries and growing paranoia. Milovan Djilas, a Yugoslav Communist, commented that in 1948 the formerly quick-witted Stalin began to act "in the manner of old men." Khrushchev reported that in Stalin's last years, "He trusted no one and none of us could trust him. He would not let us do the work he was no longer able to do." Regardless of his deteriorating health, Stalin still was capable of many things. Among them was keeping everyone around him on the edge of a cliff, including several would-be successors. For example, beginning in 1946 Andrei Zhdanov appeared to be Stalin's right-hand man. Yet Zhdanov's death in 1948 was followed by a massive purge of his Leningrad organization. About 2,000 people were executed in this "Leningrad Affair," allegedly for participation in an "anti-party" group.

Zhdanov's demise raised the stock of two other top Stalin lieutenants— Lavrenty Beria and Georgy Malenkov, the men who conducted the Leningrad purge. Yet they were unnerved by the executions of high-ranking officials close to Zhdanov. So were other members of Stalin's inner circle, all of whom, their scheming against each other notwithstanding, now did what they could to keep Stalin calm and moderate his suspicions. Beria had performed a long list of important services for Stalin and joined the Politburo in 1946. By 1951, however, his star was dimming because of his alleged involvement in another of Stalin's concoctions, the "Mingrilian Affair," a nonexistent web of crimes named after a region in Stalin's and Beria's native Georgia. Nor could Molotov, formerly the Soviet Union's prime minister and its foreign minister since 1939, rest easy. Stalin removed him as foreign minister in 1949 and sent his wife, who happened to be Jewish, to a labor camp. It was, in fact, one of Stalin's long-established practices to arrest immediate relatives of his closest aides, which may explain why Molotov's wife once greeted an acquaintance at a function with the remark, "Ah, Sasha, haven't you been arrested yet?" Stalin also publicly called both Molotov and Voroshilov British spies. Other ministers to lose their jobs were Anastas Mikoyan (whose son had been arrested) and Nikolai Bulganin. Nikita Khrushchev, a tough purger and administrator who served Stalin in the Ukraine and in Moscow and as a Politburo member since 1939, seemed to be a rising power. Yet he too ran into trouble, first in 1947, when he temporarily lost his post as first secretary of the Ukrainian party organization, and again in 1951, when his scheme to consolidate the *kolkhozy* into huge "agro-cities" was rejected. The best bet in this thoroughly confusing situation was Malenkov. The youngest of the group—he was only fifty in 1952—his power base was in the Secretariat. The clearest sign of his ascendancy appeared at the Nineteenth Party Congress in

1952, when he became the first person other than Stalin to deliver the main report to the Congress since Zinoviev did it nearly thirty years before.

THE NINETEENTH PARTY CONGRESS

The Nineteenth Party Congress was the first one Stalin had called in thirteen years, party regulations that called for a congress every three years notwithstanding. The aging dictator, whose physical appearance had noticeably deteriorated, did not speak until the last session of the congress. Still, despite the prominence accorded Malenkov, Stalin appeared to be using the meeting to dilute the powers of his top lieutenants. The congress abolished the old Politburo and Orgburo in favor of a new "Presidium." The Presidium was a bulky body of thirty-six members, in contrast to the trim Politburo's eleven. The Secretariat was expanded from five to ten members. The implication of these changes undoubtedly was not lost on Stalin's top aides, since packing party bodies had been one of his most effective techniques for undermining rivals in his struggle for power in the 1920s. Stalin also continued his war on the Bolshevik past. In 1946, he had changed the name of the government from the Council of People's Commissars, its revolutionary title, to the more conventional Council of Ministers. Now he changed the party's official name from the All-Union Communist Party (Bolsheviks) to the Communist Party of the Soviet Union. The term "Bolshevik" now joined the dreams it once represented and the many people who had proudly embraced that label in the huge historical graveyard Stalin had built for them all.

THE LAST PLOT

Stalin did not long survive the Nineteenth Party Congress, a fortunate development for his nervous lieutenants. In all likelihood he had been planning another purge, one that almost certainly would have engulfed most of them. The Doctors' Plot, announced to the world in January 1953, accused a group of physicians of murdering Zhdanov and of being in the clutches of the CIA, British intelligence, and the Joint Distribution Committee, a Jewish social welfare organization. Aside from what evil that boded for the Soviet Union's Jewish population, these revelations and the enormous security lapses they implied suggested nothing good for Beria and Malenkov, among others. However, except for two doctors who died under torture in prison, everyone survived. The underlings lived because this time it was the boss who died. After suffering a stroke on March 1, 1953, Stalin, who normally had the best of everything, could not be treated by his personal physician, who was under arrest in the Doctors' Plot. Stalin died on March 5, 1953.

STALINISM IN HISTORICAL PERSPECTIVE

Stalin's death ended one of the most murderous regimes in human history. The total number who died will never be known, in part because after March 1953 many of the relevant police records were destroyed and cemeteries and burial grounds either plowed under or covered with fresh soil. A reasonable guess is that collectivization, dekulakization, the Stalin famine, the purges, the labor camps, the executions, the wartime military policies, and the deportations claimed at least 20 million lives, and possibly more. It was said in the eighteenth century that Peter the Great built his city of St. Petersburg on bones; in the twentieth century Stalin built his socialist society on them. It goes beyond human reason and sensibility that anything could justify such apocalyptic human suffering. Yet the student of history must assess and evaluate what the Stalin regime built and accomplished between 1929 and 1953 against at least two standards: Russia's historic struggle to catch up economically and militarily with the West and the professed goals of Marxism and the Bolshevik Revolution.

In terms of cold statistics, the economic growth of the Stalin years was substantial, even spectacular. After centuries of lagging behind the West, Soviet Russia in a generation became the world's second leading industrial power, trailing only the United States. Despite the destruction of World War II, overall production grew by four times and heavy industrial production by nine times. The gap in the ability to fight modern warfare was overcome by increasing the funds available to the military by twenty-six times between 1928 and 1952. All of this translated into enormous power that gave Soviet Russia greater security from foreign attack than ever before. In short, under the "man of steel," Soviet Russia's position in the world underwent a profound and fundamental improvement.

These gains look much less impressive in a broader perspective. Despite all the *Sturm und Drang*, overall growth under Lenin and Stalin was no greater on a per year percentage basis than it had been during the last fifty years under the tsars. Most Western estimates place the annual industrial growth rate for Stalin's great industrialization drive (1928–1940) at between 9 and 12 percent, a range that exceeds but certainly does not dwarf what Witte achieved in the 1890s (about 8 percent annual growth). Nor can the Soviets boast vis-à-vis the Japanese. Their average annual rate of growth in gross national product (GNP) matched Russia's for the 1928–1940 period as a whole, while their annual rate of industrial growth was reasonably close (8.9 percent versus between 9 and 12 percent) for the 1931–1940 period. Between 1950 and 1973, Japan's annual GNP increase averaged 10 percent, a record of long-term growth unmatched in the Soviet Union before, during, or after the Stalin era. In light of the enormous waste, inefficiency, and human suffering Stalin's methods entailed, as well as the existence of other records of achievement and the alternative methods suggested within the Communist Party prior to Stalin's revolution from above, the evidence is compelling that the industrial growth achieved under Stalin could have been attained with far less pain by other methods.

If the record in terms of quantity is ambiguous at best, it is clear in terms of quality, at least as defined by traditional Marxist and socialist ideals. The socialist and Marxist vision was of a classless, egalitarian society held together by voluntary cooperation, a situation that supposedly would eventually render the old oppressive state superfluous. That vision promised prosperity, freedom, and the end of human alienation. Under Stalin, the people of the Soviet Union were oppressed more than ever before by a state that became larger and more powerful than ever before. Despite economic growth, the standard of living plummeted for most Soviet citizens. A new elite replaced the old. Djilas called that elite the "New Class." Under any name, it monopolized the fruit of the nation's labor for itself, much like the old aristocracy or any other ruling class. It is true that capitalism and private property were abolished in the Soviet Union, but this in itself, especially when accompanied by tyranny, did not constitute socialism or communism to Marx. Plekhanov, the father of Russian Marxism, had called this control of the masses by an all-powerful elite "Inca Communism" and had warned strenuously against it. When measured against the traditional Marxist assumptions of what a socialist society should look like, the Stalinist social order would seem to be its political, economic, and social opposite.

Despite its formidable record in terms of heavy industry and military power, the Stalinist system was yet another catastrophe, possibly the worst, that has befallen the people of Russia in their troubled history. As historian Robert Conquest has noted: "Stalinism is one way of industrialization, just as cannibalism is one way of attaining a high protein diet."[3] In 1953, there was nothing anyone could do about Stalin's methods. What counted after March 5, 1953, was what his successors would do with the impoverished and brutalized society his methods had left them.

NOTES

1. For these and related statistics in this chapter, see Nicolas Werth, "A State Against Its People: Violence, Repression, and Terror in the Soviet Union," in Stéphane Courtois et al., *The Black Book of Communism*, translated by Jonathan Murphy and Mark Kramer, consulting editor Mark Kramer (Cambridge, Mass., and London: Harvard University Press, 1999), pp. 235–238.

2. Edward Crankshaw, *Khrushchev: A Career* (New York: Viking, 1966), pp. 141–142.

3. Robert Conquest, *The Great Terror* (New York: Macmillan, 1968), p. 495.

Part V

The Socialist Superpower

Nikita Khrushchev at a meeting of the United Nations General Assembly in New York, September 1960.

16

Khrushchev: Reforming the Revolution

We removed
      him
              from the mausoleum.
  But how do we remove Stalin
            from Stalin's heirs?

—Yevgeny Yevtushenko[1]

Although Stalin's death was welcome news to many, including most if not all of his top lieutenants, it also evoked genuine mourning throughout the Soviet Union. Unrelenting propaganda over two decades had done its work; millions of Soviet citizens loved Comrade Stalin. This mourning was accompanied by fear, for Stalin's passing left a yawning gap in Soviet life in which all that was visible was the dark and foreboding unknown. At the same time, the atmosphere was heavy with relief. Life under Stalin had been unbearably harsh for the millions of ordinary Soviet citizens, who had very little, and insufferably tense and dangerous for the privileged Communist Party elite, who had everything but could lose it in a single stroke. This was as true for those at the very top of the party pyramid as it was for the tens of thousands of functionaries of lesser rank who managed the governing bureaucratic apparatus. More than anything else, these privileged but insecure people were determined to seize the first opportunity to protect themselves and stabilize their lives and careers. Stalin's last breath therefore turned into a wind of change that almost immediately began to sweep away parts of the system he had so laboriously built.

This process of change was anything but smooth, for Stalin's death added an enormous problem to those that existed while he was alive. The dead tyrant's successors knew that they could not govern as he had. Their personal security could not be achieved simply by the end of the terror from above; it also required additional reforms to avoid a possible threat from the abused and oppressed masses. The dilemma that Stalin's death presented was to determine what kind of reform the system—the Communist Party dictatorship and centralized socialist economy—could stand without being undermined. At what point would the reforms that were necessary to sustain the system begin to threaten it? No consensus existed on this crucial question. While there was considerable fear that reform might generate its own momentum and run out of control, moves toward retrenchment evoked fears of a renewed Stalinist terror.

This two-sided dilemma immediately metamorphosed into a long-lived political hydra that sprouted new heads even as Stalin's successors hacked away at the old ones. It wounded Georgy Malenkov, Stalin's unsuccessful heir-apparent; hounded Nikita Khrushchev, the eventual winner in the post-1953 struggle for power; and pestered Leonid Brezhnev, who led the coup against Khrushchev and his reforms. After Brezhnev it stalked Yuri Andropov and Konstantin Chernenko and then devoured Mikhail Gorbachev, ultimately tearing the Soviet Union itself to pieces in the process.

"COLLECTIVE LEADERSHIP"

After March 1953 Soviet political life became a sort of interlocking two-ring circus, with the struggle for power going on in the first ring and a flurry of reform activity in the second. In the first ring Stalin's former Politburo lieutenants moved to reassert the authority they as a group had lost during Stalin's last months; at the same time, as individuals they scrambled to acquire as much personal power as they could. Georgy Malenkov, the number-two leader before Stalin's death, initially cornered the positions of senior party secretary and prime minister, respectively the top party and government posts, to emerge as the apparent number one. Lavrenty Beria, Stalin's longtime enforcer and executioner, became a first deputy prime minister; more significantly, he took over the newly strengthened Ministry of Interior (MVD), which was given control over the secret police. The veteran Bolshevik Vyacheslav Molotov, one of the very few pre-1917 figures left, a Politburo member since 1925 who had served long stints as both prime minister (1930–1941) and foreign minister (1939–1949), now again became foreign minister and, like Beria, a first deputy prime minister. These three in effect formed an uneasy triumvirate ostensibly committed to what they solemnly called "collective leadership." A small step below them was Nikita Khrushchev, former party boss of the Ukraine and subsequently the first secretary of the party's Moscow organization. Along with other Stalin henchmen such as Lazar Kaganovich and

Anastas Mikoyan, Malenkov and his partners purged the Presidium (as the Politburo was called after 1952) of the newcomers Stalin had brought in to dilute their power in 1952 and emerged as Stalin's successors, the new rulers of the Soviet Union.

THE STRUGGLE FOR POWER

This new ruling order proved to be unstable. It buried Stalin without serious incident, Beria having deployed his secret police troops and tanks around Moscow to make sure that the population avoided "disorder" or "panic," but small cracks quickly appeared in the ruling group's "united and unshakable" ranks. On March 14, only nine days after Stalin's death, Malenkov was compelled by his colleagues to give up his post on the Secretariat, probably to prevent him, or anyone else, from accumulating too much power and following in Stalin's footsteps. That important job now went to Khrushchev, possibly because the three senior men did not consider him a serious candidate for supreme power. The small cracks widened quickly during the next three months as Beria showered his comrades with a series of reform proposals in a campaign clearly designed to enhance his political standing at their expense. Beria also was out in front in criticizing the recently departed Stalin. His disparaging remarks ranged from writing policy memos critical of Stalin's treatment of non-Russian minorities to calling his late mentor a "son of a bitch," "tyrant," and "bloodsucker." None of this, it turned out, saved him from being engulfed by the first political split of the post-Stalin era. On June 26, 1953, Beria, the member of the ruling group most feared by his colleagues because he controlled the secret police, was secretly arrested in his Kremlin office while army tanks surrounded the secret police headquarters. Khrushchev was the organizer of the anti-Beria coup. An immediate purge of the secret police followed, including several executions, as did a public announcement in July that Beria had been a "capitalist agent" and an "enemy of the people" all along. His secret trial and execution came in December, while trials of leading secret police officers that resulted in numerous executions continued until 1956.

Beria's removal was followed by a showdown between Malenkov and the rapidly rising Khrushchev. At first Malenkov, who stood senior to Khrushchev both before and after March 1953, appeared stronger, but several inopportune moves, including his attempt immediately after Stalin's death to monopolize the top party and government posts, hurt his standing with his colleagues. Also damaging was his public promise to raise the standard of living by producing more consumer goods at the expense of investment in heavy industry, a pledge that antagonized powerful vested interests, including the military and party leaders directly involved with heavy industry, and which Khrushchev was able to use against him. Malenkov also was hindered by habits acquired as a result of his past successes. He seemed to believe that behind-the-scenes intrigue in Moscow, which had been sufficient when Stalin's support was the crucial political factor, would still suffice in a new era of Soviet politics when there were many more flanks in the huge party bureaucracy to be covered.

Most of all, however, Malenkov lost because Khrushchev seized the initiative and won. Dynamic and outgoing, Khrushchev was skilled at using face-to-face meetings to rally support, which he busily did on factory floors and at collective farms and, far more important, in meetings with party cadres and officials. He also was adept at bureaucratic intrigue, using his old contacts from his decade as party boss in the Ukraine as a power base and his new job as first secretary (as his position on the Secretariat was called after September 1953) to place his supporters in key positions during 1953 and 1954. Thus, by 1955 Khrushchev loyalists and allies headed the Leningrad (Frol Kozlov) and Moscow (Katerina Furtseva) party organizations, the secret police (Ivan Serov), and the Komsomol (Alexander Shelepin). Khrushchev's replacement of over half of the provincial party first secretaries meant the emergence of yet more of his partisans. Khrushchev also skillfully exploited the poor conditions in agriculture and the discomfiture felt by the moguls of heavy industry and the military over Malenkov's consumerism to discredit his rival. Malenkov was further compromised by his ties to the discredited Beria. By February 1955 he was outmaneuvered. Recognizing his lack of support, Malenkov resigned as prime minister, confessing his overall "inexperience" in local work and industrial affairs and his "guilt and responsibility" for the "unsatisfactory" state of agriculture. Neither Khrushchev nor Malenkov mentioned that after World War II it was Malenkov who had successfully overseen the reconstruction of the Soviet Union's aircraft industry and managed the recovery of large areas of the country occupied during the war by the Germans, or that it was Khrushchev, not Malenkov, who had been in charge of agriculture between 1953 and 1955.

THE "THAW"

That so much changed even as the struggle for power was being played out is a measure of the enormous pressure for reform Stalin's successors faced. In fact, the struggle for power itself contributed to the reform process. That Malenkov tried to win public acceptance and support in March 1953 by publicly promising the Soviet people more consumer goods was a landmark in itself. An equally significant departure from Stalin's methods occurred in April of that year, when Beria, who apparently was willing to undertake more extensive reforms than any of his colleagues, publicly admitted that the Doctors' Plot was a hoax perpetrated by the presumably unimpeachable Soviet government. He then released the seven surviving doctors and sanctioned the arrest of the secret police officials supposedly responsible for the hoax. Of course, Beria's own arrest and the subsequent purge of the secret police produced a far greater reform as they helped bring that dreaded institution under the control of the party leadership as a whole for the first time in more than two decades. Henceforth, methods other than terror would have to be used both in the struggle for power and to govern the nation.

This was all certainly welcome news to the long-suffering Soviet public. The events of 1953 seemed to signal that some degree of personal security and an improvement in the material standard of living, two things the Soviet people desperately needed and wanted, were in the offing. There were even hints that the Soviet intellectual community might get a small measure of what it craved: a loosening of censorship. The public therefore had good reason to watch with interest, even if that was virtually all it could do as its fate was decided.

The Soviet people also received some good news about prices. During April of 1953 retail prices were cut by an average of 10 percent. The prices of some foodstuffs, such as meat, potatoes, and vegetables, were cut by even larger amounts. Though this policy led mostly to longer lines at stores because there were insufficient quantities of these goods, the announcements did represent a new interest in wooing popular support. So did the title Malenkov in August gave to his economic program, the "New Course," in which even the peasants received something. During 1953, among other good tidings, some debts and tax arrears were canceled, taxes on private plots and compulsory deliveries by the collectives to the state reduced, and higher prices paid for those deliveries.

The winds of change reached even to the deepest caverns of the Gulag, where a total of 5.5 million people languished: 2.75 million prisoners in labor camps, colonies, and prisons and an equal number of people living in exile in special settlements. Stalin's successors were well aware of the inefficiencies of Gulag labor. For example, a report Beria had commissioned in 1950 revealed that the monthly cost of housing, feeding, and guarding a forced laborer involved in building the Don–Volga canal during 1949 was 470 rubles a month whereas the monthly salary of a free worker would have been only 388 rubles. With Stalin gone, his successors acted quickly. An amnesty announced late in March, one of Beria's initiatives, freed 1.2 million camp, colony, and prison inmates serving short sentences (less than five years) within a period of just three months. Those released were mainly ordinary citizens who had run afoul of a long list of repressive laws such as "leaving the workplace" and petty criminals. Many of the latter gravitated to the cities and soon became responsible for a crime wave that made the streets of Moscow unsafe after dark. Only a tiny smattering of the Gulag's political prisoners was released during 1953. However, because most of this group were people with important connections—they included Molotov's wife and Khrushchev's daughter-in-law (the wife of his son Leonid, a fighter pilot killed during World War II)—their return to society increased the pressure for more amnesties and reform, especially as their numbers grew to 90,000, including some of Khrushchev's associates from the Stalin days, by 1955.

In 1954 an increasingly visible and active Khrushchev initiated the most dramatic economic reform of the immediate post-Stalin years, his "virgin lands" campaign. While Malenkov's attention focused on the "intensification" of agriculture, that is, on the complex and long-term effort to increase productivity on land already under cultivation, Khrushchev, an impatient man by nature, expected to achieve an immediate, spectacular expansion of the food supply (and not incidentally to boost his own political stock) by putting enormous new areas under cultivation. His plan was to farm previously uncultivated land in Central Asia and western Siberia. These areas had been left unsown because rainfall there was unreliable and often inadequate. Many party leaders therefore opposed the plan with good reason. Still, Khrushchev succeeded in launching his pet program, choosing an up-and-coming party bureaucrat, Leonid Brezhnev, to go to Kazakhstan to run it. Brezhnev was joined by 300,000 young Komsomol recruits, supposedly "volunteers," who traveled eastward on special trains to work on hundreds of newly organized state farms. Despite poor planning and considerable hardship—housing was among the amenities of life the regime neglected to provide the idealistic pioneers—they produced a decent harvest in 1954, an important year in Khrushchev's power struggle with Malenkov. Khrushchev himself toured the region in 1954 and was enraptured by the scale of his enterprise. The fields were so enormous, he recalled, that "people . . . used to say a tractor driver could have breakfast at one end of the field, lunch at the other end, and dinner back where he'd started out in the morning." A drought in 1955 caused a serious setback, a "year of despair for the virgin lands" according to Brezhnev, but good weather and millions of newly plowed acres produced an excellent harvest in 1956 that again helped the program's sponsor. Never a man to rest on his laurels, Khrushchev had also opened another agricultural front in 1955 with a campaign to increase the production of corn, a crop he believed was a key to the agricultural success and consequent high standard of living in the United States, the Soviet Union's rival and nemesis.

The post-Stalin "thaw," as it usually is called after Ilya Ehrenburg's 1954 novel of that same name, also extended to cultural affairs. In 1953 Ehrenburg felt emboldened to declare that a writer was "not a piece of machinery" but someone who required autonomy and freedom. Others echoed his sentiments, including author Vladimir Pomerantsev, who attacked the all-powerful Writers' Union by noting that "Shakespeare was not a member of a union at all, yet he did not write badly." A new and more liberal minister of culture, G.F. Alexandrov, was appointed in early 1954. Writers began to explore a number of previously taboo themes, including corruption in the party and the damage Stalin's policies had done to artistic endeavor. It once again became possible to read the works of formerly proscribed authors such as Isaac Babel and Mikhail Bulgakov from the Soviet period and Dostoyevsky from pre-revolutionary times. In science, Lysenko's unscientific genetic theories came under attack, while contacts with the West were renewed in several disciplines in both the sciences and social sciences during 1954 and 1955. But although optimism about the possibility for further reform swelled, Alexandrov's dismissal in March 1955, barely a year after his appointment, indicated there were strict limits to change.

FOREIGN AFFAIRS

Foreign policy also received something of a facelift. By the 1950s, as their Cold War rivalry continued, the United States and the Soviet Union were busily building arsenals of nuclear weapons. Fearing a possible nuclear confrontation, particularly in light of the stalemate in Korea, Malenkov upon becoming prime minister moved to defuse tensions with the West. A Korean armistice was signed in July 1953, and the next year the Soviet Union helped arrange a conference that ended the war between the French colonial forces and Communist guerrillas in Vietnam. Relations with the West were further improved when the Soviet Union agreed in May 1955 with the United States, Britain, and France to end the four-power military occupation of Austria and permit the reunification and neutralization of that country. In July Khrushchev and Nikolai Bulganin, Malenkov's successor as prime minister, met with American, French, and British leaders in Geneva. The meeting yielded few concrete results, but it did provide an impetus for the policy Khrushchev was calling "peaceful coexistence." Another conciliatory move was the return to Finland of its naval base at Porkkala.

Although certainly not insignificant, these episodes proved to be islands of cooperation in a sea of contention. They did not prevent the hardening of Europe's division into Eastern and Western blocs. Germany remained divided, and West Germany began to rearm after entering NATO in 1955. The Soviet reaction included organizing the Warsaw Pact, the Moscow-dominated military alliance with its Eastern European satellites that after 1955 stood opposed to NATO across the breadth of Europe.

The Soviets also worked to mend their fences with Communist nations in an attempt to reunite the Communist world. A 1954 treaty with the People's Republic of China acknowledged Chinese control of Manchuria, stipulated that Soviet troops would withdraw from Port Arthur, and turned over certain assets to the Chinese. But the bargaining was hard, leaving the Chinese grudgingly satisfied rather than grateful. This was followed in May 1955 with a momentous visit by a delegation of Soviet notables to Yugoslavia, the Communist country Stalin had banished from the Soviet bloc seven years earlier. The Soviet delegation was led by Khrushchev, who publicly apologized to Yugoslav leader Tito for the latter's treatment at Stalin's hands. Khrushchev also acknowledged Yugoslavia's, and by implication any nation's, right to develop socialism in its own way, another radical departure from Stalin. Tito, while pleased, kept Yugoslavia at arm's length from the Soviet fold.

The Soviet leaders enjoyed greater success in their approaches to the newly independent nonaligned nations of Asia and Africa, an area Stalin had neglected. Unlike Western Europe, where deeply rooted fears and American power were insuperable obstacles to Soviet advances, or Yugoslavia and Communist China, where the Soviets faced both old fears and new grievances, Asia and Africa represented virgin and fertile fields for the Soviet Union to sow. The United States, despite its great wealth and power, was tainted by its associations with the British, French, Dutch, and Portuguese, whose crumbling empires left a powerful residue of resentment and anti-Western feeling. The Communist regime in Beijing, a potential if not yet an actual Soviet rival, may have had a "pure" anti-Western ideological pedigree, but it was too poor to offer much more than words to the poverty-stricken emerging nations. By contrast, the Soviet Union, which seemed to provide an imposing practical example of rapid economic progress, was an arch foe of Western imperialism and, in addition, able to offer some economic and military assistance to prospective new Asian and African friends.

A signal of this new interest in the Third World was a highly publicized junket that Khrushchev and Bulganin made to India, Burma, and Afghanistan in 1955. Subsequent Soviet efforts bore fruit in India and Egypt, two of the most important nations in their respective regions of the world. They became the largest recipients of Soviet aid. Other major recipients of Soviet economic or military assistance were Burma, Afghanistan, Indonesia, and Iraq, after military officers overthrew that Arab nation's pro-Western monarchy in 1958.

OBSTACLES TO REFORM

These internal reforms and foreign-policy initiatives did not come easily; they took place against a background of instability. Within months of Stalin's death, in fact, the combination of reduced pressures and apparent indecision among the new leadership led to a major anti-Soviet outbreak in East Germany, which erupted in East Berlin in June 1953 and quickly spread to cities throughout the country. Soviet troops and tanks were required to put down the strikes and demonstrations in East Berlin. Even worse, there was serious trouble in the Gulag, including three major uprisings during 1953 and 1954. Strikes in 1953 by thousands of prisoners at two Siberian locations, in May at the Norlisk labor camp complex and in July at the Vorkuta coal mines, were suppressed with great loss of life. Even more menacing to the regime was an uprising at the prison complex at Kengir in Kazakhstan that began in May 1954 and lasted for forty days before it was crushed by troops equipped with tanks.

Resistance to reform and doubts and hesitation by the would-be reformers themselves further constricted the process of change. Molotov, for example, strongly opposed a conciliatory foreign policy in general and Khrushchev's overtures to Tito in particular. Khrushchev himself circumscribed some of the regime's agricultural reforms by increasing party supervision of the collectives and raising the peasants' work obligations. The first secretary even played the role of anti-reformer when certain proposals conflicted with his political goals. He spoke against Malenkov's plans to increase consumer goods production at the expense of heavy industry, for example, thereby winning the support of key party elements who favored the traditional economic priorities.

Nonetheless, even the political struggle of 1953–1955 proved to be part of the process of reform. Its bloodless denouement in February 1955, which marked Khrushchev's triumph over Malenkov, was a major milestone in Soviet political history. Malenkov was demoted, not liquidated. He even remained on the party's ruling Presidium and in the government as minister of electric power stations. He was succeeded as prime minister by Bulganin, a technocrat rather than a top-ranking political power.

NIKITA KHRUSHCHEV: STALINIST AND ANTI-STALINIST

Although the events of February 1955 seemed to clarify the issue of who was in charge, a great many important issues remained unresolved. The reforms of the past two years were incomplete, to say the least. The basic structure of the economy remained unchanged, with old inefficiencies persisting and productivity still lagging. An increase in wages had produced both long lines for unavailable consumer goods and rising black-market prices for food, which remained in short supply. These discrepancies between supply and demand forced the government to raise prices in 1955. Many prisoners had been released from the Gulag, but millions remained behind barbed wire. Meanwhile nervous bureaucrats at all party levels, including those in the Presidium, feared the consequences of further reform and resisted it. A bottleneck seemed to have been reached.

The stage thus was set for Nikita Sergeyevich Khrushchev, the peasant-born, poorly educated worker from the grain fields of southern Russia and the coal mines of eastern Ukraine who had joined the Communist Party in 1918, supplemented his formal education by attending a party school for politically reliable workers, and built himself a remarkable career. An early protégé of Stalin's collectivizer and troubleshooter Lazar Kaganovich, Khrushchev was one of the generation that rose to prominence during Stalin's purges, an ascent, he later admitted, that left him "up to the elbows in blood." He ran the Ukraine for Stalin for about a decade after 1938, winning the dictator's favor by efficiently carrying out repressive policies that included Russification, deportation, and the general suppression of dissent. During World War II Khrushchev served with the Soviet army as a political officer, attaining the rank of major general, and saw the war's dreadful carnage firsthand. In 1949 he moved to the center of power in the Moscow party apparatus. Khrushchev was ruthless and tough, but crude; perhaps it was the latter characteristic that led his rivals to underestimate him after 1953. Whatever the reason, Khrushchev skillfully negotiated the post-Stalin political rapids, emerging as first secretary in September 1953 and as the victor in the struggle for power barely eighteen months later.

His surprising victory accomplished, Khrushchev soon provided other surprises. He was folksy and down to earth (sometimes excessively so, as numerous embarrassing public outbursts, such as pounding his desk with his shoe at the U.N. General Assembly, testify). While others in power remained remote from the population, Khrushchev was known for going out among the people and was often at his best when surrounded by crowds of ordinary workers and peasants. Khrushchev's contact with the people distinguished him from both his dead mentor and his living rivals, despite what he had done as one of Stalin's henchmen. His continual trips to the collectives and factories, both before and after 1953, gave him firsthand knowledge of conditions there and direct contact with the people's suffering. This apparently kept alive in him a spark of sympathy that dated from his youth and had made him a revolutionary in the first place.

Khrushchev also had been a horrified witness to some frightening consequences of Stalin's methods, especially the mass desertions and surrenders that occurred during the early days of World War II by Soviet citizens desperate enough to seek help from the invading Germans. This experience seems to have convinced him that the regime had to reach an accommodation with the general population if it was to survive. Beyond that, Khrushchev was convinced that the Soviet Union could never overcome the inefficiency and incompetence that weighed so heavily on the economy unless it first overcame public apathy and alienation. Only with popular support could the bountiful promises of socialism, and ultimately the even more bountiful promises of communism, be realized. And Khrushchev, for reasons of both personal vanity and genuine concern for the Soviet people, was determined to deliver on those promises, to bring about real progress in his own time and to receive the credit for it. Yet Khrushchev also reflected his Stalinist background and was not a democrat in any sense of the word. Therefore he inevitably undermined his own reform efforts. He wanted the people to participate and contribute but not to have any real power, and, like Stalin, was determined to bend the party to his will.

Khrushchev, then, urgently wanted change. The great obstacle to change remained Stalin, or rather Stalin's ghost, since his name still lent important legitimacy to those in the party opposed to further change. To be sure, Stalin's reputation had been tarnished slightly between 1953 and 1956, and his name was invoked far less frequently. Lenin's accomplishments were stressed at the expense of Stalin's, and a few of Stalin's victims were, as the euphemism went, "rehabilitated" posthumously. Yet, though slightly tarnished, Stalin's reputation still stood imposingly astride the Soviet Union, like the thousands of statues of him and monuments to him that littered the country's landscape.

THE TWENTIETH PARTY CONGRESS, KHRUSHCHEV'S SECRET SPEECH, AND DESTALINIZATION

All of that changed the night of February 24–25, 1956. The Twentieth Party Congress, the first since Stalin's death, was nearing the end of its deliberations. Just when most of the delegates thought the congress had finished its work, Khrushchev called them together for a closed session. The congress already had a respectable list of credits. The Sixth Five-Year Plan it approved promised increased investment in agriculture and more consumer goods. Khrushchev endorsed the doctrine of "peaceful coexistence" with the capitalist world, although he added that he expected the process of decolonization would provide ample opportunity for the spread of socialism and Soviet influence. There was even some criticism of Stalin in a speech by the old party veteran Anastas Mikoyan.

Nothing, however, had prepared the delegates for Khrushchev's four-and-one-half-hour tirade, a political trumpet blast heralding reforms in the Soviet system that would come to be called "destalinization." The Communist closet burst open and the skeletons came tumbling out. Khrushchev accused the deceased leader of being a brutal dictator. Stalin, the first secretary revealed, had ravaged the party by murdering thousands of its best people, including over 70 percent of the Central Committee at his own 1934 "Congress of Victors." The "Generalissimo" was a blunderer whose errors during World War II had cost enormous losses in lives. His bloodletting and mistakes had damaged vast areas of Soviet life, from governmental administration and economic performance to the nation's very ability to defend itself against the Germans. Adding insult to injury, Stalin had promoted a "personality cult" that glorified him beyond recognition and gave *him* credit for what so many others had done. Khrushchev documented it all with many long horror stories about particular individuals.

Although this sort of criticism was unprecedented, Khrushchev also left out a lot. He ignored the millions of peasants killed during collectivization and the suffering that accompanied the brutalities of the industrialization drive. The party itself, as distinguished from its leader, was left above criticism. Equally important, so was everything Stalin did prior to 1934, which according to Khrushchev amounted to a "great service" to the proletarian revolution. None of Stalin's major opponents of the 1920s were exonerated, nor did the millions of *non*party victims of the purges receive their due. Lenin and all he did still stood pristine and pure; the party remained the infallible vanguard of the proletariat; and Khrushchev emerged as the most loyal servant of the people, the party, and the beloved prophet Lenin.

IMPACT OF THE SECRET SPEECH

Khrushchev's "secret speech" did not remain secret for long. For one thing, copies were distributed to local party organizations across the Soviet Union. A copy soon reached the West, and its contents were released to the public by the U.S. State Department. In the Soviet Union, where it was not published until 1989, word of Khrushchev's earthshaking speech spread quickly. It proved to be a many-edged sword, cutting most deeply into Malenkov, Molotov, and Kaganovich, who stood closest to Stalin's throne while the worst crimes were being committed. Khrushchev therefore had helped himself in his campaign to discredit his most formidable opponents and consolidate his power.

Yet the speech also cut dangerously into the system that Khrushchev was determined to save and revitalize. After all, Stalin had ruled for almost twenty-five years with barely a breath of opposition from Khrushchev or anyone else in the leadership. Once Khrushchev cast doubts on Stalin, the party's symbol of truth for so long, he inevitably cast doubt not only on the party's future policy, but on its very legitimacy to rule. Using Khrushchev's speech, a good case could be made for condemning the entire party for permitting such terrible crimes.

Since the evidence and damage from Stalin's "crimes" were visible everywhere, the pressure for more reform built once news of the speech and its explosive contents spread throughout the Soviet Union and its satellites in Eastern Europe. Inside the Soviet Union, several million prisoners were released from the Gulag and many of the camps and other facilities closed down during 1956 and 1957. The reintegration of these people into Soviet life further intensified the pressures for an accounting of what had happened under Stalin and for those still in office to answer for what they had done prior to 1953. Some officials even received light rebukes—for example, Ivan Serov, who was fired as head of the secret police in 1958. But to accede to demands for accountability in any meaningful way would have been suicidal for the party leadership and probably for the system as a whole. Khrushchev had let a tiger loose simply by making his secret speech, as he quickly found out.

THE POLISH UPHEAVAL AND THE HUNGARIAN UPRISING

Developments in the satellites first raised the specter of a Communist collapse. The combination of oppressive, Moscow-imposed Communist dictatorships and nationalist feeling became an explosive compound when stirred by Khrushchev's catalyzing secret speech. Poland and Hungary, two nations with little love for Russia, burst out of control in 1956. In Poland, bloody riots occurred in June. By October the pressures on the old-line Stalinist rulers were great enough to force a major change. Wladyslaw Gomulka, an independent-minded Communist recently released after serving five years in prison for "Titoism," crowned his political comeback by being elected first secretary. Although Gomulka made no attempt to pull Poland out of the Soviet orbit, he was determined that his country enjoy a measure of independence. He stood up to immense Soviet pressure, including an angry visit from Khrushchev and the threat of military intervention, to finally win Soviet acquiescence to his rule and program. A Pole replaced the Russian designated by Moscow to head the Polish armed forces, and Gomulka dismantled most of the hated collective farms.

If the pot boiled over in Poland, it exploded in Hungary. There, reform sentiment in late October 1956 facilitated the return to power as prime minister of Imre Nagy, a Gomulka-type Communist, or so it seemed. Nagy's reemergence pushed a button that set events into fast-forward. Within a few days of becoming prime minister of a government in which he included several non-Communists, Nagy requested that Soviet troops withdraw from Budapest, Hungary's capital. Then came the real bombshell. On October 31, Nagy announced that Hungary would no longer be a one-party dictatorship and would leave the Warsaw Pact and the Soviet bloc to become a neutral state like Austria. Khrushchev and his colleagues now drew their line in the sand. The Soviet regime had no intention of letting a satellite state achieve any measure of real independence, a development that could easily set off a chain reaction that might sweep Eastern Europe and possibly cross the Soviet frontiers. On November 1 Soviet reinforcements began crossing the border into Hungary, and three days later Soviet troops and tanks poured into Budapest and other Hungarian cities. The Western powers, preoccupied by the Suez Canal crisis in the Middle East, could do nothing but watch from afar. Thousands of Hungarians were killed in bitter but futile resistance to a quarter of a million Soviet troops equipped with 3,000 tanks. More than 200,000 Hungarians fled to the West. Nagy and several colleagues, after being promised safe conduct, left their refuge in the Yugoslav embassy and were seized and taken to Moscow. They were executed in 1958.

THE ANTIPARTY GROUP

The Polish "October" and the Hungarian uprising were nearly politically fatal to Khrushchev as well. They provided ample grist for those in the party opposed to his reforms. Whether to strengthen his own position or because his own enthusiasm for reform had cooled, Khrushchev now made it clear to intellectuals at home that he would not tolerate the type of open discussion and criticism that had helped spark the events in Poland and Hungary. Some of those who did not get the message were arrested. But this new hard line was not enough. On June 19, 1957, a coalition in the Presidium led by Malenkov, Molotov, and Kaganovich, joined by old Stalin cronies like Voroshilov and Khrushchev's own prime minister, Nikolai Bulganin, secured a majority to remove the first secretary. Aside from their concerns about events in Eastern Europe, Khrushchev's opponents were opposed to his economic schemes, particularly an administrative reorganization that would have greatly strengthened his political loyalists at their expense. But the seven-to-four majority in the Presidium turned out to be insufficient. Khrushchev, citing party rules, demanded that the dispute be decided by the full Central Committee. The first secretary received critical help from his minister of defense, Georgy Zhukov of World War II fame, who provided the military aircraft that brought in Khrushchev's supporters from the provinces, where his greatest strength lay. While this helped put Khrushchev and his allies in control from the start, there was no shortage of drama in what became an eight-day-long plenum. Malenkov, Molotov, and Kaganovich were denounced for their direct responsibility in the arrests and executions of party cadres. Some speakers provided statistics, and Khrushchev himself cited figures for those arrested and executed during the terrible days of mid-1937 to late 1938. It was, as Khrushchev biographer William Taubman has observed, "the closest Stalin's henchmen ever came to a day of reckoning."[2] That reckoning, of course, never came: too many party leaders leveling accusations, most notably Khrushchev himself, were themselves complicit in Stalin's crimes. The proceedings of the meeting were kept secret. All that the general Soviet population knew was that the first secretary had triumphed in the June 1957 showdown at the Central Committee.

Khrushchev's opponents, unceremoniously dubbed the "antiparty group," soon were scattered to the four winds, as Malenkov, Molotov, and Kaganovich were dismissed from the Presidium and their government posts. Still, they survived. Molotov was sent to apply his diplomatic skills as ambassador to Outer Mongolia. After several years he received a more congenial posting as the Soviet representative to the International Atomic Energy Commission in Vienna and later retired on a pension. Malenkov was dispatched to manage a remote power station in Kazakhstan. Kaganovich, Stalin's ex-hatchet man who after his defeat had tearfully called Khrushchev to beg for his life, was allowed to retire on a pension. Since it would have been awkward to dismiss Khrushchev's own prime minister just yet, Bulganin temporarily remained at his post as window dressing. Zhukov was rewarded by being promoted from candidate, or nonvoting, to full member of the Presidium. The significance of these events transcended the individual winners and losers. Just as Khrushchev had triumphed over his opponents, the new, less murderous politics had triumphed decisively over the old. Only four years after Stalin's death Soviet political life had changed a great deal.

Khrushchev followed up his June victory by securing his flanks. In October he eliminated a potential rival by removing Zhukov, an ally too powerful for Khrushchev's comfort, from the Presidium. Zhukov was replaced as minister of defense with a trusted Khrushchev associate, Rodion Malinovsky. In March 1958 Bulganin followed his colleagues into political oblivion. Khrushchev now became prime minister as well as first secretary, thereby duplicating Stalin in holding both the top party and government posts, though not matching Stalin's power.

KHRUSHCHEV'S REFORM AGENDA

Political victory over his opponents did little to solve Khrushchev's other problems. One major difficulty was that his agenda was much too large. Khrushchev had defeated Malenkov in 1955 in part because he criticized his rival's emphasis on producing consumer goods and insisted that heavy industry must maintain its traditional priority, an orientation reflected in the grandiose goals of the Sixth Five-Year Plan approved by the Twentieth Party

Congress. This plan called for oil and electricity production to double, for steel production to rise by 50 percent, and so on. Khrushchev was also committed to increasing the production of food and consumer goods and thereby raising the Soviet standard of living until it equaled that of the United States. Early in 1957 Khrushchev even promised that the Soviet Union would outproduce the United States in milk, meat, and butter within four years, a promise that required a huge increase in agricultural production. Khrushchev intended to accomplish all this while keeping the voracious Soviet military machine fed and making enormous investments in space technology. To his sorrow, there simply were not enough resources to realize these grand ambitions.

Along with his self-imposed tasks, Khrushchev was burdened by his methods. He was in such a terrible hurry that he turned to panaceas, as with the virgin lands program and his various reorganization schemes. Panaceas, of course, rarely work; moreover, as time went by, Khrushchev's increasingly embarrassing failures eroded his base of support. Khrushchev also did himself little good when he resorted to threats, a tactic that alarmed the governing bureaucracy that so cherished its newfound security. Finally, both Mother Nature and foreign adversaries refused to cooperate in the long run. Khrushchev, prime minister and first secretary or not, was left with ever steeper mountains to climb.

KHRUSHCHEV IN CONTROL

Whatever his eventual difficulties, Khrushchev enjoyed considerable success during his early years in office. He won friends in various ways. The millions released from the Gulag became his strong supporters. Another popular measure was the abolition of Stalin's worst labor laws. It once again became possible in the workers' state to change jobs without permission and be absent from work without being subject to criminal prosecution. A minimum wage was introduced, pensions were raised, and the workweek was reduced.

More controversial was the economic reorganization of early 1957, a measure that helped galvanize the "antiparty group" to move against him. Khrushchev's goal was to combat the inefficiency and lack of initiative that resulted from centralizing all planning and economic decision making in Moscow. Since the Moscow planners seldom knew or understood conditions in the provinces, their decisions and targets often were unrealistic and counterproductive. Khrushchev therefore abolished over 140 ministries on both the national and union republic levels. Instead of having individual ministries that dealt with a single industrial sector either throughout the entire USSR or in a single union republic, Khrushchev divided the country into 105 economic units called *sovnarkhozy*, each responsible for the overall economy within its geographic jurisdiction. Presumably decisions made locally would better reflect the available economic resources and requirements and therefore produce more rational policies and better results. Not incidentally, this massive administrative upheaval enabled Khrushchev as first secretary to remove and appoint thousands of officials and thereby strengthen his political base.

Good weather and bumper harvests in the virgin lands during 1957 and 1958 further strengthened Khrushchev's support. He could also take satisfaction in the expansion of state farms relative to collective farms, a development favored by the party leadership because it facilitated greater state control over agriculture and, presumably, economies of scale as smaller inefficient collectives were amalgamated into larger, more viable units. The year 1958 also witnessed the abolition of the Machine Tractor Stations, which eliminated the burden the collective farms carried in paying exorbitant rental fees for the machinery they needed. However, because the collectives were compelled to buy certain machines regardless of their needs or wishes, many were saddled with equipment they could not use or repair and debts they could not pay. Maintenance problems occurred in part because many skilled MTS employees had absolutely no interest in the dreary prospect of becoming a member of a collective farm and left the countryside for the cities and towns.

Khrushchev also enjoyed other successes. Industrial growth rates, benefiting from the huge investments made under Stalin, remained high until the end of the 1950s. Housing, an area grossly neglected under Stalin, required a change in priorities. Khrushchev considered housing an urgent matter. It disturbed and embarrassed him that in the 1950s it was common for entire families in urban areas to live in one room of a communal apartment in a crumbling old building. In his memoirs he admitted "it was painful for me to remember that as a worker under capitalism I had much better living conditions than my fellow workers now living under Soviet power." It was unacceptable that "Soviet man," who had sacrificed so much to build socialism, should live "in a beehive." To get Soviet men, women, and children out of beehives and into apartments, Khrushchev turned to prefabricated housing, which permitted what he called "industrial-velocity" methods of construction. From 1955 to 1959 the first secretary doubled housing construction. By 1964, the year he left office, the Soviet Union had twice as much housing as had existed in 1950 and more than 100 million of its citizens were living in new apartments. To be sure, much of the housing so hastily built under Khrushchev was poorly constructed and became the butt of jokes, but it did help to ease a severe crisis.

One problem that proved intractable was the appetite of the enormous military establishment, which left few resources for developing the civilian sector of the economy. Between 1955 and 1958, the Soviet leadership tried to control the defense budget by demobilizing more than 2 million troops. However, the funds saved went into military modernization, in particular developing and deploying technologically advanced weapons such as ballistic missiles and nuclear-powered submarines. Indeed, between 1957 and 1959 expenditures on advanced weapons rose dramatically, and with them the defense budget as a whole. In 1960 Khrushchev announced further manpower cuts, both to pay for advanced weapons and to ease the labor shortage in the civilian economy. While these cuts made economic sense, they were resented by the military, especially since no provisions were made for thousands of demobilized military officers who suddenly found themselves deprived of both their careers and homes. Another attempt at economizing was the decision to defer extensive deployment of the first generation of intercontinental ballistic missiles (ICBMs) developed during the 1950s.These missiles were impractical as weapons because they took so long, about twenty hours, to prepare for launch. This compared unfavorably with American intercontinental missiles available at the time, which used a different fuel and could be prepared for launch in fifteen minutes. The Soviet leadership opted to wait for a new, more practical generation of missiles currently being developed. This decision made economic and military sense, but it also left the Soviet Union at a disadvantage in terms of deployed intercontinental missiles vis-à-vis the United States that lasted until the end of the 1960s.

That was not the case in a closely related high technology area. Beginning in 1957, the Soviet Union scored a series of stunning triumphs in space exploration, a major dividend of Khrushchev's policy of encouraging and even pampering the scientific elite. Among the beneficiaries of that largesse was the brilliant rocket designer Sergei Korolev, who had been released from the Gulag in 1944 and later put to work designing a missile powerful enough to hit the United States with a nuclear warhead. Korolev's passion, however, was not weapons of war but space flight, and his skill at bureaucratic infighting helped divert significant resources toward that end, despite opposition from influential officials who wanted all resources focused exclusively on weapons development. It was Korolev's good fortune that if one version of his huge R-7 intercontinental missile could carry a nuclear warhead to the United States, another could launch an artificial satellite into space. In late August 1957 the R-7 successfully delivered a dummy atomic warhead to a target 4,000 miles from its launch site. Just six weeks later, on October 4, 1957, Korolev used an R-7 to launch *Sputnik*, the world's first artificial satellite, into orbit, stunning the United States and thrilling his fellow Soviet citizens. An ecstatic Khrushchev told reporters, "The Americans have told the whole world that they are preparing to launch a satellite of the earth. . . . We, on the other hand, have kept quiet but now have a satellite circling the planet." A series of space firsts followed, each of which brought the Soviet Union additional prestige as the world leader in space. Among them, in 1959 a Soviet rocket circled the moon and took the first photographs of its "dark side." Two years later, on April 21, 1961, Yuri Gagarin thrilled his Soviet comrades and commanded worldwide attention when, squeezed into a cramped capsule perched atop a modified R-7 rocket, he became the first human being to be launched into space and orbit the earth. Given Korolev's priorities, it is perhaps fitting that because of technical characteristics, including the extreme volatility of the fuel it used, the R-7 was not a practical weapon of war. It was, however, a remarkably successful vehicle for space exploration. The R-7 gave the Soviet Union a lead, albeit temporarily, in the space race and more than vindicated Korolev's advocacy of space flight and Khrushchev's crucial support of the Soviet space program.

Back on the ground, Khrushchev crisscrossed the country, meeting, encouraging, exhorting, and often charming his countrymen. He was a refreshing change from the remote and foreboding Stalin, who for a generation had ruled the Soviet Union holed up in the Kremlin or hidden away in one of his country homes.

WINDOWS TO THE WEST

Reform inside the Soviet Union was inseparable with opening the country, albeit cautiously and on a limited basis, to contacts with the West, most notably with the United States. After Stalin's death the Soviet government permitted the publication of translated works by a number of major American writers. It also allowed the Soviet public to enjoy selected American films, mainly musicals, comedies, and adventure movies. These films were enormously popular with Soviet audiences. Although carefully vetted to screen out ideologically unacceptable messages, they turned out to be subversive nonetheless, especially when it came to a small but significant group of educated Soviet young people, many of whom came from privileged backgrounds. To them the contrast between the excitement that came out of Hollywood and the tedium of state-controlled cultural life and entertainment available at home was a revelation, "a window onto the outside world from the Stalinist stinking lair," as novelist Vasily Aksyonov later recalled. On a more down-to-earth level, these films revealed to millions of Soviet citizens that, unlike them, Americans owned their own cars, did not live in communal apartments, and did not have to stand in line when they shopped for food in well-stocked grocery stores and supermarkets. The United States was not, as Soviet propaganda would have it, a country divided between the few fabulously rich and the many wretchedly poor. Meanwhile, the U.S. government's Voice of America radio broadcasts, accessible via shortwave radio despite Soviet jamming efforts, further seduced Soviet youth with the rhythms of American jazz and rock 'n' roll.

In the summer of 1957, as part of a "peace offensive" designed to overcome the bad press from the suppression of the Hungarian uprising, the Soviet Union sponsored the sixth World Youth Festival. More than 30,000 young people from all over the world, including Western Europe and the United States, were invited to Moscow, presumably to be impressed by the achievements of Soviet socialism. It turned out to be a big mistake, as historian Vladislav Zubok has put it, to bring "the world to Moscow."[3] So many young people accustomed to living in free societies were impossible to control, especially given the eagerness of Soviet youths to learn about them. What the latter encountered were free-thinking, stylishly dressed contemporaries who shared none of the fears that so pervaded Soviet society. As the poet and future dissident Vladimir Bukovsky later recalled, after the World Youth Festival "all this talk about 'putrefying capitalism' became ridiculous." These impressions were compounded in 1958, when Khrushchev and his colleagues began a program of scientific and academic exchanges with the United States. Four decades later, Oleg Kalugin, who unlike Aksyonov and Bukovsky did not become a dissident but rather a high-ranking secret police official, commented that for the Soviet Union these exchanges were a "Trojan horse" that "kept infecting more and more people over the years." None of this registered with Khrushchev, whose confidence in the superiority of socialism over capitalism never wavered and who in any event had a long list of more immediate concerns to worry about.

THE SOVIET UNION AS A GLOBAL POWER

Those concerns included foreign affairs, where results were mixed. Late in 1958, the Soviet Union increased Cold War tensions when it put pressure on the Western powers to abandon their position in West Berlin and recognize East Germany. These efforts failed. Still, relations with the United States improved enough to allow Khrushchev to visit the bastion of capitalism in 1959. The trip produced little that was durable; the "Spirit of Camp David" that supposedly emerged from Khrushchev's meeting with President Dwight D. Eisenhower at the American presidential retreat in Maryland proved to be ephemeral. Khrushchev nonetheless did surprisingly well with the American public and media and added to his prestige at home.

A more lasting development occurred in 1959 when Fidel Castro came to power in Cuba and proceeded to align that island nation, only ninety miles from the Florida coast, with the Soviet Union. Soviet diplomatic initiatives and careful use of foreign aid also won friends in the strategic Middle East.

In Egypt, the Soviets benefited from the 1956 Suez Canal crisis. In late October of that year, in an effort to end years of Egyptian-sponsored raids into its territory in which terrorists killed civilians and destroyed property, Israel attacked Egypt in the Sinai desert. Meanwhile, Britain and France, cooperating with Israel but acting according to their own agenda, landed troops near the Suez Canal in an attempt to undo Egypt's nationalization of that strategic waterway. Soviet threats against Britain, France, and Israel were empty gestures—Moscow had problems enough in Poland and Hungary at the time—but they were welcomed in Egypt and the rest of the Arab world. The Soviets further strengthened their ties with Egypt, the most populous Arab country, by agreeing to build the Aswan High Dam when the United States pulled out of the project. Soviet influence also grew in Asia. India, looking for a counterweight to China and grateful for Soviet economic aid, proved to be a receptive object of attention. There were also some successes in sub-Saharan Africa as it emerged from European colonial rule. Overall, under Khrushchev the Soviet Union increasingly made its weight felt as a global power.

PROBLEMS AT HOME AND ABROAD

Khrushchev reached his high-water mark in 1958 and 1959, though by the latter year there were signs the tide was beginning to recede. In January and February of 1959, when the party met at its Twenty-First Congress, Khrushchev, as usual, was full of promises. His new Seven-Year Plan, he assured everyone, would increase both investment in heavy industry and consumer goods and enable the Soviet Union to surpass the United States in per capita production by 1970. What he did *not* say publicly was that the Sixth Five-Year Plan had been scrapped after only one year because widespread shortfalls made it impossible to realize any of its goals. The congress, of course, adopted the Seven-Year Plan, but, significantly, it did not, as Khrushchev wanted, demote some survivors of the "antiparty group," notably Voroshilov. A far more serious setback occurred later in 1959 when the grain harvest was poor.

More bad news followed the next year. The long-simmering differences between the Soviet Union and the People's Republic of China finally burst into the open. At the same time relations with the United States were cooling. A planned summit meeting between Khrushchev and President Eisenhower was aborted in May 1960 when the Soviets shot down an American U-2 spy plane deep inside their country just two weeks before the summit conference was scheduled to open. When another American plane, this time in the Arctic, was downed in July, American–Soviet relations chilled further still. They did not improve when Khrushchev, having come to New York in September to attend the annual meeting of the U.N. General Assembly, shocked everyone with his unruly conduct, most notably by taking off his right shoe and pounding it on his desk to protest a speech in which a Philippine delegate accused the Soviet Union of colonialist oppression in Eastern Europe. The Soviet leader further angered the Americans when he met with his new friend Fidel Castro, who also happened to be in town for the General Assembly meeting.

THE TWENTY-SECOND PARTY CONGRESS

Khrushchev had no intention of retreating in the face of setbacks. At the Twenty-Second Congress of the CPSU in October 1961, the first secretary responded forcefully, almost defiantly, to his various intractable and frustrating domestic and foreign problems. The congress adopted a new party program, only its third in history (the first two were adopted in 1903 and 1919, respectively). Khrushchev's program "solemnly" assured the Soviet people that the "present generation will live under communism." By 1980, the "foundations of communism" would be built. The production of everything would be doubled, tripled, quadrupled, and so on, by then, and the high road to complete communism would be opened. For the present, Khrushchev informed his comrades that a "state of the whole people" had replaced the "dictatorship of the proletariat" and the party had become a "party of the whole people."

Khrushchev had at least two objectives in mind at the Twenty-Second Congress. Since the late 1950s the Soviet Union in general and he in particular had been under increasing attack from the Chinese Communists for insufficient revolutionary zeal. The Chinese denounced Khrushchev for his concern with material well-being—his so-called goulash Communism—and for his attempts to defuse relations with the world's main imperialistic dragon, the United States. Khrushchev was determined to reclaim the undisputed leadership of the world Communist camp both for his country and for himself. He also wanted to rekindle mass enthusiasm and idealism at home in the hope that such revolutionary spirit would help overcome the growing obstacles to economic progress.

These goals demanded, Khrushchev believed, a crushing denunciation of Stalin far beyond anything said in 1956. This would pull the rug from under the Chinese, who were Stalin's staunchest defenders as they railed against the "revisionist" Khrushchev. It would also strike a powerful blow at the various conservatives and bureaucrats at home who were resisting or sabotaging Khrushchev's reform efforts.

This time there was no secret speech; Khrushchev spoke in open session before the world. A chorus of speeches by Khrushchev and his top associates pointed to Malenkov, Kaganovich, Molotov, and Voroshilov as Stalin's accomplices. The crescendo of denunciation apparently reached even the Marxist afterworld, for one venerable delegate rose to announce that she had asked "Ilyich," as she fondly called Lenin, for advice, and he had answered that Stalin should be removed from the mausoleum the two dead leaders shared because, the unhappy Ilyich complained, "I do not like lying beside Stalin, who inflicted so much harm on the party."

An appropriate resolution was passed, and Stalin was removed from the mausoleum the next day and reburied in an area near the Kremlin wall reserved for dignitaries of the second rank. Perhaps Khrushchev and his associates felt like the remarkable young poet Yevgeny Yevtushenko, who wrote:

> Grimly clenching
> > His embalmed fists,
> he watched through a crack inside,
> > just pretending to be dead. . . .
> He has worked out a scheme,
> > He's merely curled up for a nap.
> And I appeal
> > to our government with a plea
> to double
> > and treble the guard at this slab,
> so that Stalin will not rise again
> > and with Stalin—the past.[4]

At any rate, they buried Stalin not under six feet of earth but under several truckloads of concrete. A new round of destalinization, spearheaded by a wholesale renaming of places and things, followed. Not even Stalingrad, the scene of the tyrant's civil war adventures and his momentous victory over Hitler during World War II, was spared. It became Volgograd.

KHRUSHCHEV UNDER SIEGE

Unfortunately for Khrushchev, burying Stalin physically was not enough. The first secretary could not bury many of the problems Stalin had left behind or the new ones that had developed since his death. Probably the most serious was agriculture. Things had been going wrong since 1958. Poor weather reduced the 1959 grain harvest, both in the virgin lands and in the older agricultural regions. Khrushchev's mismanagement and authoritarian methods made things worse. The poor weather in the virgin lands was predictable, since unreliable rainfall was the main reason this area had not been farmed prior to Khrushchev's brainstorms. Even worse, the agricultural methods used in the virgin lands were totally unsuited to the dry climate. In 1963 these faulty methods combined with dry weather and windstorms to turn large areas into a huge dust bowl. Millions of tons of irreplaceable topsoil were blown away. In the older agricultural regions, Khrushchev's Machine Tractor Station reforms often left the collectives with equipment they could neither afford nor maintain. Khrushchev's corn campaign also took its toll, since at his insistence corn was grown in areas totally unsuited to that crop such as southern Siberia. Pressures to produce more meat led to excessive slaughtering, which consequently hurt both long-term meat *and* milk production. It also led to fraud as ambitious or desperate provincial first secretaries strove to meet or exceed their targets. Meanwhile, the refusal to let supply-and-demand mechanisms set sensible prices added to the damage. Prices for farm goods set by the state consistently failed to reflect the real costs of production or actual demand. This led to milk and meat being sold at a loss, much to the detriment of the already hard-pressed collective farms. When the peasants turned to their private plots to make up the difference, Khrushchev responded with fiscal penalties and other types of pressure, all of which reduced productivity on those plots and hence the availability of food.

In 1962 the rising cost of agricultural goods forced the state to raise food prices sharply. This led to numerous protests, riots, and strikes. The worst incident occurred in the city of Novocherkassk, where a procession of strikers carrying portraits of Lenin was fired upon by army troops, who killed twenty-six demonstrators and wounded almost ninety. The drought of 1963 led to a genuine food shortage because the government had no grain reserves to make up for the resulting shortfall. It also caused a decline in livestock herds. Since the days were gone when the regime could ignore or tolerate widespread hunger, the Soviet Union had to undergo the humiliation of buying grain from the supposedly declining capitalist countries.

By 1963 agriculture was only one of several anchors dragging the Soviet economy down. The centralized planning methods inherited from Stalin were unable to coordinate and manage an increasingly complex economy. Khrushchev's division of the country into 105 *sovnarkhozy* had not helped; instead, it created new webs of conflicting interests, as *sovnarkhozy* competed against one another for resources and often were unable to get what they needed from distant areas. Khrushchev therefore reduced the number of *sovnarkhozy* to forty-seven. Meanwhile, factories still produced to meet the all-important plan targets (e.g., producing excessively heavy sheet metal to meet gross weight requirements) rather than to supply what their customers—whether other producers or ordinary consumers—needed. The list of similar difficulties could go on almost endlessly. Increased military expenditures after 1961 added to the strain, with the result that in 1963 and 1964 industrial growth rates registered their worst peacetime performance since 1933.

TROUBLES ABROAD

Foreign policy difficulties, especially vis-à-vis the polar opposites of the United States and the People's Republic of China, were another area of concern. The dispute with China had deep roots, some going back to nineteenth-century tsarist territorial expansion at the expense of the weakened Chinese Empire. Other causes were of more recent vintage. The People's Republic of China was a militant have-not nation, while the Soviet Union, its revolution far in the past, was behaving more like a country with something to lose. In 1958, when China's Mao Zedong launched his "Great Leap Forward," a quixotic attempt to jump directly from backwardness to communism by organizing gigantic "communes," and not incidentally leapfrogging the Soviet Union in the process, he was in effect challenging Khrushchev for leadership in the Communist world. (The Soviets were delighted when the Great Leap Forward was a disastrous failure.) That same year Khrushchev refused to help Mao drive the Nationalist Chinese from two tiny islands just off the Chinese coast for fear of a conflict with the United States. This infuriated Mao, as did Khrushchev's refusal to help the Chinese develop an atomic bomb. In 1960 the Soviet Union suddenly withdrew all its advisors and technicians from China, and in 1962 it refused to support the Chinese in their border war with India. There were other incidents as well, none of which were helped by Khrushchev's bombastic personality. Border incidents began as early as 1960, and in 1963 the Chinese made their first public call for revisions of the Sino-Soviet borders that were the result of tsarist Russia's expansion at the expense of the Chinese Empire during the second half of the nineteenth century.

None of this intra-Communist tension precluded friction with the Americans. The same sour note that closed Soviet relations with the outgoing Eisenhower administration in 1960 sounded again in 1961 with the incoming Kennedy administration. When Khrushchev met Kennedy in Vienna in June 1961, he used the opportunity to demand once again a Western withdrawal from West Berlin, one of eight conditions Khrushchev set regarding the German problem as a whole, and in general attempted to test the young American president. These demands were quickly rejected by the Western powers. For his part, Kennedy came back from Vienna determined never to be bullied by Khrushchev again. As he put it, "If Khrushchev wants to rub my nose in the dirt, it's all over. The son of a bitch won't pay attention to words. He has to see you move."

Kennedy soon had more reasons to show how he and the United States could move. During the summer of 1961 the Soviets and their East German puppets acted to stop an accelerating exodus from the German Democratic Republic (East Germany) that had reached thousands of people per week and threatened to cripple that Communist state. The bulk of the exodus was via Berlin, a city divided politically but with no physical barrier separating its Eastern and Western halves. Then, on August 13, 1961, one suddenly appeared: a barbed-wire fence through the center of the city that soon became the concrete, barbed-wire-and-broken-glass-topped Berlin Wall. The exodus from East Berlin virtually ceased. In September Khrushchev ended the Soviet Union's voluntary ban on atmospheric nuclear testing. Since the United States and Britain also had refrained from atmospheric nuclear testing, Khrushchev's decision ended a moratorium that, with the exception of several French tests, had left the world free of these tests and their dangerous radioactive fallout for almost three years. The subsequent series of Soviet tests included the detonation of a fifty-seven-megaton device, the largest man-made explosion in history.

THE CUBAN MISSILE CRISIS

Then Khrushchev reached too far. His boasts about Soviet military power notwithstanding, as the 1960s began the Soviets lagged behind the United States in strategic military capability, in part because under Khrushchev resources had been diverted to nonmilitary priorities in industry and agriculture. The Soviet deficiency was most disturbing with regard to intercontinental ballistic missiles, the newest and literally unstoppable vehicles for mounting a nuclear attack. In the fall of 1960 Khrushchev had bragged that the Soviet Union was producing missiles "like sausages from an automatic machine, rocket after rocket." In fact, while at that time the Soviets had a significant number of shorter-range missiles, it had only four operational intercontinental missiles, which were the ones that really mattered in terms of strategic balance because they were the only Soviet missiles that could reach the United States. A year later that number had inched upward to ten. By contrast, the United States in 1961 had more than sixty, was adding new ICMBs to its arsenal faster than the Soviet Union, and had a vastly superior long-range bomber force as well.

As was his wont, Khrushchev tried to bridge the huge gap in one stroke. If the Soviet Union could place its medium-range (1,200 miles) and intermediate-range (2,500 miles) ballistic missiles close to the United States, he reasoned, those missiles could hold the line and give the appearance of greater strategic nuclear equality between the two superpowers until the intercontinental missiles the Soviets were developing were ready. Such a stroke also would help the first secretary fend off his critics at home and in Beijing. Khrushchev's proposed new launching pad was conveniently available in Cuba, only ninety miles from the U.S. east coast, where he also wanted to protect Fidel Castro's Communist regime in the wake of the American-backed invasion by Cuban exiles in 1961, the ignominious Bay of Pigs fiasco.

The result was the Cuban Missile Crisis of October 1962. This episode reflected one of the fundamental flaws in the Soviet decision-making process. Khrushchev, unlike Stalin, was not an absolute dictator and could not unilaterally make any decision he wanted. He often had to line up support from various powerful constituencies and sometimes did not get his way or had to compromise in order to implement parts of his agenda. At the same time, as first secretary and prime minister he had enormous power and latitude in many areas, and his colleagues on the Presidium, who might have acted as a brake on bad decisions, were reluctant to challenge him lest they jeopardize their own positions. Khrushchev's emphatic refusal to consider cautionary advice once he decided to place missiles in Cuba meant that this initiative was never seriously debated by the small group of men who made the key decisions in the Soviet Union. So in June 1961 the Presidium acquiesced to a plan that was reckless in the extreme and poorly thought out. In its final form (the weapons list grew longer in September) the plan called for delivering over a period of several months an enormous quantity of military hardware—including the medium-range and intermediate-range missiles and their warheads, short-range missiles and their warheads, jet fighters and bombers, antiaircraft missile batteries, and a vast range of support material—and 42,000 troops to Cuba. Although the Americans were carefully watching Cuba, regularly flying U-2 spy planes over the island, somehow Khrushchev and his colleagues assumed they could carry out their plan without being discovered. Making matters worse, Khrushchev and his colleagues ignored an American statement issued in early September that "the gravest issues would arise" if the Soviets attempted to base offensive weapons, including ground-to-ground missiles in Cuba.

The Soviets actually succeeded in getting an astounding amount of equipment to Cuba before the Americans discovered what was happening and reacted. Aside from all the scheduled intermediate-range missiles *and* their warheads, Soviet weaponry in Cuba by early October included short-range (twenty-five miles) battlefield missiles and their nuclear warheads that could have been used to destroy an American invasion force as it landed on Cuban beaches. Given the sequence of events, these probably were the weapons most likely to have sparked a nuclear war, even though Khrushchev twice during the course of the crisis specified that Soviet commanders in Cuba required approval from Moscow before using any nuclear weapon. As it turned out, the Soviets could not hide their huge missiles or the construction sites where they were being installed from the Americans, certainly not, as the planning called for, by covering the missile warheads with palm leaves to disguise the missiles as palm trees. American intelligence planes spotted the construction sites before any missiles could be made operational. President Kennedy then ordered a naval blockade around Cuba and demanded that the missiles on the island be withdrawn. For several days the United States and the USSR stood, as the American Secretary of State Dean Rusk put it, "eyeball to eyeball," and, as Rusk noted, it was the Soviets who "blinked." They had little choice in the face of Kennedy's determination and American air, land, and sea military superiority. The face-saving formula that resolved the crisis, under which the Soviets agreed to remove their missiles from Cuba in return for a public American guarantee not to invade the island in the future and a secret unofficial promise to remove obsolete American missiles in Turkey, accomplished Kennedy's announced objectives and gave Castro the security he needed. But the agreement did little for Khrushchev's security. Nor did two important agreements reached in mid-1963: the agreement establishing a direct teletype "hot line" between the White House and the Kremlin, and the partial nuclear test-ban treaty signed by the United States, the USSR, and Great Britain banning all above-ground nuclear tests. Despite their value to the Soviet Union and to the United States, these measures simply were too little and too late for the first secretary in the wake of his defeat in Cuba.

The hotline and partial test ban agreements reflected the chastening effect of a crisis that brought the world to the brink of nuclear war. Both sides now wisely drew back. However, the Cuban Missile Crisis was a disaster for Khrushchev. It exposed him as a reckless bluffer and added the Soviet military to the growing list of powerful elements inside the Soviet Union dissatisfied with his policies. Compounding his difficulties with the economy and with China, the Cuban Missile Crisis added yet another albatross to those already hanging around the neck of the embattled Nikita Khrushchev.

THE DILEMMAS OF DESTALINIZATION

Khrushchev carried another albatross—his own ambivalence about how far to go with reform. That ambivalence at times turned him into a political Dr. Jeckell and Mr. Hyde. As much as he hated certain aspects of Stalinism, Khrushchev still *was* a Stalinist in the sense of being committed to the bulk of the system created by collectivization and the industrialization drive of the 1930s. Khrushchev the Stalinist constantly constricted or countermanded what Khrushchev the reformer did. When this self-sabotage was added to the resistance to change by large parts of the bureaucracy, Khrushchev's reformist policies were further damaged. This led Khrushchev the reformer to more drastic, desperate, and usually ill-conceived schemes that disrupted more than they solved and added to his growing list of opponents. This pattern, which began as early as 1955, had become more pronounced and therefore more damaging by the early 1960s.

The pattern of reform and reaction was clearly visible with regard to cultural policy. Here it was a genuine roller coaster ride, with steep ups and downs sometimes following each other from month to month. One peak, the publication in 1956 of Vladimir Dudintsev's *Not By Bread Alone*, a ringing indictment of party corruption, was followed by a crackdown after the Polish and Hungarian upheavals. Dudintsev fell from grace. Then came Boris Pasternak's *Doctor Zhivago*, which focused on the individual's fate during revolutionary upheavals and raised serious questions about the nature of the Bolshevik Revolution. Denied publication in the Soviet Union, it was published abroad in 1957 and won the Nobel Prize for literature in 1958. An avalanche of party-orchestrated abuse fell on Pasternak, who felt compelled to turn down the award for fear of having his citizenship revoked. Yet in 1959 Dudintsev was restored to good standing. Then, in 1961, the young poet and Pasternak admirer Yevgeny Yevtushenko published "Babi Yar," a stunning denunciation of Soviet anti-Semitism, while in the fall of 1962 Khrushchev personally intervened to secure the publication of Aleksandr Solzhenitsyn's *One Day in the Life of Ivan Denisovich*. This literary bombshell exposed the horrors of Stalin's labor camps to public view as never before. However, before the year was out reaction began to set in. In November Khrushchev visited an exhibit of avant-garde art in a large exhibition hall near the Kremlin, where he both insulted and threatened the artists. One of the artists who had organized the exhibit, a former paratrooper turned sculptor named Ernst Neizvestny, firmly stood up to the first secretary, even telling him that he was being used by people who were exploiting his ignorance about art. Khrushchev defended himself and added more insults, but took no further action, ending the conversation by shaking Neizvestny's hand. Still, the cultural atmosphere remained tense. In early 1963 Khrushchev coldly warned Soviet intellectuals that "My hand will not tremble" if they went too far. December of that year witnessed the arrest and trial of poet Joseph Brodsky. At the same time, the Brodsky case produced public and spirited protests from many major Soviet cultural figures, something that would have been suicidal under Stalin.

The same pattern was repeated in other areas. Khrushchev had reversed many of Stalin's Russification policies and permitted some of the ethnic groups Stalin had exiled to return to their homes. There also were legal and judicial reforms and additional limits placed on the powers of the secret police, which beginning in 1954 became known as the KGB, the Russian initials for the Committee for State Security. But after 1960 antireligious propaganda and repression were intensified. The Khrushchev regime released millions of political prisoners and attempted to give more authority to popular, nonparty institutions in dealing with common crime. That did not necessarily mean progress toward the rule of law, since these so-called "people's guards" often turned into unruly vigilante gangs that themselves committed violence and blackmail against ordinary citizens. Meanwhile, certain crimes became punishable by harsher penalties, including execution. Capital punishment became common for so-called economic crimes, among them speculation and diverting state resources to private ends. The group most singled out for committing alleged economic crimes was the Jews, as Khrushchev after 1960 reversed the more tolerant policies of 1953–1957 vis-à-vis that religious minority.

MORE ECONOMIC PROBLEMS

Khrushchev's reversals of policy did the most harm in economic affairs. He was well aware that industrial policy had to be made more flexible, and there was considerable discussion about what to do, both in terms of expanding the role of market forces to make enterprises more efficient and the use of modern mathematical and programming techniques to improve planning. But very little was done. More damaging were Khrushchev's reversals of policy in agriculture. Some of his policies, such as lowering taxes and abolishing the Machine Tractor Stations, helped the peasants, but Khrushchev then turned around and curtailed the cultivation of private plots, forced the collectives to buy machinery they did not want, and told the peasants what crops to raise. Khrushchev even restored Lysenko and his discredited theories to prominence. He pushed through a program to expand the production of chemical fertilizer, only to see much of it wasted because of inadequate storage and shipping facilities and the lack of machines to spread what did reach the farms. What he did *not* do was allow the peasantry to use its experience and expertise to decide for itself what to grow and when to grow it. His bitter reward was agricultural stagnation. After a 40 percent growth in agricultural output during his early years in power, output rose only about 3 percent between 1958 and 1963. Hunger and massive imports were the disastrous result.

SPLITS, FUSIONS, AND DISLOCATIONS

By the fall of 1962 too many of Khrushchev's reforms, campaigns, and inspirational harangues had backfired. He responded in typical fashion by instituting his most radical reform of all: he split the Communist Party in half. Henceforth one branch of the party would be responsible for agriculture and the other for industry. This division of responsibility meant that each half tended to ignore the needs of the other, to the detriment of both. Suddenly it was impossible to tell who was in charge of a locality, since there were now two "first" secretaries, or who had ultimate responsibility for such neutral but vital services as education, police protection, or health care. This administrative nightmare developed at about the same time that Khrushchev ordered the number of *sovnarkhozy* reduced from 105 to 47. Since the new, larger economic boundaries that resulted from these fusions did not conform to the older political–regional ones, the bureaucratic tangle worsened. This tangle came on top of earlier and equally disruptive schemes, such as relocating the national ministry of agriculture from Moscow to a rural area sixty miles away, where it was supposed to set up and run a large model farm. (The agricultural ministries of several national republics also were relocated to state farms.) This may have facilitated Khrushchev's aim of having bureaucrats "dirty their hands" by doing various farm chores in addition to their regular work, but it was disastrous in terms of efficiency. For example, because of inadequate facilities it was almost impossible to place the telephone calls necessary to coordinate ministry affairs. As for morale, three-quarters of the ministry's staff quit within a year.

KHRUSHCHEV'S FALL

Soon Khrushchev was out of a job as well. He had thoroughly antagonized a majority of the party from top to bottom. The state bureaucracy was equally disenchanted. Khrushchev had few friends left in the military as a result of his earlier efforts to hold down military budgets and his failure in the Cuban Missile Crisis. Finally, he had failed by his own standards. He had promised rapid economic progress and delivered far too much chaos. In October 1964, while on vacation at a Black Sea resort, Khrushchev was suddenly called back to Moscow. This time there was no room for maneuvering. His opponents had prepared carefully, both in the Presidium and the Central Committee. Nikita Sergeyevich was informed of his "request" that he be relieved of his duties because of ill health. Although not intentional, there was an element of truth to the official rationale, since Khrushchev, at a minimum, was worn out. As his son Sergei later recalled:

> My seventy-year-old father was tired, tired beyond measure, both morally and physically. He had neither the strength nor desire to fight for power. Let everything take its course, I won't interfere, he had obviously decided.[5]

A terse official announcement followed. Khrushchev then became the latest beneficiary of his own reforms. Although relegated to private life and obscurity—public mention of him ceased—and subject to constant surveillance, the former first secretary lived in comfort, retaining a Moscow apartment, a country house outside Moscow, the use of a car and a chauffeur, and other luxuries until his death in 1971. It is in a sense fitting that although no member of the Central Committee attended his funeral, several of those he rescued from the Gulag showed up. After Sergei Khrushchev delivered a simple but eloquent eulogy, one of them spoke, thanking her "dear comrade" Nikita Sergeyevich for his role in releasing millions from the camps and restoring the reputations of millions more who did not survive. The Khrushchev era, so full of sound and fury, ended without a bang or a whimper.

THE LEGACY OF THE KHRUSHCHEV ERA

In the end, Khrushchev's fate was that of an idiosyncratic historical figure only partially in touch with his time. His success both in rising to power and in using it to implement change between 1953 and 1958 grew out of an impulse for reform that had broad appeal within the Soviet elite. The drive for reform was powerful because it involved something as basic as personal and professional security and because it had been denied for so long by Stalin's presence. The reform impulse also included a new concern for perceived public desires, specifically a higher standard of living and an easing of general police and bureaucratic controls, as public acquiescence was considered vital to the security of the governing elite. The reform impulse included attempts to ease international tensions because such steps also contributed to that security.

Yet the reform impulse was a limited one. The Soviet elite did not want to erode or undermine those aspects of the Stalinist system that had provided it with so much status and power. It was also an ambiguous impulse. There was no precise agreement about what should be done beyond dismantling Stalin's terror machine. In that sense Khrushchev was out of touch with the predominant conservative sentiment among the Soviet elite of his time. Because of his impatience and belief that only through *active* participation of the whole population could the system work, and because of his sympathy for ordinary Soviet people, Khrushchev wanted to change the system more than his colleagues did. This accounts for measures and behavior that in a nondictatorial environment would be considered populist. Khrushchev attempted to open up higher education to children of workers and peasants, an effort that met with only marginal success. He invited nonparty members of the intelligentsia to Central Committee meetings. He reformed the party rules at the Twenty-Second Party Congress to require a substantial periodic turnover of leadership at the various levels from the Central Committee on down, a measure that angered many party officials and cost him significant support in powerful circles. Khrushchev even encouraged activity by ordinary people outside the party to make the party more responsive to the population at large. Thus his *sovnarkhozy* reform was discussed at over 500,000 meetings attended by over 40 million citizens, while almost 1 million meetings attended by 70 million people served as forums to discuss his proposed Seven-Year Plan. Of course, Khrushchev intended that popular pressure would be applied to approve *his* programs. Instead, his populism got him into trouble with his colleagues. They either sabotaged his reforms or increasingly turned against him until he fell from his political perch.

Khrushchev lagged behind his colleagues in one respect. Nikita Sergeyevich frequently acted like a dictator, albeit at times a generous and paternal one, with a cult of his own. He was thus *too* Stalinist for his time. He was not satisfied to act as a representative of the ruling oligarchy, but rather wanted to bend it to his will. So rather than providing additional security for the party elite who staffed the upper layers of the nation's vast bureaucracy, as the times demanded, Khrushchev, the vestigial Stalinist, threatened them. However, without Stalin's implements of terror, he lacked the power to overcome them completely. With each passing year that elite became more deeply entrenched and better able to act cohesively to defend its interests. And in the end, the party elite, rather than Khrushchev, prevailed.

Yet both the Soviet elite that removed him and the population at large that greeted his downfall so indifferently owed Nikita Khrushchev a considerable debt. He did not, needless to say, alter the fundamental structure of Soviet society. Nor did he want to, for as biographer William J. Tompson has observed, "Khrushchev's fundamental faith in the system that he inherited—and had helped to build—prevented him from seeing the extent of its deformity."[6] When Khrushchev was pushed into retirement in 1964, a single party still ruled, the economy remained highly centralized, censorship and thought control remained pervasive, and so on. But Khrushchev nonetheless played a pivotal role in removing the most unbearable part of the Stalinist inheritance. The secret police terror was ended, the Gulag was dissolved and the bulk of its slave-labor camp network dismantled. A serious and reasonably successful effort was made to raise the nation's miserably low standard of living. When Stalin in the 1930s said that life had become "better" and "more joyous," he was lying. Under Khrushchev Soviet life did become better and, if not joyous, at least much less sorrowful. That accomplishment may not deserve accolades, but there have been many famous leaders who achieved far less.

NOTES

1. Yevgeny Yevtushenko, "The Heirs of Stalin," in *Twentieth Century Russian Poetry*, selected, with an introduction, by Yevgeny Yevtushenko (New York: Doubleday, 1994), p. 808.

2. William Taubman, *Khrushchev: The Man and His Era* (New York and London: Norton, 2003), p. 323.

3. Vladislav M. Zubok, *A Failed Empire: The Soviet Union in the Cold War from Stalin to Gorbachev* (Chapel Hill: University of North Carolina Press, 2007), p. 175.

4. Yevtushenko, "The Heirs of Stalin," pp. 807–808.

5. Sergei Khrushchev, *Khrushchev on Khrushchev: An Inside Account of the Man and His Era*, edited and translated by William Taubman (Boston: Little, Brown and Company, 1990), p. 125.

6. William J. Tompson, *Khrushchev: A Political Life* (New York: St. Martin's Press, 1995), p. 284.

17

The Brezhnev Era:
The Graying of the Revolution

Order is Heav'n's first law.

—Alexander Pope

*Make the Revolution a parent of settlements,
and not a nursery for future revolutions.*

—Edmund Burke

Khrushchev's removal from power marked the coming of age of the bureaucratic Soviet ruling class. In 1953, although privileged, the Communist Party elite was stunted by Stalin's suffocating terror and therefore lacked the cohesiveness necessary to defend its interests. The tyrant had to die before his court could secure its privileges. In 1964, having thrived on eleven years of political air unpolluted by terror, the party elite was sufficiently mature to depose Khrushchev, whose egalitarian schemes, ill-conceived reforms, policy errors, and dictatorial tendencies threatened its security interests. The successful plot of October 1964 gave the Soviet Union a new leadership team headed by Leonid Brezhnev, Khrushchev's successor as first secretary.

THE COMMUNIST OLIGARCHY

Aside from Brezhnev, the new Soviet leadership team initially included Alexei Kosygin, the new prime minister; Nikolai Podgorny, after 1965 the president of the Soviet Union, or official head of state; and Mikhail Suslov, the most powerful party secretary aside from Brezhnev, and the party's chief ideologist and kingmaker. Henceforth that leadership operated within the parameters of the political consensus that brought it to power. That consensus did not create anything like a democratic Communist Party—the leadership was not responsible to the party as a whole. It *did* mean that both the top leadership and the party as a whole shared a commitment to a specific set of unwritten political ground rules that no single person could successfully defy. Those rules sanctioned efforts to make the economy more efficient and raise the national standard of living, as well as attempts to expand the Soviet Union's influence worldwide and overcome its strategic military imbalance vis-à-vis the United States. Above all, however, they guaranteed the security of the party and state bureaucracies by ending the arbitrary assaults that were a constant, terrifying part of life under Stalin and a haphazard, unwelcome intrusion under Khrushchev. So intent was the Soviet elite on reinforcing stability that it proved unwilling in the long run to undertake reforms necessary to end stagnation in many key areas, including the economy. Such reforms were forbidden because they might have threatened the job security or status of important constituencies of the Soviet party-state.

The prime directive of security and stability determined the nature of leadership in the Soviet Union. During 1965 and 1966 Brezhnev prevailed in a struggle for power over two serious rivals—Podgorny and Alexander Shelepin—and emerged as the leading figure on the Presidium. Shelepin's fate was particularly instructive. Although more than a decade younger than his colleagues, Shelepin, nicknamed "Iron Shurik," had played a major role in the plot against Khrushchev and in November 1964 became a full member of the Presidium without having to pass through the normally obligatory candidate stage. He had headed the secret police for two years under Khrushchev and was a tough law-and-order advocate and hard-liner regarding foreign policy who had disapproved of Khrushchev's attempts to ease tension with the United States. Shelepin's unbridled authoritarianism and apparent ambition to accumulate more power than his colleagues thought safe, as well as his close ties both with the old-line Stalinists Khrushchev had pushed aside and with the secret police, evoked uncomfortable memories among the Presidium membership. His political eclipse thus reinforced the principle that the new party leadership, while prepared to restore certain practices from the Stalin era that Khrushchev had ended, was determined to chart a course between the Scylla of a dangerous new Stalin and the Charybdis of another destabilizing Khrushchev.

Brezhnev, a generally moderate man and centrist politician who disliked confrontation, was far preferable to the top party leadership than Shelepin and was a skilled political infighter as well. By 1966 he had eclipsed his colleague Kosygin and taken the newly restored title of general secretary, the same title Stalin had once held. But the new general secretary was a far cry from the old one, as was the office itself. Although Brezhnev became the most powerful man in the Soviet Union, he used his power and that of his associates to protect the interests of the various branches of the party–state bureaucracy, not to impose policy on them. Rather than being a dictator—by the mid-1970s his accumulated offices and honors put him far above any of his colleagues—Brezhnev was an enormously powerful manager. His long tenure—he remained in office eighteen years, until his death in November 1982—resulted from doing his job to the satisfaction of his colleagues and staying within the new boundaries of power. As Brezhnev put it, albeit with undeserved self-flattery, "I am a leader, not a ruler." Fedor Burlatsky, an advisor to Khrushchev, assessed Brezhnev rather less kindly but not altogether differently by observing that the type of power the Soviet elite wanted for its leader fit Brezhnev so perfectly "that he wore it for eighteen years without any fear, conflict or horror. His immediate retinue desired one thing only: that he live forever, as they were doing so well out of it."[1] In short, the Brezhnev years completed the transition from rule by a single dictator to oligarchic rule by the upper layers of the Communist Party bureaucracy.

Brezhnev and his colleagues were well suited to restoring order to the system that Khrushchev had disrupted. Born in the twentieth century (Brezhnev in 1906, Kosygin in 1904, Suslov in 1902), this new generation of leaders had spent its formative years in the party under Stalin, not, like Khrushchev and his generation, under Lenin. An ethnic Russian, Brezhnev was born in the northern Ukraine, an area of mixed Ukrainian and Russian population, into a working-class family. He studied both land surveying and metallurgy and became an engineer. Brezhnev was admitted to the party as a full member in 1931, at the height of the collectivization drive, when tough recruits were in great demand. From the late 1930s on, Brezhnev gained wide experience in a variety of posts in the Ukraine, Moldavia, Moscow, and Kazakhstan, ultimately rising through the ranks as a protégé of Nikita Khrushchev. During World War II he served in the army as a political commissar, seeing combat and reaching the rank of major general. As party chief in Kazakhstan from 1954 to 1956, Brezhnev was instrumental in carrying out Khrushchev's virgin lands campaign in its critical formative years. A Central Committee member from 1952, Brezhnev became a full member of the Presidium in Khrushchev's triumphant year of 1957. He was considered a Khrushchev supporter, but alienated by both Khrushchev's failures and his methods, Brezhnev played a leading role in deposing his benefactor in 1964.

"DEKHRUSHCHEVIZATION"

Khrushchev's fall was accompanied by accusations in the Soviet press that he had been guilty of "hare-brained schemes," "hasty decisions divorced from reality," "bragging and bluster," "attraction to rule by fiat," and more, all of which allegedly led to a rash of domestic and foreign difficulties. Not surprisingly, "dekhrushchevization" was not long in coming. It is symptomatic of how isolated Khrushchev had become that aside from a few of his closest cronies, like his son-in-law, none of the party elite followed its ex-leader down the memory hole. By November 1964 what was generally viewed as Khrushchev's most ill-conceived scheme was undone: the bifurcated Communist Party was reassembled into its previous unitary form. In September 1965 another signature Khrushchev policy was reversed when the *sovnarkhozy* were abolished and the centralized ministerial system for running the economy was restored, while in 1966 Khrushchev's rule requiring the regular turnover of party officials was dropped. Destalinization, at least in terms of expanding cultural and literary freedom, also fell victim to dekhrushchevization. An offensive against literary and cultural expression already was well under way by 1965, as was a quiet campaign, in the interest of stability, to restore at least a part of Stalin's battered reputation. Dekhrushchevization also meant the end of utopian promises such as the deposed leader's pledge to build the "foundations of communism" by 1980. Instead, the Soviet people were given the more modest assurance that as of the mid-1960s they were enjoying life in a stage of economic development variously dubbed "developed," "mature," or "real existing" socialism.

TINKERING WITH THE ECONOMY

Public assurances notwithstanding, the first priority for Brezhnev and his colleagues was the faltering Soviet economy. Policies to rejuvenate agriculture included easing restrictions on private plots and livestock holding, expanding the markets in which peasants could sell their privately produced foodstuffs, canceling debts of poorer collective farms, raising prices for required collective farm deliveries to the state, and reducing prices for industrial products the farms required such as tractors, trucks, and electricity. Equally important, in 1966 collective farm peasants finally were guaranteed a minimum wage and made eligible for pensions. Investment in agriculture increased considerably, eventually rising to about 27 percent of total investment. This was a 50 percent higher share than Khrushchev, supposedly the great friend of agriculture, had permitted.

All this produced mixed results. Grain output climbed from an average of 88 million tons during 1951–1955 to more than 180 million tons during 1971–1975 and over 200 million tons during 1976–1978. The production of milk, meat, vegetables, and eggs approximately doubled between the early 1950s and the late 1970s. But those apparently glittering figures glossed over some serious weaknesses. Agricultural production during the early 1950s was appallingly low. Growth thereafter reflected massive new investments, not the increased productivity that was so desperately needed. The collectivized and state peasants generally remained lethargic and indifferent workers. Centrally planned investment, its size notwithstanding, continued to neglect urgent problems such as poor roads and inadequate local storage facilities in favor of grandiose projects such as irrigation works that impressed bureaucrats in Moscow but did not answer the peasants' needs. As a result, waste continued to plague the system throughout the 1970s; for example, a fifth of the grain crop, a quarter of the sugar beets, and a third of the potatoes spoiled or were otherwise lost before reaching the consumer. Equally serious, the initially impressive 21 percent growth in agricultural production achieved under Brezhnev from 1966 to 1970 dropped to 13 percent from 1971 to 1975 and to 9 percent from 1976 to 1980. Poor weather added to the losses and shortfalls in 1965, 1969, 1971, 1972, 1974, 1975, and each year between 1979 and 1982, helping to make massive grain imports a permanent part of Soviet life.

A major reform effort was also made in the industrial sector. The goals were the same as with agriculture: increased productivity and reduced waste and inefficiency. This effort was supervised by Kosygin, an able and experienced administrator who held responsibility for the economy as a whole. Kosygin's reforms reflected discussions that had begun under Khrushchev, particularly concerning the ideas of economist Yevsei Liberman. In the early 1960s, Liberman had advocated that managers of industrial enterprises be allowed to make decisions in such areas as hiring, the percentage of factory resources devoted to wages, and the mix of goods a given enterprise would produce. A manager's performance would be judged by his factory's profitability. Presumably this would lead to improved quality and efficiency since in order to be profitable a factory would have to produce goods that customers actually wanted to buy. This daring innovation would supersede the traditional Soviet system under which a factory received production quotas calculated in terms of quantity, weight, and other easily measurable categories (as well as detailed instructions on whom to hire, what wages to pay, what materials to buy, etc.) and was rewarded simply for meeting those quotas, regardless of whether anybody could *use* the goods produced. The traditional system often led to quotas being met by shirts without buttons, trucks without starter motors, sheets of steel too heavy for many uses, and the like. The Brezhnev team also set lower and more realistic economic growth targets, both for its first five years and for the subsequent decade.

Despite their sensible provisions, the Kosygin reforms never made it off the ground. Because of the conservatism pervading the power structure, the new methods were not introduced on a scale wide enough to acquire what economist Marshall Goldman has called a "critical mass."[2] Because that vital threshold was not reached, a factory operating according to the new system inevitably became entangled in the old system. For example, it might want to improve its product by using a new material but would be unable to procure that material because no factory was either free to produce it under the Kosygin reforms or authorized to do so by the central planners. Widespread opposition from party bosses concerned over losing much of their authority hamstrung the reforms, as did the central planners' refusal to allow prices to fluctuate according to the dictates of supply and demand.

The Soviet economy nonetheless managed impressive quantitative growth, mainly because Brezhnev and his central planners continued to favor heavy industry over light industry and investment over consumption. By the late 1970s Soviet industry produced seven times more than thirty years earlier, and the Soviet Union led the world in the output of such basic items as steel, oil, machine tools, and heavy military hardware. The annual rate of increase in the gross national product even grew from 1966 to 1970 as compared to the previous five years, inching upward from 5 percent to 5.2 percent.

THE SOVIET ECONOMY SLOWS DOWN

But then an inexorable decline set in, as the annual growth rate slipped to 3.7 percent between 1971 and 1975 and then to 2.7 percent between 1976 and 1980. Innovation lagged; much of the Soviet Union's equipment was obsolete. Also, the Soviet Union did not produce many of the finished industrial goods that in Japan, Western Europe, and the United States formed the basis for increased productivity and a far higher standard of living than Soviet citizens knew. Even when the Soviet planners committed additional resources to producing consumer goods, as in the Ninth Five-Year Plan covering 1971–1975, a variety of complications and the continued investment priority enjoyed by heavy industry and the military derailed their intentions.

Economic stagnation occurred in large part because the revolution's past began to catch up with it. The Brezhnev regime made a serious, and very expensive, effort to improve lagging agricultural productivity by giving that sector, for so long subject to Stalin's exploitation and Khrushchev's unworkable panaceas, about 25 percent of all investment funds between 1966 and 1975. But the infusion into agriculture was a drain on the industrial investment pool. Meanwhile, there was no significant structural reform: the *kolkhoz/ sovkhoz* system that largely caused the problem remained a sacred cow, and the agricultural sector remained unable to meet the nation's food needs. The growing price of food imports, including grain to feed cattle, and the cost of food subsidies that were required to keep the price of food affordable to consumers added tens of billions of rubles to the soaring cost of keeping the Soviet agricultural system intact, without doing anything to improve it.

Equally important, the central planning system became increasingly unable to cope with the growing complexity of the Soviet Union's industrial economy. The problem was not simply coordinating the requirements of tens of thousands of individual economic units, each with its own schedule and problems; it included managing the competition among these units and among whole industries and entire regions for resources of all kinds. There was also the vexing inability to introduce new products and technologies into an enormous and unwieldy economic system, particularly when innovation carried the nightmarish risk that haunted most managers and bureaucrats: the failure to produce the number of units, kilograms, square meters, cubic meters, or whatever was required by Moscow's master plan. Another shibboleth of the Stalin era—the primacy of the military—continued to absorb vital human and material resources in prodigious quantities, dragging down growth rates for the economy as a whole. In fact, the military's share of the total economy increased substantially during the Brezhnev era. Meanwhile, the Soviet economy was being deprived of two formerly abundant resources upon which it had become dependent: cheap labor and cheap natural resources. The huge pool of cheap labor that had fueled Soviet industrialization began to dry up as urbanization and higher levels of education, themselves products of the revolution, drove down birthrates among Slavs and other European peoples, who together formed over 80 percent of the USSR's population. The labor shortage was made worse by the wasteful use of what was available, as huge numbers of excess workers unproductively passed the time on factory floors where they were not needed or went through the motions in the poorly tended fields of collective and state farms. Likewise, the cheap and easily exploitable raw materials west of the Urals that had been so vital to both prewar and postwar economic growth were being depleted. The Soviet Union still possessed enormous natural resources, but many of them—including vital oil and natural gas deposits—were deep in Siberia and required large long-term investments to make them exploitable. In the short term, these investments represented another expensive anchor weighing down the economy as a whole.

Despite these problems, the old Stalinist economic structure still had enough momentum to enable the standard of living to rise from its 1964 level. Real wages rose 50 percent between 1965 and 1977. By the late 1970s the majority of Soviet families owned radios, refrigerators, and even washing machines. Yet, just as the overall economic growth rate declined, so inevitably did the growth rate in the standard of living. In 1981 per capita consumption grew by less than 2 percent; the 1982 figure was 1 percent. The housing situation remained unsatisfactory, to say the least; in 1981 the Soviet Union could not meet minimum standards that had been set by the government in 1928, and 20 percent of all urban families still shared kitchen and bathroom facilities. Repair and personal care services remained exceedingly difficult to obtain. Between 1965 and 1978 the percentage of the budget devoted to health care dropped despite increased need for health services. Soviet infant mortality rates increased during the 1970s, and the Soviet Union gained the dubious distinction of being the first industrialized country to see its life expectancy drop. Worst of all, Soviet per capita consumption in the late 1970s remained one-third that of the United States and less than half that of France and West Germany. Another bitter truth was that the economy's best postwar performance in terms of annual growth was during 1951–1955, *before* most of the reforms, experiments, and efforts of the Khrushchev and Brezhnev years. Finally, what made all the post-1950 consumption figures look so good was the abysmally low standard of living in the immediate postwar era. In short, the performance of the Soviet economy under Brezhnev was impressive for a developing country but not for an advanced socialist society, which the Soviet Union claimed to be.

REACTION IN CULTURAL AND INTELLECTUAL LIFE

If the Brezhnev record was mixed regarding economic performance, it was clear and consistent when it came to intellectual and cultural freedom. Destalinization was over. In 1965 a few ripples of the receding destalinization tide continued to wash up on Soviet shores: a collection of Boris Pasternak's poems; Alexander Nekrich's *June 22, 1941,* an exposé of the devastating effects of Stalin's purges on the Soviet military prior to World War II; and the release of poet Joseph Brodsky after he had served two years of his five-year sentence. However, these small ripples were swamped by a far stronger and growing incoming tide. Several months before Nekrich's book appeared, influential figures in both the military and political bureaucracies, worried that Khrushchev's debunking of Stalin had undermined the party's authority, began to press for Stalin's partial rehabilitation. While those favoring this step hardly wanted a return to a Stalin-style personal dictatorship, they saw a revival of Stalin's reputation as helpful in imposing tighter controls on Soviet cultural and intellectual life. Brezhnev himself was a prime mover in this campaign. At the same time, much of what Khrushchev had done away with could not be restored. Several important intellectuals protested directly to Brezhnev about any further rehabilitation of Stalin, while the party itself was deeply divided on the issue. The result was a typical Brezhnev compromise. Stalin was not rehabilitated at the Twenty-Third Congress (March–April 1966) as had been rumored. The congress did revive two terms from the Stalin era, however, as Brezhnev was designated the *general* rather than first secretary and the Presidium again became the Politburo. Stalin once again was called an outstanding party leader, albeit one with some faults. Eventually a bust was placed over his grave.

Whatever precise things were done or said about Stalin personally, the most dramatic events that set the limits to destalinization involved other names. In September 1965 two writers, Andrei Sinyavsky and Yuli Daniel, were arrested. Their "crime" was having published abroad (under the pseudonyms Abram Tertz and Nikolai Arzhak, respectively) literature critical of the Soviet Union. These arrests sent out a shock wave since Sinyavsky and Daniel were under attack simply for their writing, not for any overt act of defiance. Following the courageous and dramatic precedent set by Brodsky, Sinyavsky and Daniel refused to admit any guilt; they were tried in early 1966 and sentenced respectively to seven and five years at hard labor.

THE DISSIDENT MOVEMENT

These sentences stunned the intellectual community, but what followed surely must have stunned the Soviet leadership even more. The specter of Stalinism revived was too much for many intellectuals and even ordinary citizens to stand. Despite the threat of harsh reprisals, they engaged in an unheard of response: public protest. Not only such well-known writers as Solzhenitsyn and Yevtushenko, but also prominent figures across the spectrum of Soviet intellectual, cultural, and even scientific life signed petitions of protest. Among them was Andrei Sakharov, the country's leading physicist and the father of the Soviet hydrogen bomb. Many others of humbler status joined in with protests of their own. It mattered little that at the Twenty-Third Congress Brezhnev denounced the protesters, that others soon followed Sinyavsky and Daniel into prison or exile, or that the regime quickly added two new articles (190–1 and 190–3) to the criminal code of the RSFSR to use against dissidents. Soviet intellectuals cherished the small gains that had been made between 1953 and 1964 and hoped to expand them. The end of Stalin's terror meant that those with extraordinary courage might speak out and survive. Vocal dissent certainly exposed its practitioners to the threat of harassment or arrest, but the days of untrammeled secret police arrests for the slightest offense—real, suspected, or imagined—were over. Under these new, if hardly benign, conditions, the attempt to strangle the budding efforts at self-expression gave birth instead to the dissident movement.

This phenomenon has been designated a "movement" for lack of a better word. In reality it was a diffuse, diverse, and disorganized flotilla of largely self-contained vessels, sometimes cooperating, frequently operating independently, often with radically different goals, and sometimes even at odds. Although that flotilla had lacked a flagship, several distinguished intellectuals provided it with a series of beacons, most prominent among them being Sakharov, Solzhenitsyn, and two brothers, Roy and Zhores Medvedev. An important common link among the various dissident groups was the remarkable phenomenon of *samizdat* (literally "self-publication"), the underground publication of materials that developed into an invaluable source of information about the movement, both for the dissidents themselves and for their sympathizers in the West. The most important of these publications was the *Chronicle of Current Events.* It first came out in 1968 as a bimonthly, was suppressed in 1972 (along with another important journal, the *Ukrainian Herald*), and was successfully revived in 1974. Many other *samizdat* journals appeared across the Soviet Union espousing different causes for varying periods of time, adding up to literally thousands of documents. They were supplemented by writings smuggled to the West and published there without official authorization (*tamizdat*) and by illegal tape recordings of songs for secret distribution at home (*magnitizdat*).

SAKHAROV AND SOLZHENITSYN

The two outstanding individuals of the dissident movement were Andrei Sakharov and Aleksandr Solzhenitsyn. Ironically, despite their enormous stature as individuals, their deep disagreements and the difficulties they shared in reaching the Russian people made them symbolic of the weakness of the dissident movement as a whole. Sakharov, a modern-day "Westerner," advocated reform of Soviet society along Western democratic lines. His 1968 manifesto, "Thoughts on Progress, Peaceful Coexistence, and Intellectual Freedom," called for freedom of thought and expression and a multiparty system in the Soviet Union. Sakharov warned that without these freedoms the Soviet Union would decline into a second-rate power. Two years later he was one of the founders, with Valery Chalidze and Andrei Tverdokhlebov, of the Moscow Committee for Human Rights. Sakharov vigorously supported the right of Jews to emigrate from the Soviet Union. In 1975 he was awarded the Nobel Peace Prize, which Soviet authorities prevented him from accepting. Although Sakharov endured harassment, some of it quite cruel and damaging to both his and his wife's health, because of his international reputation he remained immune from the more severe punishments generally handed out to other dissidents. In 1980, however, the KGB seized Sakharov and exiled him to Gorky, a city several hundred miles from Moscow and closed to foreigners.

Solzhenitsyn, a towering figure blessed with equal measures of literary talent and personal courage, took it upon himself to assault the entire Soviet system, not just as it stood in the 1960s and 1970s, but all the way down to its Leninist roots. This he did with thunderous power in his novels *The First Circle* and *The Cancer Ward* and in his groundbreaking history of the Soviet labor camp system, *The Gulag Archipelago*, works that were denied publication in the Soviet Union and had to be published in the West. Unlike Sakharov, however, Solzhenitsyn did not look to the West as a model for reform. A classic Slavophile, Solzhenitsyn urged his country to return to what he considered its ancient Russian roots. Western influences, Marxism being the most pernicious, should be rejected in favor of values derived from Russia's Orthodox and peasant traditions. Solzhenitsyn, winner of the 1970 Nobel Prize for Literature, was, like Sakharov, protected by his international reputation for a time. By 1974, however, he had become such a painful thorn that the Soviet authorities, while not daring to imprison him, seized him, put him on a plane, and banished him to the West, a fate that Solzhenitsyn at times may have considered worse than prison in his beloved native land.

NATIONALITY AND DISSENT

Dissent in the multinational Soviet Union inevitably also reflected the suppressed aspirations of non-Russian ethnic nationalities and groups. The deep wellspring of national feeling in the Ukraine again bubbled to the surface in the 1960s. Ukrainian intellectuals protested, among other things, Russification and pervasive discrimination. Given the Ukrainians' status as the Soviet Union's second most populous nationality (after the Great Russians) and the region's immense strategic and economic importance, the regime cracked down hard. Among the many who went to prison between the mid-1960s and the early 1970s were Ivan Dzyuba, author of *Internationalism or Russification?*; Vyacheslav Chornovil, who chronicled the persecution of Ukrainian dissidents; and Valentin Moroz, author of *A Report from the Beria Reservation*, an exposé of the shocking conditions in the post-Stalin labor camps. Higher up the ladder, Pyotr Shelest, the Ukrainian party first secretary, was removed from office in 1972 for failing to suppress local nationalist sentiment. The Ukrainian pattern was repeated in other national republics. The problem was the most serious in the Baltic republics, where at one point in Lithuania alone there were a dozen *samizdat* journals, and in the Caucasus.

Dissent also took on a religious cast. Roman Catholics had a number of clashes with the regime, particularly in largely Catholic Lithuania, where religious faith converged with national sentiment. Some Protestant groups pushed for religious freedom, the most active of them being the Baptists. A few stirrings even occurred within the usually pliant and somewhat privileged

Russian Orthodox Church, but these were rather small and easily contained, largely by the church hierarchy itself.

The most successful of all dissident groups was the Jewish movement. The Jewish activists owed their surprising success to several factors. They received support from Jewish communities abroad, the most influential of which was in the United States, as well as from dissidents at home, including Sakharov. They were inspired by the achievements of the state of Israel—first and foremost by its very existence, but also by its triumphs in the 1967 and 1973 wars against far larger, Soviet-equipped Arab armies—and unified by ever-present anti-Semitic harassment at home. The crucial point, however, is that most Jewish dissidents were not primarily concerned with changing Soviet society; their goal simply was to leave it. Most of the movement's founders and leaders were eager to emigrate to Israel, which was equally eager to welcome them. Having a country willing to accept them also distinguished the Jews from most groups trying to win the right to emigrate. Aided especially by U.S. pressure at a time when the Soviet government wanted improved relations with the West, Soviet Jews succeeded in convincing the Brezhnev regime to let some of them go. Over 200,000 Jews left the Soviet Union during the 1970s. But even this small success was highly qualified. Hundreds of thousands of others who also wanted to emigrate were either denied permission to leave, prevented from even applying to leave, or intimidated so they dared not apply in the first place. Meanwhile, renewed difficulties in Soviet–American relations led the Soviets to reduce the emigration flow. In late 1974 a new American law required the Soviet Union to make a formal commitment to continued high levels of Jewish emigration in return for liberalization of the 1972 American–Soviet trade agreement. Moscow responded by canceling the trade agreement and curtailing emigration considerably. After a brief revival in the late 1970s, during which the number of emigrants peaked at 50,000 in 1979, deteriorating Soviet–American relations contributed to the Soviet decision in the early 1980s to reduce to a trickle the flow of Jewish emigration.

As a whole, the Soviet dissidents had occasional spurts of activity and some small successes. Periodically a dramatic event led to an upsurge in activity. The 1968 Soviet invasion of Czechoslovakia, for example, exerted a powerful influence on Sakharov and others working for democratic reform. Many dissidents interested in democratic reform or in emigration found renewed vigor in August 1975 when the Soviet Union signed the Helsinki Accords, which pledged all signatories to guarantee a broad range of human rights to their citizens. "Helsinki Watch Groups" were formed in several Soviet cities after the accords were signed. More frequently, however, state repression debilitated the movement as dissidents were sent to prison, "exported" abroad, or left the Soviet Union by choice. However, the most fundamental reason for the movement's precarious standing was that aside from a few examples where the dissidents had an ethnic base and a very limited goal, as with the Jewish movement or the movement of ethnic Germans to emigrate to West Germany, the dissident movement, particularly the segment interested in democratic reform, could not reach a wide audience. The barriers of traditional Russian apathy in the face of authority, the strength of the KGB and other organs of repression, and the enormous social gap separating Soviet intellectuals from the average Soviet citizen were insurmountable. During the early 1980s dissident activity was at a low ebb. By then most of the well-known dissidents for one reason or another were out of commission. Many were in prison or internal exile: people like Sakharov, Yuri Orlov, Alexander Ginzburg, Anatoly Shcharansky, and Yuri Galanskov, who died in a labor camp due to lack of proper medical care. Others were abroad, some having gone there directly (such as Solzhenitsyn and Chalidze) and some after serving prison terms (Sinyavsky, Vladimir Bukovsky, and others).

Yet dissent continued to exist. Often a nuisance, at times an embarrassment, always a source of discomfiture, the dissident movement under Brezhnev became something like a chronic but narrowly confined case of social psoriasis on the Soviet body politic, unable either to spread outward or bore inward and thereby become an immediate threat, but short of amputation à la Stalin, not subject to complete eradication either.

THE 1977 CONSTITUTION AND DEVELOPED SOCIALISM

None of these problems was reflected in the new Soviet constitution adopted in 1977. It proclaimed that the Soviet Union was a "developed socialist society" in which "All power . . . belongs to the people." The new document, which replaced Stalin's 1936 constitution, also contained a long list of economic and political rights due each Soviet citizen. These included the peasantry's right to farm private plots and the right of all citizens to engage in a strictly limited range of private economic activity. Most significantly, however, the 1977 constitution made the Communist Party the final arbiter of virtually everything of importance, including whether individual Soviet citizens could actually enjoy their constitutionally mandated rights. Unlike the 1936 constitution, which did not emphasize the party, the 1977 document stressed the role of the party as the predominant force in the Soviet Union. Overall, the new constitution, its genuflections to Marxism notwithstanding, did not reflect the Marxist ideal of the state withering away but rather the older Russian tradition of the state waxing stronger and controlling society.

THE MILITARY BUILDUP

While the Soviet state was bringing its power to bear on its citizens, it also was building up its strength against its foreign rivals, particularly the United States. Soviet defense spending grew at an annual rate (adjusted for inflation) of about 4 percent from 1964 to 1976. Thereafter the rate of growth dropped to a still imposing 2 percent per year. Despite this slowdown, a reasonable estimate is that under Brezhnev about a quarter of the Soviet Union's gross domestic product eventually was devoted to the military, in contrast to the American figure of 6 percent. It was a staggering burden on the economy as a whole. About half of all Soviet industrial enterprises and between one-half and three-quarters of the country's scientific and technical personnel were linked in one way or another to the military effort. By 1981 Soviet defense dollar outlays were 45 percent higher than those of the United States. The result was that Soviet preponderance in conventional arms increased considerably, at least in quantitative terms. In 1981, for example, the Warsaw Pact had more than three times the main battle tanks, three times the artillery and mortars, and over three-and-a-half times the armored personnel carriers and infantry fighting vehicles than did NATO. At the same time, the American strategic nuclear superiority that had loomed so large during the Cuban Missile Crisis was overcome. By the late 1970s, the Soviets led the Americans in the number of ICBMs, submarine-launched missiles, nuclear submarines, and total nuclear megatonage, although the United States continued to lead in the total number of nuclear warheads and in the accuracy and quality of its missiles. Meanwhile, the Soviet navy developed from an essentially coastal force under Stalin and Khrushchev into a major vehicle for projecting Soviet power worldwide by means of long-range submarines and aircraft carriers.

The direct military effort was complemented by a comprehensive space program, although the Soviet Union suffered an irreplaceable loss when Sergei Korolev died in January 1966 because of an improperly performed operation. The death of the man known in life only as the "Chief Designer" because of his country's obsession with secrecy—his many official honors came only posthumously—effectively ended any chance the Soviet Union could beat the United States in the race to land a man on the moon. Still, while the Soviets could not match the American achievement of manned lunar landings, their program did manage several impressive "firsts," while also providing valuable technological services to the military. Overall, the military sphere was one area where Brezhnev and his colleagues could claim to have achieved a solid success, although they probably preferred not to mention the burden the military effort placed on the Soviet people and the damage it did to their inefficient and overtaxed economy.

DÉTENTE

Under Brezhnev, as under Stalin and Khrushchev, the Soviet Union's major foreign policy concern remained the United States. Despite their ideological hostility, other considerations such as the threat of nuclear catastrophe, the mounting burden of the arms race, and the difficulties each superpower was having with third parties—especially Moscow, which was becoming increasingly worried about Communist China—impelled the U.S. and USSR to seek some sort of accommodation, or "détente." Supporters of détente in the Kremlin saw it as a vehicle for gaining access to Western technology and the financial credits the country needed to pay for high-technology and other necessary imports. They also saw it as the best way to win formal recognition from the United States of the Soviet Union's status as a superpower and equal.

The path to détente was not a smooth one, especially in the halls of the Kremlin. Although the Soviet leadership as a whole supported détente, some important figures, most notably Politburo members Nikolai Podgorny and Mikhail Suslov, opposed or at a minimum deeply mistrusted the policy, as did the country's military leadership. The pragmatic Alexei Kosygin cautiously supported détente because of its potential technological and economic benefits but shared reservations about overdoing what skeptics called the "détente waltz." These concerns extended to détente's centerpiece, nuclear arms negotiations known as the Strategic Arms Limitation Talks (SALT), which began in 1969. The crucial and most consistent supporter of improving relations with the United States was Brezhnev, who between 1968 and 1972 worked long hours to build and maintain a consensus for détente in general and the SALT negotiations in particular. Other important pro-détente leaders included Foreign Minister Andrei Gromyko and KGB boss Yuri Andropov. It was in dealing with this contentious issue that Brezhnev came closest to fulfilling his self-described role as a "leader." His steady efforts on behalf of détente culminated in a secret Central Committee meeting held in May 1972, just before President Richard M. Nixon's scheduled arrival in Moscow to complete the SALT negotiations, at which the general secretary won decisive support for his policies.

Brezhnev's summit meeting with Nixon then yielded the SALT I accords, which put the first restraints on the nuclear arms race. SALT I included two treaties, one dealing with defensive, or antiballistic, missiles (ABMs) and the other with intercontinental and submarine-launched ballistic missiles (ICBMs and SLBMs). The ABM treaty limited each superpower to a total of 200 interceptor missiles equally divided between two separate sites. In effect this meant that neither country could defend itself against a nuclear attack by the other and, the thinking went, therefore neither would begin a nuclear war for fear of catastrophic retaliation. The other treaty placed a five-year interim ceiling on each country's arsenal of ICBMs and SLBMs. Because of American technological superiority, Moscow was allowed more of both types of missiles than Washington, a total of 2,558 versus 1,710. Other positive signs for détente during 1972 and 1973 included large Soviet purchases of American wheat, a dramatic increase in overall trade with the West, and Brezhnev's June 1973 visit to the United States.

There nonetheless remained many sources of tension between the two superpowers. The most serious difficulties involved Vietnam, where the United States was committed to protecting anti-Communist South Vietnam against the Soviet-backed campaign to overthrow it by the Communist North Vietnam. The Americans and Soviets also clashed in the strategic and oil-rich Middle East as they backed opposite sides in both the 1967 and 1973 Arab–Israeli wars. All of these issues slowed the pace of détente until 1973 when the Americans, suffering from deep and painful wounds, withdrew from Vietnam. The pace of détente then began to quicken.

The next several years constituted the high-water mark of détente. In June 1974 President Nixon returned to the Soviet Union, and in November, after Nixon was forced from office by the Watergate scandal, President Gerald Ford and Brezhnev met in the Siberian city of Vladivostok and signed an agreement that provided a framework for the next stage of nuclear arms talks, known as SALT II. The Vladivostok agreement covered long-range, or strategic, bombers as well as the strategic ballistic missiles covered by SALT I. It allowed each country to deploy an arsenal of 2,400 such weapons, which would consist of a mix of intercontinental ballistic missiles, submarine-launched ballistic missiles, and long-range bombers. The two powers even met in space when an American Apollo space vehicle docked with a Soviet Soyuz craft in July 1975. In August, the Soviets and Americans, along with more than thirty other nations, signed the Helsinki Accords. These finalized the post–World War II boundary changes in Europe, a longtime Soviet goal. All signatories also agreed to respect a list of basic human rights, something that would cause the Soviets some subsequent embarrassment but that at the time seemed a small price to pay in return for the legitimization of their postwar expansion.

Notwithstanding its agreements with the United States to manage the nuclear arms race, during the détente years the Soviet Union was considerably less forthcoming regarding other nonconventional weapons. In 1973, four years after the United States publicly renounced the use of biological weapons, and in violation of an international agreement the Soviet Union had recently signed, Brezhnev and his colleagues began a massive new secret program to develop biological weapons. This was on top of programs the Soviets already had. While many motives certainly were involved, it appears that the Soviet leadership did not believe the United States was being truthful in its renunciation of these weapons and was convinced the United States still had an offensive program, assumptions that in fact were incorrect. Soviet leaders also apparently feared that their country lagged far behind the West in genetics and molecular biology and therefore had to catch up. The expanded Soviet biological weapons program was carried out by the newly created Chief Directorate for Biological Preparations, or Biopreparat. Biopreparat included about 50 sites and at its peak probably employed at least 40,000 people, 9,000 of whom were highly trained scientists and technicians. Its facilities were hidden from foreign intelligence by being placed inside civilian biotechnology and pharmaceutical enterprises. Biopreparat scientists weaponized a wide range of agents including brucellosis, Marburg virus, tularemia, typhus, Q fever, smallpox, plague, and anthrax. Altogether, they studied more than 50 biological agents. Genetic engineering was used to develop new generations of biological agents more deadly and better suited for weapons use than anything known in the West. Tons of smallpox agents were produced and weaponized by placing them in intercontinental missiles capable of reaching the United States. Anthrax and plague agents also were prepared for use against the United States and its allies.

The Soviet Union succeeded in keeping the Biopreparat program secret during the détente era and for a long time thereafter. Finally, two defections by top Biopreparat scientists, the first in 1989, seven years after Brezhnev's death, and the second in 1992, a year after the Soviet Union collapsed, exposed the program. Its scope and sophistication left Western intelligence agencies in shock. Biopreparat, whose facilities supposedly were dismantled beginning in 1986, left behind a grim legacy of environmental pollution and skilled, unemployed scientists who might sell their services to anyone willing to pay, as well as troublesome questions, unanswered to this day, as to whether it was completely dismantled or whether some parts of the largest and most dangerous biological weapons program in history are still secretly in operation.

In any event, even with Biopreparat safely hidden from Western eyes, détente did not prove to be durable. The 1974 flap over Jewish emigration and trade led the Soviets to cancel a number of agreements along with the trade agreement in question. Soviet intervention in Angola via Cuban proxies and, more important, the Soviet Union's 1979 invasion of Afghanistan (which soon tied down more than 100,000 troops) left détente in a shambles. Among the casualties was the SALT II, signed by both parties in June 1979 but never ratified by the U.S. Senate. The United States then led a boycott of the 1980 Moscow Olympics, a gesture that provided more insult than injury. Relations reached a new post-détente low in December 1981 when, under immense pressure from Moscow, the Polish government proclaimed martial law and forcibly disbanded the independent labor movement, Solidarity, which in 1980 had grown out of a massive series of strikes to become the first independent union in the history of the Soviet bloc.

INTRA-COMMUNIST CONFLICTS

Aside from capitalist America, Communist China caused the Soviet Union the most problems. A short-lived Soviet attempt to patch up relations immediately after Khrushchev's fall ended in failure. In 1965 the Soviet Union requested military facilities and air transit rights in China in order to transport supplies to North Vietnam. The Chinese refused. Then came Mao's "Cultural Revolution," a rabid attack on everything Mao felt was hindering China's march to communism, a rogues' gallery that included Soviet "revisionism" no less than the pernicious influence of the West. China was thrown into turmoil for three years. The Cultural Revolution was framed by China's refusal to attend the Twenty-Third Congress of the CPSU in 1966 and the bloody border incidents that erupted along the Chinese–Soviet frontier in 1969. When the turmoil ended, the Soviets were dismayed to find that the Chinese, unnerved by the Soviet Union's military buildup and aggressiveness, were beginning to develop a détente of their own with the United States. Henry Kissinger's secret trip to Beijing in July 1971 was followed by the United States dropping its objections to the Beijing regime's admission to the United Nations and assumption of the "China" seat in the Security Council formerly held by the Nationalist regime on Taiwan. In 1972 President Nixon made a landmark visit to the People's Republic. In 1979 Washington ended its thirty-year-long policy of refusing to recognize the Beijing regime, and normal Chinese–American diplomatic relations were established.

Meanwhile, Soviet–Chinese relations had failed to improve. The most successful Soviet effort vis-à-vis the Chinese involved strengthening relations with China's neighbors. In August 1971 Moscow signed a treaty of friendship with India; in November the Soviets backed predominantly Hindu India in its successful war against Muslim Pakistan. Continued economic aid further solidified Soviet–Indian relations. Moscow also successfully wooed two Communist states that bordered on China—Mongolia and North Korea—and worked to improve relations with Japan. But the Soviet refusal to return four small islands seized from Japan at the end of World War II remained a thorn in Soviet–Japanese relations, as was the improvement in Sino-Japanese relations that occurred in the late 1970s.

The Sino-Soviet rivalry was further reflected in the intra-Communist conflicts that engulfed Indochina after the American withdrawal from South Vietnam. After North Vietnam overran South Vietnam in 1975, ending a struggle for control of Vietnam that dated from the 1940s, the regime in Hanoi that now controlled the entire country tilted clearly toward the Soviet Union and against China. This was not surprising since Vietnam has traditionally feared China, its huge neighbor directly to the north. However, the Communist victory in Cambodia (renamed Kampuchea) that same year led to a pro-Chinese regime there; this also was not a surprising turn of events since the Cambodians feared Vietnam, their traditional rival and powerful neighbor. Soon there was war again in Indochina, but unlike what occurred from the 1940s through the mid-1970s, the combatants were all Communists, albeit Communists of different nationalities. In December 1978, Vietnam invaded Kampuchea in order to oust its homicidal pro-Chinese regime, which had slaughtered between a fifth and a quarter of the country's entire population—the death toll may have reached 2 million people—in its macabre campaign to build its version of a communist utopia. But the Vietnamese quickly became bogged down in a guerrilla war—their own "Vietnam"—that dragged on for a decade. In February 1979 China responded to Vietnam's invasion of Kampuchea by starting a short, bloody war of its own with Hanoi. As the war strained and weakened China and turned the Vietnamese increasingly toward Moscow, the Soviet Union reaped the benefit. However these gains were largely offset by China's development of a nuclear arsenal that included hydrogen bombs and medium-range ballistic missiles. By 1980 the Chinese had also begun to test intercontinental missiles.

DÉTENTE WITH WESTERN EUROPE

The Soviet Union's difficulties with Communist China stood in contrast to its successes in capitalist Western Europe. After French President Charles de Gaulle, chafing under American leadership, withdrew French military forces from the unified NATO command in 1966, albeit without taking France out of NATO itself, Brezhnev responded by inviting him to visit the Soviet Union and making him the first Western head of state permitted to visit a Soviet space facility. This was followed by increased Soviet–French economic cooperation that included the French building of a huge truck factory in the Soviet Union. The Soviets also did reasonably well with West Germany. In a series of treaties beginning in 1970, the West Germans accepted the post–World War II boundaries with Poland, renounced the use of force against the Soviet Union, and recognized East Germany. These improved relations with the two leading capitalist nations on the European mainland, along with the signing of the Helsinki Accords, represented a considerable enhancement of the Soviet position in Western Europe. So too did the scrapping of the American plan to deploy in Western Europe the so-called neutron bomb—an effective potential counter to the Warsaw Pact's tank superiority over NATO—and the 1982 decision of several of America's NATO allies, anxious to decrease their dangerous dependence on Middle Eastern oil, to help the Soviet Union build a huge pipeline to transport Soviet natural gas to customers in the West.

The Soviets did not, however, succeed in breaking up NATO or weakening the Common Market. Instead, it was their influence over the Communist parties of Western Europe that began, if not to unravel, then at least to fray around the edges. Widespread general revulsion toward the 1968 Soviet invasion of Czechoslovakia damaged Western Europe's Communist parties. They were further hurt by their continued demeaning subservience to the Soviet Union and their adherence to the Soviet doctrine of "proletarian dictatorship," a euphemism that to many Europeans meant police-state oppression and the destruction of political pluralism. The unpleasant result for the Soviets was Eurocommunism. The major European Communist parties—the most important being in France, Italy, and Spain—began to assert their independence from Moscow, criticize the suppression of human rights in the Soviet bloc, and stress the right of each nation to chart its own path toward socialism.

THE PRAGUE SPRING

Whatever the Soviet Union's difficulties with regard to Western Europe, at times it seemed that it had more problems with Communist Eastern Europe. During the Brezhnev years the most serious crises arose in Czechoslovakia and Poland. Czechoslovakia was the only Eastern European country to maintain a democratic form of government during the period between World War I and World War II. After the war it reestablished a democratic regime. The Soviet Union extinguished that solitary flame in 1948, installing in its place a Communist regime that became one of the most brutal and incompetent in Eastern Europe. It remained rigidly Stalinist even when the Soviet Union was changing under Khrushchev. Rigidity finally turned into brittleness, and in 1968 the system cracked under the pressure of a moribund economy and swelling dissent. In January, Antonin Novotny, the old-line local satrap who was both the Communist Party boss and head of state, was removed from his more important position as party first secretary and replaced by Alexander Dubček, a leading reform advocate.

What followed thrilled many in the West and horrified the Soviets. The reform impulse, fed by Czechoslovakia's lingering democratic tradition, spread with astonishing speed. Novotny was ousted from the presidency in March 1968 and replaced by war-hero General Ludvik Svoboda (the general's last name means "freedom" in both Czech and Russian). The new leadership meanwhile abolished censorship, established freedom of the press, committed itself to civil liberties, and took steps to sanction a genuine multiparty political system. Dubček, unlike the Hungarian Nagy in 1956, went out of his way to assure the Soviet Union that Czechoslovakia would remain a socialist state and member of the Warsaw Pact. But his "socialism with a human face" was a Medusa to Brezhnev and his Politburo; they worried that Czechoslovakian ideas might spread to other Eastern European satellites or even to the Soviet Union and cause incalculable damage. On August 20, 1968, after neither pressure nor threats could turn Dubček around, Czechoslovakia was invaded by more than 400,000 Soviet, East German, Hungarian, Polish, and Bulgarian troops. The West was outraged, as were many European Communists and Soviet dissidents. None of that helped Czechoslovakia.

The matter did not stop with the successful invasion. The entire Soviet bloc was promptly informed that the Soviet Union would use force to eliminate any threats to "the course of socialism." This "Brezhnev Doctrine" thus proclaimed the impossibility of any fundamental change within the Soviet bloc, no less than the impossibility of secession from it. In fact, the invasion of Czechoslovakia and the Brezhnev Doctrine did far more to divide the world Communist movement than to unify it. The shockwave created by hundreds of thousands of Soviet soldiers on the move shook and frightened Beijing and pushed the Chinese leadership toward reconciliation with the United States. Albania and Yugoslavia, Eastern European Communist states that were not part of the Soviet bloc, denounced the invasion and Brezhnev's justification of it. Albania, a tiny state protected from Soviet military forces by Yugoslavia to its east, continued to support Communist China in the increasingly bitter Sino-Soviet conflict. Romania, a Soviet bloc member that shared a border with the Soviet Union, feared it might be next on Brezhnev's invasion list. The country was ruled by the ruthless Nicolae Ceauşescu, who maintained an orthodox and repressive Communist dictatorship. No Soviet troops were stationed in Romania, and Ceauşescu refused to permit the Soviets to correct the oversight, using it instead as a wedge to carve out a small measure of independence for his country. Romania had been the only Communist state to maintain diplomatic relations with Israel after the 1967 Six-Day War. It not only refused to participate in the invasion of Czechoslovakia, but refused to allow Warsaw Pact troops to cross Romanian territory in order to enter Czechoslovakia. Aside from antagonizing the Soviets over the invasion, Romania leaned toward Yugoslavia and China on certain intra-Communist issues and consistently resisted Soviet attempts at closer integration of the Soviet and other Warsaw Pact economies.

The Kremlin paid a heavy price for its actions in Czechoslovakia. Western European Communist parties almost unanimously condemned the invasion.

At home, the invasion angered and depressed Soviet intellectuals and was an important factor in the growth of the dissident movement. Roy Medvedev, an independent-minded Marxist, spoke for many of his peers when he maintained that the invasion of Czechoslovakia was "not in 'defense of socialism' but a blow against socialism in Czechoslovakia and throughout the world."

These unwelcome reactions did not prevent the Soviet Union from reinforcing its control over most of its Eastern European satellites. Its main methods were increased integration of various Communist-bloc economies through COMECON (the Council of Mutual Economic Assistance) and increased military integration under the aegis of the Warsaw Pact.

POLAND AND SOLIDARITY

In the long run, no thorn in the Soviet side caused more pain than Poland, a country that never accepted tsarist or Soviet domination despite an almost unbroken string of bitter disappointments in numerous attempts to reestablish its independence during the nineteenth and twentieth centuries. After breaking free from Russian control after World War I, Poland enjoyed two decades of independence before being wiped from the map yet again by the Nazi–Soviet pact of 1939. It reemerged as a nominally independent state in 1945, but as a Communist satellite of the Soviet Union. Since 1956 Poland had enjoyed a small measure of local autonomy under Wladyslaw Gomulka, but not nearly enough to satisfy most of its people. In 1970 incompetence and repression sparked food riots that led to Gomulka's dismissal. As the Soviets watched, with ominous concern, Gomulka was replaced by a nondescript functionary, Edward Gierek. Matters stayed under control for a decade, although the Polish government continued to mismanage the economy and alienate its people. In 1980, their poverty standing in ever-starker contrast to the privilege of Poland's utterly corrupted Communist Party, the Polish people could stand no more. Widespread riots centered in the industrial city of Gdansk raged out of control. Eventually they led to something hitherto unknown in the Soviet bloc since the earliest days of the Bolshevik Revolution: a genuine trade union responsible to its members. Called Solidarity, the union was born in the Lenin Shipyards in Gdansk. It was led by Lech Walesa, an electrician who became a national hero. Solidarity soon counted 8 million members out of a population of 30 million and beyond that clearly had the support of most of the Polish people. Again the Soviets threatened invasion, holding back largely because they feared armed Polish resistance. The Polish Communist Party was virtually paralyzed. The best it could do was replace Gierek with Stanislaw Kania, another undistinguished functionary, and then replace Kania with Wojciech Jaruzelski, an army general who also served as defense minister and prime minister. Soviet pressure finally got Jaruzelski to do the necessary dirty work. In December 1981 he declared martial law, arrested Solidarity's leaders, and drove what was left of the union underground. The best anyone in the West could do was to award Walesa the Nobel Peace Prize in 1983.

QUAGMIRE IN AFGHANISTAN

Jaruzelski's actions were doubly welcome to the Kremlin, because by December 1981 it had concluded it could not risk invading Poland. By 1980 the Soviet Union was involved in a costly intervention in Afghanistan, a Muslim country bordering on largely Muslim Soviet Central Asia. The Soviet road into this quagmire began in 1978 when a pro-Soviet Marxist group seized power in Afghanistan in a bloody coup that surprised Moscow no less than Washington. By early 1979 armed resistance by Afghan guerrillas fired by fundamentalist Islamic beliefs had put the entire venture in deep trouble. Unable to stem the guerrilla tide, the Afghan regime pleaded for Moscow to send troops. The Soviet leadership was well aware that its Afghan clients were brutal fanatics with little common sense and few supporters among the population. At a Politburo meeting in March, Andrei Kirilenko, a member of that body since 1962 and one of Brezhnev's closest associates, urged restraint, complaining that the Afghan regime had "executed innocent people for no reason." He warned his comrades against trying to rescue the "kind of Marxists we have found here." Prime Minister Alexei Kosygin also strongly opposed intervention. When Afghan leader Nur Mohammed Taraki came to Moscow to plead his case, Kosygin, in the presence of Foreign Minister Andrei Gromyko, bluntly told Taraki that if Soviet troops entered Afghanistan,

> the situation in your country not only would not improve, but would worsen. One cannot deny that our troops would have to fight not only with foreign aggressors, but with a certain number of your people. And people do not forgive such things.

Nikolai Ogarkov, the head of the Soviet general staff, also opposed intervention. Nonetheless, after months of hesitation, and after Taraki had been murdered and replaced by the even more extreme Hafizullah Amin, the Politburo decided to intervene in Afghanistan. It acted largely on the dubious grounds that the collapse of the Afghan regime would be a serious defeat for the Soviet Union and, in addition, somehow leave Afghanistan under the influence of the United States. Soviet paratroopers invaded Afghanistan in December 1979, murdering Amin and replacing him with a more moderate figure, Babrak Karmal. That turned out to be the easy part. Soviet forces met determined guerrilla resistance, while the Afghan army was virtually use-less as unwilling conscripts deserted faster than they could be replaced. At Brezhnev's death in 1982, an army of over 100,000 Soviet troops was still struggling against worsening odds to protect and prop up a decrepit regime utterly lacking in popular support. The Soviet Union, not without warning from some of its top leaders, and for defensive rather than offensive reasons, had blundered into a disaster—its own "Vietnam"—that over the course of a decade would weaken the country internationally and, more important, do-mestically, much more than Washington's unsuccessful struggle in southeast Asia had weakened the United States.

SOVIET GLOBAL REACH

Despite its domestic problems and troubles in Poland and Afghanistan, the Soviet Union after 1964 found the resources to engage in a far-ranging foreign policy. Moscow was active in the Middle East, where its goal was to weaken Western influence in the region containing the world's largest oil reserves. The Soviet Union therefore supported the region's nineteen Arab states—a collection of authoritarian regimes of various sorts that included conservative monarchies, reactionary sheikdoms, one-party nationalist dictatorships, and a lone Marxist dictatorship—and the Palestine Liberation Organization (PLO) against Israel, even though, unlike the PLO and the Arab states, Moscow offi-cially recognized Israel's right to exist. Soviet support of the terrorist Palestine Liberation Organization and the militantly anti-Western regime of Muammar Qaddafi in Libya strengthened destabilizing forces in the region. This in turn threatened such oil-rich but politically fragile Arab states as Saudi Arabia, Kuwait, and the United Arab Emirates, upon which the Western powers and Japan were so dependent for energy supplies. Soviet influence was particularly strong in Marxist South Yemen and also in Iraq and Syria, both recipients of huge quantities of Soviet arms notwithstanding that their governments effectively and brutally suppressed local Communists. However, in 1972 a major setback occurred in Egypt, a pro-Soviet power during the Khrushchev era, when President Anwar Sadat, fearing excessive Soviet influence in his country, reversed his predecessor's policy and expelled 20,000 Soviet advi-sors. Sadat then oriented his country toward the West, particularly the United States. After the 1973 Yom Kippur War, Sadat in 1979 made Egypt the first (and, until Jordan became the second in 1994, the only) Arab state to sign a peace treaty with Israel, further increasing American influence in the region at Soviet expense.

The year 1979 did, however, see a significant gain of sorts for the Soviet Union in the Middle East when an Islamic fundamentalist revolution led by the Ayatollah Khomeini overthrew the pro-American regime of the Shah of Iran. The fanatical Khomeini regime was hardly pro-Soviet, but Khomeini's victory in Iran, by replacing the Shah with a virulently anti-American regime, did weaken American influence in the Middle East and along the Soviet Union's southern frontier.

Sub-Saharan Africa, a region of desperately poor countries torn by tribal and ethnic strife, provided a setting for Soviet advances during the Brezhnev years. The foundations of Soviet policy had been laid by Khrushchev, who established good relations with three rulers of newly independent nations— Kwame Nkrumah of Ghana, Sékou Touré of Guinea, and Modibo Keita of Mali—though Nkrumah (in 1966) and Keita (in 1968) were overthrown not long after Khrushchev's own downfall. The region's many conflicts and the dissolution of the Portuguese sub-Saharan empire, the last Western colonial empire in Africa, created new openings for Soviet penetration. Over 15,000 Cuban troops enabled the pro-Soviet faction to win a three-way civil war in the former Portuguese colony of Angola in 1976, although recently released documents indicate that the Cubans initiated the intervention and that the Soviets were dragged into it by their Caribbean clients. Meanwhile a Marxist regime established itself in another major former Portuguese colony, Mozambique. The Soviets enjoyed a brief period of influence in Somalia, a Muslim nation on the strategic Horn of Africa, upon signing a treaty of friendship and cooperation in 1974. Three years later, however, the Somalian president, Siad Barre, upset over Soviet aid to the newly installed Marxist regime in neighboring Ethiopia, abrogated the treaty. The Soviets thereupon increased aid to Ethiopia, which included paying for a large contingent of Cuban troops. Moscow also built bridges to several other sub-Saharan countries. Though the rapidly shifting winds of sub-Saharan politics precluded guarantees of longevity for any alliances or agreements, Brezhnev and his colleagues could take credit for making the Soviet Union a significant factor in that region for the first time.

Soviet foreign policy under Brezhnev also found new vistas in Latin America, the backyard of the United States. In 1960 the Soviets had diplomatic relations with three Latin American nations and trade of $70 million; by 1980 this had expanded to diplomatic relations with nineteen nations and trade of over $1 billion, including large wheat purchases from Argentina that helped minimize the impact of the U.S. grain embargo against Moscow after the 1979 Soviet invasion of Afghanistan. The jewel in the crown remained Cuba, where Fidel Castro longed to carry the revolutionary torch from his Communist island outpost to all of Latin America. In return for massive Soviet aid to prop up its sagging socialist economy, Cuba provided troops and technicians to support pro-Soviet regimes and forces not only in Latin America but also in the

Middle East and Africa. Another source of Soviet satisfaction was Nicaragua, where in 1979 Marxist Sandinista rebels deposed an American-backed dictatorship and established a pro-Soviet regime. The Soviets did suffer two major setbacks in Latin America, however: the failure of Castro's attempt to export his revolution to Bolivia in 1967 and the 1973 U.S.-sponsored overthrow of the government of Salvador Allende, an independent Marxist who had been elected president of Chile with Communist support.

During the Brezhnev years, then, the Soviet Union expanded its role in world affairs. In its relations with the United States, Moscow could take pride in having overcome America's nuclear superiority, while also signing arms limitation agreements with the Nixon and Ford administrations. However, relations chilled noticeably during the latter part of the Carter administration and became positively frigid during Brezhnev's last two years, when the Soviets were dealing with the administration of President Ronald Reagan. Détente was over, and the talk increasingly was about a "New Cold War." Overall, Soviet foreign policy under Brezhnev had its successes (improved relations with West Germany and France, and the establishment of pro-Soviet regimes in Angola, Mozambique, Ethiopia, South Yemen, and Nicaragua) and failures (continued difficulties with Eastern Europe, Afghanistan, and the People's Republic of China, and anti-Soviet developments in Egypt and Somalia) on a worldwide scale. Only the United States could match the Soviet Union in world influence, an unprecedented achievement in the history of the Russian state. But such grandeur abroad had been bought at a high price. By 1980 Cuba alone—an expensive jewel indeed—was costing the Kremlin $4 billion per year. The annual tab for Vietnam was $1 billion, and several billion more went to clients, Communist and non-Communist, in Asia, Africa, and Latin America. Eastern Europe was another financial black hole, mainly in the form of exported oil sold to the Warsaw Pact nations at low subsidized prices in order to prop up failing local economies and keep the populations quiet. At home the ravenous military budget cannibalized the civilian economy. The price to society, in terms of unmet human needs, untreated social and economic ills, and unrealized reforms, was soaring with each passing year. Brezhnev left it to his successors to pay that price.

THE SOVIET GERONTOCRACY

On November 10, 1982, Leonid Brezhnev, in bad health for years and increasingly enfeebled, died of a heart attack. In what was considered by many in the Soviet Union as a triumph for the system, it took only fifty-four hours for Yuri Andropov to emerge as Brezhnev's successor. But the smooth succession from Brezhnev to Andropov did nothing to solve a far bigger succession crisis—the transfer of power from one generation to another. The leadership that had ruled the Soviet Union since Stalin's death had become a gerontocracy as well as an oligarchy, a development that owed much to Brezhnev's stress on stability. Between 1964 and 1982, this meant not only maintaining a coalition of various bureaucratic interests, but keeping the same people in their posts. While under Khrushchev 62 percent of the Central Committee was reelected at the Twentieth Congress and only 49 percent at the Twenty-Second Congress, under Brezhnev the figures jumped to 79 percent at the Twenty-Third Congress, 76.5 percent at the Twenty-Fourth Congress, and 83.4 percent at the Twenty-Fifth Congress. By 1980 the average age of the Politburo membership had climbed to seventy years, as opposed to fifty-five in 1952 and sixty-one in 1964. Shortly before Brezhnev died in office, his septuagenarian colleagues Kosygin and Suslov died, the former just after his retirement and the latter while still in office. By 1982 Brezhnev's foreign minister, Andrei Gromyko, his defense minister, Dmitri Ustinov, and his prime minister, Nikolai Tikhonov, were all in their mid- or late seventies.

THE RISE OF YURI ANDROPOV

Yuri Andropov, at sixty-eight, was only seven years younger than his predecessor. Nonetheless, the party at least had a tough and intelligent functionary as its new general secretary. An authentic product of the purges, Andropov rose rapidly through the ranks of the Komsomol during the worst years of Stalin's bloodletting and became a member of the Communist Party in 1939. His early years as a local party functionary in Karelia, a region bordering on Finland, were distinguished by a close association with the secret police in managing the Gulag forced-labor system. Andropov subsequently became ambassador to Hungary, where he actively participated in crushing the 1956 uprising. In 1957 he was transferred to Moscow to head the Central Committee's foreign affairs department and in 1962 became a Central Committee secretary, an important step up the party ladder. After supporting Brezhnev in the post-Khrushchev struggle for power, he was appointed head of the KGB in 1967. He served in that post for fifteen years, upgrading the KGB's sophistication, the quality of its personnel, and its overall capabilities. It was under Andropov that the KGB first recruited top university students and developed new and less visibly brutal tactics for dealing with dissidents—including "exporting" them abroad instead of resorting to the criminal trials and harsh sentences that often antagonized the West. His entry into the party's ruling circle came in 1973, when he was elected a full member of the Politburo.

During Brezhnev's declining years Andropov used his position at the KGB to undermine the general secretary and his inner circle, mainly by circulating embarrassing stories about corruption in high places. Andropov positioned himself for an eventual bid for power when he gave up his KGB post and took over the powerful ideology portfolio in the Secretariat after Suslov's death early in 1982. Having also cultivated allies in the military and among other important interest groups, Andropov won the top job in November of that year, beating out Konstantin Chernenko, the man Brezhnev preferred as his successor.

THE ANDROPOV AGENDA

Andropov came to power in a Soviet Union suffering from poor leadership and inertia. In his last infirm years Brezhnev could not respond to problems such as an economy and a standard of living that had been stagnant since 1976. He used what energy he had to support the expanding Soviet military establishment and a coalition of bureaucratic interests essential to overall political stability. Corruption grew enormously in those days, reaching even to Brezhnev's own family; his daughter was implicated in schemes involving diamond smuggling, bribery, and currency speculation.

The new general secretary was expected to change all of this. One of his first actions was to launch a campaign to prove that a new age of efficiency and honesty had dawned. Shoppers taking time off from work were arrested. Andropov even sent his police into the Moscow public baths and bars to collar delinquent workers. Thousands of people involved in illegal economic activities, as well as corrupt officials, were arrested, and a number of harsh sentences, including capital punishment, were handed out for corruption. Andropov also started a well-publicized propaganda campaign to spur productivity.

There were a few signs indicating that thought was being given to genuine changes in how the country was run. During 1983 a plan surfaced to allow farmers more freedom to raise livestock on their private plots. An up-and-coming young Politburo member named Mikhail Gorbachev made a speech suggesting the state use long-term contracts to encourage increased peasant productivity. A new law permitted some worker input in industrial management through so-called workers' collectives. Most far-reaching was a remarkable document called the "Novosibirsk Report," put together by a group of academics based in that western Siberian city. The report, which was leaked to an American journalist, was shockingly blunt. It urged a "restructuring that would reflect fundamental changes" in the economy and a greater reliance on "market relations," code words for a free market. Although the report caused a sensation, it produced no immediate policy changes. Andropov continued to stress "socialist discipline," essentially using the old stick rather than a new carrot to get Soviet citizens to increase their efforts at work and to toe the line in all their other pursuits. Repression of dissidents became even more severe than under Brezhnev, while Jewish emigration fell to less than 1,000 per year.

POLITICAL RENEWAL, ECONOMIC REVERSALS

The one area where there was significant renewal was in political life. Death and retirement removed some of Brezhnev's old cronies and allowed Andropov to promote to the Politburo three younger men who averaged in their spry late fifties. One level down the ladder, Yegor Ligachev, the efficient, reformist-minded Tomsk regional first secretary, became one of several new Central Committee secretaries, while major personnel changes took place in the Secretariat apparatus and the Council of Ministers. One-fifth of the Central Committee was removed. Aided by Gorbachev and Ligachev, who functioned like two political archangels around the general secretary's throne, Andropov replaced about one-fifth of the regional party secretaries, the work proceeding apace even as Andropov's kidneys were failing and he was confined to a sick bed.

Andropov's efforts helped give the economy a temporary boost in 1983. Industrial output rose by 4 percent, and a large jump in investment in modern technology, including a doubling of investments in industrial robots, testified to a more vigorous campaign to bring the economy up to date. Agriculture showed some improvement from its dismal 1982 performance, as overall output rose by 10 percent and grain output by about 20 percent. Yet all this was hardly cause for rejoicing. Most of the increases were attributable to better weather, including a mild winter, rather than to any systematic improvements in the collective farm system. Although grain production rose from 180 million to 200 million metric tons, the total was far short of the official target of 238 million metric tons. Meanwhile, in the vital oil industry production actually declined during the last quarter of 1983.

Equally troublesome, Andropov's much heralded program for industry, designed to increase factory efficiency by giving managers more authority and incentives, proved to be quite limited in scope—far more limited, in fact, than the Kosygin reforms of the 1960s. The new workers' collectives that were supposed to participate in industrial management had little power. There was entrenched and powerful opposition to even these limited reforms. It also proved impossible, even for the ubiquitous Soviet police, to end the absenteeism and lax work habits of tens of millions of workers. They continued in their old ways, which was reflected in a popular motto: "They pretend to pay, we pretend to work."

FOREIGN DIVERSIONS

Much of Andropov's energy was diverted by foreign affairs crises in Afghanistan, Lebanon, Central America, and the Caribbean. In Afghanistan, the war against anti-Communist Muslim rebels dragged on as Western commentators began to refer to the Soviet Union's "Vietnam." In the Middle East, the Soviets easily and cheaply checkmated American peacemaking efforts in Lebanon by providing diplomatic and military backing to the Syrians, who occupied most of their weak neighbor and whose real interest was *de facto* if not *de jure* control of that small country. Another Soviet–American sore point was in Central America, where the United States, troubled by growing Communist influence in its own backyard, stepped up efforts against the activities of Cuba and the Marxist Sandinista regime in Nicaragua. Concerned that the Cubans and Nicaraguans were aiding the pro-Communist rebellion in El Salvador, the United States put increasing pressure on Nicaragua in particular to stop that assistance, pressure that included support for guerrillas fighting the Sandinista regime. Washington's concern regarding developments in Central America was one factor behind its invasion of the Caribbean island nation of Grenada in October 1983, which overthrew the radical Marxist regime whose leaders themselves had recently seized power in a bloody coup against slightly less extreme Marxist colleagues. The large Cuban contingent that had been providing various types of assistance to the deposed regime was expelled and Soviet influence in the area was diminished.

The Kremlin's relations with the United States meanwhile continued to deteriorate. During 1983 the Americans responded to the Soviet deployment of new SS20 intermediate range missiles by beginning their own deployment of new and extremely accurate Pershing II and cruise missiles in Western Europe, the massive Soviet propaganda effort to get America's NATO allies to refuse the missiles having failed. The Soviets then walked out of three sets of arms control negotiations: the talks to limit intermediate-range missiles in Europe, the Strategic Arms Reduction Talks (START), and the decade-long East–West talks on reducing conventional arms in Central Europe. For the first time in twenty years the Soviet Union and the United States were not even *discussing* the arms race. The new Cold War appeared to be developing rapidly into a dangerous deep freeze.

THE WANING OF THE OLD GUARD

Soon it became evident that the sixty-nine-year-old Andropov did not have as much energy as advertised. During the summer of 1983 he allegedly caught a cold, after which he disappeared from view. In fact, Andropov was suffering from kidney failure and was undergoing dialysis treatments. He did not reappear to help quell the international uproar after the Soviets shot down an off-course Korean Air Lines jumbo jet that had strayed into Soviet airspace at the cost of 269 lives, an act which helped drive Soviet–American relations to a post-détente low. The official job of explaining Soviet actions went to General Nikolai Ogarkov, the chief of the general staff. Nor could the annual November celebration of the Bolshevik Revolution—an event so important that even Brezhnev staggered through it just days before he died—prompt Andropov's return. In December Andropov missed two other important events: meetings of the Central Committee and the Supreme Soviet, the country's parliament. On February 4, 1984, Yuri Andropov died after only fifteen months in office, the shortest tenure up to then of any Soviet leader.

In the second smooth transfer of power in as many years, Andropov was succeeded by Konstantin Chernenko, the elderly bridesmaid in 1982. The seventy-two-year-old Chernenko was the oldest man ever to assume leadership of the Soviet Union; on the day he took power he already had lived ten years longer than the average Soviet male. His health was poor: he suffered from emphysema, was rumored to have heart trouble, and in 1983 had been hospitalized for two months with pneumonia. At Andropov's funeral he looked frail and exhausted, barely able to get through his obligatory speech and unable to raise his hand high enough to give a proper salute, a pathetic exhibition viewed live on television by millions of his fellow citizens. The next several months were no better; it was painfully evident that the new general secretary often needed assistance simply to walk.

Chernenko, rejected by his colleagues barely a year before, made it to the top because Andropov's main protégé and heir-apparent, Mikhail Gorbachev, was still unable to muster the Politburo votes to become general secretary himself in the face of opposition by conservative Brezhnev-era holdovers. The struggle and indecision were reflected in the four-day lapse between Andropov's death and the announcement of Chernenko's election. The compromise that broke the deadlock made Chernenko general secretary but placed enough power in Gorbachev's hands so that *Pravda* at one point referred to him as the "second secretary." One sign that Chernenko was viewed purely as a stopgap leader was that no changes took place in the Politburo that strengthened his position during his entire term in office. Chernenko's tenure in office amounted to a thirteen-month-long pregnant pause. The reform process slowed and in some cases stopped. Examples of this were loss of steam by the anticorruption campaign and the failure of a special Central Committee meeting on agriculture to accomplish anything. A symbolic antireform occurred when Stalin's loyal servitor Vyacheslav Molotov, well into his nineties and utterly unrepentant, was rehabilitated and given back the cherished party membership taken from him by Khrushchev. On several occasions Gorbachev failed to speak at policy meetings, an indication that in those cases he was not getting his way.

There was little consistency regarding the poor state of Soviet–American relations. In the spring of 1984 the Soviets boycotted the Olympics being held in the United States. A renewed effort was made at limiting contacts between Soviet citizens and visiting foreigners, and emigration rates continued to fall. Yet 1984 also saw the demotion of General Ogarkov, a vocal advocate for diverting more resources to the military for modernizing Soviet conventional forces facing NATO troops in Europe. At the end of the year, with Chernenko's health failing and Gorbachev increasingly visible, the Soviets and Americans reached an agreement to resume suspended arms negotiations.

In December, while Gorbachev was impressing the West during a tour of Great Britain, another member of the Brezhnev old guard, Defense Minister Dmitri Ustinov, died. Three months later, in March of 1985, Chernenko followed his comrade to the grave. He had been in office barely a year, even less time than Andropov.

THE ERA OF STABILITY

Chernenko's departure finally solved the Soviet Union's basic succession problem by transferring power to a younger and more vigorous generation. That transfer appeared to set the stage for making the reforms necessary for building on what the Brezhnev regime, notwithstanding its serious faults, had accomplished. During the 1960s and 1970s, the Soviet Union had achieved unprecedented international power and, most important to Soviet citizens, security from foreign invasion. Brezhnev's greatest domestic success was to maintain stability while he was in office. He did this by satisfying the various elite constituencies that controlled the vital sectors of the Soviet party-state—the party's central apparatus; its numerous union republic, provincial, and local tentacles; the military; the police; and the scientific and technical establishments, among others—while providing at least some improvements for the population at large. Although housing, availability of consumer goods, medical care, and many other amenities of life were substandard by Western criteria, the three decades since Stalin's death, including almost two under Brezhnev, had provided a much better life for the average Soviet citizen. Per capita consumption of all goods increased three times between 1950 and 1980. Food consumption doubled over the same period and also improved in quality with the addition of more meat, vegetables, fruit, and dairy products. Clothing consumption rose fourfold, durable goods fourteenfold. Extensive housing construction under both Khrushchev and Brezhnev had enabled millions of families to move from shared to individual—albeit poorly constructed—apartments. Most citizens enjoyed a broad range of social welfare benefits, from free (if badly flawed) medical care and cheap (although severely cramped) housing to pensions and job security. By the 1980s, the Soviet educational system provided a respectable secondary education for most children and higher education at more than 70 universities and 800 technical institutes for about 5 million full- and part-time students. Although teaching methods often stressed rote learning, and subjects like history and literature were highly politicized by the infusion of Marxist dogma, the Soviet educational system excelled in the teaching of mathematics, science, and technical subjects. The Soviet Union, to be sure, had not closed the standard-of-living gap vis-à-vis the West, but the elites who were in the best position to compare life at home with that abroad were pampered in order to minimize dissatisfaction that could prove dangerous.

The social mobility of those decades had given millions a stake in the system. The CPSU alone had over 16 million members, having grown by 50 percent under Khrushchev and an additional 40 percent under Brezhnev. It enrolled about one-third of Soviet citizens with a higher education and 44 percent of all males with ten years or more of schooling. The Komsomol, the party's youth wing, enrolled about 40 million potential new party recruits. Tens of millions more, including more than 100,000,000 trade union members, belonged to a dense web of organizations tightly controlled by the party. These organizations were both a means of control and a mechanism to gather and occasionally respond to popular complaints. Stability was further enhanced by the long-standing Soviet and Russian tradition of valuing order and fearing change and chaos, a frame of mind forged by the cruel pressures of Russian history. These pressures also produced a deep mistrust of foreigners and a willingness to accept abuse from the government in return for security from outsiders.

When the regime could not count on popular support, it could count on the KGB, the world's largest security apparatus, employing about 250,000 well-armed troops as well as a million technicians, agents, and informers scattered across the country. The regime also had a prison system, pared down drastically from Stalin's time, but still a grim netherworld into which dissidents and other undesirables could be cast. Finally, despite a host of problems, until the early 1980s the various wellsprings of dissent and discontent remained relatively isolated and therefore manageable currents rather than converging into a single uncontrollable torrent. For example, while workers and intellectuals had their respective complaints, the gap between these two social groups remained unbridged. The economy had faltered, but the memory of harder times lingered. Non-Russian nationalities had their grievances, but they often were directed against each other and were counterbalanced by ethnic Russian nationalism when they were not. Meanwhile, the non-Russian elites had largely been co-opted into the Soviet system, which rewarded them well for preaching the party line to their constituents about the benefits of being part of the Russian-led Soviet family of nations.

THE ERA OF STAGNATION

The overriding problem with the Brezhnev era was that stability had turned into stagnation. Unlike Stalin, who threatened everyone with prison or death, or Khrushchev, who rocked the boat with his egalitarianism, appeals to popular sentiment, and utopian or unworkable schemes, Brezhnev guaranteed the elite's status, privileges, and lifestyle. Consequently, the Soviet Union was rendered impervious to reform. Almost two decades of inertia under Brezhnev meant that the Soviet Union entered the 1980s with many serious and festering problems, some of which were becoming critical. The most important domestic ones concerned the faltering economy, pervasive corruption and alienation among the citizenry, and the so-called nationality problem: the rising percentage of non–Great Russians and non-Slavs in the country's overall population. There were also several vexing foreign policy problems. And it took until Chernenko's death in 1985 to transfer real power from the aging and immobilized Brezhnev cohort to a new generation of leaders prepared to deal with them.

The post-Stalin but still Stalinist economy of the Brezhnev era may have provided reasonably well for its citizenry compared to conditions thirty years earlier, but those conditions formed an abysmally low base of comparison. Furthermore, the unreformed Soviet economy entered the 1980s with institutions basically unchanged in fifty years. The Stalinist model with its centralized planning, extreme emphasis on heavy industry, and collectivized agriculture may have been a viable, although dreadfully brutal and enormously wasteful, method of industrialization; it was not, however, an effective way of running a complex industrial economy. In glaring contrast to the economies of the industrialized capitalist powers, the 1980-vintage Soviet civilian economy generated almost nothing on its own. Hamstrung by central planners, factory managers lacked the authority and incentive to use new methods or technologies or to introduce new products for either factories or consumers. Planners continued to rely almost exclusively on easily computable quantitative standards, rewarding those who met production quotas whether or not the goods themselves were useful or needed. Innovation was stifled because it involved risks that traditionally conservative bureaucrats, whose charge was to meet production targets rather than make profits, were unwilling to take. The absence of a free market in which products competed for customers, with some succeeding and others failing, meant that there was no way to weed out inefficient production methods and shoddy goods.

Yet central planning remained untouched by the series of economic reforms introduced under Brezhnev in 1965, 1973, and 1979, and under Andropov in 1983. Strong opposition to change came from the planning bureaucracy and party bosses, whose power blunted or buried every reform impulse. The Soviet economy therefore rang up large output numbers while producing enormous quantities of useless goods. Waves of advances in technology—including the electronic and computer revolution—that generated so much growth in the West and Japan barely touched the Soviet Union's shores, leaving its government compelled to buy or steal much of the technology the country needed for both civilian and military purposes.

Nor was there improvement in agriculture, the economy's weakest sector. One late-1970s campaign, the "Ipatovo method," developed in the Stavropol region (where Gorbachev was the local first secretary at the time), was typically Soviet; it involved the massive use of machines (combines and trucks) and workers to speed up the harvest. After initial glowing reports, the Ipatovo method ended up a fiasco. It did speed up the harvest in the Stavropol region, shortening it from several weeks to nine days, but only by employing such enormous and prohibitively expensive human and material resources that it could not be applied to more than a few selected areas at any given time. Brezhnev's last effort, his highly publicized "Food Program," was no better. It was the "largest, most expensive document ever produced on agriculture," according to agricultural expert Zhores Medvedev, who added, "it has not worked because it is not a *reform.*"[3] After fifty years of collectivization, the failure to build proper storage facilities and adequate rural roads, among other deficiencies, meant that between one-fifth and one-third of many crops, ranging from fruits and vegetables to potatoes and grain, spoiled or were otherwise lost before reaching the consumer.

Meanwhile, the Soviet Union's traditional methods of overcoming economic difficulties—mass mobilization of cheap labor, exploitation of readily available and cheap raw materials, and concentration on a few key areas—were rendered obsolete in the face of a limited labor supply, scarcer and therefore more expensive raw materials, and an economy increasingly too complex for the old "storming" methods. As a result, the standard of living stagnated. This was unwelcome news in a country where, despite undeniable improvements, the life of the average citizen remained drab. A contemporary witticism summed up what the Soviet people regularly experienced and how frustrated they were becoming:

> A man enters a fish store and asks for meat. Upon being told he is in a fish store he stubbornly asks for meat again. Finally he is told: Go to the store across the street. *That* is where there is no meat.[4]

In the mid-1970s the Soviet press reported that its citizens spent 30 billion man-hours each year just buying merchandise. People walked around with large quantities of cash so they could join a line at a moment's notice if some scarce product were being sold, whether they needed it or not. Lines literally one-mile long were not uncommon. A Western journalist described one monstrous Moscow line whose very existence, however exceptional, was testimony to what people living under the Soviet Union's "developed socialism" were prepared to endure:

> Some friends of ours . . . watched and photographed a line that lasted for two days and nights, four abreast and running all through an apartment development. They guessed that there were 10,000–15,000 people signing up to buy rugs, an opportunity that came only once a year in that entire section of Moscow. Some burned bonfires to keep warm out in the snow and the crackling wood and din of constant conversation kept our friends awake at night.[5]

Meanwhile, about 30 percent of working-class families still lived in communal apartments where they shared kitchen and bath facilities, while newlyweds often lived for years with in-laws before securing an apartment of their own. Life in communal apartments was laced with friction rather than a sense of community. As sociologist Basile Kerblay observed:

> For these people [living in shared apartments], relations with their neighbors must be regulated. They take turns to clean the shared portions of the apartment, they have a timetable for doing laundry, etc., although even this does not entirely preclude conflict. Each family's living space is marked off by sideboards and cupboards, and family gatherings have to be held in a restaurant as there is no dining room.[6]

Medical care, though free, was hampered by obsolete equipment and shortages of the most basic supplies, so that those among the elite with connections often went abroad for treatment of serious health problems.

One of the most scandalous problems in a country that claimed to have achieved "developed socialism" was the persistence of poverty. Estimates in the early 1980s suggested that two-fifths of the nonpeasant labor force earned less than what the Soviets themselves considered the minimum necessary for small urban families. The statistics were even worse when larger families, peasants, and pensioners were included. The peasants were especially deprived. Although their income varied widely, statistics show that many collective farm workers in the mid-1970s still made less than the minimum wages set for state enterprises. Peasants also often worked unusually long hours, largely because of the time spent on the private plots that were so vital to their welfare.

THE NOMENKLATURA

Life offered far greater opportunity for the Communist Party elite. They did not eat what they disdainfully called "town stuff"; their food came from special stores stocked with high-quality meats, fruits, vegetables, and a wide range of imported delicacies. A half century after an official announcement that the country's exploiting classes had been eliminated, the Soviet elite's specially built apartment houses, in which they lived free of charge, were staffed by servants and complemented by country homes (ranging from cottages to genuine mansions) and expensive cars (often complete with chauffeurs). Of course, it was hard to compete with Brezhnev himself, whose personal automobile fleet included a Mercedes-Benz, a Rolls-Royce, and a Cadillac. While the masses coped as best they could, the Soviet elite enjoyed their own restaurants, ticket agencies, and medical facilities—even their own graveyards. They received their jobs, the fountainhead from which all privileges flowed, from a special list controlled by the party, the secretive *nomenklatura*. The nomenklatura dated from the 1920s. It included not only the key party positions at every level, but the key positions in all important Soviet institutions. To be eligible for nomenklatura posts required more than the proper technical qualifications; it required the proper political credentials, which in effect meant that with the exception of jobs demanding the most sophisticated technical skills or special talents, all important positions were reserved for party members. Indeed, a nomenklatura position was the first major step in advancing a party career. Overall, the nomenklatura lists (the term also referred to the list of individuals filling those posts) included a total of about 750,000 individuals who, along with their families, constituted a social class of approximately 3 million people that controlled the country and enjoyed its bounty. Because the Soviet Union supposedly was a "developed socialist society," as opposed to the capitalist inequality-ridden societies in the West, efforts were made to enjoy the good Soviet life discreetly. But most Soviet citizens were aware of the discrepancy between ideology and reality; as one humorist noted, "We have everything, of course, but not for everyone."

THE "SECOND" ECONOMY AND CORRUPTION

Because the Soviet economy produced so little of what most people needed and wanted, especially after the military and heavy industrial sectors took their hefty shares, a "second" economy evolved and grew to enormous proportions. It was here that Soviet citizens exchanged goods and services under the table on a barter basis; it also was here where enormous corruption developed. Some daring entrepreneurs became millionaires by operating illicit factories producing goods such as quality clothing right inside state factories. The bribes these people paid at every turn in the production and distribution process did not exhaust their considerable profits; there was no shortage of consumers willing to pay high prices for these so-called left-handed goods, for to do without them meant forgoing fashionable clothing, decent shoes, and other high-quality items. What was diminished, as vast quantities of materials were stolen and skilled personnel did private work while on the public payroll, was the ability of the state-run economy to do its job. The bureaucratic web that enveloped the country further encouraged corruption; it simply was virtually impossible to survive without breaking the rules. A factory manager could not get what he needed for his plant without extensive bribery. Those who accepted bribes did so because it was the rule, whether they were policemen who took bribes not to give tickets, professors who charged their students for good grades or just for the right to take examinations, or surgeons who charged for operations supposedly covered by the state's free medical program, this after the patient first bribed his way into a good hospital. Bribery had become a way of life in the Soviet Union.

Sooner or later most people got involved in this rampant illegality, which is one reason why the lethargic Brezhnev did nothing about it. Another is that the second economy and the corruption that made it work actually served the regime by filling some of the huge gaps left by the malfunctioning state economy. That in turn helped reduce popular discontent and let Brezhnev and his colleagues avoid the dreaded alternative: reform of the centrally planned Soviet economy that might upset the status quo.

The position of the party was another source of the corruption pervading Soviet society. Party bosses, immune from public control, consistently abused their power. In some places—the Caucasian republics of Georgia and Azerbaijan probably were the most extreme examples—local ministerial posts regularly were bought and sold. Even when central authorities attempted to bring the matter under control, as they did by purging most of the ruling apparatus in Georgia in 1972 and 1973, those removed from office often suffered no further punishment. Prosecuting and jailing large numbers of prominent party leaders would have struck too directly at the myth of the party's infallibility and hence at its legitimacy. Beyond that, any systematic attack on corruption would have threatened too large a percentage of the party elite to be consistent with Brezhnev's prime directive of maintaining stability. As for Andropov, who was unwilling to accept pervasive corruption, he was not around long enough to make more than a tiny dent in the huge problem.

THE WITHERING AWAY OF MARXISM

Corruption and the frustrations of daily life in turn helped breed demoralization and alienation; the general attitude by the early 1980s was that the system was there to be beaten, not improved. Those who had given up on the system often responded by anesthetizing themselves to it. Chronic drunkenness increasingly was one of the most serious social problems in the Soviet Union; between 1965 and 1979 per capita consumption of alcoholic beverages grew by 50 percent, and alcohol abuse was linked more frequently to crime, birth defects, automobile accidents, and other troubles. It also was linked to the corruption that pervaded everyday life. Along with carpenters, plumbers, mechanics, and a host of other people with marketable services who illegally plied their trades during their spare time or on government time in the second economy, uncounted thousands of enterprising illicit brewers made a good living producing illegal drinking alcohol, called *samogon,* in their kitchens for sale to millions of eager consumers.

One important victim of this cynicism and loss of confidence was Marxism itself. Although it was the official ideology of the state, fewer and fewer Soviet citizens took its revolutionary and messianic doctrines seriously. Its predictions and promises about equality and abundance were simply too much at variance with the realities of Soviet life. Popular humor had an ordinary Soviet citizen going to the doctor for ear and eye problems. "I keep hearing one thing and seeing another," he complains. Artists and writers, while stopping short of being overtly anti-Soviet, often infused their work with themes incompatible with official Marxist ideology. They included the distinguished director of Moscow's Taganka Theater, Yuri Lyubimov, whose productions of plays by Shakespeare, Pushkin, Gorky, Chekhov, Brecht, and many others infuriated Soviet censors for almost two decades before he left the Soviet Union in 1983. One of Lyubimov's most brilliant actors, Vladimir Vysotsky, achieved his greatest fame as a counterculture poet and balladeer. Singing in a haunting, gravelly voice one critic described as "torn from despair,"[7] Vysotsky chronicled the fates of the down-and-out of Soviet society. His music, recorded and distributed on illegally made tapes, reached millions and made him both a superstar and a revered icon before he died of drug and alcohol abuse in 1980. Another eloquent critic of Soviet values was the writer Valentin Rasputin, whose work juxtaposed the emptiness and alienation of modern Soviet life with the community and spirituality of the traditional Russian village. Rasputin focused on the devastating impact of Soviet industrialization and modernization on the environment and rural life of his native Siberia. He made his point with gripping poignancy in his novella *Farewell to Matyora,* in which he describes the death of a three-hundred-year-old village on Siberia's mighty Angara River as it is about to be inundated by water rising behind a giant hydroelectric dam.

Another measure of the drabness and spiritual vacuity of late 1970s and early 1980s Soviet life was the growth of overt religious expression in a country where religion was condemned and its observance, if discovered, could damage one's career. One Soviet study concluded that in some regions 25 percent of the population exhibited "religious influence." This disturbing phenomenon was of particular concern when religion and ethnic or national feeling coalesced, as they did among Catholics in Lithuania, Muslims in Central Asia, and Independent Orthodox in Georgia. The regime was further disturbed by the sharp increase in church weddings, although a state wedding remained a legal requirement, and by the crowds of young people who gathered each year for midnight Easter services. Perhaps even more worrisome was the popularity of rock 'n' roll, and especially of the Beatles. Their music, despite the regime's best efforts, had been infiltrating the Soviet Union since the mid-1960s via Western radio broadcasts, reel-to-reel tape recordings made from those broadcasts, and records smuggled into the country by athletes, sailors, and other Soviet citizens able to travel abroad. To the Soviet regime, all rock 'n' roll was subversive, and indeed degenerate, but the Beatles' irresistible music with its antiestablishment message was especially pernicious. Beatles music circulated far and wide, often on underground recordings made from old x-ray plates. Public telephones were vandalized so thousands of aspiring Soviet rock musicians, making Beatles music in secret, could use their receivers to build electric pickups for homemade guitars, as were public loudspeakers destined to become amplifiers for those guitars. To millions of urban young people, already left jaded by their strictly regulated Soviet surroundings, John Lennon and the Beatles had much more to say about how life should be lived than Vladimir Lenin and the Bolsheviks ever had or could. As art critic Artemy Troitsky put it years later, by which time the Soviet Union had collapsed, "The thing is that the Soviet regime couldn't offer the kids anything. The Beatles clicked in the hearts of my generation." By the early 1980s, that clicking had contributed significantly to the alienation felt by many Soviet "kids," some of them by then well into their thirties, from most things Marxist or Soviet.

Many party members were little different from ordinary citizens in their lack of commitment to Marxism. They endured the indoctrination sessions in order to safeguard privileges available only to those considered reliable. However, most Soviet citizens still could not see beyond the system. They depended on the social contract, which included benefits such as socialized medicine and guaranteed employment, they associated with the Soviet state. A majority remained leery of democracy, a concept they did not understand, and opposed a multiparty political system. The fear of authority remained very strong, as did suspicion of open dissenters. If Marxism as a belief system indeed had begun to wither, the space it left in Soviet life had not been filled, leaving a vacuum with regard to values and thus creating a serious problem for those inclined to reform the system along more humane or democratic lines.

THE NATIONALITIES PROBLEM

The greatest threat to the Soviet Union's long-term stability was its nationalities problem. For the non-Russian nationalities, the "Union of Soviet Socialist Republics" was old Russian wine in a new Soviet bottle. The Soviet Union remained the last of the great European empires forged between the sixteenth and nineteenth centuries. Official ideology to the contrary, the non-Russian nationalities continued to be dominated by the Great Russian majority, which held all the levers of power in the "Union." As of 1980, no non-Russian served as Central Committee secretaries. Only three non-Slavs held any of the top 150 positions in the armed forces. The hope from Lenin to Stalin to their successors was that the Soviet Union's non-Russians would gradually accept the Russian language and culture and become more or less assimilated into a new "Soviet" nationality. In some cases this appeared to be happening, but in most it was not. Despite the thick layer of repression that coated the Brezhnev regime's nationalities policy, ethnic ferment occasionally broke through to the surface. In 1972 demonstrators in Lithuania openly called for freedom from Moscow; in 1978 angry protests in Georgia forced authorities to back down on a plan to give the Russian language equal status to Georgian in that southern Soviet republic; and in 1980 there were street demonstrations against Russification in Estonia.

Ironically, Soviet policy had contributed to the persistence of national identities. The federal structure of the state was originally designed to pacify national feeling while gradually encouraging assimilation. Instead, the Soviet Union's formal federal structure reinforced local national identity. Each of the largest national groups was managing many of its own affairs within a clearly defined geographic and political entity. Also, while improved education created local elites who were weaned away from many local traditions, those same elites developed a modern national feeling, much like their counterparts throughout the underdeveloped world.

Demographics added to the nationalities problem. The birthrate among certain non-Russian minorities, most notably Central Asian Muslims, continued to be far higher than that among the Great Russians or their Ukrainian and Belarusian cousins. By 1970 the Great Russians were barely 53 percent of the Soviet Union's overall population; by the year 2000 their share was expected to be less than 50 percent, while the Muslim share was projected to rise from 14 to 23 percent. This posed many problems for the new leadership generation, including pressures to divert development away from the traditionally favored Slavic parts of the country. More troubling was the projected increase in the percentage of non-Russian and possibly non-Russian-speaking army recruits, a military commander's nightmare in terms of both efficiency and reliability.

THE INSECURE SUPERPOWER

Finally, Brezhnev and his two immediate successors left the new generation with serious problems abroad. As it became one of the world's two superpowers, the Soviet Union largely subordinated the worldwide revolutionary ambitions of its founders to the more limited and therefore more attainable goal of expanding the international power and influence of the Soviet state, a change in priorities that actually began under Stalin in the 1920s. The Soviets, to be sure, retained an important element of their old Marxist heritage, remaining fundamentally hostile to the West and actively trying to undermine Western strength and resolve and to promote the fortunes of like-minded regimes in both hemispheres. However, in its deep mistrust of the outside world and its unrelenting quest for unassailable security guaranteed by superior military power, the post–World War II Soviet Union followed a foreign policy evoking the policies of tsarist Russia. Its confrontation with the West in the 1970s and early 1980s had much in common with the traditional rivalries between great powers. Like its rivals, the Soviet Union had interests and commitments that made it a power with a great deal to lose. This tended to make its foreign policy, despite its pronounced expansionist component, cautious and pragmatic in general and designed to avoid direct confrontation with the United States in particular. In some parts of the world the Soviet Union even struggled to preserve the status quo, something, as its great rival the United States knew all too well, that is not easy to do.

By the early 1980s the Soviet Union most of all wanted to preserve the status quo in Eastern Europe. Its dominance there provided a buffer against the West and was an important source of reassurance and confidence at home. But persistent national feeling was an ineradicable source of instability, while economic stagnation turned the region from an exploitable semicolony into an expensive liability. Poland, at heart a Catholic rather than a Communist country, remained especially hostile to everything Russian or Soviet and, despite the suppression of the Solidarity trade union movement late in 1981, was in a state of open, if passive, rebellion.

To the east was the People's Republic of China, a hostile power over a billion strong. Fifty Soviet divisions, about one-quarter of the country's ground strength, guarded the long Sino-Soviet border. To the south Afghanistan continued to bleed the Soviets of soldiers (the death toll passing 10,000 in 1984), money ($1.7 million per day), and prestige. In the Western hemisphere Cuba, though a valuable ally and a thorn in America's side, was a considerable economic burden. By 1985 the price of supporting Cuba and Vietnam had climbed to more than $5.7 billion per year. Finally, the Brezhnev generation left Soviet–American relations worse than they had been for years.

It was against this background that the leadership baton was finally passed. It was passed in neither a timely nor a graceful fashion, but fumbled and then spasmodically thrust into the hands of the Soviet Union's first leaders to reach adulthood in the post–World War II era. Despite the collective sigh of relief reaching from Moscow to Europe to Washington that this transfer finally had been accomplished, expectations regarding decisive and fundamental change were guarded at best. Soon both the speed and the direction of change made it clear that despite more than six decades of Soviet rule, at least one fundamental thing had not changed in Russia: its uncanny ability to surprise itself and the entire world.

NOTES

1. Fedor Burlatsky, *Khrushchev and the First Russian Spring: The Era of Khrushchev Through the Eyes of His Advisor*, translated by Daphne Skillen (New York: Charles Scribner's Sons, 1988), p. 210.

2. Marshall Goldman, *USSR in Crisis* (New York and London: Norton, 1983), p. 49.

3. Zhores Medvedev, *Soviet Agriculture* (New York and London: Norton, 1987), pp. 408–409.

4. Cited in David K. Shipler, *Russia: Broken Idols, Solemn Dreams* (New York: Times Books, 1983), p. 173.

5. Hedrick Smith, *The Russians* (New York: Ballantine Books, 1976), p. 83.

6. Basile Kerblay, *Modern Soviet Society*, translated by Rupert Swyer (New York: Pantheon Books, 1983), pp. 63–64.

7. Quoted in W. Bruce Lincoln, *Between Heaven and Hell: The Story of a Thousand Years of Artistic Life in Russia* (New York: Viking, 1998), p. 445.

18

Gorbachev: From Restructuring to Deconstruction

Our society is ripe for change, and the need for change has cleared its own road.

—Mikhail Gorbachev, 1987

Workers of the world, we're sorry.

—Sign at a counterdemonstration during the seventy-second anniversary celebration of the Bolshevik Revolution in Moscow, November 7, 1989

*Half measures
can kill
when,
chafing at the bit in terror
we twitch our ears,
all lathered in foam
on the brink of precipices,
because we can't jump halfway across.*

—Yevgeny Yevtushenko, 1989[1]

On March 11, 1985, Mikhail Sergeyevich Gorbachev was elected general secretary of the Communist Party of the Soviet Union. Gorbachev's election was a signal that the winds of change, which had swirled under Andropov, only to subside under Chernenko, were again rising in Moscow. The question remained how strong those winds would be and precisely in what direction they would blow.

Gorbachev was an Andropov protégé, and Andropov had begun making changes during his brief tenure as general secretary. But there was nothing in Andropov's program that could be called radical or that promised fundamental changes in any of the major institutions of Soviet life. Gorbachev was young;

he had just celebrated his fifty-fourth birthday. Yet among Soviet leaders this made him an exception only to the two sickly senior citizens who had preceded him. What Gorbachev would try to do, and to what degree he would succeed where he tried, therefore were open questions.

THE RISE OF MIKHAIL GORBACHEV

While Gorbachev's personality was unusually outgoing and attractive for a Soviet political leader, his personal background was conventional. Like any man since the death of Stalin with a serious chance of becoming general secretary, Gorbachev was an ethnic Russian. He rose through the system, albeit more quickly than usual, along a classic trajectory. He was born in 1931, at the height of collectivization, in a small village in the Stavropol region of the North Caucasus, a prime agricultural area extending eastward from the Ukraine between the Black and Caspian seas. His maternal grandfather was a party member who served as the first chairman of a local collective farm. Gorbachev therefore was born into the new Soviet rural elite, which helps explain both his survival at a time when so many peasant children were dying and the educational opportunities he subsequently received. Yet, like tens of millions of Soviet citizens regardless of their status, Gorbachev did not live through the terror-filled 1930s unscathed. Both his grandfathers were arrested, and although they somehow survived and returned home, both sides of Gorbachev's family suffered.

After his graduation from secondary school in 1950, Gorbachev was admitted to the law faculty at Moscow State University. Shortly before receiving his degree in 1955, he married Raisa Titorenko, a bright and attractive fellow student from the Urals. After graduation Gorbachev returned to Stavropol to take a job with the Komsomol. He soon switched to the Communist Party apparatus, working his way up the ladder over a period of about fifteen years until he became first secretary of the Stavropol region, a post he held from 1970 to 1978. That position earned him a place on the party's Central Committee in 1971.

In 1978 Gorbachev was called to Moscow to serve in the powerful Secretariat as the top party official responsible for agriculture. There he presided over a string of poor harvests. His survival must be attributed both to his political skills and to Andropov's protection. Gorbachev became a candidate member of the Politburo in 1979 and a full voting member in 1980. Under Andropov he became the general secretary's right-hand man, often chairing Politburo meetings in the ailing party leader's absence. Under Chernenko, Gorbachev again often stood in for his sick superior and became the de facto second secretary of the party. His election as general secretary came with the unanimous if not altogether enthusiastic support of the aging Politburo. In nominating Gorbachev, veteran Foreign Minister Andrei Gromyko, in stressing the candidate's fitness for the job, opined that he "has a nice smile but iron teeth."

There was nothing concrete in Gorbachev's professional career to suggest that he would turn into the bold and dynamic reformer he became. Had there been, it is safe to say that his career, which was largely made under Brezhnev, would have quickly stalled. Making it in the Soviet system during the Brezhnev era required playing strictly by the rules; initiative was desirable only in quantities large enough to demonstrate a degree of competence. In other words, one of Gorbachev's indispensable talents as he climbed up a slippery ladder was his ability to mislead his colleagues and superiors. Still, in retrospect, one can see dim glimmers of originality and faint streaks of independence against the gray background of a successful Soviet bureaucrat's career. As a university student, speaking in confidence to a close friend, Gorbachev challenged the rosy official version of collectivization, no doubt on the basis of his own childhood experiences. In Stavropol he was known for getting out among the people and making on-the-spot visits to farms, factories, and other institutions under his jurisdiction. He was influenced by the reformist spirit of the Khrushchev era, and after becoming general secretary even referred to his generation as the "children of the Twentieth Party Congress." During the 1970s in Stavropol Gorbachev tried to improve collective farm efficiency by allowing the peasants increased freedom to organize their work and to sell more of what they earned at market prices rather than at the low prices paid by the state. Once he returned to Moscow in 1978, Gorbachev became part of the reformist group Andropov was collecting around him.

But even all of this would still leave Gorbachev within a framework that he certainly outgrew. The best that one can say about his remarkable political evolution is that prior to 1985 Mikhail Gorbachev had the intelligence and adaptability to transcend conventional Soviet bounds. After he became general secretary, the realization of the enormity of the problems his country faced and the courage to face them broadened Gorbachev's outlook and made him a political figure of international stature and genuine historical importance.

Actually, the events of March 1985 and their aftermath during the next several months brought more than a new general secretary to power. They ended the Soviet Union's succession crises by bringing a new political generation to the helm of the ship of state. Unlike the older Brezhnev generation, Gorbachev and his colleagues did not work in the industrialization drive, participate in and survive the purges, or, in most cases, fight in World War II. For them industrialization was an established fact; their formative political activities took place during Khrushchev's destalinization era and they were influenced by the spirit and possibilities of those times. They were the first Soviet leaders, with the exception of Lenin and several of his lieutenants, to have a formal university education. The Gorbachev generation also benefited from the rising Soviet standard of living during the 1960s and 1970s. Some of them had the opportunity to visit and learn about the West from direct experience; Gorbachev himself made unescorted trips to France and Italy with his wife during his younger years. These experiences made Gorbachev and his colleagues relatively comfortable with Westerners and more ready than previous leaders to borrow both methods and ideas from the United States and Western Europe.

MODERN SOVIET SOCIETY AND THE COMMUNIST DICTATORSHIP

The new party leadership presided over a society that had undergone a fundamental change in the past generation: the process of urbanization. Urbanization, of course, antedated the Soviet era; it had been going on since Russia's industrialization began in earnest during the nineteenth century. Urbanization accelerated to record levels during Stalin's industrialization drive of the 1930s and continued at a rapid pace after the dictator's death. But although the Soviet Union became increasingly urbanized as it industrialized, it took a very long time for it to become an urban *society*, to overcome what historian Moshe Lewin has called the "rural nexus" of Soviet life.[2] This is true both in terms of raw statistics—that is, the percentage of Soviet people who actually lived in cities—and even more so in terms of the *quality* of life in those cities. It took until 1960 for the proportion of Soviet citizens living in cities to reach 49 percent, which means that despite its industrial growth the Soviet Union remained a rural society until almost the end of the Khrushchev era. In 1972 the urban population reached 58 percent; it passed the two-thirds mark in 1985, the year Gorbachev came to power. The Soviet Union therefore did not become a *predominantly* urban society, like the advanced states of Western Europe and the United States, until the middle of the 1970s.

Urbanization is a process of cultural change that alters how people live, what they know, and what they are capable of doing and demanding from their government. Thus over time peasants flooding Soviet cities abandoned their rural habits and acquired an urban sophistication and state of mind. One important aspect of that transformation was a dramatically increased level of education, which the government promoted for reasons of its own.

Urban citizens are in many ways more difficult to manage than rural populations. The Stalinist state, for example, was able to mobilize and manipulate peasants and proletarianized peasant workers during the 1930s not only because it used overwhelming force but also because it was dealing with relatively simple social institutions. Another important factor was the kind of work these people were being mobilized to do, which for many years was largely manual labor. But industrialization required highly trained specialists, and over the years this led to the creation of a large and well-educated group of people who lived and worked in the cities. Their presence gradually began to change the character of Soviet urban life. The number of people with a specialized or technical education increased from about 2.4 million in 1941 to 8 million in 1960 to more than 30 million in the mid-1980s. Meanwhile, the millions of ordinary workers in the cities also became better educated, as did the shrinking minority of Soviet citizens still on the farms; the proportion of workers and peasants with only an elementary education dropped from more than 90 percent in 1959 to less than 20 percent thirty years later.

Urban society, with its complexity and concentration of people with sophisticated skills and intellectual resources, is not amenable to the same controls that can regulate a rural village. In the anonymity of the modern city, people with special skills more easily find their way around governmental attempts to control them as, in the words of one observer, they "rush about like the unplottable electrons in an atom."[3] One example of this in the Soviet Union was what happened to the state's ability to control the flow of information, which from 1917 on was a crucial factor in maintaining the one-party Bolshevik dictatorship. During the 1960s tape recorders, often smuggled in from abroad, became an effective way of transmitting information both within the country and abroad. This information could be a statement from a dissident confined to prison or a rock song the authorities refused to record in state-controlled studios. The telephone and automobile also increasingly enabled citizens to slip between the multiple tentacles of the Soviet state. New technologies—such as computers and videocassette recorders—made control even more difficult. Although the authorities tried to limit the distribution of these devices, they nonetheless became available in ever-larger numbers because without them the increasingly industrialized and complex Soviet Union could not function.

It was in the cities that networks of unsanctioned activity multiplied exponentially, beyond the control of even the KGB. Millions of urban dwellers of varying degrees of sophistication found niches to pursue private interests. These were as varied as the city dwellers themselves, ranging from small groups who played jazz or rock music or organized unsanctioned art exhibitions, to youths who dodged the draft, to illegal entrepreneurs who thrived in the burgeoning second economy. This phenomenon, the direct product of urbanization, itself the product of the Soviet state's modernization and industrialization policies, undermined the ability of the state to control society. It produced a nonsocialist, nonparty twilight zone in the Soviet universe where individuals made decisions free of official control and formed organizations to implement those decisions. While in the West such activity has long been considered normal and is the basis of how Western democratic societies function, it ran counter to everything in official Soviet ideology.

By the late 1970s legions of skilled specialists—scientists, engineers, economists, and experts in many other fields—had become vital to managing the country. Their existence and essential skills in effect meant that some power had slipped away from the Soviet bureaucracy and, hence, from the Communist Party itself. Stultifying central controls over the economy and gross incompetence and mismanagement became increasingly intolerable to these specialists. They could not suffer a level of censorship that made it difficult to get information vital to their work, not to mention to read, view, or listen to what they wanted in their private time. This development did not threaten the political power of the Communist Party, even as late as the first years of the Gorbachev era. But alongside the Soviet Union's other serious problems, it created enormous pressure for reform. The frustration these skilled specialists felt regarding the party's incompetence, the country's lagging standard of living, and the limits on their personal aspirations also led to alienation and pessimism, thereby adding new straws to the Soviet camel's back.

From the outside, as its economic growth slowed and its social problems grew, the Soviet Union during Brezhnev's later years appeared frozen in place. But like barren ice covering a Siberian lake, the frost was only a surface phenomenon. Beneath the sterile surface of the Communist Party there was vibrant and growing life. None of this registered with Brezhnev and his aging cohorts. As one observer put it, "The country went through a social revolution while Brezhnev slept."[4] But in the early 1980s that life began to reach the surface as the Communist Party under Andropov haltingly committed itself to change. It broke through visibly after 1985 with the advent of Gorbachev.

An example of this process was the emergence of what can genuinely be called public opinion, which even before 1985 was able to influence government policy. An early beneficiary of this was Lake Baikal, Siberia's "sacred sea," according to the native people who live near its shores, and the largest freshwater lake in the world. Pressure from scientists and intellectuals to prevent pollution of the lake by new industries began in the mid-1960s and helped convince the government to institute corrective measures. Public opinion also mobilized during the early 1980s against a plan to divert several Siberian rivers, which flow northward into the Arctic Sea, southward to Central Asia for irrigation purposes, a scheme Gorbachev scuttled in 1986.

Gorbachev, then, was not the initiator of change; it had already swept Soviet society in several crucial ways. The problem was that while *society*

Society

had changed a great deal, the *party* hardly had changed at all, and through its extensive control levers the party was preventing further progress that was necessary to make Soviet society in general and the economy in particular competitive with the West. Gorbachev's job, at least as he first saw it, was to get the party to catch up with the times and become an agent of progress.

This was not going to be easy, especially if one looked at the Soviet Union in rigorous Marxist terms, as Gorbachev might have been expected to do. During the next several years, especially as he undertook more radical reforms, Gorbachev would turn to what he considered Leninist formulations, in particular the policies of the NEP, as opposed to what he condemned as Stalinist distortions of Leninism, to justify his policies and proposals. This approach was based on an idealization, actually a fictionalization, of Lenin, whom Gorbachev for his purposes chose to transform into a moderate socialist and tolerant political leader. Fictionalizing Lenin was nothing new; it had been going on in the Soviet Union for sixty years. However, Gorbachev never seems to have gone beyond his rose-colored Leninist visions to a serious Marxist analysis of the problems he faced in trying to overhaul Soviet society. Had the general secretary done so, what he would have found might have given him pause. In Marxist terms, by the 1980s the Soviet Union's mode of production (its "substructure," upon which everything rests) was in crisis because its two components—means of production and relations of production—were at loggerheads. Specifically, the means of production— the resources, technology, skills, and workers—had outgrown the relations of production, in this case the centrally controlled Soviet economic system. Among the many telling signs of this development was the Soviet system's inability to integrate the most modern technology into most branches of the economy or to control a whole range of activities that made up the illicit second economy. According to Marx, increasing pressure from the evolving means of production inevitably shatters the old relations of production, at which point a society's "superstructure"—the system of ideology, law, and government based on the mode of production—comes crashing down. The society in question, proclaimed Marx, is doomed, and there is nothing anyone can do about it.

THE GORBACHEV AGENDA

Gorbachev did not become general secretary with a comprehensive program for solving the Soviet Union's problems. Something resembling a strategy with many interrelated programs, albeit with many gaps when it came to specifics, emerged over a period of about two years. That strategy as a whole was called *perestroika*, or "restructuring." The word perestroika actually was used in two contexts. Initially it applied primarily to the economy, which from the beginning was Gorbachev's central concern. Perestroika reflected the assumption that the Soviet economy would have to be overhauled if it was to become sufficiently modern and efficient to maintain the Soviet Union as a superpower. The key point was to find a way compatible with socialist principles to reduce the role of central planning and administration and allow the managers of factories, mines, and farms room for initiative so they could increase productivity.

Over time the term perestroika came to refer to the entire scope of Gorbachev's reform program. As an overall program of revitalizing the Soviet Union, perestroika ultimately included three policies that extended far beyond the confines of economic reform. Soon after taking office Gorbachev concluded that he could make little progress restructuring the Soviet economy without what he called *glasnost*. Glasnost, usually translated as "openness," was precisely that: the opening of the Soviet Union to an unprecedented range and variety of information, personal and artistic expression, and genuine public debate. It included the drastic reduction of censorship in literature, art, news reporting, and the like. Glasnost was essential to Gorbachev and his overall program of perestroika for several reasons. The Soviet Union's obsession with secrecy had led to innumerable absurdities, among them Soviet economists waiting impatiently for the annual publication of *American* estimates on the Soviet economy because Soviet statistics were either unavailable or unreliable. Glasnost was necessary to inform the party leadership properly because so much had been covered up over the years by bureaucrats protecting their fiefdoms. It was also demanded by many members of the Soviet elite, who could not work effectively unless they had access to new ideas and information, both at home and from abroad. Beyond that, the Soviet Union's most educated citizens were disgusted by censorship that prevented them from enjoying the best of what both domestic and foreign artists produced, whether it was literature, art, film, or anything else. But Gorbachev's glasnost was not an inalienable right of citizens to enjoy the freedom of information and expression as known in the West. Rather it was one of the leadership's instruments of reform, and while the limits on public expression were broadened dramatically, the Gorbachev regime intended to determine what those limits would be and made this clear on several occasions. In mid-1987 the general secretary announced that glasnost must "serve the interests of socialism." In October of 1989, in a more menacing comment on glasnost, Gorbachev angrily attacked the press for undermining his efforts.

Another key element of perestroika involved a word few people associated with the Soviet Union or its Communist Party: *demokratizatsia*, or democratization. Once again, the term did not mean what it does in the West, at least not to Gorbachev and the Soviet leadership. Gorbachev did not want a multiparty political system in which the Communist Party could be forced to share power or be voted out of office. To him democratization meant that the Soviet political system would be made more flexible: most notably, that in factory elections, in elections to government bodies, and even in party elections there would be a choice of candidates. The hope was that glasnost and democratization, even in their limited Soviet versions, would entice ordinary citizens to pitch in voluntarily to help the reform effort. This was crucial because Gorbachev understood that without active popular support no substantial economic reforms would be possible.

Finally, there was *novoe myshlenie*, or "new thinking." Although this term also could be applied to all of Gorbachev's reforms, it referred most specifically to foreign policy and in particular to the Soviet Union's relationship with the West. New thinking implied a radical change in Soviet–Western relations, which for so long had been marked by hostility. Soviet expansionism in Eastern Europe after World War II had been the key factor in provoking the Cold War with the West and its concomitant arms race. Although "peaceful coexistence" became the official Soviet policy in the 1950s, it existed alongside an aggressive policy of "class struggle" with the capitalist powers that fueled the expensive arms race. For over fifty years the Soviets assumed that security could be bought with military power and, therefore, committed huge resources to building the world's largest military establishment. The trouble was that military spending absorbed between a quarter and a third of the country's productive resources and was one of the heaviest anchors dragging down the Soviet economy. Gorbachev knew he had to shift resources to the civilian sector in order to rebuild the Soviet economy. This helps to account for the steady stream of arms control proposals, some serious and others for public relations purposes, that flowed from the Kremlin after 1985. Gorbachev eventually argued that all nations had to work together to solve growing mutual challenges, chief among them being the world's deteriorating natural environment.

ACCELERATION

Gorbachev's lack of a comprehensive program when he took office reflected a number of factors. Other than a general agreement that change was necessary, no consensus existed among the new leadership about exactly what to do. Equally important, and as one would have expected from a lifelong party bureaucrat, Gorbachev initially was committed to the narrow Andropov approach, which focused almost entirely on tightening economic management and combating corruption. That is why calls for *uskorenie*, or acceleration of economic activity, and increased discipline in the workplace, both associated with Andropov, dominated Gorbachev's early months as general secretary. In addition, Gorbachev simply did not understand how bad conditions were; he and his colleagues talked only about a "pre-crisis" situation, not one that could in any way threaten the regime. After all, glasnost had not yet shed light on the country's problems. Gorbachev himself admitted several times his initial failure to grasp the grave difficulties he and his colleagues faced. For example, in 1988 he observed: "Frankly speaking, comrades, we have underestimated the extent and gravity of the deformations." This helps to account for the shocking overconfidence of Gorbachev's first year, when the Soviet leadership seemed to think that some economic tinkering and arresting a few corrupt officials would be enough to turn the economy around and get the situation in hand.

All this made 1985 a year of small deeds and hints of more to come. Gorbachev could be pleased that he did not stumble while taking his first steps into the economic, political, cultural, and foreign policy minefields that lay before him. His very modest forays into economic reform included experiments at two factories that were permitted to retain their profits to finance their own development without funds from the central authorities. There was also some administrative reorganization, most notably the consolidation of six agricultural ministries into one "super ministry." However, none of these measures loosened the deadening grip of the Moscow central planners on the economy. The agricultural reform in fact did the opposite and soon was recognized as a bureaucratic boondoggle that had to be undone, a correction not made until 1989.

The rest of Gorbachev's 1985 economic program followed Andropov's pattern. It consisted mainly of attempts to tighten discipline in the workplace by firing incompetent managers and combating alcohol abuse. As under Andropov, the assumption seems to have been that there was slack in the system and that judicious tightening could make it perform significantly better. However, a faint trace of glasnost was visible on the cultural horizon. The important literary journal *Novyi Mir* published a prose poem by Yevgeny Yevtushenko that graphically discussed several sensitive or even forbidden themes including abuses under Stalin, the fate of Leon Trotsky, and current Soviet neofascism. Yevtushenko also delivered a dramatic speech calling for openness and honesty in Soviet life, and two plays about corruption in the party played to full houses in Moscow.

BATTLING THE GREEN SNAKE

The most notable domestic initiative by the new Soviet leadership was to attack what the Russians call the "green snake": the problem of alcoholism. Once again this policy was a continuation of Andropov's, except that Gorbachev put teeth into it. He closed down two-thirds of all liquor stores, cut the hours of those that remained, reduced the production of alcoholic beverages, and increased the fine for public drunkenness tenfold. During the 1986 new-year celebrations, for the first time in memory, soft drinks were sold on Moscow's streets rather than the traditional alcoholic beverages. For his efforts, the public dubbed the new general secretary the "mineral water secretary," a title that probably reflected equal measures of admiration and anger.

But the public did not respond the way Gorbachev hoped. There was considerable support for the campaign among women wearied by the chronic drunkenness of their men. Elsewhere enthusiasm waned, as the Soviet Union's heavy drinkers displayed considerable ingenuity in getting around the new rules. There was a huge increase in the number of underground stills, which often produced toxic brews. Sugar, used in the brewing process, disappeared from store shelves. When home brew was not available, desperate drinkers turned to brake fluid, after-shave lotion, and similar dangerous and frequently poisonous liquids. Adding financial insult to social injury, the decline in revenue from alcohol sales pushed the Soviet budget further into the red. Such problems forced a reversal of several of these policies, beginning as early as 1986.

COMMON DENOMINATORS

Like domestic policy, Soviet foreign policy under the new general secretary initially was marked by only slight adjustments, more of style than substance. Gorbachev announced a unilateral ban on all nuclear tests that lasted from August of 1985 to February of 1987, a measure that raised his stock in Western European antinuclear circles when the United States continued its testing. He told Western Europeans that they and the Soviet Union shared "our common house," in part to try to loosen their ties with the United States, and he wooed both Communist and non-Communist Asian nations with references to what he called "our common Asiatic heritage." However, the United States, the world's capitalist superpower, remained the central Soviet foreign policy concern. Even before becoming general secretary, Gorbachev had moved to raise Soviet–American relations from the low point to which they had fallen in the early 1980s. During Chernenko's last months, by which time Gorbachev was making many major decisions, the Soviet Union and the United States agreed to resume arms control negotiations. Once Gorbachev was in power the two sides inched toward each other, not only by sitting down at the negotiating table but by renewing cultural exchanges suspended by the Americans after the 1979 Soviet invasion of Afghanistan. In November of 1985 Gorbachev and

President Ronald Reagan held their first summit in Geneva, a get-acquainted meeting without any serious business on the agenda.

GORBACHEV'S COLD PURGE

Gorbachev's most substantial gains during his first year in office involved consolidating his position, a logical task on which to focus. Election as general secretary guaranteed neither job security nor the ability to carry out significant change. The Politburo was dominated by Brezhnev-era holdovers unsympathetic to serious reform, as was the Central Committee. The party bureaucracy at the middle and lower levels was still staffed by bureaucrats whose status and material well-being depended on the old way of doing things. Against this background, Gorbachev did a remarkable job of consolidating and broadening his power base. The old guard's grip on Soviet political life, loosened under Andropov but slightly retightened under Chernenko, was finally broken. The most notable high-ranking official removed from office was foreign minister Andrei Gromyko. Gromyko was eased out of office by being kicked upstairs to become president of the Presidium of the Supreme Soviet, a ceremonial post whose occupant served as the Soviet Union's official head of state but wielded no power. Gorbachev's "cold purge" extended down both the party and state ladders to four of the union republic party chiefs, about 40 percent of the Council of Ministers, and almost a third of the regional party secretaries. At lower levels thousands of party and government officials were replaced.

Several new men became full Politburo members during the spring of 1985, although this did less for reform than it first appeared. The most powerful was Yegor Ligachev, who had worked closely with Gorbachev during the Andropov days. Ligachev became the secretary in charge of party personnel and the politician second in rank to Gorbachev. Within a year he also emerged as Gorbachev's main rival when Gorbachev began to explore more radical strategies of reform. Ligachev was a moderate reformer ready to continue the type of programs Andropov had started. However, he firmly opposed going beyond them and overhauling or possibly abolishing any of the basic institutions of Soviet life. Thus, as Gorbachev began to advocate more radical measures in all areas of Soviet life, Ligachev in effect became the leader of the general secretary's conservative opposition. More open to new ideas was Boris Yeltsin, a newcomer to Moscow from the provincial city of Sverdlovsk. He took over the post of Moscow party chief and became a candidate Politburo member. Shortly thereafter Eduard Shevardnadze, a staunch Gorbachev and perestroika supporter, joined the Politburo. Shevardnadze, the former first secretary of Georgia with a reputation as a corruption fighter, also replaced Gromyko as foreign minister. Another important new face was Alexander Yakovlev, the former ambassador to Canada. Although in 1985 he was only head of the Central Committee's propaganda department, he became Gorbachev's closest advisor. Probably the strongest advocate among the Soviet leadership for radical reform during the first two years of Gorbachev's tenure, Yakovlev has been called the architect of perestroika. He rose quickly, becoming a Central Committee secretary in 1986, a candidate Politburo member early in 1987, and a full member by the end of the year.

THE TWENTY-SEVENTH PARTY CONGRESS

The Twenty-Seventh Party Congress, which took place in early 1986, produced more political changes. Gorbachev fixed its opening for a significant date: February 25, 1986, thirty years to the day after Nikita Khrushchev gave his secret speech. The housecleaning continued. Almost 40 percent of the Central Committee members elected at the congress were new, and several reformers were added to the powerful Secretariat. Among them was Alexandra Biryukova, the first woman since Khrushchev's time to join the top party elite.

The Twenty-Seventh Congress also instituted new party rules that made it easier to move against corrupt officials, although Gorbachev was thwarted in his attempt to revive Khrushchev's controversial rule number 25, which limited the tenure of party officials to three terms, or fifteen years. This defeat was symptomatic of a larger division of opinion and lack of consensus at the congress. There was general agreement that reform was necessary but sharp disagreement on what type of reform and how drastic it should be. This dichotomy emerged during the congress debates. That there were real debates at all was a historic change; the Twenty-Seventh Congress was the most open party congress since the rise of Stalin. As a media event the congress was a stunning success and a demonstration of change. But it left unanswered the questions of Gorbachev's long-term security as general secretary, the degree of unity at the top, and the nature and direction of future reform.

CHERNOBYL

Shortly after the congress closed, another problem literally exploded in the Soviet Union's face. On April 25, 1986, the peaceful spring routine of the Ukraine was shattered by thundering noise, roaring flames, and searing heat. What must have seemed like the devil's work was in reality the poorly executed work of human beings. An explosion had destroyed one of the reactors at the Chernobyl nuclear power plant, sending radioactive poisons in unprecedented and disastrous amounts upward into the atmosphere and outward across the countryside.

Chernobyl recalled a Soviet nuclear disaster in 1957 in the Urals. This new disaster, however, was far worse. Air currents carried the nuclear poisons into Central and Western Europe. The political fallout for Gorbachev and glasnost was also serious. The Soviet government fell silent. No announcement of the explosion came until radiation was detected in Western Europe. It took three days for an official response and fifteen more before Gorbachev himself spoke publicly. Meanwhile, the government was irresponsibly slow to respond to the catastrophe itself. It delayed evacuating the civilian population from around the smoldering reactor. Thirty-six hours after the explosion, children were still playing in the streets of Pripyat, five miles from the stricken reactor. It took a week to evacuate the town of Chernobyl, slightly further away.

Only truly heroic action by local firefighters, many of whom would die from radiation sickness, prevented a far greater disaster. That was poet Andrei Voznesensky's point in "Thoughts on Chernobyl," in which he spoke of the debt the Soviet people owed to each of the small band of men who "Went into the object, / Who put out the reactor fires." The price each man had paid, and the debt owed, Voznesensky continued, was in the highest currency:

> He did not save himself
> He saved Kiev and Odessa. . . .
> We both stayed alive, you and I,
> Because that was a real man.[5]

Having failed so badly at first, the Kremlin struggled to recover its credibility by issuing a long and comprehensive report. A few officials directly responsible for the Chernobyl facility later went to jail. Yet nothing could prevent billions of dollars in damage to water, crops, and farm animals, not only in the Soviet Union but in European countries to the west. Officially, the immediate death toll—mainly those near the explosion and those who fought the ensuing fire—was put at 31, although unofficial sources cited higher numbers. The total number of long-term deaths attributable to the Chernobyl accident, according to a United Nations report issued in 2005, is likely to be about 4,000. Chernobyl also caused extremely serious long-term environmental damage in the Ukraine and Belorussia, the regions most contaminated by the fallout from the explosion.

NUCLEAR ARMS NEGOTIATIONS

As the radioactive and political fallout from Chernobyl dispersed, Soviet and American attention shifted to a greater nuclear danger: nuclear weapons. Both sides wanted a substantial agreement that would put a real brake on the arms race. In January 1986 the Soviets had agreed to the American demand that strategic and intermediate arms talks be separated. In the course of the next few months, Gorbachev first linked, then unlinked, and then linked again progress on intermediate range missiles to American research on a space-based antimissile system known as the Strategic Defense Initiative (SDI). In the fall of 1986 came the surprising announcement that General Secretary Gorbachev and President Reagan would meet again in Reykjavik, Iceland, to try to work out a major arms agreement. Amid a whirlpool of near euphoria and serious skepticism, Reagan, Gorbachev, and their advisors spent October 11 and 12 in intense negotiations. They reached tentative agreements on several major issues, including a 50 percent mutual cut in strategic weapons. But the agreements and the summit ran aground on the rock of SDI. Gorbachev demanded strict limits on SDI research that Reagan refused to accept. The result was the worst Soviet–American summit failure in twenty-five years.

SOVIET WOMEN IN THE 1980s

When Gorbachev went to Reykjavik, in fact almost wherever he went, he was accompanied by his wife, Raisa. Before 1985 the wives of Soviet leaders stayed in the background, if they were visible at all. Raisa Gorbachev was not only highly visible, but she was clearly audible. In effect she became an attractive, modern, educated, and articulate role model for the more than 50 percent of the Soviet Union's population that had never had one. Persistent rumors that Raisa influenced her husband on matters of policy shocked and offended many Soviet citizens in a country where traditional views of a woman's role in society persisted and where women's needs, despite official rhetoric dating from 1917, remained sorely neglected. By the mid-1980s women in the Soviet Union had access to many careers—about 85 percent of all women were in the workforce—but in most fields the prestigious positions were still held by men, while women remained disproportionately concentrated in lower-paying jobs. And Soviet women did double duty because they received little help at home, either from their husbands or from the mostly outdated appliances they had to use. Soviet socialism did not provide adequate day care for preschool children, leaving Soviet mothers with yet another burden. Families headed by women received scant extra help from the state, while the number of these families had risen as the Soviet divorce rate soared during the 1970s and 1980s. Soviet women spent endless hours shopping in interminable lines and found their needs were poorly attended to when they required medical attention. For example, because contraceptives were generally unavailable Soviet women had one of the highest abortion rates in the world, so high that abortions in the Soviet Union exceeded live births. The abortions themselves often took place in clinics that lacked proper anesthetics, a situation that likewise frequently was the case when Soviet women entered hospitals to give birth. Women made up over a quarter of the Communist Party membership but were increasingly scarce at the higher ranks. While Raisa Gorbachev's charisma and outspokenness had little immediate impact on all of this, her presence at Gorbachev's side, and Alexandra Biryukova's rise to the Secretariat in 1986 and the Politburo as a candidate member in 1988, stood as symbols that times were beginning to change.

PRELUDE TO PERESTROIKA

In truth, despite the considerable political movement, most aspects of Soviet life remained unchanged even after the Twenty-Seventh Party Congress. The economy, Gorbachev's main area of concern, was stuck in neutral. The greatest movement concerned glasnost, where the pace picked up considerably during 1986. Censorship of literature was eased. Some previously banned works began to reappear on the shelves, and reformist-minded editors emerged at a number of newspapers, magazines, and journals. Anatoly Shcharansky, the human rights activist and Jewish movement leader, was released from prison in February and allowed to emigrate to Israel; in December, Andrei Sakharov was freed from internal exile and allowed to return to Moscow.

Meanwhile, the pervasiveness and persistence of social and political problems carried over from the Brezhnev era began to convince Gorbachev that economic progress depended on curing many other ills in Soviet society. An alienated, demoralized, and frustrated population was not going to make the effort needed to revive the economy. What was needed was a program of systemic reform across the full spectrum of Soviet life. Gorbachev began to grow impatient with the slow pace of progress in the economy, a feeling that was probably reinforced and deepened by the complaints he read in the press and heard directly during his tours around the country. At the beginning of 1986 Gorbachev called only vaguely for "radical economic reforms." By August he both extended and clarified the lines of his new thinking when he called for reform of

> not only the economy but all other sides of life: social relations, the political system, the spiritual and ideological sphere, the style and work methods of the Party and of all our cadres. Restructuring is a capacious word. I would equate restructuring with revolution . . . a genuine revolution in the hearts and minds of the people.

The years 1985 and 1986 have been called the "prelude to perestroika."[6] Gorbachev's statement during the summer of 1986 and subsequent policy initiatives in 1987 marked the transition to the real thing.

PERESTROIKA AND HALF-MEASURES

By 1987 Gorbachev in effect had become radicalized, but he still had to contend with entrenched opposition before he could move further. One significant source of resistance was the military leadership, which opposed having its resources diverted elsewhere. In May of 1987 Gorbachev got some help from an unexpected source when a young West German flew a single-engine plane through the Soviet Union's vaunted air defenses and landed in Red Square, right at the Kremlin wall. That embarrassment enabled Gorbachev to launch a major housecleaning of Brezhnev-era military holdovers. He fired the minister of defense and the air defense commander immediately, quickly following that up with dozens of dismissals. He also passed over about twenty higher-ranking officers to make Dmitri Yazov the new defense minister.

A month later the Central Committee endorsed what Gorbachev called a comprehensive program for economic renewal based on what was termed "market socialism." On paper the changes mandated by Gorbachev's "Enterprise Law" looked large; when it took effect in January 1988 it would limit central planning to long-range guidelines, cut the power of the economic ministries, put factories on a self-financing basis and require them to produce quality goods at a profit, tie workers' wages to performance, expand the peasantry's private plots, and so on. However, the key to any economic reform was to end the system in which the government set the prices for most goods. This radical proposal was extremely controversial and dangerous because it would eliminate the subsidies on food and other necessities so vital to ordinary Soviet consumers. And it was at this key point that, despite his radical rhetoric, Gorbachev held back; price reform was put off, and with it any real economic change.

Gorbachev held back again at another Central Committee meeting in October 1987, when Boris Yeltsin stunned his colleagues and the world by publicly denouncing the slow pace of reform. Yeltsin lashed out at Gorbachev but reserved his harshest words for Ligachev, the leading critic of Gorbachev's recent policies and proposals. Faced with a choice between an emerging group of radicals represented by Yeltsin, who would push him into the unknown, and entrenched conservatives symbolized by Ligachev, who wanted to keep him within the old confines, Gorbachev tilted away from the radicals. He rebuked Yeltsin and a month later removed him from his positions as head of the Moscow party organization and as a candidate member of the Politburo.

While all this made Yeltsin the big loser, the October 1987 Central Committee blow-up also hurt perestroika and the general secretary himself. Along with opponents on his conservative flank, Gorbachev now had critics on his radical flank. It was at this point that Gorbachev, who previously had been close to the cutting edge among the reformers, moved to a more centrist position, beginning a delicate and often dangerous balancing act between his conservative and radical critics that lasted until the collapse of the Soviet Union in December 1991.

Yeltsin's outburst meanwhile emboldened the conservatives, who could now raise the specter of perestroika running out of control. Giving substance to that warning was an explosion of ethnic violence in the Caucasus, where two neighboring union republics, Armenia and Azerbaijan, confronted each other over control of Nagorno-Karabakh, a region with an Armenian majority that was part of the Azerbaijan. Gorbachev's performance at the seventieth anniversary celebration of the Bolshevik Revolution in November seemed to reflect a sense of discomfort. His long-awaited speech was expected to fill in some of what he called the "blank pages" of Soviet history. He did so, but with uncharacteristic timidity, attacking Stalin, to be sure, mouthing kind words for Bukharin, as everyone expected, but also repeating standard canards against Trotsky, which darkened those "blank pages" once again with falsehoods rather than enlightening them with accurate information.

NEW THINKING IN FOREIGN POLICY

The year 1987 nonetheless ended on a positive note, at least in terms of foreign policy. In December Gorbachev went to Washington for his third summit with President Reagan. The two men signed the Intermediate-Range Nuclear Forces Treaty, which required the elimination of all Soviet and American land-based nuclear missiles with ranges between 300 and 3,400 miles. It was a small step toward ending a massive arms race; these missiles represented only about 4 percent of the superpowers' nuclear arsenals. Still, for the first time an entire class of nuclear weapons was to be destroyed. The Soviets also accepted what are called asymmetrical reductions: because they had more of these weapons, they had to destroy more than the Americans. They also agreed that British and French missiles would not be included in the treaty. Meanwhile, Gorbachev used his four days in Washington to meet representatives of America's elite—artists, scientists, business leaders, and congressional representatives—making a highly favorable impression on them and, through television and other media, on the American people. He also seized an opportunity to meet directly with a group of ordinary American citizens when, while riding in a motorcade, he ordered his car stopped and forged into a crowd of onlookers gathered at the curb. Before his stunned security guards could react, Gorbachev briefly worked the crowd as well as any American politician.

The next year Gorbachev provided further examples of his "new thinking" in foreign policy. He announced in February of 1988 that the Soviets would withdraw their troops from Afghanistan, and to the surprise of many skeptics the withdrawal was completed on schedule. On February 15, 1989, the last Soviet soldier, General Boris Gromov, left Afghanistan with the comment, "Our nine-year stay ends with this." That "stay" had cost the Soviets 15,000 lives, tens of thousands of wounded, and a loss of international prestige. Eight months later foreign minister Eduard Shevardnadze denounced the Soviet intervention in Afghanistan as illegal and immoral.

Meanwhile, in December of 1988, Gorbachev came to the United Nations in New York to explain to the world how his "new thinking" applied to the arms race and global peace. He rejected the old Soviet assumption of security based exclusively on military power, asserting that modern technology made achieving security at the expense of others impossible; rather it could best be achieved by recognizing nations' mutual interdependence and their need for cooperation. Gorbachev then announced the Soviet Union would unilaterally cut its armed forces by 500,000 men, about 10 percent of its total strength, and by 10,000 tanks. A large part of these reductions would be from forces in Eastern Europe, which Gorbachev claimed should reduce the perceived threat the West felt about a potential Soviet invasion. These cuts were not popular everywhere; Sergei Akhromeyev, the Soviet chief of the general staff, resigned over the issue.

THE SPREAD OF GLASNOST

Gorbachev's triumphant U.N./U.S. visit was cut short by a devastating earthquake in the Armenian SSR. But that massive human tragedy was only one of the many domestic problems with which Gorbachev had to deal. The strains caused by the reform effort were showing. One reason for the tension was that the country was being stretched unevenly in many ways, in part because some areas of reform were advancing faster than others. Glasnost set the pace; the light it let in as a glimmer in 1985 became a steady beam in 1986 and a glaring beacon thereafter, shining in many different directions at once. In 1988, more than three decades after it was published in the West, Boris Pasternak's Nobel Prize–winning novel *Dr. Zhivago* was published in his native land. Soviet citizens were able to read Anatoly Rybakov's *Children of the Arbat* and Vasily Grossman's *Life and Fate*, which explicitly compares Stalinism to Nazism. Some of Vladimir Nabokov's writings were published in a magazine. Overall, the newspaper *Izvestia* reported that by the end of 1988 over 6,000 book titles previously confined to "special collections" had become available to the public. In 1989 came the stunning announcement that Solzhenitsyn's *The Gulag Archipelago* was scheduled for publication in the Soviet Union.

Glasnost let the Soviet people see films like *Repentance* in 1987, three years after it was made. This exposé of Stalin's crimes played to over 700,000 people in Moscow in *ten days*, before being released all over the country. It was only one of 100 formerly banned films released between 1985 and 1988. In 1989 came *Little Vera*, a film about the frustration and hardship of Soviet working-class life. While dealing frankly with topics like alcoholism and terrible living conditions, *Little Vera* also focused on youthful sexuality in a number of explicit scenes that broke all the rules Soviet censors had once enforced. The film—which one citizen called "the first Soviet sexual act"— actually was part of a widespread erosion of puritanical Soviet strictures that ranged from the publication of a scholarly text on sexology and a sex manual for young couples (which became an immediate best seller) to occasional nudity on television and a striptease revue playing regularly in Moscow.

Glasnost reverberated in music as well. The liturgical tones of Sergei Rachmaninoff's *Vespers*, silenced for decades by official hostility, filled a Leningrad concert hall during the 1987 Easter season. Rock and roll, once denounced as a "crime," emerged from the underground. Aquarium, the best-known Soviet rock group, finally was allowed to record and release an album. Without a single advertisement, 200,000 copies sold out within hours; the album's sales soon topped 3 million. Soviet officials even got together with ex-Beatle Paul McCartney, who in 1988 released an album called *Back in the USSR* for distribution exclusively in the Soviet Union.

Religious observance became easier under glasnost. In 1988 public celebrations of the one-thousandth anniversary of Russia's conversion to Christianity symbolized the relaxation of restrictions on the Russian Orthodox Church. Roman Catholics, Muslims, and Jews also benefited from the more tolerant atmosphere. Catholics in Lithuania received more bishops and Muslims in Central Asia more mosques. In 1989 the Lithuanian parliament declared Christmas to be an official state holiday in that Baltic republic, a status it had not enjoyed since the Soviet Union annexed Lithuania in 1940. Jews were permitted to open their first rabbinical school since the 1920s and allowed to emigrate to Israel in greatly increased numbers. While these changes did not create complete religious freedom, they were a major improvement from pre-glasnost days.

One of the most sensitive areas glasnost touched was history. Mikhail Shatrov's plays *The Brest Peace* and *Onward, Onward, Onward* portrayed not only Nikolai Bukharin but Leon Trotsky in a favorable light. Bukharin was rehabilitated and posthumously restored to membership in the party, exactly fifty years after his execution in 1938. Bukharin's rehabilitation had a special significance, as the economic ideas he articulated in defending the NEP against Stalin in the late 1920s had resurfaced sixty years later in the economic programs of Mikhail Gorbachev. Restored posthumously to grace with Bukharin were Grigory Zinoviev, Lev Kamenev, and hundreds of other old Bolsheviks and purge victims. Leon Trotsky's 1923 attack on Stalin and the growth of authoritarianism in the party, *The New Course,* was serialized in a magazine. It joined hundreds of works by political figures as varied as Alexei Rykov (the Soviet head of state until purged by Stalin), Provisional Government head Alexander Kerensky, and anti-Soviet General Anton Denikin on the long list of political literature restored to open shelves. In 1989 the Soviet government even admitted the existence of the notorious secret clauses of the Hitler–Stalin pact of 1939 that divided Poland and other parts of Eastern Europe between Germany and the Soviet Union. That year it also published the text of Nikita Khrushchev's secret speech at the Twentieth Party Congress. These and many other revelations emerged so quickly that in 1988 history texts in the schools had to be withdrawn and history examinations canceled.

Attacking Stalin, while difficult for many conservatives to stomach, became almost respectable under Gorbachev. More serious difficulties arose when the rising tide of criticism spilled over the limits that Gorbachev wanted maintained and washed over Lenin. It did not take long for a few brave souls to point out Lenin's role in setting up the first Soviet labor camps and his repressive policies, which paved the way for Stalin, remarks that virtually no Soviet officials, Gorbachev included, wanted to hear. What turned out to be too much for the general secretary was the suggestion on a popular television show in April of 1989 that Lenin's embalmed remains finally receive a proper burial. This quickly led to the "retirement" of the head of the agency in charge of television and radio broadcasting. There also were other limits to glasnost such as the continued ban on independent cooperatives publishing and printing books, magazines, or newspapers. Some tried to do so anyway, including a group of dissidents who in 1987 began publishing a journal called, fittingly, *Glasnost.* It found little favor with Soviet officials, who denounced it with the observation that the country needed "only one glasnost." Commenting along broader lines, Yegor Ligachev warned that via glasnost "Western bourgeois values" were infecting the country.

Glasnost nonetheless continued to cast its probing light on Soviet reality. Soviet citizens, once privy mainly to information about how well their country was doing, instead heard about corruption, poverty, murder, drug addiction, inflation, and prostitution. They heard immediately about current disasters, such as when a Soviet nuclear submarine sank in 1989, and long-evolving scandals, such as how an entire peninsula in northern Siberia was so poisoned by nuclear tests that its residents had a life expectancy of only forty-five years. But glasnost, it turned out, also had a dark underside, best symbolized by an organization called *Pamyat*, or memory. *Pamyat* expressed the old ideas of extreme Russian nationalism, including a mean streak of anti-Semitism and a pronounced hostility toward the West. Although it operated without official endorsement, *Pamyat* was rumored to have supporters in high places.

PROBLEMS IN ECONOMIC RESTRUCTURING

While glasnost brought movement and excitement to the Soviet Union, restructuring of the economy yielded disappointment and frustration. As Gorbachev and his allies tried to implement change, they were resisted by powerful party conservatives, who in turn were backed by literally hundreds of thousands of bureaucrats whose status and livelihood rested on the status quo. The reformers also were hurt by their own inconsistencies, which included scaling back or even reversing policies, and their own lack of experience. Nor did they have sources that might provide guidance; no one had ever before attempted a thorough overhaul of the Soviet economy. The job was monumentally large and intricately complex. The basic structure of the Soviet economy, dominated by its massive central planning apparatus, dated from the early 1930s. It was grossly inefficient and would have been hard enough to change had everyone pulled in the same direction. Soviet industry was so technologically backward and unproductive that many leaders worried how it could sustain a military machine modern enough to compete with the West. The country's 50,000 collective and state farms had become a swamp into which a third of all investment sank without enabling the nation to feed itself. Meanwhile the multibillion-ruble second economy continued to illegally supply Soviet citizens with necessities, and even a few luxuries, unavailable from the moribund official socialist economy.

Gorbachev's initial stress on the "human factor"—firing incompetent managers, attacking alcoholism, replacing ministers, all to promote increased discipline and efficiency within the existing economic institutions—soon demonstrated its inadequacy. By 1987 his program was far more radical, the emphasis having shifted to changing or even abolishing the Stalinist institutions that simply did not work. But what was in theory intended to be radical change in practice produced many piecemeal, erratic, and sometimes contradictory policies. Early in 1987 a series of laws allowed cooperatives and even private businesses to engage in a range of economic activities that included operating restaurants, repair services, taxis, and small-scale manufacturing plants, although restrictions on private business in matters such as hiring remained stricter than on cooperatives. Later the range of opportunities open to cooperatives was expanded to include activities such as banking and foreign trade. By 1989 there were over 77,000 cooperatives employing over 1.4 million people in the Soviet Union; by 1990, 3 million workers, about

2.4 percent of the workforce, worked for cooperatives. But there were many problems, including mixed signals from the government. No sooner had the cooperatives been given the go signal when they were hit with impossibly high taxes, levies so excessive that they had to be lowered. In 1989 cooperatives and private businesses were hit by new rules that limited their activities and installed price controls. Cooperatives and private businesses also found they had to struggle to get supplies and materials from a socialist system that could not meet their needs because of either ineptitude or hostility. Some cooperatives and private businesses nonetheless were quite successful. At the same time, they ran up against public resentment in a country where enforced equality had been drummed into the national consciousness by seventy years of Soviet rule and, before that, centuries of communal peasant life. Worse still, many businesses had to pay protection money to criminal gangs. Those gangs were the building blocks of the expanding world of organized crime. As communism was fading away, criminality was taking its place.

While policies dealing with cooperatives and private businesses involved only a tiny percentage of the Soviet economy, equally vexing problems plagued Gorbachev's Enterprise Law, which covered the bulk of Soviet industry. Although the new law technically precluded economic ministries from telling an industrial enterprise what to produce, the ministries did what amounted to the same thing by using their leverage as customers to place orders for as much as 70 to 80 percent of production. In some cases the orders actually exceeded certain firms' total output. Another problem arose when the failure of many factories to produce goods of acceptable quality led to lower earnings for their workers. In January of 1987, for example, a large tractor factory failed to produce even one tractor that met the new standards.

A similar pattern of erratic radicalization marked Gorbachev's agricultural reforms. This was an area he knew especially well; he had earned a degree in agronomy in 1967 and had attempted to implement reforms during his term as Stavropol first secretary. As Soviet general secretary he began modestly. A 1986 decree increased incentives for collective farms by allowing them to sell part of their production on the free market. During mid-1988 and early 1989 Gorbachev moved from tinkering with Stalin's system to preparing to dismantle large parts of it. Declaring that the time had come "to return the man back to the land as its real master," Gorbachev won approval for a program under which peasants would be permitted to lease land, which in effect would have restored a form of private farming. The key task was finding suitable farmers after generations of what Gorbachev himself called "depeasantization" had driven the best farmers from the land and destroyed the initiative of many of those who remained. But current policies also were a part of the problem. One reason some peasants refused to step forward into the uncertain field of private farming was the regime's continued prohibition on land ownership. As late as 1990, Gorbachev himself told *Pravda* that "I . . . do not accept private ownership of land whatever you do with me." It therefore should not have been surprising that as of mid-1990 there were only 20,000 private farms in all of the Soviet Union; 12,000 were in Georgia and 5,700 in Latvia, while all of the RSFSR had 240 and the Ukraine—exactly 4 private farms.

Gorbachev and his colleagues tried many other tactics to jump-start the economy. They encouraged foreign companies, with some success, to establish joint ventures with Soviet firms. They negotiated several large loans from Western European banks. Soviet specialists traveled to the West to study management techniques. A start was made in converting some military factories, generally the best supplied and most efficient in the Soviet Union, to produce goods for civilian use. But the economy simply did not respond. Gorbachev found this out for himself in dramatic fashion during a Siberian tour in the fall of 1988. At a stop in Krasnoyarsk he was surrounded by angry citizens who told him, "Go to the store, Mikhail Sergeyevich; there is nothing there." To his promise to get results came the shout, "That won't happen." And, for the most part, it did not. Soviet harvests continued to be poor; the 1988 harvest was 40 million tons short of the target and the worst in three years, while overall agricultural production fell by 2 percent. Losses between the time crops ripened in the fields and orchards and reached consumers continued to be enormous. Industrial production rose slightly, but production in key industries continued to lag behind targets. The technological lag in key industries also remained; for example, a 1988 American intelligence report estimated a lag of eight to ten years in microcircuits and nine to fifteen in mainframe computers. Basic consumer goods such as tea, cheese, sausages, and salt were in short supply, and some were being rationed. In 1989, in part to prevent its diversion to the illegal production of spirits, sugar was rationed in Moscow for the first time since the end of World War II. The budget deficit soared, swollen by lost revenues from alcohol sales. In 1989 the government responded to consumer outrage by setting up an emergency fund to import a range of consumer goods from cassette tapes and soap powder to razor blades and pantyhose. To stem the flow of budgetary red ink, Prime Minister Nikolai Ryzhkov announced plans to cut the military budget by 33 percent by 1995. The government also announced it was scaling back its manned space program to save money.

NEW NATIONS RISING

Gorbachev's other major domestic concern was the minority nationalities question. While the roots of the Soviet Union's nationalities problem were embedded in the legacy of the multinational empire created by the tsars and preserved by the Bolsheviks, Gorbachev's policies inadvertently helped turn a serious situation into an uncontrollable crisis. As glasnost and democratization made the Soviet Union less repressive, ethnic grievances previously bottled up by police-state controls burst into the open. When they did, the new openness allowed them to expand and feed one another in a chain reaction of major and minor incidents that became impossible to manage.

Gorbachev's own words provide a good measure of how poorly he was prepared to deal with the nationalities question and how quickly the situation he faced escalated into a crisis. Shortly after coming to power, he referred to his country as "Russia" during a speech in Kiev, the capital of the Ukraine, correcting himself by referring to the "Soviet Union" only after being prompted by an aide. In his book *Perestroika*, written in 1987, Gorbachev penned the incredible remark that the "revolution and socialism had done away with national oppression and inequality" and that in the Soviet Union the nationalities question had been "solved in principle." He soon found out how terribly wrong he was. Where he saw economic and social integration and a commonly held Soviet identity, many non-Russians saw an empire based on oppressive rule. During 1987, as disturbances had already swept the country from the Baltic coast to Central Asia, Gorbachev remained optimistic, expressing his understanding of the notion that "every people wants to understand its roots," and answering "Of course not" to the question of whether this was at variance with socialism. By 1988 a subdued Gorbachev labeled the nationalities problem "a crucially important, vital issue in the USSR" and called for a "very thorough review of our nationalities policy." By 1989 a worried general secretary was denouncing "this multivoiced choir" from which he heard "threats of approaching chaos and talk of a threatened coup, and even of civil war."

The first serious signs of trouble occurred in December of 1986 in Kazakhstan when Gorbachev fired the longtime local party chief, an ethnic Kazakh known for his corruption, and replaced him with an ethnic Russian. This affront to national pride produced a full-fledged riot, complete with several killings, destruction of property, and attacks on militia troops. Far more serious trouble soon erupted along the Baltic coast and in the Caucasus. In 1987 in the tiny Baltic republics of Latvia, Lithuania, and Estonia, where memories of the short interwar period of independence lingered, there were demonstrations against the 1939 Nazi–Soviet pact that had ended that era. Soon the spontaneous shouts of "freedom, freedom, freedom" heard in demonstrations evolved into organized political movements called "Popular Fronts" in all three republics. In 1989 Lithuanian legislators declared the Soviet annexation of their country null and void, while the Soviet Ministry of Justice declared an Estonian voting law that discriminated against ethnic Russians to be unconstitutional. By the fall of that year, the fiftieth anniversary of the notorious pact, calls for economic autonomy and even independence echoed along the entire Baltic coast. In a stunning demonstration of solidarity, 2 million people linked hands in an unbroken line from Tallinn, Estonia, in the north through Latvia to Vilnius, Lithuania, in the south.

If the situation in the Baltic States was serious, at least it was bloodless. The same was not true in the Caucasus, where national hatreds, not for Russians, but for each other, pitted local populations against one another. The most serious problem was in the autonomous region of Nagorno-Karabakh, populated mainly by Christian Armenians but part of the largely Muslim Azerbaijan SSR. Beginning in early 1988 huge demonstrations and riots resulted in numerous deaths as Armenians demanded the territory be transferred to the neighboring Armenian SSR. The compromise solution, ruling the region directly from Moscow, satisfied no one. Moscow had to station over 50,000 troops there to keep the peace. In the summer and fall of 1989, taking advantage of the fact that Armenia received many of its supplies via a railroad line that crosses Azerbaijan, the Azerbaijanis clamped a blockade on their fraternal Soviet neighbor that lasted for two months. For good measure they blockaded Nagorno-Karabakh and did not lift the blockades until Moscow threatened to use the army to open the rail lines.

In Georgia, another Caucasian union republic, anti-Russian riots in the spring of 1989 led to several fatalities and a national scandal when troops used poison gas against the demonstrators. By the end of 1989, interethnic conflict in the Caucasus and in Central Asia had caused hundreds of deaths and created tens of thousands of refugees. But most disturbing were nationalist stirrings in the Ukraine, home of the largest non-Russian Soviet minority and producer of one-fourth of the nation's food and a third of its heavy industrial output. Tsarist and Soviet leaders alike always had come down especially hard on Ukrainian nationalism because of the region's strategic importance. In the summer of 1989, when Ukrainians were forming their Ukrainian Popular Movement, they were careful to say their goal was "rebirth" rather than independence, a tenuous distinction that did not significantly ease growing concerns in the Kremlin.

An old joke has it that the USSR was really the "Union of Silently Swallowed Republics." With the arrival of glasnost, they were not silent any more. As the 1980s waned, nationalism among non-Russians rivaled economic troubles on Gorbachev's worry list, having become a threat not only to Gorbachev and perestroika but to the Soviet Union itself.

NEW POLITICAL STRUCTURES

These developments took place against continued tension between Gorbachev and his conservative critics. While Gorbachev was on a foreign visit in March

1988, a leading Soviet magazine published a letter allegedly written by a Leningrad chemistry teacher named Nina Andreyeva but in fact inspired by Ligachev and other conservatives. The Andreyeva letter was a Stalinist attack, complete with anti-Semitic slanders, against Gorbachev's policies. More disturbing than its appearance was the paralysis in the perestroika camp. Without Gorbachev on the scene, the old fears, supposedly gone since 1985, reappeared again to haunt Moscow; nobody found the courage to defend perestroika, and the silence continued even after Gorbachev returned home. It took three weeks for Gorbachev to mount his counterattack, but when it finally came it was vigorous and included a rebuke to Ligachev from the Politburo.

Gorbachev's counteroffensive continued at the Nineteenth Party Conference in June 1988. Party conferences were second in importance only to congresses, although none had been called since 1941. The main business of the conference was the structure of the Soviet government: Gorbachev wanted to strengthen the state apparatus at the expense of the party, where he continued to face strong opposition to his reforms. In fact, if applause is any measure, the delegates decisively preferred Ligachev and his ideas to Gorbachev and his. Still, after heated debate the general secretary got his way. The conference voted to abolish the Supreme Soviet, the old Soviet parliament, and replace it with a 2,250-member Congress of People's Deputies, henceforth "the country's supreme body of power." Elections to this body would feature a radical innovation: there would be a choice of candidates. The Congress of People's Deputies would then elect a smaller body to conduct the nation's day-to-day business. It would have the same name—the Supreme Soviet—as the parliament that had just been abolished. While these changes lay in the future, one innovation was immediate: the conference debates were broadcast on Soviet television for all to see. As Gorbachev understated it, "I think we will not err from the truth by saying nothing of the kind has occurred in the country in six decades."

Gorbachev pressed his advantage in September at a Central Committee meeting. He removed Andrei Gromyko, the last powerful Brezhnev-era holdover, from the Politburo. A few days later Gromyko's government post as Soviet head of state went to Gorbachev. Although this was only a ceremonial position, Gorbachev increased his prestige by becoming his country's official leader. Ligachev meanwhile was weakened by being shifted from his post as Central Committee secretary responsible for ideology to the thankless agriculture slot.

In the spring of 1989 Gorbachev led the Soviet Union into the rough and uncharted waters of multicandidate electoral politics as voters chose their new Congress of People's Deputies. The elections, held in late March, were not completely democratic. One-third of the seats were reserved for the party and a variety of party-dominated "social" organizations. Old-line party bosses often kept reformers and dissidents off the ballot, so there were almost 400 seats for which only one candidate stood for election. Nonetheless, it was the most democratic election the country had seen since 1917, complete with campaign literature, boisterous rallies, and television debates. The results stunned everybody: 15 percent of the winners were not Communist Party members. This tendency was especially pronounced in several non-Russian republics. Outright dissidents, including Andrei Sakharov, won seats. Nor did the election of certain party members necessarily give the leadership comfort. In Moscow, Boris Yeltsin, so recently rejected by the party leadership, did better with the people: he won 89 percent of the vote. Yeltsin now began to emerge as a challenger to Gorbachev in two ways. First, he stood for increasing the pace and expanding the scope of reform. Second, unlike Gorbachev, who in the selection of the congress took one of the seats reserved for party officials, Yeltsin was elected directly by the people, which gave him a mandate the general secretary lacked. Of more immediate concern and most embarrassing for the party, some of its leaders running *without opposition* managed to lose when they could not garner 50 percent of the vote. Among these notable losers were the head of the Leningrad party organization, the mayor of Moscow, and the mayor of Kiev. Whatever he really thought, Gorbachev hailed the "people's power" that emerged from the election. Yet he must have been worried lest conservatives again accuse him of allowing perestroika to run out of control, as he quickly moved against them. In April, in another "cold purge," Gorbachev engineered the removal of 110 members of the Central Committee, including 74 full members. In their place 24 reformers became full members. Once again the military lost strength, its representation declining by 40 percent.

The Congress of People's Deputies met for the first time in late May 1989. Aside from being a historic political event, that initial meeting was the largest media hit in Soviet history. It was covered live on television across the country and watched by 70 percent of the population. One American observer compared it to the World Series in the United States. And there was a lot to see. Deputies of varying opinions spoke bluntly: Sakharov, for example, warned against allowing Gorbachev to accumulate too much power, and a former Olympic star lashed out against the KGB. The congress elected a 542-member Supreme Soviet, the country's new parliament, amid protests by dissidents at the congress that their members were being frozen out. The congress then elected Gorbachev to the post of chairman of the Supreme Soviet, the country's head of state, or president, under the newly established political system. Gorbachev received more than 95 percent of the vote, but not before he stood in front of the delegates to answer hard questions, respond to pointed criticism, and solemnly promise, "I will never allow the things that happened in our past to happen again."

Many others were determined to play their part in realizing Gorbachev's promise, even without his approval. During its six-week inaugural session in July and August, the Supreme Soviet showed surprising independence for a body whose membership was overwhelmingly Communist. Toward the end of its session, to Gorbachev's public dismay, a number of dissidents led by Yeltsin set up what they called the "Interregional Group," whose membership also included several hundred delegates from the larger Congress of People's Deputies. The Interregional Group, which within two days had established its own newspaper, in effect was the first formal opposition to the Communist Party the Soviet Union had seen in more than sixty-five years. Beyond that, it reflected the movement of some dissidents to a position where the agenda was no longer to reform the Soviet system, but to replace it with a genuine democracy.

PERESTROIKA FROM BELOW

These events were paralleled by the revival of another phenomenon not seen since the 1920s: a massive series of labor strikes. They began in July 1989 in the Kuznetsk Basin (the Kuzbas) of central Siberia, a major coal mining and industrial region first developed during the industrialization drive of the 1930s. Coal miners in the Kuzbas had long endured low wages, poor equipment, and meager supplies of food and other necessities. The issue that finally broke the camel's back was, of all things, soap. Miners in the Kuzbas, who spent their days hundreds of feet underground, had no soap to wash the dirt and grime off their bodies after a hard day's work. A wave of strikes spread to every mine in the Kuzbas in less than a day, and from there north to the Arctic Circle, west to the Ukraine, and east to Sakhalin Island. Within two weeks over 500,000 miners were on strike, seriously threatening the nation's coal supply at a time when economic conditions already were bad. Desperate to end a potentially crippling crisis, the government promised a package of improvements including pay raises and increased availability of food, medical supplies, and other consumer goods estimated to cost between $5 billion and $9 billion. While these concessions were enough to get the miners back to work, many mines maintained their strike committees to make sure the government delivered on its promises.

All of this caught the general secretary unprepared. Gorbachev's program of reform had begun as an initiative from the top, with every intention on the part of those in charge to keep all the controlling strings in their hands. Though different in content and more humane, Gorbachev's "reform from above" was in the Russian/Soviet tradition of change initiated and controlled by the state that ran from Stalin back to the days of the tsars. Peter the Great, Russia's first systematic practitioner of reform from above, would have recognized the general secretary's statist approach. But by mid-1989 something fundamental had changed in the Soviet Union. The rapid spread of glasnost, the explosive upsurge of minority nationalism, the surprisingly independent behavior of the Congress of People's Deputies and the Supreme Soviet, and the miners' strikes of 1989 that brought the Soviet working class into the picture as an active participant—none of which Gorbachev could control—marked the beginning of what amounted to a "revolution from below." This was neither an expected nor a welcome development to the architects of perestroika. As the revolution from below merged and inevitably clashed with their reform from above, it caused continual disruptions that made it ever more difficult for Gorbachev to keep a grip on events. After mid-1989, the general secretary and his colleagues, forced to become reactive rather than proactive, found it increasingly difficult to implement coherent policies or hold a steady course.

In September 1989 Gorbachev reinforced his position within the Communist Party by getting the Central Committee to remove several conservatives from the Politburo. However, in restaffing the Politburo Gorbachev ran directly into a growing problem he either overlooked or refused to see: party regulars who between 1985 and 1987 favored limited Andropov-style reforms were becoming convinced by 1989 that change in the Soviet Union was threatening their power and should be stopped and even reversed. This dilemma did not have a better symbol, or more dangerous personification, than Vladimir Kryuchkov, head of the KGB, who with Gorbachev's support vaulted over candidate status to full Politburo membership in September 1989. Almost exactly two years later, Kryuchkov was one of the party leaders, all of whom Gorbachev had promoted or supported, who tried to overthrow him and reverse perestroika.

THE COLLAPSE OF COMMUNISM IN
EASTERN EUROPE

Gorbachev's most urgent problems in 1989 were with Communist leaders outside the Soviet Union's borders. The one initiative that went reasonably smoothly was his visit to the People's Republic of China in May, ironically just before authorities there brutally massacred students in Beijing's Tiananmen Square who were demanding the same kinds of political reforms Gorbachev was instituting in the Soviet Union. In Eastern Europe it was Communist governments rather than the people that became the casualties of change. The first regime to fall was in Poland, where in April the Communist Party, desperately trying to shore up its popular support, legalized Solidarity and agreed to relatively free parliamentary elections. The Communists were routed by Solidarity-backed candidates when the elections were held two months later. In August this led to the formation of the first non-Communist-dominated government in Eastern Europe since the Communist takeover of Czechoslovakia in 1948. Gorbachev himself had pressured his Polish colleagues to allow this drastic step in light of their election defeat. Although Soviet troops were stationed in Poland and local Communists still controlled the country's military and police, the Communist hold on Poland was slipping away.

Meanwhile, 1956 began to repeat itself as Hungary took its cue from Poland. In May 1989 hundreds of miles of barbed wire came down as Hungary opened its border with the West. The following month Imre Nagy, the leader of the ill-fated 1956 revolt whom the Soviets had executed along with other leaders of the rebellion, was officially declared a national hero. In October Hungary's Communist Party abolished itself and became the Hungarian Socialist Party. A few days later the Hungarian People's Republic became the Republic of Hungary, a multiparty democracy that intended to hold its first elections the following spring. It turned out that the dreams of 1956, once dismissed as dead, had only been deferred.

Next the East European political earthquake hit East Germany, where it quickly reduced the country's hard-line regime, along with the Berlin Wall it had built, to rubble. East Germany, a bastion of Teutonic order and Communist orthodoxy, was supposedly the most successful Communist state in Eastern Europe. But no sooner did Hungary open its borders with the West in May than several thousand East Germans, mostly young and educated, and therefore a critical part of their country's future, crossed the Hungarian frontier into Austria. In September, as the flight of thousands of East Germans to the West continued, huge demonstrations on East German soil, the largest since the anti-Soviet uprising of 1953, demanded reforms. On October 18, party leader Erich Honecker resigned due to "ill health" after eighteen years in office. His replacement was Egon Krenz, at fifty-two the youngest of the old-line leaders and to most East Germans the perfect example of old wine in a new bottle. Krenz's promises of reform and his plea to his "dear fellow citizens" that "we need you all" (two weeks earlier the government had called the protesters "neo-Nazi thugs") were greeted with demonstrations that reached half a million strong, while tens of thousands continued to stream to the West.

Then what only weeks before had seemed unthinkable happened. The flood of refugees fleeing abroad, the thunder of protest of those staying put, and quaking political ground underneath the East German leadership combined to topple the Berlin Wall. On November 9, 1989, twenty-eight years after it built the wall to stop an earlier flood of refugees, the East German government announced the end of all travel restrictions to the West, including those via Berlin. The Berlin Wall—singular symbol of the Cold War; scene of spectacular escapes and fatal failed attempts at flight; dead zone of over 100 miles of concrete, steel, barbed wire, watchtowers, and minefields surrounding all of West Berlin; place of mourning for over a generation of Germans—suddenly became a place of jubilant celebration with thousands of people crossing back and forth at its checkpoints, drinking champagne, banging at the hated edifice with hammers, chisels, and sledgehammers, and literally dancing atop its concrete blocks. The irony was that at its festive death the wall remained what it was at its funereal birth: a giant monument to the failure of Soviet-style socialism in Eastern Europe.

The day after the Berlin Wall was opened Todor Zhivkov resigned after thirty-five years as the undisputed strongman in Bulgaria. Two weeks later, surrounded by reform in East Germany, Poland, and Hungary and pressured by political forces ranging from huge crowds in Prague's Wenceslas Square to Mikhail Gorbachev and his comrades in Moscow's Red Square, the hard-line Czechoslovakian Politburo resigned. By the end of December, Czechoslovakia had its first non-Communist government since 1948, headed by former dissident playwright Vaclav Havel, while Alexander Dubček, the tragic hero of his country's ill-fated 1968 precursor to perestroika, emerged in triumph as chairman of the national parliament. Back in East Germany Egon Krenz and his entire Politburo resigned. Change also finally came to Romania but, unlike elsewhere in Eastern Europe, only after extensive violence. In mid-December Nicolae Ceaușescu's secret police forces brutally attacked thousands of pro-democracy demonstrators. But the demonstrations continued, and when the Romanian army refused orders to kill the people it was supposed to protect and joined them instead, protest became revolution. Several days of bloody fighting followed, during which Ceaușescu and his wife Elena, were captured while trying to flee and executed. A quickly formed National Salvation Front then took power and promised a multiparty political system and free elections. By the end of December, all the presumed Soviet allies in Eastern Europe—Poland, Hungary, East Germany, Czechoslovakia, Bulgaria, and Romania—had changed their laws to deprive their respective Communist parties of a monopoly on political power. As 1989, Europe's "year of the people," came to a close, the end also came for the Communist satellite system and security zone that was the Soviet Union's great prize from World War II and a cornerstone of its foreign policy since 1945.

Moscow did nothing to stop the continental Communist collapse. In effect, the Gorbachev regime seemed to have quickly revised the Soviet Union's security formulas and written off the control of an increasingly expensive and unreliable Eastern Europe in favor of achieving security through normalized relations with the United States and Western Europe.

GERMAN REUNIFICATION

The new year, 1990, ushered in a new decade, with new expectations and concerns. Whereas in 1985 there were few in either the Soviet Union or the West who thought the Soviet regime, despite its problems, was in danger, by 1990 it was visibly beginning to totter. The process of change clearly was not merely accelerating; it was careening out of control and turning into chaos, the most dangerous developments being the unraveling economy and the spreading and increasingly violent ethnic strife. Gorbachev, the internationally acclaimed political sorcerer, was being turned by events into a sorcerer's apprentice, unable to manage the upheavals his policies had unleashed.

The one area where Gorbachev could still claim success was in foreign policy, as relations with the West continued to improve. But even there, Soviet policy was looking to critics at home more like a headlong retreat from superpower status and an unending acquiescence to Western demands. During the early part of the year, the Soviet Union reached agreements with Czechoslovakia and Hungary for the withdrawal of its troops. It also restored relations with the Vatican after a break of sixty-seven years. Far more significant, the fall of the Berlin Wall had raised the question of whether Germany would be reunified. That question was answered during the autumn of 1990. But that settlement was based on Western, and especially German, terms, not Soviet ones. There was in fact no great enthusiasm in the West for immediate German reunification, but both Soviet opposition and Western hesitancy proved unable to derail the blitzkrieg diplomatic campaign launched by West German Chancellor Helmut Kohl, who lavished assurances about Germany's peaceful intentions on leaders from Washington to Moscow. In the end, Gorbachev accepted both German reunification and a united Germany's membership in NATO, the latter condition representing a repudiation of Soviet policy that dated from the formation of NATO in 1949. In return, the Germans agreed to limit the size of their army to 370,000 troops; to renounce chemical, biological, and nuclear weapons; and to provide the Soviet Union with about $8 billion in desperately needed aid. Germany's formal reunification, and with it the liquidation of the Soviet role in Eastern and Central Europe, took place on October 3, 1990.

THE END OF THE COLD WAR

The reunification of Germany was followed within a month by a NATO/ Warsaw Pact arms agreement limiting conventional arms in Europe. Two days later, on November 21, 1990, the United States, Canada, the Soviet Union, and every European nation except Albania signed the Charter of Paris, which proclaimed the end of the Cold War. It seemed anticlimactic and not a touch ironic that this titanic struggle, which had brought the world to the brink of nuclear destruction, spawned the greatest arms race in history, divided the European continent in two, and consumed one of the world's two superpowers and weakened the other, was concluded with the short, bland statement that the "era of confrontation and division of Europe has ended."

The Soviet Union became the first beneficiary of the Cold War's demise when Western European nations and the United States began sending emergency aid to cope with urgent shortages of essentials, including food. Meanwhile, the Kremlin was already abandoning old Cold War habits by supporting the international effort to force Iraq, which had invaded and occupied Kuwait in August 1990, to withdraw from its oil-rich neighbor. After economic sanctions failed to budge the Iraqis, the Soviets did not interfere when a U.S.-led coalition used military force early in 1991 to expel their former client from Kuwait. While this development was welcomed in the West, it did not sit well among Gorbachev's conservative critics in Moscow, who viewed his foreign policy, especially his readiness to give up Eastern Europe, as capitulation rather than cooperation. They were not impressed when on October 15, 1990, the Norwegian Nobel Committee announced that the 1990 recipient of the Nobel Peace Prize was Mikhail Sergeyevich Gorbachev. The Soviet old guard suffered another blow, symbolic but still painful, when the Warsaw Pact formally disbanded on July 1, 1991. Nor was Gorbachev's performance a few weeks later at a meeting with the world's seven leading capitalist industrial nations sufficient tonic for his ailing reputation at home, as he failed to win any solid commitments for large-scale economic aid. On July 31, Gorbachev and President Bush signed another breakthrough arms reduction treaty, the START I (Strategic Arms Reduction Treaty) agreement, which called for the Soviet Union and the United States to reduce their long-range nuclear weapons by 30 percent. But by then, as the world soon found out, time was rapidly running out not only for Gorbachev, but for the Soviet Union itself.

GORBACHEV AND YELTSIN

By early 1990 the Soviet political arena provided increasing evidence that Gorbachev was both losing control of events at home and failing to adjust to new political conditions. In February and March local elections across large parts of the Soviet Union saw Communist Party candidates rejected en masse. This trouncing included the loss of majorities in the Moscow, Leningrad, and

Kiev city councils to non-Communists. Gorbachev's conduct as these events unfolded was a good example of what Yevgeny Yevtushenko called "half measures" in his poem of that name. In February Gorbachev appeared to be making necessary adaptations when, after a bitter debate, he convinced the Central Committee of the Communist Party to agree to the repeal of Article 6 of the Soviet constitution, which guaranteed the party's monopoly on political power. In mid-March, again at Gorbachev's urging, the Congress of People's Deputies formally repealed that article. However, Gorbachev then retreated back to the old politics. When the Congress of People's deputies repealed Article 6, it also heeded Gorbachev's call to establish a strong executive presidency, a head of state who would be elected directly by the people. But rather than risk going to the people for the mandate he so desperately needed, Gorbachev had the congress bypass the new direct election statute and elect him president of the Soviet Union; a direct election by the people would have to wait until 1995. To be sure, as president, Gorbachev now had more power than before, but neither he nor the Congress of Deputies could give the presidency the authority and respect that could come only from its occupant being chosen by the people.

For the time being, that failing did not affect Gorbachev's well-established ability to manipulate the Communist Party, although that was not always an easy task. At the party's Twenty-Eighth Congress in July, conservative delegates denounced what Ligachev called Gorbachev's "blind radicalism." Still, Gorbachev was able to push Ligachev into retirement and keep the conservatives in check. He convinced the delegates to create a new post—deputy general secretary—responsible for supervising the day-to-day party operations while General Secretary Gorbachev concentrated on his presidential duties. The delegates also approved Gorbachev's plan to overhaul and weaken the Politburo. Its new membership, with the exception of Gorbachev himself, contained no prominent politicians, turning that body into what one observer called "a long list of nobodies." In that banal way, in July of 1990, the Politburo's role in governing the country, a role it had played since March of 1919, quietly came to an end. Overall, Gorbachev seemed to be trying to get away with yet another half measure: slowly pushing the party aside and gradually distancing himself from it, but without pushing too fast or far or completely cutting his ties to what increasingly looked like a sinking ship.

Gorbachev's failure to adjust to the emerging new political culture and get a direct mandate from the people compared unfavorably with the approach of his new rival, Boris Yeltsin. Yeltsin had triumphantly revived his political fortunes in 1989 when the people of Moscow elected him to the Congress of People's Deputies with the largest majority of any candidate. In the 1990 local elections Yeltsin was elected once again, this time to the new parliament of the Russian Republic. In May 1990 he overcame Gorbachev's backing of a rival candidate and was elected by parliament as the president of the Russian Republic. Yeltsin's best act of political theater occurred in July 1990 at the Communist Party's Twenty-Eighth Congress, when he dramatically announced his resignation from the party after a short speech and strode out of the hall, leaving 4,700 stunned delegates and the old Soviet politics behind while simultaneously planting both feet firmly in the new political arena forming outside the party. He was followed out of the party by a number of other radicals, including Leningrad mayor Anatoly Sobchak and Moscow mayor Gavril Popov. Gorbachev remained behind, both physically and politically, to manage what was left of the dispirited party.

RETREAT FROM REFORM

While these high-level meetings were taking place in Moscow, the regime's authority was crumbling across the country. On March 11, 1990, Lithuania, where anti-Soviet nationalists had won an overwhelming victory in local elections, declared its independence. Although the declaration lacked practical significance—it was revoked three months later after immense pressure from Gorbachev that included moving troops into the Lithuanian capital of Vilnius—it was an important symbol of defiance. By December 12, when the small Central Asian republic of Kyrgyzstan made its announcement, all fifteen Soviet republics, including Russia, had declared their "sovereignty," a term sufficiently vague to avoid a reaction from Moscow but still indicative of how low the Kremlin's authority had sunk.

In the meantime, Gorbachev was retreating from reform. In October 1990 he rejected a radical economic reform program dubbed the "500 Days Plan," which would have moved the Soviet Union to a market economy over a period of about sixteen months. The Soviet president seems to have been motivated by three factors: his perception that growing chaos threatened the country's survival; the fear that the short-term hardship caused by economic reform—especially the sharp rise in the prices of food and other necessities—would lead to dangerous public unrest; and nasty rumblings from powerful conservative forces, including the military. Then on December 2, 1990, Gorbachev stunned and demoralized the pro-reform camp when he removed reformer Vadim Bakatin, his interior minister (and as such the official in charge of the police), and replaced him with Boris Pugo, a hard-line conservative. Less than three weeks later, Eduard Shevardnadze resigned as foreign minister with a chilling warning: "The reformers have headed for the hills. Dictatorship is coming." Shevardnadze's warning gained credibility in January 1991 when elite Soviet army troops equipped with tanks and machine guns stormed the central radio station and television station in Vilnius, Lithuania, killing 13 people and injuring over 200. Gorbachev denied he knew anything about plans to strike against the Lithuanians, but he also refused to condemn the action. Despite angry public protests he continued his retreat during January and February. He appointed Valentin Pavlov, a staunch conservative, as prime minister, authorized army patrols of Soviet cities to reinforce local police, and called for a law limiting the freedom of the press. By early 1991 almost all of Gorbachev's old perestroika team—including Shevardnadze, Yakovlev, economic advisor Stanislav Shatalin, and Bakatin—had left or been dropped from the government. They were replaced with conservatives, men like Pugo, Prime Minister Pavlov, and KGB chief Vladimir Kryuchkov. Perestroika had become Janus-faced, as it seemed to be turning from reform to reaction.

None of these actions had any noticeable effect on the spreading revolt of the minority nationalities and the collapsing economy, twin threats that continued to undermine both Gorbachev and the Soviet Union itself. On the nationalities front, the fifteen declarations of sovereignty of 1990 were followed in early 1991 by two referenda, in Lithuania and Georgia, in which local voters overwhelmingly cast their ballots for independence. Inter-ethnic hatred continued to fester and occasionally explode across the country, as in the Armenian/Azerbaijani conflict, rioting in Georgia between Georgians and Ossetians, and violence in the Uzbek and Kyrgyz republics.

The economic news for the first half of 1991 was no better. The year began with widespread food shortages, as the collapse of the old central distribution system left a large part of the 1990 grain harvest rotting either in the fields or while en route to market. Inflation rose, state shops remained empty, national income dropped by about 10 percent, and production fell in key industries. The transition to private agriculture, one of the main hopes for economic renewal, proceeded at a snail's pace, and the forecast for the coming harvest was gloomy. In Moscow, the city council began rationing meat, grain, and vodka. A major cause of these difficulties was Gorbachev's search, dating from 1987, for a workable economic program that could appeal to both the conservatives on his right flank and the radicals on his left. He had started dismantling parts of the old Stalinist command system but not taken the radical steps necessary to permit the development of a market economy. The result was summed up by one distressed official who observed that "We have completely destroyed the old system and proposed nothing in its place."

GORBACHEV'S LAST GAMBIT

It was against this background that Gorbachev tried his last major gambit as Soviet president: he turned away from the conservatives and back to the reformers. In March 1991 the nation held its first-ever referendum when citizens voted on Gorbachev's question as to whether the Soviet Union should continue to exist as a united country. Gorbachev got the answer he wanted: three-quarters of those voting on the vaguely worded question answered "yes." However, that figure was less impressive than it looked because six republics, including all three Baltic republics, boycotted the election. The March voting yielded another "yes," but one that Gorbachev did not want: Yeltsin supporters asked voters in the Russian republic if they wanted to elect their president directly instead of through their parliament. After 70 percent of the voters answered affirmatively, Yeltsin swept to victory in June 1991 with over 57 percent of the vote, as compared to 17 percent for Nikolai Ryzhkov, the Communist Party candidate. On July 10, in a ceremony in which he spurned the Communist Party while accepting the blessing of the Russian Orthodox Church, Boris Yeltsin was inaugurated as the first freely elected leader in Russia's history. Yeltsin, whose personal mandate now spanned the Soviet Union's largest republic, had eclipsed Gorbachev.

The Soviet president, however, continued to push forward into a growing storm. In April 1991 he and the leaders of nine Soviet republics, including President Yeltsin, worked out what was called the "nine plus one" agreement for a new union treaty. This was an attempt to hold the union together by giving the individual republics considerable power to run their own affairs. But by the middle of 1991 the center was no longer holding. On one flank conservatives were denouncing Gorbachev openly and gathering their forces against him, determined to prevent the new union treaty, which would have cut many of the central government's powers and hence their own, from taking effect. On the other flank, Yeltsin, his supporters, and other radical reformers had given up on Gorbachev. Early in August, Alexander Yakovlev, the godfather of Gorbachev's perestroika, warned of an impending coup against his former colleague. By then Gorbachev had left Moscow for a vacation in the Crimea, his last, it turned out, as president of the Soviet Union.

THE AUGUST COUP

On the morning of August 19, 1991, the world awoke to the shocking news that Mikhail Gorbachev had been removed from office, allegedly "for health reasons." A group of hard-line Communist Party leaders, officially led by the new "president" Gennady Yanayev, announced that it had taken control of the country. Despite all warnings, the coup still came as a shock to most observers, who had been worried more about food shortages during the coming winter than about a coup d'état during the summer. As Gorbachev sat stunned under house arrest in the Crimea, he learned that he had been betrayed by the same men he had recently promoted and sponsored. They included Pugo and Kryuchkov (the two central conspirators), Defense Minister Yazov, Vladimir Ivashko (the man Gorbachev had just made the party's deputy general secretary), and, most painfully, Anatoly Lukyanov, Gorbachev's friend and associate from his university days, who knew about the plot even though he did not actively join in it.

The technical reasons for the failure of the coup are well known. The coup leaders, two of whom were drunk while critical events unfolded, did not begin with mass arrests of potential resistance leaders, notably Russian President Boris Yeltsin. This allowed Yeltsin to rally the resistance from a perch atop a tank in front of his newly established headquarters, the Russian parliament building (called the White House) in the center of Moscow. The plotters did not make sure that vital military and KGB troops were prepared to follow orders, and in fact they waited six hours before deploying troops and tanks in Moscow. By the time the conspirators were ready to use force, crowds had gathered around the White House. Among the luminaries who joined them were Moscow's mayor Gavril Popov, former foreign minister Shevardnadze, poet Yevgeny Yevtushenko, and Elena Bonner, the widow of Andrei Sakharov. The crowds that defied the plotters were not massive by the standards of major historical events, never numbering more than 150,000 in Moscow and 200,000 in Leningrad; the crowds that defied the Eastern European Communist regimes in far smaller cities were several times larger. Most Soviet citizens, in fact, stayed on the sidelines and waited.

Yet Yeltsin's hundreds of thousands were enough, even though their barricades were, as one Soviet commander put it, "like toys" that his troops could have overcome in "fifteen minutes." The price, however, would have been a bloodbath, and this the military refused to pay. The soldiers would not defy a sign hanging near Yeltsin's headquarters that told them "Don't Shoot Your Mothers" or shoot at a crowd that stuffed flowers into the gun barrels of their armored vehicles. Individual tanks, paratroopers, and entire units defected to the resistance at the start. The KGB elite troops refused to attack Yeltsin's headquarters. Yeltsin's personal ties with the troops and their commanders paid off when the commander of the air force opposed the coup. Meanwhile, opposition to the coup spread across the country. Leaders of several republics rallied against the coup, and coal miners struck against it. Finally, support for Gorbachev and Yeltsin came from abroad, most importantly from the United States, which refused to recognize and legitimize the new government. By August 21, 1991, it was all over, and the plotters were under detention. On August 22, a pale and visibly shaken Mikhail Gorbachev returned to Moscow, once again the president of the Soviet Union.

These are the surface details. The fundamental reasons for the coup's failure lie deeper. It was undertaken to reverse the process of change in the Soviet Union but failed because the change perestroika had unleashed already had gone too far. For example, by 1991 the conspirators had to base their actions on some sort of legal norms or risk a potentially dangerous public reaction. One of the reasons the conspirators did not begin with a campaign of mass arrests that would have included Yeltsin is that they wanted to avoid overt illegality. To bolster their legal credentials they cited Article 127 of the Soviet constitution, which justified removing the president if he proved unable to perform his duties because of health problems. In other words, the new conditions in Gorbachev's Soviet Union created what one observer has called the need for "legal cover,"[7] but getting it in turn helped to undermine the coup and contributed to its failure. At the same time, the country had changed enough so that soldiers refused to fire on their countrymen—this in a country where at one time children were expected to betray their parents. The Soviet Union also had changed to the point where fear no longer could immobilize everyone. As recently as 1988, the Andreyeva letter had paralyzed the reformers until Gorbachev, their knight in shining armor, returned from abroad to rally his frightened legions. But in August 1991 there were hundreds of thousands of ordinary citizens who were not afraid to stand up against dictatorship, a small force in a country of 290 million, but just enough to thwart the coup. They succeeded in part because since 1985 the continual waves of change had hollowed out the Communist Party (about one-fifth of its membership had already quit) and demoralized the army, two essential pillars of the order the conspirators hoped to save. Those waves also had eroded the foundations of the Soviet Union itself, which by the summer of 1991 was so weakened that it collapsed with barely a shove a few months later.

In short, despite its obvious failings, perestroika had succeeded in its most important task: to make it impossible to turn the clock back. In August 1991 Boris Yeltsin was the hero of the moment. But even though he was unable to join the pivotal August battle, Mikhail Gorbachev remained, to paraphrase Russia's great nineteenth-century poet and novelist Mikhail Lermontov, the hero of that time.

THE END OF THE SOVIET UNION

Prior to the August coup, Soviet Communism had been dying a slow death; the coup pulled it off life support and killed it. Yeltsin immediately banned the Communist Party in the Russian Republic, while Gorbachev resigned as its general secretary and ordered that party property be seized. The top leaders of the KGB and army were dismissed, and many of them were arrested. Central ministries of the government were closed down and their functions transferred to the republics. The Komsomol dissolved itself. A wholesale renaming of cities and towns began, the most symbolic of which was Leningrad's change to St. Petersburg. On November 7, 1991, there was no official celebration of the Bolshevik Revolution.

As Communism collapsed inside the Soviet Union, the union itself disintegrated. Early in September, Lithuania, Latvia, and Estonia won Soviet recognition as independent countries. Gorbachev then undertook a last-ditch attempt to hold the rest of the Soviet Union together. His effort was futile. In a referendum on December 1, 1991, the Ukraine voted overwhelmingly for independence. A week later, Boris Yeltsin and the leaders of the Ukraine and Belorussia banged the last nail into the Soviet Union's coffin when they announced the formation of what they called the Commonwealth of Independent States (CIS). The CIS was vaguely projected as a loosely organized body of fully independent nations. Despite Gorbachev's vocal opposition, less than two weeks later the CIS was formally constituted by eleven of the former Soviet republics. The three Baltic states and Georgia remained outside its loose embrace.

On December 25, 1991, Mikhail Gorbachev resigned as the president of the nonexistent Soviet Union. At 7:32 P.M., moments after he finished his resignation speech, the red Soviet flag was lowered from over the Kremlin for the last time. The official end came at midnight, December 31, 1991. The Union of Soviet Socialist Republics, the embodiment of a bold and brutal social experiment that once had claimed to own the future, now belonged to the past.

THE GORBACHEV LEGACY: SUCCESS IN FAILURE

Mikhail Gorbachev came to power determined to reform, and thereby preserve, the Soviet system. He wanted to purge it of what he considered the Stalinist perversions of Leninism and put the country back on what he believed was the true Leninist path. His objective was to build a humane form of socialism consistent with Marxism and Leninism as he understood them. In these goals he was very much like Khrushchev, and like Khrushchev he failed. Instead of reforming the system, Gorbachev's policies destabilized it and hastened its demise. Gorbachev could not easily accept what had happened; even after the failed coup he argued against both the banning of the Communist Party and the dissolution of the Soviet Union. As late as mid-December 1991, when there was nothing of the old order left for him to save, he warned his countrymen that "We are destroying a state that needs to be reformed."

It was the statement of an authentic Marxist true believer, one of the last, albeit one of the most dynamic and charismatic, of a dying breed. It was also the statement of a political figure Karl Marx would have scorned for desperately trying to use intellect and political will to accomplish the most un-Marxist objective of reconciling incompatible economic and political elements in a new society. In making that attempt, Gorbachev the politician had set for himself a task even more formidable than what modern physicists try to do with their cyclotrons. The physicists are satisfied to create new transuranic elements for an instant simply for study; Gorbachev wanted to create a durable trans-capitalist, trans-Communist society to be lived in. But that society was to be composed of the economic and political equivalents of matter and antimatter, particles that cannot coexist and in fact annihilate each other on contact. In Gorbachev's new perestroika universe, individual initiative in a genuine marketplace was to meld with a planned, state-owned economy to produce "market socialism." Genuine political democracy was to combine with the rule of the Communist Party and create "socialist pluralism." And non-Russian nationalist aspirations were to be reconciled with the continued existence of a cohesive political entity inside a "Union of Sovereign States." It was a vision grand enough to match any of the idealistic schemes of non-Marxist socialist thinkers that Marx and Engels so contemptuously dismissed as "utopian" more than 140 years earlier in *The Communist Manifesto.*

But if Gorbachev's vision proved to be a mirage, in the broader historical sense his achievements dwarf his failures, both in the possibilities his leadership created for the people of the Soviet Union and in the example he provided as a statesman. What made Mikhail Gorbachev an outstanding political leader is that he possessed the vision to see further and wider than other Soviet party leaders and had the courage to try new policies, despite the opposition of powerful entrenched forces and the danger that untested policies could fail and backfire. Trapped with his country in a dark tunnel seven decades long, Gorbachev had the will and strength to lead his people toward the light. As he did so, often stumbling in the treacherous darkness, sometimes reversing his field, but always returning to the original course, his policies made possible the end of the Cold War. Those same policies also gradually freed the Soviet people from the fear that had silenced them since Stalin's terror, which is why the conspirators of August 1991 were thwarted by hundreds of thousands of demonstrators, by soldiers who would not kill their fellow citizens, and by politicians who were prepared to defend the gains of the previous six years. This process of liberation from fear took time, which Gorbachev provided with his six-year daredevil high-wire political balancing act that showcased his remarkable political skills. In short, although in 1991 Gorbachev was unable to break with the old system, his policies created the conditions that allowed others to do so.

Given the realities of the Soviet system, none of the weak and scattered groups of dissidents that predated Gorbachev's election as general secretary could budge or dent the party dictatorship that controlled the country. Only an extraordinary member of the Communist Party power structure could have led the country out of the totalitarian quagmire in which it still was trapped in 1985 to the point where it could finally break free from that system, and do so with a minimum of bloodshed. Mikhail Gorbachev was that man, and he therefore is deserving of the title one Russian intellectual bestowed on him: "the one great Russian reformer." As Archie Brown has observed in his biography of Gorbachev:

> He presided over, and facilitated, the introduction of freedom of speech, freedom of the press, freedom of association, religious freedom, and freedom of movement, and left Russia a *freer country* than it had been in its long history.[8]

Gorbachev also will be remembered as a leader who recognized that his goals of making society freer and more humane precluded the use of certain methods. As political scientist Michael Mandelbaum put it:

> Mikhail Gorbachev's character, however flawed, was marked by a basic decency missing in every previous leader of the Soviet Union and indeed in every ruler of imperial Russia before that. He refused to shoot. He refused—with the exception of several episodes in the Baltics and the Caucasus in which civilians were killed—to countenance the use of violence against the citizens of his country and of Eastern Europe. . . . For this alone he deserved the Nobel Peace Prize he received . . . and deserves as well the place of honor he will occupy in the history of the twentieth century.[9]

Perhaps the most compelling tribute of the many one could cite came from Boris Yeltsin, Gorbachev's rival and the man who eventually pushed him out of the Kremlin:

> What he has achieved will, of course, go down in the history of mankind. I do not like high-sounding praise, yet everything Gorbachev has initiated deserves much praise. He could have gone on just as Brezhnev and Chernenko did before him. . . . He could have draped himself with orders and medals. . . . Yet Gorbachev chose another way. He started by climbing a mountain whose summit is not even visible. It is somewhere up in the clouds and no one knows how the ascent will end: Will we all be swept away by an avalanche or will this Everest be conquered?[10]

THE LEGACY OF TOTALITARIANISM

That said, there are several basic reasons why Gorbachev, his immense political skills notwithstanding, could not save the Soviet system. First of all, he really never fully understood the forces his policies had unleashed, especially how they were affecting the Soviet people and their attitudes toward perestroika in general and him in particular. Both his lack of knowledge about economics and his unwillingness to implement essential market reforms led to policies that killed the old economic system but could not give birth to a new one. As the old economy collapsed, shortages of food and essential consumer goods hit the general population hard, causing Gorbachev's popularity, so essential to his ability to carry out his program, to plummet. Respected and lionized abroad, especially in the prosperous West, he was increasingly disliked and ridiculed at home by ordinary people whose economic condition rapidly went from bad to worse. Gorbachev was also blind to the nationalities problem for far too long. Even after non-Russians began to raise their voices in the era of glasnost, Gorbachev failed to listen to them and so did not comprehend how resentful they were. As late in the day as December 1991, he was shocked when the Ukraine voted to leave the USSR. There were also serious limits to Gorbachev's understanding of freedom and democracy, which is why he thought that he could allow just a little glasnost and democracy and then perhaps dole out some more bit by bit at times of his own choosing. But following the logic of openness and freedom, both glasnost and democracy rapidly took on lives of their own and raced ahead beyond the bounds Gorbachev wanted, becoming a radical and uncontrollable genie out of the bottle rather than Gorbachev's desired manageable servant of socialist reform. Gorbachev, ultimately a product of a dictatorial system, reacted to this development with imperious disdain and anger. Each passing day, especially after 1989, left him more and more out of step with the times and therefore unable to respond effectively to new and unfamiliar challenges.

Gorbachev's foreign policy played a major role in undermining Communism at home. As he moved away from the Cold War, he deprived the Soviet system of the implacable outside enemy needed to justify its Marxist ideology, its low standard of living, and the dictatorship it imposed on the people. In addition, when Gorbachev permitted the Communist regimes in Eastern Europe to collapse without a protest, a chain reaction began that did not stop until it reached the Kremlin itself and shook down its Communist walls. No invader from the west, not even Napoleon or Hitler, ever swept eastward more relentlessly from the Polish frontier into the Russian heartland, brushing aside all opposition as it bore down on Moscow and the Kremlin, than did the idea of overthrowing communism after the Eastern European revolutions of 1989.

The core reason that Gorbachev failed, and what ultimately rendered his hope of reforming the system futile, lies deeper, however, than any specific policy error or misjudgment. It lies in the totalitarian nature of Soviet society. The Gorbachev era was a revelatory event regarding the fundamental nature of the Soviet Union for many people, including Western specialists in Soviet affairs. For example, the claims made during the 1980s by some revisionist historians that the number of deaths caused by the Stalin regime had been grossly overestimated—one revisionist number-cruncher miraculously reduced the toll in Stalin's great terror to "thousands"—and that the fear caused by Stalin's great purge and terror did not grip the entire country, have been laid to rest and buried under an avalanche of personal testimony, archival records, and physical evidence that has emerged since 1985. The most grisly "documentation" is what might be called the Gulag Archipelago's subterranean islands, a series of mass graves scattered, as the camps themselves once were, throughout the country. Just two of them, burial grounds at Kuropaty near Minsk and at Bykovna near Kiev, contain at least 50,000 and 30,000 victims of Stalin's terror, respectively, and possibly several times that number. Far more widespread among Western scholars than any absurd revisionist diminution of the scope of Stalin's terror was the idea that the Soviet Union after Stalin was not a totalitarian state but rather an "authoritarian" society where a variety of interest groups shared power. This school of thought also has tended to deemphasize Lenin's responsibility for the development of Stalinism and draw a sharp distinction between Lenin's and Stalin's respective regimes. But while the totalitarian view of the Soviet Union does not always account for every twist and turn in Soviet history—what can?—it does explain the essence of Soviet society and what made it different from other systems. As historian Geoffrey Hosking has observed, the concept of totalitarianism

> is capable of affording us a more complete view of Soviet society than any alternative yet propounded. . . . Remove the term "totalitarian," and it is not obvious how the Soviet Union differs from, say, Spain under Franco or Chile under Pinochet. But these differences are crucial.[11]

These differences certainly were not lost on Soviet leaders and commentators of the post-1985 era, who regularly used the term "totalitarian" to describe the system they were trying to dismantle more than thirty years after Stalin's death. Thus in his resignation speech, Gorbachev summed up his accomplishments by noting that the "totalitarian system that long ago deprived the country of an opportunity to succeed and prosper has been eliminated," while in his autobiography Yeltsin thanked Gorbachev for embarking on reform rather than being satisfied to "have lived the well-fed and happy life of the leader of a totalitarian state."

And it is precisely the totalitarian structure of Soviet society that best explains both how resistant it was to Gorbachev's reforms and why it collapsed so quickly and completely as change finally began to take root. It was not a variety of interest groups, but the Communist Party that ran Soviet society. The party dominated the economy, the state, and the social institutions of the Soviet Union. As scholar Theodore Draper observed, "this system was held together by the total control of the Communist Party."[12] Gorbachev's reforms undermined the party; that is why they were so destabilizing to a system that until 1985, whatever its problems, both appeared to be and indeed was relatively stable, even as it stood on corroded foundations. Once the party's power began to crumble from the relentless erosion caused by Gorbachev's reforms, the entire Soviet system began to disintegrate. Or, as historian Martin Malia succinctly put it, "such a total collapse could only proceed from a total society."[13]

The collapse was total because it did not stop at the demise of Stalinism— that is, those aspects of Soviet society that could be traced directly to the Stalin era—as Gorbachev had hoped and as those who would decouple Leninism and Stalinism might have expected. Nor could it because Leninism, while it did not feature the mad, murderous terror of Stalinism, was the totalitarian foundation upon which Stalinism was built. Lenin, not Stalin, gave the Soviet Union the one-party dictatorship, buttressed by its secret police, that claimed total control over all aspects of life in the new socialist world. To Lenin's work Stalin added the centralized command economy and an expanded secret police apparatus to carry out his terror and consolidate his personal dictatorial rule. With the important exceptions of Stalin's terror and the Gulag, the entire Lenin–Stalin edifice remained in place after Stalin's death to serve the party dictatorship of his successors for more than three decades. The institutions created under Lenin's Bolshevik dictatorship of the 1920s and Stalin's personal dictatorship of the 1930s were inextricably fused and part of the same structure, and that is why they collapsed and were swept away together when the tidal wave of freedom washed over them. Nothing could better symbolize that basic fact than what occurred in Moscow and Leningrad, the Soviet Union's two main cities, immediately after the defeat of the August coup. In Leningrad, the citizens repudiated their city's Bolshevik name and restored the name, St. Petersburg, given to it by its founding tsar. In Moscow, the first thing to come down was the huge statue of Felix Dzerzhinsky, one of Lenin's most loyal supporters and the founder of the secret police, set up by the Bolsheviks barely a month after they came to power and used to entrench and protect their dictatorship. The people, to whom Marxists are supposed to appeal as the ultimate authority, were not drawing fine distinctions. When an elderly Moscow woman watching the removal of the hated "Iron Felix" told an

American reporter, "We are sick of all Communists. They have been strangling us for seventy years," she was not limiting her critique to Stalinism.

The Russia that emerged from the stranglehold of failed communism and the debacle of the fallen Soviet Union was still a giant, in some ways even a colossus, but a badly wounded one. It was plagued by ominous political, economic, and social problems that required urgent attention. Although still the world's largest country in terms of area and its second-ranking nuclear power, as well as the inheritor of the former Soviet Union's seat on the U.N. Security Council, Russia could no longer be called a superpower and was shorn of most of the empire it had ruled for centuries. Its future, while potentially promising, contained equal potential for turmoil. In short, after more than seven decades on a revolutionary path that many Russians bitterly called the "road to nowhere," the country had come full circle. Amid the rubble of a fallen regime and in the face of extremely difficult conditions, Russia faced the unenviable task of beginning again.

NOTES

1. Yevgeny Yevtushenko, "Half Measures," in *Twentieth Century Russian Poetry: Silver and Steel*, selected, with an introduction, by Yevgeny Yevtushenko, edited and translated by Albert C. Todd (New York: Doubleday, 1994), p. 818.

2. Moshe Lewin, *The Gorbachev Phenomenon: A Historical Interpretation* (Berkeley and Los Angeles: University of California Press, 1988), p. 24.

3. S. Frederick Starr, "Soviet Union: A Civil Society," *Foreign Policy*, No. 70 (Spring 1988), p. 30.

4. Martin Walker, *The Waking Giant: Gorbachev's Russia* (New York: Pantheon, 1986), p. 175.

5. Andrei Voznesensky, "Thoughts on Chernobyl," in Walker, *The Waking Giant*, p. 245. The poem originally was published in *Pravda* on June 3, 1986.

6. Seweryn Bialer, "The Changing Soviet Political System," in *Inside Gorbachev's Russia*, edited by Seweryn Bialer (Boulder, Colo. and London: Westview Press, 1989), p. 122.

7. Robert Kaiser, *Why Gorbachev Happened: His Triumphs, His Failure, and His Fall* (New York: Simon and Schuster, 1992), p. 426.

8. Archie Brown, *The Gorbachev Factor* (Oxford and New York: Oxford University Press, 1997), p. 318.

9. Michael Mandelbaum, "Coup de Grace: The End of the Soviet Union," *Foreign Affairs*, Vol. 71, No. 1 (Winter 1991/92), p. 193.

10. Boris Yeltsin, *Against the Grain: An Autobiography*, translated by Michael Glenny (New York: Summit Books, 1990), p. 139.

11. Geoffrey Hosking, *The Awakening of the Soviet Union* (Cambridge, Mass.: Harvard University Press, 1990), p. 7.

12. Theodore Draper, "Who Killed Soviet Communism?" *New York Review of Books*, June 11, 1992, p. 12.

13. Martin Malia, "Leninist Endgame," *Daedalus*, Vol. 121, No. 2 (Spring 1992), p. 60.

Part VI

The Russian Federation

Matryoshka dolls of Russian and former Soviet leaders. Vladimir Putin (labeled with the letters KGB), Boris Yeltsin, Mikhail Gorbachev, Leonid Brezhnev, Nikita Khrushchev, Joseph Stalin, Vladimir Lenin, Nicholas II, Catherine the Great, and Peter the Great. (Photograph by Brandt Luke Zorn, Wikimedia Commons.)

19

The Russian Devolution

Wandering between two worlds
one dead,
The other powerless to be born.

—Matthew Arnold

There is nothing more difficult to take in hand, more perilous to conduct,
or more uncertain in its success, than to take the lead in the introduction
of a new order of things.

—Machiavelli, 1514

The king reigns, but does not govern.

—Jan Zamoyski, Polish nobleman, to his country's parliament, 1605

I want to ask your forgiveness.

—Boris Yeltsin, December 31, 1999

Post-Soviet Russia, which officially began its existence as the Russian Federation on January 1, 1992, was considerably downsized from both the pre-1917 Russian Empire and the Soviet Union. Gone was Ukraine, taking with it Kiev—the ancient "mother" of Russian cities—as well as about one-fifth of the former Soviet Union's industrial plant, a variety of important mineral resources, a rich belt of black earth that produced about one-fourth of Soviet agricultural goods, and the sunny Black Sea shores of the Crimea. Gone also were the grasslands of Moldova, long contested with Romania; the forests and marshes of Belarus, contested even longer with Poland; most of the Baltic coast, where Lithuania, Latvia, and Estonia—once again free of Russia's imperial grasp—eagerly looked westward; the soaring mountains and picturesque valleys of the Transcaucasus, where the tiny and troubled republics of Georgia, Armenia, and Azerbaijan uneasily calculated their unsettled, complex ethnic scores; and the vast steppe, deserts, and mountains of Central Asia, a politically unstable region divided among sprawling Kazakhstan, arid Uzbekistan and Turkmenistan, and diminutive Kyrgyzstan and Tajikistan. In short, with the collapse of the Soviet Union, Russia lost most of its conquests of the past 250 years. Its borders, with some variations, now approximated those of the Russian Empire at the death of Peter the Great.

Yet the Russian Federation was still roughly three-quarters the size of the defunct Russian Empire and Soviet Union, about 6.6 million square miles spread across northern Eurasia, or close to twice the size of any other country on the planet. It retained a vast, if somewhat reduced, treasure-trove of natural resources, including oil, gas, iron, rare metals, timber, and coal; its most serious losses were the oil and gas reserves in the Caspian Sea region, which fell within the borders of Azerbaijan, Kazakhstan, and Turkmenistan. The reduction was far greater in terms of population: the Russian Federation's 148.3 million people were barely half of those who had lived in the former Soviet Union. However, over 80 percent of Russia's population, as opposed to just over 50 percent of the Soviet Union's, consisted of ethnic Russians. Another 25 million Russians lived as a minority population scattered throughout the other fourteen independent states that emerged along with Russia from underneath the rubble of the collapsed Soviet Union.

RUSSIA'S PROBLEMS

Russia's problems were as immense and complex as the country itself. One of the most costly legacies of seventy years of Soviet totalitarianism was that once it collapsed it left so little on which to build. By contrast, when non-Communist authoritarian regimes collapsed in European countries such as Greece, Portugal, and Spain, or in Chile in South America, they left behind social and economic institutions that had been permitted to operate independently of the state so long as they did not interfere with the existing political dictatorship. These institutions, where people functioned autonomously according to well-established customs and legal codes, traditionally formed the basis for what in the West is known as civil society, and they provided an essential foundation for rebuilding formerly undemocratic societies on a democratic and free-market basis. In addition, the former authoritarian countries of Europe and the Americas did not face the multiplicity of problems that simultaneously confronted Russia. These problems fell into four general categories: making the transition from a socialist to a free-market economy; building a democratic political system; crafting a foreign policy that would define Russia's place in the world; and forging a Russian, as opposed to an imperial or Soviet, national identity.

The most pronounced contrast between Russia and former authoritarian countries involved the economy. Countries such as Greece and Chile began their new eras with reasonable facsimiles of market economies. Even in the former satellite states of Eastern Europe, where Communism had been imposed only after World War II, there were people who retained habits and attitudes from the old days. No such legacy existed in Russia, whose economy had been totally deformed by three generations of Soviet totalitarian socialism. No Russian entrepreneurial class was available to undertake the countless activities necessary for the functioning of a market economy. No class of independent farmers remained from before collectivization to overhaul and revitalize Russia's moribund agricultural sector. No system of laws and customs essential for conducting business in a manner that was simultaneously orderly and competitive existed. The bulk of the population, including most of the country's elite, looked askance at private property.

Against this background, building a market economy required taking several difficult and interdependent steps. First, even though the old centralized socialist economy was falling apart, in late 1991 most prices still were set by the state. Prices had to be freed from state control and allowed to fluctuate according to the demands of the marketplace. Second, state-owned factories, farms, and shops, which amounted to virtually the entire economy of the country, had to be privatized. This was a monumental task in a country that had not known private property for seven decades and had no body of law that established the right of private ownership of economic assets. Third, Russia needed a stable currency that would enable the domestic economy to function and permit it to join the world economy, from which it had been largely isolated since Stalin's First Five-Year Plan. Along with these tasks, Russia had to start converting to civilian uses its enormously bloated military industries, whose high-technology and resource-hungry factories produced little to meet the needs of the general population. It had to find a way of creating competitive market conditions in a country where industrial production was so highly concentrated that a single gigantic factory or factory complex often produced 100 percent of a given manufactured product. All of this, and more, had to be done while production and the standard of living were plummeting, and unchecked corruption and theft were draining the country of its wealth.

Along with its formidable economic agenda, Russia faced the equally daunting task of building a new political system. Once again, there was virtually nothing from the Soviet system that could be retooled for the new era if Russia's new government was to be based on democratic principles. The Soviet-era constitution that the Russian Federation inherited had been a mask for a one-party dictatorship and was useless as a framework for a workable government. In particular, despite numerous amendments during the Gorbachev years, the constitution left unclear the relationship among the key branches of government, most significantly between the president and the parliament, and between them and a third branch, the constitutional court created in July 1991. Russia had no experience with institutions vital to democratic life such as genuine political parties accustomed to legislative give-and-take and compromise. In addition, the collapse of centralized Communist Party control destabilized the relationship between Russia's new central government and the country's various regions and ethnic republics. The power vacuum and resultant separatism that emerged threatened the country's unity. This problem was most acute with regard to the several non-Russian ethnic republics that were demanding extensive autonomy or even complete independence, the most militant being Tatarstan and Chechnya.

Russia's relationship to the outside world was one area where the new regime under President Boris Yeltsin did not have to start from scratch. Between 1985 and 1991 Mikhail Gorbachev's "new thinking" had repudiated the Marxist-Leninist tenets of Soviet foreign policy and forged a new approach that stressed normalized relations with the West and a mutual concern for dealing with major international problems. One of the architects of the new policy was Andrei Kozyrev, who served in the Soviet foreign ministry until he became the foreign minister of the Russian Federation in October 1990. With Russia's independence, Kozyrev and President Yeltsin continued their pro-Western, or "Atlanticist," policy. Its basic premise was that Russia's national interests were best served by cooperating with the United States and its allies, as this would help integrate Russia into the Western world and, not incidentally, guarantee a flow of Western aid that would help Russia rebuild. However, it was not long before this approach was challenged by elements less friendly to the West than Yeltsin and his supporters. These groups had deep disagreements: their views about how Russia should be run ranged from traditional Communist to neofascist. But they were in harmony in rejecting the Yeltsin–Kozyrev foreign policy. They saw it as subservient to the West and a betrayal of Russia's national interests, particularly with regard to the newly independent states of the former Soviet Union, which Russians now called the "Near Abroad," and the former Soviet satellites in Eastern Europe. These domestic pressures had their effect, as Russia's foreign policy and attitude toward the West hardened noticeably by 1993.

Russia's attitude toward the West and the rest of the world reflected a deeper dilemma that grew out of its unresolved sense of national identity. While there were many conceptions of how post-Soviet Russia should view itself, two core issues stood out. First, for centuries Russia had been associated with empire, first under the tsars and then, for a shorter period, under the Soviets. This association held sway across the political spectrum. Not only unrepentant Communists and neofascists, but moderates and liberals as well, were shaken when the Soviet Union collapsed. The loss of Central Asia's alien Muslims may not have been hard to take, but the defection of the Ukrainians and Belarusians, fellow Slavs who were viewed as "brothers," caused shock and dismay. Suddenly it was necessary to accept Russia existing within a much smaller space and playing a far more modest role in the world. Second, a new version of the old Westerner/Slavophile debate reared its head. Russians were asking themselves to what degree Russia was a European nation and how much it should strive to be like Europe. Did Russia have its own uniquely Orthodox Eurasian civilization, and if it did, to what degree should it seek its own path of development? Furthermore, post-Soviet Russia, which presumably aspired to be a democratic society, had to accommodate within its new identity the aspirations and sensibilities of its non-Russian minorities, a concern unknown during the country's authoritarian past. How these questions were answered had direct implications for urgent policy matters, among them how Russia should treat the Near Abroad and how it should build its federal structure at home.

As if all these problems were not enough, Russia emerged from the Soviet era bearing other heavy burdens. The country's environment—its polluted cities, its poisoned lakes and rivers, its vast stretches of ruined countryside—amounted to what Yeltsin correctly called an "ecological disaster." Russia also faced a growing health crisis and a swelling crime wave, as well as a host of other severe social problems. Yet somehow there was a feeling of optimism, even euphoria, in the air, an expectation that Russia could make the transition from a socialist dictatorship to a capitalist democratic regime relatively quickly and with a tolerable level of pain. That shimmering mirage quickly dissipated as Russia's grim new reality became starkly clear. Russia's post-Soviet era began not with triumph, but with turmoil.

YELTSIN AT THE HELM

The man at the center as Russia began its post-Soviet era was Boris Nikolayevich Yeltsin, the former Communist Party apparatchik turned radical reformer. Yeltsin was the scion of generations of peasants, who, he recalled, "had plowed the land, sown wheat, and passed their lives like all other country people." He came from a village in the Ural Mountains near the city of

Ekaterinburg (called Sverdlovsk during the Soviet era), where Europe and Asia meet. Yeltsin's 1987 Central Committee outburst, which cost him his job as Moscow party chief, was not the first such incident in his life; he had broken the strict rules governing Soviet society on several occasions, but had always survived the consequences. He became a civil engineer and eventually entered the Communist Party apparatus, where he rose through the ranks to the Moscow post from which he fell with such suddenness in 1987. As 1992 dawned, having just completed his most remarkable comeback yet, Yeltsin now faced the greatest challenge of his life: leading Russia as it struggled to build a new social order based on Western political and economic principles.

Yeltsin actually formed Russia's new government in November 1991 while the Soviet Union officially still existed. He also convinced Russia's parliament, elected the year before, to grant him emergency powers for one year, including the right to enact economic reform by decree. (The full 1,040-member Russian parliament, like the post-1989 former Soviet parliament, was called the Congress of People's Deputies. It elected a smaller 248-member body called the Supreme Soviet to function as Russia's day-to-day legislature.) President Yeltsin then became his own prime minister and appointed several academics, all advocates of radical economic reform, to key government posts. Two of the most important were Yegor Gaidar and Anatoly Chubais. Gaidar, an economist who in 1990 had helped craft the stillborn 500 Days Plan, began as Yeltsin's deputy prime minister responsible for economic affairs and then became acting prime minister. Chubais became minister of privatization. Yeltsin clearly was looking for new ideas and turning to the younger generation for them: both Gaidar and Chubais were in their mid-thirties. Significantly, two tough politicians, Alexander Rutskoi and Ruslan Khasbulatov, who had stood prominently with Yeltsin during the August coup, now were excluded from his inner circle. Rutskoi, Russia's vice president and a highly decorated Afghanistan war hero, had been Yeltsin's running mate in the June 1991 election. His courage was unquestioned, but his vanity and ambition exceeded his political talents. Khasbulatov, an ethnic Chechen and former economics professor, had been Yeltsin's ally in Russia's parliament and, after Yeltsin's election as president, had succeeded him as chairman of the Supreme Soviet. Arrogant and manipulative, Khasbulatov from the start displayed his cravings for power and luxurious living. It would not be long before both men emerged as bitter opponents of Yeltsin and his policies.

CAPITALISM FROM ABOVE

Russia began the immensely difficult project of rebuilding and turning itself into a democratic, free market country with a president who in important ways was ill prepared for leading that effort. Notwithstanding his position as Russia's first democratically elected leader, Boris Yeltsin was no democrat. He drew on his long experience as a Communist Party boss for the core of his political style. President Yeltsin intended to govern and institute reforms by decree from on high in the Kremlin. In this regard, he was acting both as an old party boss and in concert with Russia's tradition of reform and revolution from above that stretched back to Peter the Great, a ruler he admired. In addition, Yeltsin was literally and figuratively a provincial man. He had spent most of his life in the Urals, had never been abroad, and had little understanding of Western democracy or free-market economics. Never having lived in a democratic society, Yeltsin did not appreciate the need to build popular support for his economic reforms. He therefore rejected the idea of early parliamentary and local elections, which might have strengthened his mandate for change. Not unlike a tsar, Yeltsin also emphatically placed himself "above politics" and made no effort to organize a political party around himself and define a clear political platform, measures that might have helped him to deal with the parliament. Nor did Yeltsin use the prestige he had in late 1991 and early 1992 to press for a new constitution to replace the unworkable Soviet document with its unclear division of powers. Finally, while charismatic, a gifted showman, and capable of enormous bursts of energy, Yeltsin also was prone to alcoholic binges and long bouts of depression. And, like so many other Russian leaders at the time, he was eminently corruptible by the exercise of power and the access to luxurious living that power provided.

All that said, Yeltsin knew Russia and had defensible reasons for not forming a new political party or focusing on constitutional change. He understood that the Russian people, after decades of Communist Party rule, mistrusted any political party, and he wanted to act as president of all the people. As for constitutional change, Yeltsin and his closest advisors considered it a distraction from their most important task. They were convinced they had to move ahead quickly on the economic front, both because Russia's economy was in such dire straits and because they believed they had to seize the "window of opportunity" that had opened up with the defeat of conservative forces during the August coup. That defeat had been anything but total; many of the nomenklatura bureaucrats who had staffed the ministries of the defunct Soviet Union remained entrenched in Russian government offices. Yeltsin's main goal during 1992 was to destroy the Soviet centralized economy once and for all and to create a constituency of pro-capitalist property holders before political opposition to market reforms had a chance to coalesce. Devoid of experience with the type of massive economic overhaul they were attempting, as was everybody else in Russia and in the West, Russia's radical reformers believed that if they moved decisively, their country could get its market economy working in the shortest possible time and thereby keep the economic pain to a minimum. Yeltsin and Gaidar appeared to expect that the worst would be over within a year, before the population as a whole rebelled against the unavoidable economic hardship. This unrealistic optimism was based in part on prognoses presumptuously provided by a group of Western economic advisors, including several prominent Americans, who had been working with Gaidar and his team since the summer of 1991.

There was another, and peculiar, assumption underlying the Yeltsin/Gaidar economic program: that an operational free-market capitalist economy would somehow automatically generate the rule of law, civil society, and democratic institutions characteristic of Western societies. Ironically, this assumption of the primacy of economics dovetails with Marxist teachings. According to Marxism, it is the economic substructure, or mode of production, that matters. All the rest—law, values, religion, and the like—is merely the superstructure that reflects and reinforces the mode of production. Turning Marx, the prophet of the end of capitalism, on his head, this analysis could suggest that if one created a capitalist free market in Russia, it in turn would produce political democracy and all its accoutrements. This type of deterministic thinking, which ignored, among other factors, the cultural context within which any economic system operates, was understandable from a man like Yeltsin, whose intellectual horizons had been limited by Marxist dogma for most of his life. It was even understandable from Yeltsin's youthful economic advisors such as Gaidar and Chubais, who, after all, as students during the Soviet era, presumably were thoroughly drilled in Marxism before they learned about and enthusiastically embraced Western free-market economic theories. But it is harder to understand how this thinking seduced the Russian government's Western advisors and, for that matter, policy makers in Washington who were formulating the U.S. response to events in Moscow. Still, it did, and the results earned little credit for any of those who accepted it.

SHOCK THERAPY

The Yeltsin/Gaidar program of drastic steps was called "shock therapy," an unfortunate name from a public relations point of view. Yeltsin plunged ahead with the crucial first step on January 2, 1992, by doing what Gorbachev had not dared: ending price controls on most goods. Only a few necessities were exempted to protect low-income people. They included bread, milk, medicines, public transport, and vodka, the last item providing a telling and depressing commentary on the importance of alcoholic beverages in Russian life. Although oil and gas prices were raised, they remained regulated at about 20 to 30 percent of world prices. At the end of January another Yeltsin decree lifted all restrictions on private trading. For the first time since the 1920s, all Russians legally could engage in the business of buying and selling.

The first stage of shock therapy yielded some modest positive results. It destroyed what was left of the old Soviet central planning system. At the same time, thousands of Russians responded to the price and trading decrees by setting up small stands known as kiosks on the streets of Russia's cities and towns. However, the immediate negative effects of price liberalization decidedly outweighed the positive ones. The kiosks sold mostly imported consumer goods such as liquors, canned foods, and cigarettes, generally at prices ordinary workers and people on fixed incomes could not afford. Uncontrolled prices soared, rising much faster than wages; food prices climbed 300 percent in a month and more than 2,500 percent by the end of 1992. Unemployment, unknown during the Soviet era, made its grim appearance; by mid-year almost one million Russians were jobless. Millions of Russians saw their savings, accumulated over decades of stable prices, wiped out by inflation. The Russian economy, already in decline during the last years of perestroika, continued to contract, and the number of people living in poverty rose. By 1993 over one-third of the population was classified as living beneath the poverty line, with 10 percent classified as "very poor." Among the worst off were the elderly, who generally lived on modest fixed pensions that quickly lost most of their purchasing power.

The reaction to shock therapy was not long in coming, particularly from Yeltsin's opponents in parliament, who ranged from moderate centrists to unrepentant Communists and overt neofascists. During 1992 Rutskoi and Khasbulatov increasingly found common ground with Yeltsin's hard-line opponents in parliament, whose strength was growing along with the country's economic hardship. A sign of that strength was the formation of the National Salvation Front, which brought under one umbrella former Communists still loyal to the cause and hard-line nationalists whose views shaded into neofascism, a combination soon dubbed the "red–brown alliance." Among the front's goals was the restoration of the Soviet Union with its old borders.

PRIVATIZATION

In the meantime, Yeltsin and Gaidar pushed ahead with the second key part of their economic program: privatization of the more than 200,000 state-owned enterprises that dominated the Russian economy. The goal was a transfer of wealth of unprecedented scope and size: the shifting of the ownership of hundreds of thousands of enterprises—not only small shops but also gigantic factories—from the state to individual owners. This was, said Yeltsin, the "ticket to a free economy." Just as important,

privatization was to be the vehicle for creating a class of property owners and a strong middle class—"millions of owners, not a small group
of millionaires," in Yeltsin's words—that would provide the basis for a
democratic society. In effect, it was a modern-day version, albeit in support of a different type of political regime, of Peter Stolypin's wager on
"the sober and the strong."

Progress was extremely slow until October 1992, when Yeltsin, in the face
of strong opposition in parliament, began his "voucher" program. Managed by
Anatoly Chubais, the program distributed vouchers worth 10,000 rubles—by
then worth only $33 because of inflation—to each Russian citizen. The vouch-
ers could be used, either on an individual basis or by joining an investment
company, to buy shares in businesses that were being privatized. In deference to anti-reform forces in parliament, the program was modified to enable
workers to gain control of the enterprises where they were employed. While
this preference for worker ownership appealed to egalitarian sentiments that
were still strong in Russia, it also left many enterprises under the control of
people who, to protect their jobs and security, were unlikely to take measures,
such as shedding excess workers, that were necessary to make those businesses efficient and profitable. Another more serious problem with Yeltsin's
privatization program was that well-placed members of the old nomenklatura
were able to use their connections and positions to gain control of valuable
state enterprises. They then often sold off assets and turned themselves into
instant millionaires, thereby negating Yeltsin's promise that his program
would benefit a broad spectrum of the population rather than a privileged or
unscrupulous few. In other words, the process of privatization was corrupted
by insider manipulation from the start. It was also compromised when many
bewildered or desperate people sold or traded their vouchers to satisfy immediate needs or wants. In a sense what took place was Esau's bad bargain
(exchanging one's birthright for some porridge) on a mass scale, made worse
when many Russians exchanged their vouchers—diminished by inflation to a
value of about $3 by 1993—for a bottle or two of cheap vodka. Some people
did still worse by making no bargain at all, having simply lost their vouchers
or thrown them away. A widespread and legitimate complaint among Russia's hard-pressed masses was that Yeltsin's policy amounted not to genuine
privatization, or what had been trumpeted as "people's privatization," but to
"nomenklatura privatization."

The results of privatization were most positive in the area of retail trade,
77 percent of which was outside state control by December 1993. There was
less progress in other areas, including agriculture. Although most collective
and state farms officially underwent reorganization, in practice they were
little changed. People who withdrew from the collectives to establish private

farms faced many difficulties, including getting good land to farm and securing necessary equipment and financing. They also faced resistance from the
majority of collective farmers, who considered private farming a threat to the
only way of life they knew. By December 1993 Russia had about 270,000
private farmers. However, they farmed only about 6 percent of the land, and
some of them were failing; more than 14,000 private farms went out of business during 1993.

PRIVATIZATION OR "GRABITIZATION"?

The main beneficiaries of shock therapy and privatization fell into three broad
groups. The first, mentioned above, were the nomenklatura managers who used
their insider connections to turn chunks of former Soviet enterprises into their
private property. Probably the most successful representative of this group was
Viktor Chernomyrdin, former head of the Soviet natural gas industry and, as
of mid-1992, one of Yeltsin's deputy prime ministers. Chernomyrdin ended
up with 1 percent of the shares of Gazprom, Russia's partially privatized
but still government-controlled natural gas monopoly. This deft maneuver
made the former Communist official and future (December 1992–March
1998) Russian prime minister a billionaire. Once they had their piece of the
privatization pie, these ex-managers turned shareholders rarely tried to retool
their enterprises for competition in the marketplace. Instead, they made instant fortunes by using government credits for personal gain, exporting raw
materials and profiting from international prices that far exceeded domestic
prices, selling off assets, and resorting to other underhanded schemes. The
second group of beneficiaries, as historian Dmitri Simes has noted, "emerged
very quickly, literally from nowhere."[1] They were entrepreneurs and hustlers
who had made money in other businesses, often during the Gorbachev era,
and then became what they called bankers, a term that fit them only loosely.
The key to their success was using connections to get government funds
deposited in their banks and using that money for dubious but enormously
profitable financial transactions. A normal banking system, in which banks
take in deposits and turn them into loans to foster genuine economic development, did not develop in Russia. The third group that did well from shock
therapy and privatization was made up of criminals, who often got their start
in the corrupt second economy of the Brezhnev era or during the disorder that
accompanied perestroika. They used violence to run a wide range of rackets
and take over legitimate businesses. Most of the activities undertaken by all
three groups occurred quite openly, which was one reason millions of Russians used the word "grabitization" to describe the process that supposedly
was creating a market economy.

"OUR OCTOBER REVOLUTION"

Against this background of rapid change and growing economic hardship, the political conflict between Yeltsin and his opponents in parliament again came to a head in December 1992. The result was a tenuous compromise. Yeltsin thwarted an attempt to limit his powers, but only at the price of sacrificing Gaidar, the architect of his economic program, who was replaced as prime minister by Chernomyrdin. The deadlock between Russia's president and parliament continued until tension reached the breaking point in the fall of 1993. On September 21, declaring that the parliament was making reform impossible, Yeltsin dissolved it and called for an entirely new parliament to be elected in December. The Supreme Soviet, the country's day-to-day legislature, responded by voting to remove Yeltsin from office and ordering security troops not to obey his commands. To noisy applause, it swore in Alexander Rutskoi as Russia's acting president. Several hundred supporters of the revolt gathered outside the parliament building, the White House, where they built bonfires and barricades.

This time neither side drew back from the brink. On October 2 stone-throwing demonstrators opposed to Yeltsin battled police in the center of Moscow. The well-organized crowd forced police to retreat as Rutskoi, calling himself the "president of the Russian Federation," issued a statement proclaiming a "struggle against dictatorship." The next day an enormous mob wielding clubs, metal pipes, and wooden planks smashed through police lines to rally at the White House. Armed parliamentary guards seized the office of the mayor of Moscow by driving trucks through plate glass doors. The Russian flag at the office was ripped down and replaced by a red symbol of Communism amid shouts of "It's our October Revolution" (a reference to the Bolshevik Revolution) and "Hang that bastard Yeltsin." At Rutskoi's urging, another crowd tried to storm the building housing Russia's main television complex. By the end of the day at least twenty people were dead. It was the worst street violence in Moscow since the Bolshevik Revolution of 1917.

On October 3 Yeltsin declared a state of emergency. His position was precarious. In August 1991 the military had refused to back the coup against Gorbachev, rallying instead to Yeltsin and helping him to emerge as the hero of the struggle against reaction. In October 1993, aware that the military was demoralized and hurt by cutbacks in funding since 1991, Rutskoi, Khasbulatov, and their allies calculated that this time the army would turn against Yeltsin. They were mistaken. Minister of Defense Pavel Grachev and the troops he commanded remained loyal to Yeltsin. By the early morning of October 4, tanks and troops were in position at several key locations in Moscow, including the White House. So were television crews from around the world, allowing millions of viewers in

Russia and abroad to look on in fascination and horror. Near the White House, Russian citizens, some perched in trees, watched events unfold with a calmness that seemed out of place for a country on the brink of civil war.

Shortly after 9:00 A.M., pro-Yeltsin troops seized the first two floors of the building. As the battle raged, Yeltsin spoke frankly to his "Dear Compatriots," the people of Russia, and told them, "I bow to you from my heart." The tone of his speech was a reminder of how, at least in certain respects, Russia had changed since 1985. By noon, clouds of black smoke billowed from the White House as the army's most powerful tanks pounded the building. Soon the top half of the White House was engulfed in flames. The overwhelming firepower was decisive. The rebels inside the White House began to surrender at 5:00 A.M., and an hour later it was all over. A stunned Rutskoi, Khasbulatov, and other rebel leaders were taken from their smoldering headquarters to prison. According to official reports, about 150 people were killed and 600 wounded in the abortive revolt.

A NEW CONSTITUTION AND A NEW PARLIAMENT

With the parliament dispersed and his leading opponents in prison, Yeltsin moved quickly to strengthen his position. He banned eight political parties, fired several high-ranking government officials who had failed to support him, and suspended Russia's regional and town councils, many of which had sided with his opponents. Another presidential decree mandated that when Russian citizens elected a new parliament in December they would also vote on a new constitution, a hastily prepared draft of which was published in early November. The proposed new constitution vastly strengthened the president's powers at the expense of parliament. Parliament's lower house, called the State Duma, would have 450 seats, half elected from single-seat districts and half according to proportional representation, with each party winning over 5 percent of the vote getting seats corresponding to the percentage of votes it received. The upper house—the Federation Council—would have 178 members: 2 representatives from each of Russia's 89 territorial divisions, which included 21 republics for ethnic minorities and a hodgepodge of nonethnic regional divisions with an assortment of statuses and names.

The short election campaign provided many unpleasant surprises for Yeltsin and his supporters. Yeltsin officially refused to endorse any of the contending political parties, focusing instead on selling his new constitution, although he clearly favored Yegor Gaidar's party, Russia's Choice (later Russia's Democratic Choice). However, Russia's Choice and several other political parties identified with Yeltsin and economic reform did poorly. In the party-preference voting for the Duma, a neofascist group misleadingly named the Liberal Democratic Party (LDP) and headed by a nasty but charismatic demagogue named Vladimir Zhirinovsky led the pack with 23 percent of the vote. Zhirinovsky's ultranationalist and anti-Semitic campaign appealed to a demoralized public with attacks on Yeltsin's economic policies ("Can I do it worse than they have? Can you honestly believe that I can do it worse?" he asked rhetorically) and posters that proclaimed "I will bring Russia off its knees." Another unpleasant surprise for Yeltsin was that a revived Communist Party of the Russian Federation (CPRF), led by a former party bureaucrat named Gennady Zyuganov, won 12 percent of the vote, while its close ally, the Agrarian Party, took another 8 percent. Against these totals, Russia's Choice mustered only 15 percent. Taken together, Russia's Choice and other reform parties took about 34 percent of the party-preference vote, while red–brown parties opposing Yeltsin garnered about 43 percent.

Despite the strong showing of red–brown parties, the December 1993 elections were a milestone. For the first time in Russia's history its people freely voted for a parliament and president as well as a constitution. Moreover, Yeltsin could find some solace in the electoral results from the single-seat districts. Russia's Choice won enough of those seats to be overall the largest single party in the State Duma, just ahead of Zhirinovsky's LDP. Yeltsin also won a majority, albeit a narrow one, for his constitution. Russia's new constitution was a lopsided document. The president's enormous powers included the right to appoint the prime minister, issue decrees with the force of law under certain conditions, dismiss the State Duma in specific circumstances, and call for referenda. While the new presidential powers suited Yeltsin's immediate needs, some critics justifiably worried that those powers were undemocratic and could be very dangerous in the hands of the wrong president.

Even with his new powers Yeltsin had to bow to the reality of a public clearly disenchanted with the results of his economic program. Of the preelection cabinet's leading economic reformers, only Anatoly Chubais, the man in charge of privatization, remained. In place of the departed reformers were ministers who favored a slower pace toward a free market economy. As Prime Minister Chernomyrdin put it, "the period of market romanticism is over." At the same time, again responding to popular sentiment as expressed in the election, both Yeltsin and Foreign Minister Kozyrev began taking a harder line toward Russia's immediate neighbors in the Near Abroad and toward the United States and its NATO allies. Yeltsin also started talking tougher regarding social issues such as crime. In short, in making policy the Yeltsin regime clearly had an ear tuned to the popular discontent reflected in the parliamentary elections. The Duma itself quickly indicated its attitude toward Yeltsin when in February 1994 it declared an amnesty for all participants in the abortive coups of August 1991 and October 1993.

MONEY PRIVATIZATION AND THE OLIGARCHS

Yeltsin's political problems did not change the basic thrust of his economic program. Voucher privatization lasted from late 1992 to mid-1994. It was succeeded in 1995 by a second round known as money privatization. The goal was to raise cash for the government by selling, at competitive auctions, large enterprises of which the government still held full or partial control. Again the process was corrupted from the start. The auctions were manipulated, and hundreds of valuable properties ended up being sold to insiders at bargain basement prices. Uralmash, the huge machine-building plant in Yeltsin's home city of Sverdlovsk, sold for less than $4 million. Unified Energy Systems, a power-generating company worth billions, was bought for less than $200 million. The story was the same for telephone companies, munitions factories, shipping companies, and other properties.

In the summer of 1995 money privatization evolved into the worst scandal yet, the so-called "loans for shares" scheme. Loans for shares, the brainchild of one of Russia's new bankers, grew out of the government's increasingly desperate need for cash to balance its budget. It called for private banks to loan the Russian government money. The collateral consisted of large blocks of shares of some of the most valuable assets of the former Soviet economy— assets that, because of their strategic importance, had not yet been privatized. These "crown jewels" included companies that controlled natural resources, such as oil and metals, and vital industries such as telecommunications. In the extremely likely event that the government failed to repay the loans— which was in fact exactly what happened—shares would revert to the banks; in other words, they would gain control of the companies. The key issue was which banks would get to make the loans. This was settled in a new series of auctions in which banks bid for the shares, the bank offering the largest loan winning the right to hold the shares. Of course, the auctions were decided by insider deals, and huge chunks of Russia's prize assets were sold at fire-sale prices. Those properties included Norilsk Nickel, the largest nickel producer in the world and the producer of 90 percent of Russia's cobalt and all of its platinum; Lukoil, Russia's largest oil producer; and Yukos, the country's second largest oil company. Ownership of three-quarters of Yukos cost one banker about $159 million; at the time the company was worth about $5 billion, and in 1999 it produced 44.5 million tons of crude oil worth $8 billion. In early 1996 another oil company, Sidanko, went to a bank for $20 million; less than two years later, British Petroleum bought 10 percent of the company for $571 million. Sibneft, an oil producer worth $3 billion, was privatized for $100 million. Making matters even more outrageous, the banks often provided their "loans" from government funds that they were holding as deposits. It all was a scandal of monumental proportions that came as close as anything ever has to vindicating the French anarchist Pierre Proudhon's dictum that "property is theft."

The loans for shares scam enriched a small number of bankers and business-men who henceforth were justifiably known as the "oligarchs." As the 1996 presidential election would demonstrate, their enormous wealth and control of large parts of the media had made them not only economic moguls but kingmakers in the political arena as well.

YELTSIN'S CHECHEN WAR

One of Yeltsin's main goals in 1993 was to strengthen the central government and assert Moscow's control over the country's territorial divisions. Russia emerged from the wreckage of the fallen Soviet Union officially divided into eighty-nine administrative units, including twenty-one republics that were supposed to provide a degree of autonomy for non-Russian ethnic minorities. In reality, in only five of the republics was the titular nationality actually a majority. Ethnic Russians made up about 45 percent of the total population of the republics and constituted a majority in nine of them. Nonetheless, the Yeltsin government was immediately faced with demands for genuine au-tonomy from several of the republics with large non-Russian populations, and three of them—Tatarstan, Bashkortostan, and Chechnya—openly threatened secession. Yeltsin also had plenty of trouble with nonethnic administrative units, several of which echoed demands for autonomy and even withheld tax revenues they were supposed to send to Moscow.

Russia's new constitution legally strengthened the central government vis-à-vis the country's eighty-nine administrative units. While by itself this did not solve any practical problems with the restive republics and regions, during 1994 most of them at least accepted Russia's new constitutional order. The exception was Chechnya, a strategically located republic near the Caspian Sea and Caucasus Mountains with a population of about 1.3 million, most of them ethnic Chechens. Chechnya was one of several small republics with predominantly Muslim populations in this part of Russia, which is known as the North Caucasus. The president of Chechnya was a ruthless and reck-lessly ambitious former Soviet air force officer named Dzhokhar Dudayev. After seizing power in Chechnya in the fall of 1991 and confirming his status in a rigged election, Dudayev declared the territory independent. He further kicked sand in Moscow's face by allowing Chechen gangs to base their illegal operations in what one Russian official called Dudayev's "free economic-criminal zone." Among these illicit activities were arms smuggling and narcotics trafficking.

However, Yeltsin did not move against Chechnya because it was a hub for criminal activity or because it represented a potential threat to Russian territorial integrity. In fact, by 1994 there were signs that Dudayev's grip on Chechnya was weakening. Yeltsin had other imperatives. He was convinced by advisors on his National Security Council that he needed to steal some of Zhirinovsky's nationalist thunder if he expected to be reelected president in 1996. These advisors, the so-called "party of war," included the minister of the interior, the head of the Federal Security Service (FSB, the main successor agency of the KGB), and Defense Minister Grachev. They guaranteed Yeltsin a victory in a matter of weeks. Grachev suggested that Chechnya, which had resisted Russian conquest for decades during the nineteenth century, could be disposed of "in two hours by a single paratroop regiment."

The invasion of Chechnya began on December 11, 1994, and immediately turned into a bloody and humiliating fiasco for the Russian army and for Yeltsin's government. The operation was poorly planned, and the first inexperienced and unprepared troops sent into the Chechen capital of Grozny—which means "terrible" in Russian—were slaughtered. Eventually 40,000 Russian troops fought in Chechnya. Although Grozny was bombarded and shelled until it was a shattered hulk, the Russians did not establish secure control over the city until March 1995.

By mid-1995 Russian forces held most of the key points in Chechnya's lowlands but faced a protracted guerrilla war against Chechen fighters holding out in their mountain bastions. The Chechens also took the war to Russian territory with two spectacular and deadly terrorist raids. In June, at Budyonnovsk in the Stavropol region, about 100 Chechen fighters seized a hospital, killed more than 100 people, and took over 1,000 hostages. After negotiating with Prime Minister Chernomyrdin, they released the hostages and retreated in triumph to Chechnya. In January 1996 the Chechens mounted a second deadly raid, this one into the neighboring republic of Dagestan. In April the Russians succeeded in killing Dudayev, but their triumph was short-lived. In August the Chechens stormed back into Grozny, routing the unprepared and demoralized Russian defenders. By then the death toll had reached 100,000, the large majority being Chechen civilians.

Yeltsin's only real remaining option was to seek an agreement that would mask Russia's disastrous defeat. That job went to retired general Alexander Lebed, a highly respected soldier and Afghanistan war hero. On the last day in August 1996, Lebed signed an agreement that called for a withdrawal of Russian troops from Chechnya but left the issue of Chechen independence unresolved, specifying only a five-year transition period before the people of the republic would decide its final status.

The war in Chechnya was a disaster for the Yeltsin regime. Its enormous financial cost drained Russia's budget and fueled inflation, thereby undermining Yeltsin's economic reforms. It embarrassed Russia internationally and humiliated its army, which still bore deep scars from the Soviet military's defeat in Afghanistan. Sold to Yeltsin by his advisors as a way of rescuing his presidency, the war in Chechnya instead undermined Yeltsin's popularity at home and weakened his ability to govern. It also drove a wedge between Russia's president and leaders in Russia's democratic camp, most of whom opposed the war.

CRIMINAL RUSSIA

Against this background of wrenching economic change and political turmoil, in its first post-Soviet years Russia also was beset by a crime wave of staggering proportions. Yeltsin called Russia's criminal element a "superpower," adding that "crime has become problem number one for us." Millions of ordinary Russians agreed with him. A 1994 poll found that 91 percent of all Muscovites feared for their lives and that one in three had been in a life-threatening situation involving criminals during the past year. They had good reason for their fears: in 1994 Moscow, once considered an extremely safe city, was the scene of more than 1,800 murders.

By far the most dangerous element of Russia's new lawlessness was organized crime. Russia's organized criminal gangs had their origins in the Brezhnev era, when the illegal second economy developed to supply the people with goods the Communist system did not provide. Hundreds of criminal gangs dominated large parts of the second economy, often in collusion with corrupt government officials. It was during this period that Russians first began to talk about their "Mafiya." These gangs grew stronger during the Gorbachev era, as government controls over everything weakened. They took over many of the new small businesses that sprang up during the 1980s. After 1991, as Moscow's ability to control the country further diminished, criminal gangs flourished as never before. By 1994 there were 5,000 gangs in Russia, ten times as many as in 1990. The Russian government estimated that these gangs controlled one-third of all goods and services sold in the country; the CIA reported that criminal organizations controlled 40,000 Russian enterprises. Criminals dominated as much as 50 percent of all private business. Organized crime also played a major role in the transfer of billions of dollars of vitally needed capital from Russia to foreign banks. It discouraged foreign investment in Russia and hampered the expansion of legitimate private business. Making matters worse, as criminal gangs infiltrated Russia's emerging market economy, they extended their tentacles to government officials at every level, strangling efforts to build democratic institutions.

A NORMAL GREAT POWER?

While juggling all these domestic problems, the Yeltsin regime simultaneously struggled to formulate a post-Soviet foreign policy. The challenge for the Russian government was to emerge from the shadow of seven decades of Soviet hostility toward the West while maintaining what it regarded as Russia's vital security interests as a great power. Foreign Minister Kozyrev summed up that goal when he said he expected Russia to play the international role of a "normal great power."

Despite its territorial losses, Russia still had a legitimate claim to great-power status. It inherited the defunct Soviet Union's place in many international bodies, including its permanent seat and veto on the U.N. Security Council. It also inherited most of the Soviet Union's nuclear arsenal, which left it, along with the United States, one of the world's two dominant nuclear powers. The remaining Soviet nuclear arms were located in the territories of Ukraine, Belarus, and Kazakhstan.

One of Yeltsin's most urgent objectives was to continue the progress on nuclear arms reduction that began with the landmark Soviet–U.S. START I agreement of 1991. In January 1993 Russia and the United States signed START II, which stipulated yet deeper cuts. However, before the Yeltsin government was prepared to implement even START I, it wanted guarantees that Ukraine, Belarus, and Kazakhstan, which possessed arsenals that included both short-range and long-range (strategic) weapons, would give up their nuclear weapons. After difficult negotiations and under heavy pressure from the United States and its NATO allies, Ukraine, Belarus, and Kazakhstan transferred all short-range weapons to Russia in 1992. It proved more difficult to resolve the question of strategic weapons. This required that the three nations sign and ratify both START I and the Nuclear Non-Proliferation Treaty (NPT), a process that was not completed until the end of 1994.

Another major foreign policy goal was to assert Russia's influence in as much of the Near Abroad as possible. Moscow could do little with the westward-looking Baltic countries, from which all Russian troops were withdrawn by the summer of 1994. Relations with Ukraine, the most populous and economically important of the Near Abroad states, were generally tense. Russian–Ukrainian relations had several sore points, the most serious being the status of the Crimea, a peninsula on the Black Sea with a predominantly Russian population that Nikita Khrushchev transferred from Russia to Ukraine as a "gift" in 1954. Despite continued threats of secession, which found considerable sympathy in Russia, the Crimea remained part of Ukraine, albeit unwillingly. While Ukraine held Russia at arm's length, Belarus, whose dictatorial president Alexander Lukashenko dreamed of a revived Soviet Union, edged closer to Moscow in May 1995 by agreeing to a Russia–Belarus customs union. This and subsequent agreements remained largely symbolic. Their main purpose was to boost Yeltsin's sagging popularity at home and signal that Russia would resist further Western influence along its western flank. In the Caucasus region ethnic turmoil helped Russia increase its influence in both Azerbaijan and Georgia. In Central Asia thousands of Russian troops were sent to defend Tajikistan's dictatorial government of ex-Communist functionaries against a rebellion by Islamic fundamentalists, turning that troubled country into a Russian protectorate.

Russia was less able to impose its will on its former satellite states in Eastern Europe. The Yeltsin government was especially disturbed about proposals to expand NATO that included some of those states. Russian objections initially had limited success: in 1994 NATO created a stopgap compromise program called the Partnership for Peace that allowed the East European states to be associated with the alliance and cooperate with it militarily but denied them full-fledged membership. Another source of tension between Russia and the West was Moscow's $800 million deal with Iran to complete its Bushehr nuclear power plant, whose construction had been interrupted by Iran's 1979 revolution and subsequent war with Iraq. This project was certain to help that militant Islamic state and active supporter of international terrorism build nuclear weapons. Further problems arose in 1995 over NATO bombing attacks against the Serbs of war-torn Bosnia in the former Yugoslavia. Although Yeltsin generally supported U.S.-led peace efforts in Bosnia, Moscow also saw the NATO bombings as an intrusion into what had once been a Soviet sphere of influence and an attack on a people who shared Russia's Orthodox Christian heritage. Yeltsin's denunciation of the bombings also was linked to domestic politics; he understood that angry and growing nationalist sentiment at home was strengthening opponents of his government. In September 1995 the Duma demanded that Yeltsin fire Foreign Minister Kozyrev. Communist Party leader Gennady Zyuganov denounced Kozyrev as the "minister of national disgrace," while Vladimir Zhirinovsky, not to be outdone in militancy by any Russian politician, announced the time had come to "start the motors of Russian tanks and bombers" and send them to the war zone.

Zhirinovsky's proposal was not only politically outrageous but also militarily impossible. By the mid-1990s Russia's military was in bad shape. Its total strength of 1.2 to 1.5 million men was a fraction of the former Soviet Union's armed force. It was receiving less than a quarter of the material resources that it consumed during the Soviet era, leaving it with few funds for research and development or the procurement of new weapons. Only the Strategic Forces that controlled Russia's nuclear weapons were at full authorized-strength; the army, navy, and air force lacked the recruits necessary to fill their units.

RUSSIA AT MID-DECADE

Overall, the first half of the 1990s brought Russia little shelter from the cold winds of change. There was a smattering of positive news. By mid-1995 the privatization of more than 100,000 enterprises and the creation of over 1 million new businesses meant that two-thirds of the labor force worked in the private sector. Russia's major cities sported new shops, restaurants, and renovated buildings. Some newly privatized industrial enterprises, including large military firms, were producing goods for the consumer market, sometimes in joint ventures with foreign companies. Inflation, while still a problem, had dropped significantly from the stratospheric levels of 1992 and 1993. Increasing numbers of Russians, especially younger people, were making money as entrepreneurs of various sorts and enjoying the luxuries, frequently imported, their new wealth could buy.

However, Russia's post-Soviet economy was rife with discouraging statistics and images. Between 1991 and 1994 Russia's gross domestic product dropped by almost 40 percent. Investment in production was sharply down. Of particular concern was the fate of the high-technology factories of the military-industrial complex, which employed many of Russia's best engineers and scientists and produced its most advanced civilian as well as military products. By mid-1995 about 10 million Russians were unemployed. In agriculture, the grain harvest of 1994 was the lowest in a decade and private farms accounted for only about 5 percent of total farmland. The country's standard of living had fallen drastically and the inequality between rich and poor had increased.

There were many other serious structural problems as well. Privatization notwithstanding, the existence of so many huge factory complexes meant that Russia remained what one local economist called a "country of monopolies," and these monopolies ignored market forces that were supposed to make Russian industry more efficient. Market forces were further hamstrung because the state continued to own a controlling interest in many officially "privatized" industrial enterprises. In addition, Russia lacked a social safety net for its workers to replace the collapsed Soviet system and a body of law and tax policies necessary for a market economy to function. Criminal elements had become increasingly entrenched in many sectors of the new economy. As one Western financial journal reported, "Moscow's roads are busy with flashy foreign cars, driven by men in dark glasses, whose profession is invariably 'trade' or 'banking.'" Political scientist Peter Reddaway noted that the defunct state-run economy had been replaced "not by a true market economy, but by an unstable semi-market system preyed on by a growing army of parasites—mafiosi and bribe-taking officials."[2] Or, as economist Marshall Goldman observed, Russia's "bastard" capitalism "may be a market, but not one that most societies would tolerate."[3]

Russia's political situation likewise was problematic. Russia now had a popularly elected president and parliament and a voter-approved constitution, but not what can be called a functional democracy. Enormous power was concentrated in the presidency, which commanded a bureaucracy so swollen that by 1995 the Russian government actually was larger than the Soviet government had been in 1991. One tentacle of that bureaucracy that concerned democratically minded Russians was the heavily armed presidential security service headed by Yeltsin's crony General Alexander Korzhakov. With his health increasingly fragile—he had two heart attacks in 1995—Yeltsin relied more heavily on Korzhakov. Another concern of Russian democrats was the revitalized Federal Security Service (FSB). The FSB was the main internal security successor agency to the KGB, which had been divided into five separate agencies after the collapse of the Soviet Union. In early 1995, as part of Yeltsin's efforts to battle crime, the FSB was given extensive new powers to spy on Russian citizens. Meanwhile, theft by government officials and the bribes they demanded from businessmen discredited the government in the eyes of the people and may have caused greater harm to the economy than organized crime. The perks and privileges of Russia's ruling elite—including special access to cars, apartments, quality medical care, and vacation spots—increasingly recalled the lifestyle of the old Soviet nomenklatura.

This bloated, corrupt government was ineffective. The central government was so inefficient that it was able to collect only one-fourth of the taxes it imposed. Russia's social safety net was full of holes; its schools, roads, and many other public facilities and services were in disrepair or disarray. As one Western observer put it, the "reality of Russia in 1995 is that it is *undergoverned*. And an undergoverned Russia is dangerous both to itself and to others."[4]

Russia's struggle to overcome its staggering array of problems was made all the more difficult because it was losing many of its most capable people. By 1994 it was estimated that 10 percent of the country's scientists and engineers had emigrated, among them many with international reputations and the most valuable skills. This brain drain was compounded by an internal brain drain as scientific personnel abandoned their research institutes to make a living wherever they could. A typical example was a talented theoretical physicist from a major institute in Novosibirsk who gave up physics to become an officer in a bank. The man was doing well and could afford a new car, but as a former colleague asked with a touch of both sadness and contempt, "What's he producing in a bank?"

Even more debilitating and dangerous in the long term, the physical health of the Russian people was deteriorating with shocking speed. Between 1990 and 1994, the life expectancy for Russian men fell from 63.8 to 57.3 years, a plunge unprecedented in modern industrial countries. Life expectancy for women also fell, although at a slower rate. Fed by epidemic rates of heart disease, cancer, infectious diseases, and accidents, Russia's death rate was almost twice its birthrate, which languished at an all-time low. The number of live births was less than half that of abortions. Even more alarming, about 10 percent of newborns suffered from serious birth defects and about 50 percent of all schoolchildren suffered from chronic diseases. As one medical expert grimly noted, "What we have here is a disaster."

PARLIAMENTARY AND PRESIDENTIAL ELECTIONS

It was against this background that the Russian people elected a new parliament in December 1995. The voters moved away from Zhirinovsky and the LDP, but they did not move toward Yeltsin and supporters of his economic policies. Instead, they drifted toward the CPRF, which led the field with 22 percent of the vote and, with its single-district victories, took more than one-third of the total Duma seats. The leading pro-reform party, Our Home Is Russia, received 11 percent of the vote. Led by Viktor Chernomyrdin, it was less a political party with a coherent program and grassroots support than a collection of careerists with powerful backing clinging together for political gain. The only other party supporting economic reform that managed to win 5 percent of the vote was Yabloko, an independent group led by economist Grigory Yavlinsky that angrily criticized corruption in the Yeltsin regime.

The CPRF's victory soon made itself felt in January 1996, when pro-Western foreign minister Andrei Kozyrev resigned. His replacement was Yevgeny Primakov, a veteran Soviet apparatchik with little fondness for the West. Anatoly Chubais also lost his cabinet job. Meanwhile, all eyes were on the presidential elections scheduled for mid-1996. In the wake of economic chaos and the Chechnya debacle, Yeltsin's approval rating sank to 5 percent. He trailed most potential candidates in the polls, including Zyuganov, his strongest challenger, and a new face in Russian politics, Alexander Lebed. Yeltsin recovered, but only by using sordid tactics that made the election a dubious example of democracy in action. His campaign was bankrolled by millions of dollars from the oligarchs, who feared a Zyuganov victory would threaten their ill-gotten wealth. Government media outlets, joined by print and electronic media controlled by the oligarchs, pounded out a constant and deafening drumbeat of pro-Yeltsin propaganda. At the same time, the government suddenly found billions of rubles to pay workers their overdue wages and provide voters with other services unavailable before the campaign began. The president won a plurality in the first round of the elections, edging out Zyuganov by a few percentage points while Lebed finished a strong third. Yeltsin then brought the popular general on board by appointing him head of Russia's National Security Council. He also fired Korzhakov, Grachev, and several other officials associated with the unpopular war in Chechnya. In July, just after the media covered up another presidential heart attack, Yeltsin coasted to victory over Zyuganov by a margin of 54 to 40 percent.

YELTSIN'S SECOND TERM

Yeltsin's second term was a grim saga of presidential and national decline. The president was pale, shaky, and obviously ill during his short inauguration ceremony on August 9, 1996. In October, Yeltsin fired Alexander Lebed from all his government posts because he considered the popular retired general and military hero a rival. The next month Yeltsin underwent quintuple heart bypass surgery. When he returned to the Kremlin he announced, "The coming year will be better for Russia—that is the word of the president."

It was not to be, neither in 1997 nor in the years that followed. Although his heart surgery probably saved his life, Yeltsin soon deteriorated into a very old man. Despite some clear moments, he was often sick or drunk and out of touch with reality. Most of his information came from a small group collectively known as "the Family." Anchored by Yeltsin's daughter Tatyana Dyachenko, the Family included a select group of advisors and several oligarchs, among them Boris Berezovsky. Yeltsin trusted nobody outside this small circle, firing anyone in the government he thought might threaten his authority. Yeltsin's new appointments muddied rather than clarified the waters. After his reelection Yeltsin moved away from fighting corruption and promoting reform when he appointed two oligarchs—Berezovsky and Vladimir Potanin—to high government office. Both were gone by 1997. In mid-1997 the president appeared to move in the opposite direction when he brought Chubais back into the cabinet along with thirty-seven-year-old Boris Nemtsov, a vigorous and brilliant radio physicist turned politician. As the governor of the Nizhny Novgorod region east of Moscow, Nemtsov had compiled an impressive record in promoting market-oriented reforms. Chubais brimmed with confidence. He boasted that he and his colleagues "have enormous intellectual potential, the best not just in Russia, but in the whole world." Intellectual potential was not enough. Chubais and Nemtsov, Yeltsin's so-called "young wolves," had little impact on Russia's economic woes and were out of government by the summer of 1998.

These maneuvers were overshadowed by the revolving-door politics involving the office of prime minister. By early 1998, Viktor Chernomyrdin, in office since December 1992, had become a rare source of political stability at home, had won respect abroad, and was considered Yeltsin's likely successor as president. This seemed to bother Yeltsin, and in March 1998 he fired Chernomyrdin and his entire cabinet. Grigory Yavlinsky spoke for many of his shocked countrymen when he commented, "This is not democracy; it is

Byzantium." Yeltsin's choice to succeed Chernomyrdin was thirty-five-year-old Sergei Kiriyenko, a virtual unknown, whose main credential appeared to be his commitment to free-market reforms.

Kiriyenko and his team of reformers remained in office only five months. The most memorable moment of their brief tenure occurred on July 17, 1998, when Russia held a funeral for Tsar Nicholas II and his family, eighty years to the day after their murder by the Bolsheviks. Boris Yeltsin, looking and sounding presidential for a change, provided the highlight of the somber ninety-minute Orthodox ceremony with a short, moving speech in which he called for national reconciliation, for Russians to embrace "repentance and peace, regardless of political views, ethnic or religious belonging." A month later, Russia experienced its worst economic crisis of the 1990s when falling revenues and rising deficits undermined the country's currency. On August 17, 1998, the Russian government devalued the ruble and defaulted on billions of dollars of foreign loans. By international standards, Russia was bankrupt. In a week, the ruble lost two-thirds of its value. For millions of long-suffering Russians, who suddenly had to pay more for imported goods, including food (more than a third of which was imported) and many other necessities, the crisis meant yet another plunge in their standard of living. For Kiriyenko, it was the end of a short line. Yeltsin fired him and his cabinet on August 23.

Now Yeltsin's revolving door spun out of his control. He tried to bring back Chernomyrdin as prime minister, but his political opponents in the Duma, led by Zyuganov and the CPRF, refused to confirm the former leader. Yeltsin had to compromise and appoint Yevgeny Primakov, who had ties to the CPRF. Upon taking over as prime minister in September 1998 Primakov skillfully put together a coalition cabinet that included both Communists and free market advocates. Although he did little to address any major problems while in office, Primakov's steadiness and diplomatic skills had a calming effect on Russia's turbulent political life. That did the prime minister little good, as Yeltsin suddenly fired him in May 1999. Primakov's successor, Sergei Stepashin, an obscure career internal security bureaucrat whose positions since 1991 included heading the Federal Security Service, barely had a chance to settle into his office when Yeltsin's revolving door spun once again in August: out went Stepashin and in came Vladimir Putin, another virtual unknown, Russia's fifth prime minister in seventeen months.

PRIME MINISTER PUTIN

Vladimir Putin was head of the Federal Security Service when Yeltsin tapped him to be prime minister. Born in Leningrad in 1952, Putin studied law at Leningrad State University and upon graduation realized a boyhood ambition by landing a job with the KGB. The KGB became Putin's career; he would not leave the organization, having reached the rank of colonel, until a few months before the Soviet Union collapsed. In 1985 Putin was posted to East Germany, where he specialized in gathering economic intelligence. Putin returned home in early 1990 with an extensive knowledge of Western business practices. The latter was particularly useful when later that same year, while still on the KGB payroll, he went to work for Anatoly Sobchak, Leningrad's reformist mayor. As the city official in charge of attracting foreign investment and promoting business, Putin established a reputation for honesty and as a man who could help foreign businessmen cut through bureaucratic tangles. After Sobchak's electoral defeat in 1996, Putin relocated to Moscow, where he served in a variety of Kremlin jobs before being appointed head of the Federal Security Service in 1998. The former KGB colonel had returned to lead the organization in which he had made his Soviet-era career. He retained that post when Yeltsin subsequently made him head of the National Security Council. Intelligent, hardworking, and loyal, Putin apparently won Yeltsin's trust and impressed him with his toughness. He was forty-seven years old when Yeltsin, with a wave of his presidential wand, transported him from the shadow world of spying to the limelight of Kremlin politics.

Putin's appointment was sandwiched between events that soon ignited a second Russian/Chechen war. Over the past two years Chechen gangs had kidnapped hundreds of Russian citizens in the region and murdered many of them. Just days before Putin's appointment, hundreds of Islamic militants led by renegade Chechen commanders crossed the border separating Chechnya from Dagestan, a poor republic populated by thirty-four quarreling ethnic groups whose territory included more than half of Russia's Caspian Sea coastline. The invaders' stated goal was to merge Chechnya and Dagestan into an independent Islamic republic, an ambition that in Moscow raised the specter of a Muslim secessionist movement extending beyond Chechnya to other parts of the Russian Federation's southern flank. After two weeks of fighting the Chechens retreated from Dagestan, but the ensuing quiet was brief. In September a series of terror bombings in Moscow, the southern city of Volgodonsk, and Dagestan killed 300 people. These bombings, which the Russian government blamed on the Chechens, turned a limited military plan to seal Chechnya's borders into a full-scale invasion of Chechnya. Unlike in 1994, in September 1999 the Russian army was prepared. Despite harder fighting than expected and several setbacks, it took Grozny in February 2000 and drove Chechen forces southward into the Caucasus Mountains. The series of military victories made Putin Russia's most popular politician, notwithstanding the financial cost of the war and the casualties Chechen guerrillas inflicted on Russian soldiers—at least 2,100 Russian soldiers had been killed and 6,000 wounded in Chechnya by June 2000.

Putin's popularity was tested and confirmed by parliamentary elections in December 1999. Two newly formed political parties he endorsed did surprisingly well. The first, an amalgam of diverse politicians called Unity, was led by a minister in Putin's cabinet. It included liberals, nationalists (among them Alexander Rutskoi), and even Communists and finished second in the proportional representation balloting with 23.3 percent of the vote, just behind the CPRF's 24.3 percent. A second pro-Putin party, the oddly named Union of Right-Wing Forces, whose leaders included Sergei Kiriyenko and Boris Nemtsov, took 8.5 percent of the vote. Parties that lost support included Yabloko, Zhirinovsky's LDP, and Chernomyrdin's Our Home Is Russia, which faded into near oblivion.

"I WANT TO ASK YOUR FORGIVENESS"

Less than two weeks after the parliamentary election, and more than a month before Russian forces took Grozny, a surprise event in Moscow turned Putin from President Yeltsin's most recent prime minister into his heir apparent. On December 31, 1999, Boris Yeltsin resigned the Russian presidency, appointing Putin as acting president. As he bade farewell to his "Dear Russians," the proud and imperious bear of a man from the Urals who had dominated the Russian political stage since 1991, while characteristically dramatic, was uncharacteristically apologetic, and also fatherly in a peculiarly Russian sort of way that evoked the bygone era before 1917 when Russians had called the tsar their "Little Father." Yeltsin's brief emotional speech was almost like a metaphor, not only for the difficult years since 1991, but in many ways for the whole of Russia's troubled history, which is why it bears quoting at length:

> I want to ask your forgiveness. For the fact that many of our hopes did not materialize. For things which to us seemed simple but turned out to be arduous. I want to ask forgiveness for the fact that I was not able to justify the hopes of some people who believed that we would be able to move forward in one swoop from a grey totalitarian and stagnant past to a bright, rich, and civilized future. I believed it myself. But it did not work out like that. In some ways I was too naive. Problems turned out to be too complicated. . . . I felt the pain of each one of you as my own, in my heart. Sleepless nights, torments: what could I do to make life easier and better for people, even if just a tiny bit? It was my principal task. I am going. I did all that I could. . . . In bidding my farewell to you, I want to say to each and every one of you: be happy. You deserve to be happy. To be happy and live in peace. Happy New Year. Happy New Century, my dears.

It is unlikely that Yeltsin's unexpected exit, while essentially voluntary, was entirely his idea. Members of the Family anxious about their futures almost certainly pushed hard for his departure. One reason was concern over his declining health. A second and probably more compelling imperative was to ensure a succession that would protect them from being held accountable for their conduct while in power. Yeltsin's premature departure—his term had a half year to run—forced early presidential elections, thereby taking advantage of Prime Minister Putin's popularity and assuring that he, not a Yeltsin critic, would become Russia's next leader. One of Putin's first decrees as acting president, guaranteeing Yeltsin and his family lifelong immunity from criminal prosecution, probably was prearranged so as to come up with an offer that the weary Yeltsin, whose family members were linked to a number of corruption scandals, could not refuse.

THE YELTSIN LEGACY

It seems fair, if sad, to say that Boris Yeltsin's career peaked in August 1991, when he played his dramatic role in thwarting the Communist coup against Mikhail Gorbachev—that is, before he came to power. During his years in power from 1992 through 1999, Yeltsin was unable to do more than expand on his essentially negative achievement of August 1991: destroying what was left of the Communist system inherited from the Soviet era. Any of Yeltsin's other credits have less to do with any constructive achievement than with what he tried to do or managed to avoid. Yeltsin's economic policies were not successful, yet he remained committed to economic reform and kept that objective alive. He was unable to establish an effective government, but he never tried to revive Russia's authoritarian past and become a dictator. Thus, during his watch Russia had free, if flawed, elections and a reasonably unfettered press, and its citizens, whatever hardships they suffered, enjoyed an unprecedented range of civil and economic rights. In foreign affairs, although there was friction with the Western powers on several major issues, Yeltsin kept Russia on a path toward normalized relations with the West. Arms control negotiations continued, and Russia worked to carry out agreements to dismantle or otherwise eliminate specified weapons of mass destruction. Finally, despite increased regional autonomy, which at times stretched Russia's federal structure rather thin, the country did not slide into anarchy.

That was the good news. The bad news was that on the ground so much went wrong. In economic affairs, the Yeltsin era was, as economist James Millar has put it, "a decade of decline, denial, and decay."[5] The statistics are staggering. During the 1990s Russia's gross domestic product declined by almost 50 percent. Agricultural production dropped by half; the grain harvests of 1998 and 1999 were the worst in four decades. Oil production also dropped by about 50 percent. Investment in 1999, although up from the previous year, was one-fifth of the level of 1990. Total direct foreign investment in Russia during the 1990s was only slightly more than the total for Hungary, whose population is about one-fifteenth of Russia's. Most of that investment went into extractive industries, not into manufacturing, which further dimmed Russia's long-term economic prospects. Meanwhile, at least $200 billion of capital flight during the 1990s drained Russia of many times the capital that foreigners invested there or sent in aid. By 1998 under 5 percent of Russia's industrial equipment was less than five years old; the figure in 1990 had been 30 percent.

There was an economic recovery of sorts during 1999. It resulted in large part from the August 1998 economic meltdown and collapse of the ruble, which cut imports into Russia by making them more expensive and boosted Russian exports by making them cheaper. Another important factor was the rise in the international price of oil, Russia's most important export. The economy grew slightly, investment rose by 1 percent, and industrial production grew by a robust 8.1 percent. By the end of 1999 unemployment was falling. But balanced future growth capable of providing widespread prosperity still required large-scale investment and structural reform that were not taking place.

The social effects of all this were readily visible and extremely depressing. Disease and alcoholism were rampant. Drug addiction was growing at an alarming rate, especially among the young. The rate for teenagers rose by thirteen times during the 1990s. By late 1998, 2 million Russian children were living without families, two-thirds of them on the streets. Ten million children were not in school. In 1999 about 35 percent of the population was living below the poverty line, and many more people hovered dangerously just above to it. Vitamin deficiency was widespread. Russia's birthrate had dropped by one-third since 1990, and its mortality rate had risen by a quarter. The suicide rate was up 60 percent since 1989. The population continued to fall. In late 1999 it was 146 million, down more than 2 million since 1991.

Meanwhile, the Russian state, notwithstanding its bloated bureaucracy, was weak and ineffectual. The old Communist Party committee network, which formed a thick web of control reaching down to the local level, was gone and had not been replaced. The state had been further hollowed out by corruption, regional politics, and the influence of private interests, in particular those of the so-called oligarchs. The oligarchs used their enormous wealth to manipulate the electoral process, as they did in the 1996 presidential elections, and evade the law. They were powerful enough to negotiate their tax payments with regional governors. As some observers put it, during the Yeltsin era the Russian state had been "privatized." Its ability to control the country's regions, whose leaders often ignored federal law, and especially the twenty-one ethnic republics, many of which had constitutions that violated the federal constitution, was a particularly serious concern. All this left the Yeltsin regime unable to carry out most of its decisions, including any involving genuinely constructive reform.

THE TWENTIETH-CENTURY LEGACY

The end of the Yeltsin era coincided with the end of the twentieth century, a century that was unkind to Russia. Alexander Yakovlev has argued with considerable merit that the "beginning of the twentieth century is the brightest period in Russian history."[6] Indeed, during the first fourteen years of that century Russia experienced rapid industrial growth, a flowering of art and culture, a tentative beginning of parliamentary government, expanded educational opportunities for many of its citizens, and other significant progress. But after 1914 the twentieth century brought Russia two world wars and a civil war, revolution and totalitarian tyranny, famine and ecological destruction on a massive scale. Russia's Communist rulers imposed dreadful sacrifices upon the country, first to build a modern industrial infrastructure along socialist lines and then to become one of the world's two superpowers. Yet in the 1970s a process of decline began that eroded both achievements. By century's end Russia still had nuclear weapons but at best was a deeply troubled regional power. Far worse, to a significant degree the country had undergone what historian Stephen Cohen has called "demodernization."[7] Not only had Russia's industrial economy largely crumbled, but its systems of education, medical care, and public order had decayed, returning social life in many cases to preindustrial levels. The ultimate cause of this unprecedented reversal lay not, as many commentators claimed, where it reached its acute and most obvious phase—in the post-Communist 1990s—but where it began: in the era of Soviet Communism. Thus modernization carried out according to Leninist absolutist ideology and by Stalinist totalitarian methods was ultimately so deeply and dreadfully flawed that it proved to be not constructive despite the cost, as apologists for the system insisted, but destructive in addition to the cost. As a new century began, Russia in many ways had to start over, and do so under circumstances considerably less favorable than those existing in November 1917. When compared to 1914 or to the entire decade before the outbreak of World War I, Russia's condition at the start of the twenty-first century looked even worse.

NOTES

1. Dmitri Simes, *After the Collapse: Russia Seeks Its Place as a Great Power* (New York: Simon and Schuster, 1999), p. 153.

2. Peter Reddaway, "Desperation Time for Yeltsin's Clique," *New York Times*, January 3, 1995.

3. Marshall Goldman, "Is This Any Way to Create a Market Economy?" *Current History*, October 1995, p. 310.

4. S. Frederick Starr, "The Paradox of Yeltsin's Russia," *Wilson Quarterly*, Summer 1995, p. 73.

5. James R. Millar, "The De-development of Russia," *Current History*, October 1999, p. 323.

6. Alexander N. Yakovlev, *A Century of Violence in Soviet Russia*, translated by Anthony Austin (New Haven and London: Yale University Press, 2002), p. 236.

7. Stephen B. Cohen, "'Transition' Is a Notion Rooted in U.S. Ego," *New York Times*, March 27, 1999, p. A19.

20

Russia in the Twenty-First Century

Russia was created as a centralized state, and it has existed exactly this way. Thus we had tsarism, then Communism, and now the president has appeared, the institution of the presidency.

—Vladimir Putin, 2000

There is no such thing as a former Chekist.

—Soviet-era saying

There is no such thing as a former KGB man.

—Vladimir Putin, December 2005,
at dinner with Federal Security Service agents

Vladimir Putin was chosen president of Russia in an anticlimactic election on March 26, 2000. He received a majority of the votes (52.9 percent) in the first round, with Communist leader Zyuganov (29.2 percent) and nine other candidates trailing far behind. Forty-seven years old, lean, vigorous, and an expert at judo, Putin stood in sharp contrast to the tired, old former president who had anointed him three months earlier. His energy even while still only acting president underscored that contrast. During January and February of 2000 Putin fired or demoted several cabinet ministers and other Kremlin insiders closely connected with Yeltsin. In mid-April, a few weeks after his election but before his inauguration, Putin succeeded where Yeltsin had failed by convincing the Duma to ratify the START II, albeit with reservations unacceptable to Washington. That modest step helped counter the impact of a new national security doctrine Putin had approved back in January, which took a distinctly more confrontational stance toward the West than a document issued several years earlier.

THE PUTIN AGENDA

Putin officially took his oath of office on May 7. In his brief inaugural speech, the former career KGB operative pointed out that Russia had just completed the first democratic transfer of power in its 1,100-year history. He also outlined the country's "common goals": that Russia "be a free, prosperous country, a country of which its citizens are proud and which is respected in the world." Putin was not specific about how he proposed to lead Russia toward these goals, but he had already made clear that while he did not believe in Soviet-style dictatorship, he did not believe in Western-style democracy either, certainly not for Russia. In a speech marking the new millennium in January 2000, he said it was unlikely that Russia would ever become a "second edition of, say, the U.S. or Britain in which liberal values have deep historical traditions." Russia had her own traditions, including a strong state that played a far more prominent role in national life than was the case in Britain or the United States. He added, "For Russians a strong state is not an anomaly that should be got rid of. Quite the contrary, they see it as a source and guarantor of order and the initiator and main driving force of any change." Lest there be any doubt about which state institution would now direct change, a month later Putin told a group of law students that, with the passing first of tsarism and then Communism, "now the president has appeared, the institution of the presidency." Immediately upon becoming president in his own right, Putin appointed a new prime minister, forty-two-year-old Mikhail Kasyanov, a lawyer with a reputation as an advocate of free-market reforms. Putin then turned to his most urgent concern: rebuilding the power of the Russian state in general and that of the presidency in particular. To Putin a strong centralized state was both an end in itself—a vital part of Russia's historical inheritance—and the essential means to reversing the political, economic, and social disintegration of the 1990s and restoring Russia to its traditional place as a great power. As Putin put each political building block into place, he simultaneously worked to revive the country's economy. On the one hand, that meant encouraging free market activity; on the other, it meant increasing the power of the state in key economic sectors. In economics as in politics, Russia's traditions would shape Putin's policies.

Putin began by reining in the regions and their governors, issuing a decree that grouped Russia's eighty-nine administrative divisions into seven new federal districts, each headed by a presidential appointee to be called a governor-general. Five of the seven new governors-general Putin chose were former KGB officers with close ties to him, and many members of their staffs were drawn from Russia's various security services. Directly responsible to the president, the governors-general had ultimate authority over Russia's republics and variegated regions and the job of assuring their compliance with federal policies. This gave Moscow greater control over funds from the central budget distributed to local authorities and over local tax revenues that were supposed to be turned over to the central government. The decree on federal districts was followed in August by a new law changing the composition of the Federation Council, the upper house of parliament, by removing regional governors and republic presidents from that body as of 2002. This made it more difficult for these leaders to coordinate their efforts if they wanted to defy President Putin, especially since the loss of their Federation Council seats deprived them of immunity from prosecution as members of the national parliament. The new law also allowed Russia's president to remove local presidents and governors who repeatedly violated federal laws, further enhancing the power of the central government over the regions.

During 2001 and 2002 Putin introduced several economic reforms designed to improve Russia's business climate. A new tax law that took effect in 2001 sharply lowered the income tax rate for individual taxpayers to 13 percent, the lowest rate in Europe. Another law reduced taxes on corporations from 35 percent to 24 percent, while yet another made ordinary business expenses tax deductible. The government also eased bureaucratic licensing and inspection regulations, with the result that small and medium-size businesses grew substantially over the next five years. In October 2001 parliament passed a new land code permitting the sale of commercial and residential land, a small step since it applied to only 2 percent of Russia's territory, but still an important breakthrough. In July 2002, after his supporters in parliament finally overcame years of CPRF opposition, Putin signed a law legalizing the sale of agricultural land. The law contained a number of restrictions. Most notably, it barred foreigners from owning farmland, though they could lease it for up to forty-nine years, in order to prevent wealthy foreign interests from buying up vast tracts of Russian land at bargain-basement prices. On July 1, 2002, a new criminal code came into force in Russia, replacing a Soviet-era code dating from 1960. It guaranteed a trial by jury to defendants accused of the most serious crimes, required warrants for searches, and included other Western-style rights. While these rights had been written into the 1993 constitution, the Duma had refused to pass the necessary legislation until Putin put his presidential weight behind it.

This legislation removed several major remaining socialist obstacles to free market activities and provided Russian citizens with legal rights they did not have during the Soviet era. But Putin also had his sights on the legacy of political pluralism inherited from the Yeltsin era. Thus between 2000 and 2002 the Russian government clipped the wings of two oligarchs, Vladimir Gusinsky and Boris Berezovsky, but for reasons that had nothing to do with economic justice and everything to do with restricting genuine political debate. In both cases the target was the ownership of important media outlets that had been critical of the government. In 2001 financial pressure and threats of imprisonment forced Gusinsky to give up control of NTV, the only privately owned television station in Russia whose broadcasts reached the entire country. In Berezovsky's case the prize was TV-6, a television station that reached more than half the country and most of its major urban areas, which was forced to close down early in 2002. Both men fled the country. Another station, TVS, set up after TV-6 closed, was quickly forced off the air, leaving Russia without a major privately owned television station. While Russians still had access to many international media outlets and the Internet, as well as to numerous foreign and domestic newspapers and magazines, in 2003 the respected international monitoring group Freedom House, having considered the chilling effect of these and other government actions on independent journalism, downgraded Russia's press rating from "partially free" to "unfree."

Meanwhile, the people Putin brought in to staff key posts in his administration underscored his determination to increase the power of the state in general and state control over the economy in particular. Given the trespasses and great wealth of the oligarchs, this initiative enjoyed considerable public support; indeed, polls showed that about three-quarters of the Russian people believed privatization should be at least partially reversed. They seemed to have little interest in who was being chosen to do the job. Putin consistently appointed people from Russia's intelligence services, the police, and the military—that is, people like himself—to positions overseeing important parts of the Russian economy and, simultaneously, to prominent posts on his presidential staff. Collectively known as the *siloviki*, a term derived from the Russian word for power, their growing influence also testified to Putin's intent to enhance the role of the security services in multiple areas of Russian life. By Putin's second term, between 50 and 70 percent of the Kremlin staff were *siloviki*. They also held posts such as chairman of Rosneft, the huge government-owned oil company, and positions on the boards of other large state-controlled companies in the airline, natural gas, railroad, and pipeline industries.

The Duma elections of December 2003 further eroded Russia's status as a democratic society. Two months before the elections, masked police wielding submachine guns arrested oligarch Mikhail Khodorkovsky, the owner of the Yukos oil company, the country's largest and most successful private firm. Khodorkovsky was Russia's richest man and, not incidentally, an outspoken Putin political opponent who was funding opposition parliamentary candidates and independent nongovernmental organizations (NGOs) the Kremlin found politically objectionable. Khodorkovsky was accused of tax evasion and fraud, and, as with Berezovsky and Gusinsky, most Russians did not mind seeing an oligarch stuffed with what they considered ill-gotten wealth cut down to size. But the coincidence of Khodorkovsky's arrest and his political opposition to Putin could not be missed, certainly not by other wealthy businessmen thinking of supporting opposition political groups. The point was driven home over the next eighteen months when Yukos was forced into bankruptcy and Khodorkovsky was convicted of fraud and tax evasion and sentenced to nine years in prison.

Putin's banner in the 2003 parliamentary elections was carried by United Russia, a party without a coherent political program that had been formed solely to support the president and his policies. To no one's surprise, the new party, the beneficiary of overwhelmingly positive coverage from state television and help from government officials at every level, won a solid plurality after an election campaign foreign observers generally characterized as "not fair" and "fundamentally distorted," even though the actual voting itself was reasonably free. No party considered supportive of Western-style democracy managed to reach the 5 percent threshold needed to win parliamentary seats in the proportional representation balloting. The main opposition party was the CPRF, whose representation was reduced by half compared to the previous Duma. When the Duma convened, some alliance building and political horse trading quickly gave United Russia a two-thirds working majority and with it the ability to pass any legislation the president wanted. Putin's assessment was that the election had replaced "political confrontation" with a "constructive" parliament; an independent member of that body disagreed, suggesting that the situation resembled "the pre-Revolutionary Fourth Duma, where the czar had a majority."

Several months later, in February 2004, Putin fired Prime Minister Kasyanov and the entire cabinet, thereby shedding a relatively independent prime minister who had openly criticized the assault on Khodorkovsky and Yukos. Kasyanov's replacement was a bland technocrat named Mikhail Fradkov. That done, in March 2004 Putin won a second term as president with 70 percent of the vote. The election was marred by so much one-sided, pro-Putin media coverage that it was widely regarded as a sham, even though the actual campaigning and balloting technically were declared by foreign observers to be "free and fair." Within little more than a year, two pieces of legislation tightened the presidential grip on the political process. In December 2004, a new law ended the system of electing regional governors. Henceforth they would be appointed by the president, subject to approval by local parliaments. In May 2005 single-member Duma districts, which accounted for half of that body's membership, likewise became a thing of the past when a new law mandated that all members be elected from party lists according to proportional representation balloting. This made it exceedingly difficult for independent candidates to win election to the Duma and correspondingly increased the Kremlin's control over national political life. In 2006 opposition parties found another hurdle in their path when the threshold for election to the Duma was raised from 5 percent to 7 percent. Parliamentary elections in December 2007 yielded the inevitable results. United Russia won 315 of the Duma's 450 seats, and two parties that usually support Putin's policies garnered 78 more. The only opposition party to win any seats was the Communist Party, which took the remaining 57 seats. All reformist and pro-Western parties were shut out.

ECONOMIC PROGRESS VERSUS THE RUSSIAN/SOVIET "SANDWICH"

An outstanding success of Putin's presidency was economic growth, which averaged about 7 percent per year from 2000 to 2008. Between 2000 and 2006 the income of the average Russian family almost doubled, while between 1999 and 2006 the unemployment rate fell by about half and the percentage of people living in poverty declined by even more. According to the World Bank, in 1998 Russia ranked sixteenth among the world's largest economies, just behind Mexico and several notches below the Netherlands; by 2008 it ranked sixth, just behind Germany and ahead of the United Kingdom. However, much if not most of that economic growth and prosperity was independent of anything the Russian government did. Rather it was attributable to good luck in the form of high prices for oil, Russia's most important export. Oil prices worldwide actually began to rise in 1998, while Putin was a virtual unknown running Russia's Federal Security Service. After a slight dip during 2000–2002, they rose steadily from about $23 per barrel in 2001 to more than $50 in 2005 to an average of almost $100 in 2008, the year Putin left the presidency. The price of natural gas, the second most important Russian export, also increased. This rising hydrocarbon tide lifted Russia's economic ship and significantly increased the government's tax revenues.

A positive development for which Putin did deserve some credit was an increase in foreign investment in Russian manufacturing. The automobile sector, sheltered from foreign imports by high tariffs, was notably successful in attracting foreign manufacturers. In 2001 General Motors established a joint venture with Avtovaz, Russia's largest car manufacturer, in the industrial city of Togliatti. GM opened a second plant in 2004, again with a Russian partner. Ford began manufacturing in Russia in 2002, and by 2008 Renault, Volkswagen, and Toyota had followed suit. Since several of these factories were in St. Petersburg, some Russians began referring to the city of Peter as "Russia's Detroit." Other major companies that built factories in Russia included Caterpillar, the huge U.S. manufacturer of construction machinery; Scania, the Swedish bus and truck builder; Bosch Siemens, the German appliance and electronics giant; and Coca-Cola, which in 2005 spent several hundred million dollars to buy one of the country's largest juice makers.

At the same time, long-term economic problems remained, many of them summed up in the metaphor popular in Moscow financial circles that pictured the Russian economy as a "sandwich." At the top was the vibrant oil and natural gas sector, the main driving force behind economic growth and the source of more then 60 percent of Russia's export revenues. At the bottom was the small start-up business sector, which also was doing reasonably well. The problem was the massive, decaying Soviet-era "filling" in the middle. It included thousands of struggling manufacturing enterprises, several hundred in small cities and towns—Russia's so-called "monocities"—where they were the main employer and provider of social services, and the country's largely unreformed agricultural sector. The difficulties in this large part of the economy explained why in 2003 only slightly more than half of all Russian businesses were making a profit.

Agriculture remained in dire straits. During the 1990s private family farming was considered the hope for that sector, but daunting financial barriers and a variety of other obstacles caused that vision to fade. By Putin's second term the number of private farms, about 260,000, actually was slightly below the number reached during the mid-1990s. Moribund former collective farms still controlled about three-quarters of Russia's farmland, and millions of acres of fertile land that had been farmed during the Soviet era lay fallow. Russia's grain production through 2007 hovered in the middle and upper ranges of the levels achieved in the 1990s. Even the dramatic upturn in 2008, when grain production reached 108 million tons, was less than what was achieved in 1990. To be sure, under Putin Russia did reverse the Soviet experience and become a net exporter of grain, but in effect that was borrowing from Peter to pay Paul. The sharp decline in livestock since the Soviet era meant that much less grain than before was being used as animal feed. Instead of importing grain, Russia was importing increasing quantities of beef, veal, poultry, and pork. When Putin's presidency ended in early 2008, Russia was importing more than 40 percent of its food, including 75 percent of its meat. In some of Russia's largest cities as much as 85 percent of all food came from abroad. Milk and meat production was half of what it had been in 1990, and the country's total cattle herd had fallen to where it stood back in 1918. Meanwhile, agricultural villages were dying: of Russia's 155,000 villages, by 2004 about 37,000 were home to less than 50 people, and more than 13,000 had no inhabitants left at all.

A new hope on the horizon was large-scale corporate farming. Between 2003 and 2008, large corporations increased their share of Russian farmland from about 3 percent to 10 percent. Some of these corporations were Russian companies, while others were foreign, operating through local subsidiaries or long-term leases to get around the law that barred foreigners from owning Russian farmland. These corporate farms used the most modern machinery and employed specialists to increase yields. Their success, however, was unlikely to stem the rural population decline, as a typical corporate farm employed barely a tenth of the people who had farmed the same land during the collective farm days.

These problems were compounded by an extremely unequal distribution of income by region and social class. Moscow was rich and getting richer— by 2003 it had 15 shopping malls, versus none six years earlier—and a few other cities such as St. Petersburg and Nizhny Novgorod were beginning to attract capital and prosper. But only in five of Russia's eighty-nine territorial divisions was the average income per capita as much as half of Moscow's, and all of them were oil or mining areas with very small populations. The picture was even more extreme in terms of social class. A few oligarchs were fabulously wealthy: as of 2004, 36 of them were worth at least $1 billion, a number that swelled to 53 by 2007. Russia did have a growing middle class, but there also was a sizable hard core of working people, perhaps 35 to 40 million, who struggled to get by. For example, in 2007 one expert estimated that 30 percent of all salaries were "below the minimum needed to live." Of course, many people supplemented their wages and thereby lifted themselves out of poverty with outside, often illegal, sources of income. Worse off than the working poor were millions of pensioners, veterans, and disabled people who struggled to manage on fixed incomes eroded each year by inflation. Their meager standard of living was further depressed in 2005 when the government replaced certain free or subsidized services dating from the Soviet era—such as free transportation and subsidized telephone, electrical, and housing payments—with fixed monthly cash payments certain to erode in value as inflation took its inevitable toll year after year. As Putin prepared to leave the presidency in 2008, reportedly having amassed a personal fortune worth billions of dollars, about 15 percent of the Russian population lived below the poverty line.

THE STATE AND THE ECONOMY

In light of Putin's frequent statements about the importance of the state in Russian history, it should come as no surprise that he significantly increased the role of the state in the country's economy. His most important method for achieving this was what economists have called renationalization. Renationalization began with Yukos and the oil industry. In 2004, with its owner in prison awaiting trial, the government forced Yukos into bankruptcy. Most of the company's assets were then acquired at bargain prices by the state-controlled oil giant Rosneft. The next step involved state-controlled Gazprom, the largest natural-gas–producing company in the world. Gazprom already controlled 90 percent of Russia's gas production (and therefore 20 percent of the world's), employed 300,000 people, and by itself accounted for about 8 percent of Russia's entire gross domestic product. In June 2005 the government bought $6 billion in Gazprom stock to increase its share of the company to 51 percent. That same month, Gazprom added the daily newspaper *Izvestia* to its media properties, which already included the NTV television network. A few months later, helped by government pressure on an oligarch who wisely had relocated to London, Gazprom took control of the oil company Sibneft. That multibillion-dollar deal instantly made Gazprom Russia's fifth largest oil producer. Nor were foreign companies immune from these renationalization pressures. In 2006 Royal Dutch Shell, threatened with enormous fines for allegedly violating environmental regulations, agreed to sell part of its stake in the multibillion-dollar Sakhalin-2 offshore oil and natural gas project to Gazprom. While Shell remained a participant, the deal gave Gazprom majority control of the world's largest integrated oil and gas project. These and similar activities raised the state's share of Russian oil production from about 20 percent in 2000 to 50 percent in 2007.

Meanwhile, Putin designated Gazprom, Rosneft, and other companies "national champions." Most national champions were state-controlled enterprises, although a few, such as Russia's fourth-largest oil company, Surgutneftgaz, remained largely or completely in private hands. Either way, they followed directions from the Kremlin and acted in the national interest as defined by the government. The objective was for national champion companies to dominate strategic areas of the economy such as aviation, shipbuilding, and natural resource extraction. Some national champions were formed by merging state-controlled companies into larger enterprises, most notably the arms export conglomerate Rostechnology (Russian Technologies). Along with its control of 90 percent of Russia's military exports, Rostechnology's tentacles extended into a variety of important industries including strategic metals (steel, titanium, and manganese) and automobile manufacturing, the latter by virtue of its 75 percent share of Avtovaz, Russia's largest car builder. As Putin promoted the fortunes of his national champions, he used that stone to kill a second bird as he pushed aside Yeltsin-era oligarchs, replacing them with *siloviki* loyal to him. A prime example of this new breed was Rostechnology boss Sergei Chemzov, an old KGB associate of Putin's from their days together in East Germany.

RUSSIA'S DEPOPULATION BOMB

While Vladimir Putin focused intensely on strengthening the Russian state and its control over the economy, he devoted considerably less attention to Russia's social problems, most urgently its declining population and health care crisis. The population decline, which in 2006 Putin himself called "the most acute problem in contemporary Russia," continued without letup, driven by a high death rate and low birthrate. Russia's high death rate was caused by long-term social and economic problems dating from the late Soviet and Yeltsin eras and by ingrained patterns of behavior of even longer standing, such as excessive alcohol use (Russia has 2.5 million alcoholics) and heavy cigarette smoking. Alcohol abuse was the most lethal factor, responsible through disease, violence, and accidents for half of all deaths among people in their twenties, thirties, and forties. The death rate was especially high among males between the ages of fifteen and fifty-four, who suffered from staggering rates of illnesses such as tuberculosis, HIV/AIDS, hepatitis B and C, and cardiovascular disease. Russian males were further victimized by crime and other social pathologies that cause death by violence and injury. As a result, while as of 2009 the life expectancy for a Russian woman was just over seventy-three years, about ten years less than in most Western industrialized countries, a Russian man could expect to live only to age fifty-nine, about sixteen years less than his Western counterpart. In 2007 Russia ranked 164th of 226 countries and regions listed by the U.S. Census Bureau in life expectancy, behind both Bolivia and Iraq and barely ahead of Pakistan.

As Russia's death rate rose, its fertility rate dropped 50 percent between 1987 and 1999 to 1.17 births per woman. It then inched upward to 1.41 per woman by 2009. Still, that was well below the natural replacement rate of 2.1 births per woman. Nor could it compensate for the fact that no matter what the government did the number of women of childbearing age was bound to decline after several years because of the baby bust of the 1990s. Meanwhile, by mid-2009 Russia's population had fallen to barely 140 million; most projections placed it at about 128 million in 2025 and 100 million in 2050.

Putin's response to this crisis was belated and, when he finally did respond, inadequate. In 2005 the government doubled its spending on health care, but without seriously reforming a system riddled with corruption and inefficiencies. One problem was that although health care supposedly was free, medical personnel often had to be bribed to provide proper treatment. Bribery probably accounted for 35 percent of all health care spending, making medical care unaffordable to the millions of people who needed it most. In 2006 Putin finally turned to Russia's birthrate crisis, announcing a program that doubled monthly child support benefits and provided a bonus of 250,000 rubles (about $9,200) over several years for families having a second child. That program may have slightly boosted the fertility rate.

Not until January 2009, almost a year after Putin completed his presidency, did the Russian government announce a comprehensive health-care reform plan. It replaced eleven directives announced in 2004 but never implemented. Assuming it actually is put into practice, how much this new plan will improve the health of Russia's people and counter the country's demographic decline is an open question. The current depopulation episode is Russia's fourth in less than a century. The first occurred between 1917 and 1923, when the Russian Empire collapsed and was replaced by the Soviet Union; the second between 1933 and 1934, when the Stalin regime collectivized agriculture and waged its war against the kulaks; and the third between 1941 and 1945, during World War II. All three were caused by war or government terror, and ended when, or shortly after, the violence ceased. The fourth, and current, crisis is different. It is not the result of mass violence but rather of chronic societal problems. It has lasted far longer than any of the other episodes and is taking place under generally orderly social and political conditions. Therefore, as demographer Nicholas Eberstadt has noted, "it is impossible to predict when, or whether, it will finally come to an end."[1]

CHECHNYA

One festering problem Putin was determined to overcome once and for all was armed resistance to Russian rule in Chechnya. When brutal military measures alone could not end the fighting, the Putin government added a second approach by seeking out local collaborators among powerful Chechen clan leaders. In 2000 Moscow appointed an ethnic Chechen, Akhmad Kadyrov, to run the region. Kadyrov was a Muslim cleric who at one time had fought against the Russians. He built up his own private army to enforce his will, but only the presence of about 40,000 Russian troops kept him in power. Meanwhile, in March 2003 Moscow sponsored a referendum in which Chechnya's voters approved a new constitution for their republic. It promised Chechnya considerable local autonomy while clearly stipulating that the republic was part of the Russian Federation. In October Kadyrov was elected Chechnya's president after a campaign that foreign observers criticized for its "lack of real pluralism and candidates." Seven months later Kadyrov was assassinated. In August 2004 another ethnic Chechen hand-picked by Moscow, Alu Alkhanov, was elected president of the region. Real power, however, resided with the late president's son, Ramzan Kadyrov, who like his father had switched sides and controlled a powerful private militia. A Putin protégé, Ramzan Kadyrov in 2006 officially became Chechnya's prime minister.

None of this stopped the fighting, nor did it stop the Chechen terrorism that reached across the republic's borders into other Muslim parts of the North Caucasus and beyond into ethnic Russian territory as far away as Moscow. The Chechen strategy was to use terrorism against non-Chechen civilians to force the Russian government to leave Chechnya. Hundreds of people died in these attacks, which included suicide bombings and revealed the growing influence in the Chechen resistance of radical Islamists from several Arab countries. Indeed, Shamil Basayev, the renegade Chechen warlord responsible for many of these attacks, took an Arab name and declared himself the leader of what he called the Gardens for the Righteous Islamic Brigade of Martyrs. Basayev worked closely with Ibn-ul-Khattab, an Arab probably of Saudi Arabian origin, until the Russians finally killed Khattab in April 2002. In October 2002, in the worst incident up to that time, about 50 Chechens, including 18 women, seized more than 700 hostages in a Moscow theater. Many of the terrorists had bombs strapped to their bodies. When negotiations broke down, Russian security forces, using nerve gas to incapacitate the terrorists, stormed the theater. Almost 130 hostages died in the assault, mainly from effects of the gas. In 2003 there were a dozen terrorist attacks, including one in which a suicide bomber drove a truck into a hospital and killed at least 50 people, among them many Russian soldiers wounded in Chechnya. In terrorist acts carried out by Chechens in 2004, a female suicide bomber killed 40 people in the Moscow metro, a raid into the predominantly Muslim republic of Ingushetia (Chechnya's neighbor to the west) claimed 47 lives, and explosions aboard two airplanes, again carried out by female suicide bombers, killed 89 people. Worst of all by far was the attack in September 2004 on the town of Beslan in North Ossetia, a small republic immediately to the west of Ingushetia populated primarily by Orthodox Christian Ossetians and Russians. This time about 30 terrorists, mainly Chechens but also at least 5 Arabs, took approximately 1,200 people hostage in a school on the first day of class. By the time this horrific event was over, 330 people were dead, 186 of them children. Hundreds more were wounded, many seriously. The next major raid, in October 2005 against the city of Nalchik, about 60 miles west of Beslan in the republic of Kabardino-Balkaria, went badly for the attackers, who killed dozens of people but suffered heavy losses themselves. However, the bad news for Russian authorities was that while the raid was organized by the Chechen leadership, most of those who carried it out were non-Chechen Muslim citizens of the Russian Federation, indicating that the Chechens were beginning to spread their message of rebellion against Russian rule to other Muslim groups in the North Caucasus area.

Gradually, overwhelming military force and a policy of collaboration with Chechens willing to switch sides ground down most resistance and brought an uneasy order to Chechnya. Separatist forces were isolated in southern mountain regions and unable to carry out major attacks. In July 2006 Russian forces finally succeeded in killing Shamil Basayev. In 2007 Moscow installed Ramzan Kadyrov as Chechnya's president. His governing methods relied heavily on intimidation, torture, and murder, which he used to maintain a grim stability satisfactory to Moscow. Kadyrov professed loyalty to Russia. However, while serving as prime minister Kadyrov had introduced aspects of Islamic law in Chechnya, such as the requirement that women wear headscarves in public buildings and a ban on alcohol consumption. As president he endorsed polygamy, which is illegal in Russia, as well as "honor killings," in which Muslim women are murdered by their male relatives for alleged violations of strict Islamic moral codes. All of this raised questions about the long-term prospects for Russian control of Chechnya. In April 2009 the Russian government announced that its decade-long "antiterror operation" in Chechnya had been successfully concluded. Nonetheless, even as the city of Grozny was being rebuilt and some Russian forces went home, substantial numbers of Russian troops and other security forces remained in Chechnya to deal with sporadic separatist violence, a task they performed elsewhere in the volatile North Caucasus as well.

RUSSIA AND THE WORLD

Vladimir Putin is a staunch Russian nationalist whose glorification of Russia's past extends to the expansion that took place during the Soviet era under Stalin. Indeed, in 2005 he stated that "the collapse of the Soviet Union was the major geopolitical disaster of the [twentieth] century." While he said he did not want to revive the Soviet Union, upon becoming president Putin clearly was determined to restore to Russia the worldwide influence and prestige Moscow enjoyed during the Soviet era. His foreign policy agenda included reestablishing Moscow's position of strength vis-à-vis the United States and Western Europe; assuring that the former Soviet satellites of Eastern Europe were vulnerable to Kremlin pressure; asserting Russian primacy over Ukraine, Belarus, and the former Soviet republics in the South Caucasus region and in Central Asia; and improving and deepening relations with China and Japan.

In an apparent effort to have his cake and eat it too, as he directly challenged the United States and its allies, Putin also wanted to maintain good relations with them.

Ratification of START II in 2000 and a successful summit in mid-2001 with U.S. President George W. Bush initially set a positive tone in relations with the United States. Then came September 11, 2001, when 19 Arab terrorists from the Islamic organization al-Qaeda crashed hijacked American airliners into New York City's World Trade Center and the Pentagon in Washington, killing about 3,000 people. Putin was the first foreign head of state to phone President Bush with condolences. Russia then provided the United States with important help in its campaign to destroy the radical Islamic Taliban regime in Afghanistan, where al-Qaeda was based. Cooperating with Washington enabled Moscow to play an important role in an international effort to combat Islamic radicalism in which many countries had a stake, including Russia, which sought to limit the spread of Islamic radicalism into Central Asia. It also contributed to a short-lived honeymoon in Russian–American relations. In December 2001 both powers completed the sizable reductions in their nuclear arsenals required by START I. The upswing in relations peaked in mid-2002 when the two powers signed the Treaty of Moscow, or Strategic Offensive Reductions Treaty (SORT), under which they pledged to cut their deployed nuclear forces from 6,000 to 1,700–2,200 warheads by 2012.

However, other issues already were driving Moscow and Washington apart. In December 2001 the United States announced it would withdraw from the 1972 Anti-Ballistic Missile (ABM) Treaty as of June 2002. The ABM treaty strictly limited the development of defensive missiles designed to destroy incoming nuclear-armed missiles. Moscow considered this treaty vital to its security because it left Russia and the United States equally vulnerable to nuclear attack and therefore unlikely ever to launch one against the other country. Washington was convinced that the treaty was outdated and that the United States needed a missile defense to protect itself against potential threats from rogue states with nuclear weapons programs such as Iran and North Korea. Russia countered the American ABM decision by officially withdrawing from START II, more of an angry gesture than anything else since the treaty had never actually entered into force. Russian–American relations hit another serious snag in 2003 when Moscow opposed Washington's military operation to remove Iraqi dictator Saddam Hussein from power. Another Russian–American dispute involved Putin's continued commitment, carried over from the Yeltsin era, to complete Iran's Bushehr nuclear power plant, a project Washington feared would contribute to Iran's ability to develop nuclear weapons.

NATO expansion was yet another point of contention, one that soured

Moscow's relations with the countries of Western Europe as well as the United States. In March 1999, five months before Putin became prime minister, the Yeltsin government had reacted angrily when former East European satellites Poland, the Czech Republic, and Hungary joined NATO. In April 2004 seven other East European countries, all once part of the Communist bloc, followed suit. Of the seven, Romania and Bulgaria were former Soviet satellites, Slovakia had once been the eastern part of former satellite Czechoslovakia, and Slovenia had been part of Yugoslavia until that former Communist country disintegrated in 1991. Latvia, Lithuania, and Estonia were former Soviet territories, having been annexed by Stalin in 1940. Putin and his colleagues in the Kremlin resented these developments, impervious to the notion that all of these countries still had good reason to fear a resurgent Russia and seek security under the NATO umbrella.

Meanwhile, Russia fundamentally disagreed with the United States and its allies about the 2003–2004 "Rose Revolution" in Georgia and 2004–2005 "Orange Revolution" in Ukraine. These "color revolutions," which enjoyed Western support, culminated in presidential elections that brought democratic movements to power. The new leaders of Georgia and Ukraine, along with building democratic institutions at home, were determined to orient their countries toward the West and eventually join NATO. Western efforts to promote democracy along Russia's borders infuriated the Kremlin. Russia's policy was to oppose the spread of democracy and purge American influence from Georgia, Ukraine, and the other former Soviet republics. By 2006 Putin no longer was showing any interest in friendly relations with the United States. In May 2007 he obliquely but unmistakably compared America's foreign policy to the threat once posed by Nazi Germany. Relations with the European Union, a major market for Russia's oil and natural gas exports, remained somewhat better than those with Washington.

Relations with China and Japan reflected conflicting priorities and concerns. By 2005 Beijing was Moscow's most important weapons customer and therefore crucial to keeping key Russian high-tech industries economically viable. China also was hungry for Russian oil and gas exports, and Beijing shared Moscow's desire to limit American influence wherever possible. These common economic and strategic interests helped to improve relations between the two countries, as did the signing in 2005 of a treaty resolving a long-standing territorial dispute near the eastern end of their 2,600-mile shared border. At the same time, Russia feared China's growing power and the demographic threat posed to sparsely inhabited Russian territory by tens of millions of Chinese living between Mongolia and the Pacific Ocean just south of the Russia–China border. Russia and China also competed for control of the oil and natural gas resources of Central Asia. These concerns helped to tilt certain Russian policies toward Japan, notwithstanding the unresolved dispute over four tiny islands off Japan's northernmost main island of Hokkaido seized by Moscow during the last days of World War II. The most notable tilt toward Tokyo occurred in January 2005 when Moscow decided to build a new natural gas pipeline from its Siberian fields to the Pacific coast (rather than to an inland terminus in China), from which point the gas would be shipped to Japan.

PRESIDENT PUTIN TO PRIME MINISTER PUTIN

Barred by Russia's constitution from seeking a third term, in May 2007 Vladimir Putin began his last full year in office. In December, barely three months before the presidential election, he designated his successor, Dmitry A. Medvedev, a forty-two-year-old lawyer. Mevedev's qualifications for the presidency consisted of service on Putin's behalf since the 1990s when both men worked in St. Petersburg, including positions as head of Putin's first presidential campaign in 2000, chairman of Gazprom, presidential chief of staff, and deputy prime minister in charge of social programs. Upon receiving his patron's endorsement, Medvedev immediately announced that should he be elected he would appoint Putin as prime minister. His most notable campaign poster showed him standing next to a leather-jacketed Putin alongside the slogan "Together we will win." A member of the opposition Yabloko Party described the upcoming exercise more realistically when he observed, "It might be an election, but there isn't any choice." After the inevitable landslide, in which he received 70 percent of the vote and venerable election-year punching bags Gennady Zyuganov and Vladimir Zhirinovsky received 17 percent and 9 percent, respectively, President Medvedev kept his promise, and in May 2008 Putin moved into the prime minister's office. Winning parliamentary approval, normally a three-week process, took a single day. As everyone understood, Putin's presidency had ended, but not his rule.

President Medvedev's first year in office left little doubt about the status of his prime minister. In August of 2008 the Russian army invaded Georgia, allegedly to defend Russian citizens in Georgia's secessionist region of South Ossetia. In fact, the invasion, which involved thousands of troops and clearly required extensive advance planning, was designed to realize at least three broad strategic objectives. First, Moscow wanted to cripple Georgia's democratic regime and thereby restore its hegemony in the South Caucasus, the area occupied by the former Soviet republics Georgia, Armenia, and Azerbaijan. That was one reason why after the fighting ended Russia maintained a military presence south of its borders, in effect detaching South Ossetia and Abkhazia, a second secessionist region, from Georgia. Second, by highlighting Georgia's vulnerability, it hoped to discourage the construction of twin oil and gas pipelines from the Caspian Sea through Georgia and Turkey and into central Europe that would compete with pipelines crossing Russia. Third, the Kremlin was sending a warning to Ukraine not to move closer to the West and join NATO. During the five days of fighting and in their immediate aftermath, the politician front and center in Moscow was Prime Minister Putin, not President Medvedev. In early December Putin hosted his annual TV call-in program, a three-hour nationwide broadcast he had established as a presidential tradition in 2001. Russia's new president conveniently was out of the country as its prime minister held forth, answering seventy-two questions while seated inside a ring formed by an audience of several hundred. A few weeks later, back in Moscow, Medvedev signed a new law extending the Russian presidential term to six years, a sign to many observers that Putin planned to reoccupy that office in the future.

KUDA ROSSIYA? (WHITHER RUSSIA?)

During the presidency of Vladimir Putin Russia emerged from the chaos of the Yeltsin years. By 2008 Russia had a powerful central government able to control the country's regions and ethnic republics. Even Chechnya had to operate within bounds set in Moscow. The Russian economy, boosted by oil and natural gas exports, had revived, the gross domestic product having nearly doubled since Putin's first inauguration. That economic recovery was uneven in terms of social class and region, and it was dangerously vulnerable to fluctuations in the international price of oil. Indeed, the Russian economy was more dependent on oil in 2008 than it had been in 2000, a fact painfully demonstrated when world oil prices plunged by half beginning in the fall of 2008 and the Russian economy contracted by about 8 percent during 2009. But it was strong enough to support the country's enhanced international status. Russia again was a great power, feared much more than respected but indisputably a formidable force in world affairs. Russia's great power status was largely attributable to its energy exports, upon which many European countries were heavily dependent, but it also owed something to Putin's skill as a practitioner of realpolitik, especially his ability to maximize Russia's strengths and take advantage of the differences among other powers.

There was, at least in Western eyes, a deeply troubling corollary to Russia's resurgence: the dismantling of most of its Yeltsin-era democratic institutions. By 2003, and with increasing certainty thereafter, elections did little but confirm decisions made by the ruling elite. In 2006, as it rated Russia "not free" for the third straight year, Freedom House noted that its people cannot change their government by democratic means. The parliament produced by Russia's elections functioned as little more than a rubber stamp for the president. Virtually all of the country's broadcast and print media were under state control. This did not deny Russians access to independent information, as use of the Internet remained relatively unhindered, and Russian activists could spread their messages to large audiences and keep in contact with each other via their numerous blogs. Still, by 2008 the only genuinely independent national newspaper still operating was *Novaya Gazeta*, a Moscow-based weekly partly owned by Mikhail Gorbachev. Its precarious position was demonstrated by the fate of Anna Politkovskaya, its best known reporter and a courageous critic of the Putin regime for its human rights abuses, who in 2006 was gunned down in a contract-style shooting. Politkovskaya was one of more than twenty journalists murdered in Russia during the Putin presidency under circumstances that strongly indicated government responsibility. These crimes, all unsolved, made Russia one of the most dangerous countries in the world for journalists. On the airwaves, the radio station Ekho Moskvy (Echo of Moscow) was iconoclastic and feisty but also a lonely voice. Founded in 1990 by former Soviet radio employees and then owned by oligarch Vladimir Gusinsky, the station was taken over by Gazprom in 2001, after which its status became precarious. As its editor in chief told a Western journalist in the fall of 2008, "we always have to recognize that we can be gone in a flash."

Russia was as dangerous for people directly involved in human rights work as it was for journalists who reported on their activities. Between January and August 2009 alone, for example, five Russian human rights activists were murdered gangland style. Although Chechnya, where three of the murders took place, was the most dangerous part of the country, nowhere in Russia were those who defied the regime safe. One of the two murders outside Chechnya took place near the Kremlin and the other 600 miles northwest of Moscow in a town near the Finnish border.

Nor was private property legally secure, at least not for those who dared to challenge the regime or whose assets were considered necessary for implementing state economic policy. The situation was somewhat analogous for Russia's approximately 400,000 NGOs. Although independent entities, they operated under the state's lengthening shadow by virtue of a 2006 law that gave government agencies extensive and intrusive supervisory powers over their activities. Meanwhile, Russia remained, as it had been in the 1990s, one of the most corrupt countries in the world. As President Medvedev himself admitted shortly after taking office, corruption in Russia had become "a way of life for a huge number of people." Bribery was central to that life, whether one wanted to get into a university, avoid the military draft, stay out of prison, pass examinations, get a job, run a business without harassment from government inspectors or the police, or engage in a host of other everyday activities. As the foregoing list indicates, far from being part of a potential solution to many difficulties, as ex-president Putin had promised back in 2000 when he called for "a dictatorship of law," the government itself frequently was a major part of the problem. Indeed, so-called anticorruption drives during Putin's presidency were inconsistently pursued and often targeted his political opponents. It therefore was no surprise when in 2008 Transparency International ranked Russia 147th out of 180 countries on its Corruption Perception Index, several places behind countries such as Yemen and Kazakhstan, tied with Kenya and Syria, and barely ahead of Belarus and the Central African Republic.

A decade into the twenty-first century it is clear that, in contrast to what many observers anticipated or hoped for at the start of the 1990s, Russia's emergence from Communism did not put it on a path to democracy and free market capitalism. The twists and turns of the path it stumbled onto have taken it elsewhere. Among the more common terms currently being used to describe the Russian political system, all of which mean about the same thing, are "autocracy," "bureaucratic authoritarianism," and "authoritarian model." Russia may be trending toward some form of fascism. Russia's economy resembles what is known as state capitalism, a system in which private enterprise and markets exist—at present about two-thirds of the Russian economy is in private hands—but in which key sectors are under state control, and the state is the leading economic actor and manipulates markets according to its political agenda. In addition, and perhaps most important, Russia remains in the grip of a population decline that quite literally threatens its future as a nation.

As pointed out in the prologue to this book, Russia throughout its history has had to struggle against hardships that would have defeated most other nations. The problems Russia currently faces—an authoritarian political system, an unbalanced economy, rampant crime and corruption, a ravaged environment, poor public health, and a declining population—together constitute a challenge that can reasonably be compared to the most imposing in its history. Certainly that was the view of Aleksandr Solzhenitsyn, who several years before his death in August 2008 told Russia's leaders their main task was to "preserve our people." One advantage Russia has today in dealing with its difficulties is that, unlike during the Bolshevik Revolution, the goal is not to build a utopian society. That would sit well with Soviet-era writer and dissident Andrei Sinyavsky, who after six years in a Soviet labor camp had this to say about utopias: "The fact is that ideal societies cannot be—they only cause the blood to flow." The question is whether Russia's leadership, whose ambitions until now have put considerations of power and prestige above the welfare of the people, will be able to stop the current bleeding. It can do so only by reordering its priorities.

In 1841, as he concluded the first volume of his projected, but never completed, trilogy *Dead Souls*, Nikolai Gogol asked, "Whither, then, are you speeding, oh Russia of mine? Whither?" He added, plaintively, "Answer me! But no answer comes—only the weird sound of your collar bells." The question "Whither Russia?" has been repeated often since then in the title of books, conference papers, articles, and other commentaries—to the point of cliché—but never with an answer. When Leon Trotsky, whose radical Marxism was totally at odds with Gogol's conservative Orthodox nationalism, asked Gogol's question in a book of that title in 1926, the two possible destinations he mentioned were "capitalism or socialism." Today the likely alternatives diverge much less, as Russia evidently is heading toward some form of quasi-capitalist authoritarianism. At the same time, given the immensity of its problems and the failure of its leaders to address those that matter most, Russia may be limping rather than speeding toward a dead end.

NOTE

1. Nicholas Eberstadt, "Drunken Nation: Russia's Depopulation Bomb," *World Affairs*, Spring 2009, www.worldaffairsjournal.org/2009%20-%20Spring/full-Eberstadt. html (accessed May 25, 2009). This discussion relies heavily on Eberstadt's article.

Chronology

OLD RUSSIA

9th Century	Founding of Kievan Russia
1237–1240	Mongol conquest
1462–1505	Reign of Ivan III, the Great; formal end of Mongol rule
1533–1584	Reign of Ivan IV, the Terrible

IMPERIAL RUSSIA

1682–1725	Reign of Peter I, the Great
1762–1796	Reign of Catherine I, the Great
1801–1825	Reign of Alexander I
1825–1855	Reign of Nicholas I
1853–1856	Crimean War
1855–1881	Reign of Alexander II
1861	Abolition of serfdom; start of the Great Reforms
1881–1894	Reign of Alexander III
1892–1903	Sergei Witte finance minister
1894–1917	Reign of Nicholas II
1904–1905	Russo-Japanese War
1905–1907	1905 Revolution; establishment of the Duma
1906–1911	Peter Stolypin prime minister
1914–1918	World War I

SOVIET RUSSIA

1917	
March 8–15	March (February) Revolution; formation of
(February 23–March 2)	Petrograd Soviet; establishment of Provisional Government; abdication of Nicholas II

April 16 (3)	Lenin arrives in Russia
July 16–18 (3–5)	July Days
September 22 (9)	Bolsheviks win a majority in Petrograd Soviet
November 7 (October 25)	November (October) Revolution; Bolsheviks seize power
November 8 (October 26)	Bolshevik government (*Sovnarkom*) formed; Decrees on Land and Peace
December 20 (December 7)	Cheka established

1918

January 18 (5)	Constituent Assembly holds first, and only, meeting
February 14	Russia adopts Gregorian calendar
March 3	Treaty of Brest-Litovsk
March–May	Beginning of civil war
June–September	Start of War Communism; Left SR revolt; murder of royal family; assassination attempt on Lenin; beginning of Red Terror

1919

March	Eighth Party Congress sets up Politburo and Orgburo
October–December	Decisive battles of civil war

1920

April–August	War with Poland
November	General Wrangel withdraws from Crimea into exile

1921

February–March	Kronstadt Uprising; Tenth Party Congress

1921–1922

	Famine kills 5 million people

1922

February	Cheka reorganized as the GPU
April	Joseph Stalin appointed general secretary
December	Lenin dictates his "Testament"; USSR formally established

1923

January 4	Lenin adds a "Postscript" to his "Testament"

March	Lenin publishes last article; several days later suffers incapacitating third stroke
Summer–Fall	"Scissors" crisis

1924

January 21	Lenin dies
May	Central Committee suppresses Lenin's "Testament"; Triumvirate dominates Thirteenth Party Congress

1925

January	Leon Trotsky loses position of commissar of war
December	Fourteenth Party Congress

1926–1927	United Opposition of Trotsky and Zinoviev formed and defeated

1927

November 7	Trotsky and Zinoviev lead their final street demonstrations in Moscow and Leningrad
December	Fifteenth Party Congress

1928

January	Trotsky exiled to Alma Ata
Fall	Widespread strikes against poor living conditions

1929	Bukharin and the Right defeated by mid-year
April	First Five-Year Plan adopted
June–July	Sixteenth Party Congress declares the plan will be completed in four years
December	Full-scale collectivization/dekulakization begins

1930

March 2	Stalin publishes "Dizzy with Success"

1932–1933	Terror–famine in Ukraine and other regions

1933	Second Five-Year Plan begins

1934

January	Seventeenth Party Congress ("Congress of Victors")
December 1	Sergei Kirov assassinated

1936–1938	Great Terror

1936

August	First show trial: Zinoviev, Kamenev, and fourteen others in the dock
September	Yezhov replaces Yagoda as head of NKVD

1937

January	Second show trial of seventeen former Trotsky supporters
May–June	Purge of the army: secret trial of Marshal Tukhachevsky

1938

March	Third show trial: Bukharin, Rykov, Krestinsky, Yagoda, and seventeen others in the dock
December	Beria replaces Yezhov as head of NKVD, marking end of the Great Terror

1939

May	Vyacheslav Molotov replaces Maxim Litvinov as foreign minister
August 23	Nazi–Soviet Pact
September 1	Germany invades Poland; start of World War II
Mid-September	Soviet forces occupy eastern Poland

1939–1940	Soviet-Finnish War

1940

April	NKVD murders thousands of Polish officers at Katyn Forest
June–August	Soviet forces occupy Bessarabia and Baltic states
August 20	NKVD agent murders Trotsky in Mexico

1941–1945	The Great Patriotic War

1941
June 22	Germany invades the Soviet Union
September	Siege of Leningrad begins
December	Soviet forces stop the Germans at Moscow

1942
September	Battle of Stalingrad begins

1943
February	Germans surrender at Stalingrad
July–August	Battle of Kursk

1944
January	900-day siege of Leningrad lifted
October	Churchill-Stalin percentages agreement

1945
February 4–11	Yalta Conference
May 9	Germany surrenders; end of World War II in Europe
July–August	Potsdam Conference
September 2	Japan surrenders; end of World War II
1945–1948	Soviet Union establishes satellite empire in Eastern Europe; Cold War begins

1946
March	Under Western pressure, Soviet Union announces its intent to withdraw from northern Iran
August	United States sends naval forces to eastern Mediterranean to protect Turkey from Soviet pressure; beginning of *Zhdanovshchina*

1947
March	Truman Doctrine announced
June	Marshall Plan proposed

1948
January	Solomon Mikhoels murdered; beginning of "Black Years of Soviet Jewry" (1948–1953)

February	Communist coup in Czechoslovakia
June	Stalin-Tito split; Berlin Blockade begins
August	Zhdanov dies
1949	
February	Leningrad Affair denunciations begin
April	NATO alliance formed
May	Stalin ends Berlin Blockade
August 29	Soviet Union tests its first atomic bomb
October 1	People's Republic of China proclaimed
1950–1953	Korean War
1952	
October	Nineteenth Party Congress
1953	
January	"Doctors' Plot" announced
March 5	Stalin dies; Georgy Malenkov becomes prime minister and, briefly, senior party secretary
March	First amnesty for Gulag prisoners; millions released during the next several years
June	Beria arrested
September	Nikita Khrushchev becomes first secretary
1955	
February	Malenkov resigns as prime minister
May	Warsaw Pact established
July	Geneva Conference: first postwar East/West summit
1956	
February	Twentieth Party Congress; Khrushchev's "secret speech" on night of February 24–25
October–November	Hungarian revolution
1957	
February	Khrushchev's *sovnarkhozy* reorganization scheme
June	"Antiparty" group fails to remove Khrushchev; Malenkov, Molotov, and Kaganovich forced into retirement

October 4	*Sputnik* launched
1958	
March	Khrushchev replaces Bulganin as prime minister
1959	
September	Khrushchev visits the United States
1960	
April	Sino-Soviet split becomes public
May	Soviets shoot down U.S. U-2 spy plane; scheduled Paris summit collapses
1961	
April	Yuri Gagarin is first man in space
August	Berlin Wall is built
October	Twenty-Second Party Congress; Khrushchev publicly denounces Stalin
1962	
October	Cuban Missile Crisis
November	Publication of Aleksandr Solzhenitsyn's *One Day in the Life of Ivan Denisovich*
1963	
July	Partial nuclear test-ban treaty signed
1964	
October 14	Khrushchev is removed from office and replaced by Leonid Brezhnev
1965	
September	Sinyavsky and Daniel arrested
1966	
March–April	Twenty-Third Party Congress
1968	
August	Warsaw Pact troops invade Czechoslovakia, ending the Prague Spring
1972	
May	SALT I signed in Moscow

1974
February   Solzhenitsyn expelled from the Soviet Union

1975
July   Soviet and American spacecraft dock in space
August   Helsinki Accords signed

1977
October   New constitution adopted

1979
December   Soviet army invades Afghanistan

1980
January   Andrei Sakharov sent to internal exile in the
                                city of Gorky
August   Solidarity trade union organized in Poland

1981
December   Polish government declares martial law and
                                disbands Solidarity

1982
November 10–12   Brezhnev dies; succeeded by Yuri Andropov

1983
September   Soviet air force shoots down Korean airliner

1984
February 9–13   Andropov dies; succeeded by Konstantin
                                Chernenko

1985
March 10   Chernenko dies
March 11   Mikhail Gorbachev elected general secretary

1986
February–March   Twenty-Seventh Party Congress
April 26   Nuclear disaster at Chernobyl power plant
August   Gorbachev calls for reforms in all areas of
                                Soviet life
October   Reagan-Gorbachev summit at Reykjavik

December	Gorbachev permits Sakharov to return to Moscow
1987	
November	Boris Yeltsin is demoted for criticizing slow pace of reform
December	Gorbachev and Reagan sign nuclear arms control agreement banning intermediate-range missiles in Europe
1988	
March	Andreyeva letter
June	Nineteenth Party Conference
December	Gorbachev's "new thinking" speech to the U.N. General Assembly
1989	
March	Elections to the Congress of People's Deputies
March–December	Communism collapses in Eastern Europe
May	Congress of People's Deputies meets
November 9	Berlin Wall is opened
1990	
March	Congress of People's Deputies repeals Article 6 of the Soviet constitution
July	Yeltsin resigns from the Communist Party
October	Gorbachev wins Nobel Peace Prize
November 21	Charter of Paris is signed
December	Shevardnadze resigns as foreign minister
1991	
January	Repression in Lithuania and Latvia
June	Yeltsin is elected president of the RSFSR
July 1	Warsaw Pact formally disbands
July 31	Gorbachev and President George H.W. Bush sign START I
August 19–21	Unsuccessful coup against Gorbachev
December 1	Ukraine votes for independence
December 8	Commonwealth of Independent States is founded
December 25	Gorbachev resigns as president of the Soviet Union
December 31	Soviet Union ceases to exist

THE RUSSIAN FEDERATION

1992
January 2   Shock therapy begins
October   Voucher privatization begins
December   Viktor Chernomyrdin becomes
                       prime minister

1993
January 3   Yeltsin and U.S. President George Bush sign
                       START II nuclear arms treaty in Moscow
April   Nationwide referendum supports Yeltsin and
                       his economic policies
September   Yeltsin dissolves parliament
October 2–4   Attempt to overthrow Yeltsin by opposition
                       elements in parliament ends with Russian troops
                       bombarding and seizing the White House
December   Parliamentary elections; strong showing by
                       Zhirinovsky-led LDP; Russian voters approve
                       new constitution

1994
May   Solzhenitsyn returns to Russia
December   Yeltsin orders Russian army into Chechnya

1995
June   Chechen guerrillas attack the Russian city of
                       Budyonnovsk
December   Parliamentary elections won by CPRF

1996
January   Andrei Kozyrev resigns as foreign minister;
                       Chechen raid into Dagestan
July   Yeltsin reelected president
August   Yeltsin inaugurated for a second term; Chechen
                       troops retake Grozny; Alexander Lebed signs
                       peace accord with Chechen leaders
November 5   Yeltsin undergoes heart surgery

1997
May   Russia-Belarus Union Charter signed

1998

March   Yeltsin fires Chernomyrdin and entire
                      cabinet; Sergei Kiriyenko appointed new
                      prime minister

August   Yeltsin fires Kiriyenko and his cabinet; appoints
                      Yevgeny Primakov as prime minister

1999

May   Primakov fired; Sergei Stepashin appointed
                      prime minister

August   Stepashin fired; Vladimir Putin appointed prime
                      minister

August–September Chechen guerrillas raid Dagestan; terror
                      bombings kill 300 in Moscow and two other
                      cities; Russian army again invades Chechnya

December 19   Parliamentary elections; supporters of Putin
                      do well

December 31   Boris Yeltsin resigns as Russia's president;
                      appoints Putin as acting president

2000

February   Russian army takes Grozny

March 26   Putin elected president

April   Parliament ratifies START II

May   Putin inaugurated as president; he establishes
                      seven districts to oversee Russia's eighty-nine
                      regions

2001

January 1   New tax code takes effect

April   Vladimir Gusinsky forced to give up control
                      of NTV

2002

January 21   Government forces TV-6 off the air

July   Putin signs new law permitting sale of
                      agricultural land, but not to foreigners; United
                      States officially withdraws from 1972 ABM
                      treaty

July 1   New criminal code takes effect

October   Chechen terrorists take more than 700 hostages
                      in a Moscow theater, at least 129 of whom die
                      when Russian commandos storm the building

2003

March 23	Chechen voters approve new constitution
December 7	Parliamentary elections won by United Russia

2004

February	Putin fires Prime Minister Kasyanov and his entire cabinet
March 14	Putin elected to second presidential term
May 9	Chechen president Akhmad Kadyrov assassinated
August	Alu Alkhanov elected president of Chechnya
September	More than 350 people killed, half of them children, when Chechen terrorists seize school in North Ossetian region of the Caucasus
December	New law ends election of regional governors, who henceforth will be appointed by the president subject to approval by local parliaments

2005

May	Duma single-member districts abolished, all seats henceforth to be chosen from party lists in proportional representation balloting; Oligarch Mikhail Khodorkovsky convicted of tax evasion and fraud and sentenced to nine years in prison
June	Gazprom buys controlling stake in the daily newspaper *Izvestia*; Russian government increases its stake in Gazprom to 51 percent

2006

May 10	Putin announces program to increase Russian birthrate
July 10	Russian forces kill Shamil Basayev
October 7	Anna Politkovskaya murdered

2007

March 2	Ramzan Kadyrov elected president of Chechnya
April 23	Boris Yeltsin dies

December 2	Putin's United Russia Party wins 315 of 450 Duma seats. Parties that usually support United Russia win 78 more. Communist Party wins the remaining 57 seats
December 10	Putin designates Dmitry Medvedev as his successor; the next day Medvedev announces that if elected he will appoint Putin prime minister

2008

March 2	Medvedev elected president of Russia
May 7	Medvedev inaugurated as president; the next day he appoints Putin prime minister
August 3	Aleksandr Solzhenitsyn dies
August 8	Russia invades Georgia
December	Term of Russian president extended to six years

2009

January	Russian government announces comprehensive plan to improve public health care
April	Russia officially ends its decade-long "antiterror operation" in Chechnya
January–August	Five human rights workers murdered, three in Chechnya, one in Moscow, and one in a town near the Finnish border
October	Putin's United Russia Party sweeps regional elections across Russia
November	Bomb blast derails the Moscow–St. Petersburg "Nevsky Express" train, killing and injuring more than 100 passengers

Selected Readings

PART I: THE FUNDAMENTALS OF RUSSIAN HISTORY

Berlin, Isaiah. *Russian Thinkers.* Ed. Henry Hardy and Aileen Kelly. New York: Viking Press, 1978.

Billington, James H. *The Icon and the Axe.* New York: Vintage, 1970.

Blum, Jerome. *Lord and Peasant in Russia.* New York: Atheneum, 1965.

Lincoln, W. Bruce. *The Romanovs: Autocrats of All the Russias.* New York: Dial Press, 1981.

Malia, Martin. *Alexander Herzen and the Birth of Russian Socialism.* New York: Grosset and Dunlap, 1961.

Pipes, Richard. *Russia Under the Old Regime.* New York: Charles Scribner's Sons, 1974.

Pomper, Philip. *The Russian Revolutionary Intelligentsia.* New York: Crowen, 1970.

Raeff, Marc. *Understanding Imperial Russia.* Translated by Arthur Goldhammer. New York: Columbia University Press, 1984.

Robinson, Geroid Tanquary. *Rural Russia Under the Old Regime.* Berkeley: University of California Press, 1967.

Seton-Watson, Hugh. *The Russian Empire 1801–1917.* Oxford: Clarendon Press, 1967.

Sumner, B.H. *A Short History of Russia.* New York: Harcourt, 1949.

Szamuely, Tibor. *The Russian Tradition.* Edited by Robert Conquest. New York: McGraw-Hill, 1974.

Venturi, Franco. *Roots of Revolution.* Translated by Francis Haskell. New York: Grosset and Dunlap, 1966.

Vucinich, Wayne S., ed. *The Peasant in Nineteenth-Century Russia.* Stanford: Stanford University Press, 1968.

PART II: THE END OF THE OLD ORDER

Ascher, Abraham. *The Revolution of 1905,* 2 vols. Stanford: Stanford University Press, 1988, 1992.

Berdyaev, Nicholas. *The Origin of Russian Communism.* Ann Arbor: University of Michigan Press, 1960.

Charques, Richard. *The Twilight of Imperial Russia.* New York: Oxford University Press, 1958.

Crankshaw, Edward. *The Shadow of the Winter Palace.* New York: Penguin, 1978.

Florinsky, Michael. *The End of the Russian Empire.* New York: Collier Books, 1961.

Getzler, Israel. *Martov: A Political Biography of a Russian Social Democrat.* Cambridge: Cambridge University Press, 1967.

Harcave, Sidney. *First Blood: The Russian Revolution of 1905.* New York: Macmillan, 1964.

Harding, Neil. *Leninism.* Durham, N.C.: Duke University Press, 1996.

Hosking, Geoffrey. *The Russian Constitutional Experiment: Government and Duma, 1907–1914.* New York: Cambridge University Press, 1973.

Kochan, Lionel. *Russia in Revolution, 1890–1918.* London: Granada Publishing, 1970.

Kolakowski, Leszek. *Main Currents of Marxism, Vol. 2: The Golden Age.* Translated by F.S. Fella. Oxford: Oxford University Press, 1978.

Le Blanc, Paul. *Lenin and the Revolutionary Party.* Atlantic Highlands, N.J.: Humanities Press International, 1990.

Liebman, Marcel. *Leninism Under Lenin.* Translated by Brian Pearce. London: Merlin Press, 1980.

Marks, Steven G. *How Russia Shaped the Modern World.* Princeton: Princeton University Press, 2003.

Meyer, Alfred G. *Leninism.* Cambridge, Mass.: Harvard University Press, 1955.

Montefiore, Simon Sebag. *Young Stalin.* London: Weidenfeld & Nicolson, 2007.

Poole, Randall A., Editor and translator. *Problems of Idealism: Essays in Russian Social Philosophy.* New Haven and London: Yale University Press, 2003.

Schapiro, Leonard. *Russian Studies.* Edited by Ellen Dahrendorf. London: Collins Harvill, 1986.

Service, Robert. *Lenin: A Political Life, Vol. 1: The Strengths of Contradiction.* Bloomington: Indiana University Press, 1985.

Shukman, Harold. *Lenin and the Russian Revolution.* New York: Capricorn Books, 1966.

Ulam, Adam. *The Bolsheviks.* New York: Collier, 1965.

Von Laue, Theodore H. *Sergei Witte and the Industrialization of Russia.* New York: Atheneum, 1969.

PART III: LENIN'S RUSSIA

Ascher, Abraham, ed. *The Mensheviks in the Russian Revolution.* Ithaca: Cornell University Press, 1976.

Brovkin, Vladimir N. *The Mensheviks After October: Socialist Opposition and the Rise of the Bolshevik Dictatorship.* Ithaca: Cornell University Press, 1987.

———. *The Bolsheviks in Russian Society: The Revolution and the Civil Wars.* New Haven: Yale University Press, 1997.

Bunyan, James. *The Origin of Forced Labor in the Soviet State, 1917–1921.* Baltimore: Johns Hopkins Press, 1967.

Chamberlain, Lesley. *Lenin's Private War: The Voyage of the Philosophy Steamer and the Exile of the Intelligentsia.* New York: St. Martin's Press, 2006.

Chamberlin, William Henry. *The Russian Revolution,* 2 vols. New York: Grosset and Dunlap, 1965.

Daniels, Robert V. *The Conscience of the Revolution.* Cambridge, Mass.: Harvard University Press, 1965.

Deutscher, Isaac. *The Prophet Armed. Trotsky: 1879–1921, Vol. 1.* New York: Vintage, 1965.

———. *The Prophet Unarmed. Trotsky: 1921–1929, Vol. 2.* New York: Vintage, 1965.

Figes, Orlando. *A People's Tragedy: The Russian Revolution, 1891–1924.* New York: Penguin, 1998.

Finkel, Stuart. *On the Ideological Front: The Russian Intelligentsia and the Making of the Soviet Public Sphere.* New Haven: Yale University Press, 2007.

Gerson, Leonard. *The Secret Police in Lenin's Russia.* Philadelphia: Temple University Press, 1976.

Kenez, Peter. *The Birth of the Propaganda State: Soviet Methods of Mass Mobilization, 1917–1929.* Cambridge: Cambridge University Press, 1985.

Lewin, Moshe. *Lenin's Last Struggle.* Translated by A.M. Sheridan Smith. New York: Pantheon, 1968.

Mawdsley, Evan. *The Russian Civil War.* New York: Pegasus Books, 2005.

McMeekin, Sean. *History's Greatest Heist: The Looting of Russia by the Bolsheviks.* New Haven and London: Yale University Press, 2009.

Pipes, Richard. *The Russian Revolution.* New York: Knopf, 1990.

———. *Russia Under the Bolshevik Regime.* New York: Knopf, 1993.

———, ed. *The Unknown Lenin: From the Secret Archive.* New Haven: Yale University Press, 1996.

Rabinowitch, Alexander. *The Bolsheviks Come to Power.* New York: Norton, 1976.

Schapiro, Leonard. *The Origin of the Communist Autocracy.* New York: Praeger, 1965.

———. *The Russian Revolutions of 1917: The Origins of Modern Communism.* New York: Basic Books, 1984.

Service, Robert. *The Bolshevik Party in Revolution.* New York: Barnes and Noble, 1979.

———. *Lenin: A Political Life, Vol. 2: Worlds in Collision.* Bloomington: Indiana University Press, 1991.

———. *Lenin: A Political Life, Vol. 3: The Iron Ring.* Bloomington: Indiana University Press, 1995.

Theen, Rolf H.W. *Lenin.* Princeton: Princeton University Press, 1973.

Thompson, John M. *Revolutionary Russia, 1917.* New York: Scribner's, 1981.

Tucker, Robert C. *Stalin as Revolutionary.* New York: Norton, 1990.

Volkogonov, Dmitri. *Lenin: A New Biography.* Edited and translated by Harold Shukman. New York: Free Press, 1994.

PART IV: STEELING THE REVOLUTION

Applebaum, Anne. *Gulag: A History.* New York: Doubleday, 2003.

Bacon, Edwin. *The Gulag at War: Stalin's Forced Labour System in the Light of the Archives.* New York: New York University Press, 1994.

Brovkin, Vladimir N. *Russia After Lenin: Politics, Culture, and Society, 1921–1929.* London and New York: Routledge, 1998.

Cohen, Stephen. *Bukharin and the Bolshevik Revolution: A Political Biography.* New York: Knopf, 1980.

Conquest, Robert. *Harvest of Sorrow: Soviet Collectivization and the Terror-Famine.* New York: Oxford University Press, 1986.

————. *The Great Terror: A Reassessment*. New York: Oxford University Press, 1990.

Dallin, David J., and Boris I. Nicolaevsky. *Forced Labor in Soviet Russia*. New Haven: Yale University Press, 1947.

Figes, Orlando. *The Whisperers: Private Life in Stalin's Russia*. New York: Metropolitan Books, 2007.

Garros, Véronique, Natalia Korenevskaya, and Thomas Lahusen, eds. *Intimacy and Terror: Soviet Diaries of the 1930s*. Translated by Carol A. Flath. New York: New Press, 1995.

Glantz, David M., and Jonathan House. *When Titans Clashed: How the Red Army Stopped Hitler*. Lawrence: University Press of Kansas, 1995.

Gorlizki, Yoram, and Oleg Khlevniuk. *Cold Peace: Stalin and the Soviet Ruling Circle, 1945–1953*. Oxford and New York: Oxford University Press, 2003.

Gregory, Paul, and Valery Lazarev, eds. *The Economics of Forced Labor: The Soviet Gulag*. Stanford: Hoover Institution Press, 2004.

Holloway, David. *The Soviet Union and the Arms Race*. New Haven: Yale University Press, 1984.

————. *Stalin and the Bomb: The Soviet Union and Atomic Energy*. New Haven: Yale University Press, 1994.

Ivanova, Galina Mikhailovna. *Labor Camp Socialism: The Gulag in the Soviet Totalitarian System*. Translated by Carol A. Flath. Armonk, N.Y.: M.E. Sharpe, 2000.

Jakobson, Michael. *Origins of the Gulag: The Soviet Prison Camp System, 1917–1934*. Lexington: University Press of Kentucky, 1993.

Janson, Marc, and Nikita Petrov. *Stalin's Loyal Executioner: People's Commissar Nikolai Ezhov*. Stanford: Hoover Institution Press, 2002.

Jasny, Naum. *Soviet Industrialization, 1928–1952*. Chicago: University of Chicago Press, 1961.

Khlevniuk, Oleg V. *The History of the Gulag: From Collectivization to the Great Terror*. Translated by Vadim Staklo. New Haven and London: Yale University Press, 2004.

————. *Master of the House: Stalin and His Inner Circle*. Translated by Nora Seligman Favorov. New Haven and London: Yale University Press, 2009.

Kotkin, Stephen. *Magnetic Mountain: Stalinism as a Civilization*. Berkeley: University of California Press, 1995.

Laqueur, Walter. *Stalin: The Glasnost Revelations*. New York: Scribner's, 1990.

Mastny, Vojtech. *Russia's Road to Cold War: Diplomacy, Warfare, and the Politics of Communism, 1941–1945*. New York: Columbia University Press, 1979.

————. *The Cold War and Soviet Insecurity: The Stalin Years*. New York: Oxford University Press, 1996.

McNeal, Robert A. *Stalin: Man and Ruler*. New York: New York University Press, 1988.

Medvedev, Roy A. *Let History Judge*. Translated by Colleen Taylor. New York: Vintage, 1971.

Merridale, Catherine. *Ivan's War: Life and Death in the Red Army, 1939–1945*. New York: Henry Holt, 2006.

Montefiore, Simon Sebag. *Stalin: The Court of the Red Tsar*. New York: Knopf, 2004.

Nekrich, Aleksandr. *The Punished Peoples: The Deportation and Fate of Soviet Minorities at the End of the Second World War*. New York: Norton, 1978.

Overy, Richard. *Russia's War: A History of the Soviet War Effort, 1941–1945*. New York: Penguin, 1998.

Parrish, Michael. *The Lesser Terror: Soviet State Security, 1939–1953*. Westport, Conn. and London: Praeger, 1996.

Rayfield, Donald. *Stalin and His Hangmen: The Tyrant and Those Who Killed for Him*. New York: Random House, 2005.

Saul, Norman E. *Friends or Foes? The United States and Soviet Russia, 1921–1941*. Lawrence: University of Kansas Press, 2006.

Service, Robert. *Stalin: A Biography*. Cambridge, Mass.: Belknap Press of Harvard University Press, 2005.

Shentalinsky, Vitaly. *The KGB's Literary Archive*. Translated by John Crowfoot. Introduction by Robert Conquest. London: Harvill Press, 1995.

Solzhenitsyn, Aleksandr. *The Gulag Archipelago*, 3 vols. Translated by Thomas P. Whitney. New York: Harper and Row, 1973, 1975, 1978.

Stone, David R. *Hammer and Rifle: The Militarization of the Soviet Union, 1926–1933*. Lawrence: University Press of Kansas, 2000.

Sutton, Anthony. *Western Technology and Soviet Economic Development, 1930–1945*. Palo Alto: Stanford University Press, 1971.

Tolstoy, Nikolai. *Stalin's Secret War*. Translated by George Saunders. New York: Holt, Rinehart and Winston, 1981.

Trotsky, Leon. *Stalin: An Appraisal of the Man and His Era*. Edited and translated by Charles Malamuth. New York: Grosset and Dunlap, 1941.

Tucker, Robert C. *Stalinism: Essays in Historical Interpretation*. New York: Norton, 1977.

———, ed., *Stalin in Power: The Revolution from Above, 1928–1941*. New York: Norton, 1977.

Ulam, Adam. *Stalin*. New York: Viking, 1973.

Volkogonov, Dmitri. *Stalin: Triumph and Tragedy*. Edited and translated by Harold Shukman. Rocklin, Calif.: Prima Publishing, 1992.

Werth, Alexander. *Russia at War, 1941–1945*. New York: Dutton, 1964.

Werth, Nicholas. "A State Against Its People: Violence, Repression, and Terror in the Soviet Union." In Stéphane Courtois et al. *The Black Book of Communism: Crimes, Terror, Repression*. Translated by Jonathan Murphy and Mark Kramer. Cambridge, Mass.: Harvard University Press, 1999.

PART V: THE SOCIALIST SUPERPOWER

Adelman, Deborah. *The "Children of Perestroika" Come of Age: Young People of Moscow Talk About Life in the New Russia*. Armonk, N.Y. and London: M.E. Sharpe, 1994.

Brown, Archie. *The Gorbachev Factor*. Oxford and New York: Oxford University Press, 1997.

Breslauer, George W. *Khrushchev and Brezhnev as Leaders*. London: George Allen and Unwin, 1982.

Burlatsky, Fedor. *Khrushchev and the First Russian Spring: The Era of Khrushchev Through the Eyes of His Advisor*. Translated by Daphne Skillen. New York: Scribner's Sons, 1988.

Cohen, Stephen, et al., eds. *The Soviet Union Since Stalin*. Bloomington: Indiana University Press, 1980.

d'Encausse, Hélène. *Confiscated Power.* Translated by George Holoch. New York: Harper and Row, 1982.

Desai, Padma. *Perestroika in Perspective: The Design and Dilemmas of Soviet Reform.* Princeton: Princeton University Press, 1989.

Dornberg, John. *Brezhnev: The Masks of Power.* New York: Basic Books, 1974.

Fitzer, Donald. *The Khrushchev Era: De-Stalinization and the Limits of Reform in the USSR, 1953–1964.* London: Macmillan, 1993.

Goldman, Marshall. *What Went Wrong with Perestroika.* New York and London: Norton, 1992.

Hosking, Geoffrey. *The Awakening of the Soviet Union.* Cambridge, Mass.: Harvard University Press, 1990.

Kaiser, Robert. *Why Gorbachev Happened: His Triumphs, His Failure, and His Fall.* New York: Simon and Schuster, 1992.

Lewin, Moshe. *The Gorbachev Phenomenon: A Historical Interpretation.* Berkeley and Los Angeles: University of California Press, 1988.

Linden, Carl A. *Khrushchev and the Soviet Leadership.* Baltimore: Johns Hopkins University Press, 1990.

McCauley, Martin, ed. *Khrushchev and Khrushchevism.* Bloomington: Indiana University Press, 1987.

Medvedev, Roy A., and Zhores A. Medvedev. *Khrushchev: The Years in Power.* Translated by Andrew R. Durkin. New York: Columbia University Press, 1975.

Remnick, David. *Lenin's Tomb: The Last Days of the Soviet Empire.* New York: Random House, 1993.

Richter, James A. *Khrushchev's Double Bind: International Pressures and Domestic Coalition Politics.* Baltimore: Johns Hopkins University Press, 1996.

Rubinstein, Joshua. *Soviet Dissidents.* Boston: Beacon Press, 1980.

Satter, David. *Age of Delusion.* New York: Knopf, 1996.

Smith, Hedrick. *The Russians.* New York: Ballantine Books, 1976.

Strayer, Robert. *Why Did the Soviet Union Collapse? Understanding Historical Change.* Armonk, N.Y.: M.E. Sharpe, 1998.

Taubman, William. *Khrushchev: The Man and His Era.* New York: Norton, 2003.

Tompson, William J. *Khrushchev: A Political Life.* New York: St. Martin's Press, 1995.

Voslensky, Michael. *Nomenklatura: The Soviet Ruling Class.* Translated by Erich Mosbacher. Garden City, N.Y.: Doubleday, 1984.

Yanov, Alexander. *The Drama of the Soviet 1960s: A Lost Reform.* Translated by Stephen P. Dunn. Berkeley, Calif.: Institute of International Studies, 1984.

PART VI: THE RUSSIAN FEDERATION

Gustafson, Thane. *Capitalism Russian-Style.* New York: Cambridge University Press, 1999.

Herspring, Dale R., ed. *Putin's Russia: Past Imperfect, Future Uncertain.* Lanham, Md.: Rowman & Littlefield, 2003.

Jones, Anthony, ed. *Education and Society in the New Russia.* Armonk, N.Y and London: M.E. Sharpe, 1994.

Lapidus, Gail, ed. *The New Russia: Troubled Transformation.* Boulder, Colo.: Westview Press, 1995.

Lowenhardt, John. *The Reincarnation of Russia: Struggling with the Legacy of Communism, 1990–1994*. Durham, N.C.: Duke University Press, 1994.

Lucas, Edward. *The New Cold War: Putin's Russia and the Threat to the West*. Revised edition. New York: Palgrave Macmillan, 2009.

McFaul, Michael. *Russia's Unfinished Revolution: Political Change from Gorbachev to Putin*. Ithaca, N.Y. and London: Cornell University Press, 2001.

Meier, Andrew. *Black Earth: A Journey Through Russia After the Fall*. New York: Norton, 2003.

Nelson, Lynn D., and Irina Kuzes. *Radical Reform in Yeltsin's Russia: Political, Economic, and Social Dimensions*. Armonk, N.Y.: M.E. Sharpe, 1995.

Politkovskaya, Anna. *Putin's Russia: Life in a Failing Democracy*. Translated by Arch Tait. New York: Metropolitan Books, 1995.

Remnick, David. *Resurrection: The Struggle for a New Russia*. New York: Random House, 1997.

Satter, David. *Darkness at Dawn: The Rise of the Russian Criminal State*. New Haven and London: Yale University Press, 2003.

Service, Robert. *Russia: Experiment with People*. Cambridge, Mass.: Harvard University Press, 2002.

Shevtsova, Lilia. *Yeltsin's Russia: Myths and Realities*. Washington, D.C.: Carnegie Endowment for International Peace, 1999.

_____. *Putin's Russia*. Washington, D.C.: Carnegie Endowment for International Peace, 2003.

Simes, Dmitri K. *After the Collapse: Russia Seeks Its Place as a Great Power.* New York: Simon and Schuster, 1999.

White, Stephen, Alex Pravda, and Zvi Gitelman, eds. *Developments in Russian and Post-Soviet Politics*. Durham, N.C.: Duke University Press, 1994.

Yeltsin, Boris. *Against the Grain: An Autobiography.* Translated by Michael Glenny. New York: Summit Books, 1990.

OVERVIEWS OF RUSSIAN/SOVIET HISTORY

Blackwell, William L. *The Industrialization of Russia*. New York: Crowell, 1970.

Brooks, Jeffrey. *Thank You, Comrade Stalin: Soviet Public Culture from Revolution to Cold War.* Princeton: Princeton University Press, 2000.

Daniels, Robert V. *The End of the Communist Revolution*. London and New York: Routledge, 1993.

Feshbach, Murray, and Alfred Friendly, Jr. *Ecocide in the USSR: Health and Nature Under Siege*. New York: Basic Books, 1992.

Graham, Loren R. *Science in Russia and the Soviet Union: A Short History* (Cambridge History of Science). New York: Cambridge University Press, 1994.

Laqueur, Walter. *The Dream that Failed: Reflections on the Soviet Union*. New York: Oxford University Press, 1994.

Lincoln, W. Bruce. *Between Heaven and Hell: The Story of a Thousand Years of Artistic Life in Russia*. New York: Viking, 1998.

McNeal, Robert A. *The Bolshevik Tradition: Lenin, Stalin, Khrushchev, Brezhnev,* 2d ed. Englewood Cliffs, N.J.: Prentice Hall, 1975.

Medvedev, Zhores. *Soviet Agriculture*. New York and London: Norton, 1987.

Merridale, Catherine. *Night of Stone: Death and Memory in Twentieth-Century Russia*. New York: Viking Penguin, 2001.

Nove, Alec. *An Economic History of the USSR, 1917–1991,* 3d ed. New York: Penguin, 1992.

Ragsdale, Hugh. *The Russian Tragedy: The Burden of History.* Armonk, N.Y.: M.E. Sharpe, 1996.

Reshetar, Jr., John S. *A Concise History of the Communist Party of the Soviet Union.* Revised and expanded. New York: Praeger, 1964.

Sakwa, Richard, ed. *The Rise and Fall of the Soviet Union, 1917–1991.* London and New York: Routledge, 1999.

Schapiro, Leonard. *The Communist Party of the Soviet Union.* New York: Vintage, 1964.

Sinyavsky, Andrei, *Soviet Civilization: A Cultural History.* New York: Arcade Publishing, 1988.

Suny, Ronald Grigor. *The Cambridge History of Russia. Volume III: The Twentieth Century.* New York: Cambridge University Press, 2006.

Volkogonov, Dmitri. *Autopsy for an Empire: The Seven Leaders Who Built the Soviet Union.* Edited and translated by Harold Shukman. New York: Free Press, 1998.

Von Laue, Theodore H. *Why Lenin? Why Stalin? Why Gorbachev?* New York: HarperCollins, 1993.

Yakovlev, Alexander N. *A Century of Violence in Soviet Russia.* Translated by Anthony Austin. New Haven and London: Yale University Press, 2002.

Zubok, Vladislav M. *A Failed Empire: The Soviet Union in the Cold War from Stalin to Gorbachev.* Chapel Hill: The University of North Carolina Press, 2007.

Index

Afghanistan
  Andropov administration (1982–1984),
    346
  Brezhnev administration (1964–1982),
    339–40
  Gorbachev administration (1985–1991),
    378
Agriculture
  Andropov administration (1982–1984),
    344
  autocratic state, 8, 48–49, 51, 78–79,
    85, 87
  Brezhnev administration (1964–1982),
    320–21, 322–23, 351
  famine impact, 48–49, 51, 135, 273
  food production, 135, 186
  Gorbachev administration (1985–1991),
    382–83
  grain exports, 48–49, 85, 187–88, 189,
    446
  grain production, 192, 207–8, 273, 320
  Khrushchev administration (1953–
    1964), 288, 298–99, 305–6, 312
  New Economic Policy (NEP), 147–48,
    158–59
  production (1921), 143
  Putin administration (1999–2008), 442,
    446–47
  state-run farms, 209
  World War I, 87
  Yeltsin administration (1991–1999),
    411, 418–19, 429, 437
  See also Collectivization
Akhmatova, Anna, 84, 275

Akhromeyev, Sergei, 378
Albania, 264
Alcohol consumption
  Brezhnev administration (1964–1982),
    355
  Gorbachev administration (1985–1991),
    369–70
  Putin administration (1999–2008), 449
  World War I, 87
  Yeltsin administration (1991–1999), 437
Alexander I, 20
Alexander II, 19, 22–23, 35, 39, 40, 42,
    43, 73
Alexander III, 23–25, 43, 52, 53, 58
Alexandrov, G. F., 289
Alkhavov, Alu, 451
Allende, Salvador, 342
All-Russian Council of Workers' Control,
    119
Amin, Hafizullah, 339
Andreyeva, Nina, 386
Andropov, Yuri, 284, 331, 342–43
  administration of (1982–1984), 343–47
  death of, 346–47
  economic policy, 344, 345
  foreign policy, 346
  military weapons, 346
  political leadership, 343–44, 345
  reform agenda, 344–45
Antiballistic missile (ABM), 331–32
Antiballistic Missile (ABM) Treaty, 453
Anti-Comintern Pact (1936), 251
April Theses (1917), 99–101
Armenia, 377, 385

Art, 84, 155, 224
Austria, 250
Autocratic state
agriculture, 8, 48–49, 51, 78–79, 85, 87
Alexander I, 20
Alexander II, 19, 22–23, 35, 39, 40, 42, 43, 73
Alexander III, 23–25, 43, 52, 53, 58
capitalism, 21, 35, 47–53
Catherine II, 29
cultural development, 10, 21, 37, 38, 78–79, 83–84
Decembrist uprising, 20
economy, 9–10, 27–31, 48–49, 73–74, 83, 84–85, 86–87, 88
ethnic groups, 10
event chronology, 461
final years, 73–88
industry, 31, 47, 48, 49–52, 83, 85, 87
intellectuals, 21
intelligentsia, 32–44
Ivan III, the Great, 12–13
Ivan IV, the Terrible, 12, 13, 15–16, 29
Kievan Russia, 8–12, 15
middle class, 30
Mongol conquest (1237–1240), 9–10
Moscow, 11–12
Nicholas I, 20–22
Nicholas II, 25, 45 (photo), 52–53, 76–78, 85–86, 87–88, 92, 407, 433
nineteenth-century crisis, 19–25
nobility, 12–14, 17, 29–30
non-Russian minorities, 24, 54
peasantry, 8, 17
Emancipation Edict (1861), 27–31, 39
serfdom, 11, 12–14, 22, 26–29
state peasants, 17, 26–27
Peter I, the Great, 16–18, 26, 29, 34, 407
Peter III, 19
reforms, 19–20
counterreforms, 23–25
Great Reforms, 22–23, 34
religion, 9, 12, 21, 85
Russian expansion, 14–16
Russian security, 14–16
Russification, 24, 53, 54, 80
secret police, 20–21

Autocratic state (continued)
Western European relations, 13, 16, 18
Westernization impact, 15–16, 18, 22–23, 32–33, 34–36, 38–39
working class, 30–31
labor strikes, 49, 51–52, 53, 73–74, 76, 84–85, 88
Marxism, 54, 55–57, 61–66, 68–69
1905 Revolution, 73–78, 82
Automobile industry, 445–46, 448–49
Axelrod, Pavel, 65
Azerbaijan, 377, 385

Babel, Isaac, 235, 289
"Babi Yar" (Yevtushenko), 258, 311
Bakatin, Vadim, 395
Bakunin, Mikhail, 36, 40
Banking industry, 49, 120, 423–24
Basayev, Shamil, 451, 452
Beatles, The, 356–57, 379
Belinsky, Vissarion, 21, 37, 38
Belorussia, 3, 10
Russification, 226
Soviet Union dissolution (1991), 400
World War II (1941–1945), 256
Bely, Andrei, 84
Berdyaev, Nicholas, 74, 155
Berezovsky, Boris, 432, 443
Beria, Lavrenty
Khrushchev administration (1953–1964), 284, 285, 287–88
Stalinism, 216–17, 219–20, 235, 238, 239, 242, 255–56, 274, 277, 278
Biological weapons, 332–33
Biryukova, Alexandra, 372, 375
Black Repartition, 43
Blok, Alexander, 84
Bloody Sunday (January, 1905), 76
Bolsheviks
autocratic state, 57, 66–68, 70, 71–72
bureaucratism, 162–66, 195–96
dictatorship, 149–52, 164–66
elections (November, 1917), 120–22
factionalism, 150, 151–52, 179–80, 181
foreign policy, 159–62

Bolsheviks *(continued)*
  July Days (1917), 103–5
  Kronstadt Rebellion (1921), 145–46
  Lenin Enrollment (1924), 153, 182
  New Economic Policy (NEP), 186–92,
    196–98
  1905 Revolution, 81–82
  October Enrollment (1927), 153
  one-party state (1917–1918), 118–20
  Party Unity resolution (1921), 150–52,
    181–82
  political leadership, 176–86
    leading contenders, 176–79
    power struggle, 179–80
    Triumvirate, 179–80, 182–83,
      184–85
  Reds, 126–28, 137
  revolutionary movement (1917), 96,
    100–101, 106–9, 110–13
    July Days, 103–5
    November revolution, 109–13
    party growth, 101–3
    political endorsement, 115–18
  Russian Civil War (1918–1920), 124–41
  show trials, 233–34
  societal relations, 192–96
  Whites, 126–28, 137
  See also Communist Party; Lenin,
    Vladimir; Stalin, Joseph; Trotsky,
    Leon; specific Party Congress
Bonaparte, Napoleon, 6
Bonner, Elena, 398
Bourgeois
  Marxism, 55–56
  revolutionary movement (1917), 94, 99,
    100, 102–3
Brezhnev, Leonid, 240, 284, 288
  administration of (1964–1982), 317–43
  Communist oligarchy, 317–9
  corruption, 353–55
  cultural development, 324–25
  death of, 342–43
  dekhrushchevization, 319–20
  détente, 331–34, 335–36
  dissident movement, 325–29
  economic policy, 320–24, 350–53,
    354–55

Brezhnev, Leonid *(continued)*
  foreign policy, 331–42, 358–59
    Eastern Europe, 336–39
    Indochina, 334–35
    Latin America, 341–42
    Middle East, 339–41
    Solidarity (Poland), 333–34, 338–39
    United States, 328, 330–34
    Western Europe, 335–36
  legacy of, 348–59
  Marxism, 355–57
  Matryoshka doll (photo), 407
  military weapons, 330–34
  non-Russian minorities, 327–29, 357–58
  political leadership, 317–9
  socialism, 329
  Westernization, 326–27
Brezhnev Doctrine, 337
British Petroleum, 423
Broadcasting industry, 301–2, 443, 457
Brodsky, Joseph, 311, 324
Bronstein, Lev. *See* Trotsky, Leon
Budenny, Semyon, 253
Bukharin, Nikolai, 107, 122, 131, 234,
    379–80
  Bolshevik leadership, 179, 180, 181,
    183, 186
  New Economic Policy (NEP), 190–91,
    192, 197
Bukovsky, Vladimir, 302, 329
Bulgakov, Mikhail, 289
Bulgakov, Sergei, 74
Bulganin, Nikolai, 277, 289, 296
Bulgaria, 252, 260, 264, 266
Bunge, Nikolai, 49
Bunin, Ivan, 84, 155
Bureaucratism, 162–66, 195–96
Burlatsky, Fedor, 319
Bush, George W., 393, 453

Cancer Ward, The (Solzhenitsyn), 327
Capital accumulation, 189
Capitalism
  autocratic state, 21, 35, 47–53
  backwardness, 48–49
  foreign investment, 47–48, 50–51
  foreign loans, 48, 50–51

Capitalism *(continued)*
  industrialization, 50–52, 53
  industry, 47, 48, 49–52
  New Economic Policy (NEP), 158–59
  peasantry, 48–49, 51
  state role, 47
  Witte system, 49–51
  working class, 49, 51–52, 53
  Yeltsin administration (1991–1999),
    414–16
Castro, Fidel, 302, 304, 308, 341–42
Catherine II, 29, 407
Ceauşescu, Nicolae, 337
Chagall, Marc, 84, 155
Chaliapin, Fyodor, 83–84
Chalidze, Valery, 326, 329
Charter of Paris (1990), 392–93
Chechnya
  Chechen War (1994), 424–26
  Putin administration (1999–2008), 450–52
  Yeltsin administration (1991–1999),
    418, 424–26, 434–35
Cheka
  establishment of, 118, 131
  Russian Civil War (1918–1920), 124,
    129, 130–33, 134–35, 139–40
  See also State Political Administration
    (GPU); Unified State Political
    Administration (OGPU)
Chekhov, Anton, 84
Chemical industry, 47
Chemzov, Sergei, 449
Chernenko, Konstantin, 284, 350
  administration of (1984–1985), 347–48
  death of, 348
  foreign policy, 348
  political leadership, 347–48
Chernobyl (1986), 372–73
Chernomyrdin, Viktor, 419, 422, 425,
    431, 432–33
Chernov, Viktor, 99, 104, 121
Chernyshevsky, Nikolai, 36–39, 63
Chiang Kai-shek, 249
Children of the Arbat (Rybakov), 378
China
  Brezhnev administration (1964–1982),
    334, 335

China *(continued)*
  Cold War, 269
  Gorbachev administration (1985–1991),
    389
  Khrushchev administration (1953–
    1964), 290, 304, 307
  Putin administration (1999–2008), 454–55
  Stalinism, 249
Chornovil, Vyacheslav, 327
Chronicle of Current Events, 326
Chubais, Anatoly, 414, 416, 418, 422, 431
Churchill, Winston, 254, 259, 260, 265
Cinema, 156–57
  Brezhnev administration (1964–1982),
    324
  Gorbachev administration (1985–1991),
    379
  Zhdanovshchina (1946), 275
Civil War. *See* Russian Civil War
    (1918–1920)
Coal industry, 47, 49, 51, 143, 186–87,
    274, 388–89
Coal mining, 217
Cold War
  beginning of, 264–65, 267–70
  demise of, 392–93
  Gorbachev administration (1985–1991),
    392–93
Collectivization
  Marxism, 119
  post-World War II, 273
  Stalinism, 197, 199, 202–10, 226, 244
  Yeltsin administration (1991–1999),
    418–19
  See also Land ownership
Cominform (Communist Information
    Bureau), 268
Comintern (Communist International),
    160, 162, 186, 251, 268
Commonwealth of Independent States (CIS)
Communes, 27, 28, 34–35, 79, 193
Communist Manifesto, The (Marx and
    Engels), 401
Communist Party
  April Theses (1917), 100
  Jewish section, 158
  Kronstadt Rebellion (1921), 145–46

Communist Party *(continued)*
  nomenklatura, 353–54
  social inequalities, 226–29
  Stalinism
    corruption, 226–29
    Party leadership, 238–40
  See also Bolsheviks; specific Party
    Congress
Communist Party of the Russian
  Federation (CPRF), 422, 431, 444
Constituent Assembly
  disbandment of, 151
  elections (November, 1917), 120–22
  revolutionary movement (1917), 98
Constitutional Democrats (Kadets), 74,
  77, 95–97
Constitutions
  1918, 123–24
  1924, 158
  1936, 241–42
  1977, 329
  1993, 421
Cooperatives, 381–82
Corruption
  Brezhnev administration (1964–1982),
    353–55
  Communist Party, 226–29, 353–54
  organized crime, 426
  Putin administration (1999–2008), 444,
    457–58
  Yeltsin administration (1991–1999),
    419, 423–24, 426, 430, 437–38
Council of Labor and Defense, 134
Council of Mutual Economic Assistance
  (COMECON), 269
Crime
  organized crime, 426
  Yeltsin administration (1991–1999), 426
Crimean War (1853–1856), 22, 48
Cuba, 302
  Andropov administration (1982–1984),
    346
  Brezhnev administration (1964–1982),
    341–42
  missile crisis (1962), 308–10
Cultural development
  art, 84, 155, 224

Cultural development *(continued)*
  autocratic state, 10, 21, 37, 38, 78–79,
    83–84
  Brezhnev administration (1964–1982),
    324–25
  cinema, 156–57, 275, 324, 379
  dance, 84
  Golden Age, 21
  Gorbachev administration (1985–1991),
    367, 369, 375, 378–81
  Khrushchev administration (1953–
    1964), 288–89, 311
  music, 83–84, 356, 379
  natural sciences, 224–25
  New Economic Policy (NEP), 152–57
  Silver Age, 83–84
  social sciences, 224
  Stalinism, 223–25
  theater, 84, 155–56, 379–80
  Zhdanovshchina (1946), 275
  See also Education; Literature; Social
    policy
Currency, 120, 133, 423–24, 433
Czech Legion, 125–26
Czechoslovakia, 264, 266–67
  Brezhnev administration (1964–1982),
    336–38
  Gorbachev administration (1985–1991),
    391
  Nazi Germany, 250, 251–52
  Prague Spring (1968), 336–38

Dance, 84
Daniel, Yuli, 325
Darius the Great, 6
Dead Souls (Gogol), 458–59
Decembrists, 20, 33, 38
Decree on Land (1917), 116–17
Decree on Peace (1917), 116–17
De Gaulle, Charles, 335
Dekhrushchevization, 319–20
Dekulakization (1929–1930), 205–7
Democratic centralism, 182–83
Democratic Centralists, 149
Democratization
  Gorbachev administration (1985–1991),
    367–68

Democratization *(continued)*
  Putin administration (1999–2008),
    443–44, 456–59
  revolutionary movement (1917), 110–13
  Yeltsin administration (1991–1999),
    411–12, 414–16
Denikin, Anton, 126, 127, 380
Destalinization, 293–96, 310–12
Détente, 331–34, 335–36
Diaghilev, Sergei, 84
Dictatorship
  Bolsheviks, 149–52, 164–66
  Gorbachev administration (1985–1991),
    363–66, 395–96
  Stalinism, 270
Directory, 126
Dissident movement, 325–29
Divorce, 154, 193–94, 225
"Dizzy with Success" (Stalin), 204
Djilas, Milovan, 277
Doctor's Plot (1953), 276, 278
Doctor Zhivago (Pasternak), 311, 378
Dual power, 93–96
Dubček, Alexander, 336, 337, 391
Dudayev, Dzhokhar, 424–25
Dudintsev, Vladimir, 311
Durnovo, Peter N., 86
Dyachenko, Tatyana, 432
Dzerzhinsky, Felix, 24, 129, 131, 183,
  216, 405–6
Dzyuba, Ivan, 327

Eastern Europe
  Brezhnev administration (1964–1982),
    336–39
  Gorbachev administration (1985–1991),
    389–92
  postwar (1945–1948), 265–67
  Putin administration (1999–2008), 454
  Warsaw Pact (1955), 289
  Yeltsin administration (1991–1999), 428
  See also specific country
East Germany, 289, 335
  Gorbachev administration (1985–1991),
    390–91, 392
  reunification of, 390–91, 392
Economists, 59, 60

Economy
  Andropov administration (1982–1984),
    344, 345
  autocratic state, 9–10, 27–31
    backwardness, 10, 29, 48–49
    1905 Revolution, 73–74
    pre–World War I, 83, 84–85
    World War I, 86–87, 88
  backwardness, 10, 29, 48–49, 244–45
  Brezhnev administration (1964–1982),
    320–24, 350–53, 354–55
  First Five-Year Plan, 201–5, 210–14,
    217–18, 222, 233–34, 244
  forced labor camps, 215–21
  Gorbachev administration (1985–1991),
    366–67, 368–69, 375, 376, 381–83,
    388–89, 395, 396
  gross domestic product (GDP), 429,
    436–37
  gross national product (GNP), 279, 322
  Khrushchev administration (1953–
    1964), 287, 288, 291, 297–99, 303,
    305–6, 312
  market economy
    New Economic Policy (NEP), 148
    Putin administration (1999–2008),
      441
    Yeltsin administration (1991–1999),
      411, 414–16
  1921, 143–44
  Ninth Five-Year Plan, 322
  post–World War II, 272–75
  Putin administration (1999–2008), 441,
    442, 443, 445–49
  Russian Civil War (1918–1920), 133–36
  Second Five-Year Plan, 211–12,
    214–15, 217–18, 230–31, 241–42
  Seven-Year Plan, 303, 314–15
  Sixth Five-Year Plan, 293, 297–98, 303
  War Communism, 133–36, 146
  Yeltsin administration (1991–1999),
    411, 414–19, 429, 433, 436–38
  See also Agriculture; Capitalism;
    Industry; New Economic Policy
    (NEP); Privatization
Education, 78, 154, 223–24, 364
Egypt, 290, 303, 340

Ehrenburg, Ilya, 156, 288–89
Eighth Party Congress (1919), 136, 138
Eisenhower, Dwight D., 302
Eisenstein, Sergei, 156–57, 275
Electricity, 212, 423
Eleventh Party Congress (1922), 164–65
Emancipation Edict (1861), 27–31, 39
Engels, Friedrich, 57, 62, 401
Enterprise Law (1988), 376, 382
Estonia, 137, 251, 255, 261, 271, 384–85, 400
Ethnic groups. *See also* Non-Russian minorities; *specific ethnicity/ nationality*

Factionalism, 150, 151–52, 179–80, 181
Family policy
    divorce, 154, 193–94, 225
    Gorbachev administration (1985–1991), 374–75
    women, 193–94, 374–75
Famines
    1918–1921, 135, 147
    1921–1922, 144–45
    1932–1933, 207–9
    1946, 273
Farewell to Matyora (Rasputin), 356
Fathers and Sons (Turgenev), 33
Federal Security Service (FSB), 425, 430
Fifteenth Party Congress (1927), 185, 191
Finland, 106, 136–37, 145, 251, 255, 289
First Circle, The (Solzhenitsyn), 327
First Five-Year Plan, 201–5, 210–14, 217–18, 222, 233–34, 244
Food Dictatorship Decree (May, 1918), 134
Food Requisition Detachments, 134
Forced labor camps, 215–21, 261–62
    mass arrests (1945–1947), 271–72
    prisoner amnesty (1953), 287–88
    War Communism, 134–35
Ford, Gerald, 332, 342
Foreign investment, 47–48, 50–51, 437, 442, 445–46
Foreign loans, 48, 50–51
Foreign policy
    Andropov administration (1982–1984), 346

Foreign policy *(continued)*
    Bolsheviks, 159–62
    Brezhnev administration (1964–1982), 331–42, 358–59
    Gorbachev administration (1985–1991), 370–71, 373–74, 377, 378, 389–93
    Khrushchev administration (1953–1964), 289–90, 295–96, 299–304, 307–10
    Putin administration (1999–2008), 450–56
    Stalin, Joseph, 248–52, 265–70
    Yeltsin administration (1991–1999), 424–26, 427–28, 434–35
    See also Trade policy; World War I; World War II; specific country
Fourteenth Party Congress (1925), 185
Fradkov, Mikhail, 444
France
    Brezhnev administration (1964–1982), 335
    Nazi Germany, 250, 251
    Russian Civil War (1918–1920), 125, 126
    World War II (1941–1945), 250, 251, 259–61, 264
Free market. *See* Market economy
Free trade. *See* Trade policy
Frunze, Mikhail, 129
Fundamental Laws (1906), 77–78, 80
Furtseva, Katerina, 286

Gagarin, Yuri, 301
Gaidar, Yegor, 414, 416–18, 420
Galanskov, Yuri, 329
Gapon, Father George, 76
Gazprom, 448
Georgia, 163–64, 385
    Putin administration (1999–2008), 454, 455–56
German Social Democratic Party, 59, 62
Germany
    Anti-Comintern Pact (1936), 251
    Gorbachev administration (1985–1991), 390–91, 392
    Khrushchev administration (1953–1964), 289, 307–8

Germany *(continued)*
  Nazism (1930s), 250–52
  Nazi-Soviet Pact (1939), 252–53
  reunification of, 390–91, 392
  Soviet policy (1930s), 248–49
  Treaty of Brest-Litovsk (March, 1918),
    122–23
  World War II (1941–1945), 253–63,
    264, 265
Gierek, Edward, 338
Ginzburg, Alexander, 329
Glasnost, 367, 369, 375, 378–81
Gogol, Nikolai, 458–59
Gold currency, 120, 143
Golden Age, 21
Gold mining, 217, 218
Golitsin, N. D., 88
Gomulka, Wladyslaw, 295, 338
Gorbachev, Mikhail, 284, 344, 345, 347,
    348
  administration of (1985–1991), 360–406
  alcoholism, 369–70
  August coup (1991), 397–99
  Chernobyl (1986), 372–73
  cultural development, 367, 369, 375,
    378–81
  democratization, 367–68
  dictatorship, 363–66, 395–96
  economic policy, 366–67, 368–69, 375,
    376, 381–83, 388–89, 395, 396
  family policy, 374–75
  foreign policy
    Cold War demise, 392–93
    Eastern Europe, 389–92
    German reunification, 392
    Middle East, 378, 393
    United States, 370–71, 373–74, 377,
      392–93
  glasnost, 367, 369, 375, 378–81
  legacy of, 400–406
  Marxism, 400–401, 403
  Matryoshka doll (photo), 407
  military weapons, 373–74, 378, 393
  modern Soviet society, 363–66,
    369–70
  "new thinking" reform, 368, 377–78
  non-Russian minorities, 383–85

Gorbachev, Mikhail *(continued)*
  perestroika, 366–67, 376–77, 381–83,
    388–89, 396
    prelude to (1985–1986), 375
  political leadership, 361–63, 367–68,
    371–72, 385–88, 389, 393–400
  reform agenda, 366–68
  Soviet Union dissolution (1991),
    399–400
  totalitarianism, 403–6
Gorbachev, Raisa Titorenko, 361, 374,
    375
Goremykin, J. L., 87–88
Gorky, Maxim, 84, 155, 233
Grachev, Pavel, 420, 425, 431–32
Grain
  exports, 48–49, 85, 187–88, 189, 446
  production, 192, 207–8, 273, 320
Great Britain
  Nazi Germany, 250
  Russian Civil War (1918–1920), 125,
    126
  trade policy, 143, 148, 161
  World War II (1941–1945), 250,
    259–61, 264, 265
Great Reforms, 22–23, 34
Great Russians, 3, 10, 358
Great Terror (1936–1938), 229–42
Greece, 260
Greens, 127–28
Gregorian calendar, 123
Grenada, 346
Gromov, Boris, 378
Gromyko, Andrei, 331, 339, 362, 371,
    386
Gross domestic product (GDP), 429,
    436–37
Grossman, Vasily, 378
Gross national product (GNP), 279,
    322
Guchkov, Alexander, 97, 98
Gulag
  mass arrests (1945–1947), 271–72
  prisoner amnesty (1953), 287–88
  See also Forced labor camps
Gulag Archipelago, The (Solzhenitsyn),
    327, 378

Gulag (Chief Administration of Camps), 217–21, 261–62
Gulf of Finland, 106, 145–46
Gusinsky, Vladimir, 443

Havel, Vaclav, 391
Health care, 449–50
Helsinki Accords (1975), 328–29
Herzen, Alexander, 32, 35–36, 39, 40
Historical chronology
  autocratic state, 461
  Russian Federation, 470–473
  Soviet Russia, 461–469
Hitler, Adolf
  Nazism, 250–52, 261
  Nazi-Soviet Pact (1939), 252–53
  World War II (1941–1945), 254–57
Honecker, Erich, 390
Hope Against Hope (Mandelshtam), 157
Hungarian Socialist Federated Soviet Republic, 137
Hungary, 252, 260, 264, 266
  Gorbachev administration (1985–1991), 390
  uprising (1956), 295–96
Hussein, Saddam, 453

Ibsen, Henrik, 84
Imperialism (Lenin), 69, 82
India, 334
Industrialization
  capitalism, 50–52, 53
  Western Europe, 47, 50
Industry
  Andropov administration (1982–1984), 344, 345
  autocratic state, 31, 47, 48, 49–52, 83, 85, 87
  Brezhnev administration (1964–1982), 321–22, 323
  capitalism, 47, 48, 49–52
  Gorbachev administration (1985–1991), 382, 388–89
  growth rate (1860–1910), 85
  growth rate (1890–1914), 83
  industrialization debate, 189–91, 197

Industry *(continued)*
  industrialization drive, 199, 203, 204–5, 210–15, 231, 244, 245
  Khrushchev administration (1953–1964), 299–300
  labor strikes, 144, 388–89
    autocratic state, 49, 51–52, 53, 73–74, 76, 84–85, 88
  labor unions, 84, 149, 333–34, 338–39
  New Economic Policy (NEP), 159
  post-World War II, 273–75
  production
    1921, 143
    1925, 186–87
  Putin administration (1999–2008), 443, 444, 445–46, 448–49
  World War I, 87
  Yeltsin administration (1991–1999), 411, 429, 437
  See also specific industry
Intellectuals
  autocratic state, 21
  Dissident movement, 325–29
Intelligentsia, 32–44, 194
  conspiracy, 39–41
  Decembrists, 33, 38
  liberals, 39
  Marxism, 43, 54–57
  "New Men" ideology, 38–39
  nihilism, 36
  peasantry, 33–35, 39–42
  populism, 36–37, 54
  Slavophiles, 33, 34–36
  socialism, 35–36
  student revolutionaries, 41–42
  terror tactic, 42–44
  Westerners, 33, 34–36
  Westernization impact, 32–33, 34–36, 38–39
  working class, 42
  See also Marxism
Intercontinental ballistic missile (ICBM), 300, 331–32
Intermediate-Range Nuclear Forces Treaty (1987), 377
Internationalism or Russification? (Dzyuba), 327

Iran
  Brezhnev administration (1964–1982), 340–41
  Yeltsin administration (1991–1999), 428
Iraq, 393
Iron industry, 47, 49, 274
Israel, 276, 337, 340
Ivan III, the Great, 12–13
Ivan IV, the Terrible, 12, 13, 15–16, 29
Ivashko, Vladimir, 398
Izvestia, 378, 448

Japan
  Anti-Comintern Pact (1936), 251
  Brezhnev administration (1964–1982), 334
  Putin administration (1999–2008), 454–55
  Russian Civil War (1918–1920), 125, 126
  Soviet policy (1930s), 248–49, 250, 251
  World War II (1941–1945), 264, 265
Jaruzelski, Wojciech, 338–39
Jews
  anti-Semitism, 75, 157–58, 226, 275–76
  in Communist Party, 158
  Dissident movement, 328
  pogroms, 75, 127–28
  Russian Civil War (1918–1920), 127–28
  World War II (1941–1945), 254, 256, 257–58, 261
  Zhdanovshchina (1946), 275–76
July Days (1917), 103–5

Kadets, 74, 77, 95–97
Kadyrov, Akhmad, 450–51
Kadyrov, Ramzan, 451, 452
Kaganovich, Lazar, 214, 239, 242, 284–85, 292, 294, 296–97, 304–5
Kalinin, Mikhail, 89 (photo)
Kalugin, Oleg, 302
Kamenev, Lev, 100, 107–8, 117, 118, 166, 167, 233–34, 380
  Bolshevik leadership, 179–80, 181, 183–84, 185
Kandinsky, Vasily, 84, 155
Kania, Stanislaw, 338–39

Karmal, Babrak, 339
Kasyanov, Mikhail, 441
Katyn Forest, 255
Kazakhstan, 384
Keita, Modibo, 341
Kennedy, John F., 307–8, 309–10
Kerensky, Alexander, 97, 98, 103, 104, 105, 106, 109, 380
KGB, 343–44, 425, 433–34, 442
Khasbulatov, Ruslan, 414, 417, 420
Khattab, Ibn-ul, 451
Khomeini, Ayatollah, 340–41
Khordorkovsky, Mikhail, 444
Khrushchev, Nikita, 239, 263, 273, 277, 281 (photo)
  administration of (1953–1964), 283–315
  antiparty group, 296–97
  collective leadership, 284–85
  cultural development, 288–89, 311
  death of, 313–14
  destalinization reforms, 293–96, 310–12
  economic policy, 287, 288, 291, 297–99, 303, 305–6, 312
  foreign policy, 289–90, 295–96, 299–304, 307–10
  legacy of, 314–15
  Matryoshka doll (photo), 407
  political leadership, 284–86, 290–95, 296–301, 304–5, 312–15
  political power struggle, 285–86
  reform obstacles, 290–91
  secret speech (1956), 293–95
  Stalinism legacy, 291–93
  "thaw," 286–89
Kievan Russia, 8–12, 15
Kirilenko, Andrei, 339
Kiriyenko, Sergei, 433, 435
Kirov, Sergei, 227, 230–31, 232–33, 275
Kissinger, Henry, 334
Kohl, Helmut, 392
Kolchak, Alexander, 126, 127
Kollontai, Alexandra, 149
Komsomol, 153, 154, 194
Korea, 75
Korean War (1950–1953), 269–70
Kornilov, Lavr, 105–6, 117
Korolev, Sergei, 219–20, 300, 330

Korzhakov, Alexander, 430, 431–32
Kosygin, Alexei, 240, 317–18, 319,
    321–22, 331, 339
Kozlov, Frol, 286
Kozyrev, Andrei, 412, 422, 427, 428,
    431
Krasin, Leonid, 129
Krenz, Egon, 390, 391
Krestinsky, Nikolai, 234
Kronstadt Rebellion (1921), 145–46
Kryuchkov, Vladimir, 389, 396, 398
Kuibyshev, V. V., 233
Kulaks, 79, 188, 192
    dekulakization (1929–1930), 205–7
    Russian Civil War (1918–1920), 131,
        134
Kun, Bela, 160
Kurchatov, Igor, 274
Kuwait, 393

Labor strikes
    autocratic state, 49, 51–52, 53, 73–74,
        76, 84–85, 88
    coal miners (1989), 388–89
    Petrograd (1921), 144
Labor unions, 84
    Democratic Centralists, 149
    Solidarity (Poland), 333–34, 338–39
Land and Freedom Party, 42–43
Land ownership
    communes, 27, 28, 34–35, 79, 193
    Decree on Land (1917), 116–17
    Gorbachev administration (1985–1991),
        382–83
    peasantry, 26, 28, 79, 187
    Putin administration (1999–2008), 442
    See also Collectivization
Latin America, 341–42
Latvia, 137, 251, 255, 261, 271, 384–85,
    400
Lavrov, Peter, 38–39, 41
Law Code of 1649, 14, 15
League of Nations, 251
League of the Militant Godless, 153
Lebanon, 346
Lebed, Alexander, 425, 431, 432
Left Opposition, 180, 181, 183, 190–91

Left Socialist Revolutionaries (Left SRs),
    118, 122–23
Lend-Lease program, 257
Lenin, Krupskaya Nadezhda, 166–67
Lenin, Vladimir, 89 (photo)
    April Theses (1917), 99–101
    bureaucratism, 162–66
    death of, 164, 168, 169
    Eleventh Party Congress (1922), 164–65
    intelligentsia, 36, 38
    Kronstadt Rebellion (1921), 145–46
    legacy of, 167–71
    Marxism, 57–66, 68–72, 82
    Matryoshka doll (photo), 407
    New Economic Policy (NEP), 146–48
    non-Russian minorities, 24
    "party of a new type," 60–65
    "Postscript" (1923), 166–67
    revolutionary blueprint, 68–72
    revolutionary movement (1917),
        99–103, 104, 106–9, 111–12,
        115–18
    revolutionary tradition, 57–60, 82
    Russian Civil War (1918–1920),
        124–41
    Tenth Party Congress (1921), 149–52,
        176, 181
    "Testament" (1922), 166–67, 183, 185
    Twelfth Party Congress (1923), 166–67
    See also Bolsheviks
Lenin Enrollment (1924), 153, 182
Leninism
    defined, 59
    Marxist criticism of, 65–66
Lermontov, Mikhail, 399
Liberalism, 74, 75, 80–81
Liberals, 39
Liberation, 74
Liberman, Yevsei, 321
Life and Fate (Grossman), 378
Ligachev, Yegor, 345, 371, 380, 386
Literature
    autocratic state, 21, 37, 38, 84
    Brezhnev administration (1964–1982),
        324, 325–27
    Dissident movement, 325–27
    Golden Age, 21

Literature *(continued)*
  Gorbachev administration (1985–1991),
    369, 378
  Khrushchev administration (1953–
    1964), 288–89, 311
  New Economic Policy (NEP), 154–55,
    156, 157
  Silver Age, 84
  Zhdanovshchina (1946), 275
Lithuania, 10, 137, 255, 261, 271,
  384–85, 400
Little Russians, 10
Little Vera (1989), 379
Litvinov, Maxim, 252
Living Church, 153
Lukashenko, Alexander, 427–28
Lukoil, 423
Lukyanov, Anatoly, 398
Luxemburg, Rosa, 65–66
Lvov, George, 96, 104
Lysenko, Trofim, 224–25
Lyubimov, Yuri, 355

Machine Tractor Station (MTS), 209,
  299, 306, 312
Main Repertoire Committee (MRC),
  155–56
Malenkov, Georgy, 239, 277, 278,
  284–89, 291, 294, 296–97, 304–5
Malevich, Kazimir, 84
Malinovsky, Rodion, 297
Manchuria, 75, 290
Mandelshtam, Nadezhda, 157
Mandelshtam, Osip, 156, 157, 235
Mao Zedong, 200, 269, 307, 334
March revolution (1917), 92–103, 114
Market economy
  New Economic Policy (NEP), 148
  Putin administration (1999–2008),
    441
  Yeltsin administration (1991–1999),
    411, 414–16
Marshall Plan (1947), 268
Martov, Yuli, 65, 66–67, 104, 116
Marx, Karl, 55, 62, 400–401
Marxism
  bourgeois, 55–56

Marxism *(continued)*
  Brezhnev administration (1964–1982),
    355–57
  class struggle, 55
  Gorbachev administration (1985–1991),
    400–401, 403
  intelligentsia, 43, 54–57
  revolutionary movement, 55–72
  working class, 54, 55–57, 61–66, 68–69
Masaryk, Jan, 267
Mayakovsky, Vladimir, 156, 194
Medvedev, Dmitry A., 455–56
Medvedev, Roy, 326, 338
Medvedev, Zhores, 326
Mensheviks
  autocratic state, 59, 66–68
  1905 Revolution, 76, 81–82
  revolutionary movement (1917), 94,
    95–96, 97, 98, 99, 101, 102, 103–5,
    116–18
  Tenth Party Congress (1921), 149, 151
Meyerhold, Vsevolod, 156, 235
Middle class, 30
Middle East
  Andropov administration (1982–1984),
    346
  Brezhnev administration (1964–1982),
    339–41
  Gorbachev administration (1985–1991),
    378, 393
  Putin administration (1999–2008), 453
  Yeltsin administration (1991–1999), 428
  See also specific country
Mikhailovsky, Nikolai, 38, 39
Mikhoels, Solomon, 276
Mikoyan, Anastas, 184–85, 227, 239, 242,
  277, 293
Militarization
  Gulag, 218
  Stalinism, 221–23
Military weapons
  Andropov administration (1982–1984),
    346
  antiballistic missile (ABM), 331–32
  Antiballistic Missile (ABM) Treaty, 453
  atomic bomb, 274
  biological weapons, 332–33

Military weapons *(continued)*
  Brezhnev administration (1964–1982), 330–34
  Gorbachev administration (1985–1991), 373–74, 378, 393
  intercontinental ballistic missile (ICBM), 300, 331–32
  Intermediate-Range Nuclear Forces Treaty (1987), 377
  Khrushchev administration (1953–1964), 299–300
  Nuclear Non-Proliferation Treaty (NPT), 427
  nuclear weapons, 331–34, 373–74, 377, 393, 427, 453
  Strategic Arms Limitation Talks (SALT), 331–32, 333
  Strategic Arms Reduction Talks (START), 346
  Strategic Arms Reduction Treaty (START), 393, 453
  Strategic Defense Initiative (SDI), 374
  Strategic Offensive Reductions Treaty (SORT), 453
  submarine-launched ballistic missile (SLBM), 331–32
  World War II, 222–23, 253–54
  Yeltsin administration (1991–1999), 427
Milyukov, Paul, 80, 96–97, 98, 103
Milyutin, Vladimir, 117
Molotov, Vyacheslav, 183, 242, 252, 255–56, 284, 291, 294, 296–97, 304–5, 347–48
Mongol conquest (1237–1240), 9–10
Moroz, Valentin, 327
Morozov, Pavlik, 225
Moscow, 11–12
Moscow Art Theater, 84, 155–56
Munich Conference (1938), 250
Music, 83–84, 356, 379
Muslims, 158, 226, 340–41, 385, 453

Nabokov, Vladimir, 378
Nagy, Imre, 295–96
Natanson, Mark, 40
Natural sciences, 224–25
Nazi Germany (1930s), 250–52

Nazi-Soviet Pact (1939), 252–53
Near Abroad, 412, 413, 427–28
Nechaev, Sergei, 40
Neizvestny, Ernst, 311
Nekrich, Alexander, 324
Nemtsov, Boris, 432, 435
Nepmen, 147–48, 159, 196–98
New Course, The (Trotsky), 380
New Economic Policy (NEP)
  agriculture, 147–48, 158–59
  Bolsheviks, 186–92, 196–98
  capital accumulation, 189
  capitalism, 158–59
  cultural development, 152–57
  end of, 191–192
  establishment of, 146–48
  industrialization debate, 189–91, 197
  industry, 159, 189–91
  market economy, 148
  Nepmen, 147–48, 159
  privatization, 147–48, 187, 188, 189, 190
  savings, 189–90
  socialism, 158–59
New Economics, The (Preobrazhensky), 189
"New Men" ideology, 38–39
Nicaragua
  Andropov administration (1982–1984), 346
  Brezhnev administration (1964–1982), 342
Nicholas I, 20–22
Nicholas II, 25, 45 (photo), 52–53, 76–78, 85–86, 87–88, 92, 407, 433
Nihilism, 36
Nijinsky, Vaslav, 84
1905 Revolution. *See* Revolutionary movement (1905)
Nineteenth Party Congress (1952), 277–78, 386
Ninth Five-Year Plan, 322
Nixon, Richard M., 331–32, 334, 342
Nkrumah, Kwame, 341
NKVD. *See* People's Commissariat of Internal Affairs (NKVD)
Nobility, 12–14, 17, 29–30

Nogin, Viktor, 117
Nomenklatura, 353–54
Non-Russian minorities
   autocratic state, 24, 54
   Brezhnev administration (1964–1982), 327–29, 357–58
   Dissident movement, 327–29
   Gorbachev administration (1985–1991), 383–85
   nationalities policy (1920s), 157–58
   Russian Civil War (1918–1920), 136–37
Norilsk Nickel, 423
North Atlantic Treaty Organization (NATO), 269, 289, 335–36, 392, 428, 453–54
North Korea, 269–70
North Vietnam, 332, 334–35
Not By Bread Alone (Dudintsev), 311
Novaya Gazeta, 457
November (Bolshevik) revolution (1917), 109–13, 114–18
Novgorodtsev, Pavel, 74
Novotny, Antonin, 336
Novyi Mir (Yevtushenko), 369
Nuclear disaster, 372–73
Nuclear Non-Proliferation Treaty (NPT), 427
Nuclear weapons, 331–34, 373–74, 377, 393, 453

October Enrollment (1927), 153
October Manifesto (1905), 76–77
October Revolution (1993), 420–21
Octobrists, 74, 77, 80, 96
Official Nationality, 21
Ogarkov, Nikolai, 339, 347, 348
Oil industry, 47, 212, 274, 423–24, 444, 448
Olesha, Yuri, 235
Olympic Games, 333
One Day in the Life of Ivan Denisovich (Solzhenitsyn), 311
Ordzhonikidze, Sergo, 164, 230, 242
Organized crime, 426
Orgburo (Organizational Bureau), 138, 152, 176, 179, 278
Orlov, Yuri, 329

Pamyat, 380–81
Pasternak, Boris, 156, 311, 324, 378
Pavlov, Valentin, 396
Pavlova, Anna, 84
Peasantry
   autocratic state, 8, 17
      capitalism, 48–49, 51
      Emancipation Edict (1861), 27–31, 39
      intelligentsia, 33–35, 39–42
      kulaks, 79
      land ownership, 26, 28, 79
      1905 Revolution, 74, 78–79, 82
      redemption payments, 27–28
      serfdom, 11, 12–14, 22, 26–29
      state peasants, 17, 26–27
   Bolshevik relations, 192–93
   land ownership, 26, 28, 79, 187
   revolutionary movement
      1917, 94
      1920–1921, 144
   See also Agriculture; Kulaks
Peasant Union, 76
People's Commissariat of Internal Affairs (NKVD), 217
   Great Terror (1936–1938), 232–34, 235–38
   World War II (1941–1945), 254–55, 261–62
People's Will, 43–44, 55
Perestroika, 366–67, 375, 376–77, 381–83, 388–89, 396
Perestroika (Gorbachev), 384
Pestel, Pavel, 38
Peter I, the Great, 16–18, 26, 29, 34, 407
Peter III, 19
Petrograd Soviet, 95–96, 97, 99, 101, 106
Pilnyak, Boris, 235
Pisarev, Dmitry, 37
Plekhanov, George, 57, 58, 60, 280
Pobedonostsev, Konstantin, 23–24, 30
Podgorny, Nikolai, 317–18, 331
Poland
   Brezhnev administration (1964–1982), 333–34, 338–39
   Gorbachev administration (1985–1991), 389–90

Poland *(continued)*
  Nazi Germany, 251
  Russian Civil War (1918–1920),
    128–29, 137
  Solidarity, 333–34, 338–39
  uprising (1956), 295
  World War II (1941–1945), 252, 253,
    255, 261–62, 264, 265
Politburo (Political Bureau), 138, 152,
  179, 182, 185, 186, 278, 324–25,
  371–72
Politkovshaya, Anna, 457
Pomerantsev, Vladimir, 289
Popov, Gavril, 395, 398
Populism, 36–37, 54
Poskrebyshev, A. N., 232
"Postscript" (Lenin), 166–67
Pot, Pol, 200
Potanin, Vladimir, 432
Prague Spring (1968), 336–38
Pravda, 186
Preobrazhensky, Yevgeny, 189, 191
Presidium, 278, 324–25
Primakov, Yevgeny, 431, 433
Privatization
  Gorbachev administration (1985–1991),
    381–82
  of money, 423–24
  New Economic Policy (NEP), 147–48,
    187, 188, 189, 190
  Putin administration (1999–2008), 442,
    443
  Yeltsin administration (1991–1999),
    416–19, 423–24, 429
Problems of Idealism, 74
Problems of Leninism (Stalin), 184
Proletariat. *See* Working class
Proletkult, 155
Provisional Government, 92, 93–95,
  96–99, 100, 103–6, 110–13
Provisional Revolutionary Committee,
  145
Pugachev, Yemelyan, 29
Pugo, Boris, 395, 398
Putin, Vladimir
  administration of (1999–2008), 440–59
  corruption, 444, 457–58

Putin, Vladimir *(continued)*
  democratization, 443–44, 456–59
  economic policy, 441, 442, 443,
    445–49
  foreign policy, 450–56
  Matryoshka doll (photo), 407
  political leadership, 433–35, 440–45,
    455–56
  prime minister appointments, 433–35,
    455–56
  privatization, 442, 443
  reform agenda, 441–45
  renationalization policy, 448–49
  Russian society, 442–43, 449–50
Pyatnikov, G. L., 216

Qaddafi, Muammar, 340

Rachmaninoff, Sergei, 83, 379
Radek, Karl, 150
Radishchev, Alexander, 13–14, 32
Railroad industry, 47, 48, 50, 51, 87
Rasputin, Grigory, 52–53, 88, 356
Razin, Stenka, 29
Reagan, Ronald, 342, 370–71, 374, 377
Red Army
  Russian Civil War (1918–1920),
    125–26, 128–30, 137
  World War II (1941–1945), 255,
    257–58, 259
Red Guard
  Kornilov affair (1917), 105–6
  November revolution (1917), 110
Red Terror, 130–33
Reed, John, 156–57
Reforms
  Andropov administration (1982–1984),
    344–45
  autocratic state, 19–20
    agricultural reforms, 78–79
    counterreforms, 23–25
    Great Reforms, 22–23, 34
    Stolypin reforms, 78–81, 85
  Gorbachev administration (1985–1991),
    366–68, 377–78
  Khrushchev administration (1953–
    1964), 293–96, 310–12

Reforms *(continued)*
  Putin administration (1999–2008),
    441–45
Religion
  autocratic state, 9, 12, 21, 85
  Brezhnev administration (1964–1982),
    356
  Dissident movement, 327–28
  Gorbachev administration (1985–1991),
    379
  League of the Militant Godless, 153
  Living Church, 153
  See also Russian Orthodox Church;
    specific religious group
Repentence (1984), 379
Repin, Ilya, 155
Report from the Beria Reservation, A
  (Moroz), 327
Reutern, Mikhail, 49
Revolutionary movement (1905),
  73–82
  agricultural reforms, 78–79
  assessment of, 81–82
  Bloody Sunday, 76
  Bolsheviks, 81–82
  liberalism, 74, 75, 80–81
  Mensheviks, 76, 81–82
  peasantry, 74, 78–79, 82
  Russian economy, 73–74
  Stolypin reforms, 78–81, 85
  working class, 73–78, 82
Revolutionary movement (1917)
  Bolsheviks, 96, 100–101, 106–9,
    110–13
    growth of, 101–3
    July Days, 103–5
    November revolution, 109–13
    political endorsement, 115–18
  bourgeois, 94, 99, 100, 102–3
  Constituent Assembly, 98
  democratic failure, 110–13
  dual power, 93–96
  July Days, 103–5
  Kadets, 95–97
  Kornilov affair, 105–6
  Lenin's April Theses, 99–101
  March revolution, 92–103, 114

Revolutionary movement (1917)
  (continued)
  Mensheviks, 94, 95–96, 97, 98, 99, 101,
    102, 103–5, 116–18
  November (Bolshevik) revolution,
    109–13, 114–18
  Octobrists, 96
  peasantry, 94
  Petrograd Soviet, 95–96, 97, 99, 101,
    106
  Provisional Government, 92, 93–95,
    96–99, 100, 103–6, 110–13
  Socialist Revolutionaries (SRs), 95–96,
    97, 98, 99, 101, 103–5, 116, 118
  working class, 94
Right Opposition, 181, 191
Rokossovsky, K. K., 257
Roman Catholicism, 9
Romania, 252, 260, 264, 266, 337
Roosevelt, Franklin D., 259
Rostechnology, 448–49
Russia
  climate, 4
  geographical boundaries, 4, 5–6,
    409–10
  historical chronology
    autocratic state, 461
    Russian Federation, 470–473
    Soviet Russia, 461–469
  historical invasions, 5–7, 9–10
  natural resources, 4–5
Russian Civil War (1918–1920), 124–41
  Cheka, 124, 129, 130–33, 134–35,
    139–40
  class war, 127–28, 138–41
  legacy of, 137–41
  Lenin's lieutenants, 128–30
  non-Russian minorities, 136–37
  Poland, 128–29, 137
  Reds versus Whites, 126–28, 137
  Red Terror, 130–33
  War Communism, 133–36
Russian Federation
  event chronology, 470–473
  geographical boundaries, 409–10
Russian Orthodox Church, 258
  autocratic state, 9, 12, 21, 85

Russian Orthodox Church *(continued)*
  Gorbachev administration (1985–1991),
    379
  Living Church, 153
Russian Soviet Federated Socialist
    Republic, 123–24
Russification
  autocratic state, 24, 53, 54, 80
  Belorussia, 226
  Khrushchev administration (1953–
    1964), 311–12
  Ukraine, 226
Russo-Japanese War (1904–1905), 53, 75
Rutskoi, Alexander, 414, 417, 420
Rybakov, Anatoly, 378
Rykov, Alexei, 117, 179, 180, 234, 380
Ryzhkov, Nikolai, 383, 397

Sadat, Anwar, 340
Sakharov, Andrei, 326, 328, 329, 375,
    387, 398
Savings, 189–90
Savinkov, Boris, 131
Scriabin, Alexander, 83
Second Five-Year Plan, 211–12, 214–15,
    217–18, 230–31, 241–42
Secretariat, 138, 152, 176, 181–82
Secret police, 20–21
  See also Cheka; KGB; People's
    Commissariat of Internal Affairs
    (NKVD)
Secret speech (Khrushchev, 1956),
    293–95
Serapion Brotherhood, 156
Serov, Ivan, 286, 295
Seventeenth Party Congress (1934), 230
Seven-Year Plan, 303, 314–15
Shatalin, Stanislav, 396
Shatrov, Mikhail, 379–80
Shcharansky, Anatoly, 329, 375
Shelepin, Alexander, 286, 318
Shelest, Pyotr, 327
Shevardnadze, Eduard, 371, 378, 395, 396
Shlyapnikov, Alexander, 149, 165
Show trials, 233–34
Sibneft, 423
Sidanko, 423

Silver Age, 83–84
Sinyavsky, Andrei, 325, 329, 458
Sixteenth Party Congress (1930), 201
Sixth Five-Year Plan, 293, 297–98, 303
Slavophiles, 33, 34–36
Sobchak, Anatoly, 395, 434
Social Democrats (SDs), 54, 59, 61, 62,
    63, 66–68, 81, 250
Socialism
  Brezhnev administration (1964–1982),
    329
  intelligentsia, 35–36
  New Economic Policy (NEP), 158–59
Socialist Revolutionaries (SRs)
  autocratic state, 54–55, 78, 81
  revolutionary movement (1917), 95–96,
    97, 98, 99, 101, 103–5, 116, 118
  Tenth Party Congress (1921), 149, 151
Social policy
  divorce, 154, 193–94, 225
  education, 78, 154, 223–24, 364
  family policy, 154, 193–94, 225, 374–75
  Gorbachev administration (1985–1991),
    363–66, 369–70
  health care, 449–50
  Putin administration (1999–2008),
    442–43, 449–50
  women, 193–94, 374–75
  See also Cultural development; Standard
    of living
Social sciences, 224
Solidarity (Poland), 333–34, 338–39
Solzhenitsyn, Aleksandr, 219, 236–37,
    311, 325, 326–27, 329, 378, 458
South Korea, 269–70
South Vietnam, 332, 334–35
Space program
  Brezhnev administration (1964–1982),
    330
  Khrushchev administration (1953–
    1964), 300–301
  Stalinism, 219–20
Spanish Civil War (1936–1939), 250
Speransky, Mikhail, 14
Sputnik, 300
St. Petersburg, 17
Stakhanov, Alexei, 213

Stakhanovite movement, 213
Stalin, Joseph, 89 (photo)
  bureaucratism, 164–66
  Cold War, 267–70
  death of, 278
  deportations, 271–72
  dictatorship, 270
  foreign policy, 248–52, 265–70
  general secretary post, 152, 164–65
  and Leninism, 68
  and Marxism, 249–50
  Matryoshka doll (photo), 407
  and Nazism, 251–52
  Nazi-Soviet Pact (1939), 252–53
  non-Russian minorities, 24
  personal background, 177–78
  physical health, 277–78
  political leadership, 100, 176, 177–86
  Russian Civil War (1918–1920), 138,
    140–41
  Soviet security (1930s), 248–50
  Twelfth Party Congress (1923), 166–67
  Workers' and Peasants' Inspectorate
    (Rabkrin), 163
  World War II (1941–1945), 253–62
    diplomatic leadership, 259–61
    national leadership, 258–59
    secret war, 254–55, 261–62
  Zhdanovshchina (1946), 275–76
Stalinism
  collectivization, 199, 202–10, 226, 244
  Communist inequalities, 226–29
  cultural development, 223–25
  dekulakization (1929–1930), 205–7
  destalinization reforms, 293–96, 310–12
  First Five-Year Plan, 201–5, 210–14,
    217–18, 222, 233–34, 244
  forced labor camps, 215–21
  Great Terror (1936–1938), 229–42
  historical context, 243–45, 279–80
  industrialization drive, 199, 203, 204–5,
    210–15, 231, 244, 245
  militarization, 221–23
  non-Russian minorities, 225–26
  Party leadership, 238–40
  revolution from above, 199–201,
    238–40, 243–45

Stalinism (continued)
  Second Five-Year Plan, 211–12,
    214–15, 217–18, 230–31,
    241–42
  Stalin's inner circle, 231–32, 242–43
  terror-famine (1932–1933), 207–9
  totalitarianism, 240–42, 244–45
Standard of living
  Brezhnev administration (1964–1982),
    323–24, 351–53
  Putin administration (1999–2008), 447,
    449–50
  Yeltsin administration (1991–1999),
    417, 430–31, 437
Stanislavsky, Konstantin, 84
State and Revolution, The (Lenin), 70,
  162, 169
State Political Administration (GPU),
  151
Steel industry, 187, 212, 274
Stepashin, Sergei, 433
Stolypin, Peter A., 78–81, 85
Strategic Arms Limitation Talks (SALT),
  331–32, 333
Strategic Arms Reduction Talks (START),
  346
Strategic Arms Reduction Treaty
  (START), 393, 453
Strategic Defense Initiative (SDI), 374
Strategic Offensive Reductions Treaty
  (SORT), 453
Stravinsky, Igor, 83
Strikes. See Labor strikes
Struve, Peter, 74
Student revolutionaries, 41–42
Submarine-launched ballistic missile
  (SLBM), 331–32
Sub-Saharan Africa, 341
Suez Canal, 303
Sultan-Galiev, M. G., 183
Supreme Council of the National
  Economy, 119
Surgutneftgaz, 448
Suslov, Mikhail, 317–18, 319, 331
Sverdlov, Yakov, 129
Svoboda, Ludvik, 336–37
Switzerland, 57, 100

Tambov uprising (1920–1921), 144, 151–52
Taraki, Nur Mohammed, 339
Tatars, 3, 6, 11, 12
Taxation, 193, 213–14, 442
Tchaikovsky, Peter, 83
Tenth Party Congress (1921), 145, 149–52, 176, 181
Terror
  famine (1932–1933), 207–9
  Great Terror (1936–1938), 229–42
  intelligentsia tactic, 42–44
  Red Terror, 130–33
"Testament" (Lenin), 166–67, 183, 185
Textile industry, 186–87, 195
"Thaw," 286–89
Theater, 84, 155–56, 379
Third Section of the Imperial Chancellery, 20–21
Thirteenth Party Congress (1924), 183, 185
Tito, Joseph Broz, 267, 269, 290
Tkachev, Peter, 38, 40–41
Tolstoy, Alexei, 156
Tomsky, Mikhail, 179, 180
Totalitarianism
  Gorbachev administration (1985–1991), 403–6
  Stalinism, 240–42, 244–45
  Yeltsin administration (1991–1999), 410–13
Touré, Sékou, 341
Trade policy
  Great Britain, 143, 148, 161
  military supplies, 143
  United States, 328
Transcaucasian Federated Republic, 164
Transcaucasian Soviet Federated Socialist Republics, 158
Trans-Siberian Railroad, 51
Treaty of Brest-Litovsk (March, 1918), 122–23
Triumvirate, 179–80, 182–83, 184–85
Trotsky, Leon, 379, 380
  Bolsheviks, 102–3, 109
    political leadership, 176–77, 184, 185, 189

Trotsky, Leon (continued)
  bureaucratism, 166
  Kronstadt Rebellion (1921), 145–46
  on Leninism, 66
  non-Russian minorities, 24
  Petrograd Soviet, 106
  revolutionary movement, 76, 102–3
  Russian Civil War (1918–1920), 129–30, 131, 135, 138
  Twelfth Party Congress (1923), 166–67
Truman, Harry, 265
Truman Doctrine (1947), 268
Tukhachevsky, Mikhail, 129, 144, 234
Tupalov, Andrei, 220
Turgenev, Ivan, 33
Tverdokhlebov, Andrei, 326
Twelfth Party Congress (1923), 166–67
Twentieth Party Congress (1956), 263, 293, 297–98
Twenty-Eighth Party Congress (1990), 394–95
Twenty-Fifth Party Congress (1976), 343
Twenty-First Party Congress (1959), 303
Twenty-Fourth Party Congress (1971), 343
Twenty-Second Party Congress (1961), 304–5, 314, 343
Twenty-Seventh Party Congress (1986), 372
Twenty-Third Party Congress (1966), 324–25, 334, 343
Two Tactics of Social Democracy (Lenin), 68–69

Ukraine, 3, 10, 137
  collectivization, 204, 226
  Dissident movement, 327
  Putin administration (1999–2008), 454
  Russian Civil War (1918–1920), 124, 133
  Russification, 226
  Soviet Union dissolution (1991), 400
  World War II (1941–1945), 256, 258, 261–62
  Yeltsin administration (1991–1999), 427
Ukrainian Herald, 326
Unified Energy Systems, 423

Unified State Political Administration
(OGPU), 151, 203, 217
Union of Soviet Socialist Republics
(USSR)
ethnic groups, 3, 157–58
geographical boundaries, 3
Union of Unions, 76
Unions. *See* Labor unions
United Opposition, 180, 181, 185
United States
Andropov administration (1982–1984),
346
Brezhnev administration (1964–1982),
328, 330–34
Chernenko administration (1984–1985),
348
Cold War, 264–65, 267–70, 392–93
Cuban missile crisis (1962), 308–10
détente, 331–34
Gorbachev administration (1985–1991),
370–71, 373–74, 377, 392–93
Khrushchev administration (1953–
1964), 289, 301–2, 303–4, 307
Korean War (1950–1953), 269–70
Lend-Lease program, 257
military weapons, 330–34, 346, 373–74,
377, 393, 427
Nazi Germany, 250
nuclear weapons, 331–34, 373–74, 377,
393, 427, 453
Putin administration (1999–2008),
453–54
Russian Civil War (1918–1920), 125,
126
Strategic Arms Reduction Talks
(START), 346
Strategic Arms Reduction Treaty
(START), 393, 453
Voice of America, 301–2
World War II (1941–1945), 250, 257,
259–61
Yeltsin administration (1991–1999),
412, 427
Urals-Siberian method, 192, 203
Urbanization, 363–65
Uritsky, Mikhail, 124
Ustinov, Dmitri, 348

Varga, Yevgeny, 275
Vavilov, Nikolai, 225
Vespers (Rachmaninoff), 379
Vietnam, 289
Vlasov, Andrei, 256–57
Voice of America, 301–2
Von Plehve, V. K., 75
Voroshilov, Kliment, 239, 242, 253, 303,
304–5
Voucher program, 418
Voznesensky, Andrei, 373
Vyshinsky, Andrei, 233
Vyshnegradsky, Ivan S., 49
Vysotsky, Vladimir, 355–56

Walesa, Lech, 338
War Communism, 133–36, 146
Warsaw Pact (1955), 289, 330, 335–36,
337, 338, 393
Westerners, 33, 34–36
Western Europe
autocratic state, 13, 16, 18
Brezhnev administration (1964–1982),
335–36
diplomatic policy, 159–62
industrialization, 47, 50
Marxism, 59, 62
monarchy, 13
See also specific country
Westernization
autocratic state, 15–16, 18, 22–23,
32–33, 34–36, 38–39
Brezhnev administration (1964–1982),
326–27
Dissident movement, 326–27
intelligentsia, 32–33, 34–36, 38–39
Khrushchev administration (1953–
1964), 301–2
November (Bolshevik) revolution
(1917), 112
technology, 214
Yeltsin administration (1991–1999), 412
Zhdanovshchina (1946), 275
West Germany, 289, 335
Gorbachev administration (1985–1991),
392
reunification of, 390–91, 392

We (Zamyatin), 156
What Is To Be Done? (Chernyshevsky), 38, 63
What Is To Be Done? (Lenin), 63–64, 65, 67, 68, 69
White Russians, 10
Witte, Sergei, 49–52, 53, 76–77
Women, 193–94, 374–75
Workers' and Peasants' Inspectorate (*Rabkrin*), 163
Workers' Opposition, 149–52, 182
Working class
  autocratic state, 30–31
    capitalism, 49, 51–52, 53
    intelligentsia, 42
    labor strikes, 49, 51–52, 53, 73–74, 76, 84–85, 88
    Marxism, 54, 55–57, 61–66, 68–69
    1905 Revolution, 73–78, 82
  Bolshevik relations, 195
  labor strikes
    autocratic state, 49, 51–52, 53, 73–74, 76, 84–85, 88
    coal miners (1989), 388–89
    Petrograd (1921), 144
  revolutionary movement (1917), 94
  Russian Civil War (1918–1920), 127–28, 138–41
  wages, 159, 273–74
World of Art, The, 84
World War I (1914–1918), 53, 85–88
  pre-war society
    agriculture, 85
    cultural development, 83–84
    industry, 83
    working class, 84–85
  Treaty of Brest-Litovsk (March, 1918), 122–23, 128–29, 133
World War II (1941–1945), 253–63
  diplomatic leadership, 259–61
  Grand Alliance, 254
  Great Patriotic War, 254
  Gulag prisoners, 261–62
  legacy of, 262–63
  military weapons, 222–23
  national leadership, 258–59
  Nazi Germany (1930s), 250–52

World War II (1941–1945) *(continued)*
  Nazi-Soviet Pact (1939), 252–53
  postwar policies
    deportations, 271–72
    Eastern Europe relations, 265–67
    economic recovery, 272–75
    Soviet power, 264–65
    Zhdanovshchina (1946), 275–76
  Soviet security, 248–50
World Youth Festival (1957), 302
Wrangel, Peter, 126, 137

Yagoda, Henrik, 227, 234, 235
Yakovlev, Alexander, 170, 258, 371–72, 396, 398
Yalta Conference (1945), 260, 265, 269
Yanayev, Gennady, 397
Yavlinsky, Grigory, 431, 432–33
Yazov, Dmitri, 376, 398
Yeltsin, Boris, 371, 376–77, 397, 400
  administration of (1991–1999), 409–38
  corruption, 419, 423–24, 426, 430, 437–38
  crime, 426
  democratization, 411–12, 414–16
  economic policy, 411, 414–19, 429, 433, 436–38
    capitalism, 414–16
    corruption, 419, 423–24
    money privatization, 423–24
    privatization, 416–19, 423–24, 429
    shock therapy, 416–17
    voucher program, 418
  foreign policy, 424–26, 427–28, 434–35
  Gorbachev administration, 387, 393–95, 398–99, 401
  legacy of, 436–38
  Matryoshka doll (photo), 407
  political leadership, 413–14, 420–22, 430, 431–38
  presidential resignation, 435–36
  Russian Federation, 409–10
  totalitarianism, 410–13
Yenukidze, Abel, 227–28
Yesenin, Sergei, 194
Yevtushenko, Yevgeny, 305, 311, 325, 369, 394, 398

Yezhov, Nikolai, 235, 238, 242
Young Communist League, 153
Yugoslavia, 252, 260, 264, 266, 267
  Khrushchev administration (1953–1964), 290
  Yeltsin administration (1991–1999), 428
Yukos, 423, 444, 448

Zamyatin, Yevgeny, 156
Zhdanov, Andrei, 239, 275, 277, 278
Zhdanovshchina (1946), 275–76

Zhirinovsky, Vladimir, 421–22, 428, 431, 455
Zhivkov, Todor, 391
Zhukov, Georgy, 239–40, 255, 257, 258, 296–97
Zinoviev, Grigory, 107–8, 117, 118, 131, 160, 166, 167, 233–34, 380
  Bolshevik leadership, 179–80, 181, 182, 183, 185
Zoshchenko, Mikhail, 275
Zubatov, Sergei, 73–74
Zyuganov, Gennady, 422, 428, 433, 440, 455

Michael Kort, educated at Johns Hopkins University and New York University, is a professor of social science in the College of General Studies at Boston University and has been a fellow of the Russian Research Center at Harvard University. In addition to his work on Soviet history, he is the author of *The Columbia Guide to the Cold War* (Columbia University Press, 1998), *The Columbia Guide to Hiroshima and the Bomb* (Columbia University Press, 2007), and *A Brief History of Russia* (Facts on File, 2008), and co-author of *Modernization and Revolution in China* (4th ed. 2009), published by M.E. Sharpe. He has also written more than a dozen books for young adults, including biographies of Nikita Khrushchev and Mikhail Gorbachev, a history of the Cold War, and a history of Marxism. The first edition of *The Soviet Colossus*, published in 1985, was an alternate selection of the Book-of-the-Month Club.